Masters of the Mind

Masters of the Mind

Exploring the Story of Mental Illness from Ancient Times to the New Millennium

Theodore Millon, PhD, DSc

With Contributions by
Seth D. Grossman and Sarah E. Meagher

Portraits by
Theodore Millon and Carrie N. Millon

WILEY

John Wiley & Sons, Inc.

Library of Congress Cataloging-in-Publication Data:

Millon, Theodore.
    Masters of the mind : exploring the story of mental illness from ancient times to the new millennium / by Theodore Millon : with contributions by Seth D. Grossman and Sarah E. Meagher : artistic portraits, Theodore Millon, Carrie N. Millon.
        p.   cm.
    Includes bibliographical references and index.
    ISBN 0-471-46985-8 (cloth)
    1. Mental illness—History.   I. Grossman, Seth.   II. Meagher, Sarah E.   III. Title.

    RC438.M557   2004
    616.89′009—dc22

                                                            2004043538

10   9   8   7   6   5   4   3   2   1

In honor of Tevye's Tata and Zayde
Storytellers of imagination, wisdom, generosity, and warmth

Abraham Millon

Jacob Bernstein-Millon

Contents

PART VII   PERSONOLOGIC STORIES

Prologue

The mind is unique in its interest to people from all walks of life. This interest is not new; throughout written history people have observed, described, and pondered strange behaviors and thoughts within themselves and their neighbors. The questions that people have posed about these experiences seem so simple and basic. Why do we seek to please our friends, but experience great difficulty being congenial with our families? Why do we vacillate so often between hopeful fantasy and dark despair? Why do we dream peculiar events and suffer terrifying nightmares? Why do we succumb repeatedly to foolish temptations against our better judgment? Questions such as these have puzzled and intrigued people since ancient times; they persist to challenge us today. Despite their apparent simplicity, they raise some of the most stubborn and absorbing issues facing modern psychological and medical science.

It is the undramatic and mundane problems of how the mind works, the quiet but persistent anxieties we experience, the repetitive ineffectualities and the immobilizing conflicts we encounter day after day that best represent the subject matter of the mind and its difficulties. Milder disorders of emotional and mental life usually are taken for granted as part of human nature: the promising college freshman who cannot settle down to her studies; the high school teacher who is seductive with the young boys in her classes; the father who cannot tolerate disagreement from his children and flies into a rage when they question his authority; the anxiously self-conscious young engineer who sits alone each evening; the mother who binges on food and constantly complains of fatigue or headaches for which no organic disorder can be found; the child who cannot concentrate on his homework.

The mind's mental malfunctions become more obvious if we shift our attention from these commonplace difficulties to more moderately severe mental disorders: the physician who withdraws from a successful practice for fear that he will do irreparable harm to his patients; the housewife who is unable to sleep in anticipation of someone entering her home to murder her family; the ineffectual husband who leans on his wife for every decision and cannot hold a job for more than a few months; the quiet and scholarly choir boy who steals cars; the shy graduate student who exposes himself in the college library; the alcoholic father who physically attacks members of his family and then threatens suicide to relieve his guilt.

Finally, there are the markedly mentally ill individuals whose disordered state is evident to all: the disheveled woman who walks the streets muttering to herself and cursing at passersby; the unemployed man who "knows" that others have conspired to prevent his success and are plotting to take his life; the aged grandfather who wanders at night conversing with long-dead relatives; the depressed young mother, immobilized by the responsibilities of caring for her newborn son and dreading her impulse to kill him; the socially isolated college student who seems perennially perplexed, speaks of vague mystical experiences, and shouts at persons unseen by others.

Historically, professionals and the public alike considered only markedly severe disorders to be evidence of disturbed minds. They reflected a narrow view that milder disturbances—which we know today often are the precursors of more serious disorders—were a sign, not of illness, but of "moral inferiority," vanity, or dissipation. Instead of recognizing that mild disturbances may be early stages of potentially more severe disorders, they treated them with ridicule and condemnation, censuring and exhorting those with such afflictions to desist from their foolishness and degeneracy. These archaic and inhumane views have given way in recent years to more humane and psychologically sensitive attitudes.

That the incidence of both mild and severe disorders of the mind is strikingly high in contemporary society cannot be denied. Perhaps it reflects the strain of life at the turn of the twenty-first century—what political leaders and social thinkers have noted as a time of terrorism and economic decline. Whatever its causes, the inescapable facts are that each year Americans spend billions of dollars for psychopharmaceuticals as well as tens of billions for liquor and aspirin; and they purchase enough books promising successful personal adjustment to fill a good-sized college library. At the current rate, one out of every seven or eight Americans will be involved in counseling or therapy in the coming years. And for every patient who is hospitalized, there will be 20 other less severely distressed Americans who need pharmacotherapy or psychotherapy.

Mental illness is no longer a remote province of professional study tacked on as a postgraduate specialty for interested physicians. It is a necessary part of the training of psychiatrists, psychologists, social workers, teachers, nurses, and ministers, who serve the needs of the troubled, but it is also a significant part of the curricula of all colleges. The story of the mind and its disorders can help us to understand the problems of contemporary life and may lead us to find ways of preventing these problems in ourselves and our families before they get out of hand.

A growing acquaintance with mental disturbances has resulted in changes in public attitudes. No longer are these problems of the mind viewed as a disgrace, a weird and unnatural phenomenon to be feared and avoided. We have come to realize that scientific and humane action can combat the problems of the mind.

What is new or different about this book? No one has compiled a complete history of the study of the mind, including each of the many and diverse traditions into a single volume. No single work traces and analyzes the origins of each of the several paradigms that study the mind and its disorders. This book fills that gap.

This book has been written for anyone with an interest in the field, especially those who have been puzzled by the diverse, if not conflicting, orientations of thought concerning the mind. Certainly it will also be of interest to the professionals working in clinical and mental-health-related areas.

The stories I tell are fairly straightforward. Though they begin with the history of thought in ancient times, they bring us to the busy offices of academic thinkers, researchers, and clinical practitioners working in the first decade of the twenty-first century.

As a tree with many branches, mental science has been approached with numerous traditions and paradigms: philosophy, humanism, biological chemistry, society and culture, formal psychological experimentation, and the synthesis called personology. Ideas and discoveries in recent decades have come at a breathtaking rate. It is useful, therefore, to look back and review the vast distance we have traveled from early times. Similarly, it is crucial to our aims that we separate major achievements from those of a more modest character while paying homage, in the space we have available, to as many thinkers and scientists who pioneered contemporary work as possible. Our goal here is more than academic: We need to place contemporary approaches in their historical perspective so that we can recognize the wisest paths to follow in the future.

My aim is to provide a substantial understanding of each of the several diverse stories that shed light on both the nature and expression of the mind. No less important is the desire to make this story of the mind useful to those who read it. The book also leaves a record for posterity that provides an overarching framework for understanding all major approaches to the mind and its frailties.

Why is the story of the mind an important topic? In reply, and as Cicero the early Roman scholar, wrote, "Those who know only their own generation always remain children." To preserve ideas in writing allows future men and women to ponder them when their authors are no longer around. Generating a reasonably comprehensive study provides perspective to place current ideas in contexts that enrich understanding. History illuminates the numerous mistakes our forefathers made in their ventures; becoming aware of these errors reduces the likelihood of falling into the same traps ourselves.

As noted, there is an almost infinite diversity of themes and approaches related to the mind. A historical review should help us recognize how current themes follow a limited number of fundamental assumptions and scientific concepts. As well, curiosity and discovery about where such themes originated and where they appear to be going can provide the delight and excitement of newly acquired knowledge. In addition, I hope to provide the reader with a series of interesting stories.

The task of summarizing and integrating centuries of thought and study is complex. History deals with events about which we can never be sure. Their significance is anyone's guess, making selections among the many doctrines essentially a subjective matter.

Some have argued that history should be written with detachment and objectivity. Others question whether such detachment is even possible, no less desirable. The great historian of psychiatry, Gregory Zilboorg, has written (Zilboorg & Henry, 1941), that detachment suggests a certain lack of feeling, reviewing the events of the past with the cold eye of an unconcerned and unaroused observer. The events of the past, however, derive themselves from intense human drives and passions, emotions that are charged with anxieties, loves, hatreds, ambitions, and failures. To look upon history as if they were dots on a statistical table will miss the most essential aspect of living. As Lytton Strachey, the British writer and historian, has noted (1931), to obtain joy and enlightenment from a story of life's events, one must mobilize and not anesthetize one's feelings. Being amorphously impartial is to miss the very thing that makes the story of a subject real and alive. Facts relating to the past, when collected without art, are simply compilations. And while compilations may be useful they are no more history than butter, eggs, salt, and herbs are an omelet. The art of history-telling demands intuition, enlightened intelligence, and the ability to feel the facts and, then, to absorb and reconstruct their inner character and their continuous and vivid development.

A good historical account attempts to place each component of a tradition—its central guiding principles, its surrounding culture, the impact of other contemporary thinkers of the day—in the dominant ethos of the time. Each element of a historical period and cultural value system provides a context for how other elements of that age alter every other age. As the distinguished historian of the behavioral sciences, George Stocking (1965), has noted, numerous problems can arise among those who write mental science histories. In what are referred to as *whig* histories, present approaches to a subject are seen as the inevitable consequence of progressions leading from the past. This is akin to what is termed *presentist*, a problematic model in which past history is interpreted from the standpoint of the present. An obverse problem is the *historicist* approach, which interprets historical achievements solely in terms of the contextual events of its time period and does not acknowledge prior influences or contemporary implications. Similarly problematic is the *internalist* model, which deals with events solely in terms of its own discipline, instead of seeing them as a product of the broader social and scientific context of its time. Last are stories referred to as *great man* studies, which focus on the contributions of outstanding people without recognizing the general zeitgeist of the time, or the influence of others both prior to and contemporaneous with them, either culturally or scientifically. Troublesome also are historical stories that fail to reference the work of contemporary historians. I have been attentive to these potential criticisms, seeking to obviate them in as systematic a manner as possible.

Goethe once wrote that readers have a right to expect from a historical author on science that the author inform them how the elements he presents came to be known to him, and to record what was imagined, conjectured, or assumed. To write a history of a science, he noted, is a hazardous affair because the author must admit that some things will be placed in a bright light and others in a dark shade. Like the author of this book, Goethe noted that he derived great pleasure from the prosecution of his task, but that, instead of a complete history, he merely furnished only the materials for one that he hoped, at the very least, had the merit of being made with earnestness.

Relevant to several of the chapters of the book is that I have been an active participant in numerous mental science events of the past several decades and, hence, have had the privilege of knowing many of the more recent historical figures described. I feel reasonably sure, however, that I have not portrayed inappropriate impressions or indiscreet observations.

I do have misgivings, however. I have already noted difficulties in attempts to register distant events and the inner thoughts of many others; these inevitable limitations require no further comment. But I cannot say, nor do I think, that the accounts I have written are entirely impartial or unprejudiced. I trust that this reality will not be fatal to the usefulness of the book, though readers will likely spot my partialities more clearly than I can.

A primary goal in writing this book was not only to present ideas associated with the mind and the mental sciences, but also to convey the intellectual excitement in searching for answers to some of the most puzzling questions that have faced humankind. I have tried to engage the reader in the exploration of solutions and the generation of hypotheses and speculations in the evolving major approaches to the field. It was my hope to entice the reader to travel with me in a process of discovery and enlightenment.

The curious reader can hardly travel across the threshold of the several segments of the field without noting that all is not peace and harmony under its broad-ranging tree. My intent is not to justify this or that perspective or approach, but to trace its origins, note its obscurities and inchoate character, and travel along the evolution of its best ideas. Each of these doctrines has been arranged to show its place in the unfolding constellation of perspectives that, today, still stand like invincible armies defending their approach to the mind and to mental illness. History should not boast one or another perspective, but provide a contemplative base for evaluating where we are today.

You may justly ask why I have not chosen to select and present a single systematic story of mental illness instead of the views of divergent schools of thought. Although a single doctrinaire presentation might have simplified matters, it would have been not only dishonest scientifically, but pedagogically shortsighted for those who are curious about the state of the field or who plan to explore the subject in greater depth. Readers should not develop a false sense of harmony; equally important, all must recognize that in so complex a field of study as mental illness different levels of observation, using different clinical and research techniques, are both possible and necessary. Although these different stories may be united by a common interest in understanding and treating the mind, there is room, as well as a need, for a variety of approaches. A major goal of this book is to rescue the history of the mental sciences from its warring sectarians, who make the subject, as Shorter (1997) has noted, a sandbox for their ideologies. Many zealots have seized the subject of the mind to illustrate how their approach should serve as the preeminent paradigm of the day. Instead, the mind should be viewed from each of several approaches that exist in the field; each should be traced historically, mapped logically, and regarded as a systematic, yet incomplete, way of dealing with the subject.

Contemporary readers often focus their attentions on one or another perspective, ignoring the views of others. This is a major weakness in the mental sciences today. Strength would come by embracing *all* the responsible paradigms of the mind. Toward that end, I make explicit not only the history, but also the assumptions underlying each paradigm's approach to knowledge. By making their premises clear, I hope, long after the facts are forgotten, that the reader will retain fully the essential principles of each alternative approach.

What structure or outline should I employ to provide the reader with a comprehensive, yet coherent and attractive set of themes? Assuredly, there should be a measure of chronological sequence in the account, perhaps better referred to as a quasi-chronology. Thus I follow one of the major approaches for a period and then track back and do the same with a different approach to the subject. Akin to this order are stories that focus on the contributions of major figures in history. Similarly, one could construct a useful anthology of readings that compile excerpts from many of the important writers, past and present. I have, in essence, combined these options. The result is a partly chronological account, but with a back-and-forth flow that focuses on each of the major traditions characterizing the subject. I have also emphasized the great contributors to each of these traditions or approaches and provided a smattering of quotations so that the reader can experience the character of thought of these important men and women in their own words.

The broad discipline of mental science is composed of and has emerged from numerous traditions or "stories." Each has followed parallel, yet often isolated, chronological courses. There is a fundamental communality among them, but marked differences as well; only time will tell whether these diverse orientations will lead to greater or lesser interactions with one another. As will be evident throughout this book, Thomas Kuhn's brilliant, if controversial, concept of *paradigm* characterizes the divergent patterns of thought regarding the mind and mental science (1962). Kuhn's concept recognizes that theorists and investigators articulate a set of assumptions concerning the fundamental entities that compose a subject. The paradigm also identifies questions that may legitimately be asked about such entities and the techniques that may be employed in seeking answers to these questions. Once a paradigm is established, it becomes the given groundwork for "puzzle solving," that is, the rules that scientists may employ to further elaborate their subject. Although Kuhn has described how new paradigms replace previous paradigms, he acknowledges that competing paradigms can coexist, each posing its own set of propositions, rules, and questions that followers may seek to answer.

This book outlines *seven coexisting paradigms* that thinkers and scientists have developed to understand the mind and the mental sciences. No single paradigm has been completely displaced or eradicated, but history shows that certain paradigms were more prominent at one time than another. Each approach has functioned at one time as a "mental science worldview," a semi-institutionalized model for how to think about the subject of the mind.

To complicate matters, the approach of most schools of thought concerning mental illness has not been fully articulated. Inquiring readers are often presented a wonderful array of essentially overlapping findings and concepts that are disconnected and contradictory, leaving them dazzled and confused. Without differences in each paradigm's history and orientation in mind, readers are like the young Talmudic scholar who, after immersing himself for weeks in ancient manuscripts, rose suddenly one morning, danced joyously in the streets, and shouted, "I have found the most wonderful answer; somebody please tell me the question!"

Mental health sciences, as we know them, are largely the result of an evolutionary process of haphazard variation and natural selection. The uncoordinated efforts of innumerable individual investigators continually produce variation, along with their selection, communication, and critical appraisal by peers and posterity. An inevitable characteristic of this dissemination process is that whenever one surveys the state of most fields, and notably that of mental science, one finds, from the standpoint of organization and elegance, nothing less than a sorry mess. Numerous locally grounded ideas, distinct from one another, no less from the noisy background of miscellaneous ideas and data, vie for attention. Approaches to a broad subject domain form along random, if not irrational lines, and persevere long after their purposes and boundaries, perhaps originally useful as guidelines, have hardened into separating blockades.

The discouraging state of affairs just described is not peculiar to the study of mental illness. It is inevitable that so broad a subject as this would have produced diverse viewpoints. Complex problems lend themselves to many approaches, and divisions of labor in so varied a field become not only a matter of choice but also one of necessity. Beneficially, the historical evolution of these divergent approaches has led to a broad spectrum of knowledge about the mind and clinical phenomena. Nevertheless, these random evolutions and developments have distinct disadvantages. Scientists preoccupied with a small segment of the larger field often have little knowledge of others' work. Intent on their narrow approach, they lose sight of the larger perspective, and their respective contributions become scattered and disconnected. As my early mentor and historian of psychology, Gardner Murphy, has noted (1930), until a mental science Newton or Einstein comes along, readers have no choice but to view the various branches and traditions of mental study as an interrelated, if not an integrated, unit. Until such time as a bridge is created to coordinate each approach with the others, no one perspective should be thought of as all-embracing, or accepted to the exclusion of the others. A multiplicity of viewpoints must prevail.

Scientists approach nature from different vantage points, selecting just those elements of the awesome complex of phenomena that they believe will best enable them to answer the questions they pose. Not only do chemists focus on different facets of nature than do physicists, but within each of these two disciplines, scientists further subdivide the field of study. In effect, then, each of the subdivisions of a general subject deals with a different class of empirical events. The study of the mind and mental science is no different from physics or chemistry in this regard. It, too, can be and has been studied from many vantage points. It can be observed and conceptualized in legitimately different ways by behaviorists, cognitivists, psychoanalysts, and biochemists, to name just a few.

No single level of observation or conceptualization is sufficient to encompass all the complex and multidimensional features of a field such as mental illness. The processes and structures that compose the mind may be described in terms of conditioned habits, reaction formations, cognitive expectancies, or neurochemical dysfunctions. These different levels of data and conceptualization cannot, and should not, be arranged in a hierarchy, with one level viewed as primary, or reducible to another; nor can they be compared in terms of some "objective truth value." Alternative levels or approaches merely are different; they observe and conceptualize different clinical information and lead therefore to different theories of understanding, as well as different therapies. Despite fruitless debates to the contrary, there is no intrinsic conflict between theories and therapies that focus on different kinds of information—chemical, unconscious, cognitive, and so on; they are complementary, and not contradictory, approaches to the mind. No one expects the propositions of a physicist to be the same as those of a chemist; nor should we expect those of a behaviorist to be the same as those of a neuroscientist.

One of the themes of this book is that the several approaches to understanding and treating the mind may be differentiated according to the kinds of clinical information they have elected to study. These choices are essentially pragmatic, and questions of comparative utility or validity should be asked only of approaches that deal with the same kinds of mental events. What is studied becomes the basis for clinical concepts and for the theories that coordinate them. Confusion and irrelevant controversies can be avoided by specifying the conceptual level, or the kinds of clinical data to which the information refers. Readers can then determine whether two approaches are comparable, whether they refer to different clinical information, whether different therapies apply to the same processes, and so on.

The seven historical stories that compose this book suggest a useful basis for approaching a comprehensive study of the mind. These orientations reflect not only relatively distinct traditions, but perhaps more importantly, they differ also in the kinds of issues and clinical information they have elected to conceptualize. For example, followers in the tradition of *neuroscience* focus on the anatomical or chemical substrate of mental pathology; those within the *psychoanalytic* approach address and conceptualize unconscious or intrapsychic processes; scholars within the *personologic* tradition are concerned with an integrative model comprising facets of the whole person; and those employing the *psychoscientific* approach attend primarily to experimentally verifiable behavioral or cognitive data. The seven approaches—philosophical, humanitarian, neuroscientific, psychoanalytic, psychoscientific, sociocultural, and personologic—reflect, therefore, a focus on different sources of clinical data and provide us with seven corresponding historical orientations for understanding and treating mental illness.

Useful as this sevenfold division may be, it incorporates many divergent subgroupings; for example, the neuroscientific category will include clinicians and researchers whose interests focus on genetics, biochemistry, or physiology. Nevertheless, each approach is, more or less, distinct from the others by virtue of its attention to a reasonably delimited focus, a common scientific vocabulary, and a central or guiding doctrine. To reflect these subgroupings, we have divided each approach into two chapters, each of which reflects a somewhat different focus; for example, the neuroscientific approach is divided according to those who concern themselves with the *classification* of psychiatric syndromes versus those who attend to *brain studies* and *somatic therapies*.

The plan to group the stories of the mind and mental science into seven distinct approaches may have other disadvantages. To cohere an approach without touching on partially related or incidental themes may create the misleading impression that its adherents formed a single and united group whose ideas fit tightly together and followed precisely from their antecedents. Similarly, the selection of these boundaried approaches may create the impression that the larger field of mental science is organized into seven distinct schools of thought; this impression, too, would be false. Despite these potential pitfalls, I have adopted the framework, at the risk of oversimplification, as the one most suitable to convey a reasonable understanding of the subject. It will enable readers to become acquainted with the major extant alternatives both historically and contemporaneously. Not only does each approach receive a measure of historical continuity through time, but each represents how it now plays a role in modern diagnostics and therapy.

Every chapter presents both the logic of an approach, and the story of how its main ideas came into being, what we have termed its "unfolding." All approaches are designed to guide the discovery of scientific laws, but each has a bias or orientation as to what kinds of laws should be sought, what methods should be used to discover these laws, and what kinds of clinical phenomena should be observed. Experts engage in intense debates about which of several alternative approaches is best; readers should recognize at the outset that there is no "correct" choice; no rules exist in nature to tell us which clinical approach is best or most important.

The following chapters describe the seven stories or approaches in considerable detail. By arranging these orientations according to the data they observe and conceptualize, one can understand better the definitions of mental illness that have been developed. From this basis also arises a sound foundation for comparing the varied concepts and explanatory propositions that have been formulated about the development and therapeutic modification of these disorders.

Any discussion of the mind or mental illness raises the question of defining these subjects. It should be obvious from the foregoing that no single definition conveys the wide range of observations and orientations with which these subjects may be explored. In detailing each of the seven approaches, I have covered their chronology, definitions, data, as well as their main historical figures. Where relevant, the text traces their evolution from antiquity to the beginning of the twenty-first century, presenting the most significant ideas, theories, and investigations that have led to contemporary thinking about the mind and mental illness.

In this work, I have sought to do more than present stories as if they were from disembodied minds, free from the constraints and values of time, place, society, and culture. Where possible, I have tried to connect the work of several of the major figures to their life history, to the ebb and flow of their careers, and to the cultural communities in which they lived. I have attempted to humanize the many paradigms described in the book by enriching these stories with reference to certain dominant and significant personalities. As a consequence, certain lesser figures have been omitted so that those I have selected receive the space required to make them come to life.

As Boring has written (1929), the story of the mind has been an intensely personal one; the key people involved have mattered a great deal to the advancement of their tradition. Such figures have exemplified their schools of thought and have shaped the character of its research and clinical ideas. Thus, this book is more than just a survey of themes and contrasts issued from intangible phantoms. Of course, I have traced the intellectual antecedents of each major figure, as well as his or her impact on those who came in later days. But beyond my concern with the affiliation of ideas, I have attended where possible to the cultural context of each approach and have tracked how they developed. In articulating the ebb and flow of each of the seven stories, I have noted why and how each approach evolved in terms of the zeitgeist of its time. The two themes—the core ideas of each approach and the major contributors to its progress—are not mutually exclusive subjects but both sides of the coin of historical progress.

Above all, I have sought to present engaging stories that are vivid and continuous in representing each of the major approaches. Although each fact or figure should contribute and be meaningful in itself, it should intimate the larger truth of its overall story. The reader, I hope, will experience a three-dimensional appreciation of the subject, beginning with a tradition's origins, evolving through its substantive and personal developments, and ending with where we stand today; that is, where the contemporary public sees current mental sciences and clinical practices. I have sought to create both depth and texture to each pattern, a series of melodic lines in a contrapuntal orchestration leading to unrealized themes.

Not all of mental science's great contributors are men, as is the impression in many other histories I have read. Women have been both influential in and influenced by the course of understanding and treating the mind; this has been especially true in recent decades. Among the most prominent of the gender are Dorothea Dix, who was instrumental in the development of the American State Hospital system in the mid-nineteenth century, and Jane Addams, who fostered a concern for protective Settlement Houses and helped establish the social work profession in the early twentieth century. The creative ideas of Anna Freud and Melanie Klein, distinguished analysts each, set the groundwork for treating children in England in the mid-twentieth century. In recent decades, the fertile contributions of Virginia Satir, Lorna Benjamin, and Marsha Linehan, have advanced brilliant approaches to contemporary therapeutic methodology.

In closing this prologue, let me emphasize that there is no such thing as a definitive history. The stories set out in the following chapters were selected from the stream of life's events; they reflect my biases and interpretations. I have been too much a skeptic through my professional life as a clinician, scientist, and writer to believe that a complete history can ever be written, especially when one deals with the distant past. This limiting reality does not absolve one from a diligent effort to represent as best as possible the disparate approaches to mental science, as well as to keep one's perspectives toward the future open instead of closed.

Many minds have been involved in my personal education, thereby contributing greatly to my having produced a book of this magnitude. I note in the book's dedication my affection for both my father and grandfather, kind men of considerable intellect who generously guided my earliest history. The spark for many of the themes and ideas of the book owes much to teachers in my past who first sowed the seeds for this book. At the elementary level, I record for posterity the warmth and encouragement of Martin Greenspan; in junior high, I remember the creative stimulus and assurances of David Oberman; in senior high, I note the well-honed ideas and exhortations of Albert Freilich. College days were reinvigorating owing to the words and guidance of William Schultz, Max Smith, and Stanley Chapman. At the graduate level, I think first of Gardner Murphy, a person of immense erudition, generosity of spirit, and intellectual open-mindedness; of Lawrence Frank who cheered me on and taught me to appreciate the values and methods of social compassion; of Kurt Goldstein who showed me that the "organic" approach was neither sterile nor antithetical to humanistic goals; and of Ernst Kris who guided me as I explored the circuitous labyrinths of my mind and released whatever creative impulses lay therein.

To these persons must be added a host of notable clinicians, philosophers, and scientists from whose writings and personal friendships I have profited greatly; their silent instruction pervades the pages of this book. I think here of Franz Alexander, Gordon Allport, Nancy Andreasen, Aaron Beck, Leopold Bellak, Lorna Benjamin, Norman Cameron, Paul Costa, Helene Deutsch, Erik Erikson, Hans Eysenck, Glen Gabbard, Merton Gill, Adolf Grünbaum, John Gunderson, Carl Hempel, Karen Horney, Otto Kernberg, Gerald Klerman, Heinz Kohut, Marsha Linehan, Alexander Luria, Abe Maslow, Paul Meehl, Robert Merton, Henry Murray, Theodor Reik, Melvin Sabshin, Meyer Schapiro, B. F. Skinner, Michael Stone, Drew Westen, Roger Williams, and Joseph Zubin.

Opportunities to share my ideas with international colleagues have led me to learn from clinicians and researchers of diverse talent, notably Robert Abraham, Bengt Armelius, Morten Birket-Smith, Ronald Blackburn, Thomas Bronisch, Vincent Caballo, Sidney Crowne, Mircea Delehan, Jan Derksen, Herman Groen, Masaaki Kato, Nestor Koldobsky, John Livesley, Franz Luteyn, Cesare Maffei, Gunilla Øberg, Joel Paris, Bent Rosenbaum, Erik Simonsen, Hedwig Sloore, Fini Schulsinger, Niels Strandbygaard, Svenn Torgersen, Rolf Trautmann-Sponsel, Per Vaglum, Wim Van den Brink, and Robert Weinryb.

I am pleased also to record several persons in the United States who have played a constructive role for me through their friendship, talents, and ideas: Peggy Alexander, Mike Antoni, Tracey Belmont, David Bernstein, Paul Blaney, Caryl Bloom, Neil Bockian, Robert Bornstein, Joan Bossert, Jim Choca, Bob Craig, Roger Davis, Darwin Dorr, Josh Epstein, Norma Epstein, Len Eron, Luis Escovar, George Everly, Myra Fischman, Leila Foster, Ray Fowler, Allen Frances, Jill Gardner, Addi Geist, Naomi Grossman, Clyde Hendrick, Bridget Herd, Christine Herdes, Aubrey Immelman, Theo Jolosky, Sally Kolitz-Russell, Jo Ann Lederman, Marty Lerman, Jeffrey Magnavita, Joseph McCann, Robert McMahon, Robert Meagher, Jo Ann Miller, Edward Murray, Aaron Pincus, Herb Reich, Paul Retzlaff, Elsa Ronningstam, Vivian Ross, Tracie Shea, Marshall Silverstein, Steve Strack, Jeffrey Sugerman, Melvin Swartz, Shelly Taylor, Robert Tringone, Carol Watson, Irving Weiner, Larry Weiss, Rod Wellens, Rose Wilansky, and Leonard Zwerling.

Last, it is a pleasure to record the work of recent graduate students who have been valued research associates and have contributed first drafts for several sections of this book, namely, Seth Grossman and Sarah Meagher.

Relevantly and more personally on a day-to-day basis, I have been aided immeasurably by the able and kind assistance of Donna Meagher and Rowena

Ramnath in facilitating my time and work at the Institute for Advanced Studies.

Especially important to me through the years have been my now-adult children, Diane, Andy, Adrienne, and especially Carrie, who has been a major partner in several of my academic endeavors, as well as contributing her artistic talents to several of the portraits scattered throughout this book. Finally, my wife, Renée, as before, has contributed her good nature, tolerance, intelligence, and editorial talents into making my writing more grammatical, lucid, and humane.

And now, onward to an extensive and, it is hoped, enlightening excursion into the subject of the mind.

Orientation	500 BC	0	300 AD	1500	1600
Early Philosophical Contributors	Pythagorus Socrates Hippocrates Plato Aristotle Asclepiades Aretaeus Soranus Galen Aurelianus				F. Bacon
Early Humanitarian Contributors				J. Vives J. Weyer F. Plater T. Garzoni	
Early Neuroscience Contributors				Paracelsus A. Vesalius J. Huarte M. Montaigne	R. Burton
Early Sociocultural and Psychoscience Contributors					

	1700	1800	1890

T. Hobbes
  R. Descartes   D. Hume   J. Herbart
    B. Spinoza   Voltaire   E. Condillac   S. Kierkegaard
      J. Locke   J. J. Rousseau   I. Kant
        G. W. Liebniz

W. Tuke   J. Esquirol   D. Dix
  B. Rush   J. Conolly   I. Ray
    P. Pinel   J. P. Falret   T. Kirkebride
    V. Chiarugi   S. Woodward   P. Earle
    J. Reil   J. Guslain   J. Galt

                                   E. Feuchtersleben   T. Meynert
T. Willis   W. Battie   B. Morel   C. Wernicke
T. Sydenham   F. De Sauvages   R. Krafft-Ebing   H. Maudsley
        G. Stahl   W. Cullen   W. Griesinger   A. Alzheimer
                               J. Haslam   P. Broca   R. Cajal
                               J. Heinroth   J. Breuer
                                        J. Charcot
                                       K. Kahlbaum
                                       V. Magnan

G. Hegel   A. Comte   G. Lebon
H. Helmholtz   K. Marx   G. Simmel
F. Galton   H. Spencer   M. Weber
W. Wundt   I. Sechenov   J. Cattell
J. Müeller
E. Weber
G. Fechner

Orientation	1900	1910	1920	1930	1940
Modern Philosophical Contributors		E. Husserl M. Heidegger			K. Popper
Modern Humanitarian Contributors		C. Beers	L. Binswanger K. Jaspers	E. Minkowski	
Modern Neuroscience Contributors	E. Kraepelin H. Jackson C. Sherrington	P. Chaslin E. Bleuler	A. Meyer H. Head S. Franz W. Cannon	E. Kretschmer K. Schneider E. Kahn	V. Cerletti E. Moniz L. Meduna M. Sakel
Modern Psychoanalytic Contributors	S. Freud	P. Janet A. Adler C. Jung K. Abraham S. Ferenczi O. Rank		K. Horney A. Freud H. Hartmann F. Alexander O. Fenichel H. Deutsch W. Reich	E. Fromm S. Rado M. Klein W. Fairbairn E. Kris K. Menninger T. Reik
Modern Psychoscience Contributors	I. Pavlov H. Ebbinghaus E. Thorndike	E. Titchener J. Watson	M. Wertheimer K. Koffka W. Kohler	B. Skinner C. Hull E. Guthrie E. Tolman J. Piaget	
Modern Sociocultural Contributors	E. Durkheim F. Boas T. Veblen J. Addams	G. Mead C. Cooley W. McDougall A. Kroeber	B. Malinowski E. Sapir	J. Moreno S. Slavson	R. Benedict M. Mead K. Lewin F. Allport B. Whorf
Modern Personologic Contributors	A. Binet W. James T. Ribot E. Meumann	J. Dewey J. Angell G. Hall G. Heymans	L. Terman L. Vigotsky H. Rorschach R. Woodworth	W. Stern L. Thurstone	G. Allport H. Murray D. Wechsler B. Klopfer

1950	1960		1970	1980	1990
J. Sartre M. Ponty	H. Feigl E. Nagel C. Hempel		A. Grünbaum		
A. Deutsch V. Frankl	C. Rogers A. Maslow R. May	R. Felix	I. Yalom		
D. Hebb J. Delay K. Goldstein K. Lashley W. Freeman	R. Sperry J. Papez P. Maclean F. Kallmann		N. Geschwind S. Kety	E. Kandel S. Snyder	
E. Erikson D. Rapaport M. Mahler E. Jacobsen			H. Kohut O. Kernberg		
N. Miller H. Eysenck W. Estes K. Spence	J. Wolpe J. Rotter G. Miller H. Simon N. Chomsky G. Kelly		A. Bandura A. Staats A. Ellis A. Beck L. Kohlberg		
T. Parsons S. Slavson H. Sullivan G. Bateson	R. Merton A. Kardiner L. Festinger N. Ackerman T. Leary D. Riesman	M. Bowen V. Satir E. Goffman	S. Minuchin J. Haley	L. Benjamin D. Kiesler	
G. Murphy A. Luria S. Hathaway	R. Cattell P. Meehl		A. Lazarus J. Exner	T. Millon C. R. Cloninger L. Siever	P. Wachtel H. Gardner R. Sternberg M. Linehan

PART I

PHILOSOPHICAL STORIES

CHAPTER

1

Demythologizing the Ancients' Spirits

Current theories and known facts about personality and behavior are the product of a long and continuing history of human curiosity and achievement (Millon, 1969). Although dependence on the past is always appropriate, progress also occurs because dissatisfaction with the "truths" of yesterday stimulates our search for better answers today. Such perspectives on the historical development of our current thinking enable us to decide which achievements are worthy of acceptance and which require further investigation.

This and subsequent chapters look back over the long history of the mind and mental science studies, exposing patterns of progress and regress and brilliant leaps that have alternated with foolish pursuits and blind stumbling. Significant discoveries often were made by capitalizing on accidental observations; at other times, progress required the clearing away of deeply entrenched, erroneous beliefs. Despite these erratic pathways to knowledge, philosophers, physicians, and scientists have returned time and again to certain central themes. What are the causes of human behavior? How can we best classify the varieties of psychic pathology? Do just a few basic elements or processes underlie all forms

1

of personal functioning and pathological behavior? What are the best treatment methods for alleviating disorders of the mind?

It is to answer such questions that we have written this book. We must begin at the beginning, however, with ideas that characterized the ancients, those who lived and wrote in the first millennium, B.C. Here we first encounter the sacred notion of primitive societies, which slowly gave way to the early sophisticated and naturalistic thoughts of philosophers and physicians in the Orient, Greece, Rome, and the Middle East.

The Philosophical Story: I

Before undertaking a systematic analysis of the diverse traditions of study and treatment of mental disorders, we must probe their historical origins and evolution. Efforts to understand and resolve problems of the mind can be traced through many centuries in which solutions have taken unanticipated turns. They have become enmeshed in obscure beliefs and entangled alliances that unfolded without the care and watchful eye of scientific methods. We remain today, a relatively young science; however, many techniques and theories of our time have long histories that connect current thinking to preexisting beliefs and systems of thought. Many of these connections are intertwined in chance associations, primitive customs, and quasi-tribal quests. The path to the present is anything but a simple and straight line; it has come to its current state through values and customs of which we may be only partly aware. Many are the product of historical accidents and erroneous beliefs that occurred centuries ago when mysticism and charlatanism flourished.

The movements and traditions of today are not tight systems of thought in the strict sense of scientific theories; they certainly are neither closed nor completed constructions of ideas that have been worked out in their final detail. They are instead products of obscure lines of historical development, often subject to the confusions and misunderstandings of our remote past when disaffection with complexities typified life. Nevertheless, interest in ourselves, in our foibles as well as our achievements, has always been central to humans' curiosity. The origins of interest in the workings of the mind were connected in their earliest form to studies of astronomy and spiritual unknowns. Even before any record of human thought had been drafted in written form, people asked fundamental questions such as why we behave, think, act, and feel as we do. Although primitive in their ideas, ancient people were always open to the tragic sources in their lives. Earliest answers, however, were invariably associated with metaphysical spirits and magical spells. Only slowly did people formulate more sophisticated and scientific ideas.

It was not until the sixth century B.C. that humans attributed their actions, thoughts, and feelings to natural forces, that is, to sources within themselves. Philosophers and scientists began to speculate intelligently about a wide range of psychological processes, and many of their ideas turned out to be remarkably farsighted. Much of this early imaginative and empirical work was forgotten through the centuries, slowly stumbled on, and rediscovered time and again through careful or serendipitous efforts. In the seventeenth century, John Locke described a clinical procedure for overcoming unusual fears; the procedure he set forth is similar to the systematic desensitization method developed this past century by Joseph Wolpe. Similarly, Gustav Fechner, founder of psychophysics in the mid-nineteenth century, recognized that the human brain was divided into two parallel hemispheres that were linked by a thin band of connecting fibers, what we now term the *corpus collosum*. According to his speculations, if the brain was subdivided, it would create two independent realms of consciousness, a speculation confirmed and elaborated in the latter part of this past century by Roger Sperry, in what has been referred to as *split-brain* research.

The earliest conceptions of the mind and its disorders started with a sequence of three prescientific paradigms that may broadly be considered *sacred:* the animistic, the mythological, and the demonological. These prehistoric phases of history slowly came to an end with the emergence of philosophically sophisticated and medically logical approaches. Certain beliefs dominated every historical period ultimately winning out over previously existing conceptions while retaining elements of the old.

As the study of mental science progressed, different and frequently insular traditions evolved to answer questions posed by earlier philosophers, physicians, and psychologists. Separate disciplines with specialized training procedures developed. Today, divergent professional groups are involved in the study of the mind (e.g., the neuroscientifically oriented psychiatrist with a clear-eyed focus on biological and physiological processes; the psychoanalytic psychiatrist with an austere, yet sensitive attention to unconscious or intrapsychic processes; the personological psychologist with the tools and techniques for appraising, measuring, and integrating the mind; and the academic psychologist with a penchant for empirically investigating the basic processes of behavior and cognition). Each has studied the complex questions generated by mental disorders with a different focus and emphasis. Yet the central issues remain the same. By tracing the history of each of these and other conceptual traditions, we can learn how different modes of thought today have their roots in chance events, cultural ideologies, and accidental discoveries, as well as in brilliant and creative innovations.

It seems likely that future developments in the field will reflect recent efforts to encompass and integrate biological, psychological, and sociocultural approaches. No longer will any single and restricted point of view be prominent; each approach will enrich all others as one component of a synergistic whole. Integrating the disparate parts of a clinical science—theory, nosology, diagnosis, and treatment—is the latest phase in the great chain of history that exhibits an evolution in mental science professions from ancient times to the new millennium. Intervening developments, whether successful or unsuccessful, were genuine efforts to answer humankind's ceaseless efforts to understand more fully who we are and why we behave the way in that we do. The complexity of human functioning makes the desire to know who we are an unending challenge. New concepts come to the fore each decade, and questions about established principles are constantly raised. Perhaps in this century, we will bridge the varied aspects of our poignant, yet scientific understanding of mental diagnosis and therapy, as well as bring the diverse traditions of the past together to form a single, overarching synthesis.

Unfolding of Key Ideas

Primitive man and ancient civilizations alike viewed the unusual and strange within a magical and mythological frame of reference. They attributed behavior that they could not understand to animistic spirits. Although both good and evil spirits were conjectured, the bizarre and often frightening behavior of the mentally disordered led to a prevailing belief that demon spirits must inhabit them. The possession of evil spirits was viewed as a punishment for failing to obey the teachings of the gods and priests. Fears that demons might spread to afflict others often led to cruel and barbaric tortures. These primitive therapies of shock, starvation, and surgery have parallels in recent history, although the ancients based them on the more grossly naive conception of demonology.

If, by chance, the disordered behavior was viewed to signify mystical powers (as was epilepsy among the early Greeks), patients were thought to be possessed by sacred spirits with which the gods had honored them. This favorable view of mental affliction, although still based on a demonic mythology, evolved into a more uniformly sympathetic approach to the ill. Egyptians and Greeks erected temples in which physician priests augmented prayers and incantations with kindness, advice, recreation, and herbs. In the haven of the Egyptian hospice, priests interpreted dreams and suggested solutions both to earthly and heavenly problems. The Grecian Asclepiad temples of the sixth century B.C., were located in remote regions away from family, trade, war, and stress. Here the sick were comforted, fed well, bathed and massaged, given calmative drugs, and surrounded by harmonious music. Despite these promising interludes, the notion of demon possession persisted and those unable to benefit from humane treatment were cast among the evil to be flogged and chained.

Psychological treatment was first recorded in the temple practices of early Greeks and Egyptians in the eighth century B.C. During the fifth century B.C., Hippocrates suggested that exercise and physical tranquillity should supplant the more prevalent practices of exorcism and punishment. Asclepiades, a Roman in the first century B.C., devised measures to relax patients and openly condemned harsh therapeutic methods such as bloodletting and mechanical restraints. The influential practitioner Soranus (A.D. 120) suggested methods to exercise the mind by having patients enlist memorable images and participate in discussions with philosophers who could aid them in banishing their fears and sorrows. Although doubting the value of love and sympathy as therapeutic vehicles, Soranus denounced the common practices of keeping patients in fetters and darkness and depleting their strength by bleeding and fasting. The philosophical discussions espoused by Soranus may be viewed as a forerunner of many contemporary psychological therapies.

Humane approaches to the treatment of the mentally ill were largely abandoned during medieval and postmedieval times when witchcraft and other cruel and regressive acts were employed as therapy. In the early years of the Renaissance, medical scientists were preoccupied with the study of the body and its workings and paid little attention to matters of the mind or the care of the mentally ill. Institutions for the insane were prevalent throughout Europe, but they served to incarcerate and isolate the deranged, not to provide medical or humane care.

Primitive Sacred Notions

What has been called the sacred approach in primitive times may be differentiated into three models, according to Roccatagliata (1973): animistic, mythological, demonological. These divergent paradigms shared one point of view, that mental processes and disorders were the expression of transcendent magical action caused by external forces. The *animistic* model was based on prelogical and emotional reasoning derived from the deep connection between primitive beings and the mysterious forces of nature. From this viewpoint, events happen because the world is peopled by animated entities driven by obscure and ineffable forces that act on one's mind and soul. The second phase, characterized by *mythological* beliefs, transformed the animistic conception so that indistinct and indefinable forces were materialized into myths. Every fact of life was imbued with the powers of a particular entity, and every symptom of disorder was caused by a deity that could, if appropriately implored, benevolently cure it. In the third, or *demonological* phase, the transcendent mythological deities were placed into a formal theological system such as the Judeo-Christian. In this latter model, two competing forces struggled for superiority. One was creative and positive, represented by a good father or God; the other was destructive and negative, represented by the willful negation of good in the form of demonic forces of evil. These three conceptions followed each other historically, but they overlapped with elements of one appearing in the others at times.

It was about 100,000 years ago when Paleolithic man wandered the earth during an early glacial period. Even then, humans tried to explore treatments for those who suffered psychic pain or behaved peculiarly (e.g., the surgery

known as *trephining,* boring a hole through the skull to clean out bone fragments or to relieve head pressure, dates back to the Stone Age). Sundry
amulets were employed to drive away demons that purportedly possessed the
mentally distressed (e.g., the vertebrae of snakes and the teeth of animals
have been found in pouches carried by medicine men).

Magic and supernatural concepts helped early humans make sense out of the
many unfathomable and unpredictable aspects of prehistoric life. Weighted
with life's painful realities and burdensome responsibilities, these beliefs gave
order and pseudologic to fears of the unknown, a repository of unfalsifiable assumptions in which the supernatural filled in answers for what they could not
understand. Ultimately, supernaturalism became the dominant worldview for
objectifying and comprehending the mysterious experiences of life. Priests and
wizards became powerful by capitalizing on the fears and peculiarities of the
populace to undo spells, "heal" the physically ill, and "purify" the mentally distressed. To them, the eccentric or irrational were assuredly touched by spirits
who possessed superhuman powers to induce psychic pathology. Almost all
groups permitted healing to fall into the hands of priests and magicians, a situation that exists today in some societies. Living in a world populated with
imaginary beings, these spiritual forces could often calm man's worst anxieties
and expunge the ever-present terrors of life. Despite extensive archeological
analyses, knowledge of primitive times is no more than fragmentary. Nevertheless, we may assume that primitive humans saw a world populated with spirits
that were essentially illusions created by their own anguish and perplexity.

Healers in primitive times had more active and extensive community roles
than physicians do today. Not only did they address the current health and welfare of their people, but they also were fully acquainted with the mystical history
and customs of the tribe. Patients placed their hopes more in the person of the
healer than in his techniques or medications; thus the healer's personality was
the principal agent of any cure that might have occurred. Some healers employed rational methods that reflected their knowledge or skill. Others were magicians whose effects stemmed from their persuasiveness or prestige. A third
group was religious in orientation, assuming the role of saviors who energized
patients into self-healing behavior. The training of primitive healers was passed
down through families from ancestors who possessed a body of secret knowledge
and traditions. Healing events were mostly collective affairs in which patients
were accompanied by relatives who sat nearby during treatment procedures; occasionally a ceremony took place with a larger but select group of participants.
The distinction between body and mind in primitive times was not in any sense
clear-cut. Most healing methods were essentially psychological, given the fact
that "medications" were biologically inert and mystical in power.

Treatment was dedicated to ridding the patient of metaphysical uncertainty
and undecipherable fear, instead of dealing directly with realistic problems.
Practical solutions to emotional and mental difficulties were also achieved by

empirically based, but simplistic deductions. For example, mental irrationalities were relieved by lying in a bath of cold water, or by rubbing one's head with warm mud, or by sucking snake venom to poison infectious spirits. Initial attempts to explain mental illness were equally simplistic and empirical. All disorders were derived from sources outside the patient, usually ascribed to the malignant influences of mysterious supernatural phenomena that were best treated with magic or sorcery. The casting out of evil spirits was attempted initially through prayer, incantation, sharp noises, foul odors, and bitter concoctions. If these failed, the body of the afflicted was made unwelcome for the spirits by flogging and starving it. These primitive therapies of shock, starvation, and surgery are paralleled in recent history (e.g., electroconvulsive therapy, lobotomy), although the ancients based them on grossly naive conceptions of demonology.

Nascent Asian and Middle-Eastern Notions

The historical development of treatment and diagnosis in ancient times was not as focused as in later periods. The earliest records concerning the treatment of mental illness in China show that magic and sorcery were practiced in the twelfth century B.C. Throughout its feudal period, which lasted for more than 25 centuries for most of China, the courts guided folk-intuitive medical practices. This court-centered system established a socially oriented outlook for Chinese science and medicine.

The first written records of mental illness in Chinese literature were discovered on bones dating back to the fourteenth century B.C. Carvings on the bones asserted headaches and other head disorders reflected malevolent agencies in the wind. These so-called diseases of the wind persisted for centuries; the belief led to the establishment within the Imperial College of Medicine in the eleventh century A.D. of a department devoted specifically to the study of wind disorders.

In the eighth century B.C., the *Kuan Tzu* recorded that "there are institutions where the deaf, blind, dumb, lame, paralyzed, deformed and insane are received when they are ill so as to be cared for until they recover." The Chinese favored a broad social welfare policy that grouped all dysfunctions and disorders that required custodial care and treatment. Not until the arrival of Western medical missionaries in the nineteenth century were specific psychiatric institutions established in China. The *Nei Ching* and *Cha I Ching*, among the earliest works in Chinese medical literature, included brief descriptions of epilepsy, hallucinations, amnesia, and irrational crying and laughing, each of which was presumably a consequence of an overabundance of angry emotions; all were subjected to systematic acupuncture therapies. In the fourth century B.C., the *Shan Hai Ching* listed 20 or so drugs that could be used for diminishing anger and emotions such as fear and jealousy. Also recorded was the need for balance between the so-called vital elements of life. For example, attitudes of social optimism and moderation in thought and behavior could foster an "even distribution of mood"; a calmness of mind would ostensibly ensure the preservation of health.

Acupuncture treatments for psychiatric problems were employed with some success in the Ming dynasty of the fourteenth and fifteenth centuries A.D. Etiology was attributed to dysfunctions in Yin and Yang and Confucius's "Five Elements." During this later period, the *Shen Cher Men* ("Approach to the Mind"), described insanity as follows:

> The insane person is somewhat violent, sometimes stupid, singing and laughing or sad and weeping. He gets no better even after months and years. The name for this impairment is "wind in the mind." Others are boisterous, raving, stubborn and violent, abusing everyone indiscriminately. These persons may attach themselves to any eminence, sing at the top of his voice, take off his clothes, run wildly, climbing over walls or roofs in ways that no normal person could. Some persons are subject to fits, become dizzy or cannot recognize people they have known. They may fall to the ground, have convulsions and suffer from jerky behaviors over which they have no control.

Whereas Western traditions focus on the individual, Chinese culture is historically "situation-centered." The social context assumed predominance over individual wishes. For several millennia, China was governed by an all-powerful court bureaucracy established by merit and examination. Philosophical traditions stressed harmony as the natural order of life. Laws served to establish homeostatic patterns and social balance, and any disturbance—behavioral, mental, or physical—called for resolutions designed to preserve and establish harmony. Each individual was given a role and place, a purpose, and a feeling of continuity within Chinese history and its contemporary culture. Traditions and cultural institutions dealt with personal relationships and set boundaries of acceptable and unacceptable behavior, circumscribing the outer limits for interpersonal disturbances and abnormal thoughts.

Five archetypal Confucian elements established a framework for much of Chinese philosophical, ethical, social, and medical thought: Those of relationships encompassed ruler to subject, father to son, husband to wife, brother to brother, and neighbor to neighbor. Social responsibilities and proper behaviors were clearly defined in terms of one's place in the social web. In fact, ancient Chinese philosophies were dominated by ideas tied to the number five. Somewhat akin to Hippocrates and Empedocles in Greece, the Chinese believed that the universe was composed of five basic elements: wood, metal, fire, earth, and water. In parallel form, they concluded there were five basic sense organs: the eye, the ear, the nose, the mouth, and the body. Corresponding to these five organs were the sensations of vision, hearing, smell, taste, and touch. Once again, using the model of five variants, there ostensibly were five tastes: salt, sour, bitter, sweet, and acidic. Basic colors also comprised five elements: green, red, yellow, black, and white. As for psychological processes, the earliest Chinese classification categorized the basic emotions as sorrow, fear, anger, desire, and joy.

Among the more distinguished Chinese philosophers of this early period, we find **Hsun Tzu (298–212 B.C.).** In a manner similar to Aristotle, Tzu was oriented to natural phenomena and sought to identify patterns of regularity and orderliness in nature. In contrast to most philosophers of his time, he argued that rational thought and empirical procedures were more significant than superstitious beliefs. In contrast, many Chinese ideas were tied to the concepts of *yin* and *yang,* viewed initially as opposing cosmic forces; they were seen in later times as complementary as well. Balance or equilibrium between yin and yang was viewed as essential to psychological well-being and to proper social functioning.

Although it is problematic to find a clear beginning to *Hindu* medical writings, there are reasons to believe that Indian medicine was an original system that developed independently of other cultures and times. It may very well be that Hindu thought, preceding those of Persia, Greece, and Rome—and in many ways innovative and potent—traveled over several centuries across the Asian continent to the Middle East and into Europe. There are numerous similarities between Hindu and Greek writings, but as Zilboorg and Henry (1941) have stated, "Some coincidences would appear rather to be that of observers of the same facts, than of borrowers from the same books" (p. 31). Mental disorders, in the Hindu system, remained essentially within the domain and responsibility of priests and their metaphysics.

Many contributions of the Hindus are associated with the name *Susruta* who lived 100 years before Hippocrates. His works follow the traditional beliefs of his day about possible demoniacal possession. However, Susruta suggested that the passions and strong emotions of the mentally disordered may also bring about certain physical ailments that call for psychological help. Anticipating the significance of temperament or innate dispositions, Hindu medicine proposed that three such inclinations existed: wise and enlightened goodness, with its seat in the brain; impetuous passions, the source of pleasure and pain sensations, with its seat in the chest; and blind crudity of ignorance, the basis of animalistic instincts, with its seat in the abdomen.

In the Middle East, the ancient civilization of *Babylonia* was not only a vast geographic expanse, but the foundation of philosophical thought for most nations in the Mediterranean region. Many of the traditions discussed among the Greeks and Romans can be traced to ideas generated initially in the Babylonian Empire. Babylonians were oriented toward astronomical events; superstitions regarding the stars produced numerous gods, a result largely of their intellectual leaders' fertile imaginations. They sought help from the gods through magical rites, incantations, prayers, and the special powers of physicians or priests. The Babylonians assigned a demon to each disease; insanity, for example, was caused by the demon *Idta.* Each was to be exorcised through special medicines (primarily herbs and plants), confessions, and other methods to help restore a balance between conflicting supernatural forces. As the Babylonians saw it, invariable tensions existed among the gods but, more importantly, between a more-or-less rational, as opposed to a super-stitious, explanation of psychic ailments.

There is evidence that in *Egypt,* as in other early civilizations, the heart was thought to be the center of mental activity. Egyptians also had difficulty in separating prevailing supernatural beliefs from that which they could observe and modify in nature. Astronomical phenomena were the primary objects of worship. The mystical powers of the gods were usually favored over natural qualities. Over the course of a century or two, Egyptian philosophers and physicians began studying the brain, ultimately recognizing it as the primary source of mental activity. Egyptians recognized that emotional disorders could be described in line with explanations proposed by the Greeks. Thus *hysteria* was the Greek term for *uterus,* and as the Egyptians saw it, the word denoted a wandering uterus that had drifted from its normal resting location; the task of the physician was to bring the uterus back to its normal setting. This explana-tion for hysteria continued until the late Middle Ages.

The *Persian Empire* was established about 900 B.C. and flourished until about 600 B.C. Aligned with most primitive civilizations of that time, Persians considered all physical diseases and mental disorders to be the work of the devil. Moreover, they felt that treatment should be based on a supernatural point of view that employed incantations and exorcism, as well as magical and religious rites. To them, humans were creatures in which the forces of good and evil were struggling for the future of mankind. The rigid religious system and illiteracy of the common person together limited reflective growth in both Persia's philosophy and science.

The Generative Character of Greek Philosophy

Among advances in thought between 700 B.C. and 400 B.C. were the specula-tions of a number of philosopher-physicians, most notably Thales, Pythagoras, Aesculapius, Alcmaeon, and Empedocles. These forerunners laid the ground-work for the great Greek physician Hippocrates and the great Greek philoso-phers Socrates, Plato, and Aristotle.

In the earliest periods of Greek civilization, insanity was considered to be a divine punishment, a sign of guilt for minor or major transgressions. Therapy sought to combat madness by various expiatory rites that removed impurities, the cause of the psychic disorder. Priests mediated the ill person's prayers to the gods to assure his or her cure. Thus, with divine help, the person's heart could be purified of its evil.

Albeit slowly, Greek scholars realized that little of a rational nature charac-terized their thinking about mental pathology. To them, external, but unseen, agents could no longer serve as a logical basis for a genuine understanding of mentally troublesome phenomena. A fundamental shift began to take place, not merely in describing different types of mental disorder, but in providing a sounder basis for thinking about ways to alter these aberrant behaviors. To treat mental disorders, they began to recognize the necessity of understanding how and why mental disorders were expressed in the natural world: Only then could they successfully deal therapeutically with the tangible symptoms of everyday mental life. Instead of leaving the treatment of mental disorders to the supernatural and mystical, a more concretely oriented perspective began to emerge. This transition was led by imaginative thinkers in the fifth and sixth centuries B.C.

A central intellectual effort of Greek philosophers was the desire to reduce the vastness of the universe to its fundamental elements. Most proposed that complexities could be degraded to one element—be it water, air, or fire. Their task was to identify the unit that composed all aspects of the universe. Among the first philosopher-scientists to tackle this task was **Thales (652–588 B.C.),** born in the seventh century B.C. What little we know of Thales comes largely from the writings of later Greek philosophers, notably Aristotle, Plato, and the historian Herodotus. This nimble-witted Greek believed that the fundamental unit of the universe was a tangible and identifiable substance—water. Some philosophers disagreed with the notion that the universe was composed of a simple and permanent element. **Heraclitus (530–470 B.C.),** for example, proposed that fire was the component that constitutes all nature. He asserted, however, that the universe was composed of no lasting substance: nothing stable, solid, or enduring. Things real and tangible inevitably vanish, change their form, even become their very opposites.

In a similar manner, **Anaxagoras (500–428 B.C.)** asserted that a reduction to the basic elements could not explain the universe. He differed from Heraclitus in that he did not believe the universe lacked an enduring substance. He asserted that there was an endless number of qualitatively different elements. It was the organization or arrangement of these diverse elements that was central to the structure of the universe. Anaxagoras's novel belief that the character of these constituents could not be explained except through the action of human thought is similar to the view of the *phenomenologists* and the *gestaltists.* Some centuries later, they claimed that the structure of objective matter was largely in the interpretive eye of the perceiver.

Later, the philosopher **Democritus (460–362 B.C.),** following **Leucippus (ca. 445 B.C.),** proposed that the universe was made of variously shaped atoms. These small particles of matter were in constant motion, differing in size and form, but always moving and combining into the many complex components that composed the universe. This innovative speculation endures to the present time. Extending the theme proposed a century earlier by Anaxagoras, Democritus stressed that all truths are relative and subjective. As noted, he asserted that matter consisted of invisible particles called atoms, a term coined by Leucippus, who had proposed the concept some half-century earlier. Each atom was composed of different shapes that combined and were linked in numerous ways.

This purely speculative idea remains essentially correct to this day. The physical thesis of contemporary times known as the *Heisenberg principle* finds its origins in the surmise of Democritus.

Returning to Thales for the moment, it should be noted that though he was not the prime forerunner of a modern understanding of mental processes, he was a radical thinker. He redirected attention away from mysticism, recognizing that psychic disorders were natural events that should be approached from a scientific perspective. As a pivotal figure in his time, he ushered in an alternative to earlier supernatural beliefs. Equally significant was Thales's view that scientific thinkers should try to uncover the underlying principles on which overt phenomena were based. Oriented to find these principles in physical studies and "geometric proportions," he turned to "magnetic" phenomena, convinced that the essential element of all life was its animating properties. To Thales, action and movement, based on balanced or disarrayed magnetic forces, was what distinguished human frailty. He further derogated the view that external supernatural forces intruded on the psyche; instead, the source of pathology was inherent within persons themselves.

Paralleling the views of Thales, **Pythagoras (582–510 B.C.)** reasserted the importance of identifying the underlying scientific principles that may account for all forms of behavior. He differed from Thales in that he retrogressively used ethics and religion as the basis for deriving his scientific principles. More progressively, however, he was the first philosopher to claim that the brain was the organ of the human intellect, as well as the source of mental disturbances. He adopted an early notion of biological humors, or naturally occurring bodily liquids, as well as positing the concept of emotional temperament to aid in decoding the origins of aberrant passions and behavior. The mathematical principles of balance and ratio served to account for variations in human characterological styles (e.g., degrees of moisture or dryness, the proportion of cold or hot). Balances and imbalances among humoral fundamentals would account for whether health or disease would be present. Possessing a deep regard for his "universal principles," he applied his ideas to numerous human, ethical, and religious phenomena. Though he believed in immortality and the transmigration of souls, this did not deter Pythagoras from making a serious effort to articulate the inner equilibrium of human anatomy and health.

Pythagoras considered mental life as reflecting a harmony between antithetical forces: good-bad, love-hate, single-plural, limited-unlimited. Life was regulated according to his conception of opposing rhythmic movements (e.g., sleep-wakefulness, inspiring-expiring). Mental disorders reflected a disequilibrium of these basic harmonies, producing psychic impairment. To him, the soul could rise or descend from and to the body. The more the soul was healthy, in balance, and without psychic symptoms, the more it resembled solar energy. Pythagoras spoke of the soul as composed of three parts: *reason*, which reflected truth; *intelligence*, which synthesized sensory perceptions; and *impulse*, which derived from bodily energies. The rational part of the soul was centered in the brain; the irrational one, in the heart. Incidentally, Pythagoras coined the term *philosophy*, putting together the words *philo* meaning "love" and *sophia* meaning "wisdom."

Ostensibly through his father, the god Apollo, **Aesculapius (ca. 550 B.C.)** gained his understanding of mental disorders by the divination of dreams, which he then transmitted to his sons, Machaon and Podaleirius. A series of descendents, called Asclepiadeans, established long-enduring "medical temples" and a distinguished cult. It is unclear historically whether Aesculapius existed in fact or whether his ideas should properly have been attributed to Pythagoras. As the Aesculapian cult spread throughout the Greek empire, numerous temples were erected in the main cities of the Mediterranean basin, including Rome on the Tiber Island in 300 B.C.

What may be best known about Aesculapiad temples today is the *symbol* of medical knowledge they employed: a serpent wrapped around a rod. Medicine gradually evolved into a branch of philosophy in the sixth and seventh century B.C. No one of that early period achieved the mythic stature of Aesculapius— the presumed founder of temple-based hospitals. They were designed to execute the healing traditions in which he believed, notably a rest from life's stressors with opportunities for positive mental growth. Located in peaceful and attractive settings, these temples encouraged patients to believe that there were good reasons to want to recover. Included among the treatment techniques were a balanced diet, a daily massage, quiet sleep, priestly suggestions, and warm baths, all of which were thought to comfort and soothe patients.

Also of value also during this early period was the work of **Alcmaeon (557–491 B.C.),** possibly the son or favorite student of Pythagoras, carried out in the fifth century B.C. Alcmaeon, a philosopher-physiologist, asserted that the central nervous system was the physical source of mental activity and that cerebral metabolism was based on the stability of "the humoral fluxes." If imbalanced or unstable, the humors would create shifts in cerebral tissue functioning, leading then to various mental disorders. Metabolic fluxes were caused by a disequilibrium between the nervous system's qualities of dry-moist and hot-cold.

Most notable were Alcmaeon's efforts to track the sensory nerves as they ascended to the brain. He articulated, as perhaps no one else before him had done, the structural anatomy of the body through careful dissection. No less significant was his conviction that the brain, rather than the heart, was the organ of thought. Like Aesculapius, he also anticipated the work of Empedocles and Hippocrates in believing that health called for a balance among the essential components of life—coolness versus warmth, wetness versus dryness, and so on. The notion of fundamental elements in balance became a central theme in the work of Aesculapius and Alcmaeon; it also served to guide the views of their disciples. Alcmaeon's biological model, based on the concept of metabolic harmony called *isonomy*, took the place of early mythological theology in

Greece and was an extension of the growing secular and democratic spirit in its sixth century B.C. culture.

Empedocles (495–435 B.C.) adopted the homeostatic model generated in the work of Pythagoras, Aesculapius, and Alcmaeon. Most significant was his proposal that the basic elements of life (fire, earth, air, and water) interacted with two other principles (love versus strife). Empedocles stressed that a balance among the four elements could be complicated if they combined in either a complementary or a counteractive way. Love and strife represented human expression of more elementary magnetic processes such as attraction or repulsion. All the elements/humors could be combined, but Empedocles wondered what the consequences would be if they were organized in different ways. He set out to weave the several threads of his theory and concluded that the force of attraction (love) would likely bring forth a harmonic unity, whereas repulsion (strife) would set the stage for a personal breakdown or social disintegration.

To Empedocles, blood was a perfect representation of an equal mix of water, earth, air, and fire. He therefore suggested that persons with problematic temperaments and mental disorders would exhibit imbalances within their blood. Among his other contributions, Empedocles posited a rudimentary model of an evolutionary theory that anticipated Darwin's by 2,000 years. As he phrased it, "Creatures that survive are those whose blood elements are accidentally compounded in a suitable way," whereas a problematic compounding will produce "creatures that will perish and die." To him, nature created a wide variety of healthful and perishing blood configurations, that is, different combinations of the four elements.

A contemporary of Democritus—born the same year—became the great philosopher-physician who set the groundwork for sophisticated clinical medicine for the ensuing centuries. The fertility of this wondrous period of Grecian thought cannot be overestimated, ranging from the brilliant ideas of Democritus and Socrates to the creative foundations of scientific medicine by Hippocrates.

Hippocrates (460–367 B.C.) was born on the island of Cos, the center of an ancient medical school. He was the son of an Aesculapian priest from whom he acquired his first medical lessons and whose philosophy he would follow in his own future therapeutic efforts. In Hippocrates, who was the inheritor of his father's tradition and the humoral concepts of Pythagoras and Empedocles, mental disorders progressed from the magical and mythical realm, and the demonological and superstitious therapeutic approaches of an earlier era, to one of careful clinical observation and inductive theorizing. He synthesized the practical and sympathetic elements of the Aesculapian cult with the more biological proposals of Pythagoras, blending these elements to elevate mental processes and disequilibria into a clinical science.

Thus in the fifth century B.C. truly radical advances supplanted the superstitions of temple medicine. The astuteness and prodigious work of Hippocrates highlighted the naturalistic view that the source of all disorders, mental and physical alike, should be sought within the patient and not within spiritual phenomena. For example, the introductory notes to the Hippocratic book on epilepsy state:

> It seems to me to be no more divine and no more sacred than other diseases, but like other affections, it springs from natural causes. . . . Those who first connected this illness with demons and described it as sacred seem to me no different from the conjurers, purificators, mountebanks and charlatans of our day. Such persons are merely concealing, under the cloak of godliness, their perplexity and their inability to afford any assistance. . . . It is not a god which injures the body, but disease.

Like many of his progenitors, Hippocrates emphasized that the brain was the primary center of thought, intelligence, and emotions. It is only from within the brain, he asserted, that pleasures and joys and laughter arise, as well as sorrows, grief, and tears. It is, he elaborated, this very same source that makes us mad or delirious, inspires us with dread and fear, and brings sleeplessness, inopportune mistakes, aimless anxieties, absentmindedness, and other acts contrary to the person's habitual ways. All of these stem from the brain when it is not healthy (i.e., when an imbalance exists between hot and cold or moist and dry).

Hippocrates

The approach of Hippocrates was essentially empirical, despite the growing eminence of philosophical thought that characterized his time. He was a practical biologist stressing the role of the humors of the body, focusing on physical treatments, notably diet, massage, and music. Remedies stressed the value of sleep and rest. Central to the medical practices of Hippocrates and his followers was the crucial role of keen observation and fact gathering. Contrary to the thesis of his younger contemporary Plato, which addressed abstract hypotheses and so-called self-evident truths, Hippocrates focused his attention on observable symptoms, their treatments, and their eventual outcomes. In this regard, Hippocrates served as a model for Aristotle's empirical orientation, emphasizing facts, not abstractions.

Like many of his forebears, Hippocrates was convinced that dreams could serve as indicators of health or illness. Mental pathology stemmed from a disparity between the content of dreams and of reality. Hippocrates outlined his awareness of the character of dreams in the following:

> Dreams as represent at night a man's actions through the day, and exhibit them in the manner in which they occur, namely, as performed and justly deliberated, these are good to a man, and prognosticate health, inasmuch as the soul perseveres in its diurnal cogitations, and is not weighed down by any repletion,

evacuation, or any other external accident. But when the dreams are the very opposite to the actions of the day, and when there is a conflict between them— when this happens, I say, it indicates a disorder in the body; when the contrast is great, the evil is great, and when the one is small the other is small also.

Dream symbolism, as seen by Hippocrates, led him to anticipate later hypotheses concerning the operation of "unconscious forces." Hippocrates also established the tradition of carefully recording personal case histories, detailing the course and outcome of the disorders he observed. Through these histories, we have surprisingly accurate descriptions of such varied disorders as depression, phobias, convulsions, and migraine.

A major contribution of Hippocrates and his associates at the Cos College of Medicine in Athens was their classification of aberrant behaviors. Here, they provided a logic for differentiating the various mental ailments, not only among those we now label the *DSM-IV-TR* (*Diagnostic and Statistical Manual of Mental Disorders*) Axis I syndromes, but also Axis II personality types, the latter construed as abnormalities of temperament. Temperament was associated with the four humors model, which transformed earth, fire, water, and air into their parallel bodily elements. Individuals were characterized in terms of which one of the four elements predominated. For example, lethargic or apathetic individuals ostensibly reflected the predominance of phlegm, a dominance of water; the melancholic propensity for sadness and depression reflected excesses of black bile, a dominance of earth. Among other clinical syndromes differentiated were delirium, phobia, hysteria, and mania. Lacking precise observations of bodily structure and prevented by taboo from performing dissections, Hippocratic physicians proposed hypothetical explanations of disease. They adhered closely, however, to the first nonsupernatural schema that specified temperament dimensions in accord with the doctrine of bodily humors. Interestingly, history has come full circle in that much of contemporary psychiatry seeks answers with reference to inner biochemical and endocrinological processes.

Hippocrates identified four basic temperaments, the *choleric*, the *melancholic*, the *sanguine*, and the *phlegmatic*; as noted, these corresponded, respectively, to excesses in yellow bile, black bile, blood, and phlegm. Elaborated by the Roman, Galen, centuries later, the choleric temperament was associated with a tendency toward irascibility; the sanguine temperament prompted the individual toward optimism; the melancholic temperament was characterized by an inclination toward sadness; and the phlegmatic temperament was conceived as an apathetic disposition. Although the doctrine of humors has long been abandoned, giving way to contemporary studies on topics such as neurohormone chemistry, its archaic terminology still persists in modern expressions such as persons being *sanguine* or *good-humored*.

Hippocrates and his Cos associates were among the first to stress the need for a relationship between diagnosis and treatment. The mere description of a clinical disturbance was insufficient unless there was a clear indication as to the course that therapy should follow. Again, Hippocrates anticipated that physicians could waste much effort in specifying diagnosis, unless they followed it with a consideration of its utility for therapeutic decisions. Although naive in conception and execution, Hippocrates' approach to therapy followed logically from his view that disorders were of natural origin. To supplant the prevalent practices of exorcism and punishment, he recommended such varied prescriptions as exercise, tranquillity, diet, even marriage and, where necessary, venesection or bloodletting. Systematic in a contemporaneous sense, Hippocrates and his colleagues devised a series of therapeutic regimens to reestablish the humoral balance that he thought underlaid most diseases; he also employed surgical techniques such as trephining to relieve purported pressure on the brain.

Socrates

The Hippocratic proposals of biological causation and naturalistic treatment, together with his theory that temperamental types were exaggerations of normality were profound advances over earlier notions. With but minor revisions, their influence extended over the next 1,000 years. What must be stressed about Hippocrates' contribution was the role he played in divorcing clinical medicine from religious beliefs and superstition. Not only did he assert that diseases had natural causes instead of being the work of spiritual forces, but he did this without the foundations of biological laboratories, scientific methodologies, or experimental evidence.

Innumerable tales have been told about **Socrates (470–399 B.C.);** he was variously described as degenerate, brilliant, courageous, grotesque, and deranged. He was a pivotal figure in Greek thought, so much so that philosophy before him is referred to as pre-Socratic. Born approximately in 470 B.C. in Athens, he lived for 70 years before meeting his well-known death by drinking the poison hemlock. Socrates differed strongly from Protagerous, who posited that knowledge should be based on subjectivity. In contrast, Socrates claimed that one could obtain true knowledge only by analyzing concepts, that is, through principles and theories with high generalizability—even if they did not correspond directly with subjective experience. Socrates promoted the power of reason, believing that it is only through rational processes that one can discern that which is both objective and universal.

Socrates was far from handsome. Along with his bald head, his large round face, deep-set and staring eyes, he had a broad and flowery nose that hardly suggested he was a famous philosopher. From miscellaneous descriptions, we can imagine his ungainly figure, clad each day in the same rumpled tunic, walking leisurely through the Agora, blithely indifferent to the surrounding political bedlam. He would gather the young and the inquisitive around him, lead them into a shady nook of the temple porticos, and ask them to question their assumptions or to define their terms. The youths who flocked to him were a motley crew, curious about the meaning of life or the problems that agitated the society of their day. There were endless debates within this small band of intense thinkers and talkers who felt, as did their teacher, that a life without thoughtful discourse would be unworthy of a man. Every school of social, scientific, and political thought of later centuries was generated first in these dialogues, which were perhaps the source of many later philosophical movements as well.

As Durant (1953) asked: Why did his pupils reverence him so? It may have been because he was a man as well as a philosopher, modest in his bearing and his wisdom, seeking to know and to question as a deeply loving participant in their shared dialogues. As he said time and again, philosophy begins when one learns to doubt, particularly to doubt one's cherished beliefs, dogmas, and axioms. Socrates pried into all facets of human existence, uncovering man's assumptions and questioning certainties. He asked: What do you mean by those abstract words with which you judge the problems of life? What do you mean by notions such as honor, virtue, morality, or patriotism? Many who suffered Socrates' insistence on clear thinking and accurate definitions would often object that he asked more than he answered and left men's minds frequently confused and puzzled instead of settled and sure. Socrates questioned every assumption concerning nature's phenomena as well as the beliefs of the common man, doubting what appeared to be obvious, turning his talents to ridicule cant and political arrogance. He took no fees for his lectures and attracted the loyalty and devotion of the most able young minds of his day.

Socrates was consider by those in power as intentionally offensive and disdainful, and was ultimately convicted of heresy and the corruption of Greek youth. To the very end, he argued the meaning of justice and the need for law, no less the rule of reason over power and wealth. He lived his last years in a tumultuous time during which the Athenian empire was reduced to shame and shambles. Bureaucrats and political connivers rose to power, devaluing and imprisoning the insubordinate and intellectual, and launched into an early witch hunt. Socrates became the most famous of those to suffer in this period of rapid decline and social deterioration.

It is notable that Socrates wrote down nothing tangible by himself; his thoughts and ideas come to us through recorded dialogues written by Plato, many of which likely represent Plato's own thinking in articulate and dramatic form. Satisfied to live materially poor and shabby, often barefoot and unkempt, Socrates preferred a life of thought and conversation to the physical comforts that others sought. He was not an ascetic, however, often joining those of greater wealth in many of the pleasures of a good life. Nevertheless, he was a man of moderation and control, contending that he was not wise or all-knowing, as others claimed him to be, but rather a "midwife of thought," who knew little but sought to aid others in giving birth to their own ideas. Socrates did not rely on formal lectures; he posed questions that led his students step-by-step to observe and discover ideas for themselves. To Socrates, knowledge already existed within his students; it merely needed to be brought forth through careful provocation and reasoning.

Despite the profundity of his thinking, Socrates began with the idea that human beings must take care of their souls and must purify themselves from the evil influences of their bodies. A deep believer in intelligence and reason, he asserted that a person, though moved by inner demons, could be guided through purification by self-knowledge. To him, a person with a pure soul was healthy and wise, and a person with a corporal soul was ill and ignorant. Mental symptoms arose when the originally divine soul submitted to the forces of the body: "Raving, fear, disorderly passions, folly, are due to the body." To have a pure soul required a long process of self-analysis because truth and folly were mutually exclusive: Folly must be fought with words so that the passions may be made impossible by knowledge. When man is driven by physical passions, he may seem happy, but self-analysis would convince him that his belief was far from truth. According to Socrates, ignorance was not a consequence of a lack of technical knowledge, but of a lack of knowledge about one's inner mental life. "Know thyself" was a guiding principle, and knowing that one knows was an even higher principle.

Known as **Plato (429–347 B.C.)** (meaning *broad* in Greek), a designation given him as a young wrestler, he was born in Athens to an aristocratic family of wealth and accomplishment. By happenstance, he heard Socrates speaking at a public forum and was captivated by the subtlety and range of Socrates' ideas, as well as by the philosopher's calm serenity and manner. He immediately cast aside his aspiration to be a poet, becoming instead a dedicated student of philosophy, serious in manner, ultimately drafting much of Socrates' discourse and colloquies from which others could learn.

Although Socrates was the master teacher, ambling from one marketplace and assembly hall in Athens to another, stirring the "unwashed" and conscienceless masses in a self-deprecatory manner that Socrates himself referred to as being a "gadfly," Plato originally knew him in childhood as a friend of his family. Some spoke of the young Plato as little more than a stenographer with a highly attuned memory, given that Plato had transcribed in his *dialogues* much of Socrates' words. In time, however, it became clear that Plato was a genius of the first order and an innovative thinker in his own right.

Following Socrates' death, Plato, age 28, abruptly left Athens to avoid a concurrent and serious political upheaval, traveling to study with other philosophers throughout the Mediterranean. On his return to Athens years later at the age of 40, authorities quickly seized him as a threat to the dictator then controlling the city. Ultimately freed through a generous ransom payment, he set out to establish a teaching academy in 387 B.C.; for over 40 years he headed this distinguished intellectual center of Grecian philosophy.

Despite undoubted brilliance, many have difficulty in understanding some of Plato's writings owing to his dexterous mix of philosophical ideas and poetic drama. One cannot always tell in which mode Plato is speaking, whether literally or metaphorically, whether addressing a topic in earnest or in jest. This blend of style and mode can leave readers baffled, for Plato was often circuitous and spoke in parables. Many passages in his writings are playful and allegorical, at times relevant only to the circumstances of his society or to fanciful representations of complex ideas.

Plato

Plato spoke of the human characteristics of those engaged in political events as flowing from three main sources: desire, emotion, and knowledge. As he phrased it, desire is centered in the loins: It is a fundamentally sexual reservoir of bursting energy. Emotion is centered in the heart: It comprises the resonance of experience as expressed in the flow and the force of blood. Knowledge is centered in the head: It serves as the pilot and eye of the soul. In characterizing the behavior of men, he spoke of some as the embodiment of desire: restless and acquisitive souls, absorbed in material quarrels and quests; they are the men who manipulate and dominate industry. Those driven by emotion possess the temple of courage: They are pugnacious rather than acquisitive, achieving pride in power instead of possession. Those who delight in knowledge and understanding yearn not for goods, nor for victory. They seek the haven of a quiet clarity in secluded thought and truth; they are persons of wisdom who often stand aside and are unused by the world of action, power, and industry.

Plato argued for a humane approach to the mentally ill and emphasized the role of sociocultural factors in creating them. However, and despite his admiration for Socrates, he failed to transcend the dominant spiritual mythologies of his time and promulgated the view that many disorders were best attributed to and treated by divine intervention. Plato did emulate Socrates in asking his students to look beneath the surface of things, to ferret out their inner essences, not their surface expressions. To Plato, the world of sensations was a world of flickering shadows, of momentary impressions instead of the undergirding fundamentals he considered essential to true understanding. Central also to this thesis was the view that knowledge would increase, not only by the depth of reasoning, but also by the use of measurement gauges and quantification. Toward this end, he sought to use mathematical principles to characterize the objective world. What was crucial to both him and Socrates was *not* that which can be immediately seen, but the elements that underlie these manifestations.

Both Socrates and Plato asserted that the manifest symptomatic picture (e.g., Axis I) of a disorder should be differentiated from the personologic system that undergirds it (e.g., Axis II). Perhaps influenced by his older contemporary Hippocrates, Plato cautioned the physician against a tendency to address only the "diseased part" instead of the patient as a whole, foreshadowing the modern approach of treating the whole patient. He stated this view as follows:

> I dare say that you have heard eminent physicians say to a patient who comes to them with bad eyes, that they cannot cure his eyes by themselves, but that if his eyes are to be cured, his head must be treated; and then again they say that to think of curing the head alone, and not the rest of the body also, is the height of folly. And arguing in this way, they apply their methods to the whole body, and try to treat and heal the whole and the part together.

Several themes relevant to the mind and its difficulties characterize Plato's work: (1) Powerful emotional forces come to the foreground and overwhelm the everyday behavior that typifies a person's life; (2) conflicts exist between different components of the psyche, recognizing thereby the personal discord that often arises between an individual's rational side, that which is desired, and the surge of emotional feelings; (3) mental disorders do not result from simple ignorance, but from irrational superstitions and erroneous beliefs. To Plato, all humans were partly animal-like; hence, all humans acted irrationally at times, some more, some less. Evidence for these conclusions could be seen, according to Plato, in dreams where bizarre events invariably occur and unnatural connections among thoughts and images are dominant.

Not to be overlooked was his contention that therapeutic efforts could modify any and all forms of mental illness. For Plato, educational procedures could dispel ignorance and uncover truth through the application of fundamental principles. No less important in therapy was Plato's use of a dialectical model to change a patient's cognitions and belief systems. In this way, Plato's philosophy provided a methodology for engaging in therapy, essentially the application of rational discussions to modify faulty cognitions (shades of contemporary cognitive therapies!).

Plato had many distinguished students; the most eminent of them was **Aristotle (384–322 B.C.).** Though his student for over 20 years, Aristotle turned sharply away from Plato and toward matters more realistic and tangible than abstract and idealistic. Some would say that Aristotle provided history's first integrated and systematic account, not only of psychological matters, but of astronomy, physics, religion, and politics. This last of the great philosophers of the fourth century B.C., Aristotle was more scientist than philosopher. He gave special attention to the need for experimental verification and sensory-based observable data.

Although questions have arisen concerning his participation in Plato's Academy, there is evidence that he entered the school at 17, and remained there until his late 30s. These are likely to have been very happy years, brilliant pupils guided by an incomparable teacher walking in the gardens of philosophy. Though Aristotle and Plato were many years apart in age, they both were geniuses in their time. And, like many geniuses who have sought to enlighten each other, their interactions were not as harmonious as one might wish or think. Plato recognized the greatness of his new pupil from the "barbarian North" and spoke of him to many at the Academy as intelligence personified. What funds Aristotle had, he spent lavishly in collecting numerous manuscripts in a vast personal library that served as a foundation for scholarship by many others of his day.

Actually, little is known of Aristotle during his years at the Academy. In personal bearing he was seen as a handsome, bearded man inclined toward elegant dress and manners. Spoken of as kindly and warm, he was a person of great popularity among his peers. Distressed that he was passed over as the successor to Plato on his death, Aristotle left Athens and wandered for years, serving as a tutor and advisor to many of the leaders of the Mediterranean nations. At 53, he returned to Athens but was again denied the leadership of the Academy, at which point he established a rival institution, which he designated as the Lyceum.

In contrast to Plato's Academy, where he obtained his own training, the Lyceum focused on biology and the natural sciences instead of on mathematics and political philosophy. To provide a foundation for his own speculative ideas, Aristotle drew on the immense botanical and zoological material that Alexander the Great had earlier instructed his hunters, gamekeepers, gardeners, and fishermen to bring to Greece from every region he had conquered. This vast collection provided Aristotle with the resources from which he built the biological sciences.

Aristotle was the first of the major philosophers to take an inductive and empirical approach in his writings. He was interested in the concrete observables of experience as registered through the senses. Although he admired the abstract rationalism of Plato, he was much more disposed to deal with the tangible world than with high-order abstractions or broad principles. To him, data should be grounded in empirical observables to minimize the risk of subjective misinterpretations. Despite these reservations, Aristotle believed that thought transcended the sensory realm. As he saw it, imagination could create thoughts of a higher order of abstraction than could sensations themselves.

Yet, Aristotle was not successful in bringing all matters within his purview. Despite growing evidence that the brain was the center of thought and emotion,

Aristotle retained the erroneous belief that the heart served as the seat of these psychological experiences. He made keen and significant observations, however, in recognizing the psychological significance of cognitive processes, dreams, and emotional catharses. It was Aristotle who said that events, objects, and people were linked by their relative similarity or their relative difference from one another. To Aristotle, things became associated if they occurred together; in this he was a forerunner of the associationist school of the eighteenth and nineteenth centuries. Aristotle viewed dreams to be afterimages of the activities of the preceding day. Although he recognized that dreams might fulfill a biological function, he judged the content of dreams to be ideal gauges of potential pathology. He had a specific interest in how physical diagnoses could be deduced from dream content.

As just noted, and unlike Plato, who emphasized the key role of the brain in mental life, Aristotle did not attribute any psychological function to this key organ. As he stated: "The brain is a residue lacking any sensitive faculty." The organ of mental life, according to Aristotle, was the heart, where all bodily sensations ultimately arrived. To him, the heart varied in its "natural heat" and served as the nucleus of the soul and of the *sensus communis*, the organ that integrated all perceptions. Aristotle asserted that heat provided the energy for the soul, and the sensus communis was its instrument. Sensory events that altered the level of natural heat could set off a mental reflex and produce a disordered symptom. Modifications in heat were the core source of Aristotle's view of psychic pathology. Wine, mandrake, and poppy juice could bring on heated blood, resulting in mental confusion; similarly, if the heart became

Aristotle

excessively cool, torpor or melancholy ensued. The brain could play a minor or secondary role in psychic life by facilitating heat homeostasis around the heart.

Aristotle's scope was exceptionally broad and inventive. It was he who wrote most perceptively of the intellectual and motivational features of the mind from the viewpoint of a natural scientist. Thus, in what might be termed a psychobiological theory, he outlined the basics of human perception and rational thought, stressing the importance and validity of sense impressions for an objective form of experimental study. Along the same lines, Aristotle articulated a series of proposals about the nature of learning, a model based on the principles of association and reinforced by what we have come to term the pleasure principle. Similarly, he emphasized the importance that early experience and education played in acquiring skills, and the role of habit and practice in forming psychological attitudes. To him, the processes of development were key themes in understanding human behavior.

When Aristotle left Athens in the year 322 B.C., following the death of Alexander the Great, he arranged to have his associate **Theophrastus (371–286 B.C.)** succeed him as head of the Lyceum. Shortly thereafter, Aristotle, alone and despondent over the turn of political events in Athens, died in exile. Theophrastus was only a decade younger than Aristotle and had come to Athens to study with Plato. He and Aristotle had been friends, joined together in their travels and in their study of nature. Theophrastus remained head of the Lyceum for some 30 years. Perhaps most significant is the attention Theophrastus paid to the study of botany, establishing him as the true founder of that science, just as Aristotle's works established the field of zoology.

Theophrastus made Aristotle's ideas more comprehensive and widespread. In matters of psychic pathology, he wrote on what became known in the nineteenth century as *neurasthenia,* which he characterized as a morbid group of symptoms composed of "unpleasant sensations in the body, tiredness, and depression with a chronic course." Among his botanical discoveries, he identified an herb ostensibly successful in stimulating "erotic potency." A lover of animals, he strongly condemned vivisection and the use of animals as sacrificial gifts to the gods. As did Aristotle, he anticipated the physiognomic ideas of later centuries, suggesting that correlations could be found between human facial features and the emotional dispositions of similarly appearing animals.

A prolific and sophisticated thinker, Theophrastus wrote no less than 220 treatises on different topics. Although this diversity of work was substantial, he became best known for a secondary aspect of his career, the writing of personality sketches he called "characters." Each of these portrayals emphasized one or another psychological trait, providing a vignette of various personality types (e.g., the flatterers, the garrulous, the penurious, the tactless, the boors, the surly).

Whether these portrayals were penetrating or poignant, Theophrastus (as well as later novelists) was free to write about his subject without the constraints of psychological or scientific caution. Lively and spirited characterizations most assuredly captured the interest of many, but they often misled the reader about the true complexities of natural personality patterns. That the facile wordplay of "literary characterology" is frequently insubstantial may be seen in the following comment by Gordon Allport in the 1930s:

> One of his characters may have "menial blood in his veins," another "a weak chin." A hand may possess "a wonderfully cruel greed" and a blond head "radiate fickleness." Such undisciplined metaphors give cadence and inspire a kind of bland credulity, but for science they are mere idle phrases. (1937, p. 62)

It is of great interest to recognize that writers of antiquity, born ages and oceans apart, describe persons frequently found in modern societies; the very portrayals sketched by Theophrastus and others can be identified as akin to those seen in everyday twenty-first century America. Nevertheless, portrayals of Theophrastus fail to encompass many variations of character seen today. Moreover, innumerable styles and disorders may be formulated on the basis of sound scientific and theoretical grounds (Millon & Davis, 1996).

Theophrastus was successful in the first 20 years of his leadership of the Lyceum, but his work was associated with a gradual erosion and deterioration in Greek philosophy. This appears to have been a consequence of the emphasis the Lyceum brought to solve practical rather than fundamental matters. The Lyceum stressed issues such as how to make life more joyful or how to enhance one's personal gains in commerce, reducing interest in the pursuit of knowledge for its own sake.

Emerging Roman Medicine

Although the beginning and ending of the Roman period cannot be sharply demarcated, it basically spanned twelve centuries, from the seventh century B.C. to the fifth century A.D., when the last of the major Roman emperors was deposed. As a formal organization, the Roman Republic dates from the fifth century B.C. to the third century A.D. In its greatest period of power and influence, the empire included all the countries bordering on the Mediterranean Sea, extending to western portions of Spain and as far east as the Persian Gulf. Northward, it included much of present-day England; its southern sphere encompassed the countries of North Africa, extending eastward to Egypt.

Romans were intensely practical, having little interest in the theoretical issues that had enticed the Greeks. Their intellectual leaders were primarily engineers and architects, who covered the hills of Rome and its surroundings with impressive buildings, roads, and aqueducts. The Romans did have a particular interest in law for the maintenance of social order and for military conquests. Although many were acquainted with the ideas of Greek science, few advanced it or explored its philosophical principles. What little there was of Roman philosophy—as represented by Stoicism and Epicurism—was oriented toward providing a way for its subjects to avoid the evils of the everyday world. Nevertheless, a small number of physician-philosophers brought forward ideas the Greeks had developed some centuries earlier. As stated by Bertrand Russell (1945), "The Romans invented no art forms, constructed no original system of philosophy, and made no scientific discoveries. They made good roads, systematic legal codes, and efficient armies; for the rest, they looked to Greece" (p. 278). For example, the prevalent belief in animistic spirits and divine interventions was gradually replaced by the distinctly naturalistic views of Hippocrates.

The more cultured classes of Rome were determined to eliminate magic and superstition in considering psychic processes. A mechanistic conception of mental disorders came to the foreground; it was fundamentally materialistic and opposed to all transcendental mythologies, which were regarded as superstitious beliefs that originated from fear and ignorance. Mental disorders were caused not by the action of mysterious forces, nor were they a product of bio-humoral movements or conflicts, but by the periodic enlargement or excessive tightening of the pores in the brain. In this corpuscular hypothesis, a derivative of the atomistic notions of Democritus of Greece, the task of the mental healer was to confirm and normalize the diameter of the pores. In certain cases, the mentally ill were seen as apathetic, fearful, and in a depressed mood, by what was called a *laxum* state. Others presented an excited, delirious, and aggressive appearance; they were in a *strictum* state. If both sets of these symptoms occurred, there was a *mixtum* state.

Although the first major Roman physician/theorist, **Asclepiades (171–110 B.C.),** was of Greek extraction, he was unable initially to practice in Rome because of the prejudice against Greek doctors. Hailed, however, after discovering that a corpse was revivable, he was permitted to practice and soon became known as a miracle physician. Despite his Greek origins, he rejected the humoral concepts of Hippocrates, but vigorously espoused the wisdom of naturalistic diagnosis and humane treatment. Further, Asclepiades stressed environmental influences and is credited as being the first to distinguish among hallucinations, delusions, and illusions, as well as to subdivide disorders into acute and chronic. Not only was he ingenious in devising methods of relaxing his patients, but his observations of the effects of bloodletting, mechanical restraints, and dungeons led him to openly and emphatically oppose them.

Asclepiades brought order and logic to the atomistic or corpuscular theory of his day, uniting its incidental fragments and forming a systematic methodology for curing the mentally disabled with an optimistic and daring approach. Based on meticulous clinical observation, he sought to achieve therapies that were joyful and were carried out quickly and well. To him, the symptoms of mental disorder stemmed from organic processes connected exclusively with the corpuscles which, when clogged and irritating to the brain, could produce severe psychic aberrations. The *canalicula* of the nervous system could be tightened or dilated by such emotions as anger and fear, or by such toxic agents as alcohol and opium. Some foreign substances could obstruct the nerves because they tightened the ducts; others dilated them. If the canaliculas was enlarged, the corpuscles could separate and spread to diffuse throughout the body, producing mental diseases. Convinced of the rationality of his corpuscular thesis, Asclepiades outlined two major disease entities: *phrenitis* and *catatonia*. Phrenitis stemmed from a *strictura* of the meninges producing a turbulent insanity displayed in delirium, agitation, and hallucinations. The rigid variant, catatonia, was evident in muscle contraction and motor negativism derived from a stricture of all the body's atoms.

Asclepiades objected intensely to physical bleeding, a common mental treatment during the early Roman period. To him, it was a form of strangulation that he said may have been appropriate for the Greeks of Athens, but would be destructive in Rome because Romans were already devastated as a result of their degenerate lifestyles. From a humanistic perspective, he considered cells and dungeons for the mentally disabled to be an abomination. These dark and terror-producing environments were scandalous, and he argued vigorously for having patients live in settings that were well-lit, pleasing, and comfortable. Although Asclepiades was certainly an innovator in the humane treatment of patients, he was also one of the first investigators to argue that biological and chemically based treatments could be exceptionally beneficial, a position that came to pass some two thousand years later.

Although a Roman, **Cicero (103–43 B.C.)** had been deeply immersed in Greek learning and believed that the Greeks provided true insight into the nature of mental disorders, especially in what we call psychopathic or antisocial personalities. He described these persons as possessing such features as being "readily carried away by gain and pleasurable lust." Notable in Cicero's writings was the recommendation that each patient draw strength from within himself; in effect, to become his own physician. Unlike many who preceded him, Cicero concluded that the senses did not distort life's perceptions, but that inner psychic forces interpreted these sensations in either a problematic or a helpful way.

Of special interest was Cicero's observation that physical illnesses often result from intense or conflicting emotions. He anticipated by over 2,000 years what has become known as the *psychosomatic* conception of bodily ailments. Cicero's approach to therapy emphasized controlling emotions by reasoning and relaxation. In accord with our current popular cognitive viewpoint, he sought to eradicate errors in thinking through instruction and thereby initiate more accurate thoughts.

It was **Celsus (15 B.C.–A.D. 30)** who reorganized the basic concepts of Hippocrates into distinct groups of disease entities. Among his original contributions to Hippocratic theory was the view that mental disorders pervaded all of an individual's functioning, not just one organ. His regressive therapeutic suggestions, however—starvation, intimidation, and bloodletting—overshadowed this enlightened contribution.

Celsus was the first Roman scholar to detail a philological translation between Greek and Latin medical terms. His writing style was guided toward practical considerations and informed by common sense. He sought to synthesize the practical orientation of Rome with the theoretical tradition of the Hellenistic schools of thought. He carried out this effort in six large volumes that presented alternative philosophies of medicine in a clear, thorough way. Commenting on the culture of his time, he spoke of the more civilized segment of his society as being more readily subject to illness and disease owing to their indolence and lust. He stated that the peasant and agricultural elements of society did not need a complex medical science because their daily activities were harmonious with nature's laws. City life and mercantile society pulled men away from natural biological homeostasis and toward activities that were the natural enemies of the body and soul.

Aretaeus (30–90) was a follower of the vitalist school of thought that adopted the concept of *pneuma,* the natural or animal spirit, the physical embodiment of the soul. He was little known in his time and rarely quoted by fellow Roman scholars, probably because his works were written in the Ionic dialect instead of in Latin or Greek. Further, his vitalistic philosophy based on the fluidity of the soul's nature, and adopted by Galen a century later, rivaled the more atomistic or solidistic corpuscular theory of his contemporary Roman thinkers. Scarcely familiar with the Greek language and its medical philosophies, Aretaeus was a born clinician who was retained as a physician for the ruling Roman classes.

According to Aretaeus, the vicissitudes of the soul served as the basis of psychic disturbances. The interconnecting linkages between solid organs, the humors, and the pneuma generated all forms of mental aberration. Anger and rage stirred the yellow bile, thereby warming the pneuma and increasing brain temperature, which resulted in irritability and excitability. Conversely, fear and oppression stirred black bile, augmenting its concentration in the blood, leading to a cold pneuma and a consequent melancholy.

Disturbances of consciousness usually resulted from the sudden diminishing of pneuma's strength around the heart. His descriptions of epilepsy were notably impressive. Aretaeus spoke of its premonitory symptoms such as vertigo and nausea, the perception of sparks and colors, as well as of harsh noises or nauseating smells. Aretaeus described the origins and characteristics of fanaticism and formulated a primitive psychosomatic hypothesis in stating that emotions could produce problematic effects on humoral metabolism, noting, "The black bile may be stirred by dismay and immoderate anger." Similarly, he formulated what we speak of as cyclothymia in describing the alternation of depression with phases of mania. He stated, "Some patients after being melancholic have fits of mania . . . so that mania is like a variety of melancholy." In discussing the intermittent character of mania, he recognized its several variants, speaking of one type as arising in subjects "whose personality is characterized by gayness, activity, superficiality, and childishness." Other types of mania were more expansive in which the patient "feels great and inspired. Still others become insensitive . . . and spend their lives like brutes."

Perceptive observations by Aretaeus strengthened the notion that mental disorders were exaggerated normal processes. He asserted that a direct connection existed between an individual's normal characteristics of personality and the expression of the symptom disorder he displayed when afflicted. His insightful differentiation of disorders according to symptom constellations (i.e., syndromes) was a striking achievement for his day.

Although Hippocrates may have been the first to provide a medical description of depression, it was Aretaeus who presented a complete and modern portrayal of the disorder. Moreover, Aretaeus proposed that melancholia was best attributed to psychological causes having nothing to do with bile or other bodily humors. He may have been the first to recognize the covariation between manic behaviors and depressive moods, antedating the views of many clinical observers in the sixteenth and seventeenth centuries. Aretaeus wrote:

> The characteristic appearances, then, are not obscure; for the patients are dull or stern, dejected or unreasonably torpid, without any manifest cause: such is the commencement of melancholy. And they also become peevish, dispirited, sleepless and start up from a disturbed sleep. . . . But if the illness becomes more urgent, hatred, avoidance of the haunts of men, vain lamentations are seen; they complain of life and desire to die.

Aretaeus was also a major contributor to the humanistic school of thought in early Rome. Most notably, he introduced long-term follow-up studies of patients. He tracked their lifetime course, their periodic disease manifestations, and their return to a more normal pattern of behavior, thereby anticipating the authoritative writings of Emil Kraepelin, who recognized that the course of an illness is a key factor in discriminating a specific disorder from others of comparable appearance. Aretaeus seriously studied the sequence and descriptive characteristics of his patients, contending that a clear demarcation could be made between the basic personality disposition of a patient and the form in which a symptomatic and transient disorder manifested itself periodically.

No less important was Aretaeus's specification of the premorbid condition of patients, viewing them as a form of vulnerability or susceptibility to several clinical syndromes. As Aretaeus phrased this, he found that persons disposed to mania are characteristically "irritable, violent, easily given to joy, and have a spirit for pleasantry or childish things." By contrast, those prone to depression and melancholia were characteristically "gloomy and sad often realistic yet prone to unhappiness." In this matter, Aretaeus elaborated those essentially normal traits that make an individual susceptible to a clinical state. As Zilboorg and Henry (1941) have noted, the melancholia of Aretaeus is still observed in our time, although under different psychiatric labels. Owing to his observation of patients over extended periods, Aretaeus proposed a series of predictions as to the general outcome of different mental conditions. More than other physicians of his day, Aretaeus not only described psychological conditions with keen sensitivity and humane understanding but, in a spirit more akin to contemporary scientific work, sought to compare clinical syndromes and illuminate ways in which they could be differentiated.

The influential practitioner **Soranus (98–135)** based much of his teachings in accord with those of Celsus and Aretaeus. Melancholia was viewed as an excess of black bile; hysteria was a disorder of the uterus; phrenitis was a feverish disease related to that part of mind located in the diaphragm (*phren*); hypochondriasis was attributed to the hypochondrium.

As with Aretaeus, he espoused a humanitarian point of view, a position held by few Roman philosopher/physicians of his day. In many ways, he laid the groundwork for ideas carried out some 15 centuries later by Pinel, Tuke, and Dix. Most significant in Soranus's writings was his critical review of the harsh and mean-spirited behavioral controls that his fellow Romans employed. The abuse of the mentally disordered aroused great sorrow and discontent in Soranus. As an alternative, he outlined a convincing number of techniques noted by therapeutic kindness and generosity. He asked his peers to remember who was ill; physicians should not view their patients as disagreeable persons who offended their self-image. Soranus went into extraordinary detail regarding the treatment of the mentally ill. To him, no effort was to be spared in ministering to their comfort and well-being. Although he recognized that restraints might be called for, he implored his medical colleagues to use bands that are "soft and of delicate texture" so that the body's joints would be carefully protected against physical harm.

In accord with his adherence to the corpuscular theory of his day, Soranus believed that the mind's functioning was based on the harmonious equilibrium of *leptomeres,* or organic atoms, and the corresponding diameter of the canalicula in which they moved. When the speed of the corpuscles or the diameter of the pores increased or decreased, it created depression, hysteria, or delirium.

Soranus was among the very first who considered culture as a factor in both instigating and treating mental patients. For example, he spelled out in detail what these patients should read during their stay in the hospitals of the day; thus, a laborer should be engaged in discussions about field cultivation and a sailor might be involved in discussions of navigational issues. Though few scientific notions characterized the contributions of Soranus, his deep and genuine humanitarian outlook led him to encourage his fellow physicians to take a caring and sympathetic attitude toward those whose mental plight was deeply painful. This attitude provided a new and generous note in Roman care.

Claudius Galenus [Galen] (131–201) was the last major contributor to adopt a psychological perspective in Rome. He preserved much of earlier medical knowledge, yet generated significant new themes of his own. Galen lived more than 600 years after the birth of Hippocrates. A Greek subject of the Roman Empire, he was born in Asia Minor about 131 A.D. During his mature years, numerous radical political and cultural changes took place in Rome.

Concurrent with the Patristic period, to be described later, as the church fathers sought to integrate pagan philosophies and barbarian rituals into Christian teaching, Galen and his medical associates set out to synthesize primitive

Claudius Galenus Galen

conceptions of disease with then-modern methods of curing the sick. Following the ideas of Hippocrates, he stressed the importance of observation and the systematic evaluation of medical procedures, arguing against untested primitive and philosophical hypotheses in favor of those based on empirical test. As a follower of Aristotle, as well as Hippocrates, Galen emphasized the data of experience instead of logical hypotheses that were devoid of factual evidence. He doubted that environmental and psychological factors could affect the course of human disease. Although Galen avoided philosophical themes concerning the nature of illness, he nevertheless proposed a principle termed *spiritus anima,* in which he asserted that humans possessed an extra-physical life-giving force, a thesis based on his efforts to distinguish organic from inorganic matter.

Galen was viewed as the most cultivated and intelligent scholar of Roman medicine. Expert in medicine, neurology, and mental illness, Galen left a vast body of original works in anatomy and neurophysiology as well. He sought to construct a unified model of all theoretical, clinical, and experimental data from a broad global perspective. Galen's father, Nicon, was an influential senator in the Roman kingdom, considered to be "a calm and just character." By contrast, his mother was an irritable and depressive woman. He was encouraged by his father to study the natural sciences, as well as medicine and philosophy. At 16, he began his medical studies, performing highly technical anatomical research. He went overseas to study neurophysiology and experimental neurology. An impulsive man, highly intelligent but a polemicist, he pursued a wide range of interests from the philosophical and historical to the moral and neurological. He also sought to systematically arrange the pharmacology of his time. Arriving in Rome at the age of 31, he soon became the family physician of the emperor and the cultivated upper classes.

Galen was a relatively free spirit, uncontrolled by the doctrines of various religio-theological viewpoints of his period. He thought of himself as a creative and courageous person; in fact, his colleagues viewed him as impetuous and frequently querulous, a man of tremendous ambition who was known for his excess rhetorical habits. Nevertheless, he reconciled disparate viewpoints concerning mental disorders. He accumulated and coordinated all the medical knowledge that his many Greek and Roman predecessors had proposed. His keen observations and astute interpretations enriched this information.

Galen's conception of psychic pathology was based on the physiology of the central nervous system. He viewed clinical symptoms to be a sign of dysfunctioning neurological structures and characterized mental diseases as "a concourse of symptoms," among which a specifically pathognomonic one could be isolated. According to his organic-functional approach, mental symptoms originated from the pathogenic action of a toxic, humoral, vaporous, febrile, or emotional factor that impacted the brain from the body and then altered certain of its psychic functions. Consonant with the beliefs of his time, Galen believed that the activities of the mind were prompted by animal spirits that carried out both voluntary and involuntary actions. Galen divided these animalistic spirits (pneuma) into two groups: those that controlled sensory perceptions and motility, whose damaging effects would cause neurological symptoms; and those that had a more directive function such as coordinating and organizing imagination, reason, and memory. To him, most psychiatric symptomatology stemmed from alterations of the second group of functions.

Broadly eclectic in his rationale, Galen encompassed a taxonomy that included most contemporary psychiatric disorders. He spoke of what we would call dysthymic syndromes based on humoral grounds; for example, black bile generated melancholia, yellow bile caused mania. He wrote of melancholy as:

> An unnatural dread . . . which is not born from a fault of the heart or from habit . . . but rather from an intemperance of the brain . . . intoxicated by the black bile . . . a humour which is thus the efficient cause of this illness . . . (feeling) as though he were carrying the whole world over his shoulders like Atlas.

Sensitive to the very forms in which melancholy was displayed, he wrote:

> Some melancholics want to die . . . others are afraid of death . . . some think they are hated by the gods . . . others are convinced that they have been turned into animals . . . others into glass objects . . . some love solitude . . . others yet have thousands of ideas and they are afraid even of being touched.

He spoke of the many types of depression, from the anxious to the delirious to the obsessive to those with depersonalization and feelings of guilt. The melancholic was abulic, lacking in vitality, especially in the morning; he woke up "not rested and refreshed" but was, without reason, "tired and lazy."

In describing catatonic psychosis, Galen suggested a paralysis of the animal spirits in which the imaginative faculty was "blocked or incomplete." As far as the syndrome of hysteria was concerned, he differed strongly with Hippocrates' uterocentric view. Galen asserted that hysteria, on the basis of his own clinical examinations, could not be a disease that reflected the uterus "wandering agitated in the body." As he saw it, the toxic action of vapors that formed in the normal uterus and vagina provoked hysterical symptoms; the toxicity arose from the stagnation of semen owing to a lack of sufficient sexual intercourse. The disease therefore signified a lack of sexual hygiene.

Galen's stature grew over the next millennium, so much so that his views were thought to be sacrosanct. His writings were summarized and commented on by many lesser physicians, most of whom were recognized as being wrongheaded, such that their books were often referred to as "wretched treatises." Some of these post-Galen compilations were not based on his work at all, but dishonestly carried his name for its ability to promote the sale of untenable or alien ideas. Although many of his notions were diluted by the passage of time, or refuted by empirical knowledge, his vast contributions must be considered significant in that no other figure in history was destined to exercise so extended an influence on the course of medicine.

Preceding St. Augustine and following Galen, **Aurelianus (255–320)** sought to extend the Hippocratic system; he translated his work into Latin and it remained in circulation, along with compilations by Galen, for centuries thereafter. Although dormant through the oppressive period of medieval demonology, humoral concepts of Hippocrates were revived anew with the Renaissance.

The concepts of Aurelianus, developed in eight well-regarded books, were a model of the atomistic proposals of Leucippus and Democritus. Democritus posited that the corporal components of the organism were composed of infinitesimal atomic structures. This view contrasted with those of the humors, the more fluid elements of the body formulated by Empedocles and employed by Hippocrates in his clinical formulations. The atomistic view also differed from the pneumatic model of vitalistic spirits with its concept of animistic vapors diffused throughout the body, a formulation also used by Galen in his conceptions of mental disorders.

Psychic symptoms for Aurelianus were based on problematic mechanical structurings instead of imbalances of fluid humors or vaporous animal spirits. Rekindling an earlier interest in the disorder catatonia, Aurelianus spoke of the body's tendency to assume unusual rigid positions as stemming from the tightening of the cerebral canalicula which led, in turn, to the suffocation of psychic life. Opposite that of catatonia were the manias, spoken of as *constrictio spiriti*. For catatonias, Aurelianus recommended therapies such as rubdowns and the wearing of warm woolen clothes as well as periodic enemas and force-feedings. For the manias, treatment included relaxing walks, and cucurites (warm mud-laden towels) placed on the head to "re-corporize the atoms."

The atomists did not use the drugs of the time because they judged that diets, massages, and baths better influenced the pathological structures of the mind. Rubdowns with cold oils, the inhalation of vile substances such as vinegar, bloodletting, and other purgatives were intended to reestablish a harmonious order of the atomic corpuscles.

Aurelianus's suggestions reflected a regressive transition from the humanism that had come to characterize early Greece and Galen's Rome. A strong effort was made to revive a supernatural belief system for understanding life's matters. This was consistent with the spirit of the time and demonstrated how much psychological medicine was diluted during the early Patristic period. Aurelianus even warned others against placing their fate in a philosophical approach to the cure of madness; he stated that too much thought might itself be a cause of madness. Specifying the causes of mental disorder, Aurelianus suggested head trauma; exposure to bright sunlight; the abuse of wine; and too much love for philosophy, glory, or money.

Formative Christian Thought

Later in Roman history, there emerged an organized church theology known as Christianity, including faith healing, magic, and superstition. Referred to as the Patristic period, the Church of Rome's early doctrine became the dominant approach to thought, medicine, and mental healing in the Western world until the seventeenth century. Most of the populace remained illiterate during this period. Education was religious, otherwise inchoate and of dubious value. The idea of a scientific basis for understanding mental disorders barely appeared on the scene. Faith was the all-powerful guide.

As the Roman Empire declined in its course of decay, diminution, and debauchery in the early centuries of the first millennium, two opposing solutions to life emerged. The first reflected a general mood of stoic resignation, indifference, and withdrawal. The second was represented by the rise of Christianity; the emergence of religious philosophies; and the belief, especially for the poor and weary peasantry, that there was a life eternal, a heavenly future that would transcend the miseries of daily life. A simple and undogmatic series of principles asserting that there was one God, that man was made to serve Him and, thereby, to live eternally in His blessed light drew the attention and strengthened the hopes of "plain folk." In its brief and simple declarations, the founders of the Roman Church provided an alternative to stoic resignation and skeptical indifference, a sinister world dominated by dreadful tyrants and abhorrent overseers. In its stead, Christianity offered believers brotherhood and an eternal life—no longer to suffer hunger, plague, and warfare, no longer to grovel in oppression and exile—faith would provide ultimate and secure redemption.

Under the leadership of the Roman Church, faith became a ubiquitous force, a rationale for how people became mentally disturbed and what should be done to cure them. For these purposes, the Church exacted a price of firm if not absolute obedience. Though Church leaders may have believed in the wisdom of faith to guide and influence the population, less reputable others took advantage of religious authority and status.

During the first two to three centuries A.D., a separation was made between psychologically normal individuals, who may have doubted the dogma of the Roman Church's ideology, and those whose peculiar beliefs arose, not out of opposition, but out of a mental affliction. Nevertheless, both groups were considered guilty of heresy and subjected to punishment. In a similarly irrational twist, others' implausible or nonsensical behavior ostensibly demonstrated their fervent adherence to religious authorities and their dogma. Such persons were venerated. The works of Aristotle and other Greek philosophers soon were condemned.

In the third century, Christianity led physicians such as Aurelianus to assume a moralistic and judgmental approach to psychic pathology. Unable to escape the growing spirit of superstition, he proposed that mental cases were definitely the product of mystical events that could not be understood in the natural world. More seriously, he adopted the ancient belief that demons often appear under the guise of confused men, and it was the job of physicians to identify and to eliminate them. In this and other similar matters, he laid the groundwork with St. Augustine for a return to the age of supernaturalism and superstitions. Along with Augustine, he was nevertheless admired until the close of the seventeenth century.

Aurelius Augustine (354–430) was a key figure in the transition from early Roman thought to the Middle Ages. Better known as St. Augustine, we can see in his readings an effort to synthesize the Greek and the new Christian perspective on mental maladies. Perhaps the most influential philosopher of his time, Augustine set the foundation and tone of Christian intellectual life for centuries to come. To him, all knowledge was based on the belief that only God can provide the ultimate truth, and that to know God is the ultimate goal. To think otherwise, as Augustine averred, would not only be vain, but would assuredly lead to error and corruption. Individuals, as children of God, would in their faith begin to understand the very nature of life, and thereby would be able to lead a life of grace and honor. These beliefs were religious rather than philosophical or medical, because a failure to assert them not only would lead to unhappiness, but would be a sin that called for retribution.

During Augustine's early education, he was enthralled with the ideas of Plato and sought to incorporate much of the great philosopher's ideas into Christian doctrine. Eager to learn and widely read, he sought out the views of numerous pagan philosophers. These readings stirred him deeply and generated increasing feelings of guilt over his wasteful lifestyle while awakening his awareness of the deterioration of the world in which he lived. Wandering in Africa, pursuing a life of celibacy and poverty, he gradually turned to the priesthood and to a quiet and withdrawn life of study and reflection. Owing to his genuine convictions and high intelligence, he was seduced into becoming a bishop at a time when Rome was overrun by anti-Christian vagabonds and warriors. Nevertheless, Augustine became a leading authority on doctrinal matters within the Catholic Church. His writings on science, however, were unsystematic, dissonant, and conflicting; on some points they were insightful, on others, confusing. Essentially, he viewed all works of science favorably when they served his religious purposes but considered them questionable when they failed to support his theological beliefs.

The early Catholic Church took over numerous practices from former established religions, such as prayers, pilgrimages, and the practice of having confessions bound by absolute secrecy. The practice of confessions exerted a major influence in St. Augustine's important book entitled *Confessions*. It may also have helped develop later therapeutic procedures, such as those employed in psychoanalysis. Priests acquired clinical psychological knowledge and systematized it to some degree in their books on moral theology. However, the very nature of the priestly secret of confession camouflaged that knowledge into abstract and impersonal forms. Centuries later, Protestant reformers abolished compulsory confession, and in its stead established a new practice intended to "cure the soul." Ministers endowed with spiritual gifts obtained voluntary confessions of disturbing secrets from distressed congregants who felt the need to share and expunge their personal anguish. These clerics, however, maintained the tradition of secrecy.

Notable were two prime sources of information that Augustine believed would enable one to understand truth. "Revelations" from supernatural sources provided the first source; the second source was accurate reflection on one's inner experiences. He asserted that freedom of the will was the key factor in enriching one's existence. To him, *willfulness* was the dominant function of the mind, a force that undergirds and transcends all other psychological functions. The mind was also composed of self-consciousness; as he phrased it, "The mind knows that it is itself." Self-perception, however, could not provide the new knowledge; for one can know directly only the experience of one's own inner world, not that which exists beyond oneself. Augustine did allow that several components of the reflective mind can be differentiated, such as will, memory, reason, and imagination; in this regard, he formulated perhaps the first notions of what later came to be known as *faculty psychology*. Though he regarded these components as part of a unitary mind, the manner in which he spoke of each suggested that he considered them to be independent entities.

Augustine's influence was the most authoritative voice of the church for the next eight centuries. Despite his seemingly disinterested search for truth, his assertions and influence induced fear and psychic constraint, personal hesitations, and self-deprecation, all antithetical to freedom, independence, imagination, and creativity. His Patristic declarations helped rescue fifth-century Rome from nihilism and skepticism, but it led to a world of fear and trembling that ultimately brought forth a period of darkness that diminished the value of life in the here-and-now. Slowly, but implacably, Christian clerical powers grew stronger and more vengeful with predictable ferocity and condemnations. The common person of this period was faced with an ever-present struggle to follow the commands of an earthly king or those of an intangible God. Patristics forced their religious requirements into every sphere of life, reducing day-to-day experiences into acts of insignificance and triviality. Virulent anti-intellectualism grew, and the political authority of the church rendered all aspects of life not controlled by them as either suspect or invalid, leading step-by-step to the eventual abominations of the medieval period.

St. Augustine's work had a far-reaching and long-lasting impact on psychological thought prior to the Dark Ages some 800 years after his death. Despite the regressiveness of many of his proposals, the accuracy with which he articulated his findings as well as his conviction of the value of the introspective approach to mental problems indicates his key role in orienting thoughts that reached their zenith in the dreadful and egregious medieval times.

As we know through history, the great empire of Rome not only declined, but was ravaged and sacked repeatedly in the several centuries following

Augustine's death. Few people stayed on in the great city of Rome; most fled its burning ruins and rubble to distant and fortified villages. Much of what had been learned of science was lost; and the laws, manners, architecture, and art of the empire were undone or destroyed. Wandering thieves ransacked what little remained of the great Roman period; invading armies from the north and east joined in its final destruction. Several centuries passed until a new order was established. In time, the Catholic Church regained its power and rights to define and establish the laws of the land. Finally, the Inquisition, established by Pope Gregory IX in the thirteenth century, sharply curtailed all forms of dissent. Timely or not, the Great Plague ensued shortly thereafter. The massive devastation of the plague killed a large proportion of the European population. The Inquisition reached its zenith in the mid-fifteenth century; Christianity became evermore vicious and condemnatory. In the next chapter, we turn to this history, and to the horrors of the medieval era.

Luminous Muslim and Judaic Physicians

Four major medical figures from the Muslim and Judaic world of the Middle East, around the end of the first millennium B.C., are worthy of note. Each proposed helpful ideas that came to represent a fresh and innovative point of view concerning mental illness: Rhazes, Unhammad, Avicenna, and Maimonides.

Rhazes (860–930) lived during the late ninth and early tenth centuries and wrote textbooks dealing with medical, psychological, philosophical, and religious subjects. In contrast to the predominant religious orientation of Baghdad, Rhazes strongly argued against the notion of a demonological concept of disease and arbitrary authority to determine what is scientific and what is not. He attacked the superstitious religious beliefs of his contemporaries and strongly favored building a rational schema for understanding all disorders. Empirically oriented, he nonetheless subscribed to the four elements originally developed by Empedocles and Hippocrates. Especially talented in discerning the characteristics of many diseases, as well as how they might be differentiated, he also recognized the relationship between good physical hygiene and the prevalence of various diseases. Among his areas of special competence was the science of chemistry and the relationship of chemical factors to several medical conditions. He also had great interest in psychological subjects, writing on the power of social influence for undergirding therapeutic effectiveness. He also offered explanations for why people eagerly allowed quacks to seduce them instead of seeking legitimate healers. Rhazes knew that legitimate healing is often a very slow process, with few visible results evident to the public. As with the Greeks before him, he stressed how important it was to distract those with mental disorders by playing music, having them reside in beautiful environments, and providing healthful nutrition. In a hospital that he oversaw during the early ninth century, Rhazes created a separate section for the mentally ill to demonstrate that theirs was a special kind of ailment that called for a more humane sensibility than other disorders might require.

Unhammad (870–925), a contemporary of Rhazes, provided intelligent descriptions of various mental diseases. The observations he compiled of his patients resulted in a nosology that was the most complete classification of mental disorders in its day. Unhammad described nine major categories of mental disorders, which, as he saw it, included 30 different diseases. Among the categories was an excellent description of anxious and ruminative states of doubt, which correspond in our thinking today with compulsions and obsessions. Other categories of mental disease were judged by Unhammad to be degenerative; a few were associated with the involutional period of a man's life. The term used by the Greeks for mania was borrowed to describe states of abnormal excitement. According to Unhammad, another category, most closely associated with grandiose and paranoid delusions, manifested itself by the mind's tendency to magnify all matters of personal significance, often leading to actions that prove outrageous to society.

A most significant and influential philosopher and physician of the Moslem world was **Avicenna (980–1037),** often referred to as the "Galen of Islam," largely as a consequence of his vast and encyclopedic works called the *Canon of Medicine.* The Canon became *the* medical textbook chosen throughout European universities from the tenth through the fifteenth centuries. However, Avicenna was not a highly original writer, but rather was a systematizer who encompassed all knowledge from the past that related to medical events. Like Galen, Avicenna noted the important connection between intense emotions and various medical and physiological states, although he fully accepted Hippocrates' humoral explanations of temperament and mental disorder. To his credit as a sophisticated scholar of the brain, Avicenna speculated that intellectual dysfunctions were in large part a result of deficits in the brain's middle ventricle, and he asserted that the frontal areas of the brain mediated common sense and reasoning. As with many philosopher-physicians of the day, Avicenna made a serious effort to preserve Aristotelian thinking regarding the soul, and sought to integrate these with Islamic rules and law.

Perhaps the greatest philosopher-physician in the Middle Ages was a Jew by the name of Rabbi Moses Den Maimuni, also known simply as **Maimonides (1135–1204).** Central to Maimonides' philosophical writings were efforts to reconcile faith and reason, a theme that many an earlier philosopher (e.g., Aristotle) had struggled to resolve. Although under pressure from Islamic leaders to convert to Islam, Maimonides preferred to avoid the constraints of religious bigotry, leaving first for Morocco and subsequently Palestine, Alexandria, and finally Cairo. Throughout, he wrote commentaries on Jewish laws and traditions, outlining a systematic treatise on the rationale of Jewish religious beliefs. His best-known work was *A Guide to the Perplexed*, a book highly admired yet intensely attacked in Christian, Jewish, and Muslim quarters. He designed the guide for sophisticated Jews who were trapped by the intellectual tensions they experienced between the rationalism of the Greeks and the religious traditions of Jewish and Islamic law, the latter two based essentially on authority and revelation. Thus, Maimonides' work reflected his effort to legitimize reason and to show that there were alternative ways of thinking about religious convictions.

Notable among Maimonides' insights was his argument in favor of moderation between the extremes of passion versus denial:

> Good deeds are such as are equibalanced, maintaining the mean between two equally bad extremes, the too much and the too little. Virtues are psychic conditions and dispositions which are mid-way between two reprehensible extremes, one of which is characterized by an exaggeration, the other by a deficiency. Good deeds are the product of these dispositions. To illustrate, abstemiousness is a disposition which adopts a mid-course between inordinate passion and total insensibility to pleasure. Abstemiousness, then, is a proper rule of conduct, and the psychic disposition which gives rise to it is an ethical quality; but inordinate passion, the extreme of excess, and total insensibility to enjoyment, the extreme of deficiency, are both absolutely pernicious.

Maimonides was a prodigious scholar and thinker; he divided his time equally between the study and writing of his many books, the active life of a physician and advisor, and as a rabbi and intellectual leader of the Jewish community. It was as a religious philosopher and exponent of rationalism that Maimonides most profoundly influenced not only Judaism, but Islam and Christianity as well. He believed deeply in the rationality of all forms of law. From his Aristotelian frame of reference, he could not believe that God would enact irrational laws. He felt it was only the human mind that at times was too limited and, hence, could not perceive God's deeper rationality. His faith in the rational powers of the human mind led him to state that seeming inconsistencies or

Maimonides

contradictory statements in the Bible could be explained in an allegorical, instead of a literal way. From his view, revelation accommodated to reason, and not vice versa. Despite his Jewish origins and leadership, Maimonides' views were judged by some to be more Aristotelian than Mosaic in their orientation. Many saw his Guide as dangerous and heretical; Jews, Christians, and Muslims alike dismissed the book.

Comments and Reflections

What patterns, trends, and directions can we extract from this early history? For one, it is likely that the reactions of any group of naive individuals faced with mental disorder in their midst would follow a parallel course to the one recorded here. At first, such a group would react with perplexity and fear, followed shortly by efforts to avoid or eliminate the disturbing behavior. Because of their lack of knowledge, their crude efforts would fail, leading to frustration and, in turn, to anger, punitive action, and hostility. In due course, the obvious helplessness and innocence of the ill would evoke protests against harshness and cruelty. A new compassion and sympathy would arise and awaken a search for methods of humane treatment. But goodwill alone would not be sufficient to deal with the illness. Proper treatment requires knowledge, and knowledge can be derived best from systematic study and research. And so, in its course of progress, this imaginary group would move step-by-step from perplexity, fear, and cruelty, to scientific analysis and humane treatment. It is at this point that we stand in our study of mental illness today. Despite periodic regressions and fads, progress toward humanism, naturalism, and scientific empiricism has continued.

The formal structures of most early ideas of the mind and mental illness were haphazard and unsystematic; concepts were vague, and procedures for deriving empirical consequences were tenuous. Instead of presenting an orderly arrangement of ideas and propositions for deriving hypotheses, most inventive clinicians of the ancient past presented a loose connection of speculative opinions and analogies. Gifted as many of these speculations may have been, they often left their followers dazzled rather than illuminated. Ambiguous proposals in archaic and mysterious theories made it impossible to derive systematic and testable hypotheses. Many early observations and ideas were brilliant and insightful, but few could be attributed to the clarity of their principles, the precision of their concepts, or their methods of hypothesis derivation.

Despite exegetic brilliance, the Talmudic habit of intricate and abstruse argument within the early philosophical community drew us into recondite intellectual territories that only tangentially explored the impact of the many psychological and social forces generative of mental illness. Splendid though their contributions were to philosophy, many of the Greek writers we have touched on in this chapter rarely digressed to speculate about the problems of how the mind worked and why mental illness occurred. Though less labyrinthine and tortuous, the ideas of the Roman physicians were usually only descriptive and of limited therapeutic utility.

Beginning in the early twentieth century, professional philosophers became increasingly involved in issues related to what has come to be called the *philosophy of science,* However, this interest has been centered primarily on questions associated with physical science advances and not with developments in sciences concerned with human behavior. In part, this reflects that there are no broad-based and generally accepted theories in the psychosocial disciplines. As is evident throughout this book, the focus of the human sciences is highly fragmented and much too complicated and varied to lend itself to a single systematic philosophical analysis. As such, only a few philosophers of science in this past century have occupied themselves seriously with the substantive study of mental illness, nor have they contributed in any significant way to clarifying the logic of psychological and psychiatric inquiries.

To raise questions about either the validity or adequacy of one or another aspect of early philosophical approaches is not to take issue with all aspects of their formulations. Much of what was proposed concerning the nature and character of mental illness had both substantive merit and heuristic value. We should be entirely sympathetic to the creative contributions of those we have just critically examined. Much of what followed in later periods has proven to be more of an addendum than a supplantum.

2

Resuscitating and Fashioning Scientific Thinking

The enlightened ideas of Hippocrates were submerged for centuries following the death of Galen and the fall of the Roman Empire. During the thousand years of the so-called Dark Ages, superstition, demonology, and exorcism returned in full force and were intensified by sorcery and witch burning. With few dissenting voices, notions of magic all but condemned or distorted the naturalism of the Greco-Roman period. Only in the Middle East did the humane and naturalistic aspects of Hippocratic thought remain free of the primitivism and demonology that overcame Europe.

Signs for detecting demonic possession became increasingly indiscriminate in the Christian world. During epidemics of famine and pestilence, thousands wandered aimlessly until their haggard appearance and confusion justified the fear that they were cursed. The prevalent turmoil, the fear of one's own contamination, and the frenetic desire to prove one's spiritual purity led widespread segments of the populace to use the roaming destitute and ill as convenient scapegoats.

As the terrifying uncertainties of medieval life persisted, fear led to wild mysticism and mass pathology that simultaneously swept up entire societies. Epidemic manias of raving, jumping, drinking, and wild dancing were first noted in the tenth century. Referred to as *tarantism* in Italy, these manias spread throughout Europe, where they were known as *St. Vitus dance*.

Though many centuries passed after the rejection of the early Greeks' naturalistic ideas, rigorous scientific thinking during the Renaissance (fourteenth to sixteenth centuries) slowly but systematically countered primitive beliefs and superstitions. This chapter recounts both the gruesome medieval and postmedieval periods and the revival of rational and naturalistic thought in the writings of diverse philosophers in the second millennium A.D. The church feared the growing belief in scientific reason, for it would crowd out the mystery that was the foundation of faith. Nevertheless, by the eighteenth century the door of the spirit began to close and that of scientific thought to open.

The Philosophical Story: II

During the early Middle Ages, before the catastrophes of pestilence and famine, few mentally ill were destitute and treatment was kindly. Monasteries served as the chief refuge for such individuals, prescribing prayer, incantation, holy water, relic-touching, and mild exorcism for cure. As the turmoil of natural calamity continued, mental disorders were equated increasingly with sin and satanic influence. Significant advances were made in agriculture, technology, and architecture during the Middle Ages, but the interplay between changing theological beliefs and naturalistic catastrophe speeded even the secular world's belief that madness and depravity were the devil's work. At first, people believed that the devil had seized the mentally ill against their will and such individuals were treated with established exorcistic practice. Soon, however, the afflicted were considered willing followers of Satan; classed now as witches, they were flogged, starved, and burned.

Feudalism broke down, albeit slowly, in the eleventh century. In part as a consequence of this change, Europe fell into intense political conflicts and religious turmoil. These culminated in the sixteenth century with the division of Western Christianity into competing sects, such as seen in the Reformation. In the period between the eleventh and the seventeenth centuries, the mythology of Satanism flourished as a central constraint in the lives of all people, but most particularly those who were mentally ill.

Among the major tenets of this medieval mythology was a belief that an international conspiracy, based on satanic forces, was bent on destroying all forms of Christianity. The agents of this widespread conspiracy were witches, who not only worshipped Satan at secret meetings, but attempted to desecrate Christian symbols and beliefs, as well as to engage in murder, cannibalism, and sexual orgies. The ideas of a demonic and satanic conspiracy existed first and foremost in the imagination of the religious leaders of the day. Pope Gregory IX established the Inquisition in 1233 to root out witches, heretics, and all other agents of Satan who, he asserted, were setting out rapidly to destroy the clerical and political orders of the church. Those with an administrative status possessed the legal right to judge which aspects of satanic witchcraft would be deemed demonic. It was not only higher-order religious leaders who conveyed this dogma to the populace; the common man took these belief systems to heart as well. From the fifteenth through the seventeenth century, demonic possession and exorcism became common phenomena among the masses. In the postmedieval period, both Catholics and Protestants believed that witches, fueled by satanic forces, would send demons to possess those judged to be undesirable. It was the task of religious authorities to coerce those possessed by demons to admit that they were witches. These individuals could justly be arrested and tortured, especially if they confessed to their involvement in these nonexistent satanic conspiracies. "Witch Finders" soon became prominent guardians of the faith, prompted by religious authorities who sought to undo the political powers of their ostensible enemies.

Symptoms displayed by those who presumably were possessed by demons varied with cultural beliefs and religious practices. For example, both Catholic and Protestant witches convulsed in distinctive sensorimotor irregularities and dysfunctions. Many Catholics believed in "indwelling" demons who often spoke in voices that differed from those normally expressed by the possessed person. By contrast, most Protestants rarely acknowledged demonic, or indwelling, selves. During the Catholic exorcism process, priests appeared to be able to communicate directly with indwelling demons. Protestants, on the other hand, rarely practiced exorcism because communication with inner demons was either shunned or regarded as sinful. Instead, Protestant demoniacs were treated with prayer and fasting, methods that were likely to release whatever demons might possess them.

Afflicted individuals frequently denied that they were possessed. Authorities, however, construed these denials as an indication of the demons' wiliness in seeking to escape their inevitable fate: divine punishment. Refusing to accept the accusation of being possessed would lead to perpetual damnation. Interestingly, punishment was meted out under the guise of being a benevolent effort to free the hapless victim of demonic control.

Encouraged by the 1484 *Summis Desiderentes Affectibus*, in which Pope Innocent VIII exhorted the clergy to use all means for detecting and eliminating witchcraft, two inquisitional Dominicans, Johann Sprenger and Heinrich Kraemer, issued their notorious manual, *Malleus Maleficarum* (*The Witches' Hammer*). Published between 1487 and 1489, this "divinely inspired" text set out to prove the existence of witchcraft, to describe methods of identification, and to specify the procedures of examination and legal sentence.

Examples of this horrendous manual's archaic and nefarious character abound. Here are just two examples:

> Although they have a thousand ways of doing harm, and have tried . . . in every way to subvert and perturb the human race, yet their power remains confined to the privy parts and the navel. Devils often lust lecherously after women, and copulate with them. (Also, some men are beholden to devils) who by their magic charms . . . turn the passions of women to lusts of every kind.
>
> Demons seem chiefly to molest women and girls with beautiful hair, either because they devote themselves too much to the care and adornment of their hair, or because they are wont to excite men by means of their hair, or because they are boastfully vain about it . . . far more women are witches than men . . . yet men are more often bewitched than women.

Maleficarum reflected the spirit of its time, even though it was published in the early stages of the Renaissance, and at the threshold of the Reformation as well. Here, the conflict between Paganism and Christianity, between magic and a monotheistic outlook, had not ceased to be a burning issue, in more than one sense of the word. As the ancient idols and deities were torn down from their pedestals, demons nevertheless retained their grip on the mind of the ordinary man. Idols and deities were relegated to the role of fallen angels, but devils and evil demons continued to reside in the world of man's unconscious, a belief embraced with wide dissemination. Women were judged to be the more devilish of the sexes, the ones who most deserved to be feared and to be punished, as recorded in the following quote:

> What else is woman but a foe to friendship, an unescapable punishment, a necessary evil, a natural temptation, a desirable calamity, a domestic danger, a delectable detriment, an evil of nature painted with fair colours! . . . A woman either loves or hates; there is no third grade. And the tears of a woman are a deception, for they may spring from true grief, or they may be a snare. When a woman thinks alone, she thinks evil.

The Witches' Hammer was an astounding document that was intensified in its tone of anger and hostility by the authors' scholarly pretensions and fanatic zeal. Historians have described it as the most prominent and authoritative volume in the vast literature of witchcraft. Given such sanction, the book served generations of inquisitioners as a ready reference for sending hundreds of thousands of innocent men and women to their death at the stake.

With torture recommended as a means of obtaining confession, and feelings of guilt and hopeless damnation characteristic of many of the afflicted, the inevitable consequence for most was strangulation, beheading, or burning at the stake. Unredeemed by good sense and wise judgment, this barbaric epidemic swept Protestant and Catholic countries alike, including several American colonies. Although the last execution of a witch occurred in 1782, the bewildering notion that the mentally ill were in league with the devil persisted in popular thought well into the nineteenth century.

Unfolding of Key Ideas

At the turn of the sixteenth century, amid superstition and inhumane treatment, emerged an outcropping of scientific questioning and courageous challenges to the demonic themes of the medieval period. Yet the fifteenth and sixteenth centuries represented a transitional era of fickle tastes and orientations between the medieval and the modern worlds. During that period, Christianity became rigidly formalized. Its humanistic origins were superseded by its faith and its rituals, now ruled by a system of convictions and beliefs whose

complexity and diversity were expressed in a wide range of architecture, literature, and philosophy. As Alexander and Selesnick (1966) phrased it, "The supernatural world still existed in man's mind, but it had lost its vitality (p. 72)."
The supernatural world of the church and the feudal lifestyle were slowly being
replaced by real-world experiences.

Numerous events of a social character occurred in European society. The
archaic feudal lifestyle that had been anchored to castle and church gave
way to a revival of city life, the development of national institutions, and the
growth of industrial trade and commerce. During the Reformation, the
church's control over men's thoughts had weakened, especially with the emergence of Protestantism. By the sixteenth and seventeenth centuries, new ways
of dealing with worldly events had to be developed as business and taxation
became a central part of everyday living. In a parallel way, intellectual thought
turned from issues of theological hairsplitting to dealing with realistic and factual solutions to daily problems. Mathematics advanced in significant and useful ways, and the emergence of scientific technology likewise progressed as
men's minds turned from theological questions to practical and economic issues. Curious and intelligent men, especially in Western Europe, began to use
decimals and logarithms as well as microscopes and telescopes to understand
the character of the world and to solve life's problems. The printing press came
into use in the middle of the fifteenth century and enabled readers to appreciate alternative philosophical viewpoints from the Greek and Roman past. In
the sixteenth century, amateur intellectuals established informal groups; so-
called invisible colleges were founded in London and Paris and given official
status as National Royal Societies. Informal networks were created throughout
the continent, as were official journals established to communicate advances
in science and philosophical thought. The finest minds of the time began to
inquire and formulate questions and answers based on the speculations of the
philosophers of Greece centuries earlier.

Philosophy, as we know it now, was largely the result of an evolutionary
process of brilliant, albeit haphazard, proposals. It was a victim of fads and
vulnerable to fashion as the uncoordinated efforts of innumerable individual
thinkers produced critical appraisals that were judged valid, wrong-minded,
or trivial by their peers or by posterity. The inevitable outcome of this historic
process is that a survey of the state of any philosophy or science finds it, from
the standpoint of clarity and organizational elegance, nothing less than a
scattered parade of movements, if not a random mess. Numerous cutting-edge
ideas, distinct neither from one another nor from the noisy background of
cultural confusions, vied for attention. The several disciplines of science,
formed along illogical lines, were virtually interchangeable and persevered
long after their tentative boundaries, originally useful as rough guidelines,
hardened in time into blockades. Of small comfort is that the discouraging
state of affairs described in the preceding sentences was not unique to the
field of mental disorders. In fact, it was inevitable that a subject as broad as

human nature would generate diverse viewpoints and traditions. Complex problems lent themselves naturally to many approaches, and divisions of belief and orientation in so broad-ranging a field became not only a matter of choice but also one of necessity.

Philosophers of this period evidenced considerable respect for the writings of the ancients. The revival of Greek learning went hand in hand with an increasing contempt for medieval scholasticism and the world of the supernatural. Philosophical sophistication, however, lacked sufficient power to free men, philosophers or not, from the authority of these lingering and antique notions. As Bertrand Russell observed, "Many have still the reverence for authority that medieval philosophers had had, but they substituted the authority of the ancients for that of the church" (1959, p. 85). This was a step toward emancipation, since the ancients—Plato, Aristotle—disagreed with each other, and individual judgment was therefore necessary to decide which one to follow. The evolution of diverging philosophical and scientific approaches resulted in a wide spectrum of psychological knowledge. Random evolutions had marked disadvantages as well. Those who were preoccupied with only a single point of view usually had little interest in the work of others. Intent on a narrow approach to the subject, they lost sight of perspective, and their respective contributions became disconnected and scattered.

Orienting European Philosophies

The fertile philosophical ideas of the thirteenth century drummed up vast followers and opened the door to further advances that achieved their highest form in the sixteenth and seventeenth centuries. The scholar, **Albert Magnus (1193–1280),** is perhaps best known for having been the first European to review all of Aristotle's then-known works, written some 1,500 years previously. This survey was most courageous, given that the Christian church judged Aristotle's writings to be heretical. Magnus ignored the church's intimidating censorship and drew his inspiration from non-Christian sources of scholarship, thereby providing a refreshing source of intellectual stimulation that had a fruitful impact on awakening others' serious and scholarly pursuits. Central to Magnus's work was his use of Aristotelian logic as a basis for rational thinking and logical inquiry. He covered wide-ranging topics, including psychology. Although he added few original ideas to those formulated by the Greeks and Romans, his revival and articulation of Aristotle's themes proved to be extremely significant. His best-known book was entitled *On the Powers of the Soul.* Here he proposed a psychology based on a human striving for goodness and an intellectual fulfillment consistent with God's wishes. As might be expected, given the time and context of this work, many of his themes used rationality as a basis for understanding God's inner intrinsic perfection. He aspired to elevate the view that human rationality could prove a source of salvation equal to that of faith.

Another medieval Aristotelian, **Roger Bacon (1214–1292),** was viewed by many as the greatest scientist/philosopher of the period. He desired to emphasize progress through systematic observation and to use mathematical techniques to describe these observations. Not only did he revive an interest in the authors of Greece, especially mathematicians such as Euclid, but he stressed, as did Aristotle, that empirical demonstrations based on careful observation would have a greater impact in advancing scientific thinking than would rational arguments. To him, agreement among observers, assisted by mathematical logic and procedures, was to be the gauge of truth. As such, Bacon reintroduced the empiricism central to Aristotle's philosophy. He differed from Magnus in that Magnus stressed the need for clear definitions and systematic classification to represent Aristotle's view. By contrast, Bacon emphasized a more inductive approach to science that rested on observable evidence. Nevertheless, Bacon agreed that both logical deduction and inductive methods could be a source of knowledge.

Bacon proposed numerous experiments in his efforts to articulate his model of empirical research. It may be useful to record a statement in which he advocated this model (1260/1928):

> I now wish to unfold the principles of experimental science, since without experience nothing can be sufficiently known. For there are two modes of acquiring knowledge, namely by reasoning and experience. Reasoning draws a conclusion and makes us grant the conclusion, but does not make the conclusion certain, nor does it remove doubt so that the mind may rest on the intuition of truth, unless the mind discovers it by the path of experience.

Both Bacon and Magnus set the stage for the acceptance of many of Aristotle's teachings, not only to help explain human psychological processes, but to show how they could be consonant with Christian thinking, where faith was the dominant force. The reconciliation of these two elements—rationality versus faith—was advanced by **Thomas Aquinas (1225–1274),** who helped establish what came to be called *Scholasticism.* His work opened the door to a life of the mind by admitting the significance of human reasoning, as long as it was balanced by a comparable acceptance of faith. Consistent with the times, he spent much time defending reason against those who believed faith alone would provide the source of truth. His efforts were akin to those of Saint Augustine, who had tried to reconcile Plato with Christian thoughts some 800 years previously. Aquinas presented Aristotle's principles of matter and form as a framework for describing the relationship that existed between the body and the soul. He spoke of the person as one composed of essences and existences. In his view, the essence of a person was universal among all people and comprised the tangible or concrete physical world; existence represented a person's immortal soul and consisted of intellect and will.

Aquinas posited two types of knowledge: *sensory knowledge*, which humans share with animals and is the source for understanding physical reality; and *human reasoning*, which provides abstractions that deal with universal principles rather than tangible sensory data. In accord with his time and position, Aquinas believed that the soul exhibited the highest and most powerful form of human activity by the process of rational thinking. According to Aquinas, it is the capacity to reason that invests humans with their uniqueness and enables them to join with God in an overarching capacity to transcend the everyday world. So successful was Aquinas that following his death, Aristotle's teachings became required reading in most Christian universities. Like his forerunners, Magnus and Bacon, he provided a strong intellectual justification for elevating reason to a level equal to that of faith as a primary source of knowledge, as described with the following statement:

> A law is a dictate of the practical reason. Now it is to be observed that the same procedure takes place in the practical and in the speculative reason: for each proceeds from principles to conclusions. Accordingly we conclude that just as, in the speculative reason, from naturally known indemonstrable principles, we draw the conclusions of the various sciences, the knowledge of which is not imparted to us by nature, but acquired by the efforts of reason, so too it is from the precepts of the natural law, as from general and indemonstrable principles, that the human reason needs to proceed to the more particular determination of certain matters. These particular determinations, devised by human reason, are called human laws. (1915, p. 110)

Aquinas was the last of the great thinkers of the thirteenth century. Following his death, Europe was racked not only with the Hundred Years' War, but with the Black Death as well as other epidemics of the fourteenth century. Scientific or philosophical reflections were cast aside as the populace returned in its desperation to superstition and mysticism. Initially, no one dared embark on a quest for alternatives. By the fifteenth century, social changes slowly came to the foreground, bringing forth a rich period of intellectual and scientific thinking. Scholars were freed from theological orthodoxy with the invention of the printing press. Learning could now take place outside church-controlled universities. People's minds were increasingly liberated from medieval thinking.

Constructing the Philosophy of Rationalism

The major contrast described in the following pages pertains to the two major contributions to ultimate scientific achievement: those elements that are deductive and drawn from a set of principles versus those that are essentially inductive and seek to draw generalizations and abstractions by generating them from the particulars of life. It is incorrect to assume that rationalism relies solely on reason, whereas empiricism relies solely on experience. Neither was rigidly formulaic in its proposals. Both played a central role, however, in establishing the basis for future philosophical thought. Rationalism starts with a major assumption about the existence of clear principles that characterize a particular class of events and then deduces consequences from those principles to portray those events. Empiricism reverses the process by focusing first on the particulars and then onto universals (e.g., from samples to populations). We set rationalism and empiricism as opposites, despite their frequent use of each other's procedures. We begin with René Descartes, the prime and earliest of the rationalists. His principles were guided heavily by a mechanistic conception of human nature.

Born in 1596 in France, **René Descartes (1596–1650)** was the son of a prominent lawyer and judge, from whom he inherited sufficient funds to support a life of study and travel. That he did not become a dilettante was a con-

Rene Descartes

sequence, we may infer, of his pervasive intellectual curiosity, perhaps his genius, and his intense hunger for knowledge. Although he was indifferent to the assertions of dogmatic authorities and sought supportive evidence for what he judged to be truth, Descartes was highly alert to the sensitivities of his Catholic religion. At various times, he wrote that he wished to prevent anything he had published from being viewed critically by the church. He was often dismayed by a conflict between his loyalty to the authority of the Catholic faith, and his passion for carefully reasoned truth. As he stated it, "I would not wish, for anything in the world, to maintain (my views) against the authority of the church."

Nevertheless, as Heidbreder has written (1933), Descartes was typical of those of his period who began a revolt against scholastic dogmatism. He was not a rebel but neither would he chance a misplaced academic piety. Candid, cautious, and extraordinarily reasonable, Descartes recognized that there was little that he knew with certainty despite his long and studious devotion to learning. As a consequence, he deliberately undertook to use his all-pervasive doubt and uncertainty as a philosophical method to vigorously doubt anything that one could possibly doubt. With this tool in hand, he found that he could doubt much of what he had learned and believed, such as the existence of God, the existence of the world, even the existence of his body. The one thing he could not doubt was the fact that he was doubting, and this certainty became the cornerstone of his philosophical thought.

In many ways, Descartes can be considered the founder of modern Western philosophy. In addition to his considerable contributions to both science and mathematics, he sought to construct a logical and deductive framework for reasoned thought, a philosophical system from the ground up, so to speak. He presented this system in his *Discoures de la Methode*, published in 1637. In his search for truth, Descartes adopted a rigorous attitude, resolving never to accept anything as true that he did not know to be such with certainty. He was especially concerned with the validity of knowledge and was sensitive to the threats that could be posed to science by the skeptical leanings of many writers of his time. As some have stated it, he sought to develop an intellectual fortress capable of withstanding the assaults of the skeptics.

More recently, **Karl Popper (1902–1994)** extended Descartes' rigor by stressing that *falsifiability* should be the *sine qua non* of a sustainable scientific theory. Essentially, a sustainable theory is one that has been subjected to and has survived efforts to falsify it through rigorous empirical tests. Popper's thesis followed a comment made by Albert Einstein in 1921 after the gravitationally induced curvature of light was successfully demonstrated to accord with his special theory of relativity. Einstein asserted that all aspects of his theories should be judged untenable if they failed to lend themselves to crucial empirical tests. Likewise, Popper believed that scientists should not focus on theory verifications but should look for tests that could refute them. Stating this thesis in his *Logic of Scientific Discovery* (1934/1959), Popper wrote:

> I do not think we can ever seriously reduce by elimination . . . competing theories since this number remains always infinite. What we . . . , should do—is to hold on . . . to the most improbable of the surviving theories . . . to the one that can be most severely tested (that is) to the severest tests we can design. (1959, p. 419)

Thus, Descartes engaged in serious efforts to question the validity of his own work. To him, the act of doubting should itself be subject to serious criteria. Thus he said, "In order to doubt, one must be able to think, and in order to think, one must exist." And this was the basis of the famous axiom attributed to Descartes: "I think, therefore I am." A more elaborate version of his reasoning on this matter follows:

> But what, then, am I? A thinking thing, it has been said. But what is a thinking thing? It is a thing that doubts, understands, [conceives], affirms, denies, wills, refuses, that imagines also, and perceives. Assuredly it is not little, if all these properties belong to my nature. But why should they not belong to it? Am I not that very being who now doubts of almost everything; who, for all that, understands and conceives certain things; who affirms one alone as true, and denies the others; who desires to know more of them, and does not wish to be deceived; who imagines many things, sometimes even despite his will; and is likewise percipient of many, as if through the medium of the senses. Is there nothing of all this as true as that I am. (1913)

Descartes posited two major categories of the mind: those composed of innate ideas, which were inborn and not dependent on experience; and those of derived ideas, which stemmed from life experiences. Among Descartes' innate ideas were those of God; conceptions of time, space, and motion; the self; as well as several geometric axioms.

As Descartes phrased it, our mind thinks, thereby deducing an open, extended, and free form of expression, but one that lacks substance. By contrast, the body is more limited in its potentials, but possesses considerable substance. Both mind and body follow different laws and functions. The body's actions are determined by mechanical principles or, as Descartes viewed it, the body is nothing more than a very complex machine, albeit a self-regulating physical one that can engage in functions without involving the mind.

His mind-body conception has come to be referred to in the literature as the *Cartesian* or *Dualist-Interactionist* view. To Descartes, both are intimately conjoined so as to "compose a certain unity." Despite his convictions on this matter, his record on the issue remained less permanent than he wished. Issues relating to mind and body continue as topics of intense inquiry for numerous philosophers to this day. They engender hypotheses on wide-ranging topics such as the nature of consciousness, the utility of brain imaging, and a host of themes concerning symbols and reality.

One such philosopher was **Georg Hegel (1770–1831).** Early in the nineteenth century, he noted that there existed three "moments" of speculation in the mind-body relationship. The first, an early period where mind and body were only vaguely differentiated, was followed by a time when mind and body were seen as sharply separated and opposed; and this led finally to a more modern period in which efforts were made to explicate the many complex and intimate connections that might exist between the two. Later in that century in the United States, **Charles Sanders Peirce (1839–1914),** drew on ideas of Schopenhauer and Nietzsche to assert a pragmatic conception of mind. He promoted the notion that any event, internal or external, must assume some function or instrumentality to acquire the status of being mental. To him, this function was achieved through signs or symbols; he stated, "Mind is a sign developed in accord to the laws of inference." Further, he argued that the body is "only an instrument of thought"; "every thought is a sign"; and a sign is a "vehicle conveying into the mind something from without." Peirce's thesis set the groundwork for *William James*'s articulation of what came to be called the *Functionalist* school of psychology (see Chapter 13), and *John Dewey*'s allegiance to what was termed the philosophy of *pragmatism*. In a somewhat similar manner, **George Santayana (1863–1952)** considered reality, be it of the body or other elements of nature, to be "essences." To him, essences become "given to knowledge" via symbols; thus, body and mind become one by virtue of their fusion through symbols.

In recent decades, the logical-empiricist philosopher **Herbert Feigl (1902–1988)** ardently and articulately defended the mind-body identity theory. To him, mental events were contingently identical with physical or neurophysiological events. He explicated this thesis as follows:

> Logical Empiricism in its present phase possesses the logical tools for a reformulation of the identity or double-language view of the mental and the physical. As in so many other issues of philosophy, this solution represents an equilibrium that has been reached only after several oscillations toward untenable extreme positions. The identity proposed is neither the reductive definitional one of phenomenalism or of behaviorism, nor is it an identity that presupposes a metaphysical realism. It is rather the hypothetical identity of the referents of terms whose evidential bases are respectively: introspective, behavioral or physiological. (1943, p. 83)

As noted, Descartes' system evidenced a clear preference for deduction based self-evident truths although he reserved a significant role for experience. However, he was not especially enthralled by experimentation. He recognized that experiments were only a single special form of observation. In this regard, his preference was to be open to free-flowing observation instead of to experimental manipulation. In effect, Descartes rejected the results of "tampered" experiments that ran counter to free observation, which was more susceptible to abstract reasoning. The role of natural experience was simply to provide authentic and unaltered material for abstract reflection. These reflections were to be based on genuine sensory experience that would provide the purest grist for the mill of scientific analysis. Without reflection, however, sensory data alone could not be trusted, for they would lead only to momentary and superficial appearances.

As is evident for Descartes, knowledge presupposes a conceptual model to guide observations. His emphasis on deduction and mathematical proofs suggest the powerful role he played in establishing rationality as the basis for a philosophy of science.

Benedict Spinoza (1632–1677) and his forebears were subjected to persecution and threats owing to their Jewish heritage. The odyssey of the Jews since their dispersion from Jerusalem in 70 A.D. is one of the epics of human religious history. They scattered by flight and trade among all nations and continents. Harshly persecuted by other great religions, such as Christianity and Islam, Jews remained peripheral members of all societies until recent time. Barred by the feudal system from owning land and by the guilds from taking part in industry, they were closeted into congested ghettos and taxed cruelly by their governors or overlords. The intense religious fervors of the late sixteenth century prompted a mass exodus of Jews from Spain and Portugal. Spinoza was one of many who fled the cruelty of the Inquisition for Holland, known as a haven of religious freedom. There is little doubt that Spinoza would have become among the greatest figures in the history of psychology had he not come to an untimely early death in his 40s. Not only was his mode of livelihood extremely stressful (grinding lenses by day and night), but he was constantly harassed, having been excommunicated both by rabbis and Christian bigots.

Though his father was a successful merchant, the youthful Spinoza had no interest in following in his father's footsteps, preferring to spend his time at the synagogue absorbing the religion and history of his people. He was a bril-

Benedict Spinoza

liant student, and the elders expected him to be a future light of their community and their faith. Reading voraciously on Jewish and Hebraic themes, the more Spinoza read and pondered, the more his certainties began to melt away into reflection and doubt. Soon he turned to thinkers of the Christian faith who had written on the great questions of God and human destiny. He quickly conquered Greek and Latin, studying Socrates, Plato, and Aristotle. Finally, and above all, he read and was deeply influenced by Descartes, the father of a rationalistic and idealistic conception of philosophical thought.

Benedict Spinoza translated much of Descartes' work in his book, *Principles of the Philosophy of René Descartes* (1663). It extended Descartes' methods in an uncompromising manner, thereby creating a conceptual groundwork for a rigorous science of human nature and human ethics. Spinoza became a leading pantheist, bringing into psychological thinking the theory of psychophysical parallelism as an alternative to Descartes' interactionism. He challenged the Cartesian notion that the mind and the body were separate substances and that these substances interact in one of the brain's minor glands. To him, mind and body were not clearly separate; rather, he viewed them to be two aspects of the same fundamental phenomenon. Thus, the mind and the body co-exist, and the world of experience and the world of behavior are but two expressions of the same thing. Psychological processes are part of the natural order of the world, and the human mind is part of nature and subject to its laws. In seeking to demonstrate the inseparability of the mind and the body, Spinoza further emphasized that it was possible to give significant weight to psychological factors in the same way one can give weight to bodily factors.

In addition to minimizing the concept of dualism between physical and psychological, Spinoza elevated the methodological importance of reason as the key to understanding all functions of nature. Central in his thoughts was the role of emotions, the role of psychopathological functioning, and the deep conflicts that often serve as dilemmas for people, thereby triggering anxiety, stress, and depression. Spinoza's psychological attributes were noted as passion, emotion, reason, and intuition. What people think of as "good and evil" are none other than the emotions of pleasure and pain. To him, joy, sadness, and desire represented the central emotions, which—with the addition of ideas and thoughts—could yield additional emotions. He believed that it is man's desire to uncover pleasure for his mind and to experience pain by its denial. In essence, Spinoza considered the ultimate goal of man's psychological being to be self-actualization, a concept rediscovered centuries later in the writings of contemporary theorists such as Kurt Goldstein and Abraham Maslow. Spinoza likewise investigated psychological determinism as well as the stresses of interpersonal relationships.

Most important, and in line with Descartes as well as earlier Platonic and Aristotelian ideas, Spinoza emphasized that rationalism and insight were the essential qualities of psychological analysis. Relating psychological functioning to deep self-preservative concerns, he elevated causality and the knowledge of antecedents to the level of major qualities in scientific study. It was his emphasis on reason, however, that had a long-term effect in shifting the focus for understanding psychological elements toward the rational and away from the irrational. A major contribution of Spinoza's philosophy was his assertion that natural revelation could be the primary means of attaining truth. To him, it was only through a rigorous rational analysis that one could ascertain truth and, in turn, find a way for knowing the nature of God. The following quotes typify Spinoza's philosophy of rational thinking (1663):

> In life . . . it is especially useful to perfect, in so far as we can, our intellect or reason, and this is man's highest happiness or blessedness—for blessedness is nothing but the contentment of the mind. . . .
>
> No life . . . is rational without understanding, and things are good only in so far as they help man to enjoy the life of the mind. . . . But those things which prevent man from perfecting his reason and enjoying a rational life—those only we call evil.
>
> Nothing is more useful to man in preserving his being and enjoying a rational life than a man who is guided by reason.

Another key to understanding Spinoza's ideas is his unrelenting effort to bring unity to disparate and opposite concepts. He therefore fought to overcome distinctions between the secular and the sacred, the mind and the body, and free will versus determinism. Moreover, he set out to deny the supernatural quality of demonology, proposing thereby a humanitarian orientation for the treatment of the mentally ill. Not only did Spinoza deny that there are devils, or that the mentally ill are possessed, but he argued that there is only one ultimate reality, and that reality prefigured the concept of God. To him, God was the one and only spiritual power—a power inherent in all aspects of nature and thus inseparable from truth. As he saw it, God was nature.

Though Spinoza and **Gottfried Wilhelm Liebniz (1646–1716)** shared a belief in the importance of reasoning to deduce the properties of life and substance, Liebniz disagreed with Spinoza's view that manifestly different phenomena were simply variations in the expression of a few universal substances. Also notable was Liebniz's rejection that determinism was not sufficient to account for how behavior and material would vary. Liebniz was a contemporary of Sir Isaac Newton, with whom he shared such creative inventions as differential calculus. It was within the area of philosophy, however, that he sought to generate a world's unity.

Liebniz was born in Leipzig, Germany, where his father was a professor of moral philosophy at the university. By the time he was a preadolescent, he was given regular access to his father's library, which brought him into contact not only with his father's work, but also the writings of other major German intellectuals. He showed an appetite for studies in many fields, notably mathematics, language, religion, and philosophy. Entering the university at the age of 15, he completed his studies for a doctorate of law by the age of 20. Although trained in the legal profession, he turned his attention to finance, becoming an advisor and administrator in the employ of German nobility, which provided him with opportunities and time for travel and leisure. He was instrumental in the founding of the Berlin Academy of Sciences and served as its first president.

A contemporary also of John Locke, Liebniz often stated that he considered Locke's "Essay Concerning Human Understanding" to be one of the most thorough and esteemed works of the period. He believed, however, that Locke's account of the human mind was mistaken. More specifically, Liebniz could not accept Locke's account of the mind's contents as consisting only of empirical experience. Liebniz stated that perhaps animals were like empty tablets at birth, filled by experience, but though humans might also be products of experience to some degree, they were not completely so. In addition to experiential knowledge, Liebniz believed that there are eternal truths with which all humans are born, the so-called nonempiric portion of the mind, or innate intellect. Locke, by contrast, believed that there was nothing in the intellect that was not first in the senses; Liebniz replied: nothing except intellect itself. As Liebniz viewed it, intellect would permit reason to construct a true science. Knowledge is therefore the essence of the human spirit. Much of life's activities may be akin to those of lower animals, based on sensory associations and physically practiced learning. However, it is in the capacity and disposition to grasp "a rule," a "knowing awareness" of the intrinsic relationship among life's phenomena, that we exhibit the distinctive quality of the human mind.

The empirically oriented philosophers of his day, notably Thomas Hobbes and Locke, made a fundamental error, according to Liebniz, when they denied the existence of inborn ideas, dispositions, and potentials. Rather than a sheet of blank paper to be written on by experience, the human mind at birth was already grained and varied in its character, indicating the presence of inborn dispositions, which lend themselves to particular and distinctive forms of behavior that are not notably affected by life's experiences.

Among other proposals were Liebniz's efforts to counter Locke's notion that the mind was passive. He suggested that the mind was replete with agents of activity, which he called *monads*. Employing monadology to describe the activity of the mind, which he defined as unextended units of force or energy, each monad was considered a separate and independent force that could act independently on all other forces of the mind. The interaction of several monads defined individuality and, in turn, produced greater compoundings that could encompass the entire universe. The monads of an individual compose his or her mind, and dispose it to be sensitive

Gottfried Wilhelm Liebniz

and responsive to its environment. Leibniz contended that monads grow and develop through life, changing at different times to deal with the tasks of different age-related experiences.

Liebniz believed that perceptions existed below the threshold of awareness, which he called *petites perceptions*. The perceptions of the conscious world, he referred to as *apperceptions*. In effect, he introduced a concept of subconsciousness centuries before Freud. Equally significant was his belief in a gradient from unconscious processes to consciousness. This gradualism, which characterized much of Liebniz's proposals, was also applied to developmental growth. Despite his observation that intellect progressed from youth to adulthood, he also recognized and emphasized the importance of how the individual's identity maintained stability in a sea of experiential change. His view that connections exist between the past, the present, and the future reinforced this theme of self-continuity. His emphasis on life's harmony and continuity oriented his readers away from archaic notions such as unanticipated miracles and intrusive supernatural phenomena.

Despite his distinction and the extensive range of his insights into complex matters pertaining to philosophy and psychology, **Immanuel Kant (1724–1804)** never strayed more than 60 miles from his birthplace in Prussia, and lived an uneventful life while serving as a professor at the University of Königsberg. Kant may represent the stereotype for the bespectacled and unworldly university professor. He became a student at his university at the age of 16 and then stayed on as a teacher and professor until the age of 73. A lifelong bachelor who followed an unvarying routine, he was a shade less than five feet in height, thin, and hollow-chested. Awakened by his servants at 5 A.M. he devoted two hours of each morning to deep and intense study, then lectured for another two-hour period and continued his writing chores until one o'clock each afternoon, following which he ate at the same restaurant each day and strolled for an hour, from 3:30 P.M. until 4:30 P.M., through a standard walkway. He was disinclined to stop and converse as he followed his daily walk.

Immanuel Kant

Each day, he read from early evening on, preparing his lectures for the following day until he retired alone in his own thoughts and dreams at 9 P.M. A creature of unvarying habits and unyielding beliefs, he remained fixed in his lifestyle until his dying days.

Kant came from a poor family that had left Scotland some 100 years before his birth. His mother was a member of a religious sect that insisted on absolute strictness and rigor in religious practice and belief. During his youth, Kant was so immersed from morning to night in his mother's religious persuasion that he inevitably rebelled, ultimately staying away from church throughout adulthood. On the other hand, the somber and strict stamp of Puritanism inculcated in him by his mother led him to preserve ever so firmly the essentially modest and temperate character of that faith. It is therefore startling that Kant ultimately proposed a radical metaphysical system for thought, an achievement that would seem the very last thing this hesitant, if not timid, professor would undertake. In fact, he wrote on his book's completion, "I have the fortune to be a lover of metaphysics; but my mistress has shown me few favors as yet." He spoke of his metaphysical work as a large, dark ocean without shores or a lighthouse, and strewn with many philosophical wrecks. He did not foresee that one of the greatest of all metaphysical tempests was of his own doing. Persevering through poverty and obscurity, he wrote his *magnum opus* over a period of 15 years. Kant may have matured slowly, but his book overturned the philosophical world.

In this great work, *Critique of Pure Reason* (1781/1991), Kant dealt a severe blow to the notion that the soul was a substance. Although rational philosophy included the soul as a central theme, to Kant the soul represented only a postulate of practical reason, a concept that served the interests of ethics and religion, and no more. To him, it was with rational philosophy that one dealt with thinking in a strictly logical and a priori fashion by pitting reasoned propositions against one another to deduce a valid conclusion. From his viewpoint, nothing of an empirical nature must enter into it; to do so would invalidate the method by forcing together that which should not be logically combined. As formulated by Kant:

> Metaphysical knowledge must contain simply judgments *a priori*, so much is demanded by the specificity of its sources. But judgments, let them have what origin they may, or let them even as regards logical form be constituted as they may, possess a distinction according to their content, by virtue of which they are either simply *explanatory* and contribute nothing to the content of a

cognition, or they are *extensive*, and enlarge the given cognition; the first may be termed *analytic*, and the second *synthetic* judgments. (trans. 1891)

At heart, Kant was a metaphysician and philosopher whose sole concern was the validity of knowledge. This contrasted with psychology, which he considered to be an empirical search for the laws of mental functioning. As Kant conceived it, the rational approach to psychological processes seeks fundamentals that derive their force and clarity from concepts and principles. The latter comprises, therefore, a form of disciplined thinking instead of a body of facts. An empirical approach deals merely with observations based on the experiences of an individual; because these are essentially subjective, the body of data so composed cannot come under the scope of a science, but simply constitutes a series of unintegrated observations and opinions. It was not Kant's goal to overturn empiricism, but to establish its limitations. To him, empirical information provided a foundation, but not explanations or causality. In his view, only logic furnishes the foundations for understanding and judgment.

While being first and foremost a philosopher, Kant laid the groundwork for many of psychology's current interests in the logical structure of thought and language, as well as those of perceptual and cognitive organization. Kant also anticipated much of the later criticism of introspection. He adhered to the notion of psychophysical parallelism, a theme that likewise was to influence psychology for years to come. His proposed interplay between the mind and the body has similarly received special attention, owing to Kant's nativistic theories of how the mind worked. Nevertheless, Wundt, founder of experimental psychology, was inclined to dismiss Kant's contributions as having been designed to diminish the possibility of "ever raising psychology to the rank of an exact natural science."

Johann Friedrich Herbart (1776–1841), successor to Kant at the University of Königsberg, is known mainly for his efforts to synthesize the rational and the empirical approach to science, especially as applied to the study and instrumentation of education. His popularity as a lecturer was immense; not many institutions had lecture halls large enough to hold the number of students who enthusiastically attended his classes. An outgoing personality who took a deep interest in his culture and his community, Herbart was somewhat erratic in his efforts to build a true metaphysical system.

As far as psychology was concerned, Herbart started where Kant left off. However, he gave little attention to the notion of independent faculties. He was interested in active processing, not in substance. He pursued the theme of forces that were inherent in each of the ideas that composed an engaged and alive mind. It was Herbart's desire to explain the most complex forms of mental activity in the simplest terms. Convinced that each idea possessed a certain measure or force within it, Herbart stressed that these forces not only could associate ideas together but could also inhibit one another. Thus, every mental idea is inclined to maintain itself and to drive out ideas with which it is incompatible. To Herbart, mental life is mainly a struggle between ideas, each of which is active and forceful and strives to maintain its place in consciousness, tending to repel all other ideas within consciousness except those with which it is compatible. In this formulation, Herbart conceived mental phenomena in terms of mechanical and quantitative forces Applying this principle, he sought to construct mathematical formulas to represent the laws of the mind. It was Herbart's efforts to build a quantitative psychology that encouraged the field to become an experimental science in the following century. Notable also was Herbart's recognition of active unconscious processes. Anticipating the central tenets of psychoanalytic thinking a century later, he conceived ideas as being active forces that persisted below the threshold of consciousness. Other ideas inhibited them there, but they always strove to gain conscious expression by fighting to overcome previously dominant forces.

In contrast to Kant, who denied that empirical psychology should possess any scientific status, Herbart proposed dealing with complex ideational processes mathematically, based on formulas that included the processes of inhibition and facilitation, as well as those of attraction and repulsion. Although his views were highly conjectural, Herbart was among the very first to propose a rigorous standard for his efforts to understand behavior. As noted, Herbart considered that ideas, once created, are never lost to the mind; hence, conscious thoughts at any particular moment would be miniscule compared with the multitude of ideas individuals may potentially be able to activate. Again, and in anticipation of Freud's thinking, Herbart asserted that certain ideas could easily move into consciousness, whereas others would resist. As he viewed it, ideas that could readily come into consciousness were those that were congruent with ideas of the mind that were already in consciousness.

The Budding of an Empiricist Philosophy

The empiricist philosophy emphasized experience and the interplay of sensory data. From these sources, one obtains the means for generating knowledge. By contrast, the rationalist philosophy turns first to generalizable principles and the process of reasoning to obtain knowledge. Rational philosophies place their emphasis on a priori knowledge, whereas empirical philosophies emphasize knowledge that is derived directly from experience. In a rational model, the mind is an active instrument in its capacity to select, organize, reject, and discriminate experiences by using its deductive processes. An empiricist philosophy, on the other hand, judges the mind as a passive receptacle, an inert *tabula rasa*, or blank slate.

The English most assuredly had their share of mystics and metaphysicians oriented to the intangible, abstract, and mysterious world that attracted philosophers on the opposite side of the Channel. On the whole, however, English philosophers were more disposed to be practical and realistic, attuned to the sober, commonplace, and empirical in striving to make sense of the human mind. Where possible, they designed experiments; otherwise, they turned to the tangible and down-to-earth elements of everyday experience instead of abstract explanations to guide their philosophical inquiries.

As noted, it would be incorrect to state that rationalism relied solely on reason, whereas empiricism relied solely on experience. Reason and experience play a significant role in both philosophies. However, in rationalism, the primary emphasis was on the deductive process, whereas in empiricism, the primary concern was on methods of induction. Rational deduction begins with a series of universal premises about a general class of events and then attempts to deduce consequences that may apply to a particular event. Induction reverses the sequence; it involves extrapolating from particulars to universals. Although these two philosophies both used empirical material and deductive reasoning, they had differing views about the nature of human behavior.

Francis Bacon (1561–1626), a leading empiricist of the late sixteenth and early seventeenth centuries, hoped to reorganize scientific studies. Born to a distinguished British family, Bacon became a prosperous attorney and Chancellor of the Realm; in 1618, he received the title of Baron from King James I. Characteristic of the times, he was forced to resign from his high office in 1621, having been charged with accepting a bribe. This was a period of great intrigue in which intense struggles for power derived from conflicts between church and throne. Nevertheless, it was also rich with intellectual thought and achievement, perhaps best illustrated in the writings of Bacon's contemporary, Shakespeare. During these years Bacon authored two major works, *The Proficience and Advancement of Learning* (1605) and *Novum Organum* (1620).

Whereas Aristotle and the Scholastics recognized the importance of both deductive and inductive reasoning, Bacon was convinced that deductive procedures were stressed at the expense of the inductive. He believed that traditional deductive approaches possessed an a priori and rigid mental set, a fixed orientation that limited the openness of future investigations. These a priori assumptions claimed, without proof, certain characteristics about humanity, but Bacon believed that the validity of these methods was so constrained by their underlying assumptions that they could rarely prove to be correct or even relevant.

In Bacon's mind, the usefulness of an activity was synonymous with its worthiness. He set forth several missions for his writings: to specify the principal bases of ignorance and disagreement; to identify the true intellectual authorities of the time; to indicate those regions of inquiry about which too little is known; to specify the basis on which efforts are worth undertaking; and, most significantly, to outline methods to achieve the preceding. Underlying each of his missions was the assumption that efforts should be expended and judged in terms of their potential benefit to the daily affairs of mankind.

Bacon believed that the human capacity to reason was sufficiently flawed and held in bondage by authorities for whom the truth was a secondary concern. To illustrate the problems in a preset or clearly oriented attitude of the mind, Bacon created a list of what he referred to as *idols*. These were phantoms of the human mind, primarily common sources of deductive error that led individuals to stray from facts, as opposed to assumptions. In what he referred to as the *idols of the tribe,* he noted that the mind could distort sensory processes that might otherwise carry experiences directly to the brain. Another distortion process was called the *idols of the cave.* These strongly preferred modes of explanation could blind people to alternative versions of the data they observed. *Idols of the marketplace* referred to the temptation to take words too seriously, or to believe that the mere naming of a thing could explain it. *Idols of the theater* referred to the power of authorities to promote belief systems that were not grounded in observable data (e.g., superstition), but nevertheless carried great weight in shaping human life.

Bacon argued that illusions and distortions did not justify a wholesale attack on all forms of deduction. Moreover, he understood that the mere accumulation of sensory data could lead to as much misinformation as could the rational philosophies he demeaned, especially when empiricists leaped to generalizations based on inadequate experimentation. But, true to his cause, Bacon vigorously condemned the rationalists and believed they intentionally divorced their methods from the data of life's experiences. It was here that he contributed to inductivism, which grounds understanding on experience instead of on preformed biases or theories.

Bacon differentiated two forms of empirical investigation. The first he termed *Experimenta Lucifera* (investigations that shed light on a topic), and the second he labeled *Experimenta Fructifera* (investigations that bear fruit). The first merely produced a sense of discovery, some potential for establishing cause or effect, one not yet definitive in its result. Those bearing fruit were designed to yield an unquestioned law of nature, results that are not merely definitive, but also of benefit to humankind.

Thomas Hobbes (1588–1679) was well acquainted with the great scholars of his time, including Descartes; an important relationship also developed with Francis Bacon, for whom Hobbes served briefly as a secretary. Provided with an Oxford education, secured largely through the generosity of an uncle, Hobbes published on wide-ranging subjects, arguing that the church should be submissive to an absolute monarch, a position that brought him great anguish in later years. In line with his empiricist orientation, Hobbes published his most famous work late in life, the *Leviathan* (1651) in which he expounded on his belief that all knowledge should be derived from sensations. He stated that nothing can exist without the senses, except matter and motion. In this latter thesis, he grounded his psychological orientation firmly in what came to be called *materialism*.

Hobbes lived in a significant period of history, during which the fundamental essence of nature radically changed from a belief in spiritualistic forces to one of naturalistic science. This renaissance took hold firmly as a result of the discoveries of Galileo, Copernicus, Kepler, Harvey, and Newton. Though living in the shadow of enduring Christian faiths, a dramatic if gradual transformation took hold that abandoned the older spiritualistic vision to pursue a vision of an omnipresent *machine*. A new metaphor emerged. Physics replaced metaphysics. The action of spiritual forces no longer caused results; universal motion was key. The movement of planets required no recourse to gods, but rather to the motions of natural forces. Movement in nature became the dominant philosophical and scientific metaphor.

According to Heidbreder (1933), Hobbes was a blunt, hardheaded British royalist whose writings centered on man's relationships to the state. His main purpose, or so it would appear, was to justify the absolute power of the ruler. To him, humans possessed a natural impulse to take what they might want and to get whatever they could, which led inevitably to conflict, to a war that every person fought with everyone else. This intolerable situation, according to Hobbes, would end when humankind, prompted by fear and self-interest, concluded that they could gain security and the goods of life by giving up their rights and receiving in return the assurance of protection by rulers with power strong enough to control all their constituents. Hence, he prescribed the need for the absolute power of an omnipotent ruler (shades of Hitler, Stalin, and Saddam Hussein).

Surprisingly, this forceful and dominating philosophy was not the expression of an unfortunate misfit who sought power for himself, but came from an energetic man, exceptionally healthy, tall and handsome, a natural royalist, as Hobbes was. He maintained close connections among many of the royalists of both England and France. Nevertheless, the bishops of England condemned him in his later years for what they judged to be his atheism and blasphemy, recommending that he be burned at the stake. Owing to his vigorous espousal favoring the preeminence of the throne, the king turned aside these condemnations; moreover, the King gave Hobbes a substantial life pension in its stead. Hobbes lived well into his 90s, a life span most untypical in his day.

John Locke (1632–1704) was brought up in country villages of England. His father, a small-town lawyer and landowner expressed a great deal of affection for his sons, but made sure that they adhered to Puritan virtues of discipline and sobriety. Locke was therefore taught to love simplicity and to shy away from excessive displays and ornamentation. He received a classical education with an emphasis on Greek and Latin. A distinguished student at Oxford, he qualified as a physician, but he did not enjoy clinical practice. Though he acknowledged that Descartes was a liberating influence on his own intellectual development, Locke being a Puritan, viewed Descartes' work with some suspicion, particularly his views concerning innate ideas and the automatic nature with which events transpired in the human mind.

As might be expected given his almost obsessive-compulsive lifestyle, Locke's visage evinced a man with a serious look, parsimonious and controlled, invariably with an even temper and an uncommonly ordered physical presence. Unlike Hobbes, who wanted to compete, argue, and demean, Locke was gentle, winsome, and approachable, easy to read and clear in exposition. As with other philosophers of distinction, he never married and may have been celibate most of his life, though he had many friends and was regarded highly by his colleagues. Meeting informally for many years at his home in Exeter, they shared opportunities to tackle complex and perplexing issues, comparing their views and seeking to find a common ground on which they could agree. Out of these discussions emerged numerous essays explaining how to acquire knowledge. Avoiding formal deductive reasoning processes, he and his associates employed their own personal experiences, including those with children, to answer which events are experienced first and in what sequence they unfold into the forms of knowledge that characterize adult mental processes.

Central to Locke's view was the existence of two primary sources of ideas. The first source included *sensations* derived from direct contact with external events and objects; the second included *reflections*, or what he characterized as the internal operations of the mind. Thus, one could think about the sensation of an experience even when an object or event was not physically present; as such, ideas could become independent of directly experienced sensations. For Locke, these two processes were the mind's only source of ideas. As Locke formulated it further, reflection could not stem from innate sources because those sources depended on earlier experiences and sensations. Among these reflections of the mind, Locke included perceiving, thinking, believing, reasoning, knowing, and willing.

Like the Greek philosophers centuries before him, Locke's concern centered on the *validity* of knowledge rather than on its processes or contents. Among Locke's major views was his position that there were no innate ideas; he held fast to the Aristotelian position, which took issue with Plato. It is unclear whether he believed there were inborn *potentialities*, not givens, that required the actualization of sensorial experience. Here, his position differed from Hobbes, who spoke directly and clearly to the effect that the mind was a *tabula rasa*, a term derived from Aristotle's writings. Locke argued strongly, however, against the belief that the mind was imprinted with extant moral, theological, and mathematical principles, which then shaped how a person would experience the world. Here, his ideas were disguised to counter the supernatural-demon mentality dominant in his day. He recognized fully that these religious prejudices could masquerade easily as preconceptions of innate ideas, which, for him, would be a disguised form of tyranny by ecclesiastical authority. As noted, he was convinced that all knowledge came from experience. Despite this assertion, he admitted that sensory impressions ultimately were transformed through reflection.

Although there were no innate ideas, according to Locke, individuals could become aware of the operations of the mind, which therefore provided its own sensory impressions. Initially composed only of elementary sensory units, the mind ultimately formed into a mental organization of complex apprehended knowledge.

Approximately in 1689, at the age of 56, Locke took a distinctly psychological turn in his writings. He wrote his "Essay Concerning Human Understanding" in 1696, then rewrote and enlarged it numerous times until the fourth edition was published in 1700. The following excerpt presents Locke's rationale for undertaking the illuminating book:

John Locke

> Since it is the *understanding* that sets man above the rest of sensible beings, and gives him all the advantage and dominion which he has over them, it is certainly a subject, even for its nobleness, worth our labor to inquire into. The understanding, like the eye, whilst it makes us see and perceive all other things, takes no notice of itself; and it requires art and pains to set it at a distance, and make it its own object. But whatever be the difficulties that lie in the way of this inquiry, whatever it be that keeps us so much in the dark to ourselves, sure I am that all the light we can let in upon our own minds, all the acquaintance we can make with our own understandings, will not only be very pleasant, but bring us great advantage in directing our thoughts in the search of other things. (1696)

Extending the ideas of Hobbes, Locke wrote in some detail about the concepts of pleasure and pain inasmuch as they were central motives for conforming to moral behavior. He wrote:

> Amongst the simple ideas which we receive both from sensation and reflection, pain and pleasure are two very considerable ones. . . . I must all along be understood to mean not only bodily pain and pleasure, but whatsoever delight or uneasiness is felt by us, whether arising from any grateful or unacceptable sensation or reflection. (1696)

In contemplating mental disease, Locke recognized that there are extended periods in which madmen behave and look normal. He stated, "Hence it comes to pass that a man who is very sober, and of a right understanding in all other things, may in one particular one be as frantic as any in bedlam." He went on to comment that "having joined together some ideas very wrongly (madmen), mistake them for truths; and they err as men do that argue right from wrong principles" (1696).

Born in Scotland and educated at Edinburgh, **David Hume (1711–1776)** failed to show much promise in his youth, causing his family worries and misgivings about his capabilities. His life was, in many respects, odd and unpredictable. Like Hobbes and Locke before him, he held no academic position, but served as a librarian and as an attaché in the Foreign Service. Owing to the initial failure of his first volume, A *Treatise on Human Nature*, he turned his attention to history, ultimately achieving more recognition as a historian than as a philosopher. Nevertheless, many of his ideas, generated in later editions of the *Treatise*,which he retitled, *An Enquiry Concerning Human Understanding*, had strong convictions that influenced the shape of later psychological thought, as evident in the following thesis:

> Man is a reasonable being; and as such, receives from science his proper food and nourishment: But so narrow are the bounds of human understanding, that little satisfaction can be hoped for in this particular, either from the extent or security of his acquisitions. Man is a sociable, no less than a reasonable being: But neither can he always enjoy company agreeable and amusing, or preserve the proper relish for them. Man is also an active being; and from that disposition, as well as from the various necessities of human life, must submit to business and occupation: But the mind requires some relaxation, and cannot always support its bent to care and industry. It seems, then, that nature has pointed out a mixed kind of life as most suitable to the human race . . . (1748)

Hume described himself as a man of modest passions. Others described him as a person of substantial girth, possessing a broad and inexpressive face, suggesting a physique more suitable to a common man than to an eloquent philosopher. He was much admired in both France and England for his stimulating conversation and liberal ideas. Though condemning others for their atheistic beliefs, he himself had serious doubts on the matter, viewing faith as "unreasonable fancies."

According to Hume, memory and imagination were not separate faculties, but simply names to describe different ways in which the mind works over its ideas. Memory is clearer, more vibrant, and tends to repeat itself on the basis of an original impression. By contrast, imagination is more diffuse and abstract, and does not follow a set of impressions. Rather it possesses a measure of freedom to be constantly reconstructed. Anticipating the associationist point of view of Hartley, Hume proposed three ways in which associations occur among sensations and perceptions: resemblance (similarity), contiguity in either place or time, and causality. Hume's empiricist position can be noted in his assertion that psychology deals merely with experience as it flows to us, a series of experiences combining and recombining in an endless chain. It is *not* the result, as the rationalists asserted, of some intrinsic logical postulate that inheres in the observer.

Most of the major figures discussed in this chapter were born in either England or Germany. ***Étienne Bonnot de Condillac (1715–1780),*** however, a distinguished contributor to *sensationalism*, was educated in a Jesuit seminary in Paris and ordained into the Roman Catholic priesthood. Nevertheless, he gradually turned his attention away from religious topics and entered into the literary and philosophical salons of Paris. He was well acquainted with the views of Descartes, a forerunner in France, as well as the English philosopher John Locke. He belongs among the empiricists of his day because of his intense conviction that only sensory experiences were the basis for a philosophy of science. In contrast to Descartes, who postulated an active, if essentially spiritual, entity, to direct life's experiences, Condillac turned to the notion of physiologically based sensations. Thus, if the contents of the mind can be reduced to their sensory bases, one need not deal with issues that arise when one separates the mind from the senses that activate it. In many ways, he viewed the concept of mind as essentially superfluous. His was a simple creation, in a way as beautiful as that found in pure mathematics. In it, we need not presuppose laws of thought. Mere variations in the quality and sequence of sensory factors were sufficient for him to account for judgments and other so-called mental functions.

The Renaissance of Psychiatric Thought

In the fifteenth century, the medieval period gradually transitioned into what we view today as the modern world. Slowly, but persistently, the importance of human emotions and strivings became a significant element to guiding intellectual thought, ultimately replacing the medieval belief that the revelations of deeper truths were beyond humans' capabilities. Psychological processes became increasingly humanized; opportunities to study man as a biological rather than a purely spiritual organism permitted these processes to be considered a natural instead of a metaphysical science. Christianity had begun to lose its spirit and vitality; although the supernatural world still existed in people's minds, it had lost much of its power, increasingly ruled by static and rigid belief systems and symbols.

Desiderius Erasmus (1465–1536) was a sincere churchman who fully asserted the new humanism. He attacked the formalism and the corruption of the church, which he judged as sterile and possessed of rituals that were divested of their purpose and humanism. As Robinson (1976) has noted, Erasmian psychology was both practical and wise, expressed with verve and clarity in his *Colloquies*. Here Erasmus pricked vanity, exorcised exorcism, lamented superstition gleefully, and guided individuals to their duty to adhere to the simple and humane lessons of Christ's life, rather than to behaviors that obscure or deceive his worthiness. In his essays and letters, Erasmus, neither scientist nor formal philosopher, addressed the everyday world, seeking to expose its vanities, follies, charlatans, and warmongers. His was the attitude of a Renaissance humanist, a fine mind and a sympathetic heart. So, too, was the humanistic outlook of the Spanish Jew **Juan Luis Vives (1492–1540),** who contributed fundamentally to educational reforms and evinced a passionate concern for the welfare of the mentally afflicted who were routinely incarcerated and maligned.

Leaving behind the horrors of the Inquisition that characterized the medieval period, in the sixteenth century threads of intelligent and humanistic thought slowly filtered upward, rising to the surface and awakening humankind from its long slumber. Zilboorg and Henry have written (1941) that for several centuries philosophers repeatedly stated that it is man who should be studied and not his soul; these scholars slowly convinced themselves by listening to their own voices. They were not physicians because physicians had turned their attention to the new anatomy and physiology of animals and cadavers, as opposed to the emotions and natural state of living humans.

The waning of Middle Ages supernaturalism and the advent of the liberating Renaissance had numerous effects on the emergence of psychological thought. The Renaissance broke the hold of medieval dogma on the mind of early clinicians. It also opened up new nonphilosophical pathways for purely psychological ventures and inquiries into the general character of human nature, as well as the substantive nature of mental disorders.

The peak of the Renaissance was associated with the birth of enlightened spirits—among them **Paracelsus (1493–1541).** He would have been an extraordinary person in any historic age but, given his time, he looms as a strange if not rare blend of both mysticism of the past and practicality of his day. The actual name of Paracelsus was Theophrastus Bombastus Von Hohenheim. Perhaps in anticipation that he would be a courageous and intrusive battler all his life, he shortened his name to Paracelsus, even if its selection was somewhat pretentious. He adopted the name to suggest that his views were superior to those of Celsus, the chief medical authority of ancient Rome. Others have suggested that he acquired this name to show that he was surpassing the encyclopedists and medical methodists of his time, that is, that he intended to blaze a new trail by his adventurous approach to mental disorders. As with most thinkers of his day, Paracelsus was a believer in divination from the stars and the healing powers of such preparations as powdered Egyptian mummy. As such, he was both an astrologer and an alchemist.

For some of his disciples, Paracelsus was the towering medical figure of the Renaissance period, comparable to other contemporary luminaries such as Leonardo da Vinci, Copernicus, and Shakespeare. Most historians today regard him as an imaginative adventurer, if not a charlatan, and are inclined to view his contributions to scientific medicine as modest at best. Among his works were efforts to test various chemical agents for the treatment of several medical conditions, a focus not unlike the activities of contemporary pharmaceutical firms. Although he made no lasting discoveries, he was an inventive and creative pioneer. Nevertheless, the whimsies he had proposed were consigned largely to the rubbish heap. Despite sound insights, he dissipated much of his energy combating colleagues who did whatever they could to make his life unbearable.

When Paracelsus interrupted his mystical flights of fantasy to deal with his medical opportunities, he spoke in a voice akin to that of a seeker of scientific truth despite his rebellious defiance of ancient traditions and scholastic dogma. Most notably, he denounced the cruelties of the Inquisition, stating, "There are more superstitions in the Roman Church than in all these poor women and presumed witches." In his rejection of the views of the clergy regarding the sources of mental disorders, Paracelsus wrote:

> In nature there are not only diseases which afflict our body and our health, but many others which deprive us of sound reason, and these are the most serious. While speaking about the natural diseases and observing to what extent and how seriously they afflict various parts of our body, we must not forget to explain the origin of the diseases which deprive man of reason, as we know from experience that they develop out of man's disposition. The present-day clergy of Europe attribute such diseases to ghostly beings and threefold spirits; we are not inclined to believe them. (1567)

Paracelsus was the first physician to lay out a systematic classification of disorders that abandoned the habit of categorizing disorders beginning with the head, then working down step-by-step to the feet. He outlined his mental health classification in a treatise entitled: "On the Diseases Which Deprive Men of Health and Reason." Here, he identified whole families of mental disorder, notably: *lunatici, insani, vesani,* and *melancholici.* Lunatici suffered from disorders stemming from their reactions to the phases of the moon. Insani suffered from disorders identifiable at birth and clearly derived from family heritage. Vesani were poisoned or contaminated by food or drink. Melancholici, by virtue of their temperament, lost their ability to reason accurately. In addition to these four forms of mental illness, he identified others as *obsessi,* that is, obsessed by the devil. In this latter formulation, Paracelsus was dissenting from the dogmatic view of earlier centuries in which a devil obsession lay at the heart of all mental disorders. As he perceived it, numerous sources of mental dysfunction existed, only one of which could be traced to demonic preoccupations, and these other disorders he saw as a problem of defective thought processes, rather than a consequence of supernatural powers.

As noted, Europe was in a period of transition in the mid-sixteenth century. Religious elements of society were still strong, as was a belief in astrology and magic. A Spanish physician, **Juan Huarte (1530–1588)** played a key role in recognizing that individual differences were critical to an understanding of man. In his highly acclaimed book, *Discovering the Difference of Wits among Men* (1575/1594), he also set out to separate psychological thought from its theological basis; in many ways, this work may be considered to be the first volume of modern psychology. Huarte offered few speculations on the nature of the soul, a concern that occupied the attention of many of his philosophical contemporaries. Central to his interest in individual differences, Huarte suggested using aptitude tests to guide the education of children so as to match those who were most suitable for different functions (e.g., physical skills, intelligence, verbal facilities, and the like). As evidenced by this, Huarte was alert to individual differences and concerned himself with the welfare and education of the common man. For example:

> . . . tis not to be denied, but that some wits that are disposed for one, are not fit for another. And for that reason, it is convenient before the child be sent to school, to discover his inclination, to find out what study is most agreeable to his capacity. (1575)

The primary dimensions differentiating individuals, according to Huarte, are three that reflect cognitive functions: understanding (wit), memory, and imagination (fancy). He approached these three prime functions in a psychogram that established criteria for each of several major professions; once properly assessed, individuals could be pointed in a direction that corresponded to their best talents or interests. He not only anticipated contemporary factor analytic efforts to identify the separate components of skills, but to use them as a guide for future work. In many ways, Huarte was the first assessment thinker, but his approach was largely programmatic and not concrete; likewise, his actual methods were nonsystematic, if not crude. It was a relevant beginning, certainly more realistic and practical than other approaches of the day, such as physiognomy. Notably, he distanced himself from believers in astrology as well as other supernatural forms of divination that characterized his time and culture, as evident in the following:

> If one did not know from where comes great intelligence and ability it would be impossible to establish an art for planning intelligent children. We must first understand the principles and the causes and arrange them in order. The Astrologers claim that children are born under the influence of the stars, and to be prudent and ingenious, with good manners and to have the thousands of desirable traits we admire one must be born under the right star. But if this were true, we would not be able to give any rules, for everything depends upon chance in this doctrine, with no choices available for man to make. (1668)

Important though his contributions were to our understanding of mental functioning, Huarte based his theory of individual differences using Hippocrates' humoral temperaments. To him, these temperaments served as a basis for age, racial, and intellectual differences. Although oriented toward the goal of establishing somatic determinants for behavior, his theoretical framework reflected a blend of Greek history, natural temperament dispositions, and a touch of Christian theology.

Born in the southwest corner of France, **Michele de Montaigne (1533–1592)** received his formal education at the University of Toulouse. Following his training, he practiced law, but by 1571 he was able to retire from public life, initiating a series of papers that he referred to as essays. It was these essays for which Montaigne became well known, and they helped establish his place in the evolution of psychological and philosophical thought. Given that he lived during the European Renaissance, Montaigne's contributions are often considered comparable in their perceptive powers to those of Freud some three centuries later. Most importantly, he sought to understand life without recourse to religious or supernatural faith.

A true skeptic, Montaigne raised serious questions about the primacy of "original sin" as the source of human suffering. In contrast to his peers, he believed that humans were filled with an unjustified vanity; this he conveyed by illustrating the many ways in which animals possessed talents far superior to those seen in humans. In line with his skepticism, he exposed obvious contradictions in the writings of prior scholars and philosophers and noted that what was proven to be true in one time period or era could readily be judged untrue in another. He wrote: "How can we be sure that what is taken as truth today will not be replaced tomorrow?" Montaigne succeeded in intensifying the doubts already produced by the religious crisis of the Reformation, the humanistic crisis of the Renaissance, and the philosophical-scientific crisis of his day.

Having introduced a new approach to psychological matters, he sought to achieve a balanced dualism that rejected a strong emphasis on the soul and on the dispositional qualities of the body. As he wrote, the first extreme orients people to a supernatural approach to understanding human events, the other to a materialistic one. In his view, it was between these two extremes that a genuine psychological approach might be able to investigate topics such as thought, motivation, and conflict. Montaigne also set out to analyze topics such as happiness, anger, fear, and folly. Although he did not attempt to tie these together in a coherent system, he exemplified each topic with great psychological insight. Of particular merit was Montaigne's recognition that total consistency in behavior within individuals is rare; in fact, he asserted that inconsistency is the rule. Montaigne also recognized that individuals follow their "appetites"—that is, their motivations, impulses, and desires—but noted that these appetites constantly change as a function of age and life circumstances. Thus, the same individual might act in a courageous and adventurous manner in one setting, but be cowardly and withdrawn in another.

Montaigne was among the very first to propose insights into deep psychological processes, long before they were developed further by Freud and his associates. His ability to describe the elements of human experience opened the door to an increasingly naturalistic study of human functioning.

Clergyman and reclusive scholar, **Robert Burton (1576–1640)** wrote a single major work of extraordinary insight and sensitivity in 1621, entitled

Anatomy of Melancholy. Burton's childhood was an arid one, lacking in warmth and care, owing to parental aloofness. Although achieving great status as an Oxford scholar, as well as recognition for his brilliant and encompassing book, Burton was basically a self-deprecatory and bitter man, often struggling with the inner torment that characterized many of the suicides of his time. He was chronically depressed and his introspective accounts of his moods contained a wealth of impressive clinical analyses. He also sought to record the behavior and emotions of others, recognizing similar patterns to his own moodiness and eccentricity. This great volume of work, despite rambling irrelevancies and inaccuracies, makes fascinating reading today, as may be judged from the following excerpt:

> It is most absurd and ridiculous for any mortal man to look for a perpetual tenure of happiness in this life. Nothing so prosperous and pleasant, but it hath some bitterness in it, some complaining, some grudging; it is all a mixed passion, and like a chequer table, black and white men, families, cities, have their falls and wanes; now trines, sextiles, then quartiles and oppositions. We are not here as those angels, celestial powers and bodies, sun and moon, to finish our course without all offense, with such constancy, to continue for so many ages: but subject to infirmities, miseries, interrupted, tossed and tumbled up and down, carried about with every small blast, often molested and disquieted upon each slender occasion, uncertain, brittle, and so is all that we trust unto. (1621)

Although limited in his perspective, Burton established a classification system that differentiated melancholy from madness, a distinction akin to our differentiation of neuroses and psychoses. He outlined the following general categories: (1) diseases emanating from the body, (2) diseases of the head (primarily the brain), (3) madness (mania), and (4) melancholy, for which Burton further distinguished melancholy of the head, the body, or the bowels, and identified the major sources of melancholy (e.g., excessive love, excessive study, intense preoccupation with religious themes).

His introspective awareness of his own personal sadness and depression led him to recognize the sources of his own melancholy. He recognized guilt as a major element, despite his exemplary lifestyle. Other causes of melancholy included bodily deterioration and old age; bad diets; sexual excesses; idleness; solitariness; and an overpreoccupation with imagination, fears, shame, and malice. Burton clearly stated that a wide range of human frailties and life circumstances could engender melancholy .

Among the many topics that Burton included in his book on melancholy, he touched on mental aberrations that we recognize today as obsessions and compulsions. Thus he wrote of an individual:

> Who dared not to go over a bridge, come near a pool, rock, steep hill, lie in a chamber where cross-beams were, for fear he'd be tempted to hang, drown,

or precipitate himself. In a silent auditorium, as at a sermon, he was afraid he shall speak aloud at unawares, something indecent, unfit to be said. (1621, p. 253)

From the viewpoint of therapy, Burton proposed the wisdom of general counseling, avoiding the magical techniques of his forebears. Most significant among his counseling methods was the suggestion that patients become involved with distracting activities, especially in companionship with others. Most important among the remedies he recommended was to be open and to confess one's sadness to an empathetic friend. Here, Burton anticipated what ultimately became the core of modern psychotherapy—engaging a patient in a dialogue with a trusted and sympathetic outsider. Not part of the medical establishment, and despite the brilliance of his book, Burton and his proposals had little effect on the course of mental health study of his time.

A man of great intensity and imaginativeness, **Thomas Willis (1621–1675)** was the son of a perfectionist who made great demands on his sons. Originator of the term *neurology*, Willis also generated the term *psychology* to designate the study of the so-called corporeal soul. Arguably the most significant founder of what came to be referred to as biological psychiatry, he considered most ailments to be disorders of nerve transmission, rather than diseases of the blood vessels. He is perhaps best known by the circuit of arteries located at the base of the brain, known today as the "Circle of Willis."

In 1664, Willis published a major book on the history of the brain sciences, entitled *Cerebri Anatome*. It was a work of great scope and insight, and was, for many decades thereafter, without equal in the field. The title suggested that the book was limited to anatomy. However, Willis, a thoroughly educated Oxford physician, concerned himself not only with brain functions, but with their behavioral consequences. Willis also proposed that vital and involuntary systems existed in the brain that were mediated not by the higher centers of the brain, but by the *cerebellum*. His detailed articulation of the functional segments of the brain, grounded in comparative anatomical precision, was enriched by his clinical observations. Drawing ideas from existing theories, his work, both speculative and empirical, stimulated many another neuroanatomist.

In his work, Willis reported his observation of a sequence in which "young persons who, lively and spirited, and at times even brilliant in their childhood, passed into obtuseness and hebetude during adolescence." Thus, Willis anticipated by two centuries an idea more fully developed by Benjamin Morel, who termed this behavioral course as *dementia praecox*. To his credit, Willis rejected the idea of a wandering womb that ostensibly led to the syndrome of hysteria. The brain functioned as the center of all mental disturbances to Willis, and the various nerves emanating from the brain served to connect this overarching organ to the rest of the body. Willis, like most others of his time, spoke of processes generated by "animal spirits" (the soul), which somehow or other could be sucked out of the brain. Also of note was Willis's observation that melancholia and mania frequently coexisted within the same person, shifting erratically from an excited state to one of depression. This observation contributed to what we now refer to as bipolar disorder and/or manic-depressive psychosis.

Willis's clinical observations were uncontaminated by formal theories. His accurate inferences were based on repeated observations of patients over time, that is, the long-term course of their difficulties. There were some 14 categories in Willis's classification system, including several that were primarily neurological. His system, published in *De Anima Brutorum* (1672/1971), specified three major impairments: orosis, mania, and melancholia, each encompassing several subcategories, as well as neurological disorders such as headache, insomnia, and vertigo.

Although the early years of humanistic thinking had come to the fore as a result of the efforts of such significant figures as Vives, Weyer, and Plater, Willis was, by contrast, a stern medical man. He approved treatment by soothing and pleasurable activities, but showed little interest in the more sensitive and caring attitudes that began to emerge in his day. In fact, he was disposed to take harsh measures when dealing with those who were "mad," advising beatings and restraints, in addition to bloodletting and purgatives. As Zilboorg and Henry (1941) have written, "He would rather beat a mentally sick man, or consider him possessed with the devil, than attempt through compassion to gain sympathetic understanding" (p. 264).

Thomas Sydenham (1624–1689), a friend of John Locke, was born in England and raised in an orthodox Puritan family. Along with his brothers, he served in Cromwell's army during England's Civil War. He studied at Oxford and received his medical degree in 1648. Along with Locke, he held strongly to the view that hypotheses should be set aside in favor of closely observing all forms of natural phenomena, such as various medical diseases. As he put it, too many writers had saddled fairly distinct diseases with excessive features that stemmed from their overblown interpretations. Sydenham did not trust books, believing only what he could see and learn from his own bedside observations. Locke preached that all reliable knowledge came from observation. In his work, Sydenham came to typify the seventeenth-century empiricist emphasis in England.

Especially informative were Sydenham's contributions to the description of hysteria. His observation of hysterical patients enabled him to recognize the variations of conversion symptoms among paralyzed and pain patients, as well as to speculate on the operation of intense but unconscious emotions. The precision of his descriptions of hysterical phenomena was so comprehensive that little could be added today to what he said three centuries ago. He recognized that hysteria was among the most common of chronic diseases and observed that men exhibit the symptom complex no less so than women. He averred that hysterical symptoms can simulate almost all forms of truly organic diseases; for example, he noted that a paralysis of the body may be caused by stroke, but may also be found in a hysterical hemoplegia "from some violent commotion of the mind." He spoke of hysterical convulsions that resembled epileptic attacks, psychogenic palpitations of the heart, and hysterical pain that might be mistaken for kidney stones. He suggested that differential diagnosis between real biological diseases and those generated by the mind was possible only by thoroughly knowing the patient's psychological state. Speculating on the elements that differentiate men and women disposed to hysteria, Sydenham wrote:

> In my opinion, disorders which we term hysteric in women and hypochondriac in men arise from *irregular motions of the animal spirits*, whence they are hurried with violence and too copiously to a particular part, occasioning convulsions and pain when they exert their force upon parts of delicate sensation. . . . Women are more frequently affected with this disease than men, because kind nature has given them a finer and more delicate constitution of body, being designed for an easier life, and the pleasure of men, who were made robust that they might be able to cultivate the earth, hunt and kill wild beasts for food and the like. (From J. D. Comrie, 1922)

Sydenham was not the only medical writer of the seventeenth century who recognized the influence of gender and psychological factors in disease, but he was among the most successful in illustrating that emotions can generate and simulate physical disorders. In his efforts to formulate a syndromal pattern for numerous hysterical disorders, he extended the range of his observations to include not only the patient's dispositions, emotions, and defenses, but the family context within which they arose. In this way, he sought to determine the overall pathogenesis of certain syndromes, based largely on both physical and psychological phenomena. What was most informative was Sydenham's recognition that a syndromal picture rarely developed from a single pathogenic agent, be it a humoral imbalance or a systemic disturbance of the body. In fact, to Sydenham, multiple influences operated simultaneously on a patient, each of which took a somewhat different turn and produced a somewhat different appearance in the same disease process. He strongly believed in syndrome complexes rather than in a distinct or singular expression of a disorder. As a consequence, and in time, all medicine men were trained to consider a wide range of elements that, together, play a partial role in generating disease. However, he believed that physicians should set aside hypotheses and philosophical systems to ensure that they observed pathological phenomena with reliability and accuracy.

Especially notable was Sydenham's belief that nature has its own healing processes. These natural remedies of the body would not invariably solve a problem because it was often delayed or displaced. Included among the healing processes of nature, according to Sydenham, were well-established "excretions, eruptions, and fevers." Sydenham's speculations were based on comprehensive observations, which comprise the most modern methods for investigating mental illness and diagnosing specific clinical syndromes. He also emphasized the importance of identifying the antecedent emotional factors that may lead to the development of mental disorders. Insightfully, he observed the interplay between personal emotions and social pressures.

Born in Germany, **Georg Ernst Stahl (1660–1734)** wrote his dissertation in his early 20s, expressing the view that the then prevalent theory of animal spirits was essentially incorrect and that the various processes of the mind stemmed from a life-giving force, to which he applied the term *soul*. Stahl's soul, however, did not consist of the supernatural phenomena that characterized ancient and medieval thinking. It represented the source of energy of all living organisms, both human and animal. This revolutionary attitude of a special force involving psychological processes was not in keeping with the views of those who preceded him, such as Willis and Descartes. Nevertheless, Stahl was a devout man, albeit often morose and bitter and, on occasion, sharp-tongued. He was convinced that his views were right, and he stated his convictions unequivocally and without restraint. This was rather unusual in a earnest-looking crusader who was otherwise inconspicuous and often depressed.

Stahl's life force was not notably different than Freud's conception of the libido. It was the sum total of the nonmaterial side of men and animals which, together with nature, had the power to effect desired cures. Hence, Stahl's soul, which in many ways equates with "psyche," was able to perform functions that either bring on or stave off various diseases. He felt strongly that this force should be considered of greater importance than beliefs such as humors or medications. If we substitute psyche for soul and recognize that psychological forces stemming from intense emotions can influence ordinary daily activities, sometimes blocking our problematic impulses, we can see that Stahl extended the range of complex thought processes to what was subsequently referred to as a dynamic analysis of behavior.

In the eyes of many, Stahl was considered to be the originator of the distinction between organic and functional mental disorders. To him, mental disorders were not the result of physical, mechanical, or supernatural forces, but were essentially psychogenic. Stahl was appalled by the sharp demarcation of body and mind. Not only did he judge this dichotomy to be unjustified in that it harmed a fundamental understanding of disease unity, but it was especially problematic in understanding the complexity of forces involved in mental diseases. It was his assertion that a synthesis be sought to integrate physical and mental phenomena. Despite his deep religious convictions, he approached the problems of mental disorders without theological preconceptions. Also, as a genuine seventeenth-century empiricist, he believed that emotions, both passions and affects, could generate and interfere seriously with recovery from physical disease. Like Sydenham, Stahl pointed out that certain irrational mental states were organic, whereas others were emotional in their origin. He noted, therefore, that similar overt symptomatology could derive from diverse physical states, mental states, or both. Although he was not honored in his time, Stahl expressed the spirit of transition from the highly mechanistic and spiritual views that prevailed among most men of authority in the seventeenth century, to that of a truly synthesized medical psychology.

Comments and Reflections

The vast number of thinkers, their conflicting ideas, and the divergent interests that have shaped the early historical course of study into mental illness are staggering. So broad a sweep as to include ancient demonology and renaissance empirical philosophy makes for a fascinating story of prejudice and cruelty, as well as thoughtfulness and brilliance. Although sketchy in detail, this two-chapter review has outlined the major trends that established the foundation for our present philosophical approach to the mind and mental illness. Its purpose is to serve as a basis from which the reader will better appreciate the various streams of thought that characterize current knowledge.

It was during the late Renaissance, with the first outcroppings of scientific thought concerning natural phenomena, that imagination turned to the idea that psychological phenomena could reflect the methods and logic of the natural sciences. As evident in the preceding chapters, influential philosophers in the seventeenth century began to systematically organize an experimental approach to logic and reasoning and then to apply these ideas to the investigation of psychological phenomena. The understanding of mental illness profited enormously as sophisticated philosophical ideas were extended to an understanding of natural as opposed to spiritual phenomena. Substantial advances were made with detailed knowledge of genuine psychological processes, such as the relationship between humankind and lower animals, the role of organic and physiological structural mechanisms, and the place of psychosocial and environmental conditions in elaborating variations in human behavior. Archaic beliefs and assumptions regarding mental illness were shown increasingly to be primitive, inadequate, and scientifically mistaken.

A summary of some of the critical themes in these first two chapters follows.

The mental illness observations and psychological speculations of early philosophically oriented thinkers cannot be confused with objective and scientific evidence. They have, however, provided useful tools of inquiry to guide later approaches to these subjects. The intricacies and complexities of mental illness have compelled clinicians and researchers to come to grips with issues that rest on distinct philosophical considerations. Similarly, philosophers who seek to understand the many dimensions of human experience in a responsible and serious manner cannot ignore the growing literature that has broadened and deepened our growing understanding of psychological and psychiatric processes.

A problem arises, however, when philosophers study mental illness. Given an intelligent person's intuitive ability to make perceptive psychological insights or speculations, we can readily be misled into thinking that these insights provide us with a scientific system. It is paradoxical, but true and unfortunate, that philosophers can learn about mental disorders quite well merely by observing the ordinary events of human life. As a consequence, philosophical speculations about the subject may lead us to think that we should and, perhaps, can shy away from the obscure and complicating, yet often fertile and systematizing powers inherent in rigorous research and formal theory.

Contemporary philosophers of science such as **Carl G. Hempel (1905–1997)** consider that mature sciences must progress from an observationally based stage to one that is characterized by theoretical systemizations. It is the judgment of such philosophers that observation and speculation alone do not make a true science, and that overt similarity among clinical attributes does not necessarily represent verifiable and true knowledge. As becomes evident in later chapters, the expectations of the founding fathers of psychiatry and psychology that their achievements would rapidly match those of the more established natural sciences have not been realized. The data and theories relating to mental illness are far from equivalent to those comprising physics and chemistry, either in their reliability or in their range and validity of explanatory power. Indeed, unlike the natural sciences, the many fields that compose the study of the mind and mental illness are marked by competing schools of thought. They differ not only in their interpretation of newly gathered research and clinical data, but are also at odds over the appropriate ways of investigating as well as interpreting phenomena that have been their subjects of study.

Proponents of competing approaches to understanding mental illness, such as those described in this book, often disagree not only on substantive issues, but also by commitments to different conceptions of what constitutes cientific knowledge and how to establish such knowledge. As **Ernest Nagel (1901–1985),** an eminent philosopher of science, has stated:

> Conceptions frequently involve gross oversimplifications and misunderstandings of the logic of inquiry in other natural sciences; in particular, they sometimes contain crude empiricistic notions of scientific research that fail to do justice to the complex substantive and methodological assumptions which enter into the collection and interpretation of empirical data. But in any event, such conceptions are commonly acquired by psychologists from parochial intellectual traditions which they imbibe in an unquestioning manner during their professional training. Accordingly, it does not seem unreasonable to suppose that the progress of psychology as a natural science would be helped, and the level of its theoretical discussions raised, if psychologists were philosophically more knowledgeable than they usually are and had, in particular, competence in the logic of theory construction. (1965, p. 26)

Certain benefits are derived from systematizing clinical data in an empirically supportable and theoretically organized fashion. Because there are countless ways of observing and analyzing clinical information, a system of formal explanatory propositions becomes a useful guide to clinicians as they sort through and seek to comprehend the stream of amorphous signs and chaotic symptoms they normally encounter. Rather than shifting from one aspect of behavior, thought, or emotion to another, according to momentary and uncertain impressions of importance, scientifically guided clinicians can pursue in a logical and penetrating manner only those aspects that are likely to be related in a meaningful order. In addition to furnishing this guidance, a scientifically oriented system provides diagnosticians with a consistent set of hypotheses concerning clinical relationships that they may not have observed before. It enlarges the sensitivity and scope of knowledge of observers by alerting them to previously unnoticed relationships among attributes and then guides these new observations into a coherent body of knowledge about the many ways in which mental illness takes form.

It is unfortunate that the number of speculative theories that have been advanced to explain mental illness is directly proportional to the squabbling that can be found in the literature. Pieties of scientific virtue and methodological purity rarely are exclaimed by scientific researchers and innovative thinkers themselves, but are by their less systematic and less creative disciples. As I have previously commented (Millon, 1969):

> Theories arise typically from the perceptive observation and imaginative speculation of creative scientists. This innovator is usually quite aware of the limits and deficiencies of his "invention" and is disposed in the early stages of his speculation to modify it as he develops new observations and insights. Unfortunately, after its utility has been proven in a modest and limited way, the theory frequently acquires a specious stature. Having clarified certain ambiguities and survived initial criticisms, it begins to accumulate a coterie of disciples. These less creative thinkers tend to accept the theory wholeheartedly and espouse its superior explanatory powers and terminology throughout the scientific marketplace. They hold to its propositions tenaciously and defend it blindly and unequivocally against opposition. In time it becomes a rigid and sacred dogma and, as a result, authority replaces the test of utility and empirical validity. Intelligent men become religious disciples; their theory is a doctrine of "truth," not a guide to the unknown. (p. 41)

No one argues in favor of philosophers, psychiatrists, and psychologists whose speculations float, so to speak, unconcerned with careful scientific procedures or coordinated clinical knowledge. Their ideas should be regarded as the fatuous achievements they are, and the travesty they make of the virtues of a truly coherent mental health science. Speculative ideas should not be pushed beyond empirically validated evidence; derivations from theory should be linked wherever feasible to consensually established research data and clinical observations. As noted in Chapter 1, even the earliest of philosophical thinkers about mental illness generated brilliant observations and insights, but few of their ideas could be attributed to the structure of a scientific system, the

precision of their concepts, or their procedures for formal hypothesis derivation and validation.

Before we turn to the innovative ideas of Kraepelin, the great classifier;
Charcot, the great neurologist; and Freud the great psychoanalyst in Chapters
5, 6, and 7, we must first recognize several early humanitarians. They were
concerned neither with issues of disease nor of diagnosis, but with responsible
and humane stewardship, as well as with caring models of treatment, and an
empathic and nurturing sensitivity to help reduce the anguishing lives of the
mentally ill.

PART II

HUMANITARIAN STORIES

CHAPTER

3

Creating and Reforming the Custodial Asylum

At the turn of the sixteenth century, convincing and courageous efforts to replace supernatural explanations of mental illness with ordinary psychological concepts gradually supplanted medieval superstition and inhumane treatment. As Karl Menninger reminded us in the 1960s, "When mental illness was regarded as the infestation of the devil or of evil spirits, or, at the very best, of sinful thoughts and sinful acts, the logical treatment was abuse, cruelty, and neglect. And this is what the afflicted got" (1963, p. 49). How did these awful circumstances come to change? What events moved this early course of indifference and brutality to one more charitable and kind? And who were the persons who initiated and led these movements toward humane care? This chapter answers these questions.

The Humanitarian Story: I

In 1917, Kraepelin drafted an essay describing the course of psychiatric history during the previous century; he explained that in prior times the plight of the mentally ill was harsh almost everywhere in Europe. At best, they were handled as if they were idlers, vagrants, or criminals. Most were subjected to punitive laws that rarely were administered humanely. Dangerous patients were restrained and kept in small rooms, or in a stall in a private house, both referred to as "lunatic boxes." The intent was to confine patients, isolate them, and render them essentially harmless. Shorter (1997) speaks of this period as follows:

> One may abandon immediately any romantic notion of the insane in past times as being permitted to gambol on the village green or ruminate idly in the shade of the oak tree. Before the middle of the nineteenth century, the people of villages and small towns had a horror of those who were different, an authoritarian intolerance of behavior. . . . Those with disorders of mind and mood that forced them to be different . . . were dealt with in the most brutal and unfeeling manner. . . .
>
> If turned out of their homes and villages, the mentally ill swelled the streams of beggars that wandered the roads of early modern Europe. Many of the "village idiots" were those who had suffered mental retardation or schizophrenia from birth trauma. (p. 2)

Louis Caradec, a knowledgeable physician practicing in France in the 1860s, reflected on the attitudes of his local community:

> If the insane person is peaceful, people generally let him run loose. But if he becomes raging or troublesome, he is chained down in a corner of the stable or in an isolated room. . . . This happens quite frequently in the country side, and often a number of years may pass before the authorities are informed of this crime. (1860, p. 335)

Such conditions persisted well into the twentieth century in some quarters. In the mid-1950s, I traveled to a hospital in one of the larger states in the Northeast to provide my students an opportunity to see the typical conditions that existed in state hospital systems. What we saw was appalling and dismaying, as well as utterly disgusting; there was little that would differentiate this institution from the "snake pits" of the fifteenth and sixteenth centuries in Europe.

The idea that special institutions should be established to confine those considered insane did not take root until relatively modern times, although there are early examples of this. Of course, such individuals were not exempt from control by authorities; thus, the early Greeks assigned guardians to serve as responsible agents to prevent the mentally ill from harming themselves or others. Plato recommended, "if a man be mad, he shall not be free to roam the city, but his family shall keep him close to them in anyway they can." For the better part of early history, the insane were considered to be domestic responsibilities. Most were overseen at home; those who were harmless were permitted to wander about, despite fears that the evil spirits inhabiting them might escape and possess others. In Christian Europe, the family had full responsibility for any consequences of their troubled member's actions. The severely deranged typically were hidden in cellars or caged in pigpens, under the control of a sturdy youth or servant. Families sent many mentally ill relatives to faraway lands, owing to feelings of shame or the family's inability to care for them.

A notable exception to this careless and cruel treatment was established in the fourteenth century at Gheel, a Flemish village that housed the shrine of St. Dymphna, a healing shrine that accepted all the mentally disabled. Comparable asylums were founded under religious auspices in Spain and Portugal. In sixteenth-century France, by contrast, the scandalous confinement of the mad and the poor led to vast "street-sweeping" efforts to round up beggars, paupers, and vagabonds but, most notably, the enfeebled and insane. Over 6,000 of these "undesirables" were confined in Paris's General Hospital alone; other hospitals of similar character and intent were established shortly thereafter in the French provinces. Houses for the mad in France treated their charges as if they were wild and deservedly caged beasts. Those who were permitted to remain in their homes were required to obtain special permission from local officials, effectively denying the person all forms of civic freedom and legal rights. "Receptacles" for the insane, such as those in France, were established throughout rural Europe. They came in all shapes and sizes; most were run atrociously; few were under medical supervision. Some patients received minimal medical attention, but the great majority were irresponsibly kept or led by corrupt officials. As Porter (2002) recounted "Asylums varied widely in quality. Reformers exposed many as abominations, riddled with corruption and cruelty, where whips and chains masqueraded as therapeutic" (p. 99).

Depending on one's perspective and the cultural values of the time, the most humane supervisors of these institutions either held fast to the supernatural/religious themes of the day or took it on themselves to fight the indifference and cruelty that characterized their time. When mental disorders were regarded as the outcroppings of the devil or of evil spirits, no less the product of sinful thought or acts, the treatment was abuse and, at best, custodial neglect. The early demonic interpretation of mental illness gradually receded, but care remained, for the most part, callous and brutish.

Reviewing the prior hundred years of psychiatry (the nineteenth century), Emil Kraepelin, the great German systematist (see Chapter 5), described conditions throughout Europe as he saw and judged them, recording a variety of reports. Thus, a medical observer in 1804 wrote:

It is indeed frightening to approach such a wretched and sorrowful place! To hear mingled shouts of exultation and despair and then to think that within are human beings once renowned for their talent and sensitivity. It is terrifying to go inside and be assailed by these filthy, ragged creatures, while others are prevented from joining in the assault only by their fetters and chains or by the jabs of their attendants.

Describing an institution in Germany, also in 1804, another observer noted:

> In the asylum in Berlin those who were stark raving mad are isolated for the duration of their madness; they are locked naked in small cages or hutches, and food and water are introduced through holes and placed in copper basins secured by chains.

A common recommendation at the time was to establish asylums in remote and isolated locales since the wailing and howling of deranged patients would disturb sane men and upset communities. Moreover, it was suggested that those who were mentally deficient, owing to the assumption that they would passively endure whatever was inflicted on them, could be mistreated since they were ostensibly insensitive to hunger, cold, and pain. As a result, their obvious suffering was seen as justified. In Vienna, a special building was established for mental patients whose features were characterized as follows:

> The dark cells and corridors, secured by massive iron doors and gates, as well as chains and locks, strongly suggests its prison-like character. . . . Doctors who visit this dungeon are greeted by its inordinate filth, by its abominable, unbearable stench, noise and howling, and by the terrifying, heart-rending cries of its inhabitants whose arms, legs and necks are cruelly shackled in heavy chains and iron rings. . . . Not even the worst menagerie would exhibit such inhumane conditions. The faces and actions of the lunatics revealed their intense pain, suffering and despair. Their meager fair and their unending physical suffering, aggravated by the senseless application of vesicants and pustulants, made their plight worse than that of the most vicious criminals and murderers. A tiny hole guarded by a heavy iron grill was the only opening through which medical attention might be accomplished. Attending physicians were greeted by weeping and wailing, by insults and imbrications. Through the same hole, brutal and unsympathetic wardens pushed food and drink to these abused madmen, as if they were wolves and hyenas.

Kraepelin went on to write that London institutions were filled with countless patients clad only in loose shrouds and chained by their arms and legs to a wall allowing them only to either stand upright or remain fixed in a seat. He went on to describe other institutions where severe punishments were mandatory to deal with stubborn, recalcitrant, or willfully filthy and malicious patients. Similarly, some superintendents asserted that "a few lashes with a birch rod could do wonders for persistent uncleanliness." Modified according to circumstances, other superintendents employed ingenious contrivances, all designed to limit the patients' freedom of movement.

Most asylums used male attendants because of their physical strength and defiant appearance. Female attendants were sought with likewise strong bones and muscles, but also with courage and a sharp tongue. Throughout Europe, the worst misfits were hired as attendants. One Berlin reporter described attendants that appeared to have been chosen from the rabble of Berlin, "for they inspire or merit such little trust that the average person would hesitate to employ them as household servants." For reasons of economy, many institutions sought to employ disabled veterans and ex-convicts.

The painter Hogarth portrayed these hospitals in grotesque detail. He portrayed the rooms in which most patients spent their days as being without light or air, windows heavily barred and doors massively bolted, solid except for small peepholes. Most patient cells were cramped, dirty, and friendless quarters, with a hutch-like bed covered with straw and stone floors with gutters to carry off the refuse. There were no adornments except what was riveted or nailed to the walls. Lazy, indifferent, or incompetent attendants could not cope with the problem of feeding the helpless or maintaining cleanliness in quarters that housed vomiting and defecating patients. Vermin thrived, and most institutions were infested with countless rats that gnawed on paralytic or imbecilic patients.

Many asylums were open to the curious public for their amusement. In 1799, Immanuel Kant warned "nervous people" against visiting such institutions out of curiosity because the sight of these patients might provoke similar disturbances in the onlookers. He said, "Avoid this if you care about your sanity."

Kraepelin concluded his review with the following comment concerning those with outward manifestations of insanity:

> Their behavior, whether ridiculous and degenerate or dangerous and terrifying, could not fail to draw attention to their plight and to cast a shadow over their relations. This accounts for the perpetuation of the notion that mental illness is not so much a misfortune as a disgrace for the patient and his family. The whole system of treatment was also predicated on the assumption that mental patients are habitually disordered, malicious, base creatures. Every attempt was made to force them to renounce their foolishness and to bring them to submission by abusing and punishing them. When abuse and punishment failed, they had to be rendered harmless. Their freedom of movement was restricted to the utmost, and they were watched over like wild beasts. (1917/1962, p. 24)

Clinicians in earlier centuries were convinced that the afflicted could be changed for the better by daily exposure to harsh treatment. Sadly, many patients likewise believed that they deserved punishment and that punitive action would have a beneficial effect. An extraordinary range of torture was inflicted on these mental unfortunates: beating, starving, and freezing, to note just a few. Even today, the lives of patients in many quarters of the world comprise tormenting and agitating daily circumstances.

Slowly, albeit inconsistently, a latent humanity emerged among clinicians who resisted the horrors of their time and began to reject oppressive methods. Instead of punishment, an initial remedy became detention and disinterest. As the great medical historian, Roy Porter (2002) noted, "The madhouse served the trade in lunacy"—but it also became a place in which psychiatry as a profession began to develop its skills. Early psychiatrists managed inmates in private madhouses. As a function of their asylum experiences, the *alienists* (the term employed for psychiatrists who worked at institutions in the nineteenth and early twentieth centuries) gradually acquired attitudes and skills by which the well-managed asylum attempted to restore the insane to health. Every now and then, an extraordinary clinician rose above the crude values and harsh methodologies of the day; such clinicians based their treatments on moral principles, compassionate care, and genuine humanity. They rejected the notion that the mentally ill were devoid of sensibilities, were possessed by the devil, or otherwise were wicked, hopeless, and incurable. It is to these early pioneers that we turn in this chapter.

Unfolding of Key Ideas

A major phase of mental treatment, termed by some as *hospital reformation* and *moral treatment,* began with the pioneering efforts of several clinicians both before and shortly after the French Revolution (1789–1791). Guided by the belief that a physically attractive environment and contact with socially kind and moral hospital personnel could rescue institutionalized patients from degradation and depravity, these reformers initiated an approach to hospital care that gradually and fitfully became commonplace. This desultory path occurred for several reasons: the persistence of archaic beliefs, a decline in medical idealism, economic difficulties that prevented staffing institutions with adequately trained or motivated workers, the frequent resurgence of fear and a distaste for those with mental difficulties, and the public's preference for simple somatic methods instead of psychologically attuned treatment. In recent years, many institutionalized patients were released from those facilities and sent to poorly staffed residential halfway houses where, at best, they received kind custodial care and, at worst, were crammed together in filthy domiciles, isolated from family life, the larger community, and genuine therapeutic activities. Even the better hospital or community settings expended little effort to see that the routines and personnel of the institution provided more than a comfortable asylum, a dull refuge from the strains of everyday existence, a place where patients withdrew quietly into themselves. Despite periodic efforts to alter the worst of these conditions, most patients, even in the late-twentieth century, sat out their lives in dreary environments, abandoned by unsympathetic families and exposed to indifferent personnel.

Any changes from inhumane to custodial to genuine therapeutic environments in the past century came about less through public outcries than through the fortuitous advent of psychopharmacological treatment. These drugs "contained" difficult patients, encouraging and enabling hospital workers to turn their attention from problems of restraint to those of periodic treatment. State legislative bodies became convinced that a massive infusion of funds for psychopharmaceuticals might ultimately unburden the taxpayer of costly long-term patient incarceration. The increased ease of patient management, together with the influx of additional funds, combined to spur a new attitude, albeit brief, on the part of both the general public and hospital personnel.

The transformation from custodialism to humanism was difficult because hospital staffs were accustomed to viewing their charges as hopelessly chronic. Only gradually did they replace the legend of chronicity with the legend of recovery and begin to think in terms of rehabilitating patients. Between the 1960s and 1990s, the well-run mental hospital was no longer a place of incarceration or simply a refuge for psychic invalids, but a therapeutic community. It was a miniature social environment that sought to simulate the life and activities of the outside world; it sought also to assist its members to replace maladaptive behaviors with more socially appropriate ones.

In the following paragraphs, we trace this humanitarian progression from the sixteenth to the end of the twentieth century.

Pathfinding Proposals in the Sixteenth Century

Indifference and brutality characterized the early treatments of the mentally ill; most patients were imprisoned within almshouses and poorhouses. These unfortunate individuals were hounded and made senseless by society's cruel notions regarding their demonic character and its causes. Most important, the prevalent therapeutic methods of the day only aggravated the plight of the afflicted.

Founded in 1247, the hospital of St. Mary of Bethlehem became an institution exclusively for the mentally ill in 1402. Not untypical for the times, it served as an entertainment showplace for the public a century or so later. As Porter (2002) recounted, *Bedlam*, the term applied to the Bethlehem hospital, was open to visitors; the sane and mad were "brought tantalizingly face-to-face." Patients were on display, as in a human zoo or freak show. In one of Hogarth's cartoons, labeled the *Rake's Progress*, two visiting ladies of fashion are seen to linger before the cell of Britain's mad monarch, with a caption "Who is really crazy?" As many a critic noted, it was often hard to tell visitors and patients apart; some thought the inmates were freer spirits than those outside the cells. In illustrating Bedlam, Hogarth's intent was to mirror life in Great Britain. His work held up a reflection to viewers: It is we who are mad; as some have asked, who are those that are more mad? To him, the world was but a larger Bedlam.

Medieval times were not congenial to thoughtful and humanistic endeavors. The fourteenth century was a tumultuous time in the history of Europe's evolution owing in part to the Hundred Years' War and pandemics such as the Black Death. It was not a period when people were inclined to explore the vagaries of human psychological functioning, either philosophically or scientifically. With few exceptions, even those who were well educated sought to explain the tragedies of daily life with reference to demonism, superstition, and astrological beliefs. Beggars and the indigent were thought to consort with the devil or to be witches possessed of the devil. Conceptions of the mind had regressed to where they had been thousands of years earlier.

Despite this, there were occasional approaches that would be recognized today as suitable and charitable. As described in Chapters 1 and 2, clinicians of courage and compassion sought to better understand these disorders and to develop more humane methods of treatment. Viewing patients sympathetically and without prejudice, these exceptional persons sought to modify existing practices and to improve the lot of those with mental aberrations. The earliest of these efforts only briefly gained a measure of acceptance; however, sporadic thinkers planted the seeds of a modern humanitarian approach to mental work.

Juan Luis Vives (1492–1540) was born in one of the most eventful years in history, when Spain was at its zenith. In contrast to his compatriots of the Great Inquisition, however, Vives spoke of the need for a humanistic attitude toward the mentally ill. Vives was a Spanish Catholic philosopher of Jewish origin who traveled to England in his early years as a tutor for Princess Mary, daughter of England's Henry VIII. Outspoken and intensely moralistic in his views, he spent time in an English prison for opposing King Henry's divorce from Catherine of Aragon. Released on the condition that he leave England immediately, he traveled extensively and devoted himself quietly to writing on numerous subjects, many of which were recapitulations of the works of Aristotle and St. Augustine. Not long after the publication of the *Malleus Maleficarum*, Vives, who had become a recluse in an orthodox monastery, began to question the role of supernatural phenomena in mental functioning. His insights and sensitivity were among the first to argue for humane compassion for those suffering mental illness.

Vives became a foe of empty Catholic formalism and dogmatic supernaturalism. His deep attachment to the moral aspects of his religious beliefs stirred him to become a relentless critic of the prevailing system of mental treatment and the primitive concepts that characterized them. Although Vives gradually abandoned the prevalent scholasticism of his country, no one would have anticipated the vigorous spirit in which he set out to counter the traditions of his time. Nor would his associates have expected him to develop so strong and courageous a personality. That his religious sincerity was genuine could not be denied; in fact, he thought his faith provided him with the inspiration for his humanistic views. The prevailing ideas to which he was exposed created a high level of inner conflict between these opposing viewpoints. Scholastic in orientation, he was well acquainted with the abstractions and intricacies of prevailing religious thought. But he found much of what he read to be devoid of substance. And, in contrast to most distinguished thinkers of his day and of earlier days, he focused on life as working and struggling men and women

actually experienced it, not on the life styles of
the powerful elitists who "oversaw" sin or were
seekers of salvation.

Vives's high sensitivity to the plight of the
poor and the wretched, including the mentally
ill, led him to preach that scholars should turn
their efforts toward the downtrodden people that
characterized the masses of his day. However, he
was not interested in fostering a sentimental and
philanthropic approach, but in activating and organizing public programs for the poor and mentally ill. He recognized that the ecclesiastic
approach, known as almsgiving, neither provided
reliable help nor solved persistent social problems. Anticipating struggles that remain with us

Juan Luis Vives

even in today's society, he felt that relief for the poor and deranged should stem
from the state municipalities rather than from the philanthropic generosity of
private citizens. He averred that it was the community's responsibility to care
for the needy, a problematic approach that we call today social welfare. He
wrote, "It is disgraceful for the father of a family in his comfortable home to permit anyone in it to suffer the disgrace of being unclothed or in rags; it is similarly unfitting that the magistrates of the city should tolerate a condition in
which citizens are hard pressed by hunger and distress."

Vives proposed a taxonomy that was anchored to the restricted body of biological knowledge in his day; here, he also drew on the work of Hippocrates
and Galen. He proposed clear definitions for his concepts and appears to have
been among the first to formulate the laws of association and of conditioning.
He stated, "When an animal enjoys something at the sounding of a tone, then
when the tone is heard again, it will expect to experience the object it enjoyed
previously." His excursions into typology were based largely on clearly written
case histories. Also notable was Vives's clarity in discussing the emotional
states, despite their religious and metaphysical character. Vives looked accurately and honestly into the emotional nature of the mind, unafraid of
acknowledging its eccentric, whimsical, haphazard, and frequently selfish
character. In anticipation of the centuries to come, he recognized that conflict
was central to many of the feelings people had toward the events and persons
of their lives; thus love was frequently seen to mix with hate. This recognition
of ambivalence, which most persons thought to be illogical, if not impossible,
was brought to the foreground in later years by theorists such as Freud and
Bleuler in their clinical studies. In this regard, he observed that painful and
long-forgotten memories could be recalled through reflective association; in
these ideas, he also anticipated modern psychoanalytic ideas.

It is to the Dutchman **Johann Weyer (1515–1588),** often referred to as
the father of modern psychiatry, that credit must go for the most effective

Johann Weyer

denunciation of medieval demonology. His major work, *De Praestigiis Daemonum* (Delusion of Witches), published in 1563, vigorously attacked the *Malleus Maleficarum*. Although his views on the existence of demons are ambiguous, he stated unequivocally that these so-called witches were ill and insisted that their treatment be medically based and humane. Not only was Weyer a courageous advocate of naturalism, but he may be distinguished by perhaps being the first physician to specialize in mental disorders. Though he formulated no broad theories of his own, his talent as a clinician was evident by his sympathetic and skillful description of disorders that we know well today.

Educated in secular schools, Weyer carried forward the ideas of his mentor, Cornelius Agrippa, in which he sought to shatter the entire religious structure that obstructed the development of a humane and knowledge-based approach to mental illness. Endowed with a quiet and courtly manner and a calm temperament, his approach received a much wider hearing than others who preceded him. Fortunately, Weyer, himself a Roman Catholic, was well protected in his militant and provocative viewpoints (e.g., from the witch hunters) by his champion and close associate Duke William III of Cleves. Weyer was a devoted physician and at the same time a loyal churchman. Nevertheless, his forceful arguments could not help but bring him into conflict with the superstitions of his day. As Weyer portrayed mental illness, diabolical possessions were more likely to indicate a disordered mind or a peculiar metabolism than the intricate workings of demons. He voiced his views in *De Praestigiis Daemonum* (1563/1991):

> My object is medical, in that I have to show that those illnesses, whose origins are often attributed to the witches, come from natural causes; and my object is legal, in that I shall speak of punishment in a manner other than the accustomed way for sorcerers and witches.

Weyer's *De Praestigiis* is filled with an impressive range of information. For example, he viewed nightmares, which had been attributed in his day to demon possession, to be the result of somatic discomforts that were elaborated through the actions of an unclear imagination. Weyer interpreted numerous other mental disturbances to be a consequence of drugs or hypersuggestibility.

Weyer was a thoughtful and softspoken man, quite different from his compatriot, the brash and outspoken Paracelsus. Nevertheless, he had the fervor of a genuine humanistic pioneer, and the courage to defy openly the cruel dogmatism of his contemporaries. Weyer was a luminous figure in establishing the foundations of psychiatric thinking; nevertheless, his clinical publications remained on the prohibited *Index of the Roman Catholic Church* for several centuries.

The Swiss physician **Felix Plater (1536–1614)** was perhaps the first person to propose the term *alienation;* for the next four centuries, psychiatrists were labeled *alienists.* In contrast to his peers, Plater went so far as to live in the dark cages and cells of the day, exploring the life experiences of those assigned to the horrid dungeons in which the retarded and mentally ill were imprisoned. Not only was he a serious and compassionate physician, but he was highly inquisitive, curious to know how these mental unfortunates fared in such dreadful conditions. From his inquiries and observations, he declared that the deplorable environments in which the mentally ill lived was of a character that no society should permit. Although intensely disposed to avoid most harsh procedures, Plater nevertheless recommended the necessity of chains or the release of mania by burning the forehead to permit demonic vapors to escape.

Trained initially as a monk and deeply imbued with the metaphysical notions of his day, **Tomaso Garzoni (1549–1589)** was a highly prolific but short-lived contributor to the humanistic orientation of the sixteenth century. He outlined both his philosophy and the symptoms of many mental disorders in his *L'Hospidale de Pazzi Incurabili* (1586). In a long series of discourses, he detailed the symptomatology of a wide range of disorders and character types, specifying differences among the melancholic, the memory impaired, the frenzied, the dumb, and the demented, to name just a few.

Perhaps of greater importance than the 30 or so disorders and syndromes he articulated was his adherence to the view that mental patients should not be assigned to depressing prison-like settings, but should be placed in hospitals for treatment by sympathetic and supportive physicians. Despite their allegiance to church dogma, Garzoni and Plater played a significant role in establishing a rationale for humane treatment of the mentally disturbed through central Europe.

Implementing Programs in the Eighteenth Century

The eighteenth century is fraught with fables and stories that memorialize the triumph of humane sensibility and medical courage over the earlier religious obscurantism and cultural mysticism, seeking thereby to obscure psychiatry's origins in a prescientific past. What history has come to us in recent times is often a series of self-promoting themes that confirm the virtuous and heroic character of the profession. Historians have noted numerous myths that have evolved to advance the professional credibility of all sciences, be it psychiatry or otherwise. For example, Pinel, identified by many as the great liberator of the insane, actually freed only a small percentage of his hospital charges, replacing their shackles with other forms of mechanical restraint. Pinel's gesture of heroism was merely a manifestation of the *zeitgeist* of the time, a public display of an idea found throughout numerous hospitals during that period in Europe. The search for valorous figures has created legends that immortalize those who contributed but a few minor steps to a broad-ranging movement of the time. As noted, the beginnings of liberating thought in psychiatry did not start in the late Enlightenment period in France or Italy, but in sixteenth-century Spain, with Juan Vives's courageous proposals, and in the Netherlands, where Johann Weyer instituted his revolutionary ideas.

Anticipating what was soon to be known as moral treatment, a number of eighteenth-century physicians and hospital superintendents sought to convince their colleagues to recognize that patients were sentient human beings and to consider their illnesses as disorders that could be cured. Moral treatment implied the use of cultural mores as modalities for therapy; for example, it was held that education was personally uplifting, as would be recreation and social comingling among peers. The thinkers to which we turn next represented a broad-based effort to create treatment environments that would be conducive to spontaneous or self-generated mental recovery. More specifically, they argued for individual care in hospitals of modest size, in which exercise, religious sermons, occupational therapy, social games, and the like, were prevalent. Each of these innovators voiced their condemnation of physical violence and emotional threats.

In the 1760s, great indignation arose in England as a result of the brutal treatment given King George III during his periods of mental confusion. Conflict among physicians engaged to treat the king led to parliamentary investigations, public attention, and eventual reforms. By 1797, a wealthy tea merchant, **William Hack Tuke (1732–1822)** established the York Retreat in England, which was a quiet refuge committed to providing humane treatment.

Although the York Retreat reflected a personal philanthropic effort on the part of Tuke, it was understandable that Tuke, a member of the Society of Friends (Quakers), would be oriented to such humanistic efforts as the abolishment of slavery, monetary assistance to the poor, and the promotion of prison reform. Tuke's ideas were modeled on an ideal bourgeois family life where patients and staff lived, dined, and worked together in settings where praise and blame as well as rewards and punishment enhanced recovery, all with the goal of restoring a healthy outlook and increased self-control. As Tuke's grandson Samuel wrote some decades later, his grandfather had sought initially to have medical authorities oversee the institute; this effort met with minimal success, leading his grandfather to establish what was termed "moral means"; essentially those of kindness and humanity within a familylike atmosphere.

On a personal level, Tuke was a merchant who had become highly distressed by the mistreatment and subsequent death of a close friend confined to an asylum. He took strong exception to the use of chains and manacles, as well as the prevalent practice of bloodletting, stressing the importance of supportive treatment and practical occupational training. He also arranged thorough educational programs for hospital attendants. Uninformed about similar developments elsewhere, especially in France under the leadership of Joseph D'Aquin and Philippe Pinel, Tuke's York Retreat created a system of reform of a highly original character, guided largely by the desires of laypersons although run by a medical superintendent. A short time after it became known that Tuke and Pinel were undertaking similar reforms, French physicians came to visit the York Retreat, and English physicians spent weeks at Pinel's Bicétre and Salpétrière Hospitals.

Joseph D'Aquin (1733–1815) was a predecessor of Phillippe Pinel. At the French hospital in Chambery, he established an approach to the treatment of mental disorders that was unusually sympathetic. Perhaps for the first time since Weyer, he sought to use the methods of medical care employed with numerous physical diseases. He also asserted that hospitals were the proper setting for treating the mentally deranged. Hospitals also were the only setting in which a sufficient number of cases could be studied intensely, thereby providing a normative base for scientific investigations.

At Chambery, he permitted patients to move about freely within the hospital's courtyards, and he selected attendants whom he judged to be humane and mild mannered. Striving to rid society of the many prejudices that characterized his time, D'Aquin wrote a book in 1791 entitled *Philosophie de la Folie*. Of special note, the book was "dedicated to all of humanity"; sadly the book was all but unnoticed, despite its strong recommendation that the chains that shackled the mentally deranged should be removed. D'Aquin's innovative text was available for every Frenchman to read and he dedicated his second edition (1804) to Pinel, so it is curious that Pinel makes no reference to the role of D'Aquin in establishing moral treatment in France before him.

Benjamin Rush (1745–1813) was born near Philadelphia, the fourth of seven children, but was raised by an uncle, a well-known Presbyterian minister. Inculcated with a firm discipline, Rush grew up to be a crusader against slavery, alcohol, and the death penalty. He was a liberating voice, not only for the humane treatment of the mentally ill, but in his advocation of public schools, educational facilities for women, and free dispensaries for the indigent.

In 1812, this "first" American psychiatrist wrote an insightful text entitled *Medical Inquiries and Observations upon the Diseases of the Mind*, in which he said:

> We are led further to lament the slower progress of humanity in its efforts to relieve (the mad people) than any other class of the afflicted . . . for many centuries they have been treated like criminals or shunned like beasts of prey; if visited, it has been only for the purposes of inhumane curiosity and amusement. (p. 14)

Earlier in his career, Rush had beseeched the managers of the Pennsylvania Hospital he superintended to provide more suitable quarters for his charges. In letters to these managers, he wrote (1810):

My attempts, which at first promised some improvement, were soon afterwards rendered abortive by the cells of the hospital. . . . These apartments are damp in winter and too warm in summer. They are moreover so constituted as not to admit readily of a change of air; hence the smell of them is both offensive and unwholesome. . . . I conceive that the appropriating of the cells any longer for the reception of mad people would be dishonorable both to the science and humanity of the City of Philadelphia . . .

. . . Many evils arise from an indiscriminate intercourse with mad people with visitors. . . . They often complain . . . in so rational manner as to induce a belief that their tales of injustice and oppression are true. . . . The anticipation of being exposed as a spectacle to idle and sometimes to impertinent visitors is a chief reason why our hospital is often the last instead of the first retreat of persons affected by madness.

Trained for an extensive period under William Cullen (see Chapter 5), Rush was convinced that insanity stemmed from neural defects or irritabilities and was not a consequence of supernatural forces. As he wrote: "The cause of madness is seated primarily in the blood vessels of the brain . . . depending on the same morbid and irregular actions that comprise other circulatory diseases" (1812, p. 11).

Although Rush was acknowledged as the father of American psychiatry, he did little, in fact, to advance the sophisticated thinking that developed later in the century in the United States. Many argued that Rush's ideas contributed to modern psychological treatment, but there is little in his writings or in his behavior to show that his ideas were truly advanced. Observers of his hospital practices commented that his patients were not managed in a manner consistent with what came to be known as moral therapy. Despite Rush's text writings about the blessings of air, light, and pleasant walks, many found his actual programs in the Pennsylvania hospital to be harsh and insensitive.

The distinguished physician and scholar, **Phillippe Pinel (1745–1826),** taking advantage of the French Revolutionary emphasis on individual freedom, was the most public of many in his time to demonstrate the success of humane treatment. The eldest of seven children in a poor medical family Pinel grew up in southwest France, studied mathematics first, and then went on to study medicine at the University of Montpellier. He wandered to Paris, became involved in revolutionary circles and, despite his modest and unsophisticated background, was engaged in liberal political matters. In short order, he became enamored of the humanitarian reforms of the rampant enlightenment psychology of his day.

Placed in charge of the Bicétre Hospital by the Revolutionary Commune, he instituted the view that the mentally ill were intractable because they were deprived of their liberty. In fact, it was the manager of the Bicétre Hospital who ordered the removal of chains at the institution. And, as noted later in this chapter, Chiarugi had preceded him in insisting that patients be freed of their constraints a decade earlier in Italy. Fortunately, be it in Italy or France, the removal of chains, the provision of sunny rooms, the institution of free access to hospital grounds, and an atmosphere of gentility and kindness resulted in many dramatic recoveries and an overall improvement in patient behavior and manageability. Pinel's writings in 1801 became a key element in establishing the notion that psychological treatment should be carried out instead of severe incarceration. He wrote:

> The hope is well justified of returning to society individuals who seem to be hopeless. Our most assiduous and unflagging attention is required for that numerous group of patients who are convalescing or are lucid between episodes, a group that should be placed in a separate ward in the hospital and provided a form of psychological treatment for the purpose of developing and strengthening their faculties of reason. (1801, p. 253)

The public success of Pinel's reformist ideals and actions led to his assignment at the larger Salpétrière Hospital where he trained personnel to assume more than custodial functions and established the practice of maintaining systematic records and case histories. The relationship that Pinel proposed establishing between physician and patient was phrased as *le traitement moral;* the phrase does *not* mean moral therapy in French, but rather, "mental therapy." Although he was given credit for establishing the concept of moral treatment, the character of the relationship it represented can be traced back to earlier periods in both England and France.

What brought Pinel to the forefront were his books, *Nosographie Philosophique* (1798) and *Traite Medico-philosophique de l'Alienation Mentale* (1801). These scholarly works were judged to be masterpieces of psychiatric knowledge. Empirically oriented and seeking scientific precision for his studies, he nevertheless failed to formulate a new classification system; in its basic parameters it proved to be a minor extension of those proposed by De Sauvages and William Cullen (see Chapter 5).

Pinel's most innovative diagnostic ideas centered on the clinical features of antisocial personalities. Psychiatrists at the end of the eighteenth century engaged in age-old arguments concerning free will and whether certain moral transgressors were capable of understanding the consequences of their acts. It was Pinel, referring to a form of madness known at the time as *la folie raisonnante,* who noted that certain patients engaged in impulsive and self-damaging acts, although their reasoning abilities were unimpaired and they fully grasped the irrationality of what they were doing. Describing these cases under the name *manie sans delire* (insanity

Phillippe Pinel

without delirium), his description was among the first to recognize that madness need not signify a deficit in reasoning powers. As Pinel (1801) described it:

> I was not a little surprised to find many maniacs who at no period gave evidence of any lesion of understanding, but who were under the dominion of instinctive and abstract fury, as if the faculties of affect alone had sustained injury. (p. 230)

Pinel was an empiricist who also sought to evaluate all therapies in terms of their outcome, an approach that resonates well with contemporary thinking. He found that bloodletting, corporal punishment, and physical confinement were not merely ineffective, but destructive. He also suggested a wide range of explanations for the etiology of mental aberrations, including "ungovernable or disappointed ambition, religious fanaticism, profound chagrin, and unfortunate love." These views asserted that insanity could not be entirely the result of physical lesions on the brain.

Though more than a decade younger, **Vincenzo Chiarugi (1759–1820)** anticipated the significant institutional changes that were widely publicized in the career of Phillippe Pinel. In 1788, Chiarugi was appointed superintendent of the Bonifazio Hospital in Italy. On assuming this role, he stated strongly and explicitly that mental patients should receive a full measure of humanitarian care, that asylums should not merely separate patients from the larger community but should serve primarily as a setting to heal them. Restraints were to be kept to an absolute minimum, recreational programs were regularly instituted, and physicians were expected to visit all patients daily in the hospital wards. As he wrote in his three-volume work, entitled On Insanity:

> It is a supreme moral duty and medical obligation to respect the insane individual as a person. It is especially necessary for those who treat the mental patient to gain his confidence and trust. It is best, therefore, to be tactful and understanding and try to lead the patient to the truth and to instill reason in him in a kind way. (1793, p. 24)

Chiarugi stated with great conviction that lashings were improper as a form of punishment, that he judged them to be "harmful, cruel, and inhumane when patients were irrational and responsive to fear, dangerous when they were rabid, and fatal under other circumstances" (1793, p. 136). He stated that threats and lashes not only were ineffective, but merely excited patients and fortified their obstinacy. As he judged it, their keepers should pamper them, consent to whatever might calm them, or laugh with them.

He asserted that it should be forbidden to make patients work for the hospital, except where it was therapeutic or served as a form of psychic relief. High standards of hygiene were imposed within the hospital; rooms and furniture were arranged to offer patients maximum comfort and protection. The only method of restriction permitted was a straitjacket reinforced with strips of cotton so as not to impair blood circulation; these restraints were to be used only with extremely unruly or delirious patients. He noted that the elimination of cruel and inhumane attitudes by hospital staff resulted in a greater measure of patient recovery than would otherwise occur. In his instructions to staff, he insisted that they pamper patients and do anything that might "calm their fevers," even joking and laughing with them when possible.

Sadly, Pinel, who received great recognition for his work, was either indifferent to or unkind in his appraisal of Chiarugi's efforts, which diminished his status as an early contributor to humanitarian reforms. Adding insult to injury, Chiarugi's work was rarely continued by his Italian followers.

Influenced by the works of Immanuel Kant, the German philosopher-physician **Johann Christian Reil (1759–1813)** is perhaps best known for introducing the term *Psychiaterie* into our modern lexicon, a new label to represent those concerned with treating the mind. Reil's professional life was centered at the University of Halle, where he both obtained his medical training and ultimately served as Chair of Medicine for over 20 years.

Despite his primary focus on medical and neurological diseases, Reil spoke of an international movement that was underway to help overcome the horrors of life among the insane. He commented that physicians in all the major nations of Europe were taking steps to vigorously improve the lot of the mentally unfortunate, to end the practice of placing them in prisons and jails, and "to wipe from the face of the earth this most devastating of pestilences." Although an educated man of considerable sophistication, Reil likely had little direct contact with mental patients. Nevertheless, he concluded that psychiatric hospitals were the preferable environment to care for the mentally ill, asserting that family care was less adequate than care provided in institutions, despite the latter's own limitations, as homes had few baths and open spaces for healthy programs of therapy.

Drawing on the contributions of Chiarugi, whose work he sought to emulate, Reil, speaking in the best style of the Enlightenment, exclaimed: "When it comes to saving others, where are the fruits of our famous culture, love for mankind, sense of community, supposed citizenship, and noble renunciation of self-interest?" (1803, p. 11). In his judgment, the "medical guild" should play a more active role than heretofore, owing to their "courage and energy." He stated that hospitals could be the one exception to the rule that the sick can be better cared for at home. He felt, however, that there should be two kinds of institutions for the insane: one for incurables, the other for curables. He specified elaborate programs for the psychotherapeutic care of the latter group, including occupational, music, and drama therapy, as well as advocating good nutrition, sufficient sleep, and sunlight.

Pinel's methods in France were continued by his student and successor at the Salpétrière, **Jean-Étienne-Dominique Esquirol (1772–1840).** In addition to establishing many new hospitals, operated in accordance with Pinel's principles, Esquirol lectured in psychiatry throughout the Continent and in

1838 published what has been judged to be the first modern treatise on mental disorders, *Des Maladies Mentales*.

Esquirol was the son of an influential French family that had been reduced to poverty following the Revolution. Searching for a career, one day he wandered into the Salpêtrière Hospital where he heard a series of lectures by Phillippe Pinel. Without hesitation, he followed what proved to be a clear direction for his future, becoming a close acolyte and reformer with the intention of carrying on Pinel's work. This he did early on with a doctoral dissertation in 1802 on the "passions" in mental illness. In 1811, he became the administrator of the hospital's major psychiatric unit. In short order, he moved to become the head physician in the Paris suburb of Charenton, using that post as a stepping-stone to institute Pinel's asylum model throughout all of France's provinces.

Esquirol wrote an impassioned letter to the Minister of Interior in Paris in 1818, where he summarized his impressions of his recent visits to nearby hospitals:

> I saw patients naked, with rags or nothing more than straw to protect them against the cold, damp weather. I saw how in their retched state they were deprived of fresh air to breathe, of water to quench their thirst, and of all the basic necessities of life. I saw them turned over for safe keeping to brutal jailors. I saw them chained in damp, cramped holes without light or air; people would be ashamed to keep in such places the wild animals which are cared for at great expense in our large cities. That is what I observed almost everywhere in France, and that is how the mentally ill are treated almost everywhere in Europe.

In addition to his institutional work, Esquirol sought to establish a hospital therapeutic community reflecting a family-like environment between patients and physicians, but separated from the patient's actual family. He believed that isolation from family and friends would aid patients by diverting them from the troublesome passions of family life, which he judged to have created many of their difficulties. Thus, he wrote (1816):

> The calm that the psychiatric patients enjoy, far from the tumult and the noise, and the mental rest conferred by removal from their businesses and domestic problems, is very favorable to their recovery. Subject to an orderly life, to discipline, to a well-calibrated regimen, they are obliged to reflect on the change in their life. The necessity of adjusting, of behaving well with strangers, of living together with their companions in suffering, are powerful allies in achieving restoration of their loss of reason. (p. 126)

Esquirol's work mirrored the work of his mentor, Pinel, so precisely that their contributions to humanistic thinking and to descriptive observations were frequently confused in the nineteenth century. Neither was preoccupied with philosophical or physiological speculations, but both centered their attentions

on clear clinical descriptions of carefully observed patients. Esquirol may be considered to
have established the tradition of descriptive
psychiatry, a framework for the classification of
disorders that remains a core element of contemporary thinking. He also spelled out numerous environmental events that he believed were
causally involved in the precipitation of clinical
syndromes. In many ways, he was the first psychiatrist to have suggested that the interaction
of external precipitants and patient personality
vulnerabilities might serve as a basis for understanding mental illness. Establishing the importance of a psychological approach, Esquirol
made a point of exploring the inner functioning

Jean-Étienne-Dominque
Esquirol

of his patients' minds, focusing, for example, on the underlying processes that
generated manifest hallucinations and deliriums. To him, inner psychic structures of affect and impulse were as significant as the patient's capacity for reason and control. In this view, Esquirol may be thought of as a forerunner of
Freud's notion of the vicissitudes between *id* impulses and their control by the
ego and *superego*.

Although Tuke quickly adopted Pinel's and Esquirol's ideas at the York Retreat (and Fricke adopted them in Germany in 1795), the policy of nonrestraint
spread slowly throughout the Western world. Many segments of the public
showed a readiness to accept this view, but forceful opposition arose within the
medical community. Thus, in England, demonstrations of successful nonrestraint by *Gardner Hill* and *Charlesworth* were vigorously condemned by their
physician colleagues.

A French teacher of the deaf, **Jean Itard (1775–1843),** extended the
ideas of Esquirol concerning the humane care of those with mental disabilities. Itard became a pioneer in the training of the mentally deficient, a work
stimulated by the discovery near Aveyron in France of a so-called wild boy, a
youngster some 10 years of age who may have been abandoned by his parents
but had managed to survive on his own in the forest. Itard studied and
worked with this seemingly unmanageable youngster over a period of five
years. The child ultimately became responsive and affectionate, engaging in
productive activities and useful tasks, but unable to acquire language skills.
Deprived of the requisite early stimulation for human language and thought,
the boy lacked the necessary substrate for complex reasoning and communication skills, and Itard was unable to compensate for these early deficiencies.
Nevertheless, along with later efforts by **Edward Seguin (1812–1880),** he
instituted a systematic, humane, and constructive approach to enable
the mentally retarded to fully realize their limited potentials. Both France
and the United States, guided by the model that Itard pioneered, established

facilities in the nineteenth century for the humane care and training of these unfortunate children.

Humanizing Care in Nineteenth-Century Europe

Pinel's and Esquirol's reforms led to the establishment of new legal requirements in the Napoleonic Code, codified in 1838. The Code required each province to either establish a public asylum or ensure the provision of adequate facilities for the insane in general hospitals. Rules were also established for the certification of the insane by medical officers to guard against improper confinement by local community politicians or families. Provincial prefects were given the power to inspect these public facilities. Other European countries passed similar legislation shortly thereafter.

Treatment in "lunatic houses" of the period focused on regimens designed to help patients acquire self-discipline so they could learn to properly minister to themselves and thereby recover more quickly. In accord with Esquirol's thesis, patients were exhorted to keep their distance from their families and to learn to behave properly with strangers, where they would experience shame should their improper behaviors be judged unfavorably. Competence would give patients feelings of hope and would lead staff to reward them with small favors, each helpful in accelerating their recovery. Asylums were to be located in lovely rustic environments, amidst brooks and lakes, hills and fields, in buildings with no bars on their windows and an indoor environment that was clean and livable.

Throughout Europe, efforts were made to replace chains for restraining delirious or violent patients. Several decades passed, however, before these brutal devices were markedly reduced and, in some quarters, totally banished. Cold baths were used increasingly throughout the mid-nineteenth century as a restraint to protect other patients from those whose behavior was precipitate, disagreeable, and potentially harmful.

In 1839, **John Conolly (1784–1860)** began removing all restraining mechanisms from the Hanwell Hospital in England, where he was superintendent. He not only renounced irons and manacles, but straitjackets and fabric cuffs as well. Appropriately trained attendants would guide daily activities designed to discipline the body and focus the mind. These steps proved remarkably successful in establishing a major revolution in the handling and care of patients. Instead of using physical restraint to repress the emotional manifestation of his patients' disorders, he sought to find constructive means of exerting a favorable influence on their lives by implementing comfortable accommodations and treating them sympathetically.

Efforts to eliminate cold douches and metal restraints were quickly introduced throughout England, a step that Conolly vigorously espoused. He sought other means than physical restraint to control the external manifestations of inner psychic turmoil. His goal was to prevent unfortunate accidents and eliminate violent tendencies by diverting patients into harmless but useful activities, such as tending livestock, raising vegetable crops, and engaging in daily laundry work. He also provided comfortable accommodations and leisure time for his patients, treated them sympathetically, consoled them, and familiarized himself with each patient's personal life circumstances. Thus, instead of forcibly suppressing symptoms by physical means, he sought to institute human love and kindness.

To achieve his goals, Conolly tried to attract and retain a dedicated hospital staff, bringing to the institution members of the community who possessed a sympathetic and open-minded attitude, as well as a willingness to adapt to the peculiarities of mental patients. He provided his staff with the financial means to present an attractive and clean appearance, and sought to teach them to win their patients' trust and respect with friendliness and thoughtfulness. So broad-based was his recognition of the importance of a capable and compassionate staff that he furnished them with both an insurance and retirement program and offered them time and opportunities to enjoy a normal family life. In Conolly's program of staff regulations, he avoided attending to potential improprieties but stressed the importance of a sympathetic attitude and the provision of wholesome hospital conditions.

Conolly's work-oriented program was adopted throughout the Continent; the asylum became a setting for work therapies. Outside the city, asylums soon became self-sufficient colonies with vast gardens, working pastures, and laundries, developed not only to achieve economy but to establish useful therapeutic activities that would help patients return to normal life. A so-called science of managing asylum life was established, including the design and architecture of the asylum buildings. Also routine were gradations among the patients; men were separated from women, the clean from the dirty, the violent from the harmless, and the incurables from those judged curable.

To no less extent than Pinel and Esquirol, **Joseph Guislain (1797–1860)**, a nineteenth-century psychiatrist, might be regarded as Belgium's intellectual successor to Weyer. What Pinel and Esquirol achieved at the Salpêtrière a generation earlier, Guislain performed with even greater success at Ghent. Spoken of by his countrymen as the "liberator of the insane," this reflective professor of philosophy and mental disease was unusually influential in his lectures on what Falret in France termed *mental alienation*. Taking special interest in each individual case, Guislain was not disposed to espouse his philosophical ideas concerning theory, but kept to the Pinel tradition of emphasizing keen observation and direct therapy.

Like many before him, Guislain recognized that familial concerns often proved to be a mixed blessing, that acts of attention and consideration could turn out to be problematic. He questioned the benefits of frequent visits by relatives since he observed that these periods often evoked consequential sadness and dismay instead of comfort and calm. Also, he took the unusual administrative position of placing similarly disordered patients in separate physical settings. He reported that groups of melancholics aggravated their common depressed state. Likewise, apathetic patients, when housed together, inhibited each other. Similarly, those with violent inclinations were in constant conflict. He arranged for patients with diverse disorders to live together, thereby balancing one another's defects and possibly producing beneficial effects.

A student of Esquirol, **William A. F. Browne (1805–1885),** served as superintendent of the Montrose Asylum in Edinburgh where he lectured frequently on the wisdom of reforming mental institutions. These lectures were published in 1837 under the title *What Asylums Were, Are, and Ought to Be.* Speaking of the ideal asylum of the future, Browne wrote:

> Conceive a spacious building resembling the palace of a peer, airy, and elevated, and elegant, surrounded by extensive and swelling grounds and gardens. The interior is fitted up with galleries, and workshops, and music-rooms. The sun and the air are allowed to enter at every window, the view of the shrubberies and fields, and groups of labourers, is unobstructed by shutters or bars; all is clean, quiet and attractive. The inmates all seem to be actuated by the common impulse of enjoyment, all are busy, and delighted by being so. The house and all around appears a hive of industry. . . . (1837b, p. 226)

Notable among his humane reforms was the initiation of drama therapy that gave patients opportunities to perform plays in which they could express their emotions and thoughts under the watchful eye of their institutional protectors. Among his visitors during the 1850s was Dorothea Lynde Dix. Drawing heavily on the diagnostic system of Heinroth and Prichard, major contributors to classification systems of the day, Browne suggested that the greatest susceptibility of women for mental illness derived from their poorer education and social inequities of the time. In his *Strong Remedies for Kindness in Custodial Care,* Browne wrote (1837a):

> There is in this community no compulsion, no chains, no corporal chastisement, simply because these are proved to be less effectual means of carrying any point than persuasion, emulation, and the desire of attaining gratification . . . such is a faithful picture of what may be seen in many institutions, and of what might be seen in all, were asylums conducted as they ought to be. (1837a, p. 229)

In the mid-nineteenth century, public commissions were set up in many nations of Europe to investigate the circumstances surrounding the care and treatment of the mentally ill. In Norway, proposals were made to build four mental hospitals in Oslo, Bergen, Trondheim, and Kristiansand; however, decades passed before funds became available for these institutions. Families with sufficient means routinely sent their afflicted relatives out of the country.

The son and great-grandson of innovative English psychiatrists, **Daniel Hack Tuke (1827–1895)** typified those who directed the institutions of the

British Islands in the mid-nineteenth century. As Zilboorg and Henry have written (1941), Daniel Tuke occupied a unique place in the English-speaking world. He made distinctive and far-reaching contributions to the welfare of the mentally sick, as well as becoming an ardent writer who, for years, guided building plans and treatment programs in both Europe and the United States. His great-grandfather, William Tuke, initiated the era of hospital re-form in England with the foundation of the York Retreat. Daniel Tuke de-voted his subsequent and later years to helping the wider British community overcome its fear and discomfort with the so-called lunatic.

No less significant were Tuke's travels in the United States, visiting numer-ous institutions along the East Coast and across the Midwest, speaking at length with many of the superintendents of the new American State Hospital system. He judged the United States to be wiser than England by planning to avoid the construction of huge asylums. Moreover, he believed American pa-tients were better fed, more warmly housed, and given more recognition and at-tention than patients in British institutions. Recording statistics available for review, he noted that only 5 percent were kept in restraints. At the Blooming-dale Hospital in New York, only two men and no women had been restrained in the preceding two-year period. Similarly, the use of seclusion and padded rooms was much less common than in Great Britain. Also notable were numerous staff appointments for women physicians. In contrast, Tuke's review of Canadian mental institutions led to severe criticisms and harsh judgments on his part.

Despite the many advances that occurred during the nineteenth century, patients throughout Europe and the United States vented intense wails of protest and disillusionment. Many claimed they were never crazy to start with or that their madness was a consequence of the barbaric hospital treatment to which they were exposed. As more and more patients were confined to insti-tutions, patient protests increased proportionately. Former inmates, seeking to vindicate their sanity and victimization by the sinister actions of their institu-tions, spoke out in numerous publications and newsletters.

Burgeoning of the American State Hospital System

As the early period of the reforms of Europe reached their peak in the early nineteenth century, their ideas crossed the Atlantic to the American commu-nity. The expansion of the state mental hospital system in the United States was a logical outgrowth of the commonly held view that people were either sane or insane. If a person was deemed insane and therefore permanently in-capable of assuming responsibility for his actions and welfare, then the kindest course of action was to remove him to a custodial asylum and let him live out his days under the guidance of others. It was not long, however, before the no-tion that mental disturbances were of an all-or-none nature became a matter of dispute among sophisticated professionals and laypersons. Early sociologists and anthropologists provided convincing evidence that a person's behavior was a product of the social environment and amenable to change if that environment could be modified. As this viewpoint grew in prominence, it was proposed that institutions be located in the social communities where patients lived, rather than in remote areas where early asylums had been built. Moreover, in their own communities, patients would be treated close to their families and near natural life conditions, rather than being isolated from them. It was an idea that took almost a century to fully implement.

Among the earliest hospital-based settings for mental patients was a ward for the insane at the Pennsylvania Hospital in Philadelphia cofounded by the Society of Friends in 1752. The humane leaders of the Society soon noted that this ward was both too small and archaic in its policies, especially in light of what its members had begun to learn from mental hospital developments in Europe. Purchasing land outside Philadelphia, the Society established the Frankford Retreat, which was modeled after the York Retreat in England. As stated in the institution's guidebook, chains were never to be used to confine patients and the "law of kindness" was to prevail at what proved to be the first formal mental institution in the United States.

Shortly thereafter, the state medical society of Connecticut, following the model set out by the Frankford and the York Retreats, established a similar institution in 1824; it was designated the Hartford Retreat. The guiding physicians, Ely Todd and Samuel Woodward, both Yale graduates, also set forth a law of kindness stipulating that the inmates were to be treated with unvaried gentleness and respect. This retreat, initially organized as semiprivate, became fully private soon thereafter; it is known today as the Institute for Living. In 1826, a psychiatric service was established at Massachusetts General Hospital; it was named the McLean Asylum, following a large monetary grant from a Boston merchant by that name. McLean's superintendent, Luther Bell, read the works of Pinel and Tuke and quickly adopted the notion of instituting amusement and work programs "to exercise both body and mind."

In 1832, Massachusetts became the first of the New England states to establish a State Lunatic Hospital for the mentally ill. Located in Worcester, the hospital opened under the leadership of **Samuel B. Woodward (1787–1850),** who had been instrumental in building the Hartford Retreat. The hospital soon acquired a national reputation, admitting a relatively large number of patients in a program designed to maximize both moral and medical treatment. In Woodward's words, "The hospital was designed to show that mental diseases were as curable, if not more curable than any other disease of equal severity." Recording his treatment program's results in the 1840s, Woodward claimed that an average of 80 to 90 percent of his patients were discharged, a finding that received considerable national attention. It also established a rationale for the founding of other state-funded hospitals throughout the country. His evidence established the value of publicly supported institutions as an instrument that could provide relatively quick and effective therapy. Shortly before his death, Woodward wrote:

The abandonment of depletion, external irritants, drastic purges and starvation, and the substitution of baths, narcotics, tonics, and a generous diet, is not less to be appreciated in the improved condition of the insane, than the change from manacles, chains, by-locks, and confining chairs, to the present system of kindness, confidence, social intercourse, labor, religious teaching, and freedom from restraint. In this age of improvement, no class of mankind have felt its influence more favorably than the insane. (1850)

Although the roots of the mental hygiene movement can be traced to the well-publicized moral treatment ideas of Phillippe Pinel and Jean Esquirol in France, the first widespread leadership in the United States came from a Massachusetts schoolteacher, **Dorothea Lynde Dix (1802–1887).** Until her investigations in 1841 into the neglect and brutality prevalent in asylums, these so-called treatment institutions for the ill were privately funded and, despite their deplorable conditions, existed only for the wealthy. Dix contended, "Insanity was a product of inhumane conditions in society; hence, society should assume full responsibility for the care of its victims."

Dorothea Lynde Dix

Dorothea Dix was a woman of strong determination who devoted her career not only to the mentally ill, but to many other distressed citizens. American women of the mid-nineteenth century had few career choices available to them. Not only did they lack political power, but they did not have the right to vote. Nevertheless, in 1843 Dix drafted a petition in support of efforts to expand the Worcester hospital, writing:

I come to place before the legislature of Massachusetts the condition of the miserable, the desolate, the outcast. I come as the advocate of helpless, forgotten, insane, idiotic men and women; of beings sunk to their lowest condition for which the most unconcerned would start with real horror; of beings retched in our prisons, and more retched in our alms houses . . . (I wish to fix) attention upon a subject only the more strongly pressing in its claims because it is revolting and disgusting in its details. (1843)

With deep passion, she averred that the state had a moral, medical, and even a legal obligation to provide the benefits of asylum care. Her devotion to the cause of the mentally ill ultimately gave her extraordinary influence in shaping the character of state hospitals throughout the country. She was often asked to recommend suitable replacements when hospital superintendencies became vacant.

Dix continued her crusade for close to 40 years, influencing the building of 30 state-supported hospitals and, more importantly, firmly establishing the modern principle of public responsibility for the mentally ill. Sadly, the product of her enlightened work, the once great state hospital system, has come to be viewed as a financial burden in current managed mental health efforts.

The first of Dix's selections of young men "with warmth and an optimistic spirit" that she encouraged to assume a major state hospital role was **John S. Butler (1803–1890),** who became superintendent of Boston Lunatic Hospital in 1839. A disciple of Samuel Woodard, then superintendent at Worcester, Butler was a man of great aptitude when dealing with both patients and hospital staff. He quickly abolished seclusion and restraint in Boston, developed occupational programs for patients, and took an active part in daily patient programs, such as organized dances and weekly plays. In 1843, Butler was asked to assume the superintendency of the Hartford Retreat, where his vigorous leadership brought it to the vanguard of mental hospitals for the next 40 years.

In his only book, *The Curability of Insanity* (1887), Butler stated: "Recent insanity in very many cases is radically curable under the prompt, persistent, and united use of medical and moral means." He claimed that separate institutions should be established for patients with acute or with chronic or long-term difficulties. In his judgment, the daily presence of chronic patients might retard progress of those in the acute phases of their illness. This position was not widely approved nor was his view that a superintendent should visit all his patients daily. Especially insightful were his writings on the central importance of prevention. He wrote:

> We can also more efficiently apply the means of insanity's prevention and remedy, when we can better measure its varied pernicious causes, such as erroneous educational and social influences, neglect of family training to reverence and obedience, sensational reading, evil habits of body and mind, and idle, aimless, or sensual lives, and learn more exactly as we shall surely learn, how very early in life the predisposing causes of insanity are planted in the child. (pp. 47–48)

Perhaps the most highly regarded of the American psychiatrists of his day, **Isaac Ray (1807–1881)** had traveled extensively in Europe before publishing in 1837 a thoughtful tract on what we now call forensic psychiatry entitled *Medical Jurisprudence of Insanity* (1837/1962). Updated and republished in six editions, this text became the standard for the mental health profession for the better part of the nineteenth century.

In 1841, Ray assumed the superintendency of the State Hospital for the Insane in Augusta, Maine, a position he held until he moved to the new Butler Hospital in Providence, Rhode Island. Despite his demanding administrative responsibilities, Ray continued to draft a wide range of papers over the next 50 years. Although concerned about the extensive limitation of physical restraints in American institutions, he was notably enlightened and humanistic in his publications, claiming that it was more considerate to constrain those of manic inclinations than to free them to harm fellow patients and staff.

In 1850, Ray drafted a document concerning legal regulations for the insane that was more advanced in its particulars than many of our laws today. He asserted:

> It will be regarded hereafter as a curious fact, that while the most of our insane hospitals have been created and more or less maintained by the State, the confinement of the insane is regulated in most, if not all the States, by no statute law whatever. . . . This condition of the law is fruitful of evil to all parties concerned (and) not in accordance with dictates of humanity or of medical science. (p. 217)

Especially sensitive to issues regarding the relationship of criminality to mental pathology, he concluded in his writings in the late 1850s that "the law of insanity, especially that relative to criminal cases, is still loose, vacillating, and greatly behind the present state of the knowledge of that disease."

Of particular interest was Ray's 350-page text published in 1863, bearing the title *Mental Hygiene*. It established a term that was to characterize a major movement fostered through the efforts of Dorothea Dix, and a half-century later, Clifford Beers. In his volume, Ray defined mental hygiene as "the art of preserving the health of the mind against all the incidents and influences calculated to deteriorate its qualities, impair its energies, or derange its movements."

Thomas Kirkebride (1809–1883) was the leader in state hospital design and construction, an achievement stimulated by Dorothea Dix's efforts to build a national system. Kirkebride served as superintendent of the Pennsylvania Hospital for more than 40 years. He articulated in considerable detail every aspect of an ideal state hospital in an 1880 book that he entitled *On the Construction, Organization, and General Arrangements of Hospitals for the Insane*. He wrote:

> . . . this volume is a contribution . . . toward securing a more elevated sentiment, and a greater harmony of thought and action, in regard to the insane, as well as a more just appreciation of the objects and the work of institutions for their care and treatment.
>
> The use of mechanical means of restraint, and the protracted seclusion of patients in their rooms—although the former may be, and I believe, is occasionally desirable, but not absolutely necessary, in the management of our hospitals for the insane—ought both always to be regarded as evils of no trifling magnitude, and to abate which, as far as possible, no effort should be left untried.
>
> Besides leading patients into bad habits, the frequent use in a ward of the means referred to, induces attendants and others to look upon them as a common resource in cases of difficulty or danger, to regard them as their grand reliance in every emergency, and to forget the great power of other measures that are entirely unobjectionable—the value of tact, and kindness and sympathy in controlling the violence and the dangerous propensities of the insane. (pp. 60–61)

Like more and more others with this responsibility, Kirkebride asserted that the chief medical officer in each hospital should see each patient every day. Moreover, the proper number of patients in an institution should never exceed 250. He urged that the interior of each building be cheerful and that the exterior of each building be comfortable to the eye. He was notably concerned with maintaining an extensive dialogue with patients' family members. Especially important was his desire to persuade the family that the hospital's choice of treatment was humane and appropriate. If hospitals were to maintain public legitimacy, a careful "moral relationship" was also to be present between community and hospital. Moreover, and wherever possible, patients were to be granted freedom to walk anywhere on the hospital grounds without supervision and, in certain cases, to walk into town upon their promise to return.

Whereas Kirkebride was the prime leader in the construction and design of state hospital buildings, **Pliny Earle's (1809–1892)** distinction lay in his contribution to the importance of accurate hospital records. Dismayed by pretensions of cure rates reported by his colleagues, Earle asserted that statistical record keeping had been notoriously inaccurate and misleading to psychiatric colleagues and the public as well. In his role as a young superintendent of the Bloomingdale Asylum in New York and later at the State Lunatic Hospital in Northampton, Massachusetts, he wrote of an unfortunate "curability delusion." He demonstrated how the hopes of his colleagues had outrun their statistical judgment, writing: "If a common formula for the statistical part of (hospital) reports could be adopted by all the asylums . . . our knowledge would be more rapidly advanced" (1838/1887). Moreover, Earle, anticipating contemporary concerns regarding descriptive classification, wrote:

> In the present state of our knowledge . . . no classification of insanity can be erected upon a pathological basis, for the simple reason that the pathology of the disease is unknown. . . . We are forced to fall back upon the symptomotology of the disease—*the apparent mental condition,* based solely on its outward manifestations.

In the latter half of the nineteenth century, psychiatry had stabilized its character and direction. For the most part, mental health professionals concentrated their efforts in the new state hospital system; these asylums had become warehouses, however, separated from the community and with little hope of adopting new approaches to treatment and remediation. Psychiatrists, in general, were not recognized as quality specialists; most were judged to be second-rate physicians. Almost all asylums in the nation were backwater institutions whose physicians had lost contact with medicine-at-large; superintendents were viewed to be more like gentlemen farmers than treatment specialists. The desolateness of the hospital environment would have shocked early reformers whose hopes were primarily forward seeking and humane. The situation throughout Europe was no less problematic. Everywhere, hospital psychiatry was viewed as the dregs of medical practice, one notch higher perhaps than working in a prison.

The mediocre and bureaucratic situation in American hospitals, however, evinced a reasonable degree of self-satisfaction among members of the American Medico-Psychological Association (the forerunner of the American Psychiatric Association), a society headed by superintendents of state hospitals in the mid-nineteenth century. This calm and complacent state of equanimity changed significantly toward the latter half of the century.

The youngest member of the association of hospital superintendents, **John M. Galt (1819–1862)** assumed the superintendency of the Williamsburg Asylum in Virginia at the age of 22, an institution with which both his father and grandfather had been associated as physicians. The most scholarly of his fellow superintendents, Galt was familiar with numerous European languages, was a botanist of notable ability, and was an avid reader of foreign literature. At the age of 27, having digested the ideas of over 75 psychiatric contemporaries in Europe, he published *The Treatment of Insanity* (1846), the most comprehensive summary of theoretical and scientific ideas in his day.

A vigorous exponent of moral treatment at his hospital, and following innovative ideas he learned from European pioneers, he instituted programs of recreational therapy, occupational therapy, bibliotherapy, and musical therapy to, "Prevent the insane from lapsing into the dull torpor of reveries and indolence into which it is the very nature of man to sink if mind and body are left in a state of vacuity from the want of means to occupy them" (1846).

Galt was the first in the United States to propose several innovations to facilitate an orderly transition of patients from asylum to community, establishing a parole system that permitted patients to live and work outside the hospital while remaining under its legal jurisdiction. Anticipating the American community mental health movement by more than a century, he sought not only to construct facilities for convalescing patients, but also set out to board chronic patients with nearby families. No less significant was his insistence on accurate record keeping and statistics, as well as his belief that state hospitals should become centers for active research. Regarding the latter, his Williamsburg institution became the first among American state hospitals to perform routine autopsies.

It was not until 1894 that the dean of American neurology, **S. Weir Mitchell (1829–1914)** seized the opportunity at the semicentennial meeting of the American Medico-Psychological Association to criticize state asylum psychiatrists for their public isolation and their indifference to the need for research on the problems of the mentally ill. In a blistering chastisement of organized psychiatry in his day, Mitchell charged them with "scientific unproductiveness."

Although care for the mentally ill had improved as a consequence of Dix's labor, more was needed than the construction of fortresslike asylums to calm the suspicions and fear of the general public. Prompted by his repeated mistreatment as a patient in three such institutions, **Clifford W. Beers (1876–1943)** wrote a penetrating account of his experiences in a famous book entitled *A Mind That Found Itself* (1908). Beers, a graduate of Yale University, had spent numerous years extricating himself from difficult business situations, followed by a suicide attempt in his late 20s. His characteristic mood alternated between deep depressions and hypermanic excitement. Hospitalized at two institutions for several years, he wrote painfully about his experiences; hoping that his manuscript would do as much for the mentally ill as he believed *Uncle Tom's Cabin* had done to popularize the cause of the abolitionists some decades earlier. Beers expressed his intense feelings toward psychiatric supervisors, especially the many attendants who took charge of him. He recorded the latter's general level of ignorance and brutality, as well as their lack of education and humane attitudes, writing:

> . . . . Their unconscious lack of consideration for my comfort and peace of mind was torture. . . . As I was rendered speechless by delusions, I could not offer so much as a word of protest. I trust that it is not now too late, however, to protest in behalf of the thousands of outraged patients in private and state hospitals whose mute submission to such indignities have never been recorded. (1908, p. 36)

When published, it aroused intense public reaction and the support of such eminent men as William James and Adolf Meyer. Meyer recommended establishing a Society for Mental Hygiene "to show people better ways of healthy living, prevention of trouble, and efficient handling of what is not prevented." With his founding of the Society shortly thereafter, Beers inaugurated a worldwide movement designed not only to encourage improved hospital conditions, but to educate the public on the importance of prevention and dispel the prevalent belief that mental disorders were incurable and a stigma of disgrace. Nevertheless, the fledgling organization he started ran into difficulties both administratively and conceptually. Information about the character and cause of mental disorders was notably rudimentary, to say the least. Treatment approaches were entirely a matter of opinion and not a result of demonstrable evidence. There were no criteria for determining effective prevention or rehabilitation. The idea of healthy living and prevention of trouble had little substance. The avowed goal of advancing mental hygiene was appealing to the public, but as a practical matter, it could not meaningfully aid the plight of the mentally ill.

Beers's specific aspiration for the care of the insane in mental hospitals was realized over the next several decades. By the beginning of the twentieth century, there were over one hundred public institutions in 40 states; by the mid-1930s there were 265 mental hospitals in the country with an overall resident population of more than a half-million people. At the start of World War II, more than two-thirds of the members of American Psychiatric Association were employed in mental hospitals, even though their goal as leaders of a progressive movement had lost its legitimacy and their institutions had become problems rather than solutions.

Among the major dilemmas of the American Psychiatric Association was the persistent and rapid growth in the number of patients in the state hospital system, a condition that overwhelmed their ability to deal with the vast hoard of the ill, whose problems of personal hygiene, self-care, and self-esteem had been eroded severely. Few could be economically self-sufficient, fewer still could be helped to overcome their severe psychological and neurological impairments. Many were the product of neurosyphilitic infections as venereal disease spread across Europe and North America. Mental illnesses associated with alcoholism had also increased, given that the average American drank almost twice as much alcohol at the turn of the twentieth century than had been the case a generation or two earlier. The number of patients classified as suffering from dementia praecox, labeled schizophrenia these days, likewise grew in vast numbers, as did an increased number of individuals who passed through forensic psychiatric services.

It was not until the close of World War II that matters began to change in a meaningful fashion in the psychiatric profession. Psychiatrists in the military concluded that mental disorders were far more pervasive and serious than had been recognized previously. Further, these younger psychiatrists observed that treatment in noninstitutional settings could produce favorable effects. This led to a growing belief that early identification of symptoms and treatment in community settings could prevent the onset of more serious disorders in later life. To prevent vulnerabilities from becoming actuated, to attack early signs of mental disorder before they flowered into clinical form, became a guiding principle for the new approach in psychiatric practice.

Combined with the nearly two decades of neglect consequent to the Great Depression of the 1930s and World War II, the American state hospital system had deteriorated to a level of severe decay. Owing to his vigorous advocacy for universal health care, **Albert Deutsch (1905–1975),** an impoverished journalist, inspected psychiatric facilities in the mid-1940s and wrote numerous graphic articles exposing the shameful plight of the nation's mental hospitals. He wrote that these institutions paid less attention to their human inhabitants than did zoos in dealing with the animals in their care, referring to oppressive crowding and depressing, dirty, and dim-lit wards, where cots were lined in corridors and restless patients were tightly strapped to them. He had taken many dramatic photographs and displayed them in his well-received book, *The Shame of the States* (1948), which visually reinforced the impact of his articles. Although he commented that many of the physicians and psychiatrists in hospitals were humane and enlightened, and some were kindly and competent, all struggled desperately to overcome the "twin diseases" of institutional overcrowding and understaffing.

Shortly after the end of World War II, the scope of federal interest in the welfare of the mentally ill broadened dramatically. Central to these efforts was the role played by **Robert H. Felix (1904–1990),** a young psychiatrist who had trained with Adolf Meyer at Johns Hopkins and then joined the United States Public Health Service. Taking over administrative responsibility as head of its Division of Mental Hygiene, Felix set out to create a federal bureaucratic structure that would expand the limiting tradition of state responsibility by employing the resources of the national government. By 1946, President Truman signed into law the *National Mental Health Act*. It established uniform policies oriented to achieve three goals: First, to support research designed to expand understanding of the causes and treatment of psychiatric disorders; second, to train mental health professionals by providing fellowships and institutional grants; and third, to provide grants to states to assist them in establishing treatment clinics and demonstration studies to deal with innovative ways of preventing, diagnosing, and treating these disorders.

Moving toward Community Mental Health and Deinstitutionalization

Novel alternatives to the hospital and asylum model for treating the mentally ill can be traced back to private institutions in Germany in the mid-nineteenth century. In the 1860s, several private hospitals in Germany established "open divisions," which permitted patients to voluntarily enter and leave as they wished. Following the Belgian community for the insane at Geel, other German psychiatrists arranged to have mental patients live as boarders in the homes of farm families, and some arranged to have wealthy patients supervised in private homes. By the turn of the century, an approach termed *Familienpflege*, or "family care," was practiced throughout central Europe. Similarly, other European hospitals established outreach outpatient clinics, a plan that several northeastern areas of the United States followed in the 1920s.

By the 1930s, England fully opened many of its asylums to the wider community, discarding all locks and keys, encouraging patients who were willing to pursue periodic outside wanderings; this "open-door" policy soon took root in the United States. At the same period in England, the concept of a *therapeutic community* was instituted, led initially by a young psychiatric resident, Maxwell Jones. Here patients ran their wards by themselves, rather than being directed top-down by the hospital staff. Some programs even developed their own *psychodramas* in which patients enacted new ways of relating to one another. By the late 1940s, the model for a *day hospital* was established and constituted a special variant of the therapeutic community. Patients could normalize their daily lives in their natural family settings while spending part of their days in a supportive hospital environment that employed treatment approaches such as group counseling and occupational therapy.

In Canada, many individuals with major mental disorders came fully out of the asylum and into the community. And, in the United States in the late 1950s, *social psychiatry* became a commonly employed term to represent an approach in which patients were to be moved from the distant recesses of state hospitals back to their community settings.

Whether the label, "the third mental health revolution," applies appropriately to the movement presented in this section may be problematic, there can be little doubt, however, that it represented a marked departure from earlier views. No longer was the individual patient's actions, thoughts, or psychic defense mechanisms the point of focus; the wider social forces that shaped and colored the patient's life—the community and the cultural setting—now took center stage. The *clinical model* was no longer salient, having been supplanted by a *public health model;* and with it came a shift toward preventive programs, therapeutic hospital communities, crisis intervention therapies, social-action research, and the like.

Beginning with Dorothea Dix's demands for public responsibility in mental health in the mid-nineteenth century and coalescing with the mental hygiene movement and the writings of sociocultural thinkers such as Emile Durkheim in Europe and Franz Boas in the United States early in the twentieth century (see Chapter 11), the foundations of the "third revolution" were well set prior to its resurgence in the United States in the 1960s. Spurred by increased support from federal sources and the growing disenchantment with traditional treatment approaches, the views of social and community theorists attracted numerous, vigorous, outspoken, and action-oriented adherents.

By the late 1950s, Harry C. Solomon, then president of the American Psychiatric Association, asserted that the large state mental hospital was "antiquated, outmoded, and rapidly becoming obsolete" (1958). Nevertheless, throughout the country in the 1950s, officials had expressed a general determination to upgrade the deteriorated state hospital system.

During the late 1950s, striking new advances were being hailed as a consequence of the so-called wonder drugs, specifically, chlorpromazine (Thorazine) and reserpine, owing to their success in moderating the intensity of bizarre and unmanageable behavior among state hospital psychotics (see Chapter 6). Similarly, a growing enthusiasm erupted that community-oriented programs could reduce the necessity of investing funds for reconstructing a hospital system in which most institutions were more than a half-century old. However, this enthusiasm was difficult to implement. The number of new patients and mental hospital budgets continued to rise. Nevertheless, early patient release and the potential superiority of community treatment continued as a belief among professionals and political leaders.

By the early 1960s, the possibility of major changes in mental health policy across the nation was highly favorable. National legislation became a reality on the inauguration of a young and vigorous president. Similarly, there was a growing recognition that state governments were not only insufficient for the task but were fundamentally retrogressive in their approach to the mentally ill. By late 1962, the recommendation to the White House was that improvement in mental health services should be carried out in the community where a "continuum of local services" could be provided. The concept of a comprehensive community mental health program was established.

The ethos of the early 1960s reflected the view that state governments were essentially reactionary in their approach to the treatment of the mentally ill and were best bypassed in favor of a direct partnership between the federal government and the communities. This approach also reflected a belief that the origins of most mental problems could be traced to problems in one's social environment. Hence, community mental health services were enacted to empower individuals and small groups on the local level in arranging the lives of the mentally ill. State hospitals were considered obsolete. As the medical historian, Gerald Grob, described this period:

> Faith in the redemptive qualities of modern psychiatry was fused with other goals: A demand for social justice; an end to structural barriers that impeded the realization of the full potentiality of individuals; and the realignment of mental health services at the community level where a professional-public partnership would function more effectively. (1994, p. 250)

By 1965, programs were established at the federal level essentially repudiating the state institutional policies that had been in place for over a century. Scores of community mental health centers started up throughout the nation; they were left to experiment on their own, free to explore programs that were not especially beneficial to those most in need: the severely mentally ill. Weaknesses in intergovernmental linkages combined with the diversity of community-based programs led to daunting problems. Program inconsistencies led to increasing confusions, for example, blurring the previously clear differentiation between mental health and mental illness.

Although the *deinstitutionalization* initiatives of the 1960s had an initial aura of success, cracks in the system began to spread as increasing difficulties appeared on the scene. At first, there was a sharp decrease in mental hospital inpatient populations, suggesting that the new community programs ultimately would replace the older state hospital system. However, as limited federal resources were diverted to establish new mental health centers, the older and more established ones fell into an increasingly precarious economic state. As the chronically mentally ill were released in ever-growing numbers, local community centers were overwhelmed and became incapable of dealing with even basic human needs.

From two contrasting quarters along the political spectrum, there was a strong desire to undermine the gothic state institutions of the past. On the one hand, those associated with left-wing politics argued against "the evils of total institutions." On the other, politicians of the extreme right, notably the political leaders in both the United States and Great Britain in the 1980s, were intensely hostile to welfarism and were inclined to cut the economic costs of state institutions in favor of "community care." Both political extremes desired to scale down, if not close, their respective national mental hospital systems.

Most troubling in these new programs was the omission of a central role for the established state institutions. No explicit linkage existed between the new community centers and state mental hospitals, a setting in which an inpatient population of over one-half million individuals had previously resided. Community centers limited their focus to the less severe and occasionally functional patients at the expense of those who were more severely and persistently ill. Moreover, seriously ill patients, temporarily alleviated from their ailments by psychotropic medications, often failed to sustain themselves in community life without close supervision and careful support. Despite well-intentioned goals, the desired result was difficult to maintain. Community programs could not be sustained owing to their failure to coordinate efforts with state hospital programs that deposited in the community an increasing number of severely ill patients it was now ill-equipped to serve.

Chronically mentally ill patients acquired a troublesome social identity in the communities where they lived. Absent family care and programmatic community deficiencies resulted in inadequate housing and emotional support for released patients that reactivated and further intensified their disorders. Deinstitutionalization led to depressing consequences. Painfully portrayed in the press and on television, the plight of the mentally ill became a reminder of years past when patients wandered the streets disheveled, bedraggled, and bizarre. Rather than being acknowledged as the troubled persons they were, the mentally ill, in the manner of centuries earlier, were judged to be unregulated, frightening, and threatening.

By the 1980s, those who advocated community programs began to concede that they did not have the ability to integrate patients into normal societal life. A comprehensive program of services was required that would create a broad-based health care system with traditional state hospitals, community clinics, and other publicly supported mental health services. As Grob has written:

> The history of the care and treatment of the mentally ill in America for almost four centuries offers a sobering example of a cyclical pattern that has alternated between enthusiastic optimism and fatalistic pessimism . . .
>
> Each of these stages was marked by unrealistic expectations and rhetorical claims that had little basis in fact. . . .
>
> For too long mental health policies have embodied an elusive dream of magical cures that would eliminate age-old maladies. (1994, pp. 309–311)

Abbreviating Therapy for the General Public

The impetus for therapeutic innovations resulted from a deep antagonism on the part of most third-party payers toward long-term approaches to psychotherapy. The role of economic influences on treatment, both physical and mental, is itself a worthy treatise. In short, the economic climate required that new variants of therapy serve more patients at lower cost than it had before. Social and financial considerations, rather than theoretical developments and empirical research, increasingly initiated new directions in treatment. Although we continue to see an explosion in the number and variety of therapies, managed care and other insurance programs have insisted on more efficient, efficacious, and socially inclusive therapies than those of the past. The message to psychotherapists became "do more, with less," meaning not only fewer sessions, but more patients, and therefore less time spent thinking about the deeper dynamics of any one patient's problems. The emphasis on efficiency became the primary impetus for the development of short-term and narrowly focused therapies across the entire spectrum of mental disorders. Moreover, these forms were forced to fit within financial constraints. Therapy became therefore more behavioral and pharmacological, less humanistic and analytic.

Whatever the economic constraints, mental illness stands squarely and intrinsically in opposition, not just to managed therapies, but to most forms of abbreviated therapy. The more concentrated Axis I clinical syndromes, such as depression and anxiety, admit to focal, and therefore briefer, interventions. The personality impairments of Axis II, however, essentially represent longstanding and pervasive disorders comprising the entire matrix of the patient and stand like stone monoliths unmoved in the face of fiscal realities.

Despite the concerns that have been recorded about the effectiveness of brief therapy, this important social and economic trend in the field warrants a short review of its history and methods. The term *brief therapy* encompasses a wide range of approaches, techniques, and philosophical orientations, often obscuring important elements more than it reveals them. Despite its relative recency, segments signifying brief approaches to treatment can be traced back to the beginning of the twentieth century.

Soon after Freud renounced the hypnotic method as a major tool of analytic treatment, he initiated a procedure of rapid diagnosis and interpretive resolution of unconscious conflicts. For example, in a series of brief treatments (4 to 6 sessions), he successfully resolved the symptoms of the orchestral conductor Bruno Walter and those of the musical composer Gustav Mahler.

Two disciples of Freud, *Sandor Ferenczi* and *Otto Rank,* followed his early model of brief treatment and formulated what they perceived to be short, but effective, therapeutic forms. Ferenczi took a vigorous stance against the passivity that had become characteristic of the analytic model by the 1920s. For purposes of a more direct analysis, Ferenczi encouraged a high measure of activity on the therapist's part to expose the unconscious conflicts and fears that patients normally avoided. To him, interpretation was insufficient to effect a cure. Concurrent with Ferenczi's active stance were similar ideas proposed by Otto Rank; these signified his progressive dissatisfaction with the slow and tentative methodology that characterized the work of his analytic colleagues. It was his judgment that setting a time period for the end of treatment was key to its effectiveness. Likewise, he emphasized the importance of exploring current life experiences instead of distant infantile memories. In his judgment, psychoanalysis was an excellent procedure for in-depth investigations of patients' psyches, but an ineffective tool for resolving their distress in an efficient and rapid manner. Anticipating methods adopted by others in later years, Rank stressed that patients assume responsibility for their life's resolutions. Further, he sought to guide patients into recognizing how their own attitudes and behaviors perpetuated their problems.

Franz Alexander conceived his own work on short-term analytic therapy to be a continuation of the ideas proposed by Rank and Ferenczi. Together with his Chicago colleague, *Thomas French* in the late 1930s, Alexander stressed the special importance of evoking an emotional experience in treatment as a counterbalance to the classical analytic focus on intellectual exploration. Alexander did not abandon the importance of understanding the early development of a patient's life. Rather, he sought to revive the emotional aspects of early conflict situations. To achieve change, Alexander sought to provide new experiences and attitudes. This he considered to be the cornerstone of successful treatment, terming this process as *the corrective emotional experience.* Another central theme to Alexander was the principle of *therapeutic flexibility.* To him, psychoanalysis was too rigid in its procedure, In its stead, he proposed that therapists use techniques designed to fit the patient's psychological outlook, as contrasted with the analytic model of selecting patients who fit their preferred and singular technique.

Reflecting the views of Alexander, *Lewis Wolberg* gave special allegiance to the importance of a high degree of therapeutic activity on the part of the clinician, and a willingness to explore therapeutic methods, rather than adhering rigidly to a single passive approach. Although espousing a broad psychodynamic perspective, Wolberg asserted that clinical evidence could not support the view that discussions regarding the past are necessarily more therapeutic than discussions of the present. Further, he was not convinced that unconscious material was necessarily more significant than that within conscious awareness. Similarly, and in contrast with traditional psychoanalytic belief, he did not judge that transference interactions with the therapist were necessarily more therapeutic than those expressed toward other significant figures in the patient's life. Also, Wolberg sought to enlist the patient to become an active participant in therapy and to agree to an initial verbal contract concerning the goals of treatment and the number of sessions to be scheduled. In summary, he felt that it was necessary for therapists to overcome "the prejudice of depth."

Along with colleagues, *Leopold Bellak* wrote that brief therapy was especially useful in dealing with both minor and major emotional problems, especially in settings such as emergency rooms in general hospitals. Here, he sought to provide immediate walk-in care, ranging from advice to the lovelorn to the amelioration of acute psychoses. Bellak stated that emergency psychotherapy, with its goal defined by whatever emotional difficulty a patient presents, can achieve more than symptom removal. He believed that it provided an opportunity to help the patient achieve a better level of adjustment than might have been the case prior to the emergency. Moreover, Bellak made an effort to achieve preventive goals by assisting patients in working through the circumstances that prompted their entrance in the emergency ward. Seeking to realize these gains in five or six sessions, Bellak believed that effective brief treatments were especially appropriate in cases of suicidal threat, marked depression, catastrophic life events, and acute psychotic states.

Given that the majority of community patients fail to show up for a second therapeutic session, it appears wise to consider the possibility that single sessions may be all that therapists have available to achieve useful goals. Although popularized by others this past decade, *Bernard Bloom* developed a creative approach to single-session therapies some 20 years ago in conjunction with the emergence of the community mental health movement. Preceded in earlier years by therapists reporting on the potential impact of single sessions, Bloom contends that therapists often overlook that valuable therapeutic consequences may be associated within the first session or two.

Comments and Reflections

The emergence of the asylum, though a well-intended development in the eighteenth and nineteenth centuries, illustrates a solution that has become a sad and ignominious failure. These institutions turned into huge warehouses, not only for the chronically ill and mentally demented, but as depositories for the poor and social vagabonds who could not find housing and a measure of solicitude elsewhere. Some were mentally ill, but others simply were lost, unable to find their way or a place in life. These hospitals became protective harbors for all social misfits and community outcasts. In France, Germany, and England, genuine efforts toward humane care repeatedly led to disappointment and hospital decrepitude. Increasing numbers and incompetent treatment programs were the hallmarks of most institutions. Despite national differences, mental health workers everywhere began their programs with the same humane intentions, only to succumb in time to inefficacy and deterioration.

Although the development of state-supported institutions for the mentally ill was an encouraging humanitarian movement, it directed attention toward custodial treatment instead of prevention. In recent decades, the trend has moved toward outpatient clinics designed to catch disorders before they intensify, and to community-based inpatient centers where disorders can be treated in normal life settings instead of in distantly located and impersonal state institutions.

The history and scope of mental illness care may seem overly broad and divided in this review, and its current state one of flux or confusion. Nevertheless, change, controversy, and uncertainty are inevitable before achieving more precise and accurate knowledge. Skepticism, curiosity, and innovation characterize scientific advances. Free of the shackles of doctrinaire views, we can hope that better ways will continue to be devised for patients' welfare.

The long history that we have traveled in this chapter on social efforts to understand and care for the mentally ill illuminates that contemporary society, more sophisticated and professionally able than in the past, continues to face the same crises it has faced before. Consider current efforts in the United States by managed care systems, insurance policies, and political shenanigans to turn the clock back and to limit public and professional services for the mentally ill, no less with programs characterized by sympathy, compassion, and efficacy.

Until the past four or five decades, institutionalized patients were provided with thoughtful custodial care, at best and, at worst, incarceration in filthy wards, shackled, and isolated from the interests and activities of the larger community. Even among the better hospitals, little effort was expended to see that the setting, routines, and personnel of the institution provided more than a comfortable asylum, a refuge from strains of everyday existence, a place where patients could withdraw quietly into themselves.

The change from inhumane to custodial to genuine therapeutic environments evolved, not through public outcries, but through the fortuitous advent of psychopharmacological treatment. These drugs contained difficult patients, encouraging and enabling hospital workers to turn their attention from problems of restraint to those of therapy. At the same time, state legislative bodies became convinced that a massive infusion of funds for psychopharmaceuticals might ultimately unburden the taxpayer of costly long-term patient incarceration. The increased ease of patient management, together with the influx of additional funds, combined to spur a community-oriented model for both the public and health-service personnel.

Juxtaposing the words *treatment* and *community approaches* may appear hopelessly paradoxical, for the notion of community mental health and deinstitutionalization undoubtedly conveys to many a long overdue action of meeting social responsibility and of departing the ivory tower for the real world. This confluence may be pragmatic at best, but professional arrogance and political chicanery taint it. This arrangement, whether seen favorably or not, has a distinctly American flavor, not surprising since the community mental health movement is typical of our national restless solution to deal naively with massive social problems. This action-oriented approach is so commonplace in the United States that some see discussions of a community model as merely a delaying tactic before doing anything worthwhile. One often hears health colleagues state that social theories have little or no relevance to mental illness; at best, they furnish an intriguing, if distorting, intellectual backdrop against which more salient and realistic physiochemical processes and psychological dynamics take place.

Nevertheless, aspects of earlier hospital custodial care did promote favorable ends. First was the simple act of removing patients from their daily environmental stresses and placing them in a quiet and tolerant setting. Safe from external sources of humiliation and hostility, and able to act out their disturbed feelings without condemnation, patients' anxieties might subside and they could begin to regain some measure of composure.

The achievement of this first goal prepared patients for a second and perhaps more important one of developing increased social and occupational competence. Every facet of hospital life (e.g., cafeteria routine, housekeeping schedules, farming, recreational programs) became a therapeutic experience. Increased competence was achieved through occupational rehabilitation, group planning, and shared activities.

In years past, hospital routines functioned to keep patients busy by using them as cheap labor to reduce the costs of institutional management. At the very least, these activities countered the tendency of patients to disintegrate into idleness and invalidism. Such limited aims were replaced with programs designed with each patient's special rehabilitative needs in mind. Training was intended increasingly to be meaningful and goal-oriented, suited to the talents and interests of the patients, and arranged to provide them with new skills that might enhance their self-esteem and prepare them to find a useful vocation in the larger social community.

The former practice of isolating patients from each other and from the larger community became a thing of the past. Modern hospitals not only began to practice open ward policies, but encouraged social contact among patients and the outside world. Patients who lived together in wards established their own "governments" through which they could plan daily routines and recreational activities. Through these self-organized and administered groups, patients began to gain a sense of citizenship and social responsibility, achieved renewed self-respect, acquired a modicum of interpersonal skills, and learned to assume a participant role in an environment that parallels the give-and-take of normal community life. Although such group ventures occasionally proved a strain on the fragile state of certain patients, it allowed the greater number to strengthen their self-control and regain the perspective of shared living that was lost during earlier phases of their illness.

Hospital therapy programs were innovative and opened the door to rehabilitating large numbers of patients who could not be handled by more formal therapeutic techniques. At the very least, programs of active stimulation and patient participation ensured that fewer patients would regress into the vicious circle of self-perpetuating invalidism and social incompetence.

Deinstitutionalization, the practice of moving patients from hospital settings into the community, rapidly shifted custodial hospital care and treatment in the 1960s to community mental health centers. The positive and negative consequences of this movement, which mental health advocates initially proposed for valid reasons, was a program and a lesson of great historic significance. Nevertheless, a 2003 editorial in the *New York Times* expressed continuing dismay with the state of care of the mentally ill in that state:

> 25 years ago, the reintegration of people with mental illness into their communities was a goal. What planners envisioned was a system more responsive to patients' needs that would provide a range of options for care. Instead there

was no place for many of the discharged patients to go, and because of the state's failure to provide adequate oversight; some fell prey to unscrupulous adult home operators.

All of this couldn't come at a worse time, given the state's budget problems. Providing adequate services won't come cheaply. Hard choices will have to be made. Eliminating the sort of waste and fraud that have been documented would be a start. The state spends a far smaller percentage of its budget for mental health than it once did. With deinstitutionalization, costs were shifted to federal disability and health care programs. The chief responsibility for mental health programs, however, remains with state government. (January 12, 2003)

Two distinguished psychiatric historians, Micale and Porter, further commented:

Over the past two decades, traditional hospital psychiatry has declined decisively in power and prestige. However, in a pattern that has not been sufficiently noted, the decrease in the institutional authority of psychological medicine has been accompanied by its seemingly endless intellectual extension. . . . We turn to the psychosciences to run our private relationships, to raise our children, to try our criminals, to interpret our works of art, to improve our sex lives, to tell us why we are unhappy, depressed, anxious, or fatigued. Over the past few generations, an immense professional structure has developed to cater to our elaborate and expanding psychological needs. Hundreds of thousands of individuals in an increasing diversity of professional forms, including psychiatrists, psychoanalysts, clinical psychologists, psychotherapists, social workers, psychiatric nurses, marriage and family therapists, sexologists, guidance counselors, and lay therapists of all sorts administer our "advanced psychiatric society." Millions of people each year receive psychotherapy in a multitude of forms, and we ingest tons of psychochemicals to alter our moods. Furthermore, the number of populations conceptualized psychiatrically and the scope of behaviors diagnosed medically continue to multiply in an apparently endless process. (1994, pp. 13–14)

4

Rekindling Sensibilities and Releasing Potentials

Modern humanitarian approaches to the mind and mental illness desire to enhance each person's capacity to relate to one's feelings, to be responsive to moral values and aesthetic sensibilities, and to develop a sense of high self-worth. Practitioners are not concerned with the causes or with removing the symptoms of mental illness. They believe this approach will ultimately enable patients to explore and test themselves in the world-at-large, without being restricted by the conventions of mass society. Liberated in this manner, patients will learn to act in ways that are congruent with their innate good nature, enabling them to achieve their inherent potentials. To promote these objectives, therapists of this persuasion view events from the patient's frame of reference and convey a caring and nonjudgmental attitude, as well as a genuine respect for the patient's intrinsic worth as a valued human being. Although this may seem to be a fanciful, modern-world ideal, the precursors of such ideas have been with us for centuries. Although this chapter touches on some of these benevolent philosophers from the past, its primary focus is on developments in the late nineteenth and early twentieth centuries that led to the contemporary *humanistic* and *existentialist* schools of thought.

The Humanitarian Story: II

The foundation for the modern movement of phenomenology, and subsequently, existentialism and humanism, may be traced to the writings of several European philosophers, most notably Søren Kierkegaard, Edmund Husserl, Martin Heidegger, and Jean-Paul Sartre. The term *phenomenology* stems from two Greek words, *phenomenon* and *logos*. In Greek, phenomenon signifies "appearance, that which shows itself or can be seen." In psychology, the term represents the data of experience that the person can describe at any particular time. The concept concerns the appearance of things, as opposed to the things in and of themselves. Kant considered the phenomenological construct as central to his philosophy, asserting that "mind" can never know the objective qualities of a thing—what he termed its *Noumenon*—but can only know a thing as it appears to us, or its *Phenomenon.*

In the nineteenth century, the term phenomenology took on the quality of a field of study, a science referring to the data of consciousness. No single phenomenological approach dominates today; it is a broad-ranging movement that encompasses different orientations surrounding a central or common theme pertaining to the methods to be employed in gathering the data of consciousness. These methods are sometimes pursued in a systematic fashion; at other times, they are gathered more capriciously or fluidly. All that is perceived, imagined, or experienced can become grist for its subject and methodology in describing, intuiting, and analyzing life's ongoing experiences.

The fundamental premises of phenomenology in the United States have been labeled the *third force,* a movement led by several theorists, notably Abraham Maslow, Carl Rogers, and Rollo May, incorporated under the title "humanistic psychology." The following brief quote from its formal organization's *Articles of Association* describes the movement:

> Humanistic psychology . . . stands for respect for the worth of persons, respect for differences of approach, open-mindedness as to acceptable methods, an interest in exploration of new aspects of human behavior. . . . It is concerned with topics having little place in existing theories and systems: e.g., love, creativity, self, growth, basic need-gratification, self-actualization, higher values, being, becoming, spontaneity, play, humor, affection, naturalness, warmth, . . . autonomy, responsibility . . . transcendental experience, peak experience, courage and related concepts.

It was the omission in the major areas of psychological science of central humanistic themes, such as creativity and love, that attracted American psychologists, especially during the 1960s and 1970s, to the field of humanistic and existential psychology and its phenomenological approach. In drafting *A Philosophy of Psychology: The Need for a Mature Science of Human Psychology* (1957), Maslow enumerated several future goals for psychology, such as the following:

> Psychology should be more humanistic, that is, more concerned with the problems of humanity and less with the guild problems of the field. . . .
>
> Psychology should turn more frequently to the study of philosophy, of science, of aesthetics, and especially of ethics and values. . . .
>
> American psychology should be bolder, more creative; it should try to discover, not only to be cautious and careful in avoiding mistakes. . . .
>
> Psychology ought to become more positive and less negative. It should have higher ceilings, and not be afraid of the loftier possibilities of the human being. . . .

Academic psychology is too exclusively Western. It needs to draw on Eastern sources as well. It turns too much to the objective, . . . the behavioral, and should learn more about the subjective, the private, the inner, the meditative. . . .

Psychologists should study . . . what does man live for? What makes living worthwhile? What experiences in life justify the pains of existence? . . .

Intellectuals tend to become absorbed with abstractions, words and concepts, and to forget the original real experience which is the beginning of all science. . . .

As we begin to know more about legitimate wants and needs for personal growth and self fulfillment, that is, for psychological health, then we should set ourselves the task of creating a health-fostering culture. (p. 30)

Husserl, whom many view as the father of phenomenology, stressed a simple research principle, that of viewing events from a totally unbiased approach. In what he termed the *epoche method* of observation, all phenomena of life were to be contemplated free from any judgment of value or intellectual consideration. Simple, and perhaps as naive as this viewpoint might be, it stimulated a wealth of psychological studies, particularly the work of the introspectionists, such as Wundt and Titchener (see Chapter 10), who dominated German and American research of the early twentieth century.

Kierkegaard stressed another aspect of what has come to characterize the phenomenological schools. In his numerous essays, he contended that individuals become what they make of themselves. They do this through a series of choices, most particularly the choice between an inauthentic and an authentic existence. Inauthentic choices are those in which individuals allow themselves to be shaped by the "tyranny of the plebs," that is, by the demands and expectations of the masses. In an authentic existence, by contrast, individuals assume full responsibility for their own fate and existence. It was Kierkegaard's belief that all people must suffer the ordeal of "existential anxiety"; this occurs when individuals struggle to free themselves from an inauthentic existence and face the awesome responsibilities for self that are required to achieve authenticity. Heidegger, and later Sartre, sought to bridge the views of Husserl and Kierkegaard by focusing on the theme that all people must approach experience on their own terms. They must contemplate the events of their lives from their unique personal perspective and make choices for the direction of their future on that basis as well.

Contemporary humanistic and existential theorists also focus on the data of consciousness and construct their concepts in terms of how the individual perceives the world, rather than how it objectively exists. Mental disorders, according to these theorists, result from a failure to actualize innate potentials and are exhibited in subjective feelings of emptiness and self-alienation. These phenomenological mental ideas are loosely formulated, however, and often take the form of discursive and idealistic commentaries instead of systematic theories of mental illness.

Phenomenologists stress that individuals react to the world only in terms of their unique perception of it. No matter how transformed or unconsciously distorted this perception may be, the way that a person perceives events determines behavior. Concepts and propositions of mental illness must be formulated, therefore, not in terms of objective realities or unconscious processes, but in accordance with how events actually are consciously perceived by the individual; concepts must not disassemble these experiences into depersonalized or abstract categories.

As will be discussed later in this chapter, as well as in Chapter 10, the phenomenon of consciousness is one of the most controversial topics in both psychological and philosophical literature. No one doubts that self-awareness exists, but how can phenomenological reality as experienced by another person be categorized, measured, or even sensed? At best, observers must adopt an empathic attitude, a sensing in one's self of what another may be experiencing. But this method is justly suspect, fraught with the observer's distortions and insensitivities. To obviate this difficulty, authors of this persuasion assume that one's verbal statements accurately reflect phenomenal reality. Any datum that represents individuals' portrayal of their experiences is grist, therefore, for the phenomenologists' mill. They contend that individuals' verbal reports reveal the most important influences on their behavior. The fact that some verbal recollections and feelings are misleading is not reason to dismiss them as useless; they summarize events in terms closest to the individual's experience of them and often embody knowledge that is not otherwise available.

Unfolding of Key Ideas

Phenomenologists believe that the distinctive characteristics of each individual's conscious experience should be the primary focus of mental science. The *existential* school represents a direct and convincing application of phenomenological philosophy to the study of mental disorders. *Humanists,* on the other hand, draw on their own experiences to illustrate central phenomenological concepts such as anxiety and self. Eminent European theorists outline the philosophical and psychological basis for this view and illustrate the particular value of their ideas in the study of feeling and emotion, arguing in a straightforward way why a patient's personal experience cannot be overlooked in the science of mental illness. During a period in which the world witnessed the brilliant scientific advances of Sir Isaac Newton and Benjamin Franklin, a major paradigm shift in the culture and philosophy of modern civilization was also under way. Perhaps the best overall characterization of this change was a movement away from unquestioned divine determinism toward an understanding of the value of each human being.

Fashioning Humanistic Philosophies

Although many earlier schools of thought impacted the development of modern humanistic movements in one way or another, two philosophers, in particular, may be viewed as the most direct influences on the subsequent movements. These two French Enlightenment scholars, François Marie Arouet de Voltaire and Jean-Jacques Rousseau, were combatants for the same great causes and fought the same foes, though the two men could scarcely agree in their philosophies of *how* to produce change. Voltaire possessed the keener intellect and wit of the two, but he lacked Rousseau's intense, passionate emotionality. Each sharply criticized and defamed the other, as two reformers with similar ideals but different ideas tend to do, yet their influence was felt not only within the French Revolution (which touted Rousseau's *The Social Contract* as its Bible), but throughout Europe and the newly developing Americas. Prior to this time, French society was passive, meek, and sickly. It was subject to the whims of a powerful, exploitative, and often sadistic monarchy augmented by a church characterized by similar doctrines. Voltaire and Rousseau, each in his own way, presented society with the notion that human beings, regardless of social status, possess inherent value.

Voltaire (1694–1778) was born François Marie Arouet in Paris. One of the most famous French writers, his works embraced many branches of literature—drama, romance, poetry, history, science, and philosophy. Though Voltaire's writings brought him fame and fortune, they also caused much trouble. He boldly advocated for the people's freedom of speech and religion and dared to question, and even verbally attack, the Catholic Church of France along with its nobility and aristocracy. These crimes against the unjust status quo twice saw his indictment and imprisonment in the Bastille, and his banishment to England. They also spurred his hatred of the French justice system and its arbitrariness, and his respect for what could comparatively be called the liberalism of England. Today, he is best known for two of his works, *The Philosophical Dictionary* (1775), which outlined his political and religious dispositions, and *Candide* (1759), considered to be among the definitive satirical masterpieces of all time.

Voltaire's philosophy might aptly be described as the "Courage to Doubt," that is, to seek truth and humanity in an age where the "Will to Believe" was imposed on the masses. The controlling powers of the monarch and the high priests in France at the time, insisted that what existed was God's will. No mortal being (the aristocracy and church leaders being the exception) should undertake to change it, or dare even wish for better circumstances. Thus, seeking medical attention, attempting to change hunger or poverty, or questioning existing conditions in any other way were regarded as sins against God's divine plan. The priests and king easily persuaded the masses, in large part, that God's way was beyond their understanding, and they gave in to this miserable lot, living out their lives in serfdom.

Voltaire, however, did not concern himself with God through the eyes of either the monarch or the priesthood. He did not quest for a place in heaven, but for the greater good and esteem of humankind within mortal existence. A driving force for Voltaire was his sense of the innate proclivity for human beings to do good, even if it included countering that which was accepted as divine will. This inner sense of positive ability was, in fact, likely to confront the accepted standard, as much of it was not actually good, but simply biased toward the privileged classes. His pen most often turned to people of importance in society, bitterly and sarcastically criticizing those who allowed and demanded this downtrodden way of life. Although he used more than one hundred different pen names in his work, almost any vitriolic correspondence or work of literature was ascribed to him.

The great earthquake of Lisbon occurred in 1755, a natural disaster that killed 30,000 people in an instant and shook Voltaire to his core. The disaster of Lisbon did not disprove the existence of God to Voltaire, especially in terms of the creation of the world. However, he was convinced by this time that the notion of a greater being watching over all humanity at all times was virtually absurd. Voltaire's philosophy espouses several themes appearing throughout more recent humanistic and existential thought. Consider, for example, his assertions that humans strive toward goodness, with his example of his own battle toward a greater good found throughout his writing, and the concept of *self-actualization* espoused by Maslow, Rogers, and other humanists. Furthermore, the poems he wrote following the Lisbon disaster explored such questions as the meaning of life, death, and a grand scheme devoid of theology. In considering the context of Voltaire's life amidst the tyranny and misery of French society before the Revolution, he also exemplified the existentialists' view of transcending the inevitable drudgery of life and finding meaning within oneself.

Jean-Jacques Rousseau (1712–1778) was born in Geneva, Switzerland. His mother died shortly after his birth, and his father fled from Geneva after committing a minor offense when the boy was ten. Thus, Rousseau spent most of his childhood with an aunt and uncle, wandered somewhat aimlessly through his young adulthood, and finally moved to Paris in 1742. Rousseau's philosophy attempted to grasp the more emotional and ardent elements of human existence. Much of his earlier writing described people as being inherently "noble savages," referring to a more natural state uncorrupted by civilization and society. Much like Voltaire, he proposed that civilization had created tyrannical governments that kept individuality at best a modest commodity. However, unlike Voltaire, he blamed much of this on the advancement of knowledge and the neglect of emotional life.

As noted in Chapter 2, seventeenth-century philosophical thinkers were strongly inclined to be intellectualistic. Both empiricists and rationalists viewed the primary business of humankind to be that of knowing, thinking, and discovering the truth. To Rousseau, however, an emotional nature was central to human existence. He considered the idea of individuals as creatures of ideas and reason to be not only a falsehood, but one that accounted in greatest measure for the evils of civilization. As Heidbreder wrote of Rousseau's thinking (1933):

> The conventions and restrictions of society were false to man's deepest being. . . . Rousseau stood out in conspicuous protest against the formalism and artificiality of his age. . . . The man who sowed seeds of revolt in the France of the eighteenth century, and who protested against cold intellectualism in philosophy and against artificial conventionality in human society, made it impossible for psychology, even academic psychology, to remain wholly inattentive to the emotional side of man's nature. . . . The field of the emotions had been conspicuously indicated and its vast importance recognized. (p. 64)

It would seem unlikely, then, that this man, who lived much of his life with reckless passion, would take such a turn in his most important work, *The Social Contract* (1762/1967a). This tome described the proper relationship between the individual and society. In this publication, Rousseau appeared to take a position contrary to his earlier philosophies, in which he painted nature as amoral and lawless, asserting that good men were born only by the force of society. Because of the uncertainty and constant struggle for survival in nature, humans were destined to turn aggressively on each other, unless they joined forces with others in a collective human presence under an agreement to live together as a society. *The Social Contract* represented this agreement, from which the following is excerpted:

> The passing from a state of nature to a civil state, produces in man a very remarkable change, by substituting justice for instinct, and giving to his actions a moral character which they wanted before.
>
> It is at the moment of that transition that the voice of duty succeeds to physical impulse; and a sense of what is right, to the incitements of appetite. The man who had till then regarded none but himself, perceives that he must act on other principles, and learns to consult his reason before he listens to his propensities.
>
> Although he is deprived in this new state of many advantages which he enjoyed from nature, he gains others of equal consequence. His faculties unfold and his whole mind becomes so enlarged and refined . . . (1791)

Rousseau's main contribution to psychology (and philosophy, for that matter) was his emphasis on the emotional aspects of humanity. In his view, humans possessed a proclivity, as social and competitive beings, to strive rationally and mechanistically to attain goals, and the repetitive nature of existence made the journey remarkably devoid of emotional or passionate content. Along these lines, Rousseau was an ardent advocate for educating children emotionally, even prior to their attainment of more abstract, intellectual knowledge. He believed firmly that the emotions were the most viable path to knowledge, and that the rational, logical philosophers to date had missed this important component.

Founding of Existential Phenomenology

Popular notions of existential thinking among the public were associated initially with Parisian bistros and American bohemians in the 1950s. In part a rebellion against contemporary social norms and cultural values, existentialism was an intellectual expression of a radical break with traditional lifestyles. Whatever its particular motives and social expressions may have been, existentialism represents a genuine philosophical paradigm that in many respects is highly technical and complex. It is an approach whose details are accessible only to those thoroughly schooled in its many abstract forms and speculative ideas.

Despite its varied forms and subtleties, existentialism attempts to deal seriously with issues and problems that philosophy in general has largely neglected. Most philosophical thinking, until recent times, focused on the essences of the external or objective world, bypassing in great measure such burning questions as the meaning of life, the place of suffering, and the inevitability of death. Most philosophical inquiries have largely ignored the problems of our everyday existence—what might be called the existential problems of life. Existentialism arose to compensate for this deficiency by focusing on individuals as they experience life and relate to their fellow citizens. Its growth is a response to the conflicts and anxieties in the Western world this past century, especially since the tribulations and horrors of recent global wars and the threat of nuclear annihilation.

Existentialists interpret life in a manner that reflects the etymology of the word itself. Thus, the word *exisisto* in Latin means "I exist," a word composed of two other Latin words, *ex* and *sistere,* meaning "to stand out, to become, or to emerge." Thus, human existence is not merely static, but involves becoming; it is continually changing and developing. Moreover, existence is not an objective state, but a flowing experience of being. Everything else is an abstraction, not life as subjectively experienced.

In great measure, existential philosophy, and the branch of psychology derived from its doctrines, grew largely out of human disillusionment with the course of life consequent to pre- and post-World War II Europe. Though its roots were in the great European philosophers who came before the two world wars, few members of the general population were prone to accept the questions these seminal thinkers were asking. By this time, the industrial age had also arrived, bringing the promise of a better way of life, yet creating greater means of destructiveness. Similarly, it brought forth individuals who were savvy enough to exploit the new technologies. World War II saw what was perhaps the worst example of societal destruction in the history of civilization.

Following this appalling and catastrophic period, many Europeans turned their backs on the world they had explored through science and technology, opting instead to focus on self-understanding. Though this dismal zeitgeist of the Continent recuperating from a brutal and morbid war might suggest that this philosophy's development would have concentrated on those members of society facing severe mental disorders, much of its major emphasis was on the behavior and personalities of "normal" people. Stimulated by the work of the earlier philosophers, Voltaire and Rousseau, existentialists portrayed a vivid picture of contemporary humans trapped in the impersonal atmosphere of a mechanistic and mass society. As a result, individuals became isolated and alienated from their "true" selves. The philosophies and techniques of existential therapists, then, were suitable for those who had experienced the drudgery of a pervasively unsatisfactory life. This approach sought to enable the patient to deal with unhappiness realistically, yet in a constructive and positive manner.

The *existential* philosophy of therapy committed to the view that to achieve a worthy measure of authentic self-realization, individuals must confront and accept the inevitable dilemma, hardship, and perhaps even anguish of life. Mental illness, according to the existential thesis, reflected more than an inability to fulfill biological urges, as Freud stressed, or to establish significant interpersonal relationships, as Sullivan and Horney stressed. Pleasure, interpersonal security, even survival itself, were viewed as subsidiary to the need to relate to self. Without self, individuals would lack an identity and could not experience what was termed *being-in-the-world*. Failing to relate meaningfully to self, individuals could not satisfy their instinctual drives and could not establish satisfying relationships with others, a theme picked up and given a central role in the developmental theory of the contemporary psychoanalyst, Heinz Kohut (see Chapter 8). Unable to sense their own inner world, individuals could not sense the inner world of others, and without meaningful social interaction, they could not break the cycle to expand experience and develop a sense of identity. As this pattern continued, individuals experienced an *ontological anxiety*, a frightening estrangement from self. This anxiety would further paralyze and isolate them from others, making effective means of altering their existence impossible, which would eventually lead to a succumbing to *nothingness* and disorder.

Though not all existential thinkers were influenced by the Danish philosopher and religious thinker **Søren Aabye Kierkegaard (1813–1855),** he is considered to be among the primary precursors to formal existential philosophy. Although his life was short, his powerful writing stirred the minds and hearts of great thinkers and is still read widely today. Born into a well-to-do family, Kierkegaard wandered throughout Europe in his early years, was thoroughly trained in philosophy, and engaged in journalism for a time before adopting a life of solitude and reflective writing. Though he considered himself religious, his ideas left their theological roots and became a penetrating analysis of humans' inner experiences; Kierkegaard was perhaps the first to employ the term *existence* in the sense that the concept is used today. Central to his philosophy was the problem of eternity and the fact that humankind's existence is temporal and finite. As he wrote, individuals seek to escape from their finitude, but cannot, and therefore must occupy themselves with trivial and temporal matters to avoid thinking about failure and death. Thus in life, individuals struggle against two opposing forces: One seeks the possibility of eternity, the other has to face life's temporality.

Formally educated at the University of Copenhagen in philosophy and theology, Kierkegaard's work responded to what he felt was the depersonalization of society. Additionally, his bold theological passages attacked the established Danish church of the time. It is possible that his disdain for Danish society and its Lutheran church may reflect his ambiguous feelings about his broken marital engagement in 1841, as well as his renunciation of a career in the church, and his coming to terms with these abrupt changes. It is also widely noted that his writings were colored significantly by melancholia, which characterized much of his short life.

The lack of connection between people set up the existential human condition of alienation. Divorced from others by this barrier of subjective perception, the individual inevitably would feel alone, isolated, and despairing. For people to develop and make sense of this condition, according to Kierkegaard, they needed to strike a balance between three stages of life. This concept offered some unity within Kierkegaard's largely disharmonious philosophies. He outlined these stages as the *aesthetic*, the *ethical*, and the *religious*, and described them as being in constant tension. The first of these, the aesthetic, referred to the egocentric and fickle quest for pleasure. The second, the ethical sphere, included the rational and organized impersonal and logical interactions between the subject and the outside world. These interactions represented longitudinal plans, general moral conduct, and interests including both the self and the community. The third, the religious stage of existence, demonstrated how true religious choice was devoid of rationality, and required a genuine "leap of faith" to commit to existential decisions.

Edmund Husserl (1859–1938), a Moravian Jew and the credited founder of the formal European school of phenomenology, spent the greatest portion of his life quietly in the Universities of Göttingen and Freiburg, prior to the Nazi control of Germany near the end of his life. Born in 1859, Husserl spent most of his earlier academic years as a mathematician, before turning his attention to the human condition, as well as to the condition of a deteriorating Europe. Often at odds with contemporary psychological logicians and empiricists, Husserl strove to develop an empirically supported philosophical framework that encompassed the real meaning, or essence, of how things and beings existed. Husserl introduced the term *phenomenology* in his book *Ideas: A General Introduction to Pure Phenomenology* (1913/1931), where he defined phenomenology as "the study of the structures of consciousness that enable consciousness to refer to objects outside itself." Because the mind could recognize and respond to both real and imagined objects, Husserl posited that one could not simply assume the existence of anything. Instead, individuals needed to put aside, or bracket, the question of the real existence of an object.

Husserl's *epoche* method (from the Greek word meaning "to abstain" from everyday beliefs) stands among the greatest of his contributions to the world of scientific inquiry. This method held that all observations had to be made from a genuinely unbiased stance; predetermined ideas, judgments, and academic proclivities about an object must be put aside to truly examine how it exists *in essence*. An ultimate goal of science may be to explain, but one must first *describe* that which needs explaining. This idea came to be accepted widely as a purely descriptive method and became the accepted standard for existential phenomenology, whether examining inanimate objects, living beings, conditions of life, or existential meaning.

Probably the most significant successor to Husserl's pioneering efforts in phenomenology was **Martin Heidegger (1889–1976).** Living most of his life in the Black Forest region of southern Germany, Heidegger, who had served as Husserl's assistant, subsequently assumed his chair at the University of Freiburg. Although owing a great deal of credit to Husserl's works, Heidegger was one of Husserl's most brilliant critics, an intellectual estrangement that was a painful disappointment to Husserl. Heidegger also became a controversial and notorious figure, owing mostly to his early involvement with the National Socialist party, an association he avoided talking about following the war, and following his "return" to conscience in the 1950s. He was banned from teaching for several years after the war due to this association.

In a revision of his most important work, *Being and Time,* Heidegger may have sought to explain his submission to the power of the German tradition in the following excerpt:

> When tradition thus becomes master, it does so in such a way that what it "transmits" is made so inaccessible . . . that it rather becomes concealed. Tradition takes what has come down to us and delivers it over to self-evidence; it blocks our access to those primordial "sources" from which the categories and concepts handed down to us have been in part quite genuinely drawn. Indeed it makes us forget that they have had such an origin, and makes us suppose that the necessity of going back to these sources is something which we need not even understand. . . . (1953/1962b, p. 43)

The emphasis in Heidegger's philosophy is on the state of existence, with his hypotheses forming the basis for what came to be known, through the subsequent psychological works of Ludwig Binswanger and Medard Boss (to be discussed shortly), as *Daseinsanalyse.* With the initial publication of *Being and Time* (1927/1962a), Heidegger introduced the notion of Dasein, or "being-there," or "being-in-the-world," as the central question of human existence. This question of Being, largely ignored by philosophers (according to Heidegger) since the pre-Socratic era, differentiated humans from other creatures, as humans were the only beings with a known conscious concern for this question. Heidegger posited an interconnectedness of humans to their environment. Humans not only existed within the world but were absorbed in it, by virtue of being "thrown" into a context. This "thrownness" created social roles, purposes, and ultimately, intentionality. For Heidegger, being thrown into the world among things was a more fundamental kind of intentionality than that revealed in thinking about objects and creating meaning from this cognitive exercise. It was this more fundamental intentionality that made possible the directness that Husserl analyzed.

To Heidegger, individuals realize that their existence is not of their own making or a consequence of their choices, but has been thrust on them and will be their lot until death. Thrown into an incomprehensible and threatening world, and then discovering that life is oriented toward an inescapable death, individuals are persistently faced with anguish and dread. To overcome these dreadful feelings, they seek to camouflage them with a life that is conventional and "inauthentic." All thoughts and acts are conformist, doing and thinking what one is expected to do, such as having to suffer through life and die. When one seeks to block that thought, to evade and camouflage this terrible reality, the individual will experience a sense of worthlessness and guilt. Only by accepting the inevitability of death and nothingness can people become authentic and be free of the consequences of an illusion they share with their fellow conformists.

Heidegger's *Being and Time* established many of the fundamental assumptions of modern existential therapy, though he did not intend this to be a direct effect at the time. At a later date, he took great interest in Binswanger and Boss's developments, but his early intentions to influence psychology were brief and incidental. Nevertheless, many of the major themes and chapters in his 1927 publication included distinctly psychological subjects; most notable among these themes was his examination of moods. His exploration of fear linked this emotion with the most central question of Being. In further discussions of anxiety, this theme of fear took shape, to become one of the guiding principles of existentialism: the notion of *existential anxiety*, defined as fear of loss of "being-in-the-world." This included not only the most obvious loss, that of death, but also loss of consequence or meaning within one's given context.

Philosopher, playwright, and novelist **Jean-Paul Sartre (1905–1980)** was among the most seminal of the existential thinkers. His 1943 philosophical work, *Being and Nothingness* (trans. 1957), stands as a cornerstone of existential philosophy as we now know it. Born in Paris in 1905 to a prominent family, Sartre was orphaned early in his childhood and came to live with his grandfather. Here, he discovered literature within his grandfather's immense library, and developed a passion for his own writing. Sartre studied philosophy both at the École Normale Supérieure and Göttingen (under Edmund Husserl), and taught for several years at Le Havre in Paris before pursuing a full-time writing career. Voracious in his productivity, Sartre did not waste a moment of any day, to the extent that he was often reprimanded for typing in front of commanding officers while in the French Army in World War II and was known to dictate to his secretary from the lavatory. Known primarily as a playwright, few have noted that Sartre's earliest works, preceding the landmark *Being and Nothingness*, were largely psychological in nature. To date, these earlier works fail to draw much attention, but the basis for Sartre's ideas about the essence of humankind may be found within these volumes.

Perhaps the best-known passage from Sartre's psychologically oriented work is from his 1946 tome, *Existentialism and Humanism* (trans. 1966), in which Sartre declared that existence precedes essence. Here, he uncovered the existential view that man is defined by his actions, not by a predetermined purpose, which followed his atheistic assumptions. Furthermore, he held that there was no particular fixed constitution or nature, only a character that perpetually redefined itself by the events and deeds of everyday life. Intentionality and purpose existed in all actions, then, rather than innate forces that predetermined behavior; human beings chose their actions and thus their character.

As with most existentialists, Sartre rejected the idea of an unconscious, or at least asserted that it was not truly an unconscious entity impinging on conscious existence. He posited that individuals were aware of, and could choose, what to fully allow into consciousness. Therefore, he explicitly stated that human beings were free to choose their actions and could not simply blame uncontrollable unconscious drives and instincts for their irresponsibility. In this light, he claimed that Freud's "censor" must be a conscious entity, as it must know what to repress.

Implicit in this philosophy was the aspect of a radical freedom, but an accompanying intense responsibility for one's situation, predicament, or character. As Sartre put it, humans are "condemned to be free" (1946/1966). This was an absolute freedom of choice, unburdened by environmental factors other than the meanings ascribed to them.

The French phenomenologist **Maurice Merleau-Ponty (1908–1961)** probably made the clearest contributions to psychology, as evidenced by his pre-1945 writings and his post in child psychology at the Sorbonne. His major contributions were in the familiar phenomena of sensation and perception, specifically in his phenomenological interpretations of them. First reconceptualizing the concept of behavior, Merleau-Ponty revitalized the idea as a modality comprising both internal and external components intertwined in a singular phenomenon. By this reconceptualization, he augmented the narrow behavioristic view of this modality. In his discourse on sensation and perception, Merleau-Ponty identified perception as the way in which people are related to the world. As an existential concept, then, he regarded perception as the act by which individuals interpret experience as it presents itself to the person.

Often at odds with his contemporary, Jean-Paul Sartre, Merleau-Ponty was more sympathetic to humans and their situations. As discussed, Sartre held the view that individuals were responsible for all occurrences in the world, no matter where they occurred; therefore, by not actively opposing a situation, people, in essence, chose it for themselves. Merleau-Ponty rejected this notion, differentiating between not actively rejecting a situation and making it a personal choice. Another difference between the two contemporaries was their respective views of Freud's work. Sartre rejected Freud thoroughly, claiming his work was speculative, at best, and incompatible with phenomenology. Merleau-Ponty did not advocate a merger between phenomenology and Freud but was much more sympathetic to it, believing that there could be a meeting of the minds, as the two distinct fields became better understood.

Launching of Existential Psychiatry

Although existential theorists share this view of the human's fate in contemporary society, they are more concerned with the pathological effects of one's estrangement from self. They contend that beneath social loneliness and isolation lies a deep and profound alienation from one's own natural feelings, although they differ on the particulars. To them, the essential problem lies in an individual's experience of futility and despair of ever being what he or she is and can be. They agree further that humankind's capacity for conscious awareness enables people to make choices and control their existence; individuals possess a unique power to transform events to suit their needs and to create their own distinctive worlds. The decisions people make determine whether they will progress toward the fulfillment of their inner potentials.

Existentialism means centering on the existing person; it is the emphasis on the human being as he or she is emerging or becoming. Traditionally in Western culture, existence has been devalued in favor of essence, the latter being the emphasis on immutable principles, truth, logical laws, and such, that are supposed to stand above any given existence. In endeavoring to separate reality into its discrete parts and to formulate abstract laws for these parts, Western science has by and large been essentialist in character; mathematics is the ultimate, pure form of this essentialist approach. In psychology, the efforts to see human beings in terms of forces, drives, conditioned reflexes, and so on, illustrate the approach through essences.

Despite their differences, existential therapists also agree on a key procedural method, that the clinician must approach the patient phenomenologically by entering and listening to the patient's experiential world without any presuppositions that may distort its meaning and understanding. As Binswanger, a leader in this movement, has noted, "There is not one space in time only, but as many spaces and times as there are subjects" (1956, p. 196). These therapists share a view that contrasts with others of a more behavioral, neuroscientific and psychoanalytic perspective, which they consider to be overly deterministic and mechanistic.

Existential therapists stress that individuals are the center of their changing world of experiences; experiences must be viewed, as noted, only in terms of their relevance to the individual. As individuals mature, a portion of their experience becomes differentiated into a conscious perception of the self-as-object. Once this self-concept is established, it influences the perceptions, memories, and thoughts of the individual. If experiences are inconsistent with the self-image, they are ignored or disowned. The phenomenological and existential philosophies at the turn of the twentieth century permeated all intellectual endeavors of the day, especially that of psychiatric thinking and practice in Europe, led notably by Ludwig Binswanger, Karl Jaspers, and Eugene Minkowski.

The psychiatrist **Ludwig Binswanger (1881–1966),** who could be described as the first true existential therapist, was born in 1881 in Kreuzlingen, Switzerland, into an active and established medical and psychiatric family transplanted from Germany after 1848. His grandfather founded Bellevue Sanatorium in Kreuzlingen, becoming its first chief medical director, followed by his father, and subsequently by Binswanger himself at the age of 30. He received his medical training at the University of Zurich, studied under Carl Jung (see Chapter 7), interned under Eugen Bleuler (see Chapter 5), and graduated as a doctor of medicine in 1907. Like his notable mentors, Binswanger showed a strong interest in the study of schizophrenia. In the final year of his medical training, Jung introduced Binswanger to Sigmund Freud, and the two psychiatrists remained friends, despite significant differences in theoretical viewpoints, until Freud's death in 1939. As the chief medical director of Kreuzlingen's Bellevue, he transformed the facility from a sanatorium to an international meeting center where scholars from medicine, psychology, philosophy, and the arts regularly attended, taught, and debated. During the 1920s, Binswanger began absorbing the philosophical works of Heidegger, Husserl, and Buber, which stimulated his increasing interest in existential theory and his departure from Europe's psychoanalytically dominated psychiatric perspective of the early twentieth century.

Binswanger described his "theory of existential analysis" in a series of books and papers published over a 40-year period. Based largely on Heidegger's principles elaborated on in his *Daseinsanalytik*, Binswanger's theory centered around three modes of experience that came to be accepted as the central facets of existential therapy: the *Umwelt*, signifying the world of biological and physical energies and entities; the *Mitwelt*, the interpersonal realm of humans in social context; and the *Eigenwelt*, the individual's inner phenomenological experience. Only through the individual's balance of these three existential elements would he or she progress and grow toward an authentic existence and experience strong mental health. Disorder, then, according to Binswanger, resulted from failure to adequately come to terms with these important factors. Despite a strong emphasis on the Eigenwelt, this existential theory demonstrated a trend toward recognizing the interaction of different modes of experience, perhaps as a preamble to the integrative perspectives of later twentieth-century personality theorists. Here human functioning was recognized not just as the individual's inner perspective, the

inherent physical and biological realities, or sociological connections, but as a synthesis of
multiple modes of experience. Being a phenomenological thinker, Binswanger stressed the importance of the *self* (the Eigenwelt), with all
other needs playing a subsidiary role. Self, in
turn, formed the basis for *identity*, which was
the cornerstone for balancing the three modalities and allowed for the experience of being-
in-the-world.

Ludwig Binswanger

What was most striking about Binswanger's
existential approach was his focus not only on
the individual's abnormalities, as in Freudian
analysis, but in the understanding of the entire
person as represented in his or her normal and
abnormal aggregate. Also, like Minkowski (to be
discussed shortly), he stressed the person-to-person encounter of physician and
patient. Far from being antiscientific, Binswanger's roots and origins were in-
veterate in psychiatry as a science. He had, however, no means of directly observing and objectifying the subtleties of a human being's inner experience
within the naturalistic sciences of the day. This gap in the ability of the scientific method to accommodate all of human experience prompted Binswanger to
turn to philosophy, in the hope of completing the picture of objective and subjective experience. Despite the fruitfulness of his study and application of existential philosophy to treatment, his concern for the future of psychiatry without
a supporting science remained a troubling unanswered dilemma throughout his
career. Aspects of his therapeutic model are illustrated in the following:

A psychotherapy on existential-analytic bases thus proceeds *not* merely by
showing the patient where, when and to what extent he has failed to realize the
fullness of his humanity, but it tries to make him *experience* this as radically as
possible—how, like Ibsen's master-builder, Solness, he has lost his way and footing in "airy heights" or "ethereal worlds of fantasy." In this case the psychotherapist could be compared to someone who is informed, e.g., a mountain
guide, familiar with the particular terrain, who attempts the trip back to the
valley with the unpracticed tourist who no longer dares either to proceed or to
return. And inversely, the existential-analytically oriented therapist seeks to
enable the depressed patient to get out of his cavernous subterranean world,
and to gain footing "upon the ground" once more, by revealing it to him as
being the only mode of existence in which the fullness of human possibilities
can be realized. (Binswanger, 1956)

Despite this self-declared shortcoming, we saw in the *Daseinanalysis* of
Binswanger several important implications for the development of mental health

treatment not necessarily limited to the existential schools. Perhaps most obvious was the relationship of Binswanger's work to the psychoanalytic schools, especially to that of Freud's psychoanalysis. Despite Binswanger's existential philosophy, he and Sigmund Freud remained friends, an unusual development considering the pattern of many of Freud's other associations. Binswanger considered Freud to be a great mentor, and despite his ambivalence regarding Freudian theory, he felt Freud had thus far provided the best chance for truly understanding the essence of what it meant to be a human being. In his opinion, what was missing, however, was a solid methodology that could support Freud's interpretations, and a more comprehensive, less biased science of humans, their biology, and their social characteristics. The challenge, then, was to integrate Freud's man-within-biology perspective into a less partial account of human anthropology, which provided a large motivation for much of Binswanger's philosophical development.

The other aspect of Binswanger's approach influenced the developing humanistic approach, soon to be discussed in more detail. This was his application of an *empathic* therapeutic stance, so much the hallmark of Carl Rogers, arguably the most prolific and influential figure of the American humanistic schools. Binswanger was an early proponent and adherent to the notion of understanding the patient in his or her own language and experience, rather than from the framework of a therapist's abstract theory. He provided a clearer understanding than that formulated by Minkowski, whose pioneering works sought to understand the patient's experience from the viewpoint of the therapist's experience. Beyond concepts of client-centered treatment or other humanistic therapies, which concentrate on what is healthy or normal about the client, Binswanger's existential treatment actively sought to develop empathic rapport and a therapeutic alliance with those parts of the patient that were sick. He felt that no part of the patient's psyche should be excluded from the physician's understanding. It was central to his philosophy that the parts of the patient's psychic structure that were sick had become dissociated from the whole person. It was not enough simply to explain this, as in psychoanalysis, or to unconditionally accept this dissociation, as in Rogers' client-centered therapy. It was necessary, instead, to bring these lost parts back to the self so they could be re-incorporated and given an authentic meaning and existence for the individual.

Karl Jaspers (1883–1969) was undoubtedly an influential founding pioneer of phenomenological and existential psychiatry, though, oddly enough, he did not consider himself a phenomenologist. His system of mental illness approached classification in a unique way: It sought to describe the patient's true subjective experience and how he or she faced mental illness instead of simply describing overt psychological syndromes as observed by the therapist. To this end, Jaspers made distinctions such as that between "feelings" and "sensations," the former being emotional states of the individual and the latter being part of the individual's reactions to and perceptions of the environment. The ultimate goal of this system was to orient and enable the therapist to be as sensitive and empathic as possible with the patient. Jaspers contended that the inexhaustibly infinite depth and uniqueness of any single individual, mentally ill or healthfully functioning, could not be completely understood and objectified, but the medical/psychological practitioner must strive for as close an understanding as possible. It was this existential aspect of humankind that set this system apart from the traditional means of diagnosis and treatment. In contrast with the psychoanalysts who attempted to probe beneath the surface of patients' verbal reports to uncover their unconscious roots, Jaspers focused on patients' conscious self-description of feelings and experiences. He believed that their phenomenological reports were the best source to achieve a true understanding of the world of the abnormal.

Karl Jaspers

Jaspers was born in 1883 of Jewish ancestry and received his medical and psychiatric degrees in 1909 in Heidelberg, Germany. In 1913, at just 30 years of age, he published *General Mental Illness*, his major work on psychopathology, which remains the cornerstone of phenomenological psychiatry. He was granted a professorship in psychology at Heidelberg in 1916 and another in philosophy in 1921. World War II and the ensuing occupation of Europe by the Nazis led to his ousting from his academic post until the end of the war in 1945. The following year, he published *The Question of German Guilt* (1946), a study of how the Nazi party led the German populace. Two years later, he moved to Switzerland to accept an academic post at the University of Basel. His other works included *Man in the Modern Age* (1931), *Philosophy* (1932), *Reason and Existence* (1935), and *Existenzphilosophie* (1938), a term he coined that became a forerunner to the term *psychiatric existentialism*.

Jaspers made great contributions to the field of psychology by recognizing the limitations of Kraepelin's system and extending accepted nosological concepts to include not only objective descriptions, but the phenomenological aspect of the patient's experience *as seen from within*:

Since we can never perceive the psychical phenomena in others directly, as we can physical phenomena, it can only be a matter of empathic understanding [*verstehen*], to which we can be directed by enumerating in each case a series of external characteristics of the psychic situation; by enumerating the conditions under which it occurs, by visual analogies, and by symbolization or by a kind of suggestive presentation. In this attempt the personal accounts [*Selbstschilderungen*] of the patients, which we can elicit and examine in personal conversation, can help us. We can develop these most fully and clearly, whereas those in written form composed by the patients themselves, while often richer in content, have simply to be accepted. Clearly, whoever has experienced the occurrence himself, has the best chance of finding the appropriate description. (1963, p. 55)

Perhaps the greatest long-term contribution of Jaspers' work was that it opened the psychiatric schools' views to the vast variety of human experience, whereas previously it had been fairly well limited to the objective, simplistic categorical structure and neat sorting of the nosological systems of the day (see Chapter 5). His inclusion of both the clinician's objective observations of the patient and the patient's subjective account of his or her experience in therapy contributed significantly to the clinician's accurate empathy with the patient's personal experience. This capacity to accurately share the patient's perspective is considered the cornerstone of phenomenological therapy. As noted, this allowed for much richer investigations into the human psyche, where individual differences and human perspective could be at the foreground of inquiry. It might be said that it set the stage not only for further existential developments, but for the humanistic movement to be discussed later in this chapter, as well.

Continuing in this unique tradition of psychiatric practice rooted in the patient's subjective realm, **Eugene Minkowski (1885–1972)** examined his patients' personal experiences in the hopes of deducing recurring themes. He was considered to be a major promoter of phenomenology and existential analysis within the French psychiatric tradition, as well as a manifest example of the lasting influence of Husserl and Heidegger. Minkowski coined the term *structural analysis* for his system of attempting to find the basic disturbance of each major syndrome. For example, it appeared to Minkowski that depressed patients were somehow incapacitated in their ability to experience time in a forward direction; this syndrome's basic disturbance, then, was an inability to think about and anticipate the future. In turn, this inability made it impossible for the patient to hope for growth or change. It could be interpreted from his major work, *Traite de Psychopathologie* (1927/1968) that what was most important to him was the *approach* to mental illness. Throughout his career, Minkowski emphasized the understanding of human process and experience, rather than the classification of disease and the demarcation of outcome goals:

A whole side of our life, and not the most unimportant one, has escaped our discursive thought entirely. The immediate data of consciousness, the most essential ones, belong to this order of facts. They are irrational. This is no reason why they are not parts of our life. There is no reason whatsoever to sacrifice them to the spirit of precision. On the contrary, one ought to catch them alive. Psychology, hitherto, a desert country, scorched by the excessively hot rays of exact science, will then perhaps be transformed into green and fertile prairies and finally approach life. (p. 65)

Minkowski's focus on inner experiences and subjective processes was not necessarily innovative; certainly by this time Karl Jaspers had paved the way for such advances. Where Minkowski made significant original contributions to existential therapy was in the time he spent with patients, as well as in understanding the dynamics of the therapeutic dyad. He frequently spent entire days and nights with the mentally ill, accruing holistic portraits of the individual with much more intact nuance and thorough contextual detail than could be found in Jaspers' more fragmentary reports. His lengthy case studies allowed for moment-to-moment accounts of thoughts, behaviors, and feelings in the patient's daily environment. Once again, instead of a straightforward account of the objectively observable facets of the patient's behavior, this phenomenological approach sought to uncover further experiential aspects that cannot be readily observed, but that are important to understanding and treatment. Experiencing life *as if* the doctor were the patient allowed Minkowski to perceive the patient's inner subjective experience with accuracy.

Medard Boss (1903–1991), an occasional collaborator with Binswanger, followed a similar career path as his fellow Swiss psychotherapist. Born in Switzerland in 1903, Boss also began by studying the analytic works of Sigmund Freud, though he did not have a personal relationship with him as did Binswanger. He also studied under Bleuler in Switzerland and shared Binswanger's passion for the writings of Martin Heidegger. He held his most significant academic post at the University of Zurich, where he established the European Center for Daseinsanalyze, a facility that still exists. It was also in Zurich that he published his landmark volume, *Psychoanalysis and Daseinsanalysis* (1957/1963).

What most distinguished Boss's therapy from Binswanger's, however, was an interest in creating an effective therapy that would incorporate the techniques and atmospheric features of Freud's psychoanalysis but would replace Freud's philosophical orientation toward human nature with that of Heidegger's. As Boss matured as a therapist, he was a proponent of the "immediate reality" of Freud's practice, but a staunch opponent of his underlying theories. A similar development happened with Jungian practice; that is, Boss was initially attracted to Jung's theories due to their rejection of Freud's abstractions and constructions, but Jung's eventual use of symbols soon proved ineffective to Boss. In line with much of existential thought, Boss concluded that what was necessary was a direct interpretation of patients' phenomena, instead of extrapolations from abstract constructs or symbols.

Despite this new perspective on psychotherapy, Boss made no claim to have formed a new method of treatment. Throughout his years of practice, he maintained Freudian methods combined with Heidegger's philosophy toward Being. Drawing on his existential guidelines, the purpose of treatment, then, was not solely to be enlightened by what was hidden (as it is in Freud's model). Instead, the patient's task was to become liberated, to experience his or her individual phenomenal field for whatever it subjectively represents. Only in this way could the individual accept this personal, subjective construct and regain authenticity of self.

For many laypersons, students, and professionals in mental health, **Viktor Frankl (1905–1997)** is probably more synonymous with contemporary existential therapy than any other person in the field. Indeed, his landmark publication, the autobiographical *Man's Search for Meaning* (1959/1992), originally published in 1959, is one of the most influential works among both academic

Viktor Frankl

and popular psychology, and may well be one of the great human documents of our time. The founder of the school of existential therapy known as *logotherapy*, Frankl drew on his personal suffering in concentration camps during World War II as the basis of his particular views and explained his system of therapy in the aforementioned autobiography by demonstrating its principles as applied to his survival of this torturous experience. Unlike his contemporaries, Binswanger and Boss, Frankl was not primarily concerned with understanding human beings in an anthropological fashion. His primary motive in logotherapy was simply to provide therapeutic influence. Considering the works of Freud and Adler to be lacking pragmatically in a *noogenic* neurosis (that of frustra-

tion of meaninglessness), Frankl set out to create the "Third Viennese School of Psychotherapy" in 1938, just as World War II was rapidly encroaching on European society.

It was not long before Frankl's method was put to the test. During the Nazi regime in Germany, Frankl, a Jewish psychiatrist, was captured and subjected to three years in Auschwitz, Dachau, and other concentration camps. Though a fully trained medical doctor and psychiatrist, Frankl spent most of his internment in manual labor, digging ground for railway lines. It was not until several years had passed, in the final weeks of his captivity, that the Nazi officers realized the potential benefit his training might have offered. During his time in the camps, Frankl lost his entire family, and there seemed to be little tangible promise of his own survival beyond the war. In these camps, described by Frankl and countless other survivors as the worst possible manifestation of humanity on Earth, he noticed something miraculous. Despite dreadful hopelessness and inconceivable suffering, many prisoners were able not only to survive, but to grow. The logical conclusion was consistent with his development of the Third Viennese School: The driving force in an individual's life was a *will to meaning*. As long as the person had reason to live, he or she could bear just about any hardship.

The meaning of life referred not to some intangible, abstract ideal, but to the given meaning in life *at each moment*. To live an authentic existence, a person must be able to identify meaning throughout daily existence. As Frankl phrased it:

> As each situation in life represents a challenge to man and presents a problem for him to solve, the question of the meaning of life may actually be reversed. Ultimately, man should not ask what the meaning of his life is, but rather he must recognize that it is *he* who is asked. In a word, each man is questioned by life; and he can only answer to life by *answering for* his own life; to life he can only respond by being responsible. Thus, logotherapy sees in responsibleness the very essence of human existence. (1992, pp. 113–114)

Frankl's logotherapy was, at its core, geared toward putting patients in touch with their specific pattern of values that would create the foundation of their meaning of life. He described three types of values—creative, experiential, and attitudinal—and worked with patients to identify the ones consonant with their individuality. The first, creative values, were ones individuals could satisfy by their own creative activity. Experiential values were more passive, but important, because they allowed individuals to enjoy art and nature. Most important, attitudinal values represented individuals' responsive qualities: They reflected how they reacted to "the inevitable suffering that limits our access to creative and experiential values" (1968, p. 101). These values allowed individuals to find meaning in virtually any circumstance, regardless of the duress they might be under. Within any given moment, knowing and living these particular values allowed the individual to retain meaning in life.

Victor Frankl's logotherapy originated a psychotherapeutic technique in 1939 that has extended to other systems of therapy, most notably to the hypnotist Milton Erickson and the strategic family therapist, Jay Haley. This was the practice of *paradoxical intention*, which asked patients to bring about, if only for a moment, the fearful symptoms that they were trying to reduce or extinguish. This technique was built on the premise of anticipatory anxiety. In a classic example of the usefulness of this technique, Frankl once cured a young physician of excessive perspiration by replacing his anticipatory anxiety with a paradoxical wish; he asked the physician to deliberately resolve to show people how much he could sweat, especially in socially precarious situations. This technique, in essence, reflects an attitudinal switch that addresses the most important of the three value types Frankl outlined in his structure of the meaning of life.

Forging American Humanistic Therapies

Existential theorists were committed to the view that individuals must confront and accept the inevitable dilemmas of life to achieve authentic self-realization. As noted, these themes were first formulated by philosophers Kierkegaard, Husserl, Heidegger, Jaspers, and Sartre, as well as existential therapists such as Binswanger, Minkowski, Boss, and Frankl. Americans, notably Rogers, Maslow, May, and Yalom have joined the fold more recently in what is known as humanistic psychology. Despite differences in terminology and philosophical emphasis, existential and humanistic variants of the phenomenological school are very similar in their approach to therapy.

It may be useful, however, to illustrate differences between the European-engendered existential approach and that of the American-generated humanistic *third force* with reference to Yalom's (1980) incisive distinction:

> The existential tradition in Europe has always emphasized human limitations and the tragic dimensions of existence. Perhaps it has done so because Europeans have had a greater familiarity with geographic and ethnic confinement, with war, death and an uncertain existence. The United States (and the humanistic psychology it spawned) bathed in a zeitgeist of expansiveness, optimism, limitless horizons, and pragmatism . . . the European focus is on limits, on facing and taking into one's self the anxiety of uncertainty and nonbeing. The Humanistic psychologists, on the other hand, speak less of limits and contingency than of developmental potential, less of acceptance than of awareness, less of anxiety than of peak experiences, and oceanic oneness, less of life meaning than of self-realization. (p. 19)

Two important social theorists, Erich Fromm (1947; see Chapter 8) and David Riesman (1950; discussed in Chapter 11), portrayed the dehumanizing and isolating effects of contemporary European and American society. They identified these effects not only in severe mental disorders but in the behavior and personality of so-called normal individuals. They painted a vivid picture of people estranged from themselves, wandering aimlessly from one meaningless relationship to another.

A central theme of existential therapy was taking responsibility and blame for choices and actions in order to experience and know all the authentic feelings of existence (including those associated with suffering). *Humanistic* therapy stated instead that humankind frequently was too harsh in self-criticism. According to this doctrine, people often blame and judge themselves far too severely, invariably damaging self-esteem. This leaves individuals' most important instrument for self-direction in life, their *sense of self*, in a compromised state. Without a healthy sense of self, individuals are unable to function in concert with their true potential. The humanistic philosophy held that a psychotherapeutic or medical expert could not adequately fix this problem by using focused techniques of behavior change, intrapsychic enlightening, or pharmaceutical treatments. Instead, it posited the question, "What could be more effective for coping and adapting to our own unique context than this innate individual resource?" Since the raw materials and ability to live a productive, mentally healthy existence lay solely within the *client* (a term humanists preferred over *patient*), the *helping professional counselor's role* was to facilitate the client's self-discovery of these abilities as well as *strength in self* through interaction with the counselor. Central to therapeutic success were the counselor's personal attributes and means of relating to the client in ways that fostered and enhanced the client's self-esteem. This, in turn, activated the client's ability for *self-actualization*, a term stressed by Abraham Maslow (to be discussed shortly), but which holds a fairly universal meaning among humanistic therapists. It represents the central quest of all human beings to strive toward goodness, effective living, positive growth, and an ideal level of functioning.

This thesis that human beings are driven to actualize their potentials, interestingly enough, did not originate within the humanistic school. References to this intrinsic drive may be found throughout history, and treatment methods founded on the patient's innate ability have been explored intermittently for many centuries. Early approximations to this concept of self-actualization may be traced to *Carl Jung* and *Otto Rank*. Jung (1916), in what is likely the earliest modern description of this concept, contended that humans possessed a singular "life urge" that craved self-realization. A decade or so later, Rank (1929) translated this idea of a self-fulfillment drive into a philosophy for therapy. To Rank and his followers—pioneers of several diverse mental health fields such as the social worker Jessie Taft and the child psychiatrist Frederick Allen—the ultimate goal of therapy was to free the patient's "will," a somewhat esoteric but powerful energy that yielded self-reliance and intrinsic vigor. According to Rank, the patient needed to become the central figure within the therapeutic relationship, becoming, in effect, his or her own therapist. In turn, the therapist was to become a catalyst to strengthen the patient's will toward growth, rather than the "omniscient expert."

Forerunners of the humanistic movement also included pioneers from biological and social psychology, beginning with the late-nineteenth-century writings of John Hughlings Jackson and Theodor von Uexkuell (see Chapter 6). These influential figures posited an intrinsic unity between biological functions and environmental stimulation, which foreshadowed the brilliant work of both Kurt Goldstein (Chapter 6) and Kurt Lewin (Chapter 12). Goldstein, an eminent neurosurgeon who had been influenced significantly by the Gestalt schools (Chapter 10), contended that the only effective means of conceptualizing an individual was as an operational whole. In his view, the study of isolated behaviors or functions was inappropriate, as the organism could not be analyzed in terms of its separate parts. Goldstein articulated numerous cases in which neurological damage to the individual led to reorganization of overall functioning instead of loss of the affected function. This reorganization enabled the individual to keep his drives and goals intact, albeit more primitively. From this evidence, Goldstein suggested that humans possessed a sovereign motive for *self-actualization*.

Most humanistic therapists have concurred that an individual's disorder must result from a clash between the individual's strivings and the values imposed by a society wishing to create a level of homogeneity and universality. Thus, disorder represents an estrangement from self, an inconsistency between attitudes that the person feels are right but that others have said are wrong. For example, a young man who had been groomed to vigorously pursue financial security and reward at all costs gained no satisfaction from this and preferred an occupation that benefited humanity but did not yield large financial gains. The inconsistency between what he phenomenologically felt to be right and the judgments of others created internal discord. This inner disharmony, in turn, led to anxiety, and anxiety produced defensive reactions that alienated the person further from his "natural" feelings. By adopting social evaluations that denied or distorted his natural feelings, the individual experienced a sense of inner emptiness and purposelessness. Therapy, then, called for the client to *lead the counselor* through an exploration of these issues; the counselor provided a supportive but nondirective stance, reflecting and helping to clarify the client's statements. Such *active listening*, along with a projection of understanding, nonjudgmental attitude, and genuine interest in the client's well-being, were the *necessary and sufficient* conditions for effective change in therapy.

Humanism and existentialism share many principles, which sometimes can blur the distinction between them. A clearer presentation emerges, however, when examining world trends and their influences on these two traditions. Though somewhat of a simplification, a thematic difference seems to be the confidence and youth of the mid-twentieth century American ethos, on the part of humanists, and the atmosphere of totalitarianism and catastrophe that plagued mid-twentieth-century Europe, on the part of the existentialists. However, such a grouping based on nationality is made for purposes of presentation; to some extent, all the pioneers in this and the preceding section were influenced by both existential and humanist principles.

The counterculture and its associated social developments in the 1960s largely spurred the humanistic movement. Problematically, the "flower children," human potentialists, and drug and sexual revolutions soon took over the movement in the United States. As Yalom, one of the leading substantive figures at the time, lamented:

> The big tent of humanist psychology was, if nothing else, generous and soon included a bewildering number of schools barely able to converse with one another . . . and countergroups, holistic medicine, psychosynthesis, soothy, and many others pranced into the arena. . . . There is an emphasis on hedonism ("if it feels good, then do it"), on anti-intellectualism (which considers any cognitive approach as "mind-fucking"), on individual fulfillment ("doing your own thing peak experiences"), and on self-actualization. . . . These proliferating trends, especially the anti-intellectual ones, so affected a divorce between humanistic psychology and the academic community. (1980, p. 20)

Despite these intellectual difficulties, a genuine academic tradition remained. It was well grounded in an existentially oriented philosophical movement that employed a strong phenomenological approach to therapy.

No one psychologist has influenced more therapists and schools of therapy in the 1960s and 1970s in the United States than the psychologist, **Carl Ransom Rogers (1902–1987).** Whether clinicians refer to themselves as "Rogerian" therapists, following the "client-centered" (or "person-centered" as it was later called) approach, they were likely to have studied (and likely adopted) Rogers' writings and views on the concept and intent of *empathy*. This concept, along with *genuineness* and *unconditional positive* regard, comprised what Rogers called the "necessary and sufficient" *core conditions* for client change (Rogers, 1951). These conditions undergird the therapeutic relationship not only in client-centered therapy, but in many other major schools of therapy as well.

Carl Rogers was born in 1902 in Illinois to a close-knit, educated, upper-middle-class Protestant family with six children. At an early age, Rogers and his family moved to a farm west of Chicago to escape some of the perils and perceived evils of city life. Characterized by the Protestant work ethic and a strong puritanical backbone, the family's value system was subtle yet suppressive, and Rogers experienced little socialization outside the family circle during childhood. Growing up on a farm, Rogers enjoyed scientific agriculture and initially pursued this major at the University of Wisconsin–Madison. He then changed his major to history in preparation for a career in the ministry, prompted by his strong inherited religious inclinations. He enrolled at the Union Theological Seminary in New York City but found counseling to be much more to his liking. By his second year in New York, he had enrolled at Columbia University's Teachers College in clinical and educational psychology, terminating his theological pursuits. He attained his doctoral degree in 1924.

Trained initially in a psychoanalytic mold, Rogers quickly found that clients at his first position at a child guidance clinic in upstate New York did not respond well to the analytic approach. This prompted him to begin formulating his own therapeutic method, which led to his first landmark volume, *The Clinical Treatment of the Problem Child* (1939). The text won Rogers national attention and a full professorship at Ohio State University. Subsequently, he published *Counseling and Psychotherapy* (1942), a synthesis of his and Otto Rank's relationship work, and fully elaborated this new construct of nondirective therapy. Rogers moved to the University of Chicago in 1945, establishing a counseling center and fully explicating his theories in *Client-Centered Therapy* (1951). Subsequent academic changes included a move to his alma mater, the University of Wisconsin, in 1957, which proved to be most trying in terms of the inflexible experimental orientation espoused by psychology in major universities at the time. In the early 1960s, Rogers published *On Becoming a Person* (1961) and moved to the Western Behavioral Sciences Institute, where he founded the Center for Studies of the Person. While maintaining a schedule of

Carl Ransom Rogers

15 to 20 therapy hours per week, Rogers remained active in areas outside psychotherapy proper. He established encounter groups, helped develop play therapy models (with *Virginia Axline*), and extended his influence to other areas including parenting skills and political/civic arenas. As a result of this extension of his philosophy, he renamed his approach *Person-Centered*, to reflect the wider breadth of this philosophy. In his later years, he became active in world peace efforts, conducting peace workshops in Moscow and initiating the Vienna Peace Project, bringing together leaders from 13 nations in 1985. He remained active in all these areas of interest until his death in 1987.

Rogers' ideas shared many themes and elements of the European existentialists, most notably a subjective phenomenological view of humankind. Both Rogers and the existentialists believed that the subjective perception of self and reality is central to an individual's mental health. Rogers, however, was a perennially optimistic and encouraging man. Moreover, unlike his psychoanalytic colleagues, he felt that therapy should attend to matters of the present and not the past. To him, people were intrinsically good and capable of working through their difficulties when encouraged to believe that they possessed the means to create their own futures. Rejecting the term *patient*, Rogers preferred the term *client*. He asserted that the latter term represented equivalence between two individuals working together in which one would guide the other to unleash that person's capacities to deal with psychological difficulties. Rogers perceived the clinician to be a facilitator, providing clients with an opportunity to explore their feelings in any way that they wished, as well as to define the goals they sought to achieve. Notably, during the time in which he developed most of his ideas, Rogers' clients were highly able and reasonably well-functioning students at the University of Chicago, and not patients seen in the wards of state hospitals, a population he later worked with, achieving minimal success.

Rogers maintained the view that all individuals were capable of self-fulfillment, whereas tragedy and pessimism characterized and colored the outlook of European existentialists. The existential paradigm held that each individual must show courage and maintain meaningfulness in life in the face of inevitable hardship and atrocity, even though the individual is not implicitly strong-minded, courageous, or moral. The Rogerian philosophy proclaimed that there is joy in living, and that each individual is intrinsically geared toward positive growth. Rogerians believe that people are disposed naturally to be kindly, self-accepting, and socially productive. Only if this innate potential is restricted, and feelings of personal worth are damaged, will individuals become ineffective, antagonistic, disturbed, or a combination of these attitudes.

This universal humanistic goal of self-actualization was prominent in Rogers' *client-centered* therapeutic approach, and the *self theory* derived from his therapy. This variant of self-image therapy was based on the premise that humans possess an innate drive for socially constructive behaviors; the task of therapy, then, was to unleash these wholesome growth forces. According to Rogers, client growth was a product neither of special treatment procedures nor professional know-how; it emerged from the quality and character of the therapeutic relationship. More specifically, it was a consequence of certain attitudes of therapists, notably *genuineness*, which refers to their ability to "be themselves" in therapy and to express their feelings and thoughts without pretensions or the cloak of professional authority. Rogers called this *unconditional positive regard*, meaning the capacity to feel respect for the client as a worthy being, no matter how unappealing and destructive the client's behaviors might be, and *accurate empathic understanding*, signifying sensitivity to the client's subjective world and the ability to communicate this awareness to the client. In line with Rogers' therapeutic model, the client assumed full responsibility for the subject and goals of therapeutic discussion; the therapist reflected rather than interpreted the client's thoughts and feelings and encouraged, but did not recommend, efforts toward growth and individual expression.

Born into a household characterized by poverty, psychosis, and emotional distance, and growing up in an environment where he was an outsider, **Abraham Harold Maslow (1908–1970)** seemed an unlikely figure to have become a founding father and major contributor to the humanistic movement in psychology. Maslow was born in 1908 to Russian-Jewish immigrants in New York City, the first of seven children. Already socially deprived at home (owing, in large part, to a schizophrenic mother), he found further difficulty within his community, moving to a non-Jewish neighborhood at the age of nine. He later described this experience as akin to being the only African American in an all-Caucasian school. Shy, neurotic, often depressed, and usually lonely during his childhood and adolescence, his home and school environments fostered a great deal of introspection, and this is likely to have

Abraham Harold Maslow

provided some impetus for his turn toward humanistic philosophy. At his father's recommendation, he first enrolled in law school but lost interest quickly. After marrying at the age of 20, the Maslows both entered the

University of Wisconsin–Madison, where Abraham earned his undergraduate and doctoral degrees by 1934.

Maslow began his career as a behaviorist, but he came to consider this approach inadequate, at least partially because of his introspective nature, but also in large part owing to his interactions with his two daughters. His first postdoctoral position was as a research assistant under Edward L. Thorndike, and he remained in this position until 1937, when he accepted an academic post at Brooklyn College. It was here that his metamorphosis really began, as prominent thinkers from many philosophies influenced him, The most significant of these ideas was Kurt Goldstein's holistic approach toward neuropsychology and his aforementioned thesis of an innate actualization potential. Maslow was invited to head a newly established psychology department at Brandeis University in 1951, a position he accepted and held for 10 years before health difficulties forced him into early retirement and a move to California. During this time, he initiated meetings among several of his friends (including Goldstein, Erich Fromm, Gordon Allport, Karen Horney, and Carl Rogers). This led to the formation of the American Association for Humanistic Psychology, a group that encouraged developing psychology as a whole, with emphasis on the person, instead of factioning off individual schools and techniques. Elected to the presidency of the American Psychological Association in 1968 but suffering from rapidly failing health, Maslow was unable to read his presidential address. After many years of heart difficulties, he died of cardiac arrest in 1970.

A proponent of the study of healthy, normal individuals, Maslow felt that a great deal could be learned from psychoanalysis, yet he criticized orthodox analysts for promulgating the notion that the unconscious was ultimately a manufacturer of neuroses. In his view, individuals' innate, or *instinctoid* propensities were essentially healthy, and therapists did not need to concentrate solely on drive reduction, as did Freud and the psychoanalysts; healthy drives could be encouraged to reach higher-order life strivings. One of the primary themes of his philosophy of psychology was motivation; to this end, he established two basic forms of human motives: "B" (growth) and "D" (deficiency). Essentially, these constructs represented motivation, which either was oriented toward compensation for something lacking in the individual (the "D" construct), or represented an improvement in what the individual already possessed (the "B" construct). Maslow further elaborated that cognitions, love, and values could be described similarly, and he introduced a model that demonstrated how to arrange these constructs. This was the well-known "Maslow's Hierarchy of Human Needs," a triangular shaped figure listing human needs from the more deficiency-oriented constructs (physiological needs, the lowest construct) to the growth constructs (*metaneeds*, or self-actualization needs, at the apex). In between these extremes, in ascending order, were safety, belongingness and love, and esteem needs. Healthier individuals tended to have few issues with the lower needs (physiology, safety, belongingness/love), but concentrated instead on improvements in esteem and self-actualization (they have ascended the hierarchy). Pathological human beings, however, were not able to pursue these higher-order needs and were frequently ensnared in fulfilling deficiencies in the lower human needs. The further down the deficiency resides, according to Maslow, the more severe the pathology (Maslow, 1968).

Attacked by his former scientific associates as having succumbed to contempt for the value of experimental truth, Maslow generated little empirical support for his humanistic constructs; some crude research does exist, however, to substantiate his description of self-actualizing individuals. Maslow posited that all humans have the potential to become fully self-actualized, yet these individuals rarely, if ever, exist. To illustrate nonneurotic individuals, free from constraints of deficiency needs and pursuing potentials to the best of their skills and abilities, Maslow turned to historical figures such as Thomas Jefferson and William James, as well as a few contemporaries who were then alive and continuing to achieve (e.g., Albert Einstein). Maslow found that all self-actualized people tended to share several qualities: They were self-accepting, flexible in viewpoint (but able to abide by their decisions), empathic, spiritual, astute in perception, creative, and unfixated in culture. Nevertheless, his critics, especially his erstwhile behavioral colleagues, accused Maslow of having substituted fuzzy-minded generalities for hard and verifiable thought.

The American psychologist **Rollo Reese May (1909–1994)** bridged the existential and humanistic philosophies. Often classified as an existentialist, May retained much of the terminology and structure established by earlier existential teachings (the threefold idea of Daseinsanalyse, authenticity-in-living, etc.). He agreed that pathology often results from the individual's estrangement from self, but he differed from these thinkers on important details. Whereas he agreed that humankind's capacity for conscious awareness enabled individuals to make choices and to control their existence, he joined the humanists in recognizing the power of *unconscious* drives, a philosophical tenet differing sharply from the existentialists. His work also is characterized by an optimism not found among the European school of existentialism. Whereas they believe that environmental misery is inevitable and individuals must use their phenomenological point of view to interpret and create meaning out of frustration and chaos, May rejects this inevitability. Not that he wasn't critical of Western civilization—he was often rigorous in his attacks on social norms—but he did not share the view that society invariably worked against human existence. Whether the environment was inherently benign or malevolent, individuals had to make difficult and anxiety-evoking decisions to progress toward the fulfillment of inner potentials; it was their task to face and choose the future with courage and hardiness.

May was born in 1909 in Ohio, and grew up in neighboring Michigan. Much of his time in early adulthood was spent in the arts, and he toured Europe as an artist following his graduation from Oberlin College in 1930.

After attending Alfred Adler's summer school during this time, he returned to the United States, pursued and attained a divinity degree in 1938, and served for a short time in the ministry. He had been exposed to existential thought during this training, but as his interests shifted to psychology, he found more interest, initially, in psychoanalysis. He began his training at the William Alanson White Institute, opened a private practice in 1946, and attained the first clinical psychology PhD awarded by Columbia University in 1949. At about this time, an unlikely metamorphosis occurred, which determined the course of his career. He contracted life-threatening tuberculosis and was confined to a sanitarium awaiting his prognosis. It was during this time that the combination of reading and dreading the possibility of nonbeing turned his attention once again to phenomenology and existential thought, and the result was a radical shift away from psychoanalysis on his fortunate recovery. He went on to write many books on his unique phenomenological theory, and became an admired and influential lecturer in academia, well beyond the realms of psychology proper. His *Love and Will* (1969b) reached best-seller status, and *The Courage to Create* (1975) became an immensely popular tome among creative artists. He remained an active lecturer and psychotherapist until his death in 1994 from congestive heart failure.

As mentioned, what set May apart from existential therapy was not only the rejection of an innate pessimism, but more fundamentally, the acceptance of the power and role played by the unconscious. Whereas the existentialists did not rule out such drives and innate forces, there was no emphasis beyond the aspect of *thrownness* (the existential idea that we simply exist within our circumstances, including our innate psychogenic makeup). Most existentialists insisted that it is largely immaterial what subconscious structures exist—they exist, but must be *transcended*. In contrast, May sought not to ignore and transcend these issues, but to actively explore and engage them with clients, seeking to have the individual master these elements. Of particular relevance was May's idea of the *daimonic*, which included both conscious and subconscious motives and innate drives, and which could be characterized as illicit or benign. This word was derived from an ancient Greek term for something that represented both divinity and evil. Psychological health required engaging in efforts to control this daimonic by understanding and accepting it, rather than by repressing it. Unlike psychoanalysts, however, May rejected the notion that unconscious defense mechanisms such as repression were parts of a complicated unconscious structure at war with itself. He took a holistic view of the entire personality failing and lacking the courage to experience authentic human emotions, even those that might be painful.

If May was to be considered a humanist, however, he most certainly differed in key areas from humanist tenets as well. Most notably, he took a stance against clinician neutrality. Many humanistic therapists (as well as most psychoanalysts—this was one of May's key dissatisfactions with psychoanalysis) retained a neutral, nonjudgmental stance, not concerning themselves with the social aspects of their client's thoughts and actions. Thus, it made little difference to most of these professionals whether an individual was becoming a more social member of society or was improving dubious antisocial skills. Most humanists operated under the assumption that humankind simply would strive to actualize; people would continuously and organically move in a direction of positive growth and would always naturally do so if they were truly free. May took a much more active stance, dismissing neutrality as a dangerous point of view. He asserted that a clear values orientation was essential for therapists, and they must remain anchored to this stance. A client may be free to disagree, but neutrality "actually separates and alienates the person from his world, removes whatever structure he had to act within or against, and leaves him with no guideposts in a lonely, worldless existence" (1969a, p. 169). What kept May within the framework of humanism was his distinction between shrugging off societal values and maintaining an orientation that might become part of the therapeutic dynamic. At no time was a value actually imposed, but the presence of the external environment was felt. This way, it became a choice for the client to accept or reject the standard set by society. Undoubtedly, this created discomfort, but the client had to face the choice with courage.

The psychiatrist **Irvin D. Yalom (1931–)** was born in Washington, D.C., to Jewish parents who had immigrated from Russia. He grew up in a poor, black neighborhood, where his only safe haven was reading. His love of fiction, as well as the opportunity to study medicine, prompted him to pursue psychiatry because people and the stories they could tell always fascinated him. In addition to being one of the leading contemporary thinkers in humanistic, existential, and group therapies, Yalom has also written intriguing works of fiction and semifiction based on psychological and existential themes, as well as his insightful experiences in psychotherapeutic practice.

Yalom is perhaps best known for his advancement of group psychotherapy. In *The Theory and Practice of Group Psychotherapy* (1975) he identified and outlined a unique *group process*, universal among the various group therapy structures and orientations, that fully differentiated the group experience from individual modalities. A professor at Stanford University School of Medicine, Yalom may have been best described as a theoretician who read "between the lines"; he differentiated between the formal structure of a theoretical approach and the extras of nontheoretical, genuine human interaction. This latter aspect of Yalom's writings has earned him a place among the pioneering thinkers of the humanistic movement.

Ironically, one of Yalom's landmark textbooks is entitled *Existential Psychotherapy* (1980), and indeed, his theoretical system might best be described as existential in content. As stated, disagreement exists about how to distinguish between existential and humanistic philosophies. For historical purposes, this author distinguishes between early-twentieth-century American and European developments. However, although the themes of Yalom's therapy were existential, his emphasis on the human therapeutic process and relationships across theories spoke also to a deeper humanistic orientation. In the introduction to *Existential Psychotherapy*, Yalom elucidated a definition that seemed to capture both perspectives: "Existential psychotherapy is a dynamic approach to therapy which focuses on concerns that are rooted in the individual's existence" (p. 5).

Yalom used the metaphor of a cooking class that he once attended to describe what makes therapy really "tick." Beyond the established recipes the instructor taught in this class, Yalom noted the additions of "off-the-record" ingredients that seemed to make all the difference. In much the same light, he spoke of the formal, sometimes orthodox structure of therapy, but also of the off-the record elements—the intuitions and genuine human (as opposed to "trained professional") responses to the patient's experiences, often happening outside the therapist's own awareness. He further maintained that experienced psychotherapists of all persuasions use these extra elements and could be said to be operating within an implicit existential framework, as they are attuned to genuine patient concerns regarding existence. It is these elements, falling outside the structure of formal theory or therapy that Yalom strove to bring to the forefront of the therapeutic arena. By no means, however, did Yalom condone an unstructured, improvisational approach, as many critics of humanistic models state it. His model of existential therapy sought to include these nonspecific, human factors within a flexible, structured milieu.

Yalom's structure extended naturally to what he identified as a *group process* that extended beyond the boundaries of his particular model of humanistic therapy and across many models and theories of group intervention. When Yalom referred to the "front" of a particular ideology of group therapy (its techniques, language, and general aura), he was distinguishing between the ways different groups run. He concentrated his efforts on examining what he referred to as the "core" of a therapy, or the bare-boned mechanisms of change and noted that these processes were similar among different groups. Originally labeling these processes *curative factors*, Yalom more recently renamed them *therapeutic factors*, a term more in concert with the realization that a psychotherapy patient is not "cured." He identified eleven therapeutic factors that effect change in any group, emphasizing the last four: interpersonal learning, group cohesiveness, catharsis, and existential factors.

Viewing much of mental illness to be a result of failing to experience or to dampen one's inner feelings, *experiential therapists* not only distrust intellectual exploration and analysis, but seek to emphasize the spontaneous experience of life events. In this regard, they carry forward ideas first articulated by Aristotle in his examination of the cathartic value of drama and demonstrated in the powerful results of Breuer and Freud's abreactive treatment. This branch of humanistic treatment, known as *experiential psychotherapy*, encompasses techniques whose focus is the release of constrained emotions. Among current contributors to this perspective are *Eugene Gendlin*, an existentially oriented student of Rogers, and two Canadian psychologists, *Alvin Mahrer*, and *Leslie Greenberg*. Although their techniques differ, they seek to facilitate an inward focus on feeling within the treatment context. It is their shared view that patients will not progress, no less actualize themselves, if they discuss their problems in a distanced, abstract, and intellectual way; similarly, little will be accomplished if they focus exclusively on the objective details and circumstances of their past.

These therapists direct primary attention to the felt or affective aspects of a patient's problematic experiences. Using a technique called *focusing*, they ask patients to look inwardly and put aside all problems for the moment. Then, they are asked to focus on a single problem. Attention is directed to how the elements of that experience feel as a whole, to see whether certain words or themes emerge from the feeling that the problem generated. It is hoped that a shift may take place such that the character of the problem will take on a new quality by virtue of its associated feeling.

In this model, the therapist's role is to use different methods to facilitate eliciting the emotional tone of a problem situation. The therapist guides the patient through these interventions, attempting to locate those methods that enhance a deep and sensitive exploration of feelings. As Greenberg has noted, the therapist can use "evocative unfolding" to explore the emotional "edges" of a problematic experience. In this manner, patients are led to discover how they actually felt and construed a situation and to better understand what led to their response to that situation. No matter how dysfunctional that response may have been, it was at least sensible in that it reflected their real feelings about the matter. Consequently, new options presumably will open up for behavioral change. For experiential therapists, treatment communication keeps the topic in-the-moment, that is, in the flow of what is being experienced within the session.

Comments and Reflections

Some therapists focus on extinguishing maladaptive behaviors or relieving pathological emotions; the aim of treatment is to bring patients back to a nonpathological state rather than to spur them to a better way of life. If growth should occur, it is expected to follow of its own accord, once the troublesome symptomatology has been eliminated. Other therapists exert their primary efforts toward developing new, more effective behaviors, considering the reduction of symptomatology to be of less significance than the acquisition of better ways of life. As they view it, current symptoms should fade of their own accord once the patient has gained alternative and more adaptive ways of resolving difficulties and achieving fulfillment. Few therapists are committed firmly to one or another of these divergent goals; however, predilections toward *symptom extinction* versus *constructive response alternatives* may be noted among different therapies.

The chief goal of treatment, according to humanitarian-existentialist approaches, is not to understand the causes or to remove the symptoms of mental illness, but to strengthen and to free patients to develop a confident expression of worth. This will enable them to explore and test their own values and needs in a problematic world, unconstrained by the turmoil and conventions of a mass society. Bolstered and liberated in this manner, patients will come to act in ways that are right for them and possibly learn to actualize their inherent potentials. To promote these objectives, the therapist will view events from the patient's frame of reference and convey both a caring attitude and a genuine respect for the patient's worth as a human being.

Two schools of therapy adopt these principles. One approach, known as the American humanistic school, is based on the optimistic premise that humans possess an innate drive for socially constructive behaviors; the task of therapy is to unleash these wholesome growth forces. The European existential school possesses a less sanguine view of individuals' inherent fate, believing that they must struggle to find a valued meaning to life; therapy attempts to strengthen the patient's capacity to choose an authentic existence.

The criticism of the behaviorist's conception of humankind (to be described in Chapter 9) as an empty automaton cannot be leveled at humanistic and existential therapists. To them, human beings are vibrant participants in life, forever shaping the course of their affairs. Far from being sluggish respondents to the whims of experience, they struggle to become their inner potential. Individuals do not succumb to maladaptive reinforcements, but are depleted by self-frustration and broken by despair. Like Shakespearean characters, individuals are restrained by inner conflicts until they are exhausted shadows of themselves.

Serious reservations exist about the philosophy that undergirds the third force. A written conference summary of the views of the distinguished philosopher-psychologist Sigmund Koch is worth mention. Insofar as Koch could see, the third force is an extraordinarily loose congeries of people who are concerned about the constriction of American psychology and are eager to embrace an alternative. To speak of this as a force was a poor use of metaphor because Koch did not judge it to be anything but a group of individuals who would have considerable difficulty communicating with each other and stood for nothing specific except disaffection from the experimental and behavioral emphases of recent American psychology. While he rejected it, Koch looked on humanism as a "wave of the future" that might expand the boundaries of psychology.

Even the distinguished psychologist Jean Piaget (see Chapter 10) registered concern about the tendency among phenomenologically oriented psychologists to ignore or minimize the work of empirical psychologists, noting that most fail to make sure that scientific support exists for their insights and observations. He asserted in his *Introduction to Genetic Epistemology* (1950) that the scientific or empirical approach can enrich the phenomenologists' revelations and that their contempt for experimental research is not only ill-founded but unwise. In this vein, excellent experimental studies were carried out by the introspectionists and gestaltists (see Chapter 10), both of whom employed systematic empirical methods to verify phenomenological discoveries. Nevertheless, as many have noted, contemporary humanists have little empirical research to confirm their imaginative ideas and speculations.

Although the existentialist's portrayal of the dilemmas of life is striking, we must distinguish between skillful literary depiction and effective theorizing. No matter how compelling and vivid a theory of mental life may be, the crucial test does not lie in elegant persuasion but in explicit hypothesis. Although humanitarians are among the most acute observers of the human condition, their formulation of these observations into a theory is sporadic and casual. Perhaps these formulations should not be thought of as theories but as a set of loosely connected observations and notions. So discursive a body of work, little concerned with integration, structure, and continuity, and lacking in tautness of systematic argument, cannot be viewed as a science at all. At best, the ideas represent a consistent point of view; at worst, they provide an ill-constructed social commentary.

Other critics object, not to the loose structure of humanitarian theories, but to what these theories propose. Particular exception is taken to their idealistic conception of humans' inherent nature. The notion that they would be constructive, rational, and socially conscious beings, were they free of the malevolent distortions of society, seems not only sentimental but invalid. There is something grossly naive in exhorting humans to live life to the fullest and then expecting socially beneficial consequences to follow. What evidence is there that one's inherent self-interest would not clash with the self-interests of others? There is something here as banal as the proverbialism of a fortune cookie that suggests, "Be thyself." Conceiving mental disorders as failures to "be thyself" seems equally naive.

Several points summarize humanitarian treatment approaches. With the exception of Rogers' client-centered procedures, few outcome and process studies have been carried out on these therapies. The little that has been done fails frequently to meet even the rudiments of proper research design and control. For the most part, humanitarian therapists have formulated their treatment procedures in a discursive and vague manner; it is extremely difficult to determine the exact techniques and sequence of steps involved in the therapeutic process. Social commentaries and philosophies are provided instead of specific and tangible recommendations for the execution of treatment. Cutting through this verbal persiflage, one often finds these techniques merely to be dressed-up variants of the more simplistic supportive procedures of modestly trained psychiatric aides. In general, what little out-come data exist are equivocal, although there is some evidence that these therapies can promote beneficial changes in some patients, usually those who start with a fairly healthy makeup. Research suggests that certain thera-pist characteristics are major ingredients of success with these procedures. Much work remains, however, before we can identify these ingredients and specify how to demonstrate their contributions and efficacy in treating men-tal disorders.

PART III

NEUROSCIENTIFIC STORIES

CHAPTER

5

Identifying, Describing, and Classifying Psychiatric Disorders

As clinics and hospitals began to record case histories and detail observations, physicians could identify syndromal groupings (clusters of symptoms) and classify them into disease entities. The success with which botanical taxonomists had systematized their field in the eighteenth century provided additional impetus to the trend toward categorizing symptom clusters into a formal psychiatric nosology.

A second major trend within biological medicine, the view that mental disorders might result from organic pathology, can be traced to the early writings of Hippocrates, Aretaeus, and Galen. With the advent of valid anatomical, physiological, and biochemical knowledge in the eighteenth century and the discovery in the nineteenth century of the role played by bacteria and viruses, the disease concept of modern medicine, including the view of mental illness as a disease, was firmly established. Efforts at developing somatic (e.g., electrical, chemical, surgical) treatment methods followed naturally. Although these three stages—diagnostic classification, biological causation, and somatic treatment—rarely proceeded in a smooth or even logical fashion, they characterized psychiatric progress and continue today to guide neuroscientists who follow the medical and biological tradition.

Nosology refers to the science of classifying clinical syndromes (Millon, 1991). Its major value for depicting the mind and its pathology is to facilitate consistent communication among scientists, who are seeking causes, and practitioners, who are recommending and executing therapy. These scientific and medical activities, however, presuppose a classification system (a taxonomy) that is not only logical but valid. Unfortunately, physicians classified diseases long before they understood their true nature. Such nosologies have persisted because of widespread or authoritative use; however, they rested most often on unfounded speculations or, at best, judicious but essentially superficial observations. Criticism of premature nosological schemes is justified, given the frequent slavish adherence to them. On the other hand, there is no reason to overlook the *potential* value of a taxonomy or to abolish a sound classification system that might fulfill many important goals. When one recognizes the complexity of the mind and its diverse forms of expression in behavior, thought, and emotion, one can well understand how difficult it has been to formulate an acceptable and durable classification schema.

The Neuroscientific Story: I

A clinical study that attempted to unravel all the elements of a patient's past and present conditions would be exhausting. To make the job less onerous, clinicians narrow their attention to certain features of a patient's past history and behavior that may prove illuminating or significant. This process requires clinicians to make a series of discriminations and decisions about the data they observe. They must find a syndromal core or nucleus of key diagnostic factors that capture the essential character of the patient's difficulties and that will serve as a framework to guide further analysis and treatment.

Diagnosticians make several assumptions in narrowing their clinical focus to a limited range of data. They assume that each patient exhibits a coherent constellation of behaviors, emotions, and attitudes central to understanding the patient's pathology; that this pattern of characteristics is found in common among a distinctive and identifiable group of patients; and that prior knowledge regarding the features of these distinctive patient groups, known as diagnostic syndromes, will facilitate clinical responsibilities and functions.

What support is there for these assumptions? Theoretical and empirical justifications must exist for the belief that people display an intrinsic unity and consistency over time in their psychological functioning. Careful study of an individual should reveal a congruency among the person's behaviors, phenomenological reports, intrapsychic or unconscious functioning, and bio-physical disposition. This coherence or syndromal pattern of functioning should be a valid phenomenon, that is, not merely imposed on clinical data as a function of theoretical biases, as often seen among diagnosticians of similar clinical persuasions. These clusters of symptoms should stem from the fact that most people, be they mentally healthy or mentally ill, possess relatively en-during constitutional dispositions that consistently color their experiences, and that the actual range of experiences to which they are exposed throughout their lives is limited and highly repetitive. In this way, individuals would de-velop a particular pattern of distinguishing prepotent and deeply ingrained be-haviors, attitudes, and needs. Once several of these diagnostic or syndromal patterns are identified among certain groups of patients, clinicians should have a good basis for inferring the likely presence in a diagnostically identified patient of many other unobserved, but frequently coexisting clinical features. If we accept that people display prepotent and internally consistent character-istics, we can then question whether certain patients evidence a commonality in their syndromal characteristics. The notion of clinical syndromes rests on the assumption that a limited number of key characteristics can identify and distinguish certain groups of patients. The hope is that the diagnostic place-ment of a patient within one of these groups will clue the diagnostician to the larger pattern of the patient's difficulty, thereby simplifying the clinical task immeasurably. Thus, once the key characteristics of a particular patient are identified, the clinician can use knowledge learned about other patients diag-nosed with that syndrome and apply that knowledge to the present patient.

Another question concerning neuroscientific classification is: Why does the possession of characteristic A increase the probability, appreciably beyond chance, of also possessing characteristics B, C, and so on? Put in a less abstract way, why do particular behaviors, attitudes, and mechanisms covary in repeti-tive and recognizable ways instead of presenting in a more-or-less haphazard fashion? Put in an even more concrete way, why do behavioral defensiveness, interpersonal provocativeness, cognitive suspicion, affective irascibility, and ex-cessive use of the projection mechanism co-occur in the same individual instead of being uncorrelated and randomly distributed among different individuals?

The answers are, first, that temperament and early experience simultane-ously affect the development and nature of several emerging psychological structures and functions; that is, a wide range of behaviors, attitudes, affects, and mechanisms can be traced to the same origins, which thereby leads to their frequently observed covariance.

Second, these initial characteristics set in motion a series of derivative life experiences that shape the individual's acquisition of new psychological attri-butes that are causally related to the characteristics that preceded them in the sequential chain. Common origins and successive linkages increase the proba-bility that certain psychological characteristics frequently pair with specific others, resulting in repetitively observed symptom or trait clusters. Illustrations of these reciprocal covariances and serially unfolding concatenations among longitudinal influences (e.g., etiology) and concurrent attributes (e.g., signs, traits) may be found in Millon (1969, 1981; Millon & Davis, 1996).

The unique characteristics of each patient are unlikely to be lost when he or she is grouped in a category or syndrome; however, differences among members of the same syndrome will exist. The question is not whether the syndrome is entirely homogeneous but whether placement in the category impedes or facilitates clinically relevant objectives. Thus, identifying a patient as fitting a category composed of key characteristics may simplify clinical understanding by alerting the diagnostician to features of a patient's past history and present functioning that have not yet been observed or deduced. If it enables a clinician to communicate effectively to others about the patient, guides the selection of beneficial therapeutic plans, or assists researchers in the design of their investigations, then these syndromal categories have served many useful purposes. Of course, no single classification schema can serve all the purposes for which diagnostic syndromes can be formed; all we can ask is that it facilitate certain relevant and important clinical functions.

The neuroscientific approach assumes that biophysical factors such as anatomy and biochemistry are the primary determinants of mental illness. As noted, ample evidence from medical science exists to justify this assumption. The following section examines the unfolding of ideas among those who have sought to identify and classify the mental disorders.

Unfolding of Key Ideas

For the greater part of history (Menninger, 1963; Zilboorg & Henry, 1941), clinicians formulated psychiatric taxonomies on the basis of clinical observation, by witnessing repetitive patterns of behavior and emotion among a small number of carefully studied mental patients. They generated etiologic hypotheses to explain these patterns of covariance (e.g., Hippocrates anchored differences in observed temperament to his humoral theory, and Kraepelin distinguished two major categories of severe mental illness—dementia praecox and manic-depressive disease—in terms of their ostensive divergent prognostic course). The elements composing these notions, however, were imposed after the fact on prior observational data, rather than serving as a generative source for taxonomic categories.

The notion that the presence of covarying symptoms might signify underlying disease entities can be traced to the seventeenth-century writings of Thomas Sydenham. In connecting this notion to recent mathematical factor analytic techniques, Blashfield (1984) commented:

> Sydenham, who promoted the concept of syndrome . . . argued that a careful observer of patients could note that certain sets of symptoms tended to co-occur.

If these co-occurring sets of symptoms were seen repeatedly across a number of patients, this observance would suggest that the syndrome may represent more than a chance collection of symptoms. Instead, the consistent appearance of a syndrome would suggest a disease with a common etiology and a common treatment. (pp. 169–170)

The diagnostic categories proposed in ancient Greece and Rome were founded on Hippocrates' observations. Mental disorders were divided into five classes: *phrenitis,* an acute disturbance with fever; *mania,* an acute disturbance without fever; *melancholia,* all chronic disorders; *hysteria,* a female disorder noted by agitation, pain, and convulsion; and *epilepsy,* the only syndrome of the group possessing the same name and meaning today. With only minor variations, Celsus, Aretaeus, Soranus, Galen, and Aurelianus adopted this system. Following the dormant period of the Middle Ages, a reawakened interest in classical writings brought about the return of the Hippocratic system.

With the waning role of supernaturalism and the advent of liberating thought during the Renaissance, enlightened thinkers of the sixteenth and seventeenth centuries began to explore ideas related to a realistic classification of mental disorders. As recorded in Chapter 2, Paracelsus classified several syndromes, such as *lunatici, insani, vesani,* and *melancholici,* to represent disorders influenced by the phases of the moon, those derived from heredity, those stemming from contaminated sources of food or drink, and those reflecting a lost capacity to reason. Similarly, Robert Burton, in his extensive text, the *Anatomy of Melancholy* (1621), differentiated categories such as those that emanated from the body, those generated by a brain dysfunction, those signifying madness, and those that featured melancholy, the latter stemming from guilt and shame. Also of note were the contributions of Thomas Willis, who anticipated a syndrome labeled two centuries later as *dementia praecox,* as well as impairments that he termed morosis, mania, and melancholia, each encompassing several subcategories. Worthy of comment also in the seventeenth century were the informative symptom pictures characterized by Thomas Sydenham, who described the disorder *hysteria* in terms almost indistinguishable from the ones used to portray the syndrome today. Notable also was Sydenham's recognition that syndromes reflected the interaction of multiple rather than singular influences, as well as his bringing to the fore the natural reparative capabilities of most illnesses. Similarly, Georg Ernst Stahl was perhaps the first diagnostician in this period to distinguish between organic and psychological disorders.

Cataloging Pre-Kraepelinian Syndromes

Picking up the thread of Renaissance psychiatric classifiers discussed in Chapter 2, **William Battie (1703–1776),** a major specialist in mental illness, wrote in A *Treatise on Madness* (1758) that reliance for treatment choice should be placed in the hands and the "sagacity of the physician." Battie, founding officer of St. Luke's Hospital in London, which opened in 1751, is thought to have been the first psychiatry teacher in England. Appalled at the conditions he found in the hospitals of his time, he vigorously argued against the common use of bloodletting in cases of so-called madness. He was conflicted, however, about treatment. For example, if periods of manic excitement did not subside on their own, he suggested employing the narcotic virtue of poppy seeds and, if this failed, administering other "time-tested" methods (e.g., blisters, caustics) to cause the patient distracting pain and discomfort.

On the positive side, Battie believed that mental disorders were curable. Thus, he asserted that "madness is no less manageable as are many other distempers . . . and yet are not looked upon as incurable; such unhappy objects ought by no means to be abandoned." Following the ideas of Hermann Boerhaave, Battie asserted that when muscular spasms of brain vessels were obstructed, the resultant nerve compressions ultimately led to delusional sensations. Nevertheless, many of Battie's views regarding mental disorders were obscure or contradictory. He based his arguments primarily on speculation instead of on observation. No more so than his colleagues of the time, he wrote about the confusing array of sources of illness, especially the conflicting nature of diverse sensations as the source of all disorders. He wrote:

> . . . from whence we collect that madness, with respect to its cause, is distinguishable into two species; the first solely owing to an internal disorder of the nervous substance, being indeed, in like manner, disordered . . . it chiefly can be attributed to some remote and accidental cause. The first species, until a better name can be found, can be called *original*, the second may be called *consequential madness*. (1758)

Perhaps the leading nosologist of his day was **Françoise Boissier de Sauvages (1706–1767).** He had completed his dissertation at the age of 20, defending the teachings of the faculty of his medical school: Montpelier. Conservative in mind but clearly distant from the demonological prejudices that were prevalent in most academic circles of his day, he thought that all mental diseases were located in distinct anatomical regions. Beyond this assertion, he believed that the will had much to do not only with the generation of mental aberrations, but also their ultimate treatment. He believed that physicians had a responsibility to shape or guide individual behaviors, fearing that otherwise there would be no social compact or personal justice.

De Sauvages followed Linnaeus in seeking to organize an encyclopedic framework for grouping the many categories of mental disorder. He outlined 10 classes, 295 genera, and 24,000 species, spending the better part of his life immersing himself in the large body of medical knowledge that had accumulated from early times. His urge to catalog the bewildering and scattered array of human disorders was likely an effort to surmount the spotty and supernatural beliefs that typified earlier thought.

De Sauvages was a botanist, besides being a physician. Most of his colleagues spent their time arranging plants and animals in a clearly articulated and evolutionary system, the latter a new departure that did not achieve its fullest impact until the work of Darwin a century later. The details of de Sauvages' presentations were first published in a small book, *Nouvelles Classes de Maladies* (1731). Included in his broad classification were such illnesses as fevers, inflammations, spasms, breathing disturbances, weaknesses, pains, and dementias. Most of the mental diseases in this book were dementias, which were organized into four types: those of extracerebral origin, disturbances of the instinctual and emotional life, disturbances of the intellectual life, and irregular eccentricities and follies.

De Sauvages completed the three-volume *Nosologie Methodique* (1771) late in life, and it was published several years after his death. In this work, de Sauvages made available to others the complete model he had constructed. This model was used as an orderly classification for decades, if not centuries, to come. In this comprehensive volume, de Sauvages organized all forms of mental illness. For example, he grouped the syndrome of melancholia into numerous species (e.g., religious, imaginary, extravagant, vagabonding, enthusiastic, and sorrowful).

In the late 1770s and early 1780s, **William Cullen (1710–1790),** a distinguished physician and professor at the University of Edinburgh, became the most influential nosologist of his day, drawing on the work of de Sauvages, but extending the Linnean themes even more comprehensively. The Frenchman, Phillipe Pinel, who played a well-publicized role in the humane movement of mental treatment, used Cullen's nosology as the basis for his scientific teachings. In contrast to most of his colleagues, Cullen became a popular educator because he refused to lecture in esoteric Latin, and instead spoke in the vernacular.

In his first major work, the four-volume *First Lines of the Practice of Physick* (1777), Cullen tried to categorize all the then-known diseases, both psychological and physical, in line with the symptoms they displayed, the methods by which diagnoses were generated, and the most beneficial therapy. Cullen was a notable pioneer of neuropathology and, consistent with his orientation, believed that most pathological conditions of the mind should be attributed to diseases of the brain. Despite this orientation, he recognized that life experiences often influenced how these biologically grounded diseases were expressed. Cullen proposed the term *neuroses* to represent neurologically based diseases. Most etiologically obscure mental illnesses were labeled neuroses, ostensibly to represent diseases of nerves that were inflamed and irritable. As he perceived it, neuroses were affections of sense or motion that stemmed from a disharmony of the nervous system. Into the general category of neuroses, Cullen subcategorized four variants: those representing a diminution of voluntary motion, those representing a diminution of involuntary activity, the regular motions of the muscles or muscle fibers, and disorders of judgment.

Along with Cullen, **Robert Whytt (1714–1766)** played a large role in providing Scottish physicians of his day with a classification system of neurotic individuals. Both proposed somewhat different schemas of mental disorder, although each adhered to a physiological grounding for these disturbances. Whytt attended to the less severe mental conditions of his time, categorizing them into three broad syndromes: hysteria, hypochondriasis, and nervous exhaustion. **George Beard (1839–1883)** subsequently referred to the latter as *neurasthenia.* This classification does not deviate much from our current diagnostic manual, although Whytt's ideas were not based on detailed psychological observations. As with Cullen, Whytt's basic theory stated that disturbed motility within the nervous system produced nervous disorders. The selection of the term neuroses made good sense, as both Cullen and Whytt assumed that different sensibilities of the nerves could be the basis for certain problematic behaviors. This belief continued for at least another century, anticipating ideas that were explored in greater depth first by Charcot, and later by Janet and Freud.

John Haslam (1766–1844), a British psychiatrist, is probably best known for the diligence and astuteness of his clinical observations. As Zilboorg and Henry have noted, "Through the sheer effort of keen observation of minute, seemingly unrelated details . . . and orderly arrangements of these details . . . a coherent clinical picture of the disease came to the fore" (1941, p. 303). Using greater care than his predecessors, Haslam provided the first clinical description of various forms of paralysis, most notably that of general paresis. Alert to the epidemic of venereal disease that spread across Europe in the early nineteenth century, Haslam wrote:

> A course of debauchery long persisted would probably terminate in paralysis . . . frequently induces derangement of mind.
>
> Paralytic affections are a much more frequent cause of insanity than has been commonly supposed, and they are also a very common effect of madness; more maniacs die of hemiplegia and apoplexy than from any other disease. (1809, p. 209)

Also of great significance was his recognition, as had Aretaeus earlier in the first century, that states of excitement and depression alternated in the same individual. This observation recorded the significance of the course of a disease in classifying mental syndromes and laid the groundwork for Kraepelin's central rationale for his nosological model almost a century later. In his 1809 book, *Observations on Madness and Melancholy,* Haslam also described cases that would subsequently be classified as dementia praecox or schizophrenia. In the following year, he published an innovative text, *Illustrations of Madness* (1810), that presented a detailed examination of an individual with diverse paranoid features.

No less significant was Haslam's sophistication in matters of nomenclature and semantics. In his 1809 text, he wrote:

Mad is therefore not a complex idea, as has been supposed, but a complex term for all the forms and varieties of this disease. Our language has been enriched with other terms expressive of this affliction . . .

Instead of endeavoring to discover an infallible definition of madness, which I believe will be found impossible, as it is an attempt to comprise, in a few words, the wide range and mutable character of a Proteus disorder. (pp. 5–6)

Important contributions were made by **Jean Esquirol,** the great French reformer whose humane achievements were described in Chapter 3. Among Esquirol's diagnostic proposals was the attention he gave to a patient's dispositions and deficits of affect and impulse in his concept of *lypemanie*. By this, he meant patients deficient in their capacity to feel or desire, a feature that encompassed patients who today would be thought of as depressed. Esquirol grouped the several variants of mental disorder into five broad classification syndromes: *lypemanie, monomanie, manie, dementia, and imbecility/idiocy,* a series of distinctions used in France for over a century. Esquirol also made significant contributions to the clarification of delusions and hallucinations. He wrote:

In hallucinations there is no more sensation or perception than in dreaming or somnambulism, when no external object is stimulating the senses. . . . In fact, hallucination is a cerebral or psychological phenomenon that takes place independently from the senses. The pretended sensations of the hallucinated are images and ideas reproduced by memory, improved by the imagination, and personified by habit. (1838, pp. 191–192)

Also notable were the contributions of **Jean-Pierre Falret (1794–1870),** another humane reformer and student of Esquirol, who articulated notions similar to his mentor's regarding delusions. He specified several instrumental factors: the state of the brain, the character of the patient, the circumstances surrounding the time the delusion began, and concurrent internal and external sensations. He expressed his conception of delusions as follows:

Delusions may reflect the most intimate preoccupations and emotions of the individual. Indeed, the features of delusions may help us recognize what aspects of the subject's organization are suffering the most. Practitioners should give attention to relationships between delusions and the character of the subject. (1862, p. 357)

Falret also contributed an early and insightful series of papers that recognized the variable character of mania and melancholy, which he called *forme circulaire de maladie mentale,* consisting of periods of excitation followed by longer periods of weakness. Presenting this theme as a facet of his 1851 lectures at the Salpetriere Hospital, he subsequently elaborated these views in a book published in 1854. Baillarger, whose work is discussed in later paragraphs, proposed these ideas almost concurrently.

A series of classifications in Germany were based on a threefold distinction among the "faculties of the mind": volition, intellection, and emotion, as well as "morbid" processes such as exaltation and depression. Among the early promoters of this schema was **Johann Christian Heinroth (1773–1843).** In 1811, at Leipzig University, he became perhaps the first physician to occupy a chair in psychiatry. He subdivided one of the major categories of mental disorder, *vesania,* into several orders, genera, and species. Designing a complex matrix combining the major faculties on one dimension and the morbid processes on the other, he proposed a classification system that comprised subtypes and became the basis of several variations throughout Germany and England in the ensuing century. Heinroth also composed a theory of mind with a tripartite structure. The basic or undergirding layer was characterized by the animalistic instinctual qualities of human beings; the intermediary layer reflected consciousness, including both intelligence and self-awareness; and, finally, a superior layer comprised what we would call conscience. Akin to later ideas proposed by Freud, he also proposed the notion of conflict when two layers became opposing forces, such as the instinctual impulses of sin, on the one hand, and the conscience's sense of moral correctness.

Especially insightful was Heinroth's recognition of the significance of the patient's affect, or passions. He specified these insights in the following quote:

> The origin of the false notions in patients is erroneously attributed to the intellect. The intellect is not at fault; it is the disposition which is seized by some depressing passion, and then has to follow it, and since this passion becomes the dominating element, the intellect is forced by the disposition to retain certain ideas and concepts. But it is not these ideas or concepts which determine the nature of the disease. (1818)

Heinroth recognized a deep connection between the human qualities of mind and the more fundamental vegetative or animal passions that undergird mental disorders, notably those of melancholy and rage. Heinroth also conceived a term akin to what today we call psychosomatics, in which he took exception to Descartes' contention of a dualism between mind and body. Health reflected harmony between these two components acting as a singular entity. He not only recognized a unity between mind and body, but considered that each person's makeup included the same elements that composed nature.

Heinroth traced the term *paranoia* some 2,000 years back in the medical literature. The word had disappeared from the medical lexicon in the second century and was not revived until Heinroth, following the structure of Kantian psychology, employed the term in 1818 to represent a variety of disorders. Those of the intellect, he termed paranoia; disturbances of feeling he called *paranoia ecstasia.* He also proposed the parallel concepts of *Wahnsinn* and *Verrucktheit* (the latter term is still in use as a label for paranoia in modern-day Germany). Griesinger, to be discussed shortly, picked up the term Wahnsinn in 1845 to signify pathological thought processes and applied it to cases that exhibited expansive and grandiose delusions. In 1863, Kahlbaum (also discussed later in this chapter) suggested that paranoia be the exclusive label for delusional states.

The British alienist **James Cowles Prichard (1786–1848),** credited by many as having been the first to formulate the concept of *moral insanity,* was, in fact, preceded in this realization by several theorists; nevertheless, he was the first to label it as such and to give it wide readership in English-speaking nations. Although he accepted Pinel's notion of *manie sans delire,* he dissented from Pinel's morally neutral attitude toward these disorders and became the major exponent of the view that these behaviors signified a reprehensible defect in character that deserved social condemnation. He also broadened the scope of the original syndrome by including under moral insanity a wide range of previously diverse mental and emotional conditions. All these patients ostensibly shared a common defect in the power to guide themselves in accord with "natural feelings"—that is, a spontaneous and intrinsic sense of rightness, goodness, and responsibility. In his opinion, those afflicted by this disease were swayed, despite their ability to intellectually understand the choices before them, by overpowering "affections" that compelled them to engage in socially repugnant behaviors.

A major figure in extending the ideas of Esquirol and Falret at the Salpetriere Hospital, **Felix Voisin (1794–1872)** was also a strong adherent of the phrenological speculations of Gall and Spurzheim (discussed in Chapter 14). His particular expertise related to the linkage between the brain and the sexual organs, in which he stressed the importance of the nervous system in generating sexual disorders of desire. Placing special attention on the pathologies of nymphomania and satyriasis, especially in relationship to hysteria, Voisin articulated a progression in these disorders from their early stages to their more severe forms, contributing to the idea that disease *course* was central to clinical diagnostics.

In his major work, *The Analysis of Human Understanding* (1851), Voisin specified three major faculties of human functioning—moral, intellectual, and animal—a division that predated and paralleled Freud's subsequent formulation of the mind's structure of superego, ego, and id. Also notable was Voisin's contribution to the moral treatment of the retarded at the Bicétre Hospital. Influenced by the British alienist, Prichard, Voisin delved briefly into criminal and forensic pathology in his later years, speaking of criminals as a product of lower-class origins and of their inevitable moral degeneration. This theme was addressed elsewhere by Cesare Lombroso and Benedict Morel, both discussed in later paragraphs and chapters.

Another contributor to French thinking of the day was **Paul Briquet (1796–1881),** who focused primarily on problems of hysteria and its ostensive connection to female maladies. In his extensive monograph, *Traite Clinique et Therapeutique a l'Hysterie* (1859), Briquet took exception to the notion posited by Plato and Hippocrates that hysteria was a consequence of sexual incontinence. Briquet specified with great clarity the multiple gastrointestinal and vague sexual and exaggerated complaints that typified the symptoms presented by his "hysterical" patients. The disorder is labeled *somatization disorder* in official nosologies today and is occasionally referred to as *Briquet's syndrome*. In contrast to prior beliefs, he recorded that married women were no more inclined to hysteria than were unmarried women, that numerous cases appeared before puberty and, most significantly, that an active sexual life was no assurance that one would not develop such symptoms.

Going beyond the assumptions of his forerunners and contemporaries, Briquet rejected the historic view that men could not develop symptoms of hysteria. He also pointed to numerous psychological influences that often contributed to the symptoms of the disorder, noting painful emotional states, such as sadness and fear, as precipitants. Moreover, he speculated on untoward developmental and life experiences as playing a pathogenic role (e.g., parental mistreatment, spousal abuse, unfavorable employment circumstances, or business failures). Recognizing that only a small subset of those subjected to these psychosocial experiences developed the hysterical syndrome, Briquet proposed *predispositions* as pathogenic factors. Aware that life circumstances often troubled his patients, he suggested that many would benefit by speaking to an empathic counselor or physician who might serve as a confidant. Briquet showed a great sensitivity in going beyond the crude medications of the day to employ a psychotherapeutic approach to his patients' difficulties.

Ernst von Feuchtersleben (1806–1849) may have been the first Austrian psychiatrist to gain a distinguished status in European circles during the mid-nineteenth century. His one major publication, *The Principles of Medical Psychology*, published in 1847, likely had a significant influence on Freud and his many disciples in Vienna. A strong critic of those who supported the Cartesian mind-body dichotomy, Feuchtersleben, like many in the twentieth-century psychosomatic movement, considered the mind and the body to be a unitary phenomenon, essentially indivisible. An exponent of the role of personality qualities in the life of mental patients, Feuchtersleben wrote with great sensitivity on the psychic sources of mental disorders. In describing those inclined to the development of depressive diseases, Feuchtersleben said:

> Here the senses, memory, and reaction give way, the nervous vitality languishes at its root, and the vitality of the blood, deprived of this stimulant, is languid in all its functions. Hence the slow and often difficult respiration, and proneness to sighing. . . . When they are chronic, they deeply affect vegetative life, and the body wastes away. (p. 135)

In what may have been the first purely psychological description of what is now referred to as the histrionic personality, Feuchtersleben depicted women disposed to hysterical symptoms as being sexually heightened, selfish, and "overprivileged with satiety and boredom." Attributing these traits to the unfortunate nature of female education, he wrote, "It combines everything that can heighten sensibility, weaken spontaneity, give a preponderance to the sexual sphere, and sanction the feelings and impulse that relate to it" (1847, p. 111).

Chauvinistic as this judgment may seem today, he at least recognized and was sensitive to the limitations Victorian society placed on women in his time. Moreover, Feuchtersleben asserted the important role that psychological factors could play in helping patients understand the origins of their difficulties. He also espoused a hopeful therapeutic attitude and recommended opportunities for patients to acquire a second education in life.

As noted in Chapter 2, the great English neurologist Thomas Willis reported having observed a pathological sequence in which "young persons who, lively and spirited, and at times even brilliant in their childhood, passed into obtuseness and hebetude during adolescence." Better known historically are the texts of the Belgian psychiatrist **Benedict-Augustin Morel (1809–1873),** who described the case of a 14-year-old boy who had been a cheerful and good student, but who progressively lost his intellectual capacities and increasingly became melancholy and withdrawn. Morel considered such cases to be irremediable and ascribed the deterioration to an arrest in brain development that stemmed from hereditary causes. He named the illness "dementia praecox" (*demence precoce*) to signify his observation that a degenerative process began at an early age and progressed rapidly.

Morel was born in an impoverished family in Germany shortly before the death of his father, following which he was sent to a religious boarding school in France. Because of his rebellious behavior, Morel was expelled from school. He wandered through Paris as a penniless bohemian and eventually shared a small studio room with Claude Bernard, who later became a distinguished methodologist and physiological theorist. Despite their meager circumstances, both young men embarked on careers in medicine. While pursuing psychiatry, Morel met Jean-Pierre Falret, who allowed him to work as a physician at the Salpetriere. Following a later period of study in an asylum for the mentally retarded, Morel became physician-in-chief, first at the Mareville Asylum near Nancy, and later at an asylum in Rouen, where he explored what he judged to be the hereditary basis of degeneration. In his first major work, *Etudes Medico-Psychologiques sur l'Alienation Mentale,* he studied and wrote about social and family aspects of mental disorders. In these investigations, Morel became convinced that so-called degeneration was pervasive in all forms of psychological pathology, especially mental retardation. In 1856, when Morel became chief physician at St. Yon Asylum, he continued to lecture and write on the inevitable sequence of deterioration, which he considered the inexorable course of all mental disorders. He spoke of the "incessant progression" of degeneration that he judged to be human destiny. Speaking of those subjected to hereditary mental disorders, he wrote:

> The degenerate human being, if he is abandoned to himself, falls into a progressive degradation. He becomes . . . not only incapable of forming part of the chain of transmission of progress in human society, he is the greatest obstacle

to this progress through his contact with the healthy portion of the population. (1857, p. 46)

Although his work secured him a niche in the history of psychiatry, Morel's views contributed to the pessimistic attitude toward mental illness then pervasive in the European public-at-large, a view that gained a horrendous following a century later in Nazi Germany.

In 1854, **Jules Baillarger (1809–1892)** and Jean-Pierre Falret summarized the results of their independent work with depressed and suicidal persons. They reported that a large portion of these patients showed extended depression, broken intermittently by periods of irritability, anger, elation, and normality. The terms *la folie circulaire* (Falret, 1854) and *folie a double forme* (Baillarger, 1853) were applied to signify this syndrome's contrasting and variable character. As might be expected, Baillarger and Falret engaged in a lengthy conflict about who was first in their syndromal description. Unknown to both, there had been earlier contributions. Subsequent to parallel descriptions by the first century Roman physician Aretaeus, the first theorist to record the notion of a covariation between impulsive and erratic moods in a single syndrome was *Theophile Bonet*, who applied the term *folie maniaco-melancolique* in 1684. In the eighteenth century, *Samuel Schacht* and *Ernst Herschel* reinforced the thesis suggested in Bonet's terminology that these erratic and unstable moods followed a rhythmic or periodic regularity of highs and lows. Subsequent clinicians only slowly recognized the frequent periodicity of the manic-depressive covariation. Notably, the case histories described by Bonet, and by Schacht and Herschel, rarely exhibited a clear-cut tandem pattern. Rather, they were episodic, erratic, and desultory in sequence, shifting almost randomly from depression, to anger, to guilt, to elation, to boredom, to normality, and so on in an unpredictable and inconsistent course. Falret's son Jules, himself a distinguished psychiatric diagnostician, sought to bridge the altercation between his father and Baillarger some decades later by recognizing the ideas of the earlier theorists.

Baillarger contributed to a wide range of psychopathological conditions beyond the syndrome known today as bipolar disorder, notably in his ideas on hallucinations and delusions, neurohistology, epilepsy, and general paralyses. He sought to distinguish the perceptual basis of delusions by recognizing that they were based on false interpretations of normal sensations, whereas illusions were distortions at the sensory instead of the ideational level. Similarly, he explored whether hallucinations were sensory or psychological phenomena. He proposed two types: psychosensory hallucination, which stemmed from the interaction of sensory and imaginal distortions, and psychological hallucination, which was independent of any sensory involvement.

Although born and educated in Germany, **Richard von Krafft-Ebing (1810–1874)** became a close follower of Morel, whose concept of degeneration struck a resonant chord in Krafft-Ebing's work and practice at the Illenau Asylum in Baden. He was convinced that the Morelian process of degeneration was the primary cause, not only of mental disorders, but also of criminality and sexual pathology. He wrote: "Madness, when it finally breaks out, represents only the last link in the psychopathic chain of constitutional heredity, or degenerate heredity" (1879, p. 439).

Moving to Graz, Austria, he became a professor of psychiatry at the university there and the director of its provincial asylum. In his major work, *Lehrbuch der Psychiatrie* (1879), he referred to the problem of progressive sexual degeneration as follows: "It is specially frequent for sexual functioning to be . . . abnormally strong, manifesting itself explosively and seeking satisfaction impulsively, or abnormally early, stirring already in early childhood and leading to masturbation" (p. 424). By the mid-1880s, Krafft-Ebing assumed the chair at the University of Vienna and wrote his most famous book, entitled *Psychopathia Sexualis* (1882/1937), where he spoke of the pervasive pathology of all variants of sexual activity other than the approved and acceptable behavior of Victorian times.

Krafft-Ebing proposed the term *masochism* as a new concept in his catalog of sexual perversions. In a manner similar to sadism, the masochism label employed the name of a well-known writer of the time, Leopold Von Sacher-Masoch. In Masoch's novel, *Venus in Furs* (1870), the hero suffered torture, subjugation, and deprecation from a female tormentor. Krafft-Ebing asserted that flagellation and physical punishment were necessary elements in the perversion but were less significant than a personal relationship that included enslavement, passivity, and psychological serfdom. Hence, from its first formulations, masochism, although centrally sexual in nature, included the need to experience suffering, and not just physical pain.

To Krafft-Ebing, the male masochist was functionally impotent except when experiencing suffering, subjugation, and abuse. In what might be called characterological masochism, typically expressed in love relationships, Krafft-Ebing wrote: "When the idea of being tyrannized is for a long time closely associated with a lustful thought of the beloved person, the lustful emotion is finally transferred to the tyranny itself and the transformation to the perversion is completed" (1882, p. 207).

The contemporary historian of psychiatry, Edward Shorter, comments that Krafft-Ebing found evidence of sexual perversion everywhere; he stamped all variants of sexual behavior other than the straight-and-narrow as degenerates, using his "scientific authority" to demonize matters of cultural preference. As a colleague wrote of Krafft-Ebing, "He was a man who was gifted in literary terms, yet scientifically and critically he was incapable to the point of feeble-mindedness" (Bendikt, 1906, p. 392).

The growth of knowledge in anatomy and physiology in the mid-eighteenth century strengthened the trend toward organically oriented disease classifications. **Wilhelm Griesinger (1817–1868),** a young German psychiatrist with little direct patient experience, asserted the disease concept in his classic text, *Mental Pathology and Therapeutics*, published in 1845 when he was barely 28 years of age. His statement, "Mental diseases are brain diseases," shaped the course of German systematic psychiatry for the next 40 years. The fact that no relationship had yet been established between brain pathology and mental disorders did not weaken Griesinger's contention that classifications should be formed on the basis of underlying brain lesions. In fact, Griesinger's own system of categories—depression, exaltation, and weakness—did not parallel his views about the importance of brain pathology. Nevertheless, he convinced succeeding generations of German neurologists, led by *Thomas Meynart* and *Carl Wernicke* that brain diseases would be found to underlie all mental disturbances.

Wilhelm Griesinger

Griesinger was born in Stuttgart, Germany, and completed his medical studies in Zurich and Tubingen. There he learned to view medicine as a science based on direct observation of patient experiences and behaviors rather than on historical speculations and philosophy. He began his formal career in psychiatry at the Winnenthal Asylum in Stuttgart. Assuming that he had gathered sufficient expertise in a three-year span, he penned his 1845 classic text on mental pathology and therapeutics. Abandoning his clinical position, Griesinger accepted an outpatient department directorship in internal medicine in Tubingen and later served as Professor of Internal Medicine in Zurich, where he set the mold for German academic psychiatry for the next 40 years. To him, the study of mental illness was integral to the study of general medicine. He conceived mental disorders like most medical diseases, to be chronically progressive. Thus, he regarded depression as beginning with a minor level of cerebral irritation, leading next to a chronic and irreversible degeneration, and ending ultimately in pervasive dementia. This path of deterioration became a central theme of Kraepelin's belief that the course of a mental disorder was its most crucial characteristic.

It was not until 1861 that Griesinger revised his psychiatric text, following which he returned to his work in psychiatry at the University of Berlin. Here he both lectured and practiced at its Charité Clinic, where he divided his patients into those with routine nervous diseases and those with nervous diseases that also exhibited psychiatric symptoms. He also initiated and assumed the editorship of a new journal, *The Archives for Psychiatry and Nervous Diseases*. In its first volume, Griesinger wrote:

Psychiatry has undergone a transformation in its relationship to the rest of medicine. . . . This transformation rests principally on the realization that patients with so-called mental diseases are really individuals with diseases of the nerves and the brain. . . . Psychiatry . . . must become an integral part of general medicine and accessible to all medical circles. (1868, p. 12)

In line with his orientation concerning psychiatric disorders, Griesinger described the criteria he would use for patients exhibiting delusions as follows:

The insane ideas of patients must be distinguished from the erroneous views of the normal. . . . They are always part of a general disturbance of mental processes; they are opposed to views formerly held by the patient, he cannot get rid of them, they resist correction by the testimony of the senses and the understanding, they depend upon a disturbance of the brain which is also expressed in other symptoms. (1882, p. 72)

Reflecting his view that mental diseases were largely based on heredity, he wrote thus of suicide:

An original anomalous position is also not to be denied in those cases of suicide where one or both parents, although not suffering under insanity, present a striking eccentricity or extravagance of character, in a morbid exaltation of the passions. . . . In those cases where several instances of suicide have occurred in near relatives . . . experience has frequently shown that the inclination to suicide, which often comes on in all the members of the family at the same age, communicates itself by hereditary descent. (1845, p. 182)

Griesinger also contemplated problems of hysteria, commenting, as did his Austrian contemporary Feuchtersleben: "[hysterical women displayed an] immoderate sensitiveness, especially to the slightest reproach [in which there is a] tendency to refer everything to themselves, great irritability, great change of disposition on the least, or even from no external motive" (1845, p. 114).

Among other distinguishing characteristics of hysterics, according to Griesinger, were their "volatile humor, their senseless caprices, and their inclination to deception, prevarication, jealousy, and malice." Perhaps he should have left psychiatry for internal medicine more permanently, given his book's rather questionable assertions about women.

Although the work of Griesinger and his followers regarding the role of the brain in mental disorders soon dominated continental psychiatry, a different emphasis regarding the basis of classification was developing concurrently. Jean Esquirol, Pinel's distinguished student, had often referred to the importance of age of onset, variable chronicity, and deteriorating course in understanding pathology. This idea became a formal part of classification in 1856 when the German psychiatrist, **Karl Ludwig Kahlbaum (1828–1899),** extended Esquirol's idea by developing a classification system that grouped disorders according to their course and outcome. It became the major alternative system to the one that Griesinger proposed. Kraepelin, noting his indebtedness to Kahlbaum's contributions, stated, "Identical or remarkably similar symptoms can accompany wholly dissimilar diseases while their inner nature can be revealed only through their progress and termination" (Kraepelin, 1920, p. 116). Kahlbaum explained how attempts to group disorders on the basis of the similarity of their overt symptomatology had been useless, as if such superficial symptom collections would themselves expose something essential about the underlying disease. He commented as follows:

> It is futile to search for the anatomy of melancholy or mania, because each of these forms occurs under the most varied relationships and combinations with other states, and they are just as little the expression of an inner pathological process as the complex of symptoms we call fever. (1874, p. 2)

Karl Ludwig Kahlbaum

Kahlbaum trained originally at the Prussian state asylum in Allenberg, where he found it difficult to adhere to the asylum director's thesis that there was but one "unitary psychosis." Moving in 1857 to the Gorlitz Clinic, Kahlbaum turned his attention to psychoses that were typical of young adolescents, focusing on the sudden emergence of mental disorientation and rapid disintegration, a pattern not unlike that described by Benjamin Morel a decade or two earlier. Similarly, reading the work of Jean-Pierre Falret and Jules Baillarger, he also directed his attention to the problems of patients whose mood disorders appeared to follow a sequential course from mania to depression and back.

In a series of monographs and books published between 1863 and 1874, Kahlbaum not only established the importance of including longitudinal factors in psychiatric diagnosis, but also described newly observed disorders that he labeled *hebephrenia* and *catatonia*, and coined the modern terms *symptom-complex* and *cyclothymia*. Kahlbaum, together with his disciple, Ewald Hecker, introduced the term hebephrenia to represent conditions that began in adolescence, usually starting with a quick succession of erratic moods, followed by a rapid enfeeblement of all functions, and finally progressing to an unalterable psychic decline. The label catatonia was introduced to represent "tension insanity" in cases where the patient displayed no reactivity to sensory impressions, lacked "self-will," and sat mute and physically immobile. These symptoms ostensibly reflected brain structure deterioration.

It was Kahlbaum also who, in 1882, imprinted current thinking on the fixed covariation of mania and melancholia, known today as bipolar disorder. Although he regarded them as facets of a single disease, which he termed *dysthymia*, following a label introduced two decades earlier by Carl Flemming, the disease actually manifested itself in different ways at different times—occasionally euphoric, occasionally melancholic, and occasionally excitable or angry. It was the primacy of the former two emotions that rigidified future conceptions of the syndrome and redirected thinking away from its more typical affective instability and unpredictability. He termed a mild variant of the illness, notable for frequent periods of normality, *cyclothymia* and designated a more severe and chronic form of the same pattern as *vesania typica circularis.*

A follower of Falret and Morel, **Valentine Magnan (1835–1916)** completed his medical studies at the University of Lyons and completed his residency at the Bicétre and Salpetriere hospitals. Following his basic psychiatric training, Magnan assumed a post at the Ste.-Anne Asylum where he examined hundreds of patients each year. He provided a well-received series of hospital-based lectures, although they evoked public ire owing to the practice of displaying actual patients for purposes of realistic instruction to staff. Remaining at Ste.-Anne until his retirement some 50 years later, he wrote in great detail on a wide variety of mental diseases, especially those that promoted Morel's concept of degeneracy. Influenced by Darwin's new and radical ideas, Magnan considered mental degenerates to be the losers in the battle of survival within the human species. As with Morel, his teachings on the consequences of mental disorders achieved a brief period of social acceptance, only to fall into the dustbin of history.

Henry Maudsley (1835–1918) described his family of origin as poor farmers, whose life was both somber and dreary. Hardly a word passed between himself, his father, or his brothers after his mother's death when he was 6 years old. Admitted to London's University College at 15, he proved to be a brilliant student, completing his medical degree at 21. Unsure about his future and lacking the means to follow an early interest in surgery, he entered the East India Company's service, spending the better part of a year as medical officer at the Wakefield Mental Asylum. Owing to his high intelligence and vigorous appearance, at age 23 he was appointed medical superintendent of the Cheadle Royal Hospital, despite a total lack of administrative experience or formal psychiatric training. Shortly thereafter, he became superintendent of the newly opened Manchester Royal Lunatic Hospital. His fame grew throughout England, and at 27 he became editor of the country's major psychiatric

Henry Maudsley

publication, the *Journal of Mental Science.* By 30, Maudsley, noting that instruction in mental diseases was a routine part of training at medical universities throughout the Continent and Scotland (e.g., Berlin, Paris, Vienna, and Edinburgh), stated in an address to academic officials that comparable training should be introduced at the University College of London, commenting that every medical man had in his practice to deal with insanity as with any other disease; and it usually fell to him to deal with it at that early stage of the disease during which there is the best hope of effecting a cure.

In his major text, *Physiology and Pathology of Mind* (1876), Maudsley attempted to redirect the philosophical inclinations typical of British clinicians and sought to anchor the subject more solidly within the biological sciences. He vigorously asserted that mind and body composed a unified organism, writing "Each part of which stirs the furthest components, which then acts upon the rest and is then reacted on by it. . . . Emotions effect every part of the body and rooted in the unity of organic life."

Shortly after he was appointed to a professorship at the University College Hospital in 1870, he wrote, consistent with comparable views by Griesinger in Germany, that "mental disorders are neither more nor less than nervous diseases in which mental symptoms predominate" (1868, p. 41). Despite this view, Maudsley had asserted earlier:

> That there is no boundary line between sanity and insanity; and the slightly exaggerated feeling which renders a man "peculiar" in the world differs only in degree from that which places hundreds in an asylum. . . . Where hereditary predisposition exists, a cause so slight as to be inappreciable to observers is often efficient to produce the disease. (1860, p. 14)

Throughout the nineteenth century, German psychiatrists abandoned what they considered to be the value-laden theories of the French and English alienists of the time and moved toward what they judged to be empirical or observational research. Among this group was **J. A. Koch (1841–1908)** who proposed replacing the label *moral insanity* with the term *psychopathic inferiority*, under which he included: "All mental irregularities whether congenital or acquired which influence a man in his personal life and cause him, even in the most favorable cases, to seem not fully in possession of normal mental capacity" (1891, p. 67).

Koch used the term *psychopathic*, a generic label employed to characterize all personality diagnoses until recent decades, to signify his belief that a physical basis existed for these character impairments. Thus, he stated: "They always remain psychopathic in that they are caused by organic states and changes which are beyond the limits of physiological normality. They stem from a congenital or acquired inferiority of brain constitution" (1891, p. 54).

Simplifying Texts of Kraepelin

Kraepelin's comprehensive textbooks at the turn of the twentieth century served as one of psychiatry's two major sources of inspiration; the other resulted from Freud's innovative contributions, to be discussed in Chapter 7.

The preeminent German systematist, **Emil Kraepelin (1856–1926)** bridged the diverse views and observations of Griesinger and Kahlbaum. In his outstanding texts, revised from a small compendium in 1883 to an imposing four-volume eighth edition in 1915, Kraepelin built a system that integrated Kahlbaum's descriptive and longitudinal approach with Griesinger's somatic disease system. By sifting and sorting prodigious numbers of well-documented hospital records and directly observing the varied characteristics of patients, he sought to bring order between symptom pictures and, most importantly, patterns of onset, course, and outcome. Kraepelin felt that syndromes based on these sequences would be best in leading to accurate identification and distinction among the different conditions that differentiated and caused these disorders. The great psychiatric historian Ray Porter (2002) summarized this contribution of Kraepelin:

Emil Kraepelin

> . . . He approached his patients as symptom-carriers, and his case histories concentrated on the core signs of each disorder. The course of psychiatric illness, he insisted, offered the best clue to its nature. . . .
>
> Kraepelin's commitment to the natural history of mental disorders led him to track the entire life histories of his patients in a longitudinal perspective which privileged prognosis (likely outcome) as definitive of the disorder (pp. 184–185).

Kraepelin was born in Germany in the same year as Sigmund Freud. A serious and diligent student, Kraepelin was exposed in medical school to several professors who were instrumental in shaping his style of thinking and research for the rest of his career. Most notable among these was Wilhelm Wundt, the founder of experimental psychology, of whom more will be written in Chapter 10. Wundt had been trained by von Helmholtz, the great physiological theorist (discussed in Chapter 6). Owing to visual difficulties that deterred him from research with microscopes, Kraepelin became oriented to psychological research, becoming one of Wundt's most distinguished students. Nevertheless, Wundt advised Kraepelin to pursue medicine rather than psychology, then a fledgling science with limited career opportunities. In 1882, he began the initial drafts of his first textbook, which later became the standard for educating psychiatrists.

After completing his formal academic training in both psychiatry and psychology, Kraepelin was offered a clinical and research position at the University of Dorpat in Estonia. Here Kraepelin established a psychological laboratory in which he employed Wundt's systematic methodology and record keeping in his study of mental patients. By the age of 35, in 1891, Kraepelin had achieved sufficient recognition professionally to be invited to the University of Heidelberg. Here he kept a card file on every patient, noting clinical symptoms, prior history, and outcome. By this time, Kraepelin began to mentor numerous German, British, and American psychiatric researchers.

His first text, a 300-page volume entitled *Compendium of Psychiatry*, was so successful that it led to several subsequent editions published under the general title *Short Textbook of Psychiatry*. By the sixth edition of what he subsequently called his *Lehrbuch* or *Textbook of Psychiatry*, completed between 1899 and 1902, Kraepelin was known throughout the Continent and the English-speaking world. In 1904, he became chairman of the Psychiatric Clinic and Laboratory, a distinguished department at the University of Munich. He was able to bring along with him from Heidelberg promising young researchers such as Alois Alzheimer and Franz Nissl, both already known for their excellent neurohistological studies and peculiar work habits. At the time of his death in 1926 at age 70, Kraepelin was actively working on a ninth edition of his textbook, which had expanded to four volumes and more than 3,000 pages.

Kraepelin did not set out initially to create the nosology for which he became so famous. Although he proposed a series of revolutionary ideas about clinical syndromes, it was the astuteness of his observations and the clarity of his writing that were central to his success. Kraepelin wrote very little about how classification should be organized; he used no formal set of principles to rationalize how a nosology should be structured. It was the implicit structure of his books (their basic table of contents) that served as his classification system. Not to be dismissed was the logic that he presented for organizing syndromes on the basis of clinical symptomatology, course, and outcome. Perhaps it was the input of his mentor Wundt's keen observation and analysis of the behavior of his subjects in his research studies that taught Kraepelin to provide such richly descriptive characterizations of his patients. Moreover, his focus centered on the overt psychological manifestations of mental disorders in contrast to his more organically and physiologically oriented contemporaries. The following paragraphs touch on only a few of his conceptions regarding the major forms of psychoses and the syndromes now termed personality disorders.

Kraepelin constantly revised his diagnostic system, elaborating it at times, simplifying it at others. In the sixth edition (1899), he established the definitive pattern of two modern major disorders: *manic-depressive psychosis* (now known as bipolar disorder) and *dementia praecox* (now known as schizophrenic disorders). These were clinically vivid syntheses of previously independent entities that Morel, Kahlbaum, and Hecker had formulated. Within the manic-depressive group, he brought together the excited conditions of mania and the hopeless melancholia of depression, indicating the periodic course through which these moods alternated in the same patient. To be consistent with his disease orientation, he proposed that an irregular metabolic function transmitted by heredity caused this disorder.

Kraepelin had considered hebephrenia, the diagnosis of adolescent psychosis, and dementia praecox to be synonymous prior to the sixth edition of his text. In his original treatise, he concluded that the diverse symptom complexes of catatonia and hebephrenia, as well as certain paranoid disturbances, displayed a common theme of early deterioration and ultimate incurability. As he conceived them, each of these illnesses was a variation of Morel's concept of dementia praecox. By subsuming the disparate symptoms of these formerly separate syndromes under the common theme of their ostensive early and inexorable mental decline, Kraepelin brought order and simplicity to what had previously been diagnostic confusion. In line with the traditions of German psychiatry, Kraepelin assumed that a biophysical defect lay at the heart of this new coordinated syndrome. In contrast to his forebears, however, he speculated that sexual and metabolic dysfunctions were the probable causal agents instead of the usual hypothesis of an anatomic lesion. In addition to the progressive and inevitable decline, the major signs that Kraepelin considered central to these illnesses included discrepancies between thought and emotion, negativism and stereotyped behaviors, wandering or unconnected ideas, hallucinations, delusions, and a general mental deterioration.

As noted, Kraepelin subsumed a wide range of previously known disorders within the category of dementia praecox. He observed the primary commonality that he felt justified a synthesis among them: Each began early in life and progressed to an incurable dementia. In his view, the cause of these disorders was biologically defective sex glands, which led to chemical imbalances in the nervous system. He believed that defects arose most often at puberty as this was a crucial period in sexual development thus accounting for the frequency with which dementia praecox occurred in adolescence.

Despite Kraepelin's rigorous application of the disease concept, he recognized, in the seventh edition of his text, that the milder disturbances of neuroses, hysteria, and fright were probably of psychogenic origin. He maintained, however, that other disturbances remained the result of constitution, infection, exhaustion, or intoxicants. Although Kraepelin's impressive synthesis of biology and clinical description gave psychiatric medicine a tremendous impetus, his view that inherent bodily defects caused most disorders encouraged a fatalistic attitude toward treatment. Because of this fatalism, others were strongly motivated to reexamine his hypotheses and ultimately, the nosological classification on which they were based. Additional criticisms of Kraepelin's system arose because his observations were limited to the overt symptoms of hospitalized patients and he lacked insight into the inner thoughts and feelings of both these patients and others with less severe symptoms.

Many of Kraepelin's predecessors believed that mania and melancholia were a single disease that manifested itself in different forms and combinations over time. Kraepelin borrowed heavily from these formulations, but separated the "personality" and "temperament" variants of the disorder from the clinical state of the disease. Nevertheless, he proposed the name *maniacal-depressive insanity* for "the whole domain of periodic and circular insanity," including such diverse disturbances as "the morbid states termed melancholia and certain slight colorings of mood, some of them periodic, some of them continuously morbid" (1896, p. 161). Like Kahlbaum, Kraepelin viewed "circular insanity" to be a unitary illness. Moreover, he conceived that every disorder that featured mood disturbances—however regular or irregular and whatever the predominant affect, be it irritability, depression, or mania—was a variant or "rudiment" of the same basic impairment. To Kraepelin, the common denominator for these disturbances was an endogenous metabolic dysfunction that was "to an astonishing degree independent of external influences" (p. 173).

Kraepelin labeled four varieties of the cyclothymic disposition: *hypomanic, depressive, irascible,* and *emotionally unstable.* He described the hypomanic type as follows:

> They acquire, as a rule, but scant education, with gaps and unevenness, as they show no perseverance in their studies, are disinclined to make an effort, and seek all sorts of ways to escape from the constraints of a systematic mental culture. The emotional tone of these patients is persistently elated, carefree, self-confident. Toward others they are overbearing, arbitrary, impatient, insolent, defiant. They mix into everything, overstep their prerogatives, make unauthorized arrangements, as they prove themselves everywhere useless. (1913, p. 221)

In describing the depressive personality Kraepelin wrote (1921):

> There are certain temperaments which may be regarded as rudiments of *manic-depressive* insanity. They may throughout the whole of life exist as peculiar forms of psychic personality, without further development; but they may also become the point of departure for a morbid process which develops under peculiar conditions and runs its course in isolated attacks. Not at all infrequently, moreover, the permanent divergencies are already in themselves so considerable that they also extend into the domain of the morbid without the appearance of more severe, delimited attacks. (p. 118)

Typically, Kraepelin considered these disorders to represent an inborn temperamental disposition characterized "by a permanent gloomy emotional stress in all experiences in life" (1921, p. 118). According to him, "the morbid picture is usually perceptible already in youth, and may persist without essential change throughout life" (p. 123).

The irascible type was ostensibly endowed simultaneously with both hypomanic and depressive inclinations. To Kraepelin: "They are easily offended, hot-headed, and on trivial occasions become enraged and give way to boundless outbursts of energy. Ordinarily the patients are, perhaps, serene, self-assertive, ill-controlled; periods, however, intervene in which they are cross and sullen" (1921, p. 222).

The emotionally unstable variant presumably also possessed both hypomanic and depressive dispositions but manifested them in an alternating or, as Kraepelin viewed it, true cyclothymic pattern:

> It is seen in those persons who constantly swing back and forth between the 2 opposite poles of emotion, now shouting with joy to heaven, now grieved to death. Today lively, sparkling, radiant, full of the joy of life, enterprise, they meet us after a while depressed, listless, dejected, only to show again several months later the former liveliness and elasticity. (1921, p. 222)

Kraepelin's autistic temperament served as the constitutional soil for the development of dementia praecox. Of particular note was Kraepelin's observation that children of this temperament frequently "exhibited a quiet, shy, retiring disposition, made no friendships, and lived only for themselves" (1921, p. 109). They were disinclined to be open and become involved with others, were seclusive, and had difficulty adapting to new situations. They showed little interest in what went on about them, often refrained from participating in games and other pleasures, seemed resistant to influence (but in a passive rather than active way), and were inclined to withdraw increasingly in a world of their own fantasies.

Among the morbid personalities, Kraepelin included a wide range of types disposed to criminal activities. He described in considerable detail the so-called shiftless, impulsive types, liars and swindlers, troublemakers, and other disreputable characters. As early as 1905, Kraepelin identified four kinds of persons who had features akin to what we speak of today as antisocial personalities. First, were the "morbid liars and swindlers," who were glib and charming but lacked an inner morality and sense of responsibility to others. They made frequent use of aliases, were inclined to be fraudulent con men, and often accumulated heavy debts that were invariably unpaid; this type proves to be descriptively similar to those we might classify today as *narcissistic* personalities. The second group included "criminals by impulse," who engaged in crimes such as arson, rape, and kleptomania, and were driven by an inability to control their urges; they rarely sought material gains for their criminal actions. The third type, he essentially referred to as "professional criminals." They were neither impulsive nor undisciplined; in fact, they often appeared well-mannered and socially appropriate, but were inwardly calculating, manipulative, and self-serving. The fourth type, the "morbid vagabonds," were strongly disposed to wander through life, never taking firm root, lacking both self-confidence and the ability to undertake adult responsibilities. Each of these latter types anticipated some of the antisocial subtypes that Millon deduced theoretically almost a century later (Millon & Davis, 1996).

Kraepelin also anticipated the contemporary notion of borderline personality in his classic text when he described the irritable or "excitable personality" temperament as a "mixture of fundamental states." The following excerpts detail this parallel:

> The patients display from youth up extraordinarily great fluctuations in emotional equilibrium and are greatly moved by all experiences, frequently in an unpleasant way. . . .
> They flare up, and on the most trivial occasions fall into outbursts of boundless fury.
> The coloring of mood is subject to frequent change . . . periods are interpolated in which they are irritable and ill-humored, also perhaps sad, spiritless, anxious; they shed tears without cause, give expression to thoughts of suicide, bring forward hypochondriacal complaints, go to bed. . . .
> They are mostly very distractible and unsteady in their endeavors.
> In consequence of their irritability and their changing moods their conduct of life is subject to the most multifarious incidents, they make sudden resolves, and carry them out on the spot, run off abruptly, go traveling, enter a cloister. (1921, pp. 130–131)

The extent to which Kraepelin's description encompasses the central diagnostic criteria of the contemporary *DSM-IV-TR* borderline personality is striking, especially with regard to impulsivity, unstable relationships, inappropriate and intense anger, affective instability, and physically self-damaging acts.

Renovating Kraepelin's Proposals

Although less successful in influencing nosological thinking in the latter half of the nineteenth and early twentieth centuries than Kraepelin, several other distinguished thinkers deserve recognition. **Phillipe Chaslin (1857–1923)** was a great French theorist whose life's work overlapped Bleuler's in Switzerland, Kraepelin's in Germany, and Freud's in Austria. A philosopher and linguist at heart, he spent the majority of his professional career at the Salpetriere Hospital in Paris where he wrote on a wide range of topics such as history, linguistics, and mathematics, as well as psychiatry. Among his central formulations was the concept of *discordance*, a notion he used to describe and explain dementia praecox. Bleuler, who originated the term schizophrenia in his 1911 treatise on the subject, stated later that he might have preferred "discordant insanity" as an alternative label had he known of it earlier.

In his major work, *Elements de Seminologie et de Clinique Mentale*, written in 1912, Chaslin conveyed ideas similar to those formulated concurrently by Freud, but with special reference to psychotic delusions. For example, he wrote:

> Delusional ideas seem to have their source in the emotions of the patient of which they are symbolic representations. . . . One could illustrate the origins of

delusions by recollecting the mechanisms of dreaming. Propensities, desires, and feelings from the waking state reappear in dreams in symbolic scenes. (1912, p. 178)

Chaslin was concerned, as were many philosophers of the day, with the failure of psychiatric language to adequately represent the disorders they diagnosed and treated. In describing the difficulties of psychopathological terminology, Chaslin exclaimed:

> I believe that the imprecision of terms is due to the imprecision of our ideas, but I also think that the inexactitude of a language may cause further inexactitude in our ideas. . . . If (the terminology) only helped to combat factual imprecisions, but the opposite is the case; it is often imagined that progress has been made simply because fancy names have been given to old things. (1912, p. 18)

Substantively, Chaslin devoted much of his theoretical writings to articulating variants of delusions and states of confusion. He spoke of the several ways in which delusions presented themselves, sometimes in isolation, sometimes combined with hallucinations, occasionally incoherent, but also at times systematic and logical, as in paranoid conditions. Regarding confusional states, Chaslin asserted that these temporary periods signified a loosening of intellectual, affective, and motivational functions. He concluded that distinctions between confusion and dementia were modest and reflected an assumption that dementia possessed a chronic and deteriorating course.

Eugen Bleuler (1857–1939) is universally recognized for his description of what is known as *schizophrenia,* the term he coined to replace the historic diagnostic label "dementia praecox," a concept Morel characterized as a syndrome in the mid-nineteenth century. The term schizophrenia is now judged by many to be unfortunate, suggesting a "splitting between segments of the mind," a concept then prevalent in French circles and a notion Janet had proposed as an alternative to Freud's conception of three levels of consciousness (see Chapter 7). As evidence now indicates, patients diagnosed with schizophrenia do not suffer any form of splitting, but instead are characterized by disordered thinking leading to delusions and hallucinations.

Bleuler was born in 1857 in a suburb of Zurich, nine years prior to Adolf Meyer, also from Zurich, to a farming family of whom few had the opportunity to rise to professional

Eugen Bleuler

careers such as medicine. Bleuler attended the University of Zurich whose professors were primarily German, as most citizens of modest Swiss backgrounds were restricted from institutions of higher education. Among his professors was Wilhelm Griesinger, the leader of the organically oriented approach of German psychiatry.

Before the age of 30, Bleuler became director of the Rheinau Mental Hospital. During his 10-year tenure, he demonstrated an unusual talent for both understanding and showing a genuine devotion to his patients. In this role, Bleuler rehabilitated the once backward institution and its neglected patients. A bachelor, he lived at the hospital, spending his days with his patients, fully participating in their treatment programs and planning their work. He was known for developing a close, personal, and emotional relationship with each patient. It was during this period that he acquired his deep sensitivity for the most intimate details of his patients' psychological life, a source from which he based his theoretical ideas about schizophrenia.

In 1898, Bleuler left to head the Burgholzli Mental Hospital, a distinguished center for the clinical study of mental illness. Bleuler daily spent hours talking with his patients, often in their own unusual dialects, searching to understand the psychological meaning of their seemingly senseless verbalizations and delusions. Most importantly, he urged his students and residents to be open-minded and to establish an emotional rapport with their patients, to develop an attitude that would enable them to track the meaning of the words their patients used, as well as the word associations that might give meaning to their utterings. In this regard, he saw the utility of Freud's new free-association methods; and on these grounds also, he instilled an interest in his young associate, *Carl G. Jung*, in the work of Freud's early psychoanalytic concepts.

Bleuler's studies of association led to his theory of schizophrenia: It reflected patients' ostensible inability to connect their thoughts with their feelings, the "loosening" or disintegration in their capacity to associate ideas and emotions, and hence, the presumed split between these two core psychic processes. Following on ideas that were then emerging in both Freud and Janet's writings, Bleuler asserted that his schizophrenic patients would display secondary symptoms that derived from the primary or fundamental thought/feeling disconnection. These symptoms evidenced themselves in an autistic separation from reality, in repetitive psychic ambivalences, and in verbal behaviors akin to dreaming. Although committed to Kraepelin's view that dementia praecox was primarily an organic disease, Bleuler emphasized the presence of psychological ambivalence and disharmony in this impairment to signify the intellectual and emotional split he believed he observed in these patients.

Bleuler's conception of schizophrenia also encompassed a wider range of syndromes than Kraepelin's notion of dementia praecox. He included several acute disturbances that Kraepelin previously judged to be independent disease entities. Moreover, Bleuler believed that those displaying acute schizophrenic symptoms could recover readily with proper intensive care before devolving into a more chronic state. After observing hundreds of dementia praecox patients in the early 1900s, Bleuler concluded that it was misleading to compare the deterioration they evidenced with that found among patients suffering from metabolic deficiencies or brain degeneration. Moreover, he judged his patients' reactions and thoughts to be qualitatively complex and often highly creative, contrasting markedly with the simple or meandering thinking that Kraepelin observed. Furthermore, not only did many of his patients display their illness for the first time in adulthood, rather than in adolescence, but a significant proportion evidenced *no* progressive deterioration, which Kraepelin considered the sine qua non of the syndrome. Thus, to Bleuler, the label dementia praecox was misleading in that it characterized an age of onset and a course of development not supported by the evidence.

Schizophrenia's primary symptoms, in Bleuler's view, were disturbances in the associative link among thoughts, a breach between affect and intellect, ambivalence toward the same objects, and an autistic detachment from reality. The several varieties of patients that displayed these fragmented thoughts, feelings, and actions led Bleuler to call them "the group of schizophrenias." Although he considered schizophrenia to be a diverse set of disorders, he retained the Kraepelinian view that the impairment stemmed from a unitary disease process that was attributable to a basic physiological pathology. To him, schizophrenics shared a neurological ailment that produced their common primary symptoms. Schizophrenics also exhibited secondary symptoms, the content of which Bleuler ascribed to the patients' distinctive life experiences and to their efforts to adapt to their basic disease. Psychogenic factors shaped the unique character of each schizophrenic's impairment, but Bleuler was convinced that experience did not itself cause the ailment.

In what Bleuler termed *schizoidie*, he recognized that some dispositions, left untreated, might evolve into a clinical schizophrenic state. In Bleuler's initial formulation of the schizophrenic concept, he described, in 1911, one of the first portrayals that approximates what we now call the *avoidant* personality. Discussing several of the contrasting routes that often lead to the psychotic syndrome, Bleuler recorded the early phase of certain patients as follows:

> There are also cases where the shutting off from the outside world is caused by contrary reasons. Particularly in the beginning of their illness, these patients quite consciously shun any contact with reality because their affects are so powerful that they must avoid everything which might arouse their emotions. The apathy toward the outer world is then a secondary one springing from a hypertrophied sensitivity. (1911/1950, p. 65)

Bleuler spoke of other personalities as being "irritable of mood" (*reizbare Verstimmung*), as did Aschaffenburg later (1922) in describing them as "dissatisfied personalities" who go through life as if they were perpetually wounded. Applying the label *amphithymia*, Hellpach (1920) also depicted a similar pattern of "fussy people," who tend to have a sour disposition, constantly fret over whatever they do, and make invidious and painful comparisons between themselves and more cheerful persons, whose simpler and brighter outlook they both envy and decry.

Adolf Meyer (1866–1950), like Bleuler, was born in Switzerland and completed his medical training in 1892 at the age of 26 following several predoctoral years in France, England, and Germany. A student of Forel at the University of Zurich, he decided to immigrate to the United States shortly after receiving his

Adolf Meyer

medical degree, having heard that Chicago was a city with numerous opportunities for young physicians. Meyer eventually served as a staff pathologist for the mentally ill at the Illinois Eastern Hospital for the Insane, remaining there from 1893 to 1895. For the next seven years, he was director of clinical research laboratories at the Worcester Insane Hospital and was associated with Clark University, both in Massachusetts. He was increasingly recognized as a major contributor to neuropathology, as well as a lecturer known for his detailed patient biographies, interviews, and note taking. Meyer was appointed director of the New York Pathological Institute in 1902, as well as professor of psychiatry at Cornell University Medical School, where he continued autopsied brain research, teaching, and administrative activities until 1910. Along with Freud and Jung, he was awarded an honorary doctoral degree at Clark University in 1909. Owing to his distinguished achievements, Meyer later became chair of a new Department of Psychiatry and director of the Henry Phipps Psychiatric Clinic at the Johns Hopkins University in Baltimore, where the school philosophy strove to blend scientific research and clinical practice. He remained for over 30 years, building a German-style psychiatric clinic akin to Kraepelin's in Munich, becoming the most influential psychiatrist in the United States and a mentor to an entire generation of both academic and clinical psychiatrists.

Meyer introduced the concept of a "constitutionally inferior" type into American literature at the turn of the century, shortly after his arrival from Germany. Although he followed Koch's ideas in the main, Meyer sought to separate psychopathic cases from psychoneurotic disorders, both of which were grouped together in Koch's "psychopathic inferiorities" classification. Meyer was convinced that the etiology of the neuroses was primarily psychogenic, that is, colored less by inherent physical defects or by constitutional inferiorities.

Meyer later became disillusioned with both Kraepelin's and Koch's approach, particularly their fatalistic view of illness and their strictly deterministic prognosis and outcome for those of a problematic temperament. Meyer turned to a view increasingly shared by psychoanalysts—discarding the disease model and viewing psychiatric disorders, not as fundamentally organic conditions, but as a consequence of environmental factors and life events. Although initially sympathetic to Freud's theories, Meyer soon became critical of the mystic and esoteric nature of psychoanalysis. Despite his break from Freud's metapsychology, Meyer shared a common view that life experiences played a central role in the emergence of all psychiatric disorders.

As early as 1910, Meyer espoused the view that therapists could derive a true understanding of patients only by studying individuals' total reaction to their organic, psychological, and social experience. Although Meyer was the most prominent psychiatrist to introduce the Kraepelinian system in this country, he believed that these disorders were not disease entities, but "psychobiological reactions" to environmental stress. Through his work, Meyer bridged the physiological orientation of the late nineteenth century and the psychodynamic orientation of the twentieth.

In 1906, Meyer asserted that dementia praecox was not an organic disease but a maladaptive way of reacting to stress, fully understandable in terms of the patient's constitutional potentials and life experiences. To him, these maladaptive reactions led to what he called "progressive habit deteriorations" that reflected "inefficient and faulty attempts to avoid difficulties" (1912, p. 98). He regarded symptoms of mental illness as the end product of abortive and self-defeating efforts to establish psychic equilibrium. His well-reasoned psychobiological approach to schizophrenia, which he called *parergasia* to signify its distorted or twisted character, was the most systematic recognition of his interactive and progressive view of pathogenesis. Of special note also was Meyer's view that parergasia could be present in dilute and nonpsychotic form, without delusions, hallucinations, or deterioration. He considered the classic psychotic symptoms to be advanced signs of a potentially, but not inevitably, evolving habit system that might stabilize at a prepsychotic level. In its nonclinical state, parergasia could be detected by attenuated and soft signs that merely suggested the manifest psychotic disorder. Meyer's proposal of a self-defeating and maladaptive reaction system (personality) that parallels schizophrenia in inchoate form was a highly innovative, but unheeded, notion.

Together, Meyer's notion of reaction types and Bleuler's focus on cognitive and emotional experience reshaped Kraepelin's original system into a more contemporary psychiatric nosology. Their classifications retained Kraepelin's clinical categories as the basic framework, and Meyer's and Bleuler's psychological notions provided guidelines to the patient's inner processes and social reactions.

Leo Kanner (1894–1981), a student of Meyer's at Hopkins, and **Hans Asperger (1906–1980)** of Germany, two child psychiatrists, made similarly observant proposals in the mid-1940s. In the United States, Kanner used the term *infantile autism* to characterize a group of socially and severely disengaged children who displayed features similar to those Asperger described concurrently in

Europe. Whereas Kanner's ideas quickly drew the attention of numerous psychologists and psychiatrists, Asperger's work remained essentially unknown until it was translated into English in 1991. According to both theorists, the key feature was the mental aloneness of these youngsters, their tendency to disregard or ignore most stimuli coming from the outside world, especially people. Other characteristics were narrow preoccupation and an intense focus on unusual objects or activities in which they appeared totally fascinated. Also noted was the poverty of facial expression and gestures, as well as a tendency to follow impulses, regardless of what transpired in the surrounding environment. If language developed, it tended to be odd in character, typified by clichés, formulaic speech, or empty chatter. Kanner judged their prognosis to be an "unmitigated disaster."

Kanner had been misled in his etiologic hypotheses because his first cases were children brought to him by highly anxious and compulsive mothers with advanced degrees who happened to work with Kanner at Johns Hopkins' medical institutions. He erroneously concluded that these children were a product of remote "refrigerator mothers." Owing to the unfortunate sample he initially encountered, it took several decades before infantile autism was recognized to be a neurological dysfunction unconnected to maternal disquiet or empathic deficits.

Formulating Official Systems

In recent years, sharp criticisms have been raised against the dominance of Kraepelinian systems. Some eminent psychiatrists have asserted that, except in organic disorders, a classificatory diagnosis is less important than a psychodynamic study of personality. Instead of fitting the symptoms into a classificatory scheme, clinicians should endeavor to understand the sick person in terms of the individual's life experience. Others have noted that too much research time is wasted and too many errors are perpetuated because investigators cling to an outdated classification. Proponents, on the other hand, have explained the viability of the Kraepelin nomenclature by the hypothesis that there is considerable truth in the system and practical implications are associated with its labels; they are still sufficiently great when compared with the predictive power of competing concepts.

A major problem facing a field as inchoate and amorphous as mental science is its susceptibility to subjective values, cultural biases, and chance events. Were the field a hard science, anchored solidly in readily verified empirical fact, progress would presumably derive from advances of a tangible and objective nature. Unfortunately, that is not the case. Nevertheless, the field has endeavored to standardize, as much as possible, the language conventions and classification rules for diagnosing mental disease.

Given this semiarbitrary task, one can readily understand why mental illness and its processes may be classified in terms of several data levels (e.g., behavioral, psychoanalytic, or phenomenological) or attributes (e.g., interpersonal conduct, mood or affect, or self-image). Beyond this, each data level lends itself to specific concepts and categories, the usefulness of which must be gauged by their ability to solve the particular problems for which they were created. The inherent diversity and the imprecision of mental illness are major reasons to hesitate narrowing the clinical data that constitute a classification to one level or approach. Each source and orientation can make a legitimate and potentially fruitful contribution. No classification in mental illness today is an inevitable representation of the real world. Current classifications—the *DSM-IV-TR* (American Psychiatric Association [APA], 2000) and the *International Classification of Disease* (ICD-10; World Health Organization, 1990)—are, at best, interim tools for advancing knowledge and facilitating clinical goals (Sartorius, 1990). They orient scientific work and function as a scheme to organize clinical experiences.

In great part, clinically based taxa gain their import and prominence by virtue of consensus and authority. Official bodies crystallize and subsequently confirm cumulative experience and tradition. Specified criteria are denoted and articulated, and they acquire definitional, if not stipulative powers, at least among those who accept the attributes selected as infallible taxonic indicators.

Not until the 1920s was an effort made to develop a relatively uniform nomenclature and classification system for medical disease in the United States. Prior to the first of a series of National Conferences on Nomenclature of Diseases, held in 1928 at the New York Academy of Medicine, each of the major teaching hospitals and university medical centers in the nation developed and promulgated their own terminology and nosology. Although these reflected the idiosyncratic needs of their place of origin, many were transplanted to other settings because former staff members and trainees were comfortable with the accustomed nomenclature and recommended its use in their new clinical milieu. Rarely could such transplants be rooted in their entirety, and most were modified to meet the particular needs of their newly adopted setting. These replantings proliferated even more diversity on an already variegated babble of medical terms and categories. To say the least, the confusion seriously compromised effective communication among clinical centers, no less useful records for epidemiological statistics and research.

To disentangle this web of obscure language and esoteric custom, the New York Academy of Medicine launched a series of conferences and trial studies designed to develop uniform nomenclatures and systematic taxonomies for each of the major medical specialties. This work resulted in the 1932 publication of the first official edition of the *Standard Classified Nomenclature of Disease*, subsequently revised several times until superseded by the *International Classification of Disease*, originally conceived in 1900 and as of 1990 in its tenth revision (ICD-10).

In appraising a new taxonomy and nomenclature, the only critical question is not whether they mirror the state of the science perfectly, or whether they provide answers to all possible questions professionals may ask, but whether they represent advances over preceding nosological systems and whether they will be employed with greater clinical accuracy and facility by future practitioners and researchers.

That the official American system published in 1980, the *Diagnostic and Statistical Manual of Mental Disorders* (3rd ed.; *DSM-III*), was well received is evident in both formal questionnaire replies and number of copies sold. More orders were received in the first six months following its publication than all previous editions combined, including their 30-plus reprintings.

Comprehensive and Systematic Description.   It is almost inevitable that more detail will be incorporated in a later form of a nosology than in earlier versions. Hence, though far from a comprehensive textbook, failing to encompass matters of theory, etiology, and treatment, the *DSM-III* was nevertheless substantially more extensive and thorough than both of its predecessors. Being exhaustive and inclusionary, however, required that information on each syndrome be ordered in a reasonably standardized and systematic format. The organizational sequence of the *DSM-III* included: essential (necessary) features; associated (frequent) features; and, where reasonably reliable data are available, age of onset, course, impairment, complications, predisposing factors, sex ratio, familial pattern, and differential diagnosis. Both the scope and organizational structure signified an important advance, for the schema not only provided a logical guide for clinicians seeking information but also established a coherent framework for systematically introducing the data of future studies.

Diagnostic Criteria.   It is reasonable to assume that greater reliability and research comparability will flow from the use of standardized diagnostic criteria (i.e., explicit and enumerated features required for each syndrome); nevertheless, these criteria offered no more than a promise and an aspiration when the manual was published. Some encouraging interjudge-reliability data were obtained in the *DSM* field trials, especially when compared with prior studies using earlier classifications. Nevertheless, most diagnostic criteria lacked empirical support. Some were inadequately explicit or, conversely, were overly concrete in their observable referents. Many were redundant both within and with other diagnostic categories. Others were insufficiently comprehensive in syndromic scope or displayed a lack of parallelism and symmetry among corresponding categories.

At best, then, the diagnostic criteria of the *DSM* represented a significant conceptual step toward a future goal when clinical characteristics of appropriate specificity and breadth would provide both reliable and valid indices for identifying the major syndromic prototypes. Given that these syndromes represented only theoretical constructs, it was sufficient for clinical and research purposes to employ this standardized, reliable, and internally coherent mosaic of criterion descriptors. To the extent that the *DSM* provided a foundation of clinical syndromes, it is fairly judged to have made an advance worthy of commendation.

Multiaxial Format.   The formal adoption of the multiaxial schema in the *DSM* signifies a reformulation of the task of psychodiagnosis that approached what Kuhn (1962) described as a paradigm shift. It represented a distinct turn from the traditional medical disease model where the clinician's job is to disentangle and clear away distracting symptoms and signs to pinpoint the underlying or true pathophysiological state. By contrast, the multiaxial assessment model not only recognized that distracting symptoms and signs were aspects worthy of attention but recorded each of them on its own representative axis as part of an interactive complex of elements that, only in their entirety, defined the pathological state.

Axis I constituted the more-or-less traditional mental disorders, labeled "clinical syndromes" in the *DSM-III*, which are often transient or florid in character. Axis II was composed of two segments, one for children and the other for adults. The child section encompassed relatively specific, albeit questionable, developmental disorders, such as maturational delays in language or speech articulation. Conceptually more significant was the innovative segregation of the personality disorders in the adult section into a separate axis, thus isolating them from the clinical syndromes that compose the other axis. This bifurcation ensured that the more enduring and often more prosaic styles of personality functioning would not be overlooked when giving attention to the frequently more urgent and behaviorally dramatic clinical syndromes. It also recognized that the lifelong coping styles and emotional vulnerabilities that comprise personality could provide a context within which the more salient and usually transient clinical states were likely to arise and be understood. Axis III described physical disorders of potential importance or relevance to understanding or managing the patient. Axis IV consisted of judgments concerning the presence and severity of *psychosocial stressors*. The official recognition that psychosocial environments play a role in the development and exacerbation of mental disorders, though patently obvious, is nevertheless an achievement of great import. Not only did it acknowledge that disturbances arising in response to stressors have better prognoses than those that do not; more impressively, it signified in an officially recorded fashion the realization that psychosocial factors establish a context within which disorders not only unfold but are sustained and exacerbated. The presence in the *DSM-III* of Axis V (the "highest level of adaptive functioning" in the past year) revealed another signal achievement: the resolve not to diagnose and potentially stigmatize individuals who are seen clinically at the time of their greatest distress as if their present behaviors were fixed and constant. Not only did the recognition of the individual's recent level of adaptive functioning serve as a useful prognostic index, but it furnished a longitudinal context within which to appraise a person's current functioning.

Further Refinements to the DSM.   The *DSM-III* Task Force served an important function in that it had the courage to break a mold that had been imposed on past classifications of psychiatric nosology. As a transition to *DSM-IV*, an interim *DSM-III-R* (revised) Work Group in 1983 began to refine and elaborate the *DSM-III*. Similarly, the ICD-9 and ICD-10 Committees judged it a higher responsibility to develop a more empirically based and clinically functional nosology than to adhere to tradition-bound concepts.

With the *DSM-III*'s radical departures safely ensconced on the shelves of mental health professionals around the globe, the *DSM-IV* Task Force in 1988 worked to retain those elements of value in *DSM-III* and *DSM-III-R*, while building bridges to future ICDs. By that time, the implementation of a multiaxial schema, the introduction of explicit diagnostic criteria, and the enhanced role assigned the omnipresent personality disorders appeared to have gained considerable acceptance in the larger international community.

During the development of the *DSM-IV*, there were proposals to introduce a so-called dimensional system to supplant or supplement the categorical model used in the existing *DSM*. The group evaluated several alternative schemas, but none achieved sufficient consensus. Nonetheless, specific modifications regarding the *DSM* criteria were introduced on the basis of a review of numerous published and unpublished statistical analyses.

The *DSM-IV* (APA, 1994) quickly became the standard nosology, and soon assumed a life of its own, used and interpreted in diverse ways by clinicians and researchers of all theoretical schools to suit their special purposes and orientations. The rationale that led to the original concepts and terminology formulated by its Task Force now plays only a small part, as *DSM* users increasingly transform the instrument to fit their own purposes. Few are satisfied with every aspect of the manual, and it is sufficiently broad in scope to permit almost any clinician, theoretician, or researcher to wish to modify one or another segment because of his or her dissatisfactions.

Refinements were made in 2000 to the *DSM-IV*, published as *DSM-IV-TR*, to correct several errors and to reflect the data of recent research investigations. Likewise, committees were established by the APA in 2000 to initiate preliminary studies regarding changes proposed for *DSM-V*, publication of which is planned for 2010. The coordination of future DSMs and ICDs continues as a major goal.

The following statement of Zigler and Phillips (1961), made in summarizing their review of the status of the field over 40 years ago, is still applicable today: "At this stage of our investigation, the system employed should be open and expanding. . . . Systems of classification must be treated as tools for further discovery, not bases for polemic disputation."

Comments and Reflections

What distinguishes a theoretically grounded taxonomy from one that provides a mere explanatory summary of known observations and inferences? The answer lies in its power to generate observations and relationships other than those used to construct it. As noted in Chapter 2, this generative power is what Hempel (1965) termed the systematic import of a scientific classification. In contrasting what are familiarly known as natural (theoretically guided, deductively based) and artificial (conceptually barren, similarity-based) classifications, Hempel wrote:

> Distinctions between "natural" and "artificial" classifications may well be explicated as referring to the difference between classifications that are scientifically fruitful and those that are not; in a classification of the former kind, those characteristics of the elements that serve as criteria of membership in a given class are associated, universally or with high probability, with more or less extensive clusters of other characteristics. (p. 116)
>
> Classification of this sort should be viewed as somehow having objective existence in nature, as "carving nature at the joints" in contradistinction of "artificial" classifications, in which the defining characteristics have few explanatory or predictive connections with other traits. In the course of scientific development, classifications defined by reference to manifest, observable characteristics will tend to give way to systems based on theoretical concepts. (p. 148)

The *DSMs* were developed intentionally and explicitly to be atheoretical. This stance was taken not from an antipathy to theory per se but to maximize acceptance of the document by clinicians of diverse viewpoints. Extolling the tenets in the *DSM* of one or another theoretical school would, it was believed, alienate those holding dissimilar perspectives and thereby disincline them from adopting and using the manual.

In recent years, sharp criticisms have been raised against the current system. Today fewer voices defend the standard nosology than oppose it. Alfred P. Noyes, an eminent psychiatric teacher and hospital administrator wrote in 1953:

> Except in organic disorders a classificatory diagnosis is less important than a psychodynamic study of personality . . . we should endeavor not so much to fit the symptoms into a classificatory scheme as to understand the sick person in terms of his life experience. (p. 17)

Roe, in 1949, noted that too much research time was wasted and too many errors were perpetuated because investigators were clinging to a classification that had long since been outlived. In contrast, Karl Menninger, the well-known American psychiatrist, emphasized that all disorders are alike. They differ only quantitatively as a function of the stage of their progress. Thomas Szasz took a different but equally critical view of the current system in 1957:

> Categories such as schizophrenic may be doubly harmful: first, such categories are unsatisfactory as readily valid concepts for purposes of classification, and

secondly, they give rise to the misleading impression that there "exists" a more or less homogeneous group of phenomena which are designated by the word in question. (p. 116)

Szasz went on to say:

I have tried to show that the notion of mental illness has outlived whatever usefulness it might have had and that it now functions merely as a convenient myth. As such, it is a true heir to religious myths in general, and to the belief in witchcraft in particular; the role of all these belief-systems was to act as *social tranquilizers*, thus encouraging the hope that mastery of certain specific problems may be achieved by means of substitutive (symbolic-magical) operations. The notion of mental illness thus serves mainly to obscure the everyday fact that life for most people is a continuous struggle, not for biological survival, but for a "place in the sun," "peace of mind," or some other human value. (1957, p. 118)

Views such as Menninger's and Szasz's raised serious questions about the utility of the traditional mental disorder nosology. Problematic as the topic may be, these responses reflected a revitalized interest and ferment on an important and age-old issue that later chapters address.

In the interim, consider a sharply different view expressed by the distinguished psychologist, Paul Meehl in 1959:

I would explain the viability of the Kraepelin nomenclature by the hypothesis that there is a considerable amount of truth contained in the system; and that, therefore, the practical implications associated with these labels are still sufficiently great, especially when compared with the predictive power of competing concepts. (p. 107)

Grievances itemizing the inadequacies of both current and historical systems of classification have been voiced for years as well as suggestions that the endeavors to refine these efforts are fussy and misdirected, if not futile and senseless pretensions that should be abandoned. Such systems are both unavoidable, owing to humankind's linguistic and attribution habits, and inevitable, owing to humankind's need to differentiate and record—at the very least—the most obvious dissimilarities among the psychologically impaired. Given that one or another set of classes is inevitable, or as Kaplan (1964, p. 279) once phrased it, "it is impossible to wear clothing of no style at all," it seems fitting that one should know the explicit basis on which such distinctions are to be made, rather than have them occur helter-skelter in nonpublic and nonverifiable ways. Furthermore, if mental illness is to evolve into a true science, then its diverse phenomena must be subject to formal identification, differentiation, and quantification procedures. Acts such as diagnosis and assessment presuppose the existence of discernible phenomena that can be recognized and measured. Logic necessitates, therefore, that psychopathological states and processes be distinguished from one another, and classified or grouped in some manner before being subjected to identification and quantification.

Whatever data provide the substantive body of a classification, syndromal, personological or otherwise, decisions must be made concerning the framework into which the nosology will be cast, the rules that will govern the classes into which the clinical attributes and defining features will be placed, and the compositional properties that will characterize these attributes and features (Millon, 1991). These issues deal with the overall architecture of the nosology: whether it is organized horizontally, vertically, or circularly; whether all or only a limited and fixed subset of features should be required for class membership; whether its constituents should be conceived as categories or dimensions; and whether they should be based on manifest observables or latent features, as well as a host of other differentiating characteristics. A few of the more significant of these elements and the choices to be made among them cannot be adequately discussed in this chapter; it is a complicated task because nothing is logically self-evident, nor is there a traditional format or contemporary consensus to guide selections among these alternatives.

Because reliable and useful classifications were developed long before the advent of modern scientific thought and methods acquired by intelligent observation and common sense alone, what special values are derived by applying the complicated and rigorous procedures required in developing explicit criteria, categorical homogeneity, and diagnostic efficiency? Are rigor, clarity, precision, and experimentation more than compulsive and picayunish concerns for details, more than the pursuit for the honorific title of science? Are the labors of differentiating clinical attributes or exploring categorical cutting scores in a systematic fashion worth the time and effort involved?

There is little question in this age of science that the answer would be yes. But why? What are the distinguishing virtues of precision in one's terminology, the specification of observable conceptual referents, and the analysis of covariant attribute clusters? What sets these procedures apart from everyday methods of categorizing knowledge? Is conceptual definition and classification possible in the domain of mental disorders? Can these most fundamental of scientific activities be achieved in a subject that is inherently inexact and produces only modest levels of intrinsic order, that is, a subject in which even the very slightest variations in context or antecedent conditions—often of a minor or random character—can produce highly divergent consequences? Because this looseness within the network of variables in psychic pathology is unavoidable, are there any grounds for believing that such endeavors could prove more than illusory? Persuasive answers to these questions that are of a more philosophical nature must be bypassed for the present.

There has been a rapid proliferation of new and powerful mathematical techniques for both analyzing and synthesizing vast bodies of clinical data. This expansion has been accelerated by the ready availability of inexpensive computer hardware and software programs. Such mushrooming has progressed more rapidly than its fruits can be digested. Consequently, Kendall (1975) commented early in this technological development: "Most clinicians . . . have tended to oscillate uneasily between two equally unsatisfactory postures of ignoring investigations based on these techniques, or accepting their confident conclusions at face value" (p. 106).

There are infinite ways to observe, describe, and organize the natural world. As a result, the terms and concepts one creates to represent these activities are often confusing and obscure. Different words are used to describe the same behavior, and the same word is used for different behaviors. Some terms are narrow in focus, others are broad, and some are difficult to define. Because of the diversity of events to which one can attend or the lack of precision in the language we use, different processes are confused and similar events get scattered hodgepodge across a scientific landscape. Consequently, communication gets bogged down in terminological obscurities and semantic controversies.

One of the purposes of formalizing the phenomena that constitute a scientific subject is to avoid this morass of confusion. Not all phenomena related to the subject need be attended to at once. Certain elements may be selected from the vast range of possibilities because they seem relevant to the solution of a specific question. To create reliability among those interested in a subject, its elements are defined as precisely as possible and classified according to their core similarities and differences.

Classifications based on clinical description alone often will group patients who, on more careful evaluation, react to life situations, including their response to treatment, in substantially different manners. Hence, given their centrality to the clinical enterprise, classification categories should embody whatever data are accessible concerning the therapeutic efforts of various treatment modalities. The *DSM* offers little concrete evidence in this regard, owing to the scanty evidence at hand for such purposes; however, its empirically oriented framework and criteria might facilitate future, systematic research. It is hoped that studies that deal with both the prediction of therapeutic response and the matching of treatment to diagnosis will become increasingly available for consideration in classifying mental illness syndromes.

Reflecting on his labors while serving as chairman of the Task Force for the *DSM-II*, Gruenberg (1969) noted that the instability of mental health diagnostic schemas over the centuries led him to wonder whether the excitement concerning the appropriateness of one or another classification might not actually reflect a deep need on the part of contributors to obscure their lack of knowledge. Engaging in fruitless but easily belabored debates over new terms and clever categories may be a simple displacement of effort in which one pretends that correct labels and taxonomies are themselves the knowledge gaps. Having participated over two intense five-year periods as a member of the *DSM-III* and *DSM-IV* committees, the author is considerably more charitable about the purposes and success with which these Task Forces met their responsibilities. He has no illusion, however, that the task was completed:

> Classifying mental illness must be an outgrowth of both psychology and medicine. Efforts to construct a taxonomy must contend with the goals, concepts, and complications inherent in both disciplines (e.g., context moderators, definitional ambiguities, overlapping symptomatologies, criterion unreliabilities, multidimensional attributes, population heterogeneities, instrument deficits, and ethical constraints). (Millon, 1991, p. 245)

Thus, we remain unsure today whether to conceive depression as a taxon (category) or an attribute (symptom), whether to view it as a dimension (with quantitive degrees of severity), or as a set of discrete types, or whether to conceive it as a neuroendocrinological disease or as an existential problem of life. Although debates on these issues often degenerate into semantic arguments and theoretical hairsplitting, it is naive to assume that only metaphysical verbiage and philosophical word quibbling are involved. Nevertheless, the language we use and the assumptions it reflects are very much a part of our scientific disagreements.

In addition to reviewing diagnostic history, this chapter illustrates that philosophical issues and scientific modes of analysis must be considered in formulating a mental illness classification (see Millon, 1991). The many considerations recommended will not in themselves achieve clear resolutions to all nosological quandaries. More likely their role will be to unsettle prevailing habits and thereby force progress, if only by challenging cherished beliefs and assumptions.

In my occasional critical comments, I have not meant to imply that the philosophies and techniques of classification today are irrelevant or that theoretical or diagnostic underpinnings of contemporary practice are valueless. I urge readers, as well as taxonomic conceptualizers, to reflect on established assumptions and formulations. Protected from convention, vogue, presumption, and cabalism, taxonomic approaches to mental illness should not be dogmatic, trivial, or formalistic. Workers in the field must continue to challenge prevailing frameworks and encourage imaginative alternatives.

CHAPTER

6

Exploring and Altering
the Convoluted Brain

Many neuroscientists believe that all matters of a psychological nature (depression, anxiety) are epiphenomena, that is, superficial outcroppings of problematic neurological or chemical dysfunctions. However, until clinicians can identify a "magic pill" to dissolve the discomforts of mental illness, patients will continue to be treated with biological treatments whose mode of action scientists only partially understand and whose effectiveness is limited. This state of unclarity and modest efficacy, unfortunately, is paralleled among the equally perplexing and mediocre achievements of the psychological therapies.

The Neuroscientific Story: II

Neuroscience has both a clinical and research tradition. Although these two traditions have begun to coalesce in recent years, their histories are somewhat different. Shorter (1997) outlined early ideas by clinicians such as Heinrich Laehr, a young German physician who followed the mid-nineteenth-century work of Griesinger and asserted that insanity is a disease against which only medical treatment can prevail. Laehr's clinical observations led him to conclude that extremely small chemical changes in the brain could generate a mental disorder. Another nineteenth-century psychiatrist, Thomas Clouston of Scotland, asserted that in the future a more comprehensive physiological conception concerning the brain and its development would provide a basis for understanding mental pathology. In the twentieth century, Emil Kraepelin led a group of neuropathologists at the Universities of Heidelberg and Munich who used microscopic analyses to document the brain's functions among the mentally ill. More recently, Stanley Cobb, the 1930s' Harvard neurologist who founded the department of psychiatry at Massachusetts General Hospital, sought

200

to build a program in which "psychobiology" would be grounded in the neurosciences. He hoped to construct thereby an undergirding foundation of biological data to make the observations and interpretations of clinical phenomena more understandable.

The other line of neuroscientific research was more basic and developed earlier and concurrently. The American science writer Morton Hunt (1993) summarized these ideas in the following:

> . . . With the emergence of physics and chemistry in the seventeenth century a few daring protopsychologists began suggesting mechanical explanations of mental processes. Lacking actual observational data, they speculated about "animal spirits" coursing through hollow nerves (Descartes), atoms streaming through the nerves (Hobbes), nerves aquiver with "vibratiuncles" (Hartley), and Julien de La Metrie, a French philosopher, even wrote a book in 1748 entitled *L'Homme Machine* (Man a Machine). (p. 107)

Many psychiatrists and psychologists today assert that a biological defect, or a subtle combination of defects, ultimately will explain all mental disorders. They create an analogy with biological medicine, in which bacteria, viruses, lesions, and other traumas foreign to normal functioning have been shown to underlie overt symptoms of disturbance. This notion has a long, if stormy, history. Speculative theories have been proposed, tested, and usually found wanting when judged by the rigor of time. Significant discoveries have been hailed with much acclaim only to sink into obscurity when reexamined by investigators other than those originally involved. Nevertheless, sufficient valid findings support a continued vigorous search.

Theorists and researchers of this persuasion believe that biophysical factors such as anatomy and biochemistry are the primary determinants of psychic functioning. Ample evidence from medical science justifies this assumption. This chapter examines the orientation and findings of several historical thinkers and researchers who share this belief.

What is the basis of mental functioning according to neuroscientific thinkers? Though by no means mutually exclusive, several camps exist.

One group contends that most forms of psychic pathology can be traced to humankind's natural biological variability; accordingly, they attempt to relate these variations to measures of mental functioning and mental illness. Scientists who follow this line of thinking may be considered to be quantitatively oriented since (1) they assume that people differ along the statistical normal curve, and (2) they seek to discover correlations between biophysical variability and psychological functioning. Some time ago, Roger Williams, a distinguished biochemist, argued the case for investigating these natural biological variations as follows (1960, pp. 9–10):

> Consider the fact (I do consider it a fact and not a theory) that every individual person is endowed with a distinctive gastrointestinal tract, a distinctive

nervous system, and a morphologically distinctive brain; furthermore that the differences involved in this distinctiveness are never trifling and often are enormous. Can it be that this fact is inconsequential in relation to the problem of personality differences?

I am willing to take the position that this fact is of the *utmost* importance. The material in the area of anatomy alone is sufficient to convince anyone who comes upon the problem with an open mind that here is an obvious frontier which should yield many insights. Those who have accepted the Freudian idea that personality disorders arise from infantile conditioning will surely be led to see that, *in addition,* the distinctive bodily equipment of each individual infant is potentially important.

At the risk of being naive, it appears that the whole story we have been unfolding hangs together. Individual infants are endowed with far-reaching anatomical distinctiveness. The same distinctiveness carries over into the sensory and biochemical realms, and into their individual psychologies. It is not surprising therefore that each individual upon reaching adulthood exhibits a distinctive pattern of likes and dislikes not only with respect to trivialities but also with respect to what may be regarded the most important things in life.

Another group of neuroscientific thinkers believe that psychic pathology stems from foreign or aberrant factors that intrude and disrupt normal functioning. Their focus of interest and observation centers on defects, dysfunctions, and diseases that may arise as a result of hereditary errors, toxins, traumas, infections, malignant growths, or malnutrition. In contrast to the first group of scientists, who deal with normal biological variations, these men concern themselves with biological irregularities.

A second question pertaining to the orientation of neuroscientific theorists is: What specific data do they employ to develop their concepts? Three classes exist: (1) heredity, (2) constitution, and (3) neurophysiology. This oversimplified tripartite division of the biophysical realm should not suggest that a theorist interested in one class of data fails to see relationships with the others. Classifying theorists in this way merely recognizes their particular sphere of interest or focus.

The disease model, as adopted from medicine and used by many neuroscientists as an analogy for mental illness, possesses two main features. According to this model, symptoms represent surface reflections of either (1) an underlying biological defect or (2) the compensatory or adaptive reaction to that defect.

The first feature of the model is illustrated in physical medicine by infections, genetic errors, obstructions, inflammations or other insults to normal functioning that may present as fevers, fatigue, headaches, and so on. Researchers made significant progress in physical medicine when their focus shifted from these surface symptoms to the underlying pathology. Those who accept this model assume that an underlying biophysical defect ultimately will be found for the superficial symptoms of mental disorders, that is, for the maladaptive behavior and poor interpersonal relations of mental patients.

The second feature of the medical disease model, that symptoms represent compensatory adaptations to the basic impairment, derives from the work of the great French biologist **Claude Bernard (1838–1878)** in the nineteenth century. He observed that adaptive reactions often are more destructive to the organism than the basic defect itself; adaptive efforts, intended as temporary and reparative, often became continuous and destructive. For example, micro-organisms infecting the lung elicit physiological reactions that counter the invasion. The magnitude of the reaction often is excessive and protracted, leading to lung congestion, pneumonia, and death.

Neuroscientists adopting the disease model are inclined to use only the first feature of the model. To them the only difference between psychological and biological disorders is that the former, affecting the central nervous system, manifests itself in mental symptoms, whereas the latter, affecting other organ systems, manifests itself in physical symptoms. The parallel they draw between biological and psychological disorders has led to serious objections, notably that adherents of the disease model (1) attribute mental illness to biological defects whose existence is questionable, (2) exclude the role of psychological and inter-personal factors in mental illness, and (3) overlook the second feature of the disease model—the individual's compensatory reaction to stress or impair-ment. The following paragraphs briefly elaborate these criticisms.

Neuroscientists account for pathology in terms of heredity and constitu-tional and neurophysiological concepts. Most of these theories are formulated as specific and limited hypotheses, rather than as complicated propositional systems. Despite their narrow formal structure, these theories attempt to ac-count for a wide variety of mental disorders.

Certainly, significant progress was made in physical medicine when it shifted its focus from surface symptomatology to the biophysical disruptions that underlie them. Extending this model to mental illness, one sees that these theorists believe that biophysical defects or deficiencies ultimately will be found for such surface symptoms as bizarre behavior, feelings of anguish, or maladaptive interpersonal relations. The major difference they see between psychological and biophysical disorders is that the former, affecting the central nervous system, manifest themselves primarily in behavioral and social symp-toms, whereas the latter, affecting other organ systems, manifest themselves in physical symptoms.

There is a clear logic to classifying syndromes in medical disorders. Bodily changes wrought by infectious diseases and structural deteriorations repeatedly display themselves in a reasonably uniform pattern of signs and symptoms. These make sense in terms of how anatomical structures and physiological processes are altered and then dysfunction. Moreover, these biological changes provide a foundation not only for identifying the etiology and pathogenesis of these disorders but also for anticipating their course and prognosis. Logic and fact together enable one to construct a rationale to explain why most medical syndromes express themselves in the signs and symptoms they do, as well as the sequences through which they unfold.

Unfolding of Key Ideas

In the Middle Ages, all progress in anatomy lapsed as the dissection of the human body was forbidden and regressive religious fanaticism prevailed. Not until *Vesalius* wrote his *De Humane Corporis Fabrica* was the possibility of cerebral localization of mental disorder reaffirmed. By the seventeenth and eighteenth centuries, scientific progress overrode the influence of both Hippocrates' humoral theories and theological supernaturalism. The great English clinician *Thomas Sydenham* asserted that the primary function of diagnosis was to identify the essential disease underlying the overt symptom, noting that in the production of disease, nature is uniform and consistent and that the same phenomena you would observe in the sickness of a Socrates you would observe in the sickness of a simpleton.

Sydenham's desire to organize accurate symptom patterns was prompted by his belief that specific diseases or bodily dysfunctions could be found to account for them. This view gained strength in the extraordinary accomplishments of the early nineteenth century by *Pierre Louis* in pathological anatomy, *Louis Pasteur* and *Joseph Lister* in infectious diseases, and *Rudolf Virchow* in cellular pathology. The thesis was stated succinctly in a commonly held view that insanity was the expression of a lesion of the nervous system, just as dyspnea, palpitations, or diarrhea were the symptoms of a disease of the lungs, the heart, or the intestines.

Historians of mid-nineteenth-century psychiatry, reviewing the state of their field, noted that a deep dialectical clash existed between organic and psychogenic conceptions of mental illness. By the second half of the century, those of a somatic orientation dismissed the metaphysical psychiatry of previous generations, considering that work to be a "contemptible prescientific stage" of the discipline. They thought of it as an undifferentiated background of mystical nonsense from which the organic approach in psychiatric medicine had to struggle and free itself to achieve its scientific form.

In the mid-nineteenth century, Hermann Helmholtz, Ernst Brücke, and Emil Dubois-Reymond established physiological research laboratories in Germany that strengthened the physical disease view and dominated the outlook of medical education well into the twentieth century. Recall the role of Wilhelm Griesinger and his students in applying this notion to mental illness, discussed in Chapter 5.

Speculating on the Brain

Archaeological evidence from early societies demonstrates the practice of *trepanation*. Skulls perforated with deliberately cut borings have been found in numerous historic sites. These findings suggest that diverse cultural societies may have believed that a relationship existed between anatomical brain regions and aspects of behavior, thought, or feeling. It is likely that trepanation was associated with tribal rituals and superstitions, but it is also possible that such operations had a primitive medical intention, perhaps that of relieving headaches or convulsions. Another reasonable assumption is that holes were created to permit the release of evil spirits that might otherwise possess an unfortunate victim.

Scattered references on the ostensible role of the brain are found in early Egyptian literatures and in ancient medical writings in India and China. In Greece, the view that mental disorders are processes of the nervous system and not abstract spiritual phenomena was first espoused by Alcmaeon in the fifth century B.C. and continued in the work of Hippocrates. In the *Sacred Disease,* Hippocrates wrote:

> Men ought to know that from nothing else but the brain come joys, delights, laughter, and sports, and sorrows, griefs, despondency, and lamentations. . . . And by the same organ we become mad and delirious, and fears and terrors assail us . . . (trans. 1952, p. 69)

Evident in Hippocrates' work was his rejection of the notion that ailments, such as seizures and paralyses, should be attributed to the action of demons. Notable also was his recognition that blows to the head often resulted in behavioral disturbances, suggesting that the brain was an element in consciousness and, perhaps, thought and reasoning.

It was not until *Galen's* work in the second century A.D. that Roman thought focused its attention on the nervous system as the possible center of psychic functioning. In his lectures on the brain, Galen articulated directives for dissecting this organ system, specifying the separate structures of the cranial nerves, sensory and motor pathways, and the localization of the cerebrum and the cerebellum. Although he failed to recognize the importance of the brain's convolutions as central to higher modes of thought, he laid the groundwork for the belief that the intellect and its correlated functions of cognition, memory, and imagination were best localized in different parts of the brain.

Next in these early speculative ideas of brain functioning were the writings of **Nemesius (390–446)** in the fourth century A.D. in which he constructed a model of the brain on the basis of what he referred to as the *ventricles.* He specified that the senses had their roots in the front ventricles, that intellect was generated in the mid-ventricles, and that memory was located in the posterior ventricles. As Nemesius wrote, the senses are impaired when the front ventricles have suffered a lesion, and the mind becomes deranged when lesions occur in the midbrain. The idea that higher functions of the mind could be localized in these three ventricular regions remained a central belief for the next several centuries.

Avicenna, the distinguished Persian physician of the tenth century, stated that the powers of perception were located in the forepart of the front ventricle, but the faculty for representing these experiences was located in the latter part of the front ventricle. Further, he spoke of "rational imagination" as centered in the middle ventricle, whereas retention was located in the rear ventricle.

In the sixteenth century, **Andreas Vesalius (1514–1564)** published a set of books that dealt with the central nervous system. Based on his careful dissections of both human and animal anatomy, he noted that all mammalian species possessed a similar number of ventricles that differed in size and organization. Disagreeing with many details of Galen's work some five centuries earlier, he concluded that ventricular localization was not a sustainable hypothesis, but he failed to recognize that cerebral convolutions were related to higher mental functions. Nevertheless, in accord with Aristotle and Nemesius, Vesalius wrote:

> . . . the brain was said to have been equipped with three ventricles. The first was in front, the second in the middle, the third behind, with names according to their position and other names derived from their functions.
>
> The first or frontal, said to lie toward the forehead, was the ventricle of "Common Sense" (*sensus communis*) since, as they believed, from it the nerves of the five senses pass to their instruments. It was by these nerves that smell, color, taste, sound, and touch were said to be led to that ventricle. Accordingly, the main use of this first ventricle was to receive the objects of the five senses of the kind that we generally call "Common Sense."
>
> This ventricle was linked to the second ventricle by a certain passage through which these objects pass. Thus the second ventricle could imagine, mediate, and consider the objects in question; for to this ventricle Thought and Reason were ascribed.
>
> The third ventricle was dedicated to Memory. The second ventricle would, according to its nature, pass to it all those things which it wished to be entrusted thereto, namely those objects upon which it had thoroughly mediated. And moreover the third ventricle, accordingly as it was more moist or dry, would either more quickly or more slowly grave those things upon itself, as upon wax or [more thoroughly] upon stone. Further, those Commentaries teach that, according to the ease or difficulty of the engraving, this ventricle would preserve that which it receives for a shorter or for a longer time. (1543/1952)

The great English surgeon **Thomas Willis (1621–1675)** drafted a key work in the seventeenth century on the structure of the brain, entitled *Cerebri Anatome* in 1664. Here, he specified with great accuracy the relationship between several brain structures and distinct spheres of psychological functioning. For example, he asserted that imagination was a cerebral function and that the cerebellum largely mediated involuntary behaviors. During the same period as Willis's work, **Francois Sylvius (1614–1672)** detailed brain *fissures* and *gyri*, that is, deeply marked grooves and ridges across the entire surface and length of the cerebrum. He tracked the course of these convoluted ridges and folds in all the major regions of the brain's structure. Similarly, the great Danish physician **Niels Stensen (1638–1686)** stressed the need to differentiate and articulate the overall structure and extremely dense character of the brain to recognize its logical order and the developmental sequence in which its regions unfold.

Picking up on Stensen's ideas in the mid-seventeenth century was the Swedish philosopher **Emanuel Swedenborg (1688–1772),** who argued that the separate functions that were carried out in different segments of the brain must ultimately be coordinated in regnant functions at the level of the cortex. Different regions that were simultaneously activated in units separated by fissures and gyri would result in chaos, according to Swedenborg, unless they were regulated. Moreover, he deduced through studies of lesions that the frontal lobes were centrally involved in these coordinating functions. Further, he surmised, albeit speculatively, that the fibers comprising these lobes must serve as the substrate for imagination and thought since it was these abilities that suffered most when the forehead of a patient was wounded.

Conceiving Cerebral Localizations

The view that the differentiated regions of the brain could serve as distinct substrates for specific psychological functions did not achieve fame and a dubious status until the problematic ideas of **Franz Joseph Gall (1758–1828),** to be discussed in detail in a later chapter. Gall's theory, labeled by his disciple **Johann Spurzheim (1776–1832)** as *phrenology*, claimed that the different capabilities of psychological functioning possessed varying degrees of dominance depending on the size of their underlying cortical brain tissue. Although a distinguished anatomist in his time, Gall accepted views expounded by **Johann Lavater (1741–1801)** that the physical shape of the body and face could be directly correlated with specific psychological attributes, such as disposition and temperament. Gall asserted that where there was variation in function, there also must be variation in its controlling structures. Thus he assumed that the cerebral cortex and its associated functions would manifest themselves in varied shapes of the skull, such as seen in its bulges and indentations. In his early-nineteenth-century work with Spurzheim, Gall asserted that 27 psychological faculties correlated with specific segments of the cortex, 20 of which could also be found in many lower mammals. Gall and Spurzheim pressed their primitive concepts forward for several decades, but their work was severely criticized by numerous more sophisticated anatomists and experimentalists of their time.

It was not until the systematic work of **Paul Broca (1824–1880)** that the concept of distinct cortical localization of function became well established. The son of a distinguished army surgeon, Broca established a respected career in medical realms early on, having shown that cancer cells often are transmitted through the circulatory system, as well as having contributed to discoveries in pathology, especially pertaining to rickets and muscular dystrophy.

In an important case study, Broca was able to demonstrate that deterioration in the frontal convolutions of the left hemisphere were crucial to the capacity of articulate and meaningful speech. In his detailed case history of a patient referred to as "Tan," he specified the exact location of speech functions, going beyond the phrenological proposals of cranial bulges and depressions into a fundamental cortical localization.

Along with his associate **Gustav Fritsch (1838–1927), Eduard Hitzig (1838–1907)** extended Broca's work by demonstrating the value of systematic experimentation in establishing cortical localization. In his early studies, he observed that electrical stimulation to the back of the head often stimulated eye movements among humans. Redirecting his attention to lower mammals, especially rabbits and dogs, Hitzig obtained striking results by directly stimulating different cortical regions. He found it especially valuable to employ a therapeutic apparatus that could generate mild electrical currents to induce involuntary motoric behavior in his experimental animals. Although others preceded the work of Hitzig and Fritsch, these two illustrated a clear-cut relationship between distinct cortical sites and specific motoric responses in their experimental animals. Notable was their evidence of the cross-lateral structure of brain functioning, that is, stimulated cortical sites produced reactions on the opposite bodily region. As they wrote: "By electrical stimulations of a motor part, one obtains muscular contractions on the opposite side of the body" (1870 trans., p. 81).

Whereas the early founders of experimental neuroscientific research were primarily located in Germany, **David Ferrier (1843–1928)** was Scottish, carrying out his studies over an extended period in London and Yorkshire. He sought to confirm and extend the experiments of Hitzig and Fritsch, but concluded with different views insofar as the major functions of the motor cortex, asserting that the evidence suggested that this region of the brain subserved both sensory and motor capacities.

Earlier work of the frontal cortex had spoken of this region as silent. However, Ferrier initiated a series of studies, akin to those carried out by Hitzig, in which he sought to explore the functional realms with which the major lobes of the cortex were involved. Employing monkeys as his experimental animal, Ferrier ablated major segments of the anterior frontal area and discovered major changes in the animal's "attentional capabilities." Ferrier, summarizing his observations, noted:

> I could perceive a very decided alteration in the animals character and behavior. . . . Instead of . . . being actively interested in their surroundings and curiously prying into all that came within the field of their observation, they remained apathetic or dull . . . they had lost, to all appearance, the faculty of attentive and diligent observation. (1876, pp. 231–232)

To Ferrier, his observations suggested that the function of the frontal lobes was to maintain attention, that is, the capacity to focus. By contrast, Hitzig believed that the anterior frontal areas mediated abstract thought.

Another innovative contributor to the notion of cerebral localization, *Leonardo Bianchi (1848–1927),* an Italian, executed a series of precise studies exploring the role of the prefrontal areas of the brain. Confirming the findings of Hitzig and Ferrier, that the frontal areas played a minimal role in sensory and motor functions, he demonstrated convincingly that bilateral lesions in that region had a marked effect on the personalities of his animals. Investing time simply living with animals, he was able to record sequential behavioral changes that were more prolonged than the result of mere postsurgical injury. In describing his early observations with one animal, Bianchi wrote:

> Her behavior is altered, her physiognomy is stupid, less mobile; the expression of the eyes is as if uncertain and cruel, devoid of any flashes of intelligence, curiosity, or sociability. Shows terror, even by shrieks and gnashing of teeth when threatened or hurt . . . she is in a state of unrest. (1895, p. 517)

Korbinian Brodmann (1868–1918) carried out careful cortical studies early in the twentieth century, in which he discriminated the structure and cellular composition of more than 50 discrete cortical areas. These were differentiated in the arrangement of their cells and highlighted variations in cellular shapes, especially within and between layers, in the overall thickness of regions across the cortex, and in a number of its horizontal laminations. Although experimenters of the cortical anatomy differed in the particulars they uncovered, clear evidence indicated subtle distinctions among the several regions of the cortex that produced corresponding functional differences.

Fathering Clinical Neurology

The tremendous strides of the nineteenth-century cerebral localizers laid the groundwork for another group of neuroscientists. These investigators sought to deduce underlying neuropathology on the basis of a patient's overt clinical signs and symptoms. Correlating external manifestations of a clinical disorder with internal anatomical pathology became a distinct reality. The accurate deductions these researchers generated led to the emergence of the field of clinical neurology.

A forerunner of Broca, *Jean-Baptiste Bouillaud (1796–1881)* was perhaps the most clinically astute French clinician of his generation. He contended that manifest clinical diseases could lead to accurate inferences regarding their underlying neuroanatomical defects. In Bouillard's judgment, careful clinical examination, particularly when followed by precise postmortem analyses, could provide tangible evidence demonstrating relationships between overt disorders and their underlying lesions. Like Broca, he accumulated a large number of case studies to ensure that he could safely generalize and confirm inferences as valid. Most significant was his observation that patients who suffered impaired speech, but were still capable of moving their tongues and lips, demonstrated defects on autopsy of the anterior lobe region. Although his observations of a distinct locale within the brain to subserve speech were primitive and imprecise, Bouillaud provided a basis for subsequent research. His data provided evidence favoring the central role of the left hemisphere in speech, but he overlooked this finding, mistakenly preferring to view cerebral distinctions from a front-to-back perspective instead of from left to right.

Many consider **Jean-Martin Charcot (1825–1893)** to be the father of clinical neurology. Open-minded, deeply curious, capable of observing subtle clinical details of his patients' behaviors, Charcot was an extraordinarily astute observer of physical defects and dysfunctions. Charcot was a senior physician at the Bicétre, and later at the deteriorated Salpetriere women's hospital, where Pinel had carried out his humane activities earlier in the century. In

Jean-Martin Charcot

1862, along with another young physician of exceptional ability, *Edme F. A. Vulpain*, Charcot studied the chronically ill women housed in its decaying wards. These two highly motivated and skilled physicians quickly recognized that more than half of those for whom they were responsible had been incorrectly diagnosed, most having been lumped together in one or two categories indiscriminately.

Charcot's first discoveries related to multiple sclerosis (MS), a significant neurological disorder that was unrecognized as a distinct disease in the 1860s. Collaborating with Vulpain, he demonstrated the classic disintegration of the myelin sheath, which characterized the anatomical feature of the disorder. Also important was Charcot's recognition of the visual problems typical of those with MS, as well as his patients' tendency to exhibit extreme fluctuations in symptomological intensity over time. Another important contribution was his distinction between MS and the "shaking palsy," or what came to be called *Parkinsonism*. Charcot identified features of the disorder that Parkinson overlooked, such as patients' blank stares, motionless and stolid expressions, and periodic and involuntary oscillation of hand movements.

Owing to Charcot's distinguished work, the Salpetriere was granted substantial funds to develop laboratory facilities for clinical research and for weekly lectures by "the master." He prepared these lectures in great detail and with careful thought, although their public presentation appeared to be spontaneous. Having achieved considerable recognition in France, Charcot's work was quickly recognized throughout the Continent, attracting disciples and students from far and wide. Of special note in his later years was his interest in *hysteria*, a label used in his day for patients with clinical signs of pathology that could not be correlated with underlying anatomical or neurological diseases. Considered by many to be a catchall—a place to assign those who could not be properly diagnosed in one or another class of standard disorders, Charcot made a valiant effort to subdivide the variants of those so categorized. He differentiated subgroups still in use, such as those with defective memories, peculiar or inexplicable losses of sensitivity, apparently (false) motoric seizures that simulated epilepsy, and so on.

Charcot contended that all hysterical patients suffered from a weak constitution, with neurological vulnerabilities that made them highly susceptible to ordinary life conditions, such as work-related stresses. Among Charcot's assertions were that these constitutionally weak hysterics were readily hypnotized; in fact, Charcot believed that only hysterics could be hypnotized, that they were impressionable individuals whose neurologically weak minds could be readily swayed by the suggestions of others. Worthy of note, however, was Charcot's recognition that hysteria could be found in men as well as women, although he asserted that secondary psychological features typically differentiated the genders.

Charcot's stature and ideas concerning hysteria attracted the young Sigmund Freud, a neurologist-in-training from Vienna, who came to study with him during the winter of 1885. Impressed with Charcot's lectures, Freud set out to translate the professor's writings for German-reading neurologists. That Freud progressed in his own innovative direction, disagreeing fundamentally with Charcot's neurological assertions about hysteria, is discussed in a later chapter.

Theodor Meynert (1833–1892), a student of Wilhelm Griesinger, may be best remembered as Freud's most impressive professor at the University of Vienna School of Medicine. Whether his strong advocacy for the somatological viewpoint, which asserted that all psychic functions could be accounted for by underlying anatomical processes, was so adamant that it evoked an oppositional reaction in his pupil cannot be assessed. Meynert ran into considerable conflict with most members of the older generation of psychologically oriented clinicians of his time. A strong exponent of the natural science model of his mentor Griesinger, his orientation was distinctly research focused, not treatment focused. He was one of the major exponents of what has come to be known as the biological-oriented psychiatry of today. Writing in 1885, Meynert said: "The more that psychiatry seeks and finds its scientific basis in a deep and finely grained understanding of the anatomical structure, the more it elevates itself to the status of a science that deals with causes" (1885, p. 5).

Though Meynert spent his entire career in Vienna as a professor of psychiatry, he was essentially a neuropathologist who drew heavily on microscopic procedures. He subtitled his notable textbook *A Clinical Treatise on the Diseases of the Forebrain* (1884), in which he explicitly protested against what he asserted to be the "wishy-washy mentalistic models of psychiatry in its day." Porter (2002) records:

It was axiomatic for Meynert that each stimulus that reached the central nervous system excited a corresponding area in the cortex of the brain; he succeeded in demonstrating certain pathways by which cortical cells communicate with one another and with deeper cells of the cerebrum; and he advanced a systematic classification of mental illness based on his histopathological studies. Theoretically the bluntest of somatists, in practice, however, when his organic neuroanatomical program ran into grave problems, he was reduced to devising some rather nebulous entities, such as the primary and secondary ego, to describe behavioral and cognitive disorders. (p. 146)

Even as a young neurologist, **Carl Wernicke (1848–1904),** who was one of Meynert's students, provided substantial clinical evidence for his mentor's speculations concerning different types of aphasia. Further, he recorded that memory loss for recent events often coexisted with an excellent memory for distant or early life events. Writing convincingly of the several variants of aphasia, he concluded on the basis of a few cases that subtle clinical distinctions could be made depending on which areas of the brain were involved. Thus, in referring to motor aphasia, Wernicke specified that damage could be attributed to one facet of the frontal cortex; these patients understood what they heard or saw in print, but could not speak. Another variant he termed "conduction" aphasia; here patients used words incorrectly and were unable to read, but had both good comprehension and superficially fluent speech. Despite the small number of cases that Wernicke presented in support of his hypotheses, he possessed insight into the likely underlying lesions that accounted for distinctions differentiating the several types of aphasia.

The initial description of *Pick's disease* was made by the Czechoslovakian neurologist **Arnold Pick (1851–1924)** in 1892. This modest and cultured man became a distinguished professor at the University of Prague and engaged in detailed neuropathological studies that identified the early clinical features of the disorder associated with his name. Patients first exhibit amnesic aphasia, followed by a slowly progressive dementia. Neurologically, the degenerative process appeared limited to the frontal and temporal lobes, but progressed to a more pervasive atrophy over several years. At first, Pick assumed that he was observing a form of presenile dementia, but subsequent studies showed that he was dealing with a distinct disorder that advanced through three separable stages.

Despite Pick's careful clinical and neurological studies, there remained considerable confusion as to how one could distinguish the disorder from others of a similar character. It was differentiated over time from Alzheimer disease, to be discussed shortly; those suffering Pick's disease gave less evidence of early memory and speech difficulties and were inclined to be apathetic and indifferent rather than agitated and restless. Similarly, those with Pick's disease often had ancestors with similar pathological histories. Also in contrast to Alzheimer disease, cortical damage in Pick's is more severe in the temporal and frontal areas than in other parts of the cortex.

In distinction to the progressive and inevitable degenerative effects of Wernicke's, Pick's, and Alzheimer's, what has come to be known as Korsakoff disease seemed to be limited in scope and was often a reversible memory deterioration. The disorder, first described in 1889 by **Sergei Korsakoff (1853–1900),** was noted as especially characteristic of chronic alcoholics; as a descriptive symptom cluster, its origins have now been traced to several etiologic agents. Owing to its characteristic symptomatology, it has also come to be known as the "dysmnesic-confabulatory syndrome," reflecting marked detriments in a patient's capacity to retain new learning, an inability to sustain attention and alertness, and a tendency to falsify recollections as a means of filling in memory gaps. Recognizing that the underlying disease may arise from different nutritional deficiencies, such as found in typhoid fever and intestinal obstructions, Korsakoff noted that the clinical picture evolved often into a generalized blunting of higher integrative capacities and a series of severe personality distortions.

In 1904, a young and charming German neuropathologist, **Alois Alzheimer (1864–1915),** working in Kraepelin's laboratories, first at Heidelberg and later in Munich, noted cerebral plaques in the autopsied brain of a patient with ostensible senile dementia. What was striking in his first case was the relative youth of his patient, who was still in middle age. He recorded that this and similarly affected "young" patients showed memory lapses and attentional problems. In a brief time, these memory problems progressed rapidly and became increasingly severe, especially for recent events; soon there was a tendency toward disorientation and confusion. On further postmortem analyses, Alzheimer noted the presence of widely scattered neurofibrillary tangles and sclerotic plaques across the upper layers of his patients' cortex, seen easily even without chemical staining. Over time, he and others ascertained several features that distinguished this new disorder from similar patterns once diagnosed as senile dementia. Thus, this new entity occurred abruptly and at an appreciably earlier age than senility, usually in the patient's 40s or 50s. Severe speech impairments, involuntary movements, and periodic convulsions distinguished it; also, degeneration was rapid, with death likely within five to seven years after the initial onset of symptoms. Accompanying these clinical signs, Alzheimer noted a sharp rise in disorganized thought, a problematic restlessness, distractibility, and a capricious emotional lability, followed by feelings of hopelessness, physical exhaustion, and a rapid psychic collapse.

Recognizing Neuroanatomical Holism

The role that neurological lesions may play in producing pathology can be grasped with only a minimal understanding of the brain's structural organization and functional character. However, naive beliefs to the effect that psychological functions can be localized in precise regions of the brain must be considered carefully. Some early theorists recognized that psychological processes might derive from complex and circular feedback properties of the entire brain and were disinclined to assume that pathological symptoms arise as a direct consequence of the specific neurological lesion.

Concepts such as perception, emotion, behavior, and thought represented complex and different processes that are subsumed under a single label to simplify their understanding. However, these conceptual labels should not be confused with tangible locales within the brain. Many students erroneously believed that these theoretical concepts corresponded on a one-to-one basis to a specifiable locus in the brain. Although certain regions of the brain may be more directly involved in certain psychological functions than others, holistic neuroscientists believe that all higher psychological functions of humans require the interaction of several brain areas. Thus, the following group of thinkers and researchers do not reject the view that a few centers of the brain undergird particular psychosocial functions. But they conceive the brain to be an overarching and complex unit with highly related structural subcomponents that work together to contribute to the expression of thoughts, feelings, and behaviors. To them, the brain is an architecture of coordinated relationships in which localized regions comprise only one element of a comprehensive system.

Charles-Edouard Brown-Sequard (1817–1894) was well aware of Broca's impressive studies localizing speech dysfunctions within specific regions of the cortex. Nevertheless, he challenged the view that cortically localized *symptoms* were the equivalent of cortically localized *functions.* In his own clinical research he cited cases in which aphasia was consequential to damage on the right rather than the left side of the brain, as well as other cases in which damage to Broca's cortical area did not result in the expected speech defects. He asserted that speech was a function of several faculties that encompassed many regions throughout the brain.

Despite his early training with Hermann Helmholtz, a major physiologically oriented theorist, **Friedrich Goltz (1834–1902)** argued vigorously that intellectual functions could not be traced to the destruction of specific parts of the cerebrum. To Goltz, it was the extent rather than the location of the cortical lesions that was critical to a diminution of intellectual functions. On the basis of his research with dogs, Goltz concluded (1881):

> In general, one may affirm that the degree of dementia is proportionate to the spatial extent of the lesion. . . . The dementia after removal of three quadrants (of the cerebral cortex) is severe and most severe of all after the destruction of the fourth quadrant. (translated in Lashley, 1963, p. 4)

The most distinguished neurologist of Great Britain at the turn of the twentieth century was **John Hughlings Jackson (1835–1911),** who joined those who argued against the assumption that localization of symptoms was identical to localization of functions. He contended that it was incorrect to claim that the ability to correlate a symptom or dysfunction with an anatomical lesion was proof that the cortically damaged region was the primary, or sole source of that function. In his own research, he concluded that overt symptoms might stem not only from the destruction of the damaged area but also from secondary and interconnected disturbed regions. In disagreeing with Broca's views concerning discrete faculties for language, he stated unequivocally that to locate a lesion that undermines the capacity for speech is not equivalent to having found a specific location for that capacity.

John Hughlings Jackson

A major contributor to understanding epileptic seizures, Jackson asserted that multiple regions of the brain become involved when epileptic activity is manifest. In his view, a progression of activation from one brain region to another occurred as successive neurocenters become engaged in the epileptic convulsion. He claimed that diverse regions of the cortex were both logically organized and interconnected.

Jackson was a close follower of Darwin's evolutionary ideas. Accordingly, he believed that the nervous system comprised progressively more complex structures throughout evolution such that advanced structures were built on top of the more primitive structures of lower species. The newer components of the nervous system were interconnected with the lower centers, but were both increasingly specialized and integrated. The primitive levels of the brain and spinal cord remained essentially intact and could engage only in simple sensory functions and stereotypic movements that were developed early in evolution. He considered the frontal lobes to be the most advanced elements of the cortex and the last to be organized. They not only served to inhibit the more primitive actions of the lower centers but also were uniquely capable of symbolic and abstract thought.

Another major British theorist with a holistic perspective was **Henry Head (1861–1940),** who viewed the cortex of the brain to be a mosaic, composed of multiple integrated regions. In Head's opinion, a primary lesion in the brain disturbs not only a specific part's function, but usually disrupts the entire interconnected system in which that part is a component. Anticipating the work of Kurt Goldstein, Head asserted that the damaged brain becomes an entirely new system; it is not the old brain minus one of its functions, but a wholly new system of altered relationships. As he wrote:

> So far as the loss of function or negative manifestations are concerned, this response does not reveal the elements out of which the original form of behavior was composed. . . . It is a new condition, the consequence of a fresh readjustment of the organism as a whole. (1920, p. 498)

Borrowing ideas developed by gestalt psychologists and the neurological concepts of Hughlings Jackson, **Baron Jacob von Uexkull (1864–1944)** vigorously contested the assumption that specific functions could be attributed to localized regions of the cortex. In proposing what he termed the *tonus valleys* of the brain's architecture, Uexkull was perhaps the first to note that external stimuli can produce diverse reactions in different brain localities depending on prior conditions in the regions involved. If stimulation in one locale is prevented from spreading, perhaps as a consequence of a brain lesion, it may spill or diffuse into other brain regions like a stream flowing into a valley. According to Uexkull, the flow of excitation is not fixed in the brain but can be displaced and proceed in new directions, yet continue to activate the entire system despite its interrupted pathway.

Uexkull further claimed that interrelationships between stimulating sources and the nervous system were both complex and interactive. In this assertion, he extended the gestalt principle of the whole being a product not only of its individual parts, but of the manner in which these parts are interconnected or aligned. Thus, as the gestaltists demonstrated in their perceptual studies, three dots will be perceived as something entirely different when they are aligned in a row, in contrast to when they are arranged as a triangle. The individual dots are the same, but their relationship has changed and has thereby produced distinctly different effects. So, too, will a stimulus event have a different impact on the nervous system depending on the state of that system when it is impacted.

Shepherd Ivory Franz (1874–1933) was perhaps the first American to disavow the notion of cortical localization. An early researcher who used apparatuses developed by experimental psychologists, Franz systematically examined behaviors not available to other neuroscientists of his day. He was able to show that habits lost following cortical destruction could be rapidly relearned and that early learned capacities remained fully intact despite the removal of the frontal lobes. Franz demonstrated also that comparable memory defects could stem from diverse lesions in the cortex. Particularly impressive were his studies demonstrating the ability of lower mammals to overcome severe frontal lesions. This capacity to compensate for serious neural damage led Franz to recognize the motivational aspects of nervous system functioning. Although he acknowledged some degree of localization at the cortical level, he asserted that the brain still functioned as a coordinated system in which all parts played a role. Franz showed repeatedly that the concept of localized functions was simplistic and that the brain was a composite of multiple interrelated capacities that can achieve numerous pathways to effective psychological functioning.

Kurt Goldstein (1878–1965) was a major follower of the German gestalt movement, as well as an admirer of Hughlings Jackson in Great Britain. A skilled neurosurgeon and a keen observer of patient adaptation to the experience of severe brain damage in World War I, Goldstein was a major neurological theorist prior to leaving the University of Berlin in the 1930s owing to the hostile attitude toward Jewish professors. Central to Goldstein's theories was an awareness that localized brain damage was but one facet of a complex system of adaptive adjustment in neurological functioning. As with Henry Head, he considered the nervous system as becoming a new entity following damage, rather than remaining a stable entity with just one missing part.

Goldstein employed the concept of a "catastrophic reaction" to signify the shock to the nervous system and the consequential struggle to compensate for a severe brain injury. He saw the patients as struggling to reconstruct themselves so as to continue functioning in an effective way within their environment. Most notable was the patient's inclination to deal with life increasingly in a concrete rather than an abstract way. Thus, the key feature of brain damage to Goldstein was the loss of an abstract attitude. Although this loss may not be evident when the patient deals with ordinary familiar and routine conditions, environmental changes or altered life circumstances that are unfamiliar or present new challenges and demands clearly show the patient's increasing rigidity, perseveration, and abstraction defects.

Kurt Goldstein

Karl Spencer Lashley (1890–1958), a zoologist, became a student of the behaviorist John Watson and, more importantly, a colleague of the leading neurophysiologist in the United States, Shepherd Franz. Because of his skill in building and using complex tools and apparatus, Lashley might have become a skilled surgeon instead of a neurophysiological theorist. Despite his early training, Lashley rejected the simplistic behavioral explanations of his forerunners and joined Franz in propounding a theory based on the novel concepts of "equipotentiality" and "mass action." They asserted the reality of the brain's complex organizational structure and viewed the cortex as providing a general framework within which individual neural impulses routinely conform.

Much of Lashley's research addressed the relationship between cortical activities and learned behaviors. His experimental approach was to train animals, especially the white rat, in a particular performance such as running a maze or making visual discriminations. He then destroyed different parts of the cortex and, after the animals had recovered from the surgery, quantified the extent to which and in what manner the learned performance had been impaired. He sought to establish definite measurements of the relationship between the impaired abilities and the location and extent of the correlated brain injuries. For the most part, he concluded that a specified location of the cortex was not invariably associated with a specific performance deficit, that is, strict localization of function was not the rule. He did find a relationship, however, between the *amount* of the cortical area destroyed and the degree of behavioral deterioration. Further, he found that complex performances required greater amounts of brain tissue than simpler tasks. Lashley wrote:

> We are dealing with a complex system in which there is an influence of every part upon every other with all degrees of intimacy in the relations and various degrees of dominance and subordination. Our problem is to discover the means by which these influences are exerted. (1929, p. 20)

Lashley defined his central findings with the following concepts:

> The term "equipotentiality" I have used to designate the apparent capacity of any intact part of a functional area to carry out, with or without reduction in efficiency, the functions which are lost by destruction of the whole. . . .
> . . . (by the law of mass action) the efficiency of performance of an entire complex function may be reduced in proportion to the extent of brain injury within an area whose parts are not more specialized for one component of function than for another. (1929, p. 24)

The distinguished Canadian neuropsychologist **Donald Olding Hebb (1904–1985)** was born in Nova Scotia and drifted into psychology after an early reading of Freud's ideas. As a student at McGill University, he was drawn toward the writings of Pavlov and his work on conditioned learning. Most significant, however, were his studies with Karl Lashley, first at the University of Chicago, later at Harvard University, and then for a postdoctoral period at the Yerkes Laboratories of Primate Biology in Florida. To Hebb, behavior derived from the nervous system operating as a whole.

Hebb published a comprehensive text called *The Organization of Behavior* in 1949. Here he sought to reconceptualize a wide range of psychological processes in neurophysiological terms. Central to his writings was his conclusion that the brain must have significant "self-governing capabilities" that are largely independent of environmental stimulation. Heavily influenced by motivational and learning theorists of the day, Hebb emphasized the existence of reverberatory circuits within the nervous system, labeling these as *cell assemblies*. These internal structures and their interconnections enabled the brain to generate thought, motivation, and action independent of external input. Describing his concept of cell assembly, he posited an intricate network of neural connections such that impulses automatically progress from one cell to any other cell within the assembly. So conceived, nerve impulses travel in a recurrent series of loops or circuits to permit sustained thought and action. Significantly, numerous alternate pathways exist within a cell assembly such that the loss of any particular cell would not render the functioning of the entire system inoperative.

The role of the *corpus callosum* had been a puzzle to theorists and clinicians for several decades prior to the impressive studies carried out by **Roger Sperry**

(1913–1994), a former student of Karl Lashley and vigorous opponent of the role of cortical localization for higher functions such as thought and memory. In the 1920s, the Russian physiologist *Konstantine Bykov*, working with Ivan Pavlov, had recognized in studies in which the corpus callosum was segmented in dogs, that learning acquired in one hemisphere failed to transfer to the other. Unfortunately, this important finding was overlooked for some 40 years. Also prior to Sperry's research, *Walter Dandy*, an eminent neurosurgeon, had argued in the 1930s that no symptoms could be found following the splitting of the corpus callosum. As he wrote in 1936, "No symptoms followed its division. This simple experiment at once disposes of the extravagant claims to function of the corpus callosum" (p. 40). Similarly, *Andrew Akelaitas* reviewed the results of a large number of "split-brain" patients in the 1940s and concluded that these patients showed no deficits on various measures of higher brain functions.

Together with his student **Ronald Meyers (1929–)**, Roger Sperry undertook a series of studies that revealed the corpus callosum's crucial character:

> Under special training and testing conditions . . . one finds that each of the divided hemispheres now has its own mental sphere or cognitive system—that is, its own independent perceptual, learning, memory, and other mental processes . . . as if the animals had two separate brains. (1961, p. 1749)

In follow-up work with his students, Sperry demonstrated several distinct roles for the corpus callosum: First, this bridge between hemispheres permitted each half to know what the other was processing and experiencing, and second, memory traces became embedded in both hemispheres, enabling each hemisphere to activate and draw on traces that were stored in the other. Moreover, Sperry, using highly sophisticated evaluative procedures, concluded that the left hemisphere was more analytical, more rational, and more verbally competent than the right. By contrast, the right was more emotional, more artistic, more imaginative, and more impulsive than the left.

TM

Norman Geschwind

Following up on the work of Sperry and Meyer was **Norman Geschwind (1926–1984)**, another neuroscientist seeking to elaborate hemispheric functions and specialization. His early work identified major structural asymmetries between the hemispheres and specified that the temporal plane was three times more extensive on the left side compared with the right side. In this surgical exploration, Geschwind illustrated the major reason the left hemisphere played a more central role in language comprehension and production than the right.

Each hemisphere was structurally and anatomically prepared to perform specialized functions, yet each member of the pair was able to share its special abilities in a coordinated and synergistic manner, akin to successful marital partners or scientific collaborators. Thus, despite their differences, Geschwind demonstrated that complex interactions existed among the centers of each hemisphere. More specifically, in exploring the interactive elements of language functions, Geschwind and his colleagues demonstrated that Broca's area was specially organized to deal with the details of grammatical structure and the means to use simple words necessary for fluent speech. However, other regions of the brain (e.g., the angular gyrus), were necessary to comprehend verbal information presented in a visual form (e.g., text readings). Similarly, Wernicke's area appeared to be structured to recognize language presented in auditory form, enabling oral communications to be translated and comprehended. Thus, both language expression and reception require visual and acoustic interactions that cross from one region of the brain to another.

Through Geschwind's work, this synthesis largely resolved the conflict between localists and holists. Language, like other psychological functions, is recorded bilaterally and is expressed bilaterally in several sections of the brain simultaneously. He emphasized that psychological processes arise from a complex network of interactions and feedbacks. All stimuli, whether generated externally or internally, follow long chains and reverberating circuits that modulate a wide range of other brain activities. Psychological functions must be conceived, therefore, as the product of a widespread and self-regulating pattern of interneuronal stimulation.

Exploring Psychophysiology and Neurochemistry

In contrast to CT and MRI scans and blood flow tools, which permit the direct visualization of what is occurring within the brain, the following procedures provide data requiring some inference. Samples of blood or urine are obtained from patients to determine whether they possess chemicals that are generally known to affect people's emotional conditions. Some tap into potential disruptions or distortions of the thyroid or adrenal glands, essentially serving to gauge the body's neuroendocrine capacity to respond to stress conditions. Other laboratory procedures are designed to explore the central nervous system's neurotransmitters, hoping thereby to identify chemical dysfunctions that may be modified by pharmacological action. Similarly, the brain is composed of a vast number of electrical circuits that continue to be activated spontaneously; here, EEG (electroencephalogram) has proven valuable since its development in the 1930s. It remains, however, a crude gauge of the brain's electrical activity in that it only summarizes the simultaneous action of billions of neurons. Its primary diagnostic value lies in identifying which parts of the brain are prone to be activated erratically and explosively in assessments of epileptic seizures. The procedure may prove in time to be a useful research tool for other clinical conditions.

Other investigators have studied chemical substances involved in normal neural transmission. This body of research centers on neurohormones, chemical secretions of nerve cells that either facilitate or inhibit synaptic thresholds. The fact that certain exogenous chemicals, known as psychotomimetics, inhibit or stimulate the action of natural neurohumoral substances, and even simulate psychotic behavior, led to speculations that natural neurohormonal defects also might underlie a wide range of behaviors and emotions.

With the advent of newly refined laboratory procedures and precision instrumentation, these discoveries spurred the twentieth-century search for other biological correlates of mental functioning. This surge of activity encompassed such diverse fields as neuropathology, psychophysiology, neurochemistry, endocrinology, genetics, and psychosomatic medicine. By the 1920s, references to physiological causes for mental disorders filled the literature. These new tools, in time, may lead to conclusive biological discoveries. J. A. Stern and MacDonald made this statement in their mid-century review of physiological correlates of mental disease (1965):

> From the electron microscope through time lapse microscopy, from looking at dendritic and nerve cell activity to the vascular bed under finger nails, from studying the web-building activity of spiders, the behavior of fighting fishes, and the rope climbing ability of rats . . . the search for a biological basis of mental disorders continues.

One point must be kept in mind lest we fall prey to past errors. Every bodily dysfunction results in diverse and far-reaching consequences as biochemical processes are involved intimately in a multitude of functions. When chemical dysfunctions of the body are discovered, the task remains of specifying exactly how they produce mental pathology. Further, the search for neurophysiological dysfunctions is handicapped by the high degree of natural physiochemical individuality among people. As noted, Roger Williams, the eminent biochemist, pointed out that each individual possesses a distinctive physiochemical pattern that is wholly unlike others and bears no relationship to a hypothetical norm. These patterns of individuality make us aware of crucial factors that must be evaluated before we can properly appraise the role of neurophysiological functions in psychic pathology.

Johannes Müller (1801–1858) was arguably the first great psychophysiologist. Born in Coblenz to a middle-class family, he was energetic and highly ambitious from the first, earning his medical degree at the University of Berlin by the age of 20, and a professorship in physiology and anatomy before he was

30. Despite suffering from a bipolar disorder, he continued for over 20 years to be a prodigious researcher, especially in his studies of sensory processes in vision and hearing. In his periods of mental illness, he struggled with the belief that the mind contained vital forces comprising the soul. Nevertheless, he generated an articulate theory in which he specified that different nerve properties characterized vision and hearing, each possessing "specific energies or qualities." The optic nerves responded only to light, the aural nerves only to sound. Unsure of certain particulars, owing to the technical limitations of the period, he noted that it was not known whether the essential cause of a peculiar energy of each nerve of sense was seated in the nerve itself, or in the parts in the brain or spinal cord with which it was connected.

Müller also countered a then prevalent belief that what the senses perceived were replicas transmitted directly to the mind: miniature representations of an object's physical qualities. Müller was able to convince his colleagues that analogs—not replicas—of the objects were transmitted. Müller's views, written in his 1838 *Handbook of Physiology,* were translated in 1912 by Rand, as follows:

> The immediate objects of the perception of our senses are merely particular states induced in the nerves and felt as sensations either by the nerves themselves or by the parts of the brain concerned with sensation. The nerves make known to the brain, by virtue of the changes produced in them by external causes, the changes of condition of external bodies. (1912, p. 543)

In the mid-nineteenth century many intelligent scientists grasped the essential elements of psychology, physiology, and physics. No one of his time understood these fields with such clarity and vision, however, as **Hermann von Helmholtz (1821–1894).** Through his research, Helmholtz demonstrated a detailed understanding of each of these fields and their interrelationships as well.

Hermann von Helmholtz

Helmholtz's studies on the eye and the ear rank among the greatest achievements of science. Their importance to the development of psychology is difficult to overestimate for he was able to demonstrate the enormous complexity of such apparently simple processes as seeing objects and hearing sounds. No less significant was his work in demonstrating the possibility of studying these psychophysical functions using scientific methods. He articulated this in great detail in two books A *Handbook of Physiological Optics* (1866/1925) and *Sensations of Tone* (1863). Heidbreder asserts the importance of Helmholtz's contributions in the following:

From the standpoint of sheer amount of work done, the achievement is stupendous. Helmholtz carefully worked over all existing knowledge on the subject, tested it experimentally, devised new experiments, discovered new facts, and suggested new theories. With equal facility, he invented apparatus, devised experimental methods, and constructed theories. He was extraordinarily gifted in dealing with both things and ideas. His powers of observation, visual and auditory alike, were said to be exquisitely accurate and sensitive. No aspect of his subject failed to interest him; his investigations ranged from the anatomy of the eye and ear to the history of the development of harmony. (1933, p. 85)

The connection between physical phenomena and psychological experience, mediated through the physiology of the organism, became his goal and his great achievement. Although his work did not extend to complex functions such as intelligence, thought, and memory, he laid the scientific basis for such fundamental processes as visual perception, color vision, and hearing. Yet, Helmholtz recognized the complex relationship that existed between the mind and perception.

Among his first and most significant investigations were studies on the speed of nerve impulse conduction. He rejected the notion that "vital forces," a rather mysterious energy, was housed in the human body. Using a rigorous scientific laboratory procedure he asserted that all organismic movements could be understood in terms of simple physical laws. Studying the motor nerves of the frog, he precisely calculated the exact time intervals from stimulus to muscular contractions, concluding that neural speed conduction was approximately 30 meters per second. This work set a foundation for later reaction-time studies that became a cornerstone of psychological research.

Helmholtz's empirical approach to the study of perception was enhanced by his invention of the ophthalmoscope, an instrument that permitted investigators to examine the retina. Notable among his achievements in this realm was the first naturalistic theory of color vision, an empirical extension of classic work carried out by Aristotle and Isaac Newton. Broadening his sphere of inquiry, Helmholtz undertook a series of original studies on the sensations of hearing, recognizing that specialized nerves enabled listeners to discriminate the timber and pitch of sound, as well as the complex harmonics generated by modern instruments.

Most significant for the young Italian scientist **Camille Golgi (1843–1926)** was his early work in developing the silver nitrate staining method for recording and tracking the pathways of neural cells, their axons, dendrites, and connected branches. Golgi received the Nobel Prize for this technique, which provided the essential tool for observing and understanding major elements of nerve structure and conduction. In Golgi's view, neural cells were intertwined in complex networks that were related by contiguity rather than continuity; the cells were not a single uninterrupted piece, but were separate, close, independently formed, and linked in interrelated sequences. Nerve cells demonstrated close and intricate contact points but were not fused.

The issue of neural cell continuity versus contiguity remained a major thorn in neurophysiological thinking in the late nineteenth century. Elaborating on the work of Golgi, **August Forel (1848–1931)** demonstrated that injured nerve cells atrophied as separate units, hence illustrating that close contact rather than absolute continuity was the more justifiable position. As he wrote in his biography: "Could not the mere intimate contact of the protoplasmic processes of the nerve cells effect the functional connections of nervous conduction just as well as absolute continuity?" (1937, p. 162).

As others ultimately demonstrated, Forel's careful research data supported the theory of simple contact, that communication among nerve cells such as between axons and dendrites could be carried out without continuity. Forel established the presence of separate cellular processes that called for a space between cells, in which communication could pass or cross over from one separate unit to another.

The Spanish scientist **Ramon Y. Cajal (1852–1934)** was born in an impoverished region near the French border and was characterized in his youth

Ramon Y. Cajal

as an obstreperous and rebellious personality, constantly involved in troublesome activities. Directed by his physician father into a profession in medicine, Cajal spent his early career struggling to find his way despite numerous illnesses and impoverishment. Fortunately, he played a significant role in overcoming the devastation wreaked by a cholera epidemic and was awarded a modern Zeiss microscope for his efforts. Using this tool, Cajal was ultimately able to improve on Golgi's silver staining methods. By sheer persistence and good fortune, he demonstrated his new techniques to an audience of histologists in Berlin, where his work was quickly recognized as exceptional. Significantly, Cajal demonstrated that nerve cells were unquestionably independent elements. Shortly after his demonstrations, *Wilhelm von Waldeyer* wrote a review in which he coined the term *neuron* to represent this anatomical unit of the nervous system; Cajal's research and Waldeyer's descriptive terminology soon resulted in the "neuron theory" or the "neuron doctrine."

A quiet and reflective British scientist, **Charles Scott Sherrington (1857–1952)** was both shy and self-effacing, despite an ever-increasing reputation as a distinguished neurophysiologist. Throughout his life, Sherrington was deeply immersed in the humanities and sciences. Like Cajal, he spent his

early years as a physician involved in the treatment of serious infectious diseases. This period
proved to be a rich phase of study, but it was
soon replaced by opportunities to engage in research on nervous system reflexes and their underlying circuitry. One of his first contributions
was investigating the functional connection
between neurons. Neuroscientists of his time
were unable to identify the nature of the space
that separated neuronal connections. Sherrington coined the term for this junction, labeling
it as the *synapsis*, later simplified to *synapse*, a
term appropriated from the Greek word meaning "to clasp."

Charles Scott Sherrington

Sherrington discovered that nerve-to-muscle
reflexes were significantly slower than the simple speed of nerve conduction
itself, a finding suggesting that the transmission process was slowed at the
synaptic junction. Work on what was to be termed "reciprocal innervation"
demonstrated that reflexes that activated one set of muscles automatically
were counterbalanced by an opposite set of muscle activity. This led Sherrington to conclude that the nervous system functioned, not discretely, but as a
unified and coordinated whole. He judged the cerebral cortex to be a complex
and integrated switchboard, arguing in favor of the holistic approach to brain
functioning.

In his late 40s, Sherrington wrote his major work, *The Integrative Action
of the Nervous System* (1906/1952). In it, Sherrington spoke of the interaction of two active processes of synaptic excitation and inhibition. He recognized that his work was merely a beginning, and that his studies of reflex
action and reaction were only a starting point for understanding the "physiology of mind."

A series of tremendous advances in the technology of nervous system research followed Sherrington's earlier work. A marked increase in electrophysio-
logical recording and biochemical analysis led to a mushrooming of knowledge.
With the invention of the electron microscope and the molecular analysis of
neurotransmitters, dramatic changes exploded in our understanding of the
mind, its biological substrates, circuitry, and chemistry.

Walter Cannon (1871–1945), an American physiologist, studied the en-
docrine system, seeking to identify connections between the adrenal glands
and the autonomic nervous system. He recognized that widespread sympathetic system changes occurred in response to stressful and life-threatening
conditions. In his early work, Cannon showed an interplay between the cortex
and lower nervous system centers. Following on early research on decerebrate
dogs, Cannon found that animals whose cortex was disconnected from the

brain stem demonstrated random and ineffective frenzied reactions he termed "sham rage."

Numerous physiologists at the turn of the century began to speculate about the mechanisms involved at what Sherrington referred to as the synapse. Along with Cannon, who recognized the importance of hormones as elements in nervous system action, several scientists proposed that chemical transmission might be involved at the synapse. In 1904, *Thomas Elliott* proposed a tentative hypothesis to the effect that sympathetic nerves might be involved in releasing adrenaline-like substances. Concluding his presentation before the Physiological Society in London, Elliott commented that adrenaline might be the substance liberated when the nervous stimulus arrives at the synapsis.

A number of years after Elliott had speculated on the possible role of chemical transmission at the synapse, an Austrian scientist named **Otto Loewi (1873–1961)** engaged in a series of inventive experiments demonstrating conclusively that a chemical process, essentially the first neurotransmitter, was central to nerve impulse transmission. A cultured and thoughtful man with strong humanistic leanings, Loewi had gravitated from early clinical work to laboratory experimentation in pharmacology, always maintaining a strong interest in complex psychological processes, as well as systematic biochemical research. In his early travels to England, he became acquainted with the young Thomas Elliott some years before Elliott's statement concerning the possible role of chemical transmission. Loewi's ideas for executing his monumental studies on neurotransmitters emerged during sleep, a random fantasy that he quickly followed up on in a series of studies with laboratory frogs. Bathing the creature's heart in a number of chemical solutions, he sought to stimulate the vagus nerve and to transfer its effects from one frog to another. He demonstrated in these studies the role of chemicals in both excitation and inhibition, concluding that natural hormones were crucially involved at the synaptic junction.

The distinguished British neurophysiologist **Edgar Douglas Adrian (1889–1977)** played a key role in using electrical recording instruments to identify the characteristics of neuroelectrical transmission. An early collaborator of **Keith Lucas (1879–1916),** Adrian carried out a series of studies designed to track the path and speed of impulse transmission in isolated long nerves segmented from the frog. He demonstrated in 1912 that nerve impulses had an all-or-none character; further, that impulses always had the same nature regardless of the strength of their stimulus source. Once triggered, nerve impulses were transmitted down the full length of the axon and then quickly returned to their initial potential after a brief rest period. In Lucas's posthumous work, *The Conduction of the Nervous Impulse* (1917), Adrian, who edited the unfinished work, specified details concerning the characteristics of the nerve impulse, its quiet periods between activation, its pattern of summation, and its all-or-nothing conduction.

In the past several decades, theorists have proposed specific areas within the brain whose functions may be associated with psychic pathology. Two sites have been mentioned repeatedly: the reticular formation and the limbic system. These two regions serve as biophysical substrates for activating and integrating motivational and emotional responses; together they alert external receptors and determine whether and how emotion-producing stimuli will be experienced.

Recent experimental and theoretical work has shown that the *reticular formation*, a previously little understood anatomical no-man's land, plays a key role in the arousal and activation of the central nervous system. The components of this complex system sweep up and down the major segments of the brain to enhance or suppress wakeful activity; it alerts or orients awareness and contributes to the selective focusing of attention. In addition to these experimentally established functions, some theorists have suggested that it also links and integrates neural connections. By its unique placement within the brain, impulses from diverse cortical and subcortical sources may readily impinge on it. As such, it is at least plausible to propose that it serves as a relay station for coordinating interneuronal circuits. If the functions of both arousal and integration are ascribed correctly to the reticular formation, lesions in this system could very well underlie many psychic disorders.

A substantial body of research has been gathered to the effect that the *limbic system*, composed primarily of the hypothalamus, amygdala, and septal regions, is deeply involved in the expression and control of both emotional and motivational processes. It has been proposed that damage to the limbic system may suppress, magnify, or otherwise distort affective reactions and lead to pathological emotions and behavior. It has been further suggested that deficient reactions either at the hypothalamic or septal regions of the limbic system may account for schizophrenic behavior, specifically that schizophrenia may be traced to endogenous disturbances of synaptic control and functional imbalances among the various limbic regions. Similarly, it has been proposed that the erratic mood swings of bipolar patients may be attributed also to dysfunctions in the limbic system. There is no direct evidence to date, however, to correlate specific limbic system defects with any of the traditional categories of mental illness.

In the 1930s, **James Papez (1893–1958),** a comparative neurologist, articulated the central role of the limbic system in both emotional expression and control. Three components of this system, the hippocampus, the hypothalamus, and the cingular gyrus were not only interconnected, according to Papez, but also served to mediate the emotional experiences and responses of the organism. Like many before him, Papez differentiated between brain structures involved in primitive emotional expression and those capable of a subjective emotional experience.

Paul MacLean (1913–1990), a researcher at both Harvard and Yale Universities, joined other colleagues who followed Papez's explorations of brain function and emotion. Papez noted that lesions in the cingulum, as well as in the inferior temporal cortex, were related to a sharp decrease in affective emotional expression. In the 1930s at the University of Chicago, other neuroscientists, notably **Heinrich Kluver (1897–1978)** and **Paul Bucy (1904–1981),** showed that bilateral temporal lobectomies in rhesus monkeys likewise resulted in a distinct loss of emotional reactions. Each of these investigations suggests a possible neurological basis for the affective deficits typically seen in patients described as schizoid personalities.

MacLean elaborated earlier speculations concerning the role of the limbic system as the primary substrate of both emotional experience and expression. Dividing the brain conceptually into three major regions, MacLean coined the term, the *Triune Brain*, holding the view that the human skull holds not one brain, but three, each representing a distinct evolutionary stratum that formed on the older layer below it. He referred to them as the *Reptilian* or primitive brain, including the structures of the brain stem, serving the basic functions of survival and ancestral memories; the limbic system or *Paleomammalian* brain, concerned with pure emotions, instincts, and reproductive behaviors; and the neocortex or *Neomammalian* brain, subserving abstract functions, subjective emotional experiences, and problem-solving abilities. All three were coordinated and in communication, but were occasionally in conflict with one another.

Arvid Carlsson (1923–   ), a Swedish scientist at the Universities of Lund and Gothenberg has, since the 1950s, given special attention to dopamine, a class of chemicals for conveying signals from one neuron to another. This synaptic messenger, once thought to be simply a chemical precursor to another neurotransmitter, proved to be a major transmitter in its own right. Carlsson's research showed that dopamine not only regulates mood and movements but plays a significant role in how the brain responds to drugs and alcohol. His work eventually led to the discovery that people with Parkinson's disease, who suffer severe movement disabilities, lack dopamine-making neurons in key brain regions. Further, he showed that a dopamine precursor called *L-dopa* often reverses many of this condition's symptoms.

Eric Kandel (1930–   ) left Austria for the United States with his family in 1939. He attended Harvard University to study the humanities. Intrigued by his reading of Freudian literature, Kandel went to medical school to pursue a career as a psychoanalyst. Early in his training, Kandel undertook work in neurophysiology in the hope of gaining a clearer understanding of how memory and emotions were biologically generated and intertwined. His early research led him to explore the hippocampus as the primary source of memory formation, but he soon turned to a simpler neurosystem for his intensive analysis. Using the Aplysia sea slug, a creature with only 20,000 nerve cells, as an experimental animal, Kandel identified a number of the biochemical changes that accompany memory formation, explicating how short-term memory involved just a minor modulation of the synapses, whereas long-term memory required new synaptic linkages. More specifically, he showed that a protein termed CREB helps the nervous system retain a memory or a learned skill for a long period of time rather than just briefly.

Their work earned Carlsson and Kandel the Nobel Prize in medicine in 2000. Together, they began to decode how the vast numbers (at least one hundred trillion) of synaptic connections in the brain are able to communicate continually as well as to alter their strength, flexibility, and function.

Working together with imaginative graduate students, **Solomon Snyder (1938–)** began his productive career at an early age, achieving a full professorship in pharmacology and psychiatry by the age of 31 at the Johns Hopkins School of Medicine. Among his first discoveries was the identification of opiate receptors in the brain, which increased our understanding of neural cell-to-neural cell communication. These studies led to a greater appreciation of active drugs such as painkillers, and of the dynamic sequences involved in narcotic addiction. His research design formula became a standard procedure for screening potential drugs with minimal use of laboratory animals. Snyder also demonstrated that nitric oxide was an integral part of the brain's communication system and revealed a role for carbon monoxide as a probable message carrier. In this work, he established that gases might be a new class of neurotransmitters. Together with Kandel and Carlsson, Snyder established an unquestioned role for chemistry in synaptic communication and learning.

Accelerating Genetic Research

The role of heredity in mental illness is usually inferred from evidence based on correlations in mental disorder among members of the same family. As further support, heredity theorists note that obvious biophysical features such as height, coloration, and facial structure are similar among close relatives, and one could extrapolate that the internal morphology and physiology of their nervous systems must also be alike. As the nervous system subserves behavior and emotion, it should follow that family members would be disposed to act and feel in similar ways.

Most psychopathologists admit that hereditary factors play a role in personality and behavior, but insist that environmental factors can substantially modify genetic dispositions. This moderate view states that heredity operates not as a fixed constant, but as a disposition that takes different forms depending on the circumstances of an individual's upbringing. Hereditary theorists take a more inflexible position. They refer to a body of impressive data implicating genetic factors in pathologies such as schizophrenia and bipolar psychoses. Although they admit that environmental conditions may produce variations in these disorders, they are convinced that these are superficial influences that cannot prevent the individual from succumbing to the hereditary defect.

Systematic genetic studies did not begin until the early twentieth century. Until then, assumptions about inheritance were based on chance observations and superstitious beliefs. The first authority to initiate a series of systematic investigations of the coincidence of disorders among relatives of mental patients was the German psychiatrist **Ernst Rudin (1874–1952).** What little Rudin had achieved was discredited, however, by his close association with the Nazi program favoring eugenics. He wrote:

> Not until the political activity of Adolph Hitler, and only through his work has a thirty-year long dream of translating racial hygiene into action finally become a reality. . . .
>
> We can hardly express our efforts more plainly or appropriately than in the words of the fuehrer: whoever is not physically or mentally fit must not pass on his defects to his children. The state must take care that only the fit produce children. (1934, pp. 228–29)

Because of Rudin's difficulty in separating the role of heredity from that of environment in his human pedigree studies, two of his German students, *Johann Lange* and *Hans Luxenburger*, devised the method of comparing identical and fraternal twins. Identical twins had identical genes, and therefore, the specific role of heredity could be isolated partially from environment. Seeking to produce an objective and unbiased population of twins, Luxenburger asked all mental hospitals in Bavaria to list their patients and to identify whether they were part of a twin birth. Over 200 twin pairs were identified, enabling Luxenburger to identify 106 cases with schizophrenia. He found that 7.5% of the monozygotic cases shared the syndrome, but none were found among dizygotic pairs.

Aaron Rosanoff (1879–1956), an American research psychiatrist, compiled a list of over 1,000 twin pairs in which one of the twins had a serious mental illness. Among monozygotic twins, both twins were found to be schizophrenic in 66.6% of the cases, but only in 15% was that so among dizygotic twins. Similar proportions were obtained for a comparison of twins diagnosed with manic-depression.

Twin studies were continued in the mid-1930s by the research psychiatrist **Franz Kallmann (1897–1965).** Trained initially at Ernst Rudin's laboratories following his medical degree from Breslau University, Kallmann later worked briefly at Kraepelin's research institute in Munich. It was during this latter period that he focused on the genetic basis of schizophrenia, concentrating his efforts on family and epidemiological studies. He published his research in *The Genetics of Schizophrenia* (1938). Kallmann left Germany for the United States in 1936 because of his opposition to the Nazi eugenics program, as well as his distant Jewish ancestry, which banned him from publishing or speaking at medical meetings. In the United States, Kallmann became acquainted with Rosanoff's studies and began a new series of twin research investigations at the New York State Psychiatric Institute. His findings indicated that schizophrenics with a traceable cotwin evidenced a correspondence in 85% of the monozygotics (i.e., they shared the disorder substantially); only 15% were equally impaired among dizygotics. Kallmann provided an amply documented argument that the coincidence of the disorder varied directly with degree of genetic similarity; he obtained these findings by comparing the frequency with which relatives were classified similarly according to the Kraepelinian nosological system.

Born in Philadelphia, **Seymour Kety (1915–   )** obtained his medical degree from the University of Pennsylvania, became scientific director of the National Institute of Mental Health, and reoriented the institute's direction toward the neurosciences rather than its prior psychodynamic studies. Following a stint at Harvard University, Kety carried out a series of genetic studies in conjunction with Danish colleagues. Given Denmark's unusually complete and detailed birth register, researchers could track the life course of mental patients from birth to death. Particularly valuable was the ability to identify the biological relatives of persons who had been adopted shortly after birth, enabling researchers to separate the impact of environmental and genetic influences. Kety's findings suggested that schizophrenia is 10 times more common among biological relatives of the schizophrenic adoptees than of those with no known schizophrenic symptomatology. Similar findings were obtained in studies of those suffering from manic-depressive disorders, notably a 66.6% concordance among monozygotics and a 20% for dizygotics (Rosenthal & Kety, 1968).

Recent work by the psychologist *Irving Gottesman* and the medical epidemiologist *Ming T. Tsuang* further reinforce the findings of earlier researchers. However, their studies indicate that a reasonably high concordance rate does not signify inevitability. Thus, for most psychiatric disorders a person can be free of illness even if his or her genetically identical twin is ill. The best guess today is that when both twins harbor the genes for a mental illness, one may be exposed to an environmental trigger whereas the other is not.

Devising Somatic Therapies

The mid-twentieth century was a period of unjustified optimism, characterized by the belief that somatic therapies, especially pharmacological "wonder drugs" would cure all mental illnesses and deplete the rolls of every clinic and hospital. The mental health field was flooded with new products, each of which was preceded by massive and tantalizing advertisements that promised a new life for the depressed or anxious patient. Despite this bewildering array of highly touted therapies, psychotherapists' offices, community clinics, and mental health hospitals are no less busy than before. Formerly agitated or assaultive patients are easier to handle, and anxious and depressed syndromes are less severe and of briefer duration; but there has been no sweeping change in the prevalence or variety of most psychopathological conditions.

Because of the varied questions that can be posed about therapeutic actions, and because of the complexity of the factors involved, theorists have had a relatively open field to speculate on why and how somatic treatments produce their effects. From early surgical successes to the recent advent of antibiotic medicines, the conviction has grown that treatment is most effective when directed at the root of a disorder and not its surface symptomatology. An assumption in psychiatric somatic therapy is that a patient's overt behaviors and feelings express an underlying biological affliction best treated at its source. The fact that few if any biological causes have been identified has not deterred the search for such therapies. In great measure, useful somatic treatments have resulted from serendipity. Perhaps the most striking fact about the history of somatotherapy is its progress through error and misconception. Speculative theories regarding new therapies were often far afield, and those who discovered effective treatment agents were usually blazing trails to other diseases. By good fortune and happy accident, alert clinical observers noted unanticipated effects that proved empirically useful for mental disorders.

Early Somatotherapeutic Procedures.   Not all ancient biological techniques should be considered forerunners of our present day somatotherapy. Trephining, a religious or magical punishment by some primitive societies to allow evil spirits to escape the possessed head of the patient, was also employed in other cultures to relieve aches and pains in the brain. The medications of lizard's blood, crocodile dung, and fly specs, prescribed by Egyptian physicians in 1500 B.C., were not disease cures, but magic potions.

Hippocrates, despite his role in specifying the brain as the locus of mental disorder, offered no biological treatment for the disorders he observed. Although the rationale for treating the underlying disease was established in the Renaissance, medical reasoning was naive. For example, fox lungs were used to treat consumption because the fox was a long-winded animal. Likewise, bear fat was prescribed as a cure for baldness. Paracelsus, in the sixteenth century, classified diseases according to the treatments that "cured" them, but universal remedies of the day included powdered Egyptian mummy, unicorn's horn, bezoar stones, and theriaca. Several potions contained more than 60 ingredients, all of which were worthless. Nevertheless, conferences were held for physicians in early times complaining of flagrant tampering with these so-called medications; failures in treatment were assumed to be the result of adulteration of "pharmaceutical" ingredients.

Not all early physicians were so naive. Many astute observers recognized the crudeness of therapies. Maimonides, in the twelfth century, said facetiously, "I call him a perfect physician who judges it better to abstain from treatment rather than prescribe one which might perturb the course of the malady." And Oliver Wendell Holmes, the physician-father of the eminent judge, said as recently as 1860 that nearly all the drugs then in use "should be thrown in the sea where it would be the better for mankind, and all the worse for the fishes." Despite commentaries such as these, patients were subjected to fright, blistering, chloroform, castration, cupping, bleeding, ducking, and twirling well into the twentieth century.

In the early 1900s, a new replacement for the straitjacket was introduced; it was referred to as *scientific hydrotherapy*. This method wrapped patients in a wet sheet pack, occasionally warm, more frequently ice-cold. They were snuggly constrained, but tied to a post if they resisted. Others were immersed in a hammock and placed in a continuously running bathtub with an open drain. A canvas sheet covered all but the patient's head; the patient was exposed to varying temperatures for periods of hours and sometimes days. This somewhat primitive procedure remained in common use in many psychiatric institutions well into the 1950s.

Somatic therapy for a disorder ostensibly required that a disease first be identified. After syphilis had been established as the cause for general paresis, **Julius Wagner-Jauregg (1857–1940),** operating more on a hunch than scientific logic, inoculated paretic patients with malaria in 1917 and successfully "cured" them of their disease. This rather reckless procedure spread rapidly and was recognized by the scientific community as the first true somatic treatment for an acknowledged mental disease. Fortunately, his effort to extend this treatment technique to other psychotic disorders failed, and he concluded correctly that the high fever induced by malarial action was specific to the paretic infection and was not a general cure-all for mental disorders. Nevertheless, von Jauregg received a Nobel Prize for this intervention, the first award for a somatic psychiatric treatment.

Electrically Based Treatments.   Electricity was used as a therapeutic instrument long before its physical properties were understood. Its first application can be traced to early Rome, where physician-priests placed live electric eels across the forehead of patients to relieve persistent headaches. Although employed by medical experimenters throughout the ensuing centuries, electricity did not attain official status as a treatment method until 1744, when the Royal Academy of Science in France initiated an annual report dealing with medical "electrotherapy." Among the early procedures recommended by the Academy were spark treatments; mild shocks transmitted by vibrators, globes, and percussive instruments; and electric baths.

"Electrical" magnetism, developed by Anton Mesmer, swept the French nation in the mid and latter part of the eighteenth century, giving rise to a brief period of pseudoscience, charlatanism, and rampant medical quackery. Although the invention of the electrical condenser in the late 1700s allowed physicians to transmit real currents to patients, it was Mesmer's intangible hypnotic magnetism that caught the eye of most psychopathologists of the day. As noted, some imaginative physicians explored the use of mild electric shocks in the 1700s for epilepsy and hysteria. And by the mid and late nineteenth century, numerous psychiatrists had experimented with electrical procedures, reporting allegedly good results with mental retardation, apathy, and depression. Needless to say, whatever benefits these treatments provided were likely to have been more the consequence of placebo suggestibility than anything else.

Ugo Cerletti (1877–1963), an Italian neurologist, along with **Lucio Bini (1908–1984),** a younger associate, experimented with electrically induced convulsions in animals for several years. Learning in 1935 of success on inducing convulsions when treating schizophrenics with the chemicals of camphor and Metrazol, they decided to investigate whether similar beneficial effects could be produced by electrical means. At no time did Cerletti and Bini believe that the electrical current per se was the essential therapeutic element. Rather, they considered electricity to be a potentially more efficient and less complicating method than Metrazol for inducing the alleged therapeutic benefits of convulsions. Hence, electroconvulsive therapy (ECT), one of the few genuine techniques to emerge from the long medical history of electrotherapy, developed not as a form of electrical treatment, but as an incidental method to induce therapeutic convulsions.

Prior to the advent of pharmacological agents in the mid-1950s, *electroconvulsive therapy* became the most widely used method of biological treatment in psychiatry. The technique of electrical convulsion, developed as early as 1900 by Leduc and Robinovitch with animals, was well known to Ugo Cerletti when he first used it with psychotic subjects in 1937. After his initial success, Cerletti formulated a theory for its effectiveness; it was quite different from the chemically induced rationale proposed by Ladislas Meduna in his use of metrazol (discussed in later paragraphs). Cerletti accepted the importance Meduna gave to the convulsive experience but did not share Meduna's notion that schizophrenia and epilepsy were intrinsically antagonistic disease entities. Meduna believed that epileptic seizures signified biophysical abnormalities that precluded the development of a schizophrenic psychosis. Alternatively, Cerletti proposed that the convulsion brought the patient close to death; this aroused extraordinary biological defenses in the form of a still unidentified substance that Cerletti termed *agonine,* which led to a generalized strengthening of the patient's adaptive capacities and, ultimately, to therapeutic recovery.

Another group of biological theories postulates that ECT destroys neural traces of recent memories to a greater extent than those of distant memories. This thesis, based on the dubious data of post-ECT retrograde amnesia, asserts that the residuals of recent experiences, attitudes, and emotions are more markedly disrupted by convulsive treatment than older and ostensibly healthier patterns. Consequently, the patient forgets current precipitants and reactions of the disorder and thereby returns to a premorbid level of adjustment.

Formulations espoused primarily by psychological theorists consider the ECT experience to be a form of expiation. According to this view, the patient is relieved of intense guilt feelings by being punished repeatedly with the electric shock. Since depressive patients often exhibit intense guilt feelings and are among those who profit most by ECT, the thesis possesses at least some measure of plausibility. Unfortunately, subconvulsive electrical procedures, which render the patient unconscious and are experienced phenomenologically as identical to ECT by the patient, do not produce equivalent therapeutic effects. Although guilt-ridden patients believe they are undergoing the punitive shock in the subconvulsive method, they fail to show the improvement evidenced in the convulsive form. No agreed-on theory of ECT action has been formulated; it remains essentially an empirical procedure, not a theoretically rational one.

Surgically Based Treatments.   *Trephining,* or chipping out a small segment of skull, may be viewed as a crude forerunner of modern-day psychosurgery. Some evidence, albeit tenuous, exists that Greek and Roman physician priests employed a procedure somewhat akin to trephining; by opening the skull, toxic humors that ostensibly caused irrational behaviors were discharged. Trephining was used in medieval times to purge the insane of demons; others used the technique to relieve head ailments or noxious poisons. These physicians made no effort to alter the brain itself, but merely perforated the cranium to "drain off" infectious matter. In the eighteenth century a young French surgeon, **Francois Quesnay (1694–1774),** introduced the idea that surgery of brain cancers should remove more than the surface lesion and enter the deeper substances of the brain tissue to extract all elements of the foreign body. He recorded that the brain itself was insensitive to the pain experience and that extraction of the entire disease area might frequently save a patient's life.

One of the many hypotheses advanced to explain the so-called successful effects of electrical therapy served to spur the further development of surgery for mental diseases. The notion that psychotic behavior might derive from abnormally fixed electrical arrangements in the brain was first proposed by **Herman Boerhaave (1668–1738)** in the early eighteenth century. He devised a special twirling cage in which patients were spun to rearrange problematic connections within the brain. This idea was approached surgically in 1888 when the Swiss psychiatrist, **Gottlieb Burckhardt (1836–1904),** removed portions of the brain cortex to rid "fixed" hallucinations in six psychotic patients. Burckhardt believed that their mental aberrations were the result of abnormally high intensities of neural activity in specific regions of the brain. He set out to relieve these neural abnormalities and their psychological correlates (e.g., impulsiveness and hallucinations) either by severing the connection between pathological and normal regions, or by excising tissue segments from the afflicted part. Although he reported success in reducing violent and hallucinatory behaviors in five cases, he abandoned his work because of adverse criticism from his medical colleagues.

Burckhardt's early studies were unknown to a group of neurosurgeons who reported the results of comparable work at the 1935 meeting of the Second International Neurological Congress in London. At these sessions, surgeons described the elimination of experimentally induced neuroses in chimpanzees following the surgical removal of large segments of their frontal lobes. At the same meetings, other researchers noted marked behavioral changes in their patients following the removal of frontal region tumors. Although these investigators stressed the serious loss of cognitive functions in their subjects, and a few conveyed fragmentary favorable consequences among patients, it revived the idea that surgical procedures might be employed to moderate pathological behaviors.

Egas Moniz (1874–1955), a Portuguese psychiatrist, reactivated this method of treatment in what he termed a *prefrontal leucotomy*. Moniz, who later won the Nobel Prize for his work, attended the 1935 Congress. He reported in later years that the ideas of the researchers at the Congress crystallized his thoughts of using a surgical procedure for psychotics that he had been mulling over for some time. Starting with the thesis that psychotics suffer from "abnormally fixed arrangements" in the brain, first formulated by Hermann Boerhaave, Moniz concluded that the destruction or isolation of these arrangements would free patients of their fixation and enable them to reorganize their attitudes and behaviors in a normal fashion.

Psychosurgery received a marked impetus in the United States in the early 1940s from the work of **Walter Freeman (1895–1972)** and *James Watts*, who reported striking results with procedures similar to those of Moniz and Lima. Patients who had for years been confined to institutions as uncooperative or utterly hopeless were reported to have become manageable, capable of working efficiently by themselves and even improved enough in some cases to take on jobs and assume a normal social life. The surgical procedure employed by Freeman and Watts, which they termed the *prefrontal lobotomy*, differed slightly from Moniz's. They refined Moniz's general statement that mental difficulties were pathologically fixed neural pathways, claiming that mental illness was a product of the patient's tendency to overelaborate, by means of the reflective processes of the frontal lobes, emotions generated in the thalamic region. In accord with this theoretical rationale, they assumed that severing the pathways between these centers would prevent patients from worrying about their emotional discomforts. Consequently, they could no longer expand minor distresses into pathological proportions. Watts severed his relationship with Freeman when the latter insisted that the procedure they developed could be employed comfortably by run-of-the-mill psychiatrists as a routine practice in their offices.

Numerous rationales had been proposed for the ostensible efficacy of surgical procedures. Most were variants of the theses formulated by Moniz and by Freeman and Watts; they were no less speculative and equally difficult to confirm or refute. Over 20,000 patients in the United States were subjected to the operation, which was quickly and appropriately abandoned when antipsychotic medications were introduced in the mid-1950s.

Chemically Based Treatments.   A number of simplistic procedures were prevalent through the nineteenth century and continued in many quarters on the Continent in the twentieth century. Leeches were commonly employed in the treatment of brain diseases to relieve "cerebral congestion." At times, these creatures were applied to the temples as a relief from epileptic seizures. Similarly, they were employed to counteract inflammations of the nerves such as those arising from amputated limbs. Some physicians of the day were also convinced that bleeding with leeches was often effective in restoring lost speech.

"Cupping," used as a milder form of drawing blood to the surface without explicit bleeding, was introduced initially in ancient Rome and Greece. In England, the art of cupping was well recognized as a procedure to be carried out by skillful surgeons; its popular use by the common man was condemned, however. Thomas Mapleson, the official cupper to the English king, wrote of cupping as especially useful for brain disorders, notably apoplexy, brain inflammation, hydrocephalus, insanity, and epilepsy. Cupping was often combined with bloodletting as a regular procedure to be carried out two or three times annually to assure good health and longevity.

Explorations to chemically modify mental illness took an intriguing turn centuries ago when laxatives were employed to purify patients with diarrhea, an endemic disorder among the asylum-based mentally ill. Next in this evolving chemical armamentarium was opium, or its extract morphine. In the mid-nineteenth century, diluted morphine was employed to overcome the anguish of patients whose behaviors were erratic or dangerous. Other alkaloids were employed to correct maniacal behaviors, either injected intravenously or administered in the form of oral cocktails. Chloral hydrate, a synthesized chemical, acquired a strong following and was used throughout Europe as a hypnotic for nonhospitalized anxious or depressed patients; many ordinary neurotics became addicts given its ready availability to the public. Similarly, various bromides became popular medications in the mid-nineteenth century, especially to control what was diagnosed as "hysterical epilepsy." By the turn of the twentieth century, numerous barbiturates were compounded and distributed under various commercial names, notably "Medinal" and "Veronal." Popular as well was phenobarbital, marketed under the name "Luminal"; the latter continues in use today. Noted earlier was the successful treatment of neurosyphilis with the antibacterial agent penicillin, but that impressive finding clearly related to a known infection and not to classical psychiatric disorders.

In the 1920s, **Ladislas Joseph von Meduna (1896–1964),** trained originally as a neuropathologist, joined the Budapest Institute for Brain Research associated with the University's Department of Psychiatry. He quickly became involved in autopsy findings of schizophrenic brains of patients who had died suddenly. His associates convinced him that the brains of patients suffering earlier with epilepsy were significantly different from those with schizophrenia. Curious about this difference, Meduna, in 1934, reported on a successful treatment of a schizophrenic by inducing convulsions with a camphor mixture, known in its synthetic form as *Metrazol.* His rationale for its presumed effectiveness was different from the one proposed by Sakel, to be discussed shortly. Meduna's thesis was derived from two observations noted frequently in the psychiatric literature: that epilepsy and schizophrenia rarely coexist, and that schizophrenic symptoms often disappear following spontaneous convulsions. This same observation had led some investigators to administer blood transfusions from epileptics to schizophrenics, without therapeutic success. Nevertheless, Meduna was convinced that these two disorders were antagonistic in their biochemistry. Subsequent research has entirely disproved Meduna's thesis. First, epilepsy and schizophrenia are neither related nor opposed. Second, clinical experience has shown convulsive treatment to be useful primarily in depressive disorders, only rarely in those diagnosed with schizophrenia.

Manfred Sakel (1900–1957) was born into a pious Jewish family, ostensibly descended from the great twelfth-century Maimonides. Finding the rampant anti-Semitism of Austria intimidating, he left for Berlin in 1925 to work at a sanitarium with patients suffering from morphine addiction. Noting that a cold turkey withdrawal with its attendant vomiting and diarrhea could be successfully managed by administering small doses of insulin, a hormone just discovered in 1922, Sakel learned from the literature that this new drug appeared to relieve diabetic patients of their attendant depression.

Insulin was first administered to mental patients to increase their weight and inhibit their excitement. Sakel took the step from this symptom-oriented approach to one based on "curing" the disease in the early 1930s. He observed that unintentional comas induced by excessive insulin benefited patients. By 1934, Sakel reported that over 70% of patients who experienced their first episode of schizophrenia had achieved a full remission of their symptoms. From this observation, Sakel was led to the extreme hypothesis that psychotic behavior resulted from an overproduction of adrenaline, which caused cerebral nerve cells to become hyperactive. This excessive adrenaline made the patient oversensitive to everyday stimulation; insulin was effective because it neutralized adrenaline and restored normal functioning. Sakel's hypothesis was a simple one and easy to test. It was soon established that psychotic patients do not overproduce adrenaline. Furthermore, adrenaline is increased, not decreased, during insulin coma. To many who followed his early work and speculations, Sakel's results were considered somewhat of a joke and many viewed him as a charlatan.

The search for biological therapies received a marked boost in 1952 when two different drugs were discovered accidentally to have beneficial effects in both anxious and psychotic patients. In France, Henri Laborit, Jean Delay, and Pierre Deniker reported on the effectiveness of a precursor of *chlorpromazine*, a chemical originally synthesized for hypertensive and surgical patients. Laborit, a pharmacist in the French Navy, had begun experimenting with what he was told was a new potentiater of anesthetics. Laborit noticed that this new medication had unanticipated desirable effects. For example, though patients became sleepy, they were markedly less anxious, clearly aware of what was going on around them, and sufficiently able to communicate their thoughts clearly. Even after major operations, patients never became excited, did not complain, and appeared genuinely to suffer less. He then approached Rhone-Poulenc, a pharmaceutical manufacturer, for a sample of a new phenothiazine they had been developing that might serve even better the anesthetic and calming functions he sought. Within a one-year period, this new drug, labeled 4560RP, subsequently termed *chlorpromazine*, was distributed to French psychiatrists as a possible calmative agent for their patients as well.

Jean Delay (1907–1991), then at the Ste. Anne Hospital, began to administer this new drug to his patients in early 1952. Delay, a professor of psychiatry at the Sorbonne, described the consequences of the drug in short order. At first, he prescribed this new medication to patients exhibiting a variety of mental disorders, including manic-depressive illness and schizophrenia. Surprisingly, not only did the drug appear to have powerful calming effects on his agitated psychotic patients, but it seemed to markedly diminish the problematic hallucinations and delusional thoughts among those diagnosed with schizophrenia. The drug did more, therefore, than merely tranquilize them; it had ameliorative effects on their psychotic symptoms. By mid-1953, Delay reported remarkable changes in all of Paris's mental hospitals, sharply reducing the use of straitjackets and wet packs. Within that very year, chlorpromazine was distributed throughout Europe and the Americas. The drug's impact was quickly recognized and evaluated experimentally by distinguished psychiatric researchers such as **Heinz Lehmann (1911–1999)** and **Nathan Kline (1916–1982)** in Canada and the United States, respectively. The results rapidly changed the course of psychiatric treatment. As Delay wrote, chlorpromazine acted like a "chemical lobotomy"; within a matter of a few weeks, scores of patients were reported as being symptom free, no longer troubled by hallucinations and delusions, and markedly diminished in their hostile and manic behaviors.

The era of psychopharmacology was strengthened when another drug, *reserpine*, a product of the Rauwolfia snakeroot that had been used since the 1920s by Indian physicians, was found to calm hyperactive and assaultive patients. Following the success of chlorpromazine, interest in reserpine quickly swept the psychiatric world. Although both possessed undeniable chemical effects, some of their initial success in treating psychotic patients stemmed from placebo action arising from the public's enthusiasm and the profession's high therapeutic expectations. When the early wave of excitement subsided, both agents, along with others since devised, took a less impressive, though still useful place in the physician's kit.

In what has been referred to as "cosmetic psychopharmacology," a bevy of new drugs rapidly spread throughout the psychiatric marketplace in the late 1950s. First among these so-called "wonder tranquilizers," designed to reduce anxiety among the mildly impaired, was meprobamate, known commercially as *Miltown* by its first pharmaceutical marketer, and as *Equanil* by another. Both drugs were prescribed and consumed at a rate greater than their manufacturers could produce them, leading to the development of a new drug produced by Swiss-based, Hoffmann-La Roche, under the name *Valium*. In short order, a sister "psychosedative drug," *Librium*, came to the market.

Despite the genuine benefits provided by these new medications, pharmaceutical companies became actively involved in borrowing and pilfering each others' chemical models and then promoting, not only new medications, but new diseases for which their ostensible medications might be marketed. In the 1970s, some drug companies sought to position their incidental chemical products as being ideal for previously nonexistent mental disorders; a notable example is panic disorder.

After some serendipitous stumbling, a series of tricyclic antidepressants (TCAs) were constituted, notably those marketed as *Elavil* and *Tofranil*. More substantive, however, were basic research results that led to what are now referred to as "selective serotonin reuptake inhibitors," (SSRIs). These drugs were designed primarily to counter depression; the most recognizable medications were marketed as *Prozac*, *Paxil*, and *Zoloft*. Also recently developed were a variety of so-called antipsychotics, such as *Clozaril*, *Risperdol*, and *Zyprexa* (Millon, 1999). Psychopharmacological medications have continued to be rapidly devised and promoted vigorously, not only to physicians and psychiatrists, but in recent years to the general public.

The genuine beneficial effects of these agents encouraged a new wave of biochemical research. The chemical action of many of these drugs was deciphered and the search for natural biochemical dysfunctions intensified. The growing expectation that a scientific rationale for somatotherapy might be found accounts in large measure for the increased strength of the neuroscientific tradition, now carried out primarily under the aegis of pharmaceutical companies rather than independent and academic neuroscientists. If the chief offense of psychological theorists is the grandiloquence of their thinking and the tenuous connection between their concepts and the empirical world, the converse may be said for pharmaceutically oriented researchers. Medical scientists propose theories of limited scope and anchor their concepts closely to the observational world. Although these features are commendable, these researchers rarely propose hypotheses that go beyond established facts and, thereby, often fail to generate new understanding.

Comments and Reflections

To repeat an earlier theme, psychology need not be committed to the view that mental disturbances are of biogenic origin in order to believe that neuroscientific therapies may be useful. Biological methods may prove efficacious in conditions in which the etiology is unequivocally psychogenic. For example, pharmacological anxiolytics such as Valium may ease psychological tension caused by the loss of a job or the death of a relative.

Further, it should be recognized that somatically oriented procedures are only one of several sets of tools that comprise the multitherapeutic armamentarium of an experienced and well-rounded therapist. They should not be employed to the exclusion of other therapeutic modalities and methods, as is too often the case. The practice of applying a single cherished treatment procedure, whether it be biological or psychological, to every form and variety of pathological condition is a sad commentary on the still-developing maturity of the profession. It is a sign of cognitive and behavioral rigidity unbefitting those who seek to aid others in achieving adaptive flexibility.

However, the availability of efficacious medications in recent decades has signaled a major advance in the transformation of somatic therapy from a hit-or-miss activity into one that has more than a marginally scientific groundwork. Whereas only four or five general groups of medications were available for treatment a decade or two ago, each of which had many side effects and diffuse main effects, newer drugs have few side effects and highly specific indications. In the past, the concurrent use of more than one class of medications often led to adverse effects: Today, a wise choice of several agents may often be employed for optimal efficacy. Neuroscientific treatments for all aspects of pathological emotion, thought, and behavior are not yet available. For example, no medications exist for the antisocial person's deficits of conscience, such as lying and stealing, but useful drugs that do exist may limit parallel symptoms, such as irritability and impulsivity.

It is troubling, further, that official diagnostic systems (e.g., the *DSM*) appear to be increasingly manipulated by pharmaceutical companies (Shorter, 1997). Occasionally, a new category of disorder (e.g., panic, social phobia) is created in the literature and introduced into the diagnostic nomenclature (as well as in magazine advertisements and TV commercials) when a chemical has been discovered to have some ostensible, ill-defined, or slightly beneficial effect on a facet of behavior or emotion. Psychiatric researchers have become so enmeshed in the pharmaceutical corporate culture as to lose some of their historic integrity as objective scientists. Owing to these and other problems of pharmacological management, it is usually wise to include one or another variant of psychotherapy to achieve optimal treatment outcomes. Medications may satisfactorily control specific symptoms, but the full range of most patients' mental and social difficulties requires a combination of several therapeutic interventions.

The search for biological causes that underlie mental illness has a long, often embarrassing, and fruitless history. Newly devised instruments and procedures, however, hold promise that whatever biological factors do exist will be identified in the near future. Because the search for biological causes has been largely unproductive thus far, somatotherapies have developed as a product of faulty logic or fortuitous accident. Rational therapies may be devised in the future as neurochemical processes associated with mental illness become better understood.

As recorded in Chapter 5, Thomas Szasz has questioned the wisdom of pursuing the "myth" of neuroanatomical defects and biochemical dysfunctions. He believes that the idea of tangible biological phenomena causing mental disorders is a myth—a false verbal analogy founded on an acceptance of the medical disease model. If Szasz's criticism is taken to mean that not all forms of mental illness can be attributed to biological causes, it is correct. But this criticism is largely an attack on a straw man, for few neuroscientists would take such an extreme position. Most neuroscientists do not deny the role of psychological factors; they merely state that certain types of mental illness can be attributed primarily to neurochemical impairments, and that even these are shaped to some extent by the unique environmental experiences they engender in the individual.

Another criticism of the medical disease model is that mental illness should be viewed as a problem of living (Adams, 1964); this view also seems irrelevant. Mental illness can be viewed as a "problem of living" *and* as a neurochemical dysfunction. These are merely different levels of analysis, not incompatible frames of reference. A deaf person may respond in a maladaptive fashion to social life because of his anatomical impairment. Which facet of his overall problem we focus on depends on the purposes of our investigation—we can stress either the person's interpersonal difficulties or the biophysical impairment. The failure to recognize that mental illness likewise can be approached from different angles and levels of analysis will lead only to fruitless controversies.

A further criticism leveled at those who have adopted the neuroscientific model is that they have overlooked the feature of the model that deals with the organism's adaptive response to impairment. This criticism perhaps is more justified than the others but may be unfair given the limited state of neuroscientific knowledge. Neuroscientists contend that they must first discover the existence of underlying defects before they can study how individuals adapt to them. Other theorists, however, feel that little will be gained from a detailed knowledge of biophysical impairments alone. According to them, mental illness is the adaptive reaction of the individual and should be the most significant part of any analyses of the person's psyche. The failure of certain neuroscientists to utilize both aspects of their interpretive model does not justify condemnation, however. A model is merely a tool, a heuristic device to stimulate clinical and theoretical ideas, as well as an orientation for empirical research. One may use one aspect of a model and overlook others. Certainly, accepting a scientific approach in toto does not assure its complete usefulness. Which aspect of the neuroscientific approach will prove most fruitful will be answered not by debate, but by research. In any event, the adaptation aspect of the neuroscientific model has not been intentionally overlooked; it can serve as the foundation for the more complex and varied theories and approaches discussed in the following chapters.

PART IV

PSYCHOANALYTIC STORIES

CHAPTER

7

Exposing and Decoding the Unconscious

The theory that unconscious psychic processes are the primary cause of mental disorders is relatively new in the history of psychiatry and psychology. An individual's chemistry and nervous system presumably function normally, according to this view, but the person's inner thoughts and feelings are nevertheless distorted and behaviors are maladaptive. Sigmund Freud effectively formulated the major theory espousing this position, known as *psychoanalysis*, at the turn of the twentieth century. Few other schools of mental functioning have had so pervasive an influence on the traditions of Western society.

Preceding the seminal contributions of Freud, however, speculative notions emerged, in part, as a reaction against the horrors of asylum care and the somatic dogmatism that characterized the mid-nineteenth century. Advances in philosophy and physics also disposed the public and the medical profession to accept novel scientific proposals. Hence, the therapeutic explorations of Franz Anton Mesmer and his followers brought forth the concept of *animal magnetism*, an ostensibly scientific thesis that could replace the metaphysical and animistic spiritualism of earlier times, a model of medical treatment that overcame hidden and troubling facets of the psyche. Well-grounded French psychiatrists of the day then investigated these speculative proposals for treating the mind. The great Jean Charcot, in turn, provided the basis for the ideas of Freud and Janet by focusing on the hidden and mysterious unconscious world, a concealed and impalpable yet profound source of power that influenced discernible and overt feelings, thoughts, and behaviors.

A review of the origin and development of Sigmund Freud's ideas is not only valuable in understanding the mind, but also offers an illuminating glimpse of the impact that one man can have on a profession. Chapters 7 and 8 trace the influence of the somewhat lessened, but once flourishing tradition of psychoanalysis.

The Psychoanalytic Story: I

Biologically oriented theories of the mind usually are limited in scope and are anchored closely to tangible and measurable data. In contrast, theories dealing with unconscious or intrapsychic processes are organized into complex conceptual systems that often lack a firm anchor to the empirical world. They rely heavily on inference and speculation and, as a result, are influenced in large measure by amorphous concepts that theorists use to guide their work. Thus, our study must begin with the conceptual orientation of psychoanalytic theorists.

As noted in the previous chapter, the neuroscientific disease model of mental functioning contains two assumptions about pathological symptoms. The first states that symptoms reflect the existence of a basic physiological dysfunction or an anatomical defect. The second assumption, generally overlooked by most medical theorists, states that symptoms also represent compensatory or defensive adaptations to the basic physical impairment. It is this second assumption that is emphasized in psychoanalysis.

Most psychoanalytic theorists substitute unconscious psychological factors for physical diseases in their model; they supplant biological dysfunctions or lesions with concepts of psychic trauma or conflict and supplant the notion of biological defenses and reactions with the concept of psychic adaptations and compensations. In the same manner as we possess biological stabilizers to correct upsetting physical defects, we possess adaptive psychological mechanisms that can moderate unconscious anxieties and conflicts. And just as defensive biological reactions occasionally prove more destructive than the original physical ailment, so, too, may psychological mechanisms prove more maladaptive than the original source of psychic difficulty. When an individual's psychic well-being is threatened, that person may invoke intricate defensive maneuvers to deny or distort awareness of the threat. The intensity and persistence of these defensive reactions will determine whether they prove to be adaptive or maladaptive.

Psychoanalytic theorists stress the importance of early life insecurities and the anxieties and conflicts they engender since these experiences may dispose individuals to a lifelong pattern of pathological adaptations. Childhood sources of distress establish deeply ingrained defensive systems that may lead individuals to react to new situations as if they were replicates of childhood occurrences. These anticipatory defenses often persist throughout life and may result in progressive and chronic maladaptations. Psychoanalytic theorists may differ in which experiences they view to be crucial to the production of distress and conflict, but all agree that mental illness arises as a result of efforts to relieve these internal discomforts and that these efforts often progress into more serious difficulties.

Consider the following example: If a young boy avoids his peers to forestall anticipated rejection, he will prevent himself from engaging in activities that might teach him how to enhance his acceptance by them. Furthermore, withdrawal will deprive him of certain future needs such as companionship, sexual gratification, and love. If, instead of withdrawal, he reacts to his peers with hostility and rage, he will evoke counteraggression and thereby intensify his rejection. As the circular pattern of maladaptation continues, he may become isolated from others entirely and develop highly idiosyncratic patterns of thought that will alienate him further from society. He may increasingly distance himself from reality, become preoccupied with his own thoughts and feelings, and be unable to avoid feelings of emptiness and confusion. A sense of futility may emerge and his defensive efforts may collapse, leading him to sink into a state of desolation, if not disorganization.

Three classes of experience have been stressed by analytic theorists as conducive to pathological mental development: (1) the extent to which the earliest and most basic needs of nurturance and protection are frustrated, (2) the conflicts with which children must deal as they develop, and (3) the general parental attitudes and familial settings in which children's experiences occur and are learned. For example:

1. When we think of how profoundly helpless infants are in meeting their own survival needs, we can appreciate their dependence on parental support and nourishment. The security children feel is tied directly to the manner and extent to which their parents supply their needs. A vital link will exist, therefore, between parental attitudes and behaviors, and children's security and comfort . This link is especially crucial during the earliest years of life when children are at the mercy of parental whims and desires. A child's persistent demand for nutrition may evoke parental balking, withdrawal, or harshness. Harsh weaning may be experienced as a sign of parental rejection, ridicule, and hostility and may undermine a

youngster's self-confidence and security. Children may handle their resultant anxieties by distorting or denying these experiences.

2. Difficulties also may arise because of children's undeveloped reasoning processes. They may be unable to grasp and separate conflicting attitudes conveyed by their parents. A child may have been admonished on several occasions to be kind and considerate to friends; at other times, the child may have been urged to be aggressive and competitive. Uncertain which circumstances call for one or the other of these incompatible responses, the child becomes confused and anxious. As a solution, the child may decide to become indifferent and disengage from others. Another child may have been taught that sexual feelings are sinful. As an adult, that individual may be unable to experience sexual satisfaction without feeling conflict and anxiety.

3. The manner and setting in which attitudes and feelings are taught often are more important than what is taught. If ridicule, intimidation, and punishment are employed to inculcate attitudes and behaviors, children will learn not only to submit to their parents' desires, but to fear and hate them. Any method of adverse training adds anxiety and conflict to what is learned. At the same time that children learn to behave, they will respond with maladaptive reactions such as anger, ambivalence, guilt, and fear.

The emphasis psychoanalytic theorists place on early childhood experience represents their contention that disorders of adulthood are a direct product of the continued and insidious operation of past events. To them, knowledge of the past provides information indispensable to understanding adult difficulties. To the question, "What is the basis of adult disorders?" they would answer: "the anxieties of childhood and the progressive sequence of defensive maneuvers that were devised to protect against a recurrence of these feelings."

Adult patterns of behavior, therefore, are not a function of random influences according to psychoanalysis, but arise from clear-cut antecedent causes. For the most part, these causes persist out of awareness; they are kept unconscious owing to their troublesome character, notably the stressful memories and emotions they contain and the primitive nature of the child's youthful defenses. Central also to the analytic viewpoint is the concept of psychic conflict. In this notion, behavior is considered to result from competing desires and their prohibitions, which only through compromise and defensive maneuver, are expressed overtly, often in disguised form. Further, all forms of behavior, emotion, or cognition likely serve multiple needs and goals—they are *overdetermined*. Behavioral expressions and conscious cognitions emerge as surface manifestations of several hidden forces that reside in the unconscious.

Psychoanalytic therapists focus on internal mediating processes and structures that ostensibly underlie and give rise to overt behavior. In contrast to cognitivists, however, their attention is directed to those mediating events that operate at the unconscious rather than at the conscious level. To them, overt behaviors and conscious reports are merely surface expressions of dynamically orchestrated, but deeply repressed emotions and associated defensive strategies, all framed in a distinctive symptomatological pattern. As these unconscious processes are essentially impervious to surface interventions, techniques of behavior modification are seen as palliative, and methods of cognitive reorientation are thought to resolve only those difficulties that are so trivial or painless as to be tolerated consciously. In their view, true therapy occurs only when these deeply ingrained elements of the unconscious are fully unearthed and analyzed. The task of psychoanalytic therapy, then, is to circumvent or pierce resistances that shield these insidious processes, bring them into consciousness, and rework them into more constructive forms.

Classical psychoanalytic therapists seek as their primary goal the total reconstruction of the individual's personality, not simply the removal of a symptom or the reframing of an attitude. Disentangling the underlying structure of personality pathology, forged of many interlocking elements that build into a network of pervasive strategies and mechanisms, is the object of their therapy. To their way of thinking, extinguishing an isolated behavior or redirecting a belief or assumption is too limited an aim. It addresses only a fraction of a formidable pathological system whose very foundations must be reworked. Wolberg (1967) illustrated this philosophy in the following analogy:

> A leaky roof can expeditiously be repaired with tar paper and asphalt shingles. This will help not only to keep the rain out, but also ultimately to dry out and to eliminate some of the water damage to the entire house. We have a different set of conditions if we undertake to tear down the structure and to rebuild the dwelling. We will not only have a water-tight roof, but we will have a better house. . . . If our object is merely to keep the rain out of the house, we will do better with the short-term repair focused on the roof, and not bother with the more hazardous, albeit ultimately more substantial reconstruction. (p. 137)

Thus, psychoanalysts accept the laborious task of rebuilding those functions and structures that compose the substance of the mental problem, not merely its facade.

Unfolding of Key Ideas

Before considering Sigmund Freud's influence on the development of psychoanalysis, we must consider those individuals whose work inspired his ideas. Not only did their work provide the foundation on which Freud based his psychoanalytic theory but, as a result of these influences, Freud set out to build a bridge between the neuroscientific and the psychoanalytic orientations. Freud anchored many of his concepts to the biological makeup of humans, a view that several of his followers rejected or overlooked. In fact, in several of his major publications Freud attempted to summarize the central features of his theoretical work by stressing two central ideas: the role and development of the biological instincts and the workings of unconscious processes.

Uncovering the Subliminal World

Awareness of the influence of unconscious processes in the human mind can be traced to the writings of numerous early Greek playwrights, as well as to the brilliant insights of writers such as Dante and Shakespeare. What Ellenberger (1970) has termed *dynamic psychiatry* had its formal beginnings with the eighteenth-century spa doctors whose attentions focused on the so-called minor nervous disorders, to the exorcist Johann Gassner, and to the physician Franz Mesmer in the mid-eighteenth century.

Whereas at this time, individuals with major psychiatric illnesses were housed in the brutal dungeons of European asylums, minor "nerve" ailments were treated primarily by general physicians and by medical practitioners who comforted patients in vacation-oriented health resorts—essentially mineral spring baths found throughout the Continent. The patients who used these spas had ill-defined and episodic ailments, largely what we today would call repetitive gastrointestinal discomforts, hypochondriasis, and variable expressions of hysteria. Health was ostensibly restored by exposure to the baths and to the powers of the waters. Wealthy patients often visited physicians of notable status and charisma, especially those in England and Scotland. Well-known at the time was **George Cheyne (1671–1742),** who wrote about the "English Malady" (patients suffering from bodily distempers). Society "nerve doctors" became popular all over the Continent; most treated women who were subject to the "vapors," a nebulous and periodically dormant force that presumably spread throughout the body and ultimately deranged the brain. Physicians of the time accredited the disorder primarily to women who led "comfortable but meaningless" lives.

Johann Joseph Gassner (1727–1779), an immensely popular healer in his day, was a talented purveyor of age-old techniques of exorcism. Despite the gradual decline of religious practices that depended on witchcraft, Gassner was an impressive exorcist, not only in relieving the ailments of church authorities, but of all subjects, both rich and poor, skeptics and believers alike. A simple priest of modest education, Gassner was born in Austria and, like Sigmund Freud, began his studies in a process of self-analysis, seeking to remedy his violent headaches and dizziness. Gassner discovered that primitive techniques of exorcism achieved considerable success in freeing him from his personal ailments.

The dramatic methods of **Franz Anton Mesmer (1734–1815),** an Austrian physician, brought to the fore the concept of the unconscious—inner thoughts and feelings beyond immediate awareness. Borrowing the notion espoused by Paracelsus of a physically based planetary magnetism, Mesmer believed that many forms of illness resulted from imbalances of universal magnetic fluids. These imbalances, he concluded, could be restored either by manipulating magnetic devices or by drawing on invisible magnetic forces that emanated from one person to another.

In 1773, Mesmer treated a patient with multiple symptoms. Employing a technique recommended by English physicians of the day, he placed a series of magnets on her body in the hope of forcing her symptoms out of her body. The patient reported that she felt that a mysterious running fluid was draining out of her and that her pains were being "swept away." Mesmer correctly concluded that the magnets could not alone produce these effects; he averred, however, that fluids that had accumulated in her person produced the magnetic streams within her body, and that he personally may have possessed the force that achieved these effects. He called this force "animal magnetism." It was this conclusion, made when Mesmer was 40 years old, that led to his mysterious method, his wide-ranging fame, and his ultimate notoriety.

An able historian of psychology, Morton Hunt, describes Mesmer's intriguing procedures as follows (1993):

> From an adjoining room comes the faint keening of music played on a glass harmonica; after a while the sound dies away, the door opens wider, and slowly and majestically there enters an awesome figure in a flowing, full-length purple robe, carrying a scepter like iron rod in one hand. It is the miracle-working Dr. Mesmer.
>
> The patients are transfixed and thrilled as Mesmer, stern and formidable with his square-jawed face, long slit of a mouth, and beetling eyebrows, stares intently at one man and commands, *"Dormez!"* The man's eyes close and his head sags onto his chest; the other patients gasp. Now Dr. Mesmer looks intently at a woman and slowly points the iron rod at her; she shudders and cries out that tingling sensations are running through her body. As Mesmer proceeds around the circle, the reactions of the patients grow stronger and stronger. Eventually some to them shriek, flail their arms about, and swoon; assistants carry them to an adjoining *chambre de crises*, where they are attended and soothed until they have recovered. (p. 98)

Owing to the increasing enthusiasm for scientific discoveries during the Enlightenment and the repugnance of the religio-exorcism methods of Gassner, Mesmer's procedures were judged initially to be powerful and scientifically grounded curative techniques. Mesmer articulated the rationale for his discovery of animal magnetism, as follows:

> In accordance with my ideas on this subject, I published at Vienna in 1766 a thesis on the influence of planets on the human body. According to the familiar principles of universal attraction, ascertained by observations which teach us how the planets mutually affect one another in their orbits, how the sun and moon cause and control the ocean tides on our globe and in the atmosphere, I asserted that those spheres also exert a direct action on all the parts that go to make up animate bodies, in particular on the nervous system, by an all-penetrating

fluid. I denoted this action by the intensification and the remission of the properties of matter and organic bodies, such as gravity, cohesion, elasticity, irritability, electricity. (1779/1948, p. 3)

Although Mesmer's fame spread quickly throughout the European world, scientists and physicians soon seriously questioned the assumption that unseen magnetic forces affected bodily function. Nevertheless, Mesmer established a successful therapeutic practice. Patients grasped iron rods protruding from a *baquet* (a tub containing "magnetic" chemicals), while Mesmer coaxed fluids into his patients by the wave of a magnetic wand. Despite the naïveté of his theory, Mesmer's patients responded in extraordinary ways, including the cure of several paralyses. Although Mesmer's success was short-lived and his mysterious methods were viewed by many as the work of a charlatan, his inadvertent introduction of what came to be seen as a *suggestion* cure led to the recognition that unseen psychological factors could influence mental symptoms.

Mesmer left Paris in 1785, having influenced numerous disciples with his startling new method of animal magnetism. Among his most notable followers were the three brothers De Puysegur, who were members of an illustrious family of French nobility. The oldest brother, Amand-Marie-Jacques de Chastenet, known as the **Marquis de Puysegur (1751–1825),** was a distinguished officer who divided his time between military life and overseeing large properties inherited from his ancestors. Puysegur proved to be an exceptionally successful mesmerist and soon developed techniques to cure numerous patients in a collective treatment format, usually held in the public square of small villages. As many as 20% of those following his magnetic procedures shed their symptoms within weeks.

What made Puysegur's work so significant was that he realized that Mesmer's thesis of an operative physical fluid was not necessary for his effects; the real agent of cure was the magnetizer's commanding will. Puysegur's fame spread swiftly, much to Mesmer's displeasure. Orthodox mesmerists clung to the belief that magnetic fluids were the source of the curative process; those who followed Puysegur concentrated on creating the induced somnambulistic state and the power of the mesmerist's suggestions.

Mesmer's ideas met with strong opposition in England until the mid-nineteenth century when a distinguished Scottish physician, **James Braid (1795–1860),** observed a demonstration in 1841 by the French magnetizer, La Fontaine. Although skeptical at first, Braid tried the experiment on his own, and quickly became convinced, as did Puysegur, that a powerful effect was present, not by activating mystical fluids, but by inducing artificial sleep. He employed a technique whereby patients concentrated on a fixed object or the movement of his hand until they fell under his spell. Braid made his method public in an 1843 book entitled *Neurhypnology: or the Rationale of Nervous Sleep, Considered in Relation with Animal Magnetism*. He wrote:

I have now entirely separated Hypnotism from Animal Magnetism. I considered it to be merely a simple, speedy, and certain mode of throwing the nervous system into a new condition, which may be rendered eminently available in the cure of certain disorders. (p. 112)

Not only did Braid refer to hypnosis as a method of inducing artificial sleep but, as with Puysegur, he stressed the importance of the hypnotist's persuasiveness in inducing his subject to do what he is commanded to do during this period of sleep. Equally important, he noted that subjects could be their own hypnotists, that is, engage in a form of *autosuggestion* or self-hypnosis.

Independent from Braid, an English surgeon, *John Elliotson,* reported on the use of "magnetic sleep" in performing painless operations on his patients. Similarly, in India, another English surgeon, *John Estaile,* reported a high degree of painless operative success with Hindu patients employing only mesmeric procedures.

By the late-nineteenth century, both magnetism and hypnotism had begun to fall into disrepute as therapeutic procedures. A modest physician working in a rural region near Nancy in France had heard of James Braid's work at a lecture and decided to explore its possibilities in his limited practice. Well-regarded in his local community, **Auguste Ambroise Liebault (1823–1904)** used a simple method of inducing sleep by suggesting to patients that they look into his eyes while he spoke to them in quiet tones. In the mid-1860s, Liebault published a small book, entitled *Du Sommeil et Des Etates Analogues* (*Sleep and Analogous States;* 1866), in which he stressed that the power of suggestion was central to successful hypnotism, as well as the primary vehicle of therapeutic efficacy.

Liebault was generally considered to be a simpleton, if not a quack, by his colleagues. Nevertheless, rumors of his therapeutic successes came to the attention of a well-regarded professor of medicine at the Nancy School of Medicine, **Hippolyte-Marie Bernheim (1840–1919)** a young, Jewish physician who had recently been appointed to this new medical institution. Bernheim had been treating a patient with sciatica for six years with minimal success. He referred this patient to Liebault, who used his methods of suggestive sleep and fully relieved the patient of the disorder within six-months. As a result, Bernheim decided to experiment with Liebault's radical hypnotic methods in his own clinic.

Jean Charcot's (1825–1893) signal importance in developing methods of clinical neurology was described in Chapter 6. By contrast, his role in fostering a psychoanalytically oriented psychiatry stems less from the intent or the originality of his work than from the incidental part he played in stimulating the ideas of others, notably Freud and Janet, to be discussed shortly. Charcot studied the diverse and confusing symptoms of hysteria at the Salpetriere hospital in Paris. Because of his neurological orientation, he viewed trances, memory losses, and bodily anesthesia to be diagnostically difficult cases of an underlying nervous system disease. It was not until his associates demonstrated that the symptoms of hysteria could be induced by hypnotic procedures that Charcot reconsidered his views of this puzzling ailment. His inability to differentiate between hypnotized and naturally produced paralyses, as well as the frequent migration or disappearance of symptoms and the anatomically impossible location of many of the paralyses, convinced him that hysteria could not be a product of a simple injury or local disease of the nervous system. Despite suggestive evidence to the contrary, Charcot could not abandon his biological perspective. To accommodate his observations, he proposed that hysteria resulted from a wide-ranging and congenital neurological deficiency and that hypnosis merely served as a precipitant that stirred and exposed the inborn defect.

Charcot presented his neurological thesis regarding hypnotism at the French Academy of Sciences in the early 1880s. Shortly thereafter, Bernheim brought to the world's attention Liebault's alternative interpretation concerning the role of suggestion in the hypnotic technique. First, Bernheim wrote that hypnosis could be employed with a variety of ailments; second, that its effects stemmed from the power of suggestion; and third, that all humans were susceptible to suggestion in varying degrees. Bernheim elaborated his views in his book on *Suggestive Therapeutics*, as follows (1900):

> We have shown that the phenomena which are present in the hypnotic and waking conditions, are not due to a magnetic fluid, to an emanation from one organism to another, but that the whole explanation lies in suggestion:—that is, in the influence exerted by an idea which has been suggested to and received by the mind. The most striking feature in a hypnotized subject is his automatism. The cataleptic condition is the result of suggestion. The subject retains the attitude in which he is placed, and continues the movements communicated to his limbs. He perceives the sensations impressed upon his mind. He believes that the visual images which are suggested, are realities, and refers them to the outer world.

Although Bernheim was an internist, and not a neurologist or psychiatrist, he vigorously disagreed with Charcot, maintaining that hysteria was primarily a state of heightened self-suggestion, and that hypnosis was an equivalent state induced by others. Moreover, Bernheim advanced the view that hysteria was essentially a psychogenic disorder, and applied the term *psycho-neurosis* for this and similar puzzling symptom syndromes. His belief that unconscious self-suggestion might underlie the symptoms of many mental disorders played a significant role in influencing Freud's thinking. In his psychoneurotic concept, Bernheim sought to parallel the medical tradition of seeking underlying biological causes for the disorder with a comparable notion of underlying psychological causes.

Josef Breuer (1842–1925) was born in Vienna where his father was a well-known teacher and author of Jewish thought. Typical of that era, Breuer adopted the views of modern or liberal Judaism and decided to follow a career in medicine, engaging in a series of experimental biological studies. An exceptionally talented researcher and teacher, he nevertheless declined the title of Extraordinary Professor at the University of Vienna, preferring to devote his primary efforts to his clinical practice. An unusually humanistic person and admirable clinician, he was a sought-after physician in Vienna and an exceptionally cultured man, a connoisseur of music, painting, and literature. Charac-

Josef Breuer

terized in the community by his extreme simplicity and personal warmth, he had many devoted friends and admirers, including the young Sigmund Freud, who served as his junior colleague in medical laboratories of the university.

Breuer helped Freud financially in his early years and, most importantly, whetted his curiosity about both hysteria and hypnosis in discussing a young patient, later to become famous under the pseudonym of Anna O. As described to Freud, the case of Anna O. was a classical example of hysteria that followed a period when the young woman had nursed her father through a major illness. Breuer employed a hypnotic technique to encourage his patient to voice her experiences and thoughts at the time her symptoms had emerged. The memories that Anna O. recalled under hypnosis were accompanied by intense outbursts of emotion that she was unable to vent at the time of her symptoms. Moreover, she became intensely attached to Breuer; uncomfortable with her affectionate feelings toward him, Breuer withdrew from the case.

Some years thereafter, Freud traveled to Paris and later to Nancy where he observed Charcot and later Bernheim using the methods that Breuer had developed. On his return from these travels in the latter 1880s, Breuer and Freud continued their discussions with a series of new cases employing hypnosis and the stirrings of emotional catharses. This work ultimately led to a series of papers and the publication of a major book, entitled *Studies on Hysteria* in 1895. In this text, Breuer and Freud formulated their idea that hysterical patients suffered from repressed memories of an emotionally traumatic event that were so distressing that the emotions they aroused could not be faced consciously when they occurred. Breuer and Freud contended that the technique for curing hysteria was to unblock the repressed and pent-up emotions in the unconscious.

Despite the originality and profundity of their observations and interpretations, Breuer was unable to deal with the intense emotional involvement of patients when pursuing the implications of their joint work. Soon thereafter, the friendship and close collaboration between Breuer and Freud began to cool. Breuer was unwilling to continue with Freud in probing the intimate emotional lives of their patients, and disagreed with the significance that Freud afforded to ostensibly traumatized sexual experiences and feelings.

Morton Prince (1854–1929), perhaps the first American explorer of the unconscious, had a strong early interest in philosophy, writing his first major work not long after graduating from Harvard. He received his MD from Harvard in 1879 and intended to follow the research studies of the great American neurologist *S. Weir Mitchell* (see Chapter 3). Prince traveled to France in the early 1890s and studied briefly with Charcot in Paris and with Bernheim in Nancy. Shortly after the turn of the century, he also became acquainted with the ideas of Janet and Freud, particularly their concepts of dissociation and the unconscious. In 1906, he founded the *Journal of Abnormal Psychology*, serving as its editor for many years. His studies of multiple personalities attracted great attention during that period from both psychiatrists and psychologists.

Morton Prince

Prince proposed a concept he termed *co-consciousness* to distinguish pathological thought processes in terms of their ostensible brain locales. He judged that losses of memory traceable to noncortical regions of the nervous system were genuinely unconscious, whereas those traceable to the cortex were readily recallable and thus referred to them as *co-conscious* instead of unconscious. Similarly, Prince introduced the concept of the *neurogram* to represent a system of intertwined neural connections where memories are stored that could be activated in varying degrees.

Pierre Janet's (1859–1947) career was an unusual one for a psychiatrist. He was born in Paris to a family that was well-known in Parisian society. Both his grandfather and great-grandfather operated a prosperous and well-respected bookstore. His father was an editor of legal papers and books. His father's brother was a distinguished philosopher and university professor. Little is known about Janet's mother, but it was said that she was a wise, sensitive, and warm person to whom Pierre was profoundly attached.

In his early career, Janet taught philosophy at a small college, the Lyceum in Chateau Roux, in the rural province of Berry, and later at the Lyceum in Le Havre, where he remained for over six years. He began his early clinical work at Le Havre mental hospital where he was assigned the task of examining all incoming hysterical women. Most of Janet's patients at Le Havre were young, fresh, and unsophisticated, unlike the usual inmates at the major institutions of France, such as Salpetriere, who had typically been examined numerous times by scores of physicians and students. By the mid-1880s, he turned to the highly esteemed studies of Jean Charcot, as well as other scholars, especially those engaged in what was known as psychical research.

Janet might have been considered the most original thinker of intrapsychic processes if he had not been overshadowed by the unusually courageous and innovative Freud. Janet evolved a theory in which neuroses resulted from an inability to integrate co-occurring psychic dynamics; this thesis foreshadowed and may have led Bleuler to his notion that dementia praecox (schizophrenia) was a split between thought and emotion. As did Freud, Janet observed that his patients could not tolerate painful experiences and undesirable impulses. In his concept of *dissociation*, Janet speculated that intolerable thoughts and feelings may take on an independent existence within the person and manifest themselves in amnesia, multiple personality, hysterical fits, and conversion paralyses. In this formulation, Janet recognized that different systems of thought could become pathologically separated, with one or another part lost to consciousness, strengthening the idea that unconscious processes may persist unmodified within the person.

Pierre Janet

In articulating his views of the hysterical phenomenon, Janet failed to recognize that the disorder may be traceable to psychic *conflict*, rather than to a neurological weakness, as Charcot had proposed earlier. In expressing his view of the source of the neurotic process, Janet wrote: "It is a special moral weakness consisting in the lack of power on the part of the feeble subject to gather, to condense, his psychological phenomenon and assimilate them to his personality" (1901, p. 502). Janet conceived these disorders as a weakness of the will and not the strength of conflicting unconscious forces, as Freud proposed.

Despite his capacity to describe his patients and their frequent exotic behaviors and complaints, Janet did not display Charcot's and Freud's relentless curiosity, nor their courage in exploring the outer reaches and deeper roots of their patients' psyche. He seemed overly cautious and circumspect, unable to plumb the depths of psychic conflict and sexual pathology. As some have characterized him, he was a "neat and well-stocked pantry, with everything in its proper place."

Proclaiming Freud

Sigmund Freud (1856–1939) was arguably the most influential psychologist and physician of the twentieth century. His reinterpretation of the observations first made by Charcot and Bernheim initiated an intellectual and cultural revolution of worldwide proportions. Like Copernicus, who forced humans to accept their peripheral place in the universe, and Darwin, who forced them to accept their nonunique and animalistic origins, Freud forced humans to recognize that their rational superiority over other animals was a delusion.

Freud and his theories have been extravagantly praised and intensely castigated. Venerated by some and condemned by others, Freud has been spoken of at times as one of history's greatest scientists, and at others as a fraudulent cult leader. Numerous historians refer to him as the greatest psychologist of all time, the profoundest of all human scientists. Others are convinced that the unconscious never existed, except in Freud's mind, and that his theories were baseless and aberrational. Some speak of him as a false prophet, others depict him as a courageous fighter for the truth. His most condemning detractors describe him as a neurotic egotist who propounded irrational and fantastic theories. More balanced historians aver that Freud's discoveries merely crystallized previously diffuse ideas of his many predecessors, such as those described in previous pages.

Personally and professionally, Freud was a man of divergent dispositions, a militant atheist and radical theorist, espousing liberated attitudes toward sexuality but, at the same time, politically conservative, usually somber and unsmil-

Sigmund Freud at 60

ing, impeccably dressed, invariably anxious about finances, clearly suffering in his midyears from assorted psychosomatic symptoms, and fearfully hesitant about modern contrivances. He always felt he was an outsider; "a godless Jew"; a free thinker, yet conservative in personal behavior, prissy, and formalistic. He did not leave his home city until forced to do so following the Nazi takeover of Austria.

Freud devoted his long and fruitful life to developing and elaborating his theories and techniques. Unlike his great German contemporary Kraepelin, who sought to classify broad groups of disorders with a common course and symptoms, Freud stressed the brightly etched inner memories, the feverish imaginations, and the unique attributes of each patient. And unlike Janet, his French contemporary, who viewed neuroses as the upshot of an underlying constitutional deficiency, Freud set out to trace the perplexing ambiguities, the afflicted emotional palette, the convoluted psychogenic origins, and the primitive passions that he perceived and explored as the unconscious source and undergirding force of each manifest disorder. It was not only the dense interplay of refracted realities in his findings that proved so epochal. The ever-dividing and sprawling new lines of his individualistic philosophy and his orientation toward the implausible and desultory character of life's realities, as well as the odds and ends of its rarefied energies, all served as a foundation for the twentieth-century understanding of humankind's complicated and intriguing nature.

Life Story.   Freud was born in the small industrial town of Freiberg in an Austrian province of Moravia in 1856. His father, Jacob, was a wool merchant who found life in the provinces to be restricted and anti-Semitic. The family immigrated to Vienna where Czech nationalism was on the rise and the small Jewish minority, primarily German speaking, was an easy target for resentments and hostilities. Nevertheless, Freud resided there for 80 years until Austria was overrun by the Nazis. These early experiences no doubt played a role in Freud's lifelong insecurities and his sense of being an oppressed outsider. Those who wrote about his early years characterized Freud as a man continuously tormented by doubts about his abilities, always in need of approval and emotional support, especially from strong and secure father figures on whom he could depend for kindness and intellectual assurances. Nevertheless, his biographers regarded him as a man distrustful of superficial amiability, who could not gloss over unpleasant facts and who insisted on merciless truth and unrelenting courage. He had no patience for cowardice or intellectual insincerity.

Freud was in the vanguard of Jews throughout Western Europe in the mid-nineteenth century. During this period, the number of Jewish lawyers, physicians, journalists, and academics grew rapidly. By 1890, over one-third of the students at the University of Vienna were of Jewish origin, and over half of the medical faculty were Jewish. Despite these opportunities for advancing by dint of diligence and capability, most Jews, like Freud, experienced an omnipresent environment of subtle hostility and anti-Semitism.

Much of Freud's insights can be traced to his self-analysis. During this process, he honestly identified his own foibles and psychic misadventures in a penetrating, expository, and revealing literary style, as noted by the biographer, Paul Roazen (1976):

> To say that his thinking was self-revelatory and an outgrowth of his self-understanding does not detract from what he achieved; that a theory originates from a subjective source need say nothing against its objective validity. Freud's strength as a psychologist lay in his use of self-knowledge in his writings; he wrote feelingly, for the sake of impersonal science, about some of his most intimate experiences. As with other great writers, it required a rich self to enable him to re-create a version of human experience out of his autobiography. Had he been any other man he would never have been able to make the discoveries that he did. (pp. 18–19)

Although Freud's ideas are often dated from his contact with Breuer and Charcot, the principles on which he constructed his theories were first shaped when he was a medical student under *Ernst Brucke* and elaborated when he was a research associate in Theodor Meynert's neuroanatomical laboratories. The physicalistic physiology formulated by Helmholtz (Chapter 6) and taught by Brucke and Meynert influenced both the language and the concepts Freud developed in his own psychodynamic theories. Brucke's lectures on physiology in the 1880s noted that the word *force* symbolizes real causes in science. Knowledge reduces them to two—attraction and repulsion. Freud, characterizing his own views in later writings, began to outline how forces assist and inhibit, combine with, and enter into compromises with one another.

Freud's consistently organized his concepts as energies interacting in a dynamic play of forces and counterforces. *Libido* was a life force struggling against *thanatos*, a death force; the *id* was an instinctual force regulated by the *ego*, a regulating and controlling force. Freud's entire metapsychology with its mental apparatus; regulating mechanisms; and dynamic, topographic, and economic modes of description, shows striking parallels with the tenets of his early neurological training. Although he abandoned his early efforts to find a physiological basis for mental processes, he was never fully emancipated from the Helmholtzian energy model.

Darwin's theories of evolution exerted a second and often unrecognized influence on Freud. Hughlings Jackson, the great English neurologist discussed in Chapter 6, extended Darwin's basic observations by proposing that the symptoms of brain disorders reflected the emergence of primitive brain functions that had been submerged during evolution. Freud, borrowing this notion, formulated the idea that emotional traumas lead to the loss of mature capacities and are followed by regression to more primitive childhood behavior. Jackson further espoused the view that organisms compensate for the loss of a biological function. He viewed these substitutive behaviors as clinically useful signs of an unobservable disease. Freud drew on this idea, first to formulate his concept of adaptive defense mechanisms, and second, to bolster his view that mechanisms are a sign of an unobservable or unconscious disturbance. Freud also adopted Jackson's view on the diagnostic value of dreams, although he later elaborated each of these ideas in an original and insightful manner.

As early as 1880, Josef Breuer, by then a well-known Viennese internist, observed that the recall of early traumatic experiences during hypnosis often resulted in therapeutic relief for hysterical patients. As recorded, Freud became further acquainted with the relationship between hypnosis and hysteria in 1885 when he was on a four-month fellowship studying diseases of the nervous system with Charcot in Paris. On returning to Vienna, Freud was convinced by Breuer, who had been a senior associate in Meynert's laboratory, that an emotional catharsis during hypnosis appeared to benefit the patient. To understand this unusual phenomenon better, Freud again returned to France, albeit briefly in 1889, to study with Bernheim.

After availing himself of Bernheim's psychological interpretations of hysteria, Freud returned to Vienna and modified the hypnotic-cathartic method Breuer espoused. After intensively treating several cases of hysteria by this technique, Freud and Breuer together reported their studies in an article in 1893, and more fully in their epochal book *Studies on Hysteria*, published in 1895. In contrast to Charcot and Janet's constitutionally oriented interpretations, which failed to explain the personal meaning of hysterical symptoms, Freud and Breuer's formulations specified a logical relationship between symptoms and the patient's psychological experiences. Their thesis was that painful thoughts and feelings were repressed into an unconscious force that exerted powerful pressures within the patient. This pressure expressed itself in symptoms that symbolically represented the repressed thoughts and feelings. Emotional catharsis, known as an *abreaction*, relieved the unconscious pressure and, in turn, eliminated the symptom that the pressure had created.

Despite the lonely years following Breuer's withdrawal, Freud remained fascinated by the obscure labyrinths of human thought and emotion he uncovered. His relentless search into these mysterious and hidden processes, notably ostensible sexual traumas in childhood, proved to be a perilous journey professionally. That he stumbled into blind alleys and held tenaciously to fruitless and obscure concepts does not diminish the courage and inventiveness of his efforts. With rare brilliance, he uncovered the inner world of humankind's psychological makeup.

Although the 1890s were an especially fruitful period in the creative ambitions that drove many of Freud's most seminal concepts, it was also the most troubled personal decade in his life. During this time, Freud recorded his painful depressions and discontents as he strove to study and analyze himself. He believed that the more he could learn about himself introspectively, the more he could understand the deepest elements of human nature, an understanding that he could then use in his treatment of patients. This self-knowledge (i.e., exploration of his own intense experiences and emotions) would serve as a foundation for communicating his ideas about the human psyche. As noted, he was not shy about exposing his inner turmoil. It is a gauge of his intellectual drive and capacities that he accomplished as much as he did, despite the painful difficulties of this period; it is especially impressive that he harnessed his neuroses into constructive directions for understanding pathology.

At the turn of the twentieth century, Freud began to gain a measure of recognition in Vienna. His followers, however, were a generation younger. Many struggled with their own neuroses, but Freud, much older and having overcome his own intense psychic troubles, remained austere and distant. His daily life was unusually orderly, filled with work and responsibilities.

His growing list of followers adhered to Freud's daily schedule, reporting on his writings and sayings with utmost devotion; few if any became as close to him as they wished. As one of his friends commented, though Freud was a good-hearted and considerate person in his private life, he was firm and relentless in presenting and defending his ideas.

Four seminal themes distinguished his contributions to what he formally termed *psychoanalysis*: (1) the structure and processes of the unconscious, that is, the hidden intrapsychic world; (2) the key role of early childhood experiences in shaping personality development; (3) the distinctive methodology he created for the psychological treatment of mental disorders; and (4) the recognition that the patient's character is central to understanding psychic symptomatology.

Focusing on Unconscious Processes.   Over Freud's 50-year career, he explored and constructed his theory of the intrapsychic world (unseen forces of the mind), which recognized the limits of conscious awareness in the face of unreason. According to Freud, humans possess hidden, yet fundamental and omnipresent biological instincts, the most important of which are the sexual or life-propelling energies known as the *libido*. These energies, together with his controversially posited survival-oriented aggressive energies, compose the *id*. A maturational sequence unfolds in which these libidinous energies shift in their primary locus from one organ or zone of the body to another; this sequence was referred to as the child's stages of *psychosexual development*. These unseen biological instincts must find outlets of expression. In attempting to gain these outlets, the child runs into conflict with reality limitations and societal prohibitions. Frustration or conflict associated with these biological drives leads to anxiety. The child learns techniques to relieve this anxiety and to gratify instinctual needs; these protective and need-gratifying techniques are referred to as the processes of the *ego*. Ego processes that develop in response to particularly intense infantile anxieties become *fixated* and may persist as lifelong *character disorders*. Experiences in later life that threaten to reactivate these repressed and unconscious anxieties lead to pathological symptoms; these symptoms represent, in symbolic form, both the repressed anxieties and the defensive techniques learned to control them.

Freud was not the first to uncover the role of unconscious processes. Perceptive thinkers have known it for ages. But Freud was the first to trace the complex manner in which unconscious motives and conflicts weave into intricate and distorted patterns of overt behavior. As he learned to unfold the strategies for self-protection and conflict resolution, such seemingly purposeless behavior as dreams, phobias, compulsions, and even everyday slips of the tongue took on meaning and clarity. Freud argued that the individual unconsciously adopted extreme defensive maneuvers to deny, falsify, or distort the pain of unfulfilled strivings and fears. He recognized that these unconscious processes occurred in normal and abnormal individuals alike. This realization helped close the gap between the study of normal behavior and mental illness.

Freud recognized that pathological behavior represents, in large measure, an adaptive strategy developed by patients in response to feelings of anxiety and threat. The bizarre and maladaptive behavior they display is not viewed as functionless or random, but as an intricate, albeit self-defeating, maneuver to relieve anguish, humiliation, and insecurity. In childhood, youngsters cope with anxiety by spontaneous strategies; they may be submissive, hostile, ambitious, avoidant, exploitive, or independent, shifting from one to the other at different times. Eventually, a dominant pattern of adaptive or maladaptive behavior emerges.

Emphasizing Childhood Experiences. Freud stressed the importance of early childhood experiences since these experiences dispose individuals to lifelong patterns of pathological adaptation. In what has been termed the *psychogenetic hypothesis,* early events establish deeply ingrained defensive systems that may lead individuals to react to new situations as if they were duplicates of what occurred in childhood. These anticipatory defensive styles persist throughout life and result in progressive maladaptations or character disorders. Subsequent patterns of behavior are not a function of random influences but arise from clear-cut antecedent causes. For the most part, these causes remain out of awareness, owing to their potentially troublesome character, notably the memories and impulses they contain and the primitive nature with which defenses and emotions are expressed. Central to the Freudian viewpoint is the concept of *psychic conflict.* In this notion, behavior results from competing desires and their prohibitions, which—through compromise and defensive maneuver—express themselves overtly. All forms of behavior, emotion, or cognition will, however, likely serve multiple needs and goals.

Freud's theory of infantile development was that children had immensely complicated emotional lives that were anchored deeply in sexual developmental stages. Freud did not work directly with children, nor was he particularly disposed to be involved with them, except for his youngest daughter, Anna. Most of his ideas were generated from retrospective reconstructions in the memories of his adult patients. He was also influenced by Jean Charcot's comments about the sexual origin of hysteria, a thought conveyed to Freud in private whispers. Freud referred to child development not only as a psychosexual progression, but as being "polymorphously perverse," often speaking of childhood sexuality and adult perversions as somewhat akin. He noted that the sexual activities of children were neglected in medicine, but those of perverts were not only recognized but judged with moral indignation, as well as with little understanding.

In his earliest writings, Freud reported that mental disorders resulted primarily from traumatic childhood experiences. His later work minimized the importance of trauma and stressed that indulgence or frustration during any of the crucial early stages of development was the major cause of disorders. The remnants of these early experiences became deeply embedded within the unconscious and not accessible to the modifying influence of changing circumstance. As the pressure of these memories persisted, individuals anticipated and recreated new experiences similar to those of their childhood. Freud specified different forms of mental illness depending on the intensity and the stage of sexual development when these difficulties arose. From this notion, he derived such disorders as the oral and anal character types.

Sexual excitation is obtained by stimulating sensitive surface areas of the body. According to Freud, the primary bodily region of maximal sexual excitation shifts as individuals mature. Freud termed this libidinal progression of erogenous zones the *psychosexual stages*. Thus, in the first year and a half of life, the lips and mouth are the primary locus of libidinal excitation; during this period sucking and eating behavior produce pleasure and gratification. The *oral* period is followed by a libidinous centering in the *anal* region, which lasts about a year; it is replaced, in turn, by an erogenous *phallic* stage in which the sensory region of the genitals serves as the basis of pleasure. These three *pregenital* stages are followed by an oedipal phase of familial conflict, partially resolved and followed, in turn, by a *latency* period, which lasts until puberty, following which the mature *genital* stage unfolds in preparation for normal adult sexuality.

During the latency period, children learn to accept the restrictions and prohibitions of their parents, establishing what Freud termed the *superego*. Henceforth, children restrain direct gratification of their instinctual impulses by their own volition. Conflicts arise now between children's ideals and their instinctual drives. If the prohibitions of the superego are too restrictive, individuals may be unable to gratify normal adult sexual needs when they emerge during the genital stage. Thus, parental teachings and religious admonishments have led numerous children to believe that it is immoral to engage in sex. This belief may be so deeply ingrained that they continue to experience tension and guilt even when sexual activities are fully sanctioned, as in marriage. To Freud, early instinctual frustrations and conflicts remain deeply anchored within the person. Although the anxieties and adaptive reactions they produce are unconscious, they persist as a mold that shapes the entire course of life. These frustrations and conflicts give rise to character formulations, identified by the developmental stage in which they occur, such as "oral characteristics," "anal characteristics," and so on.

Sigmund Freud at 75

Innovating Treatment.   In their joint studies of hysteria, published in 1895, Breuer and Freud concluded that the neurotic symptom represented a repressed painful emotion that had been converted into a symbolic bodily form. They observed that by discharging (abreaction) these repressed emotions during hypnotic sessions, the patient's hysterical symptom frequently and suddenly disappeared. This confirmed, for Freud at least, the notion that hysteria was "bound energy" stemming from a repressed emotion. The technique of its release was referred to as the *cathartic method*.

Freud explored alternative methods for achieving the cathartic effect since many of his patients were unreceptive to hypnosis. Hypnosis helped remove symptoms, but in the long run it failed to effect a cure. Thus, many patients who had been discharged as presumably cured returned months later, often with new symptoms. In these cases, Freud concluded that hypnotic procedures had failed to unearth the real cause of the patient's problem and judged hypnosis to be a superficial and inadequate tool for probing the deeper roots of the patient's difficulty. He soon discovered that he could obtain comparable results by having patients recall and ventilate emotions associated with their painful experiences. However, he encountered new complications because many patients seemed unable to bring their memories and feelings into consciousness. To overcome this obstacle, he explored a method he termed *free association*, that is, having patients relax on a couch and express orally any thoughts that crossed their minds, no matter how trivial or embarrassing they might be. This procedure appeared to circumvent many of the memory blocks that had precluded the recall of significant past events and the discharge of their associated emotions by face-to-face conversations. The procedure enabled patients to recall long-forgotten experiences that seemed to provide clues to their current difficulties. In effect, lost incidents of patients' pasts were brought to consciousness without generating any resistance, embarrassment, or discomfort. This technique brought the problematic aspects of the past into consciousness for both therapist and patient.

Freud's search for residuals of the past led him next to the discovery of dreams as the "royal road to the unconscious." As he viewed it, repressed fears and desires filtered through the patient's defenses at night in various symbolic disguises. By an introspective analysis of his own dreams, Freud was able to present a technique for deciphering the unconscious significance of typical symbols in his brilliant book, *The Interpretation of Dreams* (1900).

This book was a seminal contribution to the early stages of psychoanalysis. As he perceived his role, it was his task "to disturb the sleep of the world," an assertion that Freud voiced with revolutionary pride. He felt that he had discovered a "whole new country" and had reclaimed it from popular beliefs and ancient mysticism, judging this work a matter of good fortune that allowed him to be the Christopher Columbus of the mind. Central to his thinking was his position that dreams are an attempt at wish fulfillment, describing the images as a picture puzzle that intentionally distorts meanings. More specifically, he contrasted the *manifest* content with the *latent* content of dreams owing to the many conflicts dreams engender and represent. To him, dreams have a secret or latent meaning pertinent to the life experiences of the dreamer and no one else; dreams therefore are totally egotistic, but reflect psychic conflicts and resistances to self-knowledge. To expose the latent meaning of dreams required the use of his newly found free associative technique.

Freud's views on therapy followed logically from his theories: Replace the unconscious with the conscious, eliminate conflicts generated during the infantile stages of psychosexual development, and redress imbalances between id and superego by strengthening the resources of the ego. Maladaptive behaviors were eliminated by eliciting memories and developing insights into the past through the techniques of free association and dream analysis; the major goal was to eliminate patients' predisposition to reactivate their childhood difficulties in current life experiences. This was achieved by an analysis of the *transference phenomenon*, that is, the patients' tendency to act toward the therapist with the same attitudes and feelings that they developed in relation to their parents. Through this procedure, patients became aware of the roots and the persistence of their maladaptive behavior; with these insights, their egos could be reorganized into a more efficient and adaptive pattern. This phenomenon, which illuminated important aspects of the repressed unconscious, could be facilitated if therapists remained neutral; by assuming this passive role, therapists would force patients to attribute traits to them drawn from earlier relationships with parents or other significant childhood figures.

Characterizing Persons.   According to Freud, each stage of psychosexual development produces a distinctive set of anxieties and defenses resulting from instinct frustration and conflict. Symptoms and character traits arise from the persistence into adulthood of childhood anxieties and defenses. For example, a young boy may have experienced oral gratification only when he submitted to a rigid feeding schedule. Anxious lest he lose parental support and fearful of deviating from parental regulations, he may become a cautious and acquiescent person unable to take any step toward adult independence. This pattern of early oral frustration would dispose the individual to retreat or *regress* to this fixated pattern of early adaptation whenever he is faced with anxiety. As a freshman college student, therefore, he might develop a psychosomatic ailment if he failed to be accepted into a fraternity; faced with marital or vocational difficulties, he might turn to excessive eating or drinking as a regressive mode of oral gratification.

Freud's early disciples, notably Abraham and Reich, differentiated the oral period into two phases: the *oral-sucking* phase, in which food is accepted indiscriminately, followed by the *oral-biting* period, in which food is accepted selectively, occasionally rejected, and aggressively chewed. In their view, excessive gratifications, conflicts, or frustrations associated with each of these phases establish different patterns of adult personality. An overly indulgent sucking stage may lead to imperturbable optimism and naive self-assurance. An ungratified sucking period may lead to excessive dependency and gullibility; for example, deprived children may learn to accept anything to ensure that they will get something. Frustration experienced at the biting stage might lead to the development of aggressive oral tendencies such as sarcasm and verbal hostility in adulthood.

Difficulties associated with the anal period likewise lead to distinctive modes of adult personality. Toilet training usually occurs in the second or third year, a time when children can both control their sphincter muscles and comprehend the desires of their parents. For the first time in their lives, they have the power to actively and knowingly thwart their parents' demands; they have the option now of pleasing or foiling their desires. A battle of wits often arises. Depending on the outcome, children will adopt a pattern of attitudes toward authority that will have a far-reaching effect in shaping their adult traits. If a child's pleasure in defecation is punished and condemned, the child's assertive tendencies may be shattered, leading the child to become a compliant and conforming person, fearful of expressing independent thoughts. Conceivably, that child might accept parental condemnations of soiling behavior as right, and thereby attempt to show them how "worthy and clean" the child is. In time, the child may become not only compulsively clean and orderly, but may display harsh attitudes toward those who fail to behave in the same way. Thus, the child may seek to control others with rules and principles as severe and arbitrary as the child's parents. Other reactions to parental severity in toilet training are possible. To avoid toilet-training conflict, children may learn to hold back their feces; as a result, they may become retentive, parsimonious, and constricted individuals who forever procrastinate and always save for a rainy day. Harsh training procedures might also lead to rage and anger that could result in a withdrawal of parental demands. If successful, children may develop a lifelong pattern of self-assertion, disorderliness, and negativism.

Freud viewed conflicts during the phallic stage to be crucial to the development of mental illness. In the third and fourth year, libidinous energies center on the genitals, and are manifested in masturbation, sexual curiosity, and exhibitionism. At this time, children's attitudes toward their parents shift. Feelings toward the opposite sex become tinged with sexual desire; this is paralleled by jealousy and hostility toward the same-sex parent. A struggle ensues between children and the same-sex parent for the affection of the opposite-sex parent; Freud termed this the *Oedipus complex*. Freud considered his observation of this conflict to be a major discovery and viewed it as the nucleus of neurotic disorders. In the young boy, this conflict eventuates in an intense fear that his more powerful and jealous father will punish him for his lustful feelings. Anxieties of castration become so intense that he represses his incestuous desire for his mother and denies his hostile feelings toward his father.

Freud believed that if the entanglements of the Oedipal period were unresolved, children would forever handle sexual and aggressive impulses in a troubled manner. Sexuality might remain in conflict between seductive thoughts, on the one hand, and guilt and fear of punishment, on the other. Faulty identification with the same-sex parent could lead to a homosexual pattern. Aggressive impulses might persist, turning the individual into a bully and obstructionist.

At a later period in his exploration of personality, Freud speculated that character classification could be based on his threefold structural distinction of id, ego, and superego. Thus, in 1931, he sought to devise character types according to which intrapsychic structure was dominant. First, he proposed an *erotic* type, whose life is governed by the instinctual demands of the id.

The *narcissistic* type is so dominated by the ego that neither other persons nor the demands of id or superego can affect the individual; the *compulsive* type is regulated by the strictness of the superego such that it dominates all other functions. Lastly, Freud identified a series of mixed types in which two of the three characterological structures outweigh the third. Freud's compulsive character type has been well represented in the literature, but only in the past 30 years have his proposals for a narcissistic personality disorder gained attention (Millon, 1981, 1996).

Karl Abraham (1877–1925) was born in Bremen, Germany to a middle-class Jewish family with modest expectations for their son, despite his obvious intellectual talents. After a brief medical education with some psychiatric experiences, Abraham accepted an opportunity to work with Eugen Bleuler at the Burgholzli Asylum. Along with Carl Jung, he was among the first psychiatrists outside Vienna to become acquainted with Freud's early writings. Owing to his lifelong interest in philosophy and linguistics, Abraham brought a rich and diverse perspective to his interest in psychoanalytic work. Especially important were his contributions to the formation of character styles based on Freud's notions of psychosexual development.

A reserved and distinguished-looking man, Abraham possessed scrupulous scientific integrity and a kindly manner in both his personal and professional relationships. His students and colleagues spoke of him as realistically optimistic, a man with good, sober judgment and with a quiet and unswerving confidence in psychoanalysis. He was an incurable visionary of great maturity and exhibited a fine sense of humor and tireless kindness; he retained his buoyancy and modesty throughout his life. Apparently devoid of hateful emotions, he seemed blind to the envy and occasional hostility of those around him. A clinical observer and intense listener, he interpreted patient associations sparingly and only after giving much thought to the evidence. His greatest satisfaction appeared to be in summarizing clinical findings and then establishing connections between seemingly unrelated events.

Freud did not commend Abraham with the same enthusiasm that he gave to others in the early cliques that surrounded him. Abraham's Germanic style seemed overly formal and rigid, lacking the imaginative inventiveness and emotional spark that attracted Freud to many of his disciples. He did regret, however, not being able to draw on Abraham's communicative style of clarity, solidity, and precision. Despite his ostensible limitations, Abraham was fully devoted to psychoanalysis, perceiving much more quickly than his mentor the potentially destructive qualities that emerged in other early analytic adherents such as Adler, Jung, and Reich.

Evolving his formulation of psychosexual stage theory, Abraham gradually constructed an *oral character,* divided into two variants with appreciably different early experiences. One type was termed the *oral-sucking* or *oral-receptive* character, stemming from an early history of unusual gratification during nurturant feeding and weaning, the other he called *oral pessimists* or *oral-sadistic* characters, whose early experiences were notably frustrating. Abraham wrote of the oral-receptive character as follows:

> According to my experience we are here concerned with persons in whom the sucking was undisturbed and highly pleasurable. They have brought with them from this happy period a deeply rooted conviction that everything will always be well with them. They face life with an imperturbable optimism which often does in fact help them to achieve their aims. But we also meet with less favourable types of development. Some people are dominated by the belief that there will always be some kind person—a representative of the mother, of course—to care for them and to give them everything they need. This optimistic belief condemns them to inactivity . . . they make no kind of effort, and in some cases they even disdain to undertake a bread-winning occupation. (1924/1927a, pp. 399–400)

Following Freud's views, Abraham held closely to the relationship of psychosexuality and character development in all of his writings. Focusing on the division proposed in the oral and anal stages, Abraham identified the origins of jealousy and hostility in what he referred to as the oral-biting stage, which became a regression point for later relationships. Both negativistic and sadistic character disorders could be traced to frustrations consequent to experiences at the oral-biting and the anal-expulsive periods of libidinal development. To quote Abraham:

> The component instinct of sadism, as it exists in the infantile libido, also shows us two opposite pleasurable tendencies at work. One of these tendencies is to *destroy* the object (or the external world); the other is to *control* it. I shall later try to show in detail that the tendency to spare the object and to preserve it has grown out of the more primitive, destructive tendency by a process of repression. For the present I shall speak of this process quite in general; but I should like to say at once that psychoanalysis has given us a perfectly sound knowledge of these stages and the succeeding ones in the development of object-love. For the moment, we will confine our interest to that sadistic instinct which threatens the existence of its object. And we see that the removal or loss of an object can be regarded by the unconscious either as a sadistic process of destruction or as an anal one of expulsion. (1921/1927b, p. 428)

It was not until the writings of **Wilhelm Reich (1897–1957)** in 1933 that the concept of character appeared in its current and clearest psychoanalytic formulation. Reich asserted that the neurotic solution of psychosexual conflicts was accomplished by a pervasive restructuring of the individual's defensive style, a set of changes that ultimately crystallizes into what he spoke of as a "total formation" of character. In contrast to his forerunners, Reich claimed that the emergence of specific pathological symptoms was of secondary importance compared with the total character structuring that evolved as a consequence of these experiences. As Reich put it: "Our problem is not the content or the nature of this or that character trait" (1933/1949, p. 46). To him, the particular defensive modes acquired in dealing with early experience become stable, even ossified, or as he put it, "a character armor." As the consolidation process hardens, the response to earlier conflicts becomes "transformed into chronic attitudes, into chronic automatic modes of reaction" (p. 46).

Reich was born in a small village as the first child of then prosperous Jewish parents in a part of Galicia that belonged to the Austrian-Hungarian Empire. He claimed that his parents considered it important that he not speak the Yid-dish of his family's surrounding community, that they judged the Jewish language to be crude, and that its use would bring severe punishment. Following a series of family tragedies, Reich traveled to Vienna, a center of provocative ideas and revolutionary social movements, to begin his formal education. His original plan was to follow a career in law, but his early attraction to this profession quickly waned as he was drawn into the Social Democratic youth movement. Reich joined a number of seminars that in turn, drew him toward medicine and philosophy, as well as to the new psychoanalytic ideas. Reich eventually participated in a group of vigorous, young analysts who, though outspoken social activists, became significant contributors to this movement, notably Otto Fenichel and Erich Fromm

Wilhelm Reich

(discussed in Chapter 8). Prior to this, however, Reich attended Freud's open meetings for interested medical students and was enthralled with his concept of infantile sexuality. Some years later, Reich commented on his first contact with Freud at the seminar, noting that Freud spoke to him like an ordinary human being and that his piercingly intelligent eyes did not try to penetrate the listener's eyes, but simply looked into the world, "straight and honest."

From the very start of their relationship, Reich, one of Freud's younger and more talented disciples, was a behavior problem. He was a highly undisciplined but unusually original thinker, and many observers judged he would not likely remain fixed permanently within the master's psychoanalytic orbit. He displayed a persistent impatience with his craft; a wrenching if not incendiary temperament, and a bold, almost surrealistic attitude toward life. He was driven by numerous skewed notions of others, yet extraordinarily perceptive and insightful. He was far from being grounded, in contrast to his fellow characterologist, Karl Abraham.

Reich averred that it was not symptomatology per se that was central to the analytic enterprise but the patient's entire personality, what he referred to as *character analysis*. A Marxist in political orientation, he sought bridges between the individual focus of psychoanalysis and the social and economic focus of Marxist thought. He believed that many of the difficulties of adulthood were traceable to society's stifling of adolescent sexual impulses. In this thesis, he sought to expand on Freud's arguments favoring the "rights of the libido" by condemning the manner in which traditional societies constrain the natural and free flow of instinctual energies in youth. Reich proposed that society should be modified to prevent libidinal frustrations and oedipal conflicts, not merely analyze and cure them after they occur. In his view, what was necessary was the dissolution of the conventional middle-class family structure.

Reich made several contributions to the characterization of Freud's psycho-sexual stages, particularly the anal and phallic stages. Reich believed that so-called anal characters could be differentiated from one another depending on whether their conflict resolutions occurred during the anal-expulsive or the anal-retentive period. Characteristics emerging from the *anal-expulsive* period were primarily those of suspiciousness and megalomania, a tendency toward extreme conceit and ambitiousness, and a pattern of self-assertion, disorderliness, and negativism. Difficulties that emerge in the late anal, or *anal-retentive*, phase were associated with frugality, obstinacy, and orderliness. Anal-retentive characters exhibit parsimony and pedantry, a hairsplitting meticulousness, and a rigid devotion to societal rules and regulations.

In the phallic stage, either intense frustration or overindulgence of need for genital contact might produce conflict and defensive armoring. As a result, according to Reich, individuals would exhibit a striving for leadership, would need to stand out in a group, and would react poorly to even minor defeats. Reich depicted the traits of this *phallic narcissistic* character as vain, brash, arrogant, self-confident, vigorous, cold, reserved, and defensively aggressive. If these persons succeeded in gaining the attention of others, they often became delightful and spontaneous high achievers; conversely, if they were not greatly appreciated or sought after, they were inclined to downgrade themselves or to become exhibitionistic and provocative.

Reich's later life became especially controversial and troublesome, as he not only broke from mainstream psychoanalysis by the mid-1930s, but found himself rebuffed by former colleagues. Feeling personally beleaguered; he became a cult leader, increasingly discredited, paranoid, and scorned.

Associates spoke of an endless struggle against becoming too entangled with Reich's fierce and active ego, his strong mind, his troubled but acute psyche, his stubborn and awkward body. He constantly reached out and enveloped others with his feelings and ideas, even though most knew that he sought to satisfy his own needs and not theirs. Arrogant to a fault, he was perhaps the most tortured analyst of his time. Even early in his career, minidelusions and suspicions clouded his intelligence and persistence; in his later years, this paranoia completely possessed him. To the very end, he traded on his luminous and piercing mind with men, and on his personal misery and anguish with women, who continued to be awed by his tortured existence and intrigued by his feverish wildness.

Dissenting from Freud

Freud continually modified his theories. Although stubbornly adhering to his beliefs despite early professional isolation and ridicule, he had sufficient objectivity to modify them when convinced that they were invalid. But he jealously guarded theories that he felt were correct and tolerated few dissidents in his growing circle of disciples.

Paul Roazen (1976), recorded that Freud could not welcome others' original ideas, given his great need to continue the development of his own concepts. Despite his many eccentricities and personal pettiness, Freud perceived himself as "the" leader, upon whom others could build their ideas but not create their own. Freud's watchfulness and sensitivity made him highly resistant even to minor modifications of ideas that he himself had conceived initially. Despite his creative contributions, he was overly attuned to opinions that differed from his, frequently misinterpreting incidental criticisms as intense oppositional hostility. Although he put as bold a public face as he could on the rebellions that racked psychoanalysis, it was plain to all with whom he worked how pained he was by what he saw as desertions. On the other hand, he did not especially admire those who adhered too closely to his notions or clung dependently on his initial ideas. As he phrased this dissonance to a patient, "The goody-goodies are no good and the naughty-naughties go away." Of particular note, four imaginative thinkers and early disciples of Freud—Alfred Adler, Sandor Ferenczi, Carl Gustav Jung, and Otto Rank—became important theoretical dissidents.

Alfred Adler (1870–1937), founder of the school of Individual Psychology, became an outspoken critic of Freud's views on infantile sexuality in 1911, shortly before Jung. On the basis of his own clinical observations, Adler concluded that superiority and power strivings were more fundamental to pathology than was sexuality. Although many of his patients were not overtly assertive, he observed that their disorder enabled them to dominate others in devious and subtle ways. Phobias and hypochondriasis, for example, not only excused patients from disagreeable tasks, but allowed them to control and manipulate others. Adler hypothesized that these strivings for superiority were a consequence of the inevitable and universally experienced weakness and inferiority in early childhood. In this conception, Adler attempted to formulate a universal drive that would serve as an alternative to Freud's universal sexual strivings.

In his early years, as part of Freud's Wednesday evening circle, Adler was one of his most devoted followers, often criticizing papers by others that failed to take adequate recognition of "the professor's" central ideas. Adler joined Freud's circle in 1902, shortly after reading *Interpretation of Dreams*. He participated actively in discussions, wrote papers that furthered the cause of psychoanalysis, and prophesized and preached to others in the Viennese medical professions. As a result, Freud appointed him president of the Vienna Society in 1910. However, differences in personal style were evident in the early years. Whereas Freud was restrained and systematic, proud and imperious, Adler was highly sociable, emotionally expressive, a lover of music and art, and a born talker. In contrast to Freud, he paid little attention to writing in a meticulous and grammatically appropriate way. Moreover, as is evident in Adler's central thesis regarding compensation, he found it difficult to stand in the shadow of Freud's leadership and continually strove for his own place in the sun.

Differences between the two men were more than personal and stylistic. Freud found Adler to be overly interested in what he considered to be superficial concerns about the social difficulties of middle-class life as well as preoccupied with the ego instead of the id and with conscious instead of unconscious processes. Whereas Freud's theoretical concerns dealt with individual psychology, Adler was particularly sympathetic to those who suffered social injustices and considered it a major ambition for psychoanalysis to promote human equality and dignity. Long before his mentor, Adler was attuned to the social origins of human destructiveness such as those connected to ethnicity and race.

Alfred Adler

According to Adler, basic feelings of inferiority led to persistent and unconscious compensatory efforts. These were manifested in pathological struggles for power and triumph if the individual experienced unusual deficiencies or weaknesses in childhood. Among healthier personalities, compensation accounted for strivings at self-improvement and interests in social change and welfare. These compensatory strivings, which all individuals acquired as a reaction to the restrictions imposed by their more powerful parents, led to a general pattern of behavior that Adler called the *style of life*.

Adler's theories may have reflected his own experience. He was born in Penzing, a suburb of Vienna, in 1870. Owing to a severe case of rickets, he was unable to walk until the age of four. Soon thereafter, he developed pneumonia. Both physical difficulties were compounded further by several street accidents that might have led him to adopt a life of infirmity. Despite these ailments, Adler resolved to become a physician, spending much of his youth pursuing both botanical and biological interests, as well as reading voraciously the literature of classical and philosophical writers. That he developed his theory based on efforts to compensate for "organ inferiorities" should not have been surprising. Following his medical degree in 1895, he immersed himself in the intellectual and cultural climate of Vienna and soon became a vigorous exponent of social causes, especially with regard to the sorrowful conditions under which underprivileged laborers worked.

The cardinal concept in Adler's theory is *overcompensation,* an inborn tendency to counteract deficiencies or inadequacies through reparative strivings. According to Adler, all humans suffer an inevitable inferiority in childhood and, therefore, all individuals strive to better themselves in later life. Distinctive patterns of striving (i.e., style of life) derive from unusual shortcomings experienced in childhood. Although all individuals share the common inferiority of childhood, only those experiencing severe inferiorities become disordered.

Compensation for inferiority took the form of *fictive goals,* that is, unrealistic aspirations by which individuals could redress their shortcomings. According to Adler, these aspirations are displayed either in an overt striving for superiority, such as overly aggressive behavior and pomposity, or in a withdrawal from normal social activity, as in homosexuality and schizophrenia. Compensating strategies, which Adler termed *neurotic safeguards,* help individuals keep their fictive goals intact by various protective maneuvers. For example, by assuming the role of a hippie, a basically insecure, obese youngster asserts his superiority to "all the jocks," and displays his physical unattractiveness as a badge of his independence of "peer values."

The individual's *style of life* represents distinctive patterns of striving that derive from shortcomings and the adaptive compensations employed to cope with them. The following quote illustrates Adler's synthesis of lifestyles:

> We find individuals whose approach to reality shows, from early childhood through their entire lives, a more or less dominant or ruling attitude which appears in all their relationships. A second type, surely the most frequent, expects everything from others and leans on others, and might be called the getting type. A third type is inclined to feel successful by avoiding the solution of problems. Instead of struggling with a problem, a person of this type merely tries to side-step it, thereby trying to avoid defeat. The fourth type struggles, in a greater or lesser degree, to solve these problems in a way useful to others.
>
> The first three types mentioned above—the ruling type, the getting type, and the avoiding type—are not apt, and are not prepared, to solve the problems of life. These problems are always social problems, and individuals of these three types lack the ability to cooperate and to contribute. (1929, p. 102)

Adler reoriented characterology toward the social aspects of personal functioning. What ultimately became of his social orientation took its clearest form in the theoretical writings of Karen Horney and Erich Fromm, discussed in Chapter 8.

Sandor Ferenczi (1873–1933) was born in a small city not far from Budapest, Hungary, where his father had migrated and opened a bookstore and lending library, the largest in the area. His father also established an artist's bureau where visiting lecturers and guest artists spoke and exhibited their work. Ferenczi was one of 11 children in a Jewish family notable for its warmth and closeness. On completing his early studies at the Gymnasium, Ferenczi left for Vienna to practice medicine, with a special interest in psychic phenomena and hypnosis. In 1900, following service as a military physician, he opened an office for the practice of neurology and psychiatry. By 1907, he had published some 30 clinical papers in both Hungarian and German medical journals. Owing to his deep interest in neurotic disorders, he wrote to Freud and visited him for the first time in 1908, where he soon underwent a personal analysis with the master. A close and long-term relationship developed between the two psychoanalysts that lasted almost to the end of Ferenczi's life.

Until the few years before he died, Ferenczi was considered by his colleagues to have been the most sensitive and warm of the clinicians comprising the early psychoanalytic group. Always eager to help, expressive and poetical, Ferenczi was charming and imaginative, but invariably modest. Despite proposing numerous bold ideas, he voiced little confidence in them himself.

At the Budapest Medical Association in 1908, Ferenczi delivered an inspiring and dramatic series of talks entitled "Popular Lectures on Psychoanalysis" that quickly endeared him to Freud. A quote from these lectures on the analytic conception of psychoneuroses follows:

> In early childhood (each person) must learn to renounce a great part of his natural impulses; when he is grown up, culture requires of him that he should even regard self-sacrifice for the community as something beautiful, good, and worth striving for. The greatest sacrifice the individual has to make in the interests of society, however, is in regard to his sexual desires . . . (1908, as quoted in Ferenczi, 1926/1980, p. 19)

Freud asked Ferenczi to accompany him to Clark University in the United States in 1909. Ferenczi was recognized as an unusually talented therapist; his clinical publications and lectures also drew attention far and wide. His unusual incisive analysis into psychopathological phenomena and the quickness with which he could appraise and deal with these difficulties made him an outstanding contributor to analytic theory and its techniques. His keen observation of slight variations in patient behaviors and voice modulations provided him with a marvelous source of unconscious processes that few other therapists could emulate.

In 1920, Ferenczi stressed what many analysts referred to as a striking new departure in therapeutic technique later known as *active therapy*. Ferenczi was careful to state that his active procedure was based on Freud's own statements concerning the value of this method as a means of stirring patients to deal with their repressed feelings.

Although Ferenczi's proposals for active therapy originally aroused enthusiasm, when he published further reports concerning his active innovations, many analysts viewed his contributions as too radical and of questionable value.

Freud also came to view Ferenczi's approach as too avant-garde and deviant despite his extensive favorable contributions and friendship. Not long before Ferenczi's death, many in the analytic movement raised questions concerning Ferenczi's mental status, stating that his later writings showed "unmistakable signs of mental regression," especially in his attitude toward psychoanalytic theory and its methods.

Although chosen by Freud as his heir apparent, **Carl Gustav Jung (1875–1961)** did not agree with Freud's emphasis on the sexual nature of development and motivation and established his own system, called *Analytic Psychology* in 1913. Some years later, Jung commented on his break with Freud:

> It is a somewhat curious and remarkable fact in the history of science—although it pertains to the peculiar character of the psychoanalytical movement—that Freud, the creator of psychoanalysis (in the narrower sense), insists upon identifying the analytical method with his sexual theory, and thus has placed upon it the stamp of dogmatism. The "scientific" infallibility of this explanation caused me, in due time, to break with Freud, for dogma and science are to me incommensurable quantities which mutually interfere with one another through their confusion. Dogma as a factor in religion has inestimable value just because of its absolute standpoint. But when science thinks that it can do without criticism and skepticism, it degenerates into a sickly hot-house plant. (1920, p. 112)

Jung expanded the notion of libido, Freud's concept for the basic sexual energies, to include all life-propelling forces. The concept of racial memories, known as the collective unconscious, was proposed to suggest that instinctual forces were more than seething animalistic impulses; according to Jung, these forces contained social dispositions as well. These primitive dispositions were often expressed in folklore and mystical beliefs. When no acceptable outlet could be found for them in societal life, they took the form of symptoms such as phobias, delusions, and compulsions. Jung's belief in unconscious social dispositions led also to his formulation of two basic personality types, the *extravert* and the *introvert*. Despite these and other original contributions, Jung's views had minimal impact on mainstream psychodynamic theory and practice.

Jung was born in 1875 in the Swiss village of Kesswil, where his paternal grandfather and great-grandfather were physicians of considerable renown. His father, a parson of the Reform Church, had married the daughter of his professor of Hebrew literature in 1870. An only child until he was nine, Jung was tutored at home by his father. Thus, he was highly advanced and far beyond his contemporaries when he entered the Basel Gymnasium. An avid reader of Oriental studies and spiritualism, he showed a particular interest in philosophy prior to his turn toward the natural sciences and medicine.

Chancing on Krafft-Ebing's textbook of psychiatry, he decided to specialize in that field and began his residency in 1900 with Eugen Bleuler at the Burgholzli Asylum in Zurich. Still interested in spiritualistic séances, his medical dissertation addressed the psychology of occult phenomena, including several references to Freud's work and to an inventive methodology of word association. In 1907, he presented his significant ideas in a major book, entitled *The Psychology of Dementia Praecox*, where he sought to integrate the concepts of Bleuler, Kraepelin, Janet, and Freud. A few years earlier, he had initiated a correspondence with Freud and subsequently traveled to Vienna to speak with him at length.

Freud was delighted with Jung's interest in 1906 when he wrote to him during his theoretical and clinical work at the Burgholzli Clinic in Zurich, Switzerland. With his earlier writings, Jung had already achieved a respectable standing in the European psychiatric community, especially consequent to his dissertation on occult experiences and his word-association technique for detecting "repressed emotional complexes." Bleuler accompanied Jung to the First Congress of Psychoanalysis in Salzburg in 1908. Impressed by what he had heard there, Jung decided to resign from the Swiss clinic and devote himself entirely to Freud's psychoanalytic movement. Especially significant to Freud

Carl Gustav Jung

was Jung's book, *The Psychology of Dementia Praecox* (1907), in which he attempted to explicate the disorder in terms of Freud's neurosis theory. Jung also shared an interest in the occult with him, although Freud hesitated to voice his thoughts on the matter because he feared that a charge of mysticism would be applied to his other, more substantive theoretical ideas. Nevertheless, Freud was pleased that Jung continued these inquiries, notably his effort to explore the utility, not only of graphology and religious mysticism, but also of astrology and alchemy.

Although Jung was not a great supporter of established religions, he was respectful of religious philosophies, formally studying comparative world religions in later years. By contrast, Freud perceived religion to be a "pack of lies put over on a stupid populace." Emphasis on even the few attributes of religion was distasteful to Freud; he ultimately wrote that religion reflected mankind's collective neurosis.

Jung's lectures at Fordham University in New York in 1912 led to an eventual break with Freud. As Roazen (1976) recorded, it would have been hard to believe that Jung could have expected that Freud, especially after his recent conflict with Adler, would accept the ideas that Jung proposed publicly. Jung took strong exception to the notion of incest fantasy that marked one of Freud's major theories. Jung also believed that Freud's sexual focus on the libido would undermine what was valuable in the libido theory. In his view, obtaining pleasure was by no means identical with sexuality. Further, Jung found it therapeutically unwise to permit patients to dwell on long-past experiences, asserting that this focus cleverly drew the therapist's attentions away from the reality of current difficulties. He stated unequivocally that "the cause of the pathogenic complex lies mainly in the present moment." As others of more recent vintage have claimed, Jung was convinced that patients often invent childhood sexual traumas to escape from contemporary life difficulties.

The Analytic Congress in September 1913 in Munich not only resulted in a public confrontation but proved to be the last meeting between the two men. Freud had already expressed his discontent and feelings to others that Jung had betrayed him. Commenting on Jung's trip to New York in late 1912, he wrote to Karl Abraham that Jung was doing more for himself than for psychoanalysis, and that he, Freud, had "greatly retreated from him and had no more friendly thoughts for him." Further, he wrote that Jung's theories were bad and, moreover, they could not compensate for what he referred to as Jung's disagreeable character, especially following in Adler's wake. In a later letter, he wrote to Abraham, "Jung is crazy, but I have no desire for a separation and should like to let him wreck himself first."

Jung's break with Freud arose largely as a function of two fundamental disagreements. First, Jung asserted that libido, the life energies, consisted of several instinctual dispositions, only one of which could be called sexual. Second, he argued that instincts did not necessarily upset the individual's psychic functioning; rather, instincts could be constructive, facilitating effective and healthy growth. In both these views, he anticipated the ideas of the theorists discussed in Chapter 8. Jung believed that the instincts of human beings were oriented or goal-directed to specific objects or activities in the social environment. Thus, he proposed that the instincts possessed not only adaptive potentials, but particular goals that could fulfill these potentials (e.g., infants not only possessed ego instincts that enabled them to recognize and interact with their caretakers, but actively sought to find and relate to these need-fulfilling objects).

Jung posited that the source of a person's goal-directed energies was found in what he referred to as the *collective unconscious*, a concept representing a hypothetical pattern of inborn predispositions bequeathed by the individual's ancestral past. He wrote of this ancestral repository as follows:

> This psychic life is the mind of our ancient ancestors, the way in which they thought and felt, the way in which they conceived of life and the world, of gods and human beings. The existence of these historical layers is presumably the source of the belief in reincarnation and in memories of past lives. As the body is a sort of museum of its phylogenetic history, so is the mind. There is no reason for believing that the psyche, with its peculiar structure, is the only thing in the world that has no history beyond its individual manifestation. (1939, p. 24)

Jung viewed these racial memories as a template that shaped the direction in which the individual's general capacities would be best fulfilled; he termed these memories *archetypes*. Infants ostensibly inherited a preformed image of "mother" based on an accumulated racial history of maternal experiences; this primordial image disposed them to relate to their actual mothers in a manner similar to their inherited archetype. In Jung's opinion, archetypal images not only shaped the perception of experience, but drove individuals to find experiences consonant with their heritage. Thus, Jung spoke of the unconscious as possessing a forward or actualizing tendency.

Jung viewed failure to find adequate expression for these archetypal dispositions to be the crux of mental illness. In this formulation, Jung not only rejected Freud's position that unconscious forces inevitably conflict with reality but offered an entirely opposite hypothesis in which unconscious forces were necessary for healthy functioning. By denying, disavowing, or ignoring the unconscious, individuals would invite disorder. If these archetypal tendencies were unexpressed, they would intrude on the normal processes of perception and behavior, twisting and distorting them into pathological forms such as phobias, delusions, and hallucinations.

Many of Jung's contributions were clouded in a religious and occult mystique. In addition, Jung's notion of racial inheritance, with its implication of inborn group differences, was repellent to the humanist orientation of many in contemporary psychiatry and psychology. In fact, Jung came to be regarded as a particularly odious figure to Freud's followers in Europe and the United States, largely because Freud had such high hopes for him in earlier years. Further, Jung's contact with the Nazis during World War II intensified his disapproval among Freud's acolytes. Not only did many professionals dismiss Jungian notions, but when they discussed his contributions at all, many uniformly detested all that he represented. To this day, however, others still value and adhere to many of Jung's creative ideas.

Despite areas of dissent, subsequent theorists with little recognition of their Jungian origins have borrowed ideas that Jung first formulated (e.g., inborn constructive forces that are actualized in social relationships). Moreover, Freud's olympian role completely overshadowed the less significant, but nonetheless fertile contributions Jung made.

Otto Rank (1884–1939) had exceptional intelligence, with a strong inclination toward creative thinking and activity. Always curious about the character and qualities of the intellectual leaders of his time and the past, Rank—from adolescence onward—dreamed of being a potentially great man. In his search for an ideal father figure, Rank became deeply interested in the work of creative artists and their psychological makeup.

Like Jung, Rank had a special interest in the occult and in mythology, a theme he shared with Freud that led to jealousy among their fellow intimates in the Wednesday group. Although Freud was extremely generous with all his disciples in those early formative years, Rank was unquestionably his personal favorite. His deep affection for Rank and the increasing separation between them in the 1920s was perhaps the most difficult of all of Freud's losses among his disciples. Even as late as the mid-1930s, long after Rank had left Vienna to work and create his own group of followers in the United States, Freud wrote about his former acolyte that Rank's effort to abbreviate the length of time of psychoanalysis:

> . . . was bold and ingenious, but it did not stand the test of critical examination. Moreover, it was a child of its time, conceived under the stress of the contrast between the Post War misery of Europe and the prosperity of America, and designed to adapt the tempo of analytic therapy to the haste of American life. (1937, p. 216)

Born in Vienna in 1884, his given name was Otto Rosenfeld, but at the age of 17 he broke his attachment to his family of origin and assumed the surname of Rank. As he wrote in his diaries, life in his childhood family was not only unpleasant but frequently painful owing to a violent and irresponsible alcoholic father. His mother, a kindly and gentle woman, was forced to assume full responsibility for her three children. In his diary, he wrote that the children no longer greeted their father in their rare period of calm communication, fearing that an extended conversation would inevitably result in shouts and screams owing to the family's pervasive undercurrent of rage. Financially limited, Rank contemplated becoming a mechanic and turned to the theater as an outlet for his emotional expression and fantasy. Nevertheless, he experienced extended periods of depression with periodic thoughts of suicide; fortunately, these alternated with a desire for a joyous and creative life.

Receiving his PhD degree in 1912, Rank became the first lay analyst permitted to treat clinical patients. Together with Hanns Sachs (discussed in Chapter 8), he started the journal, *Imago,* and assumed the editorship of the *International Journal of Psychoanalysis.* After the World War I, during which he was editor of the official Austrian army newspaper, he returned to Vienna to become director of the International Psychoanalytic Publishing House. Together with Sandor Ferenczi in 1923, he published *The Development of Psychoanalysis,* in which they proposed changes that differed from classical analytic theory. They shifted from the classical focus on early experience and stated that the primary focus of analysis should be on how patients "act out" their unconscious emotions. It is here that they underscored the importance given to *transference* in psychoanalytic treatment.

The following year Rank published his *The Trauma of Birth* (1924), without discussing its content with any other member of the close-knit analytic community. Here he proposed a new conception regarding the genesis of mental development based on the separation process of birth, an almost mystical theme of resuscitated parthenogenesis. Rank asserted that a so-called primal anxiety was the main source of future development, as well as the core origin of psychoneuroses. Although he introduced technical innovations to justify his views, he provided little clinical material or details concerning this idea. Rank's proposals met with strong opposition in the analytic clique, although Freud was willing to accept the possibility that the birth trauma was a major ingredient in the later development of disorders. Nevertheless, he slowly recognized that Rank's trauma views seriously contradicted his own. At first, Rank did not wish to separate himself from the analytic movement, but after leaving for Paris in 1926, he returned to find that psychoanalytic circles received his speculations with increasing hostility. In 1935, Rank moved to the United States and worked for a while with social work disciples such as *Jessie Taft* and *Faye Karpf*, who wrote sensitively and enthusiastically about his contributions.

Freud was *not* especially pleased that psychoanalysis had taken strong root in the Americas, commenting that he was by no means happy to see that his years of effort had led to analysis becoming "the handmaiden of psychiatry." Psychoanalysis in the United States evinced little in the sophisticated theorizing he valued: It stressed the pragmatic aspects of treatment efficacy instead of the conceptual model of human nature that Freud considered to be his major contribution.

Despite his relative composure and continued creativity in the face of persistent suffering from cancer of the jaw, Freud harbored old and deep resentments until his death in the late 1930s. His pain and feelings of betrayal engendered a pessimistic view of human nature, leading to the conclusion that society had been taken over by "a wretched lot." Freud became increasingly resigned to his personal fate, judging the world to be as horrendous as one could possibly have envisioned. Forced to leave Vienna in his last years, Freud, nevertheless, found it difficult to believe that Germany could be as thoroughly cruel as it had begun to be. He viewed Hitler to be a disgrace to German history and thought that a nation that produced a Goethe could not possibly turn out to be as bad as it was under the Nazis. Nevertheless, on September 23, 1939, the month that Nazi Germany attacked Poland, Freud asked his physician to assist him through small doses of morphia to slip quietly into a final sleep.

Comments and Reflections

For the better part of the mid-twentieth century, especially in the United States, the middle class became enraptured with psychoanalysis as the prime instrument for understanding psychological problems. Likewise, psychiatry quickly adopted Freud's notions concerning unconscious conflicts and the events of one's personal past, particularly those that stemmed from the stages of psychosexual development. Furthermore, most psychiatric practitioners were delighted to shift the locus of their profession from the state hospital asylum to the private practice office. Psychoanalysis achieved a monopoly over psychotherapeutic practice from the 1930s until the 1970s; in fact, the two became virtually synonymous. Despite the emergence of psychopharmacology and its simple and direct solution to difficulties of an emotional nature, psychoanalysis, once totally dominant as an approach to psychiatry, remained a theoretical point of view of great substantive vigor and vision. However, attributable perhaps to Hollywood portrayals, many came to regard Freud's model as a costly form of self-indulgence, an outmoded treatment approach that contemporary clinical and social thinkers viewed with increasing disdain. Nevertheless, quietly, and perhaps on the sidelines of a field where drug treatment and brief therapies became the rule (see Chapter 6), many continued to consider that psychoanalysis—although an extended, costly, arduous, and emotionally stressful treatment—still offered something that could be found nowhere else. Among the intellectually elite, experiences on the couch were firmly embedded in the American culture as the best that psychotherapy had to offer. In a world of quick fixes and glib explanations for human behavior, psychoanalysis represented a commitment to nature's complexities that called for deep understandings and sophisticated treatment methodologies.

In 1909, when Freud was invited to Clark University in the United States, and later during the World War I, when his theories seemed especially fruitful in explaining combat neuroses, his views took on international significance. Notable also was the enthusiasm with which the literary Bloomsbury Group (e.g., Virginia Woolf) in England received his ideas. Intense criticism and condemnation, however, overshadowed this acclaim. As a result, Freud became particularly sensitive to criticism from within his own ranks.

Questions continue to be raised as to whether the scientific concepts of psychoanalysis can be founded on unconscious data. Psychoanalytic theories have been criticized as unscientific mixtures of metaphorical analogies, speculative notions, and hypothetical constructs because their data are anchored tenuously to the observable world. Added to this harsh judgment is the equally critical view that the methods of collecting unconscious data are both unreliable and imprecise. How can concepts of the unobservable unconscious be empirically anchored? Can one accept what patients say without corroboration from external evidence? Are patients unbiased judges, or are they motivated to agree with their all-knowing therapists? Are free associations really free, or do patients produce what their therapists implicitly suggest?

These and many other questions have been raised about the subjective and methodologically uncontrolled procedures used for the development of psychoanalytic theories. Despite these criticisms, many of which are equally applicable to other theoretical approaches, psychoanalytic processes may be a necessary part of a full study of the mind, especially aspects of pathological functioning. Although these processes are difficult to formulate according to the tenets of scientific objectivity, their existence cannot be denied or overlooked. Efforts to unravel them may fall prey to theoretical obscurity and methodological difficulty, yet the search for them is mandatory.

The distinguished American author and historian, Morton Hunt, has summarized the story of psychoanalysis as follows:

Ever since Freud began publishing his ideas, his psychology has been fiercely attacked on one ground or another. At first and for some decades many physicians and psychologists called it dirty and perverted; by the 1930s communist theorists were castigating it as decadent and bourgeois; and in the same decade the Nazis condemned it as Jewish filth and burned Freud's books.

Psychoanalysis outlived these assaults, but for many years it has been under attack of a more thoughtful kind: a number of psychologists and philosophers of science have asserted that it is not scientific. Their chief argument is that psychoanalytic research is not experimental; the psychoanalyst does not construct a situation in which he or she can control variables and manipulate them one at a time to measure their impact and so establish causal connections. (1993, p. 203)

Freud's conception of the mind has not gone unchallenged. Chapter 8 explores the work of more contemporary analytic theorists who proposed alternative explanations for the observations that Freud so keenly made.

8

Innovating the Intricacies of Intrapsychic Thought

Psychoanalysis became the major direction for much psychological thinking in the twentieth century. Variations on Freud's original ideas continued to develop well into the latter part of the century.

The Psychoanalytic Story: II

Despite the decline in the centrality and status of psychoanalysis in the 1960s, adherents of this movement continued to be highly productive and insightful. Many of the most innovative papers and books on mental disorders originated on psychoanalytic foundations. Of special significance in the United States were the contributions of the neosocial, ego-analytic, and object relations theorists, as well as proposals from earlier Freudian disciples such as Sandor Rado, Franz Alexander, and Otto Fenichel. These theorists continued their work in the United States and further illuminated and refined the understanding of Freud's original conceptions.

Variants of psychoanalytic theory also took a firm hold in many other quarters throughout the globe. In England, Freud's ideas were elaborated by Ernest Jones, Melanie Klein, and Anna Freud, the latter two in their studies of early development. W. R. D. Fairbairn, an eminent Scottish psychoanalyst, working along similar lines as Klein, extended her formulation of psychoanalysis with reference to infantile strivings for object relations. On the English scene, Sigmund Freud's daughter, Anna Freud, added her own studies of the ego and mechanisms of defense to those originally formulated by her father and Heinz Hartmann in Germany and the United States. The Swiss psychoanalysts, Ludwig Binswanger and Medard Boss, influenced by phenomenological philosophers, laid the groundwork for what they termed *daseinsanalyse*, another variant of psychoanalytic thought known also as existential analysis. Freud's ideas filtered into both psychiatric and lay thinking even before the sharp influx of

European analysts in the 1930s. In a short time, these analysts, with their great conceptual skills and extensive therapeutic experience, as well as their deep commitment, became major figures in American psychiatry. Even those who attained only a modest and undistinguished stature in Austria and Germany quickly became leaders in hospital and university psychiatric departments in the United States. Younger American analysts who had been trained in Europe quickly joined their esteemed mentors as they flooded to the United States following the Nazi assaults. No less important, American psychiatrists saw wonderful opportunities in this new clinical direction and were eager to adopt the ideas of Freud's distinguished followers.

Despite commonalities in data focus and reconstructive goals, psychoanalytic therapists parted company on several matters, notably the extent to which they emphasized the developmental roots of pathology and the particular techniques they employed in conducting treatment. A significant number of psychoanalytic therapists believe that successful treatment is contingent on the exploration and resolution of the infantile origins of adult mental illness. This necessitates probing and uncovering the conflicts of early instinctual psychosexual development and the myriad neurotic defenses that the patient has devised to keep them from consciousness.

Not all psychoanalysts share this emphasis on uprooting the past. Instead of exploring childhood experiences, some therapists focus on present-day events and relationships. They direct their efforts toward refashioning the patient's style of interpersonal behavior, rather than tracing its origins in infantile development.

Therapists who seek to revive the infantile roots of pathology depend exclusively on treatment techniques that those who concentrate on contemporary events employ only occasionally.

As noted in Chapter 7, those who focus on infantile conflicts maintain passivity in the treatment relationship; the therapist becomes a "blank screen" on which patients transfer the feelings and attitudes they acquired toward significant persons of their childhood. To further facilitate the reliving of the past, patients recline on a couch, face away from the therapist, become immersed in their own reveries and are allowed to wander in their thoughts, undistracted by external promptings. Significant childhood memories and emotions are revived during these free associations, guided only by the therapist's occasional questions and carefully phrased interpretations. These comments are employed selectively to circumvent or pierce patients' defensive resistances to the recall of repressed material.

To classical analysts, mental illness represents the persistence of repressed instinctual drives that had generated severe conflicts during psychosexual development. Not only did individuals expend energies to control the resurgence of these memories, but since the conflicts they engendered remained unresolved, they persisted into adulthood and caused individuals to act as if they were living in the past. The task of therapy was to uproot the unconscious and to free potentially constructive energies that had been tied up in the task of re-pression. To do this, classical analysts employed free association, dream inter-pretation and, most importantly, analysis of the *transference neurosis*.

Unfolding of Key Ideas

The distinctions between past and present focus and passive and active tech-niques lie on continua, with some psychoanalytic approaches at the extremes and others falling in between. There are five derivatives of these distinctions, beginning with those who adhere relatively closely to classical psychoanalysis, characterized by a reworking of infantile conflicts, and progressing through the neosocial thinkers, the ego analysts, the object relations theorists, and lastly, de-velopmental scholars.

Retaining the Core Concepts of Classical Analysis

Freud's original classical model of psychoanalysis, based largely on his instinctual-drive theory, was expanded and modified in numerous directions. Although few of the thinkers in this section adhered to Freud's classical model in every detail, most kept reasonably close to their mentor's original formula-tions. From the earliest decades of the twentieth century, devoted adherents of analytic theory began to spread Freud's ideas in both the United States and Great Britain, notably Abraham A. Brill and Ernest Jones.

Born in Austria, **Abraham Arden Brill (1874–1948)** left for the United States from Hungary, sailing alone to New York at the age of 15, essentially penniless, and knowing no more than a few words of English. Despite his mea-ger early circumstances, Brill quickly learned the language, completed his high school education within three years, graduated from the City College of New York, and acquired a medical degree from Columbia University in 1903. Deeply involved in the social conditions of his time, he specialized in neurology and psychiatry.

To expand his clinical experience and theoretical sophistication, Brill went to Paris in 1907, worked for a brief period at the Bicétre Hospital, and then traveled to Zurich to study with Eugen Bleuler. Here Brill first became acquainted with Freud's psychoanalytic discoveries, especially the uncon-scious dynamics of human behavior and the treatment techniques of hyp-notherapy and free association. During that period, he worked with Karl Abraham, an early disciple of Freud, and Carl Jung, who was a senior staff member at Bleuler's Burgholzli Clinic. While in Zurich, he traveled to Vienna to speak with Freud. They shared long walks, discussed dream analysis, and began an extended and frequent correspondence that continued for more than 30 years.

Those who worked with Brill described him as possessing a heart of gold, an easygoing personality, and a generous spirit, willing to take a lesser stature to assist others in achieving their ambitions. During medical school, he supported himself as a janitor working in bars, gave musical lessons to teenagers, and modeled for them how to succeed in America. Freud relied on Brill to take care of all matters pertaining to the publication of his books in the United States. Though dependent on Freud's support, Brill, in turn, played a major role in referring patients to other analysts beginning their own practice. Despite his kindness and willingness to render services, however, his lack of polish, problematic accent, and modest stature kept people from regarding him as a leader. When the notion was introduced to establish a training institute in New York, the group initiating the proposal told Brill that someone other than he should take on the job. Brill remained president of the New York Society, but the training institute position went to an established Berlin analyst, Sandor Rado.

A prolific writer and active lecturer, Brill wrote the first book on psychoanalysis in America, *Psychoanalysis: Its Theory and Application* (1912). In 1921, he published *Fundamental Conceptions of Psychoanalysis,* a widely read textbook for laypersons and students. By 1924, he had translated more than 10 of Freud's writings, and in 1938 he brought together these translations in a highly regarded book entitled, *Basic Writings of Sigmund Freud.*

Brill contributed numerous papers on psychoanalytic topics, notably the defensive function of neuroses, the rationale of manic behavior, the dynamics of humor and slips of the tongue, as well as the defensive function of schizophrenic verbalizations. He considered mania as reflecting a reaction of the ego that permitted the id to find expression, if only briefly. Similarly, the so-called purposeless ramblings and illogical laughter of schizophrenia, he saw as serving to protect patients against the expression of either their deep anger or their irresolvable sadness.

Brill remained an ardent exponent of psychoanalysis in the United States until his death in 1948. In his many lectures, he spoke of psychoanalysis as either an X-ray or a microscope for studying the unseen workings of the mind. To him, psychiatry without psychoanalysis would be superficially descriptive and but a barren tool for treating human personality.

Ernest Jones (1879–1958) was born in Wales, the only son of well-to-do parents who were willing to spend both time and funds for the well-being of their precocious youngster. Attracted to a scientific career early in life, he decided on medicine, where he ultimately achieved first-class honors in his graduate studies. Narcissistic and highly ambitious, he displayed an exceptional capacity for hard work, obtaining his medical degree at the age of 21.

Jones became interested in psychoanalytic ideas at the London School of Clinical Medicine in 1906 when he uncovered problems of guilt and sexual preoccupations while evaluating both normal and abnormal children. Although acquainted with Freud's name and the work of the Nancy school in

1898, he did not undertake formal analytic study until 1906, and met Freud in 1908. Owing to the hostile attitude in England at the time, especially Jones's interest in sexual instincts among children, he was soon forced to relinquish his work in London, leaving for Canada as a voluntary exile in 1910.

Following a brief didactic analysis with Sandor Ferenczi in Budapest, Jones returned to London in 1913, to become the founder and leader of British psychoanalysis, establishing the London Psychoanalytic Society later that year. The history of this first London group followed a brief and inglorious course, reflecting the continued highly ambivalent feelings of those involved in this new psychiatric movement. Conflicts rent the society despite its small membership; it took an additional six years for it to be re-formed as the British Psychoanalytic Society, meeting monthly in Jones's own offices in London. By the early 1920s, the British Society was led by Jones, J. C. Flugel, and the two Glover brothers, James and Edward. This time Jones assumed a somewhat dictatorial role in his effort to raise the quality of the organization's structure by dint of his intense personal ambition and intellectual discipline.

Jones's efforts were inexhaustible and sometimes belligerent. He was often highly suspicious of those who questioned either his mentor Freud or his own leadership and authority. Jones initially respected Jung's insights into the far reaches of the mind, but he judged over time that Jung had completely "degenerated into mystical obscurantism." Similarly, he despised Pierre Janet's "superficial analyses," and considered Otto Rank to be pathologically untrustworthy. He developed an intensely ambivalent relationship with Sandor Ferenczi, accusing him of neurotic, if not psychotic, suspiciousness and vanity. By contrast, Jones was unfailing in his admiration for Freud, finding it difficult to write critically on the few occasions where he disagreed with his mentor. His Celtic enthusiasms were rare, but he evidenced a pervasive philo-Semitism, even before his major role in protecting German and Austrian Jewish colleagues and arranging their immigration to England and the United States. He spoke of his great admiration for the moral authority and intellectual eminence of the great men of Jewish history and assisted many Jews stranded without property or funds following the rise of Hitler.

Despite his many intellectual contributions and his central role in shaping British psychoanalytic thinking, Jones was unable to build a systematic framework within which to organize his diverse writings. They remained a loosely knit collection of keen and original observations but were never exploited to their full value. Preoccupied with administrative ambitions and inclined to move hastily from one imaginative idea to another, he hoped to someday develop his work more fully; that time never came. It was his brilliant biography, *The Life and Works of Sigmund Freud* (1953/1961), for which he will be best known.

Nazism in the 1930s drove many Jewish analysts away from Europe and to the United States, where they lent their rich intellectual capabilities to America's modest psychoanalytic movement. Numerous internationally acclaimed figures brought the depth and subtlety of German analytic culture to the homespun character of American asylum psychiatry. Although this westward movement comprised no more than 50 or 60 analysts, their members included many of the most distinguished thinkers of the mid-twentieth century.

Born in Vienna, **Hanns Sachs (1881–1947)** was the son of a successful lawyer whose ancestry included numerous rabbis. This literary and artistic family was well established and secure in its community, despite its Jewish origins in an otherwise anti-Semitic world. Initially following his father's footsteps in the law, Sachs became enthralled by Freud's seminal text, *Interpretation of Dreams* in 1904. By 1909, he had joined Freud's Wednesday evening group meetings and in 1910 became a member of its executive board. One of the few nonphysicians in the group, along with Otto Rank, he became co-editor of the official analytic journal *Imago*, a position he held for 20 years.

A lively humorist, Sachs carried with him an endless supply of clever Jewish stories that he told frequently, exuberantly, and loquaciously. Plump and short of stature, he was a carefree bachelor with many women in his life; a lover of good food and wine; and a frequenter of concerts, plays, and cafés. Despite being a bon vivant, Sachs was a true disciple of Freud throughout his later years in Boston, writing a vivid account of psychoanalysis in his book *Freud, Master and Friend* (1944). Two years earlier, Sachs drafted his most important ideas seeking to explicate the creative process and to describe the elements leading to creative personalities. This search to understand the origins of imaginative literature and aesthetics was entitled *The Creative Unconscious* (1942). An indefatigable editor and teacher, he published numerous studies of Shakespeare's works, serving as a model for numerous future contributors seeking to relate literature and psychoanalysis.

Born in Galicia, then a part of Poland under Austrian rule, an area that rapidly churned between Austrian, Polish, German, and Russian control, **Helene Deutsch (1884–1982)** was raised by parents of the so-called Jewish intelligentsia. Her father was the president of the Jewish community and a scholar of international law; her mother evinced broad cultural interests in literature and learning. Helene was the youngest of four children, raised in a generation oriented to break traditions and to assert the rights of young women who sought to choose typically male careers. Despite varied interests, she enrolled in the University of Vienna Medical School, performed brilliantly, and decided to pursue a career in psychiatry. In 1916, she served as a clinical assistant to Emil Kraepelin in Munich, discovered Freudian ideas, and quickly became an enthusiast of psychoanalytic interpretations. From 1918 to 1919, she went to Freud for her own analysis, and in 1923 visited Karl Abraham for another year of training in Berlin. Admitted to full membership in the Vienna Psychoanalytic Society, she remained a close confidant of Freud for over a dozen years.

Deutsch and her husband Felix were among the liveliest members in the Vienna psychoanalytic circle. She was considered to be a superb teacher of psychoanalytic concepts and clinical analysis, able to listen to extended case presentations and then tie the major facts together clarifying their relationship with extraordinary skill and insight. She cultivated many in the younger generation of analysts in the 1920s. She led what came to be called the Saturday Night Group, where she facilitated the cultural education of numerous colleagues who then immigrated to the United States in the 1930s.

In 1933, Deutsch left for America, speaking of her Vienna period as "a glorious time." She centered her efforts at the Boston Psychoanalytic Institute, hoping to duplicate her productive Viennese experiences, especially by introducing what came to be known as the "continuous case seminar." She drafted her major work, *Psychoanalyses of the Neuroses* (1930) from her Vienna seminar presentations.

As some of her students have commented, when watching Deutsch lecture or report on a case or listening to her supervision, one was always aware of an exquisitely keen mind, empathically dedicated to her subject. She was intuitively responsive to the dynamic intricacies of the patient's material, both in its individual and personal drama and in its objective psychoanalytic significance. She was a handsome, if not beautiful, woman, with classic features, robust skin color, penetrating blue eyes, a halo of brown hair, and an overall tall figure. She invariably dressed in fashionable silks—a physical graciousness that did not conceal the strength of her character. Even the Slavic rhythm of her speech did not cloak her dramatically mobile and animated face, which, at rest, revealed both a feminine softness and kindliness.

Most notable among her contributions were her forays into interpretive ambiguity and her publications on female psychology, especially her many clinical papers on this latter topic, ultimately collected in a two-volume work, *The Psychology of Women* (1944). It included studies on sociocultural influences, female development, problems of reproduction and frigidity, as well as neurotic disturbances and deviations. Analytic historians invariably commented on her clinical acumen, the incisive brilliance of her mind, and the scope and richness of her insights into human functioning. Yet to those in later generations, her writings on the psychology of women seemed to rationalize the historically weak social position of women. Some accused her of arguing that women should give up the illusion of equivalence between the sexes, and of seeming to disparage what women such as she had accomplished.

Among Deutsch's most intriguing portrayals was the concept of an "as-if" personality, a forerunner of features seen in both schizoid and borderline character types. Central to the development of these disorders was the impersonality and formality of the child's early relationships. Learning to act with others, but devoid of the feelings or the connections that are usually part of these actions, these individuals' relationship to life "has something about it which is lacking in genuineness. . . . They do not appear to be aware of their lack of normal affective bonds, and their emotional relationships to the world appear absent or impoverished" (1942, pp. 301–302).

The third of four children born to a lower-middle-class Jewish family from Vienna, **Theodor Reik (1888–1969)** observed intense conflicts throughout his childhood between his father and his maternal grandfather. His father was a truth-seeking and tradition-rejecting free thinker who repudiated Jewish religious dogma, whereas his grandfather was pious, orthodox, and unyielding in his adherence to tradition. Following in his father's footsteps, Reik experienced repeated difficulties with academic authorities. Nevertheless, in 1909 he received the first PhD ever granted by the Department of Psychology of the University of Vienna. He met Freud in 1910, became a member of the Vienna Psychoanalytic Society, and soon was a devoted disciple whom Freud financially supported for the better part of the next decade. From 1914 to 1915, he was in a training analysis with Karl Abraham in Berlin, served as an officer in the Austrian army until 1918, and returned to Vienna for the next 10 years. Reik then moved to Berlin where he lived from 1928 to 1934, teaching at the Psychoanalytic Institute and engaging in a successful psychoanalytic practice. Moving ahead of the Nazi onslaught, he left for the Hague in 1934 and then came to the United States in 1938.

A prolific and witty writer, spiky and bookish, he had a mind that could dart hither and yon with minimal prompting. Reik served as an editor of analytic journals during most of his European years, became exceptionally productive during his American period, and published more than 10 books, beginning with *From 30 Years with Freud* (1940), *Listening with the Third Ear* (1948), and *Masochism in Modern Man* (1949). The last work is perhaps his best known and most widely respected contribution to psychoanalytic theory.

Overall, Reik's influence on the American lay public helped immeasurably to create a favorable climate for psychoanalysis in the United States. Because Reik was not a medically trained therapist, he was prevented from becoming a full member of the New York Psychoanalytic Society; nevertheless, he successfully built an active private practice and established an Institute for training other lay analysts in his adopted country. When I first met Reik in his later years, he was intense and watchful, yet with an incredibly ingratiating charm that came through his large mobile eyes and disarming smile. I learned at firsthand, however, what depths of anger, frustration, and ambivalence were buried deep within him owing to his rejection by the medical psychoanalytic community in the United States.

Like many of Freud's disciples, **Sandor Rado (1890–1972)** engaged in what he judged to be a series of modest revisions of classical Freudian theory, remaining within the basic fraternity of the master's followers, although some of his analytic cohorts did not view him as such. Rado was regarded as moving increasingly away from traditional psychoanalytic thought, even to having given up its basic tenets, yet still calling himself a psychoanalyst. Although Rado had been, in his own eyes, a faithful disciple, he felt rejected by Freud owing to several critical reviews of his work by the remaining members of the Vienna group in the 1930s. Rado contended that the classical analytic technique was overly formal and directive, asserting that its preoccupation with overcoming repressions and recalling past events was not only unnecessary at times, but would undermine the patient's capacity to develop independent action and self-reliance. He was caught up in the notion of archaic energies, considering the central achievement of his life's work, which he called *adaptational psychodynamics* to be a natural extension of Freud's basic id concepts.

Rado was born in a middle-class Jewish family in Hungary, began studies for a career in law, and received his initial degree in political science. He later turned to medicine, obtaining his doctorate from the University of Budapest in 1915. During his medical training, he became interested in Freud's ideas through Sandor Ferenczi's teachings and soon became the official secretary of the Hungarian Psychoanalytic Society, a responsibility he continued until he left for Berlin in 1920. For the next 12 years, he served as secretary of several psychoanalytic organizations. Persuasive in discussions and determination, Rado became a formidable debater—effective, logical, to the point, and often devastating—traits that did not endear him to colleagues, although his adversaries respected his intensity of purpose and brilliant cognitive abilities.

Analyzed by Karl Abraham, he was invited to join the faculty of the Berlin Psychoanalytic Institute, teaching there from 1922 to 1931. In the fall of 1931, at Abraham Brill's invitation, Rado moved to New York to organize a psychoanalytic institute on the Berlin model. In 1944, he established the Psychoanalytic Institute at Columbia University and became a professor of psychiatry, a move that the official American Psychoanalytic Association strongly resisted owing to its fear that an academic setting would dilute and compromise psychoanalytic viewpoints. Despite these early resistances, the Columbia University Psychoanalytic Institute became firmly ensconced in academia and was ultimately judged as possessing an excellent training program from the 1960s onward.

Among his major writings, Rado asserted that neuroses were essentially the result of a miscarried adaptational effort, a view not unlike a basic tenet of ego psychology, to be discussed later. Rado made a key effort to develop techniques that would actively help patients readapt following neurotic adjustment failures. He criticized his analytic peers' preoccupation with their patients' past experiences and their consequent neglect of present experiences and opportunities for change. His proposed adaptational technique shifted the classic analytic focus on undoing parental misguidance toward the acquisition of self-reliance, a reeducational process designed both to restore hope and to encourage fresh social and personal skills.

Rado addressed a wide range of clinical disorders throughout his career, several of which deserve mention. He drew on the role of rage and self-punishment as central to the self-abusive behaviors he saw in depressive characters. To Rado, depressively disposed individuals have an intense craving for love and approval. At the same time, however, there is intense ambivalence toward the object of love. To control against the expression of hostility, there is an intense sense of guilt. Self-punishment is an expiatory act, a plea for forgiveness for the rage that one feels internally.

Rado's thesis concerning the origins of obsessive traits is also well stated. Remaining true to Freud's assertion that the impact of the anal period is crucial to the development of the pattern, Rado wrote:

> If the mother is overambitious, demanding and impatient . . . then the stage is set for the battle of the chamber pot.
>
> Irritated by the mother's interference with his bowel clock, the child responds to her entreaties with enraged defiance, to her punishments and threats of punishment with fearful obedience. The battle is a seesaw, and the mother. . . makes the disobedient child feel guilty, undergo deserved punishment and ask forgiveness. . . . It is characteristic of the type of child under consideration that his guilty fear is always somewhat stronger; sooner or later, it represses his defiant rage. Henceforth, his relationship to the mother, and soon to the father will be determined by . . . guilty fear over defiant rage or *obedience* versus *defiance*. (1959, p. 330)

Rado coined the term *schizotypal*, introduced officially in the *DSM-III* in 1980, in a paper delivered in 1950 to the New York Academy of Medicine. He briefly expanded this concept in an address in 1953 to the American Psychiatric Association and further developed it in several publications in 1956 and later. Conceiving the label as an abbreviation of "schizophrenic phenotype" (indicating its ostensible representation in overt form of an underlying hereditary predisposition or genotype), Rado specified the existence of two inherited defects: an *integrative pleasure deficiency* and a *proprioceptive diathesis*.

Referring to the efforts individuals make to compensate for their innate defects as *schizoadaptation*, Rado stated that its success depends on the interplay of three reparative processes: the careful husbanding of the scarce pleasure capacity; the ability to shift the burden of adaptive tasks to others despite ambivalent overdependency; and the adequacy with which nonemotional thoughts can replace limited pleasurable feelings. He did not consider the schizotypal pattern to be inevitably fixed but an adaptive developmental process that can move forward and back between four stages: compensated, decompensated, disintegrated, and deteriorated.

Franz Alexander (1891–1964) was born in Budapest, the son of a distinguished Jewish professor of philosophy at the university, well-known for his humanistic writings and his extensive knowledge of Shakespeare. Bernard Alexander gave his son a copy of Freud's *The Interpretation of Dreams*, not only to read but to review and evaluate, before he entered his teens. Alexander was soon caught up in the catastrophic events of World War I, serving in the army and leaving for Berlin soon thereafter to complete his medical training and become the first student at the Berlin Institute for Psychoanalysis. During an analysis with Hanns Sachs, Alexander traveled to Vienna for visits with Freud.

He was deeply impressed not only by Freud's generosity of spirit, but by his devotion to the responsibilities of being a revolutionary scientist while functioning daily as a home-loving husband and father, not unlike his own intellectual father in Budapest.

Completing his analytic training in 1921, Alexander became an assistant to Karl Abraham and Hanns Sachs at the Berlin Psychoanalytic Institute where he began a career of creative and incisive publications, the first of which was *Analysis of the Total Personality* (1925/1930), and the second, a psychoanalytic study of criminology in 1929 entitled *The Criminal, The Judge, and the Public.* The following excerpt from *Analysis of the Total Personality* illustrates perhaps the first analytic exposition of the ego's dominance over instinct:

> With the discovery of the ego, there was ushered in a new era in psychoanalysis. Whereas the first era was dominated by an art of interpretation which taught us to understand the manifestations of the instincts, we now are beginning to understand these manifestations in relation to the total personality. First the human psyche was dissected into its components; now seeing the plan of its construction, we are beginning to reconstruct it. (p. 79)

Alexander was invited to the United States in 1930 to serve as the first university chair in psychoanalysis at the University of Chicago. In 1931, he established the Chicago Institute for Psychoanalysis, modeled after the Berlin Institute, where he remained director for 25 years. Alexander was a forceful and charming intellectual who breathed life into every analytic community in which he participated. Though influenced in fundamental ways by Freud, this influence was not to be measured alone by his many invitations or tributes. He was forthright in noting defects of the analytic technique, as Freud had developed it, in particular the dangers of increasing the patient's dependence and the failure of intellectual insight alone to effect changes in behavior. During this period he formulated several of his more innovative proposals for psychoanalysis.

In what he called the importance of "corrective emotional experiences," Alexander asserted that mere cognitive insight into a patient's early experiences is not sufficient to alter ingrained patterns of feeling and behavior. The task of therapy, as he saw it, was to engage the patient in a vivid reexperiencing of past emotional reactions in the setting of the patient-therapist relationship. This would thereby demonstrate the inappropriateness of the emotional reaction and the consequent need for the patient to learn new patterns to advance emotional maturation. In his book, *Psychoanalytic Therapy,* written with his Chicago colleague, Thomas French, they wrote (1946):

> In all forms of etiological psychotherapy, the basic therapeutic principle is the same: to re-expose the patient, under more favorable circumstances, to emotional situations which he could not handle in the past. The patient, in order

to be helped, must undergo a corrective emotional experience suitable to repair the traumatic influence of previous experiences. . . . (p. 12)

Of no less significance was Alexander's role in directing research in psychosomatic medicine, establishing a new journal, *Psychosomatic Medicine,* in 1939. Alexander was also a pioneer in establishing a multidisciplinary model for scientific studies undertaken in conjunction with his appointment as a professor at the University of Illinois Medical Center in Chicago in 1938. Along with his associate, Flanders Dunbar, he considered psychosomatic disorders to represent specific forms of unconscious conflict rather than symbolic conversions, as in hysteria. Any correspondence that existed between specific organs and specific psychological difficulties reflected, to him, neither a symbolic conversion process nor a personality style but rather a specific emotional conflict. Thus, specific configurations of physiological reactions were activated in conjunction with each of several types of emotional states (e.g., rage was specifically associated with cardiovascular responses, dependency needs were characteristically stimulated by gastrointestinal activity, and respiratory functions were notable when problems involved troubling social communication). To Alexander, adult psychosomatic disorders reflected the consequence of chronic reactivations of the physiological emotional reactions stirred repeatedly in childhood.

In contrast to the vast majority of traditional analysts, **Karl Menninger (1893–1990)** was a purebred American, who was born, raised, and practiced medicine in Kansas throughout most of his career. He undertook his early residency with *Richard Cabot* (1868–1939), a Harvard psychiatric researcher whose specialty was the utility or lack thereof of clinical diagnosis. Cabot demonstrated that most medical disease diagnoses, even when carried out in the very best of hospitals with the most modern equipment and a superior professional staff, were proved by autopsy findings to be frequently incorrect or incomplete or both.

Following in the footsteps of Cabot, Menninger wrote: "Gone forever is the notion that the mentally ill person is an exception. It is now accepted that most people have some degree of mental illness at some time, and many of them have a degree of mental illness most of the time" (1963, p. 33). Along with other analytically oriented psychiatrists of the day, he asserted the key role of emotional factors in all medical diseases, as well as stressing the importance of considering the patient's whole personality in any treatment program; both became central tenets of modern clinical practice and education. The great medical internist, *George Engel,* a student of Menninger, wrote in his seminal paper of 1960:

To be able to think of disease as an entity, separate from man and caused by an identifiable substance, apparently has great appeal to the human mind. Perhaps the persistence of such views in medicine reflects the operation of psychological processes to protect the physician from the emotional implications of the material with which he deals. (p. 460)

Although Menninger came to view diagnostic classification as a questionable activity, preferring to think of all mental disorders as variants of a singular mental pathology, he made useful contributions to the study of character differences in his analytically oriented early book, *The Human Mind* (1930/1945). He undertook a detailed analysis of several personality types, among them individuals suffering a deep sense of aloneness, a subgroup he termed the *schizoid*.

Menninger divided the schizoid personality into several subvarieties, five of which capture qualities akin to those judged today to be part of the personality syndrome, broadly conceived. Among these are: the *seclusive* type, encompassing those who prefer to be alone and "did never care to mix with people"; the *hard-boiled* variety, who ensure keeping their distance by being insensitive, heartless, and ruthless; the *artistic* variety, detached otherworldly type, who "submits to us fragments of their inner world"; the *stupid* type, who lacks interest in his or her surroundings, takes little part in social affairs, and manifests little or no initiative; and the *grouchy* variety, who erect a barrier to ensure seclusion.

The writings and lives of Wilhelm Reich, described in Chapter 7, and Erich Fromm, described later in this chapter, are well known even among nonprofessional readers throughout the world. By contrast, **Otto Fenichel (1898–1946)** is less recognized as a major figure in the eye of the general public, although he shared with Reich and Fromm a common past, a deep social commitment, and a high status in the analytic world that began at the Berlin Institute of Psychoanalysis in the early 1920s. The three men constituted an unusually productive, clinically astute, and politically active group of Freudian political thinkers. Fenichel remained a vigorous and scholarly exponent of the central tenets of classical psychoanalysis, whereas Reich and Fromm turned sharply from their mentor's early concepts by the mid-1930s.

Reich and Fenichel's early years were nearly identical. They were born within a year of one another; both of their families were Jews who had come from Galicia and had strongly identified with German culture. Both attended the Faculty of Medicine at the University of Vienna, completed their degrees one year apart, and delivered their first clinical papers to the Vienna Psychoanalytic Society in their early 20s. In 1934, as active politically oriented Freudians, they sought to develop an alternative to the individually oriented psychoanalytic perspective. Before they could develop their ideas in a systematic treatise, each fled to Scandinavia via Stockholm and eventually settled in Oslo for a while. Fenichel left Oslo for a post in Prague, a step that perhaps signaled the beginnings of their personal as well as theoretical and political differences. Reich's difficulties with fellow analysts, as well as with his Marxist compatriots, led Fenichel to develop a separate circle of young analytic associates, many of whom began to view Reich as suffering from a "psychic condition." Fenichel, a youth-movement activist, as well as a socialist and Jew, took over as a spokesman of the spirit of his times, not merely a passive exemplar of the difficult experiences of the period, but a leader of liberal-thinking young men and women in Germany.

Although Fenichel's life was relatively short, the sheer quantity of his published record cannot help but be impressive to any reader seriously interested in both psychoanalytic thinking and the social events of his day. He had a prodigious capacity for work, a photographic memory, and a razor-sharp intellect, drafting monthly reports for more than a decade that were circulated throughout the young analytic world; the monthly was entitled the *Rundbriefe*.

During the mid-1930s, Reich's increasing commitment to a Marxist point of view sundered the formerly close relationship between Fenichel and Reich. Fenichel played a key role as reviewer and critic of the younger psychoanalysts of his day. Although he appraised the many works of Reich and Fromm with warmth and generosity, initially commenting favorably on Reich's Marxist writings of the "social-sexual order," his reviews lacked the enthusiasm that Reich had anticipated and led to increased political squabbling between the two. Interestingly, Soviet authorities did not tolerate Reich's effort to synthesize psychoanalysis and dialectical materialism, which led to his expulsion from the Communist Party (and shortly thereafter the International Psychoanalytic Society). Reich found himself standing increasingly apart from his former colleagues, both Marxist and psychoanalytic.

Barely 35 years old, Fenichel was so highly thought of by his Berlin seniors that he was asked in 1933 to establish a Norwegian Psychoanalytic Institute; he assumed the same responsibility in Prague in 1935, and then played a key role in establishing the Los Angeles training program in 1938. The last 13 years of his life, from 1933 until his death in 1946, were beset by the turmoil of repeated exiles, not the least of which were exhausting efforts to move, to establish legal status, and to obtain medical certification in several countries. Throughout all these upheavals, Fenichel remained a prodigious list maker. Everything he did was noted somewhere, often in several places, and was then cross-listed, charted, and alphabetized. He recorded and numbered every movie he saw, every train trip, and every auto excursion, complete with destinations, stopping points, and traveling companions. From 1911 until the end of his life, he kept a catalog of his immense correspondence, receiving some 10,000 letters in his lifetime, with each incoming letter assigned a number and a note recording the writer, the date, and the origin. Despite his superorganization and compulsive control over his life events, all who knew him spoke of his zest for living, his vigor in pursuing cultural ideas, and his love of humor. Far from a dour systematizer, he was a witty conversationalist who mimicked himself and derided his own obsession for records and schedules.

Some colleagues, however, viewed Fenichel to be an uncompromising explicator of classical analytic interpretations, excessively rigid in his criticism of those views he judged as poorly formulated or in error. He was a serious defender of the then young science of psychoanalysis, but he seemed never to bear grudges. Others defended him, saying he had a passion for clarity and attacked only those whose views he considered misleading, obscure, or pretentious.

His first book, written explicitly for fellow psychoanalysts, *The Outline of Clinical Psychoanalysis* (1934), was vast in scope, closely knit and detailed in reasoning, and a highly erudite work for a man only in his mid-30s. It was followed a decade later by *The Psychoanalytic Theory of Neurosis* (1945), a text that remains today the most systematic summary of all early psychoanalytic concepts.

Fenichel demonstrated his grasp of a wide range of mental afflictions in his 1945 book. In describing the compulsion neurosis, Fenichel wrote:

> The anal-sadistic instinctual orientation of the compulsion neurotic can, as a rule, be easily recognized in the clinical picture, once attention has been directed to this point. Compulsion neurotics are generally and obviously concerned about conflicts between aggressiveness and submissiveness, cruelty and gentleness, dirtiness and cleanliness, disorder and order. These conflicts may be expressed in the external appearance and the manifest behavior. (p. 273)

Although not addressing a narcissistic character structure directly, Fenichel described what he referred to as the "Don Juans" of achievement. Developing this theme in recounting a case of his, Fenichel extrapolated to a general portrayal of these individuals, noting that they had considerable success but no inner satisfaction. Racing from one achievement to another, they seemed driven by their overwhelming narcissistic needs. Since these needs were deeply embedded in childhood, the individual could never resolve or fulfill them. In time, these persons ultimately came to realize that their repetitive searches for fulfillment only served to conceal deeper feelings of emptiness. Unsure of their real self-worth, they found that their actual, substantive achievements were only temporarily gratifying.

Frieda Fromm-Reichmann (1899–1957) was born to an orthodox Jewish family in Germany. Her parents adored her but were frustrated by the life they led together. She later noted that she grew up feeling responsible for keeping her parents calm and happy. Thus, she claimed her psychiatric career began when she was only four years old. Her biographer wrote of her serving people through psychotherapy, averring that this was a kind of *Tzedakah*, or religious commitment, that she engaged in for the purpose of social justice. In the 1920s, having just married Erich Fromm (referred to later in this chapter), Fromm-Reichmann opened a Utopian treatment community that was both psychoanalytic and deeply religious in focus. In 1933, she fled Strasburg, first to New York, and then to Maryland, where she joined the staff of a small asylum, Chestnut Lodge, which soon became a major psychoanalytically oriented hospital.

Although orthodox Freudians stated that psychotic patients could not be adequately analyzed owing to their inability to understand the difference between fantasy and reality, Fromm-Reichmann persevered courageously and forcefully. She was a therapist of incomparable intuitive sensibilities and possessed a persistent and unfailing humanistic spirit. These talents were immortalized in a thinly fictionalized novel by a former adolescent under her care, *I Never Promised You a Rose Garden*. Among her professional writings, perhaps the best known reflects her insight and aptitude in dealing with countertransference; it was entitled *Principles of Intensive Psychotherapy* (1950). In contrast with many who worked with severely regressed patients, Fromm-Reichmann retained the traditional analytic focus on verbal communication and interpretation. In her view, therapists had the task of guiding their patients in reentering the everyday and conventional world by careful and well-timed interpretations of a patient's tenuous contact with reality. She evinced the conviction of a patient's self-worth in a manner not unlike a faith, that is, the belief that all things ultimately can be made good and just.

Like the earlier phases in its European progession, schisms continued to develop as analysis moved outside the Continent to the Americas and England. Each of these new movements significantly altered and added rich dimensions to the classical Freudian point of view. Some had worked out novel systems of their own and established training institutes to educate newly stamped psychoanalysts of a neo-Freudian character. Although none totally rejected the fundamentals of Freudian thought, they newly emphasized one or another facet of Freud's original ideas. Some stressed the role of social and cultural forces, others considered the capacities of the ego and its reality orientation to be more central than originally formulated, still others focused on key aspects of the relationship of the young child to significant others, and so on.

Psychoanalytic thought attracted a new generation of creative writers, artists, and the growing modern intelligentsia in the United States. Freudian psychology greatly influenced an entire society that grew up in the 1930s, and for several decades thereafter, reaching millions of ordinary Americans through the writings of pediatricians, the phantasmagorical themes of surrealistic painters, and avant-garde political thinkers and novelists. What is truly astonishing is how few actual analysts were involved during this extraordinary period—perhaps no more than 1,000 or so. Beyond these, perhaps 10,000 or more analysands were engaged in extended treatment, many of them from the wealthy, sophisticated, and educated social classes. They, in turn, influenced hundreds of thousands if not millions through their writings and creative contributions.

Developing a Neosocial Perspective

Adler's view that the character of human development was rooted in social strivings served as a guide for Karen Horney's and Erich Fromm's ideas. Although all three took issue with Freud's biological orientation, preferring instead to emphasize sociocultural factors, Horney and Fromm regarded themselves as renovators, not deviators, from his theories. Along with *Harry*

Stack Sullivan, discussed in Chapter 12, many have referred to them as neo-Freudian social theorists, among the many of the time who were motivated to reenergize analytic thought and to forestall the danger that its central tenets might collapse altogether.

The neosocial analysts, together with the interpersonal, transactional, and family analysts to be discussed in Chapter 12, pay less heed to matters of the past than they do to the resolution of present difficulties. Moreover, they do not regard mental illness as arising from conflicts or deficiencies associated with instinctual sources, but from the character of early interpersonal relationships. In another deviation from the doctrines of Freud, they assert that adult pathology is not simply a repetition of nuclear infantile difficulties. Early experiences may be recognized as the initial basis for later problems, but intervening events are thought to modify their impact. Coping behaviors learned early in life may promote new difficulties that, in turn, may provoke troublesome adaptive strategies. By adulthood, then, an extensive series of events will have occurred, making present behaviors and attitudes far removed from their initial childhood origins. Consequently, and in contrast to classical analysts, social analysts often consider it digressive and wasteful to reconstruct either the infantile sources of neuroses stemming from the id or the adaptive deficiencies of the infantile ego. Efforts can more fruitfully be expended uncovering and resolving current unconscious attitudes and interpersonal strategies.

Born in Hamburg, Germany, the daughter of a Norwegian sea captain and a mother of Dutch descent, **Karen Horney (1885–1952)** spoke of her father as an absent, but strict disciplinarian and her mother as a sensitive and thoughtful woman. Just prior to receiving a medical degree from the University of Berlin, Karen Horney married a young attorney and gave birth to three daughters, who each achieved successful, though nonpsychiatric, careers. In her residency at a Berlin clinic during World War I, she undertook formal analytic training and was analyzed by both Karl Abraham and Hanns Sachs. She established a psychoanalytic practice in 1919 and became a faculty member at the Berlin Institute that same year. An active member of the Institute for a dozen years, she joined Franz Alexander in 1932 as associate director of the Chicago Psychoanalytic Institute, where she served for two years prior to moving to New York. Increasingly dissatisfied with prevailing psychoanalytic thought and practice and demonstrating a sensitivity to cultural influences in personality functioning, especially the problematic character of women's experiences in modern society, she resigned from the American Psychoanalytic Association in 1941 and founded an alternative analytic training program, the American Institute for Psychoanalysis.

Horney's early writings centered on the technical problems of analytic therapy, asserting that therapists should emphasize present life circumstances rather than early instinctual development. Despite her break with classical analytic practice, she impressed readers by the clarity of her thinking and her keen clinical observations. Progressively moving away from libido theory and drawing less and less on classical analytic terms and colloquialisms, her books became highly popular among the general public; many were best sellers, well known and widely discussed. She remained one of the most independent, skeptical, and questioning thinkers in analysis; nevertheless, she remained strongly devoted to such analytic themes as the importance of psychic conflict. Fully committed to seeing that the role of the social context became a key aspect in understanding neurotic disturbances,

Karen Horney

she was unwilling to swerve from the social perspective she judged necessary if analysis was to retain its standing in a complex, changing world.

Horney contended that neurotic disorders reflected cultural trends learned within the family; she minimized biological determinants and stressed interpersonal relationships. She believed that rejected children generated anxiety and repressed anger leading to feelings of helplessness, hostility, and isolation. As these children matured, they developed an intricate defensive pattern of withdrawal, acquiescence, or aggression to handle their basic anxiety. Although Horney felt that adult patterns resulted largely from early experience, she argued, in contrast with Freud, that therapy should focus on its adult form of expression. First, she averred that the intervening years between childhood and adulthood caused important changes in adaptive behavior. And second, present-day realities had to be accepted and the goals of therapy had to take them into account. Although Horney presented many of her ideas in an unsystematic and unscientific fashion, the clarity of her expositions and their appropriateness to modern life influenced the practice of psychodynamic psychiatry in the 1940s and 1950s.

Karen Horney's descriptive eloquence was without peer; nevertheless, difficulties arise when summarizing what she referred to as the major "solutions" to life's basic conflicts. Although she wrote her primary publications over a short period, she used different terms to represent similar concepts (1937, 1939, 1942, 1945, 1950). Faced with the insecurities and inevitable frustrations of life, Horney identified three emergent modes of relating: "moving toward" people, "moving against" people, or "moving away" from them. In her 1945 book, Horney formulated three character types to reflect each of these three solutions: Moving toward was found in a "compliant" type; moving against, in an "aggressive" type; and moving away, in a "detached" type. In 1950, Horney reconceptualized her typology in line with the manner in which individuals solve intrapsychic conflicts. Corresponding roughly to the prior trichotomies, she termed these solutions "self-effacement," "expansive," and "neurotic resignation." Although these sets of three do not match perfectly, they correspond to the essential themes of Horney's characterology.

Individuals who were in the moving-toward, compliant, and self-effacing orientation exhibited a marked need for affection and approval, a willingness to deny personal aspirations and self-assertion, and an assumption that love solves all problems. Self-esteem is determined by what others think, personal desires are subordinated, and tendencies toward self-accusation, helplessness, passivity, and self-belittlement are displayed. In the extreme form, a morbid dependency emerges; at a more advanced and complicated level, there is a masochistic wallowing in guilt and self-degradation.

Individuals in the moving-against, aggressive type with expansive solutions glorify themselves, and they rigidly deny weakness and inadequacy. Life is considered to be a struggle for survival; they possess a need to control or exploit others, to excel, to outsmart and belittle those who have power. Horney described three subdivisions of this solution. The first, the *narcissistic* solution, suggests that individuals believe that they are their idealized selves; and, to the extent that others reinforce this belief, they are able to maintain their sense of eliteness and superiority. The second subdivision is referred to as *perfectionism*; persons in this type believe that they are what social standards expect them to be, and they are heavily invested in repressing all indications that they may fail to live up to these standards. The third subdivision, most similar to the aggressive type that Horney described in her earlier work, was referred to as *vindictive sadism*, in which individuals arrogate to themselves all powers and rights, and seek to deny them to others. In the extreme form, such individuals endeavor to be omnipotent, invulnerable, and inviolable. They gain satisfaction by subjecting others to pain or indignity and find perverse joy in sadistically deprecating them; vindictive types feel that they restore their pride and glory through these actions.

The third of the triad is the moving-away, detached type. Employing the solution of neurotic resignation, these persons desire active avoidance of others, fearing that relationships will evoke feelings and desires that will lead ultimately only to conflict and frustration. They restrict their life, become detached onlookers, and achieve peace by curtailing needs and wishes. In extreme form, this type becomes severely alienated, moves to the periphery of life, and becomes an automaton who drifts as in a dream, unconnected to others.

Character analysis, Horney's term for her brand of psychotherapy, consists of breaking through patients' idealized self-image by exposing them to the true variety and contradictions of the impulses and attitudes that rage within them. To achieve this, the therapist puts patients through a self-disillusioning process in which the neurotic pride with which they hold their idealized self is shown to be both irrational and self-destructive.

Erich Fromm (1900–1980), a social philosopher and psychologist, was among the first of Freud's early disciples to concentrate his writings on the role of society in mental disorder. He advocated the view that the impositions of so-cial conformity force individuals to relinquish their natural spontaneity and freedom. To Fromm, neurotic behavior is a consequence of insufficient encour-agement and warmth from one's parents, which could have strengthened the individual against the demands of society. Fromm perceived the goal of therapy to be strengthening people's capacities for self-responsibility, not facilitating conformist adjustment. Fromm's interest in societal influences led him to mod-ify Freud's and Abraham's neurotic character types into social character types. Along with Horney's similar modifications, these types depicted contemporary patterns of personality functioning with extraordinary clarity.

Erich Fromm was born in Germany of liberated and educated Jewish par-ents; His early career blended psychology and sociology, and he received his PhD from the University of Heidelberg in 1922. Beginning his analytic train-ing in Munich, he completed his formal training at the Berlin Psychoanalytic Institute, studying closely the work of Karl Abraham and Karen Horney. Fromm never had a personal relationship with Freud, having been analyzed by Hanns Sachs at the Berlin Institute where he practiced subsequently for close to a decade. Here he worked with his first wife, *Frieda Fromm-Reichmann*. Both came to the United States in 1933, where Erich served briefly as a train-ing analyst at the Chicago Psychoanalytic Institute under Franz Alexander, his mentor during Berlin days. Fromm left Chicago to join Karen Horney soon thereafter in establishing the American Institute for Psychoanalysis in New York City in the mid-1930s. Fromm developed a wide following among con-temporary thinkers in the social-psychological world, analyzing prominent academics such as Robert Merton and David Riesman (see Chapter 11).

Along with Wilhelm Reich, Otto Fenichel, and other students at the Berlin Institute in the mid-1920s, Fromm had been influenced by the writings of Georg Hegel and Karl Marx and sought through most of his career to bridge a connection between Freud and Marx. Ultimately he preferred the sociopoliti-cal views of Marx, viewing them as more profound than the individual focus of Freud. Although Fromm's concepts were similar to Freud's, Adler's, and Horney's, there are differences as well. In contrast to Freud, Fromm asserted that classical psychoanalysis may lay bare the patient's problems but fail to pro-vide the patient with guidance for future solutions. Whereas Adler saw one's conflict as stemming from society's opposition to that person's superiority strivings, and Horney viewed one's struggle as that of overcoming or defending against childhood anxieties, Fromm considered the source of neuroses as stem-ming from a *fear of freedom* and a failure to find a healthy means to sustain freedom.

As with Horney, Fromm's many writings gained a wide and devoted following of American readers, beginning with *Escape from Freedom*, written in 1941. Highly sophisticated in matters of history, philosophy, and politics, Fromm be-lieved that humans are unable to tolerate the isolation and loneliness they feel when they gain opportunities to freely choose the course of their lives. Thus, freedom is frequently a negative consequence that calls for a form of escape. Healthy persons will adapt to their freedoms by uniting with others in a spirit of love and cooperative work.

Having observed the destructive consequences of the Nazi regime in Germany, Fromm concluded that most people escape from freedom in a destructive manner. He posited three unhealthy options: *authoritarianism*, a willingness to submit masochistically to powerful others or a sadistic attempt to become a powerful and controlling authority oneself; *destructiveness*, an effort to escape from isolation by destroying any person or group regarded as having created a feeling of helplessness—seen often in the violence toward society's disadvantaged classes; and *automaton conformity*, a renunciation of self and the assumption of roles that others define for oneself. A product of others' expectations, people willingly give up their identity and, not knowing who they are, leave it to others to define them. In each of these escape options, the unhealthy person only temporarily solves the problem of freedom's burdens.

Fromm placed primary emphasis on the interpersonal transactions at each developmental stage between parent and child. He believed that the compulsive pattern resulted, not from frustrations experienced at the anal stage, but from the behavioral models exhibited by a rigid and meticulous parent who imposed cleanliness and orderliness as standards for the child during toilet training.

Fromm spoke further of an existential dichotomy among humans, which he characterized as *to have or to be*. Thus, he distinguished between a having or a being orientation to life. In the *having* orientation, the person must have this and that, must work to possess one thing and then another, and must struggle in life to obtain tangible evidence of success. In effect, people are only a product of what they have. Possessions constitute a person and the person's identity. By contrast, in the *being* mode, individuals transcend material realities and are only what they existentially experience. Beyond a phenomenological purity, there is a willingness to sacrifice and give, to be directly what one is in one's relations with others, rather than what one may try to appear to be or what one materially possesses. The life focus is on love and the affirmation of living in the here and now.

Constructing an Ego-Analytic Focus

The next major analytic perspective has been referred to as neo-Freudian ego theory. Most notable among theorists of this persuasion are Anna Freud, Heinz Hartmann, Ernst Kris, Erik Erikson, and David Rapaport. This widespread school of thought minimizes Freud's focus on sexual instincts, as do the neo-Freudian social theorists. Although recognizing the significance of social and interpersonal factors, ego theorists are especially concerned with the sequence through which consciousness, perception, thought, and language unfold in the earliest periods of life. Ego theorists have retained Freud's emphasis on the role of inborn sexual instincts but, in addition, propose the existence of constructive ego instincts that enable individuals to develop in a healthy and mature fashion. Their work focuses on the course through which these naturally adaptive ego capacities emerge. In their view, most psychic disorders arise not as a function of instinctual conflicts but because these constructive ego capacities fail to develop. They believe that these adaptive and reality-oriented ego instincts are crucial to understanding pathological behavior. As a result, ego theorists concentrate their research on how learning strengthens and refines ego functions. This new emphasis widened the scope of psychodynamic theory and constructed a particularly weak link in Freud's original work.

Sigmund and Martha Freud agreed that their fifth child, Sophie, would be their last. Much to their surprise, and with mixed emotions, they learned that Martha was pregnant a sixth time. Sigmund hoped that he might have another son. He wrote to his good friend at the time, Wilhelm Fliess, that he hoped his friend would not have any objection to his calling his son Wilhelm, noting that if the child turned out to be a daughter, she would be called Anna. **Anna Freud (1895–1982)** proved to be the Freud's youngest and last child, becoming Sigmund's intellectual heir.

As Paul Roazen (1976) described her, Anna resembled her father's side of the family and was a rather unworldly young girl. In fact, her father strongly encouraged her to be more easygoing and less restless, imploring her during adolescence to relax and bask in nature's beauty. In a letter to her at that time, he said that her plans for school could wait until she had learned to take her duties less seriously, and that it would do her good to be more happy-go-lucky. The time for toil and trouble, he commented, would come for her in time, but she should enjoy life while she was still young.

Anna Freud

Nevertheless, Anna remained a shy and withdrawn adolescent with few interests outside the family. In 1918, Anna, then in her early 20s, entered into an unusual relationship with her father, that of being his analysand, with no prior formal medical or psychological training. Freud broke his own rules for the proper conduct of psychoanalytic practice by taking his own daughter into analytic treatment. Perhaps Freud's feelings of recent intellectual betrayal by Alfred Adler and Carl Jung led him to seek a trustworthy heir, who would be certain to remain faithful and become a future leader of the analytic movement.

Anna Freud's published her first analytic writings in 1922; she subsequently devoted nearly 60 years to the development of analytic techniques for children and adolescents, as well as proposing inventive ideas for the study of the ego concept. Although her primary role was as her father's chosen heir, she evolved over the years into an independent theorist exploring new psychological territories. She was not an immutable student who remained blindly devoted to her teacher's ideas, but an innovator who accomplished much that was new, perhaps with a measure of reluctance, but also with unquestionable brilliance.

Anna began attending her father's lectures and joined the Wednesday evening seminars of the Vienna Psychoanalytic Society in her early 20s. In addition, she took advantage of numerous opportunities to attend rounds in the Psychiatric Teaching Hospital under Professor Wagner-Jauregg, her father's friend from medical school years. Also notable at the time was the presence of Heinz Hartmann, who served as an assistant on these psychiatric rounds. Anna entered psychoanalytic practice in 1923 in close collaboration with her father, whom she ministered through his 16-year struggle with pain stemming from cancer of the jaw. Together with Sigmund, she left Vienna in 1938 for London following the German Anschluss in Austria.

Throughout her Vienna career, Anna focused on the evaluation and treatment of children, setting out a systematic program for appraising the developmental lines of childhood maturation. She spelled out three main dimensions of development: the *maturation* of drives and ego functions, the processes of *adaptation* to the environment and to the building of object relations, and the *organization* and integration of problematic experiences and conflicts within the personality structure. In England following the death of her father in 1939, Anna formalized and specified many of her innovative ideas. Most significant during this latter period was her contribution to the organization and development of the Hampstead Child Therapy Clinic in London, where she and her colleagues executed numerous research projects, as well as engaged in direct services to children and adolescents. It was also during this period that Anna represented traditional perspectives of analytic theory that contrasted increasingly with Melanie Klein's alternative theoretical proposals. The schism that emerged between these two perspectives cast a problematic shadow on psychoanalytic practice in England for more than two decades. It often resulted in the degeneration of theoretical disputes and the rigidifying of allegiances, on the one hand to Anna Freud and on the other to Melanie Klein.

Struggling between her loyalty to her father's work and to the powerful evidence favoring her own innovative ideas regarding child analysis and the ego functions, Anna Freud characterized her contributions as subtle refinements and clarifications, as well as minor shifts in emphasis. Nevertheless, her ideas had a profound influence on other psychoanalysts, moving her father's theories in directions he never contemplated. In her efforts to broaden psychoanalysis, she quickly recognized that the reconstruction of childhood experiences as recorded by adults was not the same as exploring children's lives as they actually lived them. Further, she found that the verbal interpretive techniques used with adults could not be employed readily with children, who were verbal and intellectual novices. Similarly, child patients typically entered therapy at the urging of their parents and did not see themselves as needing treatment, nor did they understand the role of a therapist who intruded into their lives. In effect, Anna Freud viewed child psychoanalysis as limited in usefulness unless a youngster's neuroses severely constrained further development.

Many of Anna Freud's most significant theoretical ideas were published in her classic work, *The Ego and the Mechanisms of Defense* (1936). More than any other work of the time, this text legitimized psychoanalytic interests in ego functioning. She wrote:

> If we know how a particular patient seeks to defend himself against the emergence of his instinctual impulses, that is, what is the nature of his habitual ego resistances, we can form an idea of his probable attitude toward his own unwelcomed affects. (p. 32)

Anna Freud argued that as long as a patient's ego defenses hold firm, the analyst is dealing with an essentially intact personality, who does not need therapeutic engagement. Only when patients' defenses fail and aspects of their unconscious emerges into overt thought, affect, or behavior is the analyst able to discern the character of their underlying difficulties. She stated (1969):

> So long as the defenses set up by a person's ego are intact, the analytic observer is faced by a blank; as soon as they break down, for example, when repression fails and unconscious material returns . . . a mass of information about inner processes becomes available. (p. 125)

Sigmund Freud conceived the ego as the part of the personality that served to reconcile the drives of the id to reality and to the restrictions of the super-ego. He believed that ego processes were not inborn but were learned to meet the regulatory and the defensive needs of the individual. The neo-Freudian analyst **Heinz Hartmann (1894–1970),** along with Anna Freud, considered this conception of the ego too restrictive. In a series of papers published from the 1930s to the 1950s, Hartmann proposed that the ego possessed *autonomous inborn capacities* (motility, perception, affection, and cognition) that matured independently of the instinctual drives of the id. To him, both ego and id instincts derived from a common matrix of biological potentials that differentiated into separate energy potentials.

Hartmann's family had a distinguished background in politics and academia. His paternal grandfather Moritz Hartmann, both a writer and politician, left Germany following the 1848 revolution and settled in Geneva where Heinz Hartmann's father was born and educated. Following World War I. Heinz's father became the Austrian ambassador to Germany. His maternal grandfather was a distinguished professor at the University of Vienna, where Heinz Hartmann was born and received his medical degree in 1920. Focusing on psychiatry as a career, he received analytic training at the Berlin Psychoan-alytic Institute and then worked in the Psychiatric Clinic at the University of Vienna from 1920 to 1934, also serving as a training analyst at the Vienna Psy-choanalytic Institute. Following the German invasion in 1938, Hartmann, now a Jewish émigré, moved first to the Paris Psychoanalytic Institute, and in 1941 joined the New York Psychoanalytic Institute where he became medical direc-tor, continuing in that post until the early 1950s. He served as president of the New York Analytic Society and later the International Psychoanalytic Associa-tion until 1959.

Hartmann's colleagues considered him to possess an extraordinary intellect and exceptional clinical acumen. A theorist at heart, he referred only tangen-tially to clinical data, viewing tangible observations to be of secondary signif-icance compared with conceptual frameworks or guiding theoretical models. He was well known for his urbanity and worldly manners and displayed a wide range of cultural, scientific, and artistic interests. Among his early works was a book, *Die Grundlagen der Psychoanalse*, (1927), in which he argued that psy-choanalysis should be considered to be a natural science possessing a method-ology suitable to understanding human personality and functioning. Of equal interest were papers contrasting psychoanalysis with Karl Jaspers' existential approach to psychological phenomena. Similarly, his extensive collected works were translated as *Essays on Ego Psychology*, published in 1964.

Although Anna Freud displayed reluctance in her espousal of ego theory, Hartmann approached the subject with considerable enthusiasm. He contended that psychoanalysis should be extended beyond Freud's conflict theory to ex-plore ego functions that were derived independently from the id's instinctual drives. Hartmann wrote (1939):

> We must recognize that although the ego certainly does grow on conflicts, these are not the only roots of ego development. . . . Not every adaptation to the environment, or every learning and maturation process, is a conflict. I refer to the development outside of conflict . . . and to the maturation and learning processes implicit in all (phases of development). (p. 8)

The autonomous apparatuses of the ego, as Hartmann referred to them, were preadapted to handle "average expectable environments." As infants ma-ture, innate capacities progressively unfold, each appearing in time to enable them to deal competently with the tasks and experiences that typically face youngsters of that age. Hartmann asserted that infants' innate adaptive capac-ities, if properly stimulated, enable them to develop in a healthy fashion. Al-though ego theorists accept as valid those problems articulated in Freud's id theory, which states that the seeds of pathology stem from conflicts between libidinous instincts and the demands of society, they assert that an equal if not greater cause of pathology is derived from the failure of adaptive potentials to develop adequately. Accordingly, Hartmann's ego therapy focused not only on the resolution of infantile neuroses, but also on reconstructing patients' deficient adaptive capacities.

Ernst Kris (1900–1957) was a close colleague of Hartmann. They worked together for several years at the New York Psychoanalytic Society and collaboratively wrote numerous papers on what they referred to as the "conflict-free sphere of ego-functions." Similarly, his career paralleled Erik Erikson's, in that both were deeply immersed in art and art history, and neither was formally trained in medicine, but became a major contributor to the ego concept in psychoanalytic theory.

Kris was born in Vienna to an intellectual Jewish family; his father, Leopold, was a well-known lawyer, and his mother and other relatives were engaged in art and art history, serving as major sources of inspiration for Ernst's precocious interest in pursuing a career in that field. By the age of 17, taking advantage of wartime circumstances, he actively participated in graduate seminars in art history at the University of Vienna. In the early 1920s, Kris courted a young medical student, Marianne Rie, whose father had been an associate of Freud at the university. By happenstance, Kris was asked to review Freud's collection of art objects. He became Freud's personal art consultant shortly after receiving his doctorate and following his appointment as assistant curator at the Vienna Kunsthistorisches Museum. Ernst married Marianne, who decided to pursue a career in psychoanalysis, following which he entered analysis himself in 1924 with Helene Deutsch.

By 1927, Kris became an associate member of the Vienna Institute of Psychoanalysis and served as a lecturer until 1938. Although he wished to pursue medical studies during that period, Freud requested that he forgo that desire and assume the editorship of the psychoanalytic journal, *Imago*. In 1938, the Kris family followed Freud to England where Ernst served as a training analyst at the London Institute of Psychoanalysis and was engaged in research for the BBC analyzing enemy broadcasts. In 1940, the Kris family moved again and settled in New York where he became a visiting professor at the New School for Social Research and at the College of the City of New York. He held those positions until 1950, when he moved once more to develop an interdisciplinary research group on childhood development at the Yale University Child Study Center.

Through his intensive studies of art and its history, Kris had learned the thematic sequence in which young sciences grew, developing a series of brilliant insights and hypotheses that served him well in tracing, coordinating, and disseminating knowledge of psychoanalytic theory. Together with Hartmann and *Rudolph Loewenstein*, Kris collaborated on a sequence of innovative papers that extended and integrated developments in psychoanalytic ego theory. Kris excelled at putting ideas into words and wrote all the papers they published together in the late 1940s and early 1950s. In 1946, Hartmann, Kris, and

Lowenstein wrote that the human personality is formed by more than psychic mechanisms that serve the purpose of defense. They emphasized that the instincts of the id that required defense were not intrinsically older than those developed to construct the conflict-free functions of the ego. Instead, they averred that both are products of the same intrinsic biological equipment from which they separately emerge. Kris asserted further, in contrast to the neo-Freudian social theorists, that people not only adapt to the social environment in which they live, but also participate in creating the social conditions to which they must adapt. Thus, we mold our own environment.

Kris continued his studies of creativity and art through the latter decades of his life, initiating a "gifted adolescent" project, first in conjunction with the New York Psychoanalytic Institute and later at Yale University. During my early graduate school days, I was an analysand of Ernst Kris for a brief period. As others have commented, and to which I can attest, Kris was a man of great personal warmth, charm, and human enthusiasm who sought to bring out the very best in others, enriching their thoughts and ideas far beyond what they thought they could contribute. He had an extraordinary ability to engage in numerous and diverse occupations simultaneously, yet always seemed to have time for lively conversations about a far-ranging scope of cultural and scientific matters.

Erik Homburger Erikson (1902–1994) drafted an autobiographical essay in the 1970s in which he traced the origins of his own struggle with *personal identity*, a concept central to his contributions to psychoanalytic theory (1975). Raised by his mother and her second husband, Theodor Homburger, a German pediatrician who married his mother after her first husband had abandoned her prior to Erik's birth, both mother and stepfather kept the facts of his biological origins secret until adolescence. His mother and stepfather were Jewish; his biological father was Danish. Erikson had blond hair and blue eyes, was appreciably taller than his playmates, and was often referred to as a "goy" in his stepfather's temple. As Erikson portrayed it, he grew up strikingly confused about his identity.

Erik Homburger Erikson

Owing to his unusual background and having overcome earlier struggles in his own development, Erikson stressed the importance of a concept he termed *ego strength*. In this notion, he emphasized the way in which the ego was capable not only of unifying the divergent impulses of the id, but became a crucial gauge of psychic health. To him, psychological health was not to be calculated solely in terms of identifying difficulties and symptoms, but rather by recognizing the positive capabilities that enable individuals to function and achieve. Erikson encouraged therapists to be supportive and to sanction new directions and confirm capabilities inherent in each patient. With these ideas, Erikson sought to advance analysis to extremes he judged acceptable, yet remain a respectful part of analytic tradition. Unfailingly tactful and polite, he conveyed these advanced efforts in a modest and gentle manner, in contrast to other deviants who sought more vigorously to confront and alter traditional thoughts.

Erikson constructed a sequence for the development of the ego that paralleled the stages of psychosexual development formulated by Freud. Erikson called this developmental sequence the *phases of epigenesis*. Like his ego confreres, Erikson believed that Freud's focus on psychosexuality was too narrowly conceived. He recognized a broader spectrum of sensorimotor, cognitive, and social capacities in the infant's biological equipment, and proposed the notion of *developmental modes* that represented the unfolding of genetically endowed ego capacities. Each mode was characterized by a phase-specific task for which solutions had to be found. Satisfactory solutions prepared the child to progress to the next phase; unsuccessful solutions led to chronic adaptive difficulties.

Erikson elaborated eight stages of ego epigenesis and presented the expressions, interactions, and relationships that arise during each of these phases of development. Each phase was associated with a crisis for individuals, a decisive encounter with others that shaped the course of their future development. The oral-sensory stage, or infancy nursing period, determined whether the child would develop trust or mistrust; the struggle over retention and elimination during the anal-muscular stage influenced whether the child would emerge with a sense of autonomy or with shame and doubt; initiative or guilt resulted from the success or failure of sexual assertiveness in the genital-locomotor period, and so on.

Erikson conceived an innate *mutuality* between the phases of child maturation, on the one hand, and adult phases of development, on the other. He envisioned a mutual regulation, or a *cogwheeling of the life cycles*, such that adult phase-specific tasks were innately coordinated to the phase-specific needs of the child. For example, infantile helplessness not only elicits a nurturant response from the mother, but fulfills the mother's generative-phase nurturant needs. In all cultures, according to Erikson, the basic timetable of human interaction is determined by this inborn pattern of symbiotic relationships.

David Rapaport (1911–1960) was born in Hungary to a middle-class urban Jewish family that strongly identified with Hebrew and Zionist traditions. Intellectually precocious, Rapaport possessed deep social concerns and became an accomplished political speaker and leader in his early teens, often engaging in fiery speeches that placed him in serious danger with the authorities of the day. Completing his initial education in mathematics and physics at the University of Budapest in 1933, he moved to a kibbutz in Palestine for a two-year period. Returning to Hungary in 1935 he pursued training in psychoanalysis and obtained his PhD in psychology from the Royal Hungarian University in 1938. As with other precocious young men, he served as a ghostwriter for more senior analysts who befriended him during that period. Anticipating the frightening prospects of a Hungary overrun by Germany in 1938, he immigrated to the United States where he worked briefly in New York and then in Kansas, settling at the Menninger Clinic in 1940. While he was there, he established an educational program for a number of brilliant young psychologists (e.g., Roy Schafer) and psychiatrists (e.g., Merton Gill) who became loyal followers and coauthors. Instrumental in enlarging the role of psychologists from psychometric technicians to full-fledged psychodiagnosticians, his *Diagnostic Psychological Testing* (Rapaport, Gill, & Schafer, 1946) became a standard text still used by clinical psychologists. In 1948, he left Menninger with several colleagues to establish psychology and psychiatry services and research at the Austen Riggs Center in Massachusetts.

In his papers in the 1950s on the autonomy of the ego, Rapaport proposed that the maturation of the ego's capacities depended on a *stimulus nutriment* diet, a notion consistent with ideas formulated by *Jean Piaget* (see Chapter 10) regarding the development of intellectual and cognitive functions. What Rapaport meant by this concept was that inborn capacities required periodic stimulation to develop properly. To Rapaport, social isolation or environmental deprivation led to a decline in the effectiveness of ego functions. For example, children who are overprotected by mothers who do everything for them may lack opportunities to exercise their maturing motor skills and, as a result, may fail to develop their inherent physical competencies.

Although ego analysts pay less attention to infantile id conflicts than to infantile ego deficiencies, they retain the classical psychoanalyst's emphasis on the revivification and resolution of the past. To elicit early memories and provide patients with insights into the roots of their difficulties, ego analysts adhere closely to the classical techniques of free association, recumbent position, dream interpretation, and transference analysis. In addition to these procedures, they actively promote the strengthening and expansion of patients' repertoires of adaptive behaviors. By interpretive suggestions, they seek not only to eliminate the destructive and energy-consuming consequences of id conflicts, but also to build up patients' deficient ego capacities. These analysts have not spelled out fully, however, how to do this and how to intermesh these active steps with the passive procedures required to foster transference.

Emerging of Object Relations Positions

Significant experiences from the past, especially those involving important figures of childhood, leave an inner imprint, a structural residue composed of memories, attitudes, and affects that serve as a substrate of dispositions for anticipating, perceiving, and reacting to life's ongoing events, especially those related to significant persons in one's current world. The character and specifics of these internalized representations of others from the past remain templates for interpreting and reacting to new relationships in the present. These inner templates that shape our perceptions of other persons require identification and analysis. These *object relations*, along with self-image, are the major components and content of the mind. They bridge a division between the cognitive and the psychoanalytic realms of the mind in that they are essentially unconscious images, assumptions, and emotions that persistently intrude in a person's everyday and ordinary relationships. They can usually be reactivated into awareness and thereby may be available for conscious analysis and therapeutic intervention.

Although they retain Freud's intrapsychic and instinctual approach, like other neo-Freudians, object relations theorists reject his exclusive focus on libidinous sexuality. They also go beyond ego theorists in claiming that individuals instinctively seek specific and universal social relationships and "objects"; they contend that mental illness arises when the person runs into conflicts with or is deprived of these instinctively sought social outlets.

Several major thinkers from Great Britain formulated these new object relations directions for psychoanalytic theory from the 1930s to the 1960s. Most inventive of these was **Melanie Klein (1882–1960),** one of the originators of child psychoanalysis, along with Anna Freud, with whom she vigorously differed and contended for leadership in the British analytic community. Klein's views met with intense opposition in the wider psychoanalytic world, and fierce battles raged within the English analytic society over her inventive concepts. Although a vigorous critic of more orthodox psychoanalytic thought, she believed that to emphasize the very earliest and most primitive stages of development was a natural extension of Freud's original formulations. She considered oedipal difficulties to begin as early as the sixth month of life, in which the infant projects impulses of rage and aggression toward the parent. Many seri-

Melanie Klein

ously criticized this proposal as incapable of any form of validation or confirmation. She also took Freud's concept of the death instinct seriously, claiming to be able to track its developmental sequence from infancy onward.

Klein believed that *fantasy* was a major primitive function and ability, a darker, yet implacable wilderness within the infant's psyche. Furthermore, these fantasies exhibited a clear and regular developmental sequence that basically reflected the infant's relationship with the mother. The distinctive element of Klein's object relations theory was the assertion that the mind comprised *preformed internal representations* of the infant's ultimate external relationships, or *object world*. This contrasted with Anna Freud's view that the mind possessed instinctual urges that were object-seeking, but were not preformed in their character; in Freud's formulation, objects become part of the mind only secondarily. Klein believed, however, that the mind possessed prewired fantasies, implying *unlearned knowledge* that gave shape to and prepared the child for subsequent experiences. Similar conceptions to those of Klein can be found in Jung's writings as well as, subsequently, in the views of some of her occasional followers such as Fairbairn, Winnicott, and Guntrip. Jung conceived the existence of instinctive, racially derived archetypes (essentially preformed objects), which the individual then projected on the external world.

Although aspects of Melanie Klein's origins were similar to Freud's in that she was born in Vienna and received her psychoanalytic training in Europe, other aspects of her career deviated considerably from his path and that of many of her other European colleagues. Klein did not belong to Freud's intellectual circle, she never practiced in Vienna, her theoretical ideas flourished in England rather than in Europe or in the United States, and her entire psychiatric experience, along with that of her English-speaking associates, Fairbairn and Winnicott, was unconventional and viewed by Freud's followers to signify their membership as "the outer fringe."

Klein's father was a physician whose career was limited largely to a dental practice; he was a trained student of the Talmud, and raised his children in a strict Jewish milieu. Though a poor breadwinner, he was educated and set a high intellectual standard for his children. Melanie was the youngest of four siblings; an older brother guided her early education. She set out initially to study art and history at the University of Vienna, but soon became engaged to an industrial chemist, Arthur Klein, whom she married at the age of 21. They had three children and settled in Budapest where Melanie, a chronically anxious and dissatisfied wife, began her first readings of Freudian literature. She soon entered an analysis with Sandor Ferenczi. Turning to medicine as a career, she read her first paper before the Budapest Psychoanalytic Society in 1919; met Freud and Abraham in 1920; began her own practice in Berlin in 1921, specializing in work with young children; and began a second analysis with Karl Abraham. Asked by Ernest Jones to present a series of lectures in London in the summer of 1925, she was invited to move to England in 1926 shortly after the death of Abraham in Berlin. Her work in Germany had not been enthusiastically received, but in England her ideas achieved rapid acclaim. In short order, she assumed major administrative and educational roles in the British Psychoanalytic Society. With the publication of her first major work, *The Psychoanalysis of Children* (1932), Melanie Klein gained high repute in the English analytic community. Even Edward Glover, an analytic leader and one of her severest critics in later years, wrote that this work constituted an innovative landmark comparable to many of Freud's own contributions.

Klein, and not Freud or Jung, interpreted external objects from a psychological rather than a biological point of view. In referring to internal objects, Klein meant more than internal thoughts that reflected external objects. She did not focus on images or thoughts *about* external reality, but on the intrinsic experience of an inner world that was itself as real to the child as was the world outside.

Melanie Klein's papers on *schizoid mechanisms* proposed the concept of *splitting* as a core construct of early development; this has become a major theme in subsequent object relations writings. Here she stated:

> I have often expressed my view that object relations exist from the beginning of life, the first object being the mother's breast, which to the child becomes split into a good (gratifying) and bad (frustrating) breast; this splitting results in a severance of love and hate. I have further suggested that the relation to the first object implies its introjection and projection, and thus from the beginning object-relations are moulded by an interaction between introjection and projection, between internal and external objects and situations. (1952, p. 293)

Like other analysts of her school, Klein believed the so-called schizoid process was evidenced in children who split off all intense emotional experiences from their ongoing life. Splitting was considered essentially to be a defensive maneuver against infantile persecutory anxieties that allowed infants to maintain cohesion by expelling unacceptable images into the outer world. By what she called *projective identification*, infants freed themselves of contradictory self-images; consequently, however, infants created frightening external persecutors. Thus, we observe in these persons an intense fear of others beneath the surface of what seems overtly to be a cool and composed public presentation.

Klein's therapy with children used play as its primary vehicle, with toys figuring prominently as instruments for inferring the child's inner world. Describing her technique, Melanie Klein wrote:

> I have found it essential to have *small* toys because their number and variety enable the child to express a wide range of phantasies and experiences. It is important for this purpose that these toys should be nonmechanical in that the human figures, varying only in colour and size, should not indicate any particular occupation. Their very simplicity enables the child to use them in many different situations, according to the material coming up in play. (1926/1975b, p. 135)

Klein's focus on therapeutic play elicited Anna Freud's sarcasm; according to Freud, Klein sought symbolic meaning in each and every move of the child's play. In response, and with evident irritation, Klein asserted that she would never attempt "wild symbolic interpretations," and that different meanings could be attributed to any bit of play or toy depending on the context surrounding its expression. The inevitable outcome of pitting these two bristling titans of British analysis proved to be a stalemate, albeit a perplexing and embarrassing one for the larger cause of their increasingly bedeviled profession.

Born in Edinburgh Scotland, **William Ronald Dodds Fairbairn (1889–1964)** was the only child of prosperous middle-class parents. His intensely ambitious mother raised him in comparative isolation and remained a dominant figure throughout most of his life. Called Ronald by all, he attended school in his home city, following a strict curriculum for a career in the ministry. Completing his college degree at Edinburgh University in 1911, he went on to three years of postgraduate divinity study. During World War I, however, Fairbairn decided to pursue a career in medicine with a view toward specializing in psychotherapy. He completed his initial medical training in 1923, qualified as an MD in 1927, and obtained a year's psychiatric experience at the Royal Edinburgh Hospital. He entered analysis with a Jungian psychiatrist, then drifted for the next decade, serving first as a lecturer in psychology, and as psychiatrist at the Edinburgh University Clinic for Children. He presented his first papers at the British Psychoanalytic Society in 1931, but he sought to maintain some distance between the two leading analytic thinkers of the 1930s and 1940s, Melanie Klein and Anna Freud. For the next decade, Fairbairn attempted to enrich aspects of Kleinian thinking but resisted an inclination to join her analytic clique.

At first glance, Fairbairn's ideas appear to be unrelated to Jung's; closer inspection reveals a fundamental similarity. Both rejected Freud's focus on the sexual nature of instincts, preferring to emphasize the social objects through which instincts may be fulfilled. Jung attributed the existence of these instinctive goals to racially derived archetypes that are projected on the external world throughout an individual's lifetime. Fairbairn, in contrast, proposed *infantile endopsychic objects*, that is, universal pristine images in the unconscious of children that fail to mature if children do not obtain satisfying experiences with their real-world counterparts. Deprivation of these instinctively sought-for relationships results in the loss of social capacities or in the aversion of social contacts, each of which may become a forerunner of later mental illness.

Fairbairn (1940/1952b) stressed the role of depersonalization, derealization, and disturbances of the reality-sense in a range of syndromes he variously labeled schizoid "characters," "types," "states," and "personalities." These persons sense themselves as "artificial," as having the feeling that a plate glass exists between them and others, as experiencing a strange unfamiliarity with familiar persons and, conversely, as experiencing familiarity or *déjà vu* with unfamiliar persons or situations. Among their prominent clinical characteristics are "an attitude of isolation and detachment, and a preoccupation with inner reality." Of special note to Fairbairn is their "difficulty over giving in the emotional sense" (p. 15), which they cope with by "playing roles" and by "exhibitionism." To

Fairbairn: "The significance of the exploitation of exhibitionism as defense lies in the fact that it represents a technique for giving without giving, by means of a substitute of 'showing' for 'giving'" (1940, p. 16).

Especially significant to schizoid personalities is their inability to perceive others as worthy of empathy or love. This stems not only from their unwillingness to part with what little love they possess, but because they feel that love "is too dangerous to release upon [their] objects" (p. 15).

Edith Jacobson (1897–1978) developed many themes relating Freud's original instinctual drive model to Klein's and Fairbairn's concepts, in which object-relations are seen as inherent components of libidinous development. To her, self and social relationships are equally fundamental to understanding human development and its nature. She also incorporated Hartmann's notion of primary narcissism, the earliest infantile period, preceding the development of both self and object images. She extended Hartmann's narcissism concept of an undifferentiated primary matrix from which the structures of the ego and the id emerged by asserting that object connections are also derived from the same undifferentiated matrix. In taking this position, she recast Freud's instinctual drive model to include object and relational structures. Most fully developed in her major book, *The Self and the Object World* (1964), she set forth a parallel to Hartmann's major thesis, as stated in his *Ego Psychology and the Problem of Adaptation*, mentioned earlier in the chapter. Her clinical papers on this topic were infused with the warmth and sensitivity that were her forte, but her theoretical work, especially her effort to blend the instinctual and object relations models, was at times obscure, dense, and occasionally impenetrable.

Raised in Germany in an intellectual Jewish family, Jacobson was oriented early in life toward a career in medicine and psychiatry. In the early 1920s, she became a close confidant of other young analysts-in-training at the Berlin Psychoanalytic Institute, such as Otto Fenichel and Wilhelm and Annie Reich. In contrast to her fellow Jewish peers, who quickly chose to leave for distant shores in the early years of Nazi Germany, Jacobson remained long into the 1930s and was imprisoned in a concentration camp for a period. Unlike many of her concentration camp compatriots, she escaped before the full-fledged war on the European Continent broke out. She joined her colleagues at the New York Psychoanalytic Institute, where she remained as a Training and Supervising analyst for the remainder of her career.

Throughout her career, Jacobson wrote with great sensitivity on psychotic depressions and examined numerous controversial subjects such as the differentiation between the concepts of ego and self, the emergence of undifferentiated drive energies, and the major psychic structures of self and objects. Seeking to clarify the early fusion between self and object images, Jacobson wrote (1964):

> Progress manifests itself in the child's growing desire to achieve (reality), not only through sensual gratifications and physical closeness with the love object, but also by activity of his own. However, his insufficient capacity for perception

of reality still permits him to join and to expand his images of objects and self in accordance with his wishful, magical fantasies, regardless of the love objects' and his own limitations. (pp. 43–44)

Like her followers (e.g., Kernberg), Jacobson attempted to synthesize at least two models, the Freudian instinctual theory and object relations theory, the latter a more social view of humans' nature. Though not as clearly as she might have wished, she dealt with three concurrent and reciprocally interacting theoretical systems: the biological instincts of the id, the adaptive and functional capacities of the ego, and the social and relational components of the superego.

In numerous papers and books written since the mid-1960s, **Otto Kernberg (1928–   )** developed a synthesis of drive reduction and object relations frameworks that brought considerable attention to modern analytic thought while generating considerable controversy. Seeking to bridge the work of Freud, Hartmann, Jacobson, and Margaret Mahler, Kernberg became the prime analytic theorist on the American scene in the latter part of the twentieth century. By restricting the boundaries of conventional object relations theory, Kernberg anchored his own notions to the classical metapsychological frameworks of early analytic theorists. Kernberg's goal was to accommodate both classical drive theory and contemporary object relations models. Notable as well was Kernberg's attention to severely disturbed patients, whom he has characterized in his writings on severe character disorders as narcissistic and borderline personalities.

Born in Vienna of well-educated parents of notable achievement in the Austrian intellectual and political world, Kernberg was forced to leave Europe following the invasion of Germany in the late 1930s, moving with his family to Chile where he obtained his secondary school education and medical training. He left for the United States, serving in various clinical and research services at the Menninger Clinic, where he obtained much of his advanced psychoanalytic training. An active researcher, he led this distinguished clinic in carrying out major research endeavors into the nature and treatment of severely ill patients in a modern hospital milieu. In the late 1960s, Kernberg moved to the Columbia University Psychoanalytic Training Program in New York and later became Medical Director of Cornell University's Bloomingdale Hospital in the White Plains area of New York State. Throughout this period, he was recognized as one of the major innovative thinkers in the psychoanalytic world, most recently serving as president of the International Psychoanalytic Association.

I was struck by Kernberg's enormous confidence when I met and spent a few hours with him wandering together through the gardens of a great Holland museum. He possessed a strong character, more sure of his opinions than most, certainly more than I. What some might refer to as his dogmatic analytic beliefs were concealed behind a polite and cosmopolitan manner. His dogmatism, however, seemed mostly a matter of strong convictions rather than the characterological qualities of an obstinate and rigid person. He certainly was not arbitrary in his judgments nor did he temporize or spout double-talk. Underneath his firmness appeared a formal reticence and modesty. He did speak freely, however, about the talents and quirks of his many colleagues, analytic and otherwise; he judged them fairly and quite accurately, as best as I could determine. As we strolled around the garden spotting sculptures in the distance and competitively identifying which artists created them, we told each other stories of our past and argued raucously but warmly, thoroughly enjoying the recognition we had achieved professionally, as well as the opportunity to share our views.

Otto Kernberg

Kernberg proposed original thoughts about splitting as a major defensive mechanism in schizoid disengagement. He views these individuals as having difficulty in understanding both themselves and others owing to the conflicting elements of their inner personality. Seen as one of several variants exhibiting a borderline personality organization, the schizoid's inner world, according to Kernberg, is populated by contradictory self-images, one set composed of idealized or frightening aspects of internalized others, and another split into both shameful and exalted self-images. As a result, there is a persistent state of subjective unreality and identity diffusion, leading ultimately to chronic feelings of inner emptiness.

Although numerous analytic theorists have contributed in recent years to the study of character or, as currently termed, *personality disorders*, Kernberg's work deserves special note. Taking steps to develop a new characterology, Kernberg constructed a useful framework for organizing established types in terms of their level of severity. Breaking away from a rigid adherence to Abraham and Reich's psychosexual model, Kernberg proposed a parallel but independent dimension as primary, that of structural organization. Coordinating character types in accord with severity and structural organization led Kernberg to speak of "higher, intermediate, and lower levels" of character pathology; he referred to the intermediate and lower levels as *borderline* personality organizations. To illustrate his ordering of types, Kernberg assigned most hysterical, obsessive-compulsive, and depressive personalities to the higher level. At the intermediate level of organization, Kernberg located the infantile and most narcissistic personalities. Last, he classified clear-cut antisocial personalities as distinctly of a lower borderline organization. Despite having been strongly influenced by both ego and object relations theorists, and despite the innovative nature of his proposals, Kernberg has remained anchored to the view that all pathological character types are essentially reactive in their formation, rather than conflict-free.

As noted, Kernberg's diagnostic framework for characterology deemphasizes the traditional analytic classification schema based on libidinal development. He refers to stage sequences as a means of identifying levels of instinctual maturation (e.g., pregenital, genital). The vicissitudes of maturation give rise to the clinical features, defensive operations, levels of severity, prognosis and, most centrally, the structural integration or cohesion that characterizes the individual's personality. Employing his framework of levels of structural organization as a model for constructing "a psychoanalytic classification of character pathology," Kernberg (1967) described the narcissist as follows:

> These patients present an unusual degree of self-reference in their interactions with other people, a great need to be loved and admired by others, and a curious apparent contradiction between a very inflated concept of themselves and an inordinate need for tribute from others. Their emotional life is shallow. They experience little empathy for the feelings of others, they obtain very little enjoyment from life other than from the tributes they receive from others or from their own grandiose fantasies, and they feel restless and bored when external glitter wears off and no new sources feed their self-regard. They envy others, tend to idealize some people from whom they expect narcissistic supplies, and to depreciate and treat with contempt those from whom they do not expect anything (often their former idols). In general, their relationships with other people are clearly exploitative and sometimes parasitic. It is as if they feel they have the right to control and possess others and to exploit them without guilt feelings—and behind a surface which very often is charming and engaging, one senses coldness and ruthlessness. Very often such patients are considered to be "dependent" because they need so much tribute and adoration from others, but on a deeper level they are completely unable really to depend on anybody because of their deep distrust and depreciation of others. (p. 655)

Building Renewed Developmental Models

As I wrote some years ago (Millon, 1969), arguments pointing to thematic and logical continuities between the character of early experience and later behaviors—no matter how intuitively rational or consonant with established principles they appear to be—do not provide unequivocal evidence for their causal connections; different, and equally convincing, developmental hypotheses can be and often are posited. Each explication of the origins and course of mental aberrations may be persuasive, yet each remains but one among several plausible possibilities. Among the most intriguing proposals in this regard are those articulated by relatively recent analytic theorists, such as Donald Winnicott, Margaret Mahler, and Heinz Kohut.

Donald Woods Winnicott (1896–1971) was the youngest child and only son born to simple, religious, and ostensibly diffident parents in the city of Plymouth, England. They were reasonably prosperous; his father served twice as mayor of the city, and eventually was knighted by Queen Mary. Owing to his

father's political preoccupations, Winnicott developed a strong maternal identification, became interested in becoming a physician while a student at Cambridge, and sat out World War I as a medical student. He trained in pediatrics
at Saint Bartholomew's Hospital in London and went on to serve at the
Paddington Green's Children's Hospital as pediatrician for more than 40 years.

Troubled by a notable lack of sexual desire, Winnicott entered an analysis
with a classically trained British analyst, James Strachey, and following a
10-year period shifted to Joan Riviere for an additional 6-year analytic period.
Both analysts were highly regarded publishers (Hogarth Press) and members of
the Bloomsbury literary clique, leaders in the 1920s in bringing Freud's contributions to the English-speaking world. During the 1920s, Winnicott became a
disciple of Melanie Klein, seeking her guidance in applying psychoanalysis to
his work with children. Owing to his primary affiliation in pediatrics, as well
as his general reluctance and diffident social relations, Winnicott emerged as
an independent within the British Psychoanalytic Society, remaining in the
so-called middle group between the Kleinians and the Anna Freudians during
their years of controversy. He sought to negotiate the division between the instinctual drive model and the object relations framework by sidestepping the
polemics that ensued for several decades.

A lack of a well-developed sense of identity was central to Winnicott's formulation of what he termed "false self" personalities, a character type similar
in its features to those Helene Deutsch had described. Winnicott portrayed
this unfeeling and detached person as follows:

> In the cases on which my work is based there has been a true self, hidden and
> protected by a "false self." This false self is no doubt an aspect of the true self.
> It hides and protects it, and it reacts to the adaptation failures and develops a
> pattern corresponding to the pattern of environmental failure. In this way the
> true self is not involved in the reacting, and so preserves a continuity of being.
> This hidden true self suffers an impoverishment, however, that results from a
> lack of experience. The false self may achieve a deceptive false integrity, that is
> to say a false ego-strength. . . . The false self cannot, however, experience life,
> and feel real. (1956, p. 387)

Like Winnicott, **Margaret Schoenberger Mahler (1897–1985)** took her
early medical training in the field of pediatrics, although she turned shortly to a
career with seriously ill psychotic children, gaining considerable experience
with psychoanalytic thought during her Viennese period in the 1920s and
1930s. Moving to the United States as a result of the Nazi occupation of Central Europe, she began to explore the difficulties of children recently termed infantile autistic by Leo Kanner at Johns Hopkins University. In her early writings
in 1952, and later in 1967, she differentiated children described as *autistic*, who
seemed enclosed within a shell of isolation that permitted no communication
with the outside world, from those she labeled *symbiotic*, who were excessively

attached to their mothers and could not tolerate separation. She spoke of symbiotic children as being unable to cope with change that distanced them from their mothers, acting as if both were fused as one being. She described them as unable to develop *individuation*, that is, unable to achieve sufficient security for becoming a separate individual with an autonomous identity.

Studies of problematic and normal children led Mahler to structure a picture of the first two- or three-year sequence of stages in which the child becomes a person. Here she wrote of *psychological birth*, a separation-individuation process that began at birth and fully developed toward the end of the third year of life. Her 1967 volume, *On Human Symbiosis and the Vicissitudes of Individuation*, differentiated two forerunner phases, *normal autism* (the first 2 months of life), and *normal symbiosis* (months 3 and 4); both phases provided a groundwork for individuation. The next series of phases began the process of autonomy, in which there is the *development of a body image* (5 to 9 months), a *practicing* phase of expanded locomotor capacity and exploration (10 to 14 months), followed by a *rapprochement* phase (from 14 months to 24 months), when there is an increasing awareness and acceptance of separation from mother, and a phase of *object-constancy* (from 2 to 3 years) during which there is a consolidation of individuality, and a secure sense of self separate from others. Mahler's phase model refines Freud's original formulation of the oral, anal, and genital developmental sequence. It also extends downward in time a sequence that parallels Erikson's ego development notions, which elaborate and extend forward Freud's theses into adolescent and adult life.

Mahler and her associates constructed further contributions to the understanding of developmental pathogenesis (Mahler, Pine, & Bergman, 1975). As children assert their autonomy, they challenge their "good" mother, who may seek, owing to her own life struggles, to maintain the closeness of an earlier stage. It is at this *separation-individuation* phase that children may develop an intense ambivalence toward their mothers, alternating between mothers' coercive clinging and children's negativistic withdrawal. Wishing to retain the mother's nurturance, yet desiring increasing independence, leads to a schism, a splitting process that protects children's images of the good mother from a contrasting image of a constraining and limiting force. By seeking to separate these two incompatible images, the child is unable to achieve "object constancy," and a parallel coherence fails to develop in the child's own identity. According to Mahler, this deep schism creates a fundamental structural defect that may lead to a borderline personality.

Other analysts began extensive work with infants, seeking to trace the consequences of unusual mother-child relationships. *David Levy* analyzed outcomes of relationships with excessively indulgent or domineering overprotective mothers (1941). Similarly, in England, two child-oriented analysts, **Michael Balint (1896–1970), and John Bowlby (1907–1990),** contributed to understanding other developmental vicissitudes. Balint's concept of the *basic fault* spoke of patients whose borderline characteristics appeared to be a consequence of having missed something in the first year or two of life. In his view, the fault led to one of two extreme reactions: in the *ocnophile* adaptation, the infant deals with the experience by clinging excessively to others; and in the *philobat* adaptation, children learn to distance themselves from others and rely entirely on themselves. Bowlby stressed "attachment learning," especially that resulting from the loss of a significant early relationship. He speaks of children suffering maternal loss as passing through three phases: protest, despair, and detachment. In the first stage, children evidence anger at their loss; in the second, children begin to lose hope that the mother will ever return; and finally, despair turns to disengagement in which children become depressed and unresponsive. Sharing Melanie Klein's object relations model, Bowlby asserted that the manner in which children deal with affectional deprivation will determine how they will react in later life to problematic relationships with a loved one.

Heinz Kohut's (1913–1981) views are more difficult to summarize than those of his most rivalrous contemporary, Otto Kernberg, perhaps as a consequence of their originality. Despite having been written in esoteric, if not obscure, psychoanalytic jargon, as well as having been formulated in an ingenious, if at times ponderous and tautological fashion, Kohut's work has attracted numerous disciples. A score of interpreters have sought to elucidate his metapsychological assertions, which many consider among the more imaginative advances in analytic theory.

Like many other distinguished analysts of his time, Kohut was born in Vienna, the only child of a well-to-do Jewish family. They were forced to leave Austria in 1939, shortly after Heinz completed his medical studies, arriving in England shortly after Sigmund Freud. Kohut was analyzed during his school years by a well-known Viennese child analyst, August Aichhorn. He spoke of his early years as being deficient in parental warmth and of struggling

Heinz Kohut

to find a way to be independent of his overly preoccupied and unempathetic parents. These early experiences may have served as a template that oriented his later contributions to narcissistic development and to the importance of therapeutic empathy.

Kohut's writings have had devoted admirers, but many serious critics as well. His articles are clearly written, relatively simple, and straightforward reflections on important theoretical questions in psychoanalysis. His books, by contrast, are complicated, abstractly written, and remote from what some considered to be legitimate analytic concerns. Assuredly, he had a subtle and inventive mind, but he used it more and more in his later years to create speculative and abstruse associations, even unfathomable paradoxes of tangentially related ideas. However, his imaginative eye served as an innovating vehicle for a whole range of new intellectual themes in analysis. Brilliant and agile as these theoretical excursions may have been, in the few conversations I had with him, his theories seemed to me to have more the quality of inspired intellectual improvisations than of focused and systematic thoughts.

Kohut did develop an influential variant of analytic developmental theory; it furnished a special role for the self-construct as the major organizer of psychological maturation. To him, self-psychology was the proper next step following earlier orientations of id- and ego-psychology. Kohut's primary focus was on the emergence of self, following its infantile state of fragility and fragmentation and leading to its stable and cohesive adult structure. Akin to Hartmann, he took exception to classical analytic views concerning conflict in creating pathology and asserted that disorders stemmed from deficits in the self structure. Owing to "empathic mothering" failures, the self remains fragile and enfeebled, and results in *narcissistically injured* personality disorders. As a by-product of this position, Kohut added a new group of patients that could be treated by analytic methods.

Kohut's developmental model rejects Otto Kernberg's thesis that narcissistic self-investment results from a defensive withdrawal of object-love attachments following a pattern of chronic parental coldness or vengeful spite. Kernberg's more-or-less classical view contended that narcissism resulted from developmental arrests or regressions to earlier fixation points. The future narcissist, according to standard analytic metapsychology, regresses to or fails to progress through the usual developmental sequence of initial undifferentiated libido, followed by autoeroticism, narcissism and, finally, object love. It is not the content as such but the sequence of libidinal maturation that Kohut challenged. His clinical observations led him to assert that the primitive narcissistic libido had its own developmental line and sequence of continuity into adulthood. It did not "fade away" by becoming transformed into object libido, as contended by classical theorists, but unfolded into its own set of mature narcissistic processes and structures. In healthy form, these processes might include behaviors such as humor and creativity; similarly, and most significantly, it is through this narcissistic developmental sequence that the cohesive psychic structure of self ultimately emerges.

Kohut consistently emphasized the importance of approaching an understanding of a patient's experience by viewing it from the patient's own perspective. Kohut believed that therapists could achieve this by using empathy, what he spoke of as *vicarious introspection*. Kohut regarded empathy as a mode of observation that enabled therapists to sense the affective state of patients while simultaneously retaining the stance of being objective observers (Kohut, 1959, 1971, 1977). Through this mode of observation, therapists gained all the data necessary to explain and interpret the patients' early deficiencies and could lead patients to overcome defects in their psychic structure. To Kohut, the reactivation of thwarted developmental needs became the essential driving force of the treatment process. Kohut's outlook on therapy contrasted sharply with Otto Kernberg's. Kohut emphasized the primacy of empathic understanding, whereas Kernberg considered the major task to be that of dealing with the patient's negative transferences by employing open confrontation. Perhaps their divergences reflected the different patient populations with which they traditionally dealt—for Kohut, analysts-in-training, for Kernberg, hospitalized borderlines.

Fortunately, owing to his able disciples, Kohut's early death has not resulted in his becoming a somewhat less-than-significant figure in the annals of psychoanalytic theory. Contributions by Paul Tolpin on the progressive unfolding of self, Philip Lichtenberg's theme of self-regulating motivation, and Robert Stolorow's notions of intersubjectivity in dyadic relationships continue to advance Kohut's self theory.

Comments and Reflections

Owing to numerous pragmatic considerations at the time, not the least of which were the advent of effective psychopharmacological medications and the emergence of an omnipresent community mental health movement, the balance of power within American psychiatry shifted in the 1970s rapidly and surely away from psychoanalysis. Competing approaches to psychotherapy had also mushroomed; almost all therapeutic models were considered potentially valid; most were more economical and feasible than the long course of psychoanalysis. Especially unnerving were statistical analyses that suggested psychoanalysis was not appreciably more efficacious than other treatment approaches. Likewise, with a decline in the status of analysis, psychiatric training changed. No longer were heads of departments automatically those with primary analytic interests; by the early 1980s, most department heads and training directors came from a biological and neuroscientific orientation. The supply of young physicians disposed to follow a psychiatric career began to dwindle; those students who were intrigued by the more advanced areas of modern medical science found attractive alternatives to psychiatry. Those geared specifically to the intricate mystique of psychoanalysis dwindled even more so.

The American Psychoanalytic Association, obviously alarmed at this turn of events, initiated a series of questionnaires and interviews to explore the basis of their decline and what might be done to counter it. Certainly, alternative therapeutic approaches (pharmacological, family, etc.) were seriously reducing their patient base. Likewise, insurance support for expensive and long-term treatment models was scaled back significantly. The wider culture had also turned its back on the high esteem it had formerly assigned to psychoanalysts; no longer were they seen as wise, generous, and kindly, but were depicted increasingly as mystical stumblebums. A number of legal cases added further humiliation and trouble to the ostensible effectiveness of analytic treatment. Justly or not, the view came to be that psychoanalysis was not a true methodology for treating psychological disturbances but an opportunity to enhance one's personal growth and to engage in a self-indulging interior voyage.

As Shorter noted (1997): "The retreat of psychoanalysis turned into a rout" (p. 313). Fisher and Greenberg concluded from their studies that (1977): "There is virtually no evidence that therapies labeled 'psychoanalysis' result in longer-lasting or more profound positive changes than approaches that are given other labels and that are much less time-consuming and costly." In reviewing what was wrong with psychoanalysis, critics stated that concepts such as the oedipal complex and infantile sexuality were more than objects of disbelief, not so much disproven as incapable of disproof. Some believed they should be relegated to the same scientific status as astrology. The eminent English psychologist, Hans Eysenck, asserted that just as chemistry had to slough off the fetters of alchemy and the brain sciences had to disengage themselves from phrenology, so too must psychology and psychiatry abandon the pseudoscience of psychoanalysis.

As recorded earlier, questions have been raised as to whether scientific concepts can be founded on unconscious data. Psychoanalytic theories have been criticized as unscientific mixtures of metaphorical analogies, speculative notions, and hypothetical constructs because their data are anchored so tenuously to the observable world. Added to this harsh judgment is the equally critical view, voiced by such distinguished philosophers of science as Adolf Grünbaum, that the methods of collecting unconscious data are both unreliable and imprecise. How can concepts of the unobservable unconscious be empirically anchored? Can one accept what the patient says without having it corroborated by external evidence? Is the patient an unbiased reporter, or motivated to agree with the all-knowing therapist?

These and many other questions have been raised about the subjective and methodologically uncontrolled procedures used for the development of psychoanalytic theories. Without tools such as tape-recorded therapeutic interviews, corroborative data from relatives, and experimentally controlled longitudinal studies, the probability of objectifying the concepts and propositions of psychoanalytic theories is highly unlikely. To critics, the ingenious speculations of psychoanalytic theorists are, at best, a starting point, a preliminary set of propositions that must be articulated into specifiable behaviors that can be confirmed or disproved.

Despite these criticisms, psychoanalytic processes are necessary in the study of humankind's pathological functioning. As noted, these processes are difficult to formulate according to the tenets of scientific objectivity, but their existence cannot be denied or overlooked. Efforts to unravel them may fall prey to theoretical obscurity and methodological difficulties, yet the search is mandatory.

Psychoanalytic clinicians can hardly be accused of theoretical simplicity or idealistic naïveté. They have created a highly complicated superstructure of concepts and propositions in support of their notions and, if anything, their theoretical systems can be justly criticized for their excessive complexity. In contrast to those who are humanistically oriented, many psychoanalytic theorists picture humans as inherently destructive. People, left to their own devices, generate their own hostility and sexual difficulties. This is not a sugarcoated view of life, but of humans' role in creating conflicts, tumults, and contradictions. Most analytic views contrast sharply also with the automaton simplicity of people as behaviorists conceive them. They portray individuals as a fascinating complex of seething unconscious conflicts, an intriguing and complex composite of animal drives and devious social motives.

Most psychoanalytic theories would benefit enormously from the excisions of a skillful editor. Although the intricacies and varieties of our behavior are infinite, there appears to be an excess of obscure principles and concepts to account for them. A more telling criticism, however, is the shoddy empirical foundation on which these concepts rest. Concepts and propositions were derived from uncontrolled clinical observations or patient reports, and the line of reasoning that connected these dubious facts to the theory progressed through tenuous, ambiguous steps. Not only is the source of psychoanalytic data suspect, but the sequence of reasoning that ties it to the conceptual system seems excessively involved and imprecise. Yet, to the deeply inquiring and instinctively insightful thinker, the intricate themes of mental life articulated by analysts have a richness and unquestionable accuracy about them.

PART V

PSYCHOSCIENTIFIC STORIES

CHAPTER

9

Untangling Learning and Remedying Behavior

Burrhus Frederic Skinner, the leading figure of contemporary behaviorism, phrased the position of the behavioral approach as follows (1956):

> Is the scientific study of behavior—whether normal or psychotic—concerned with the behavior of the observable organism . . . or with the functioning of mental processes under the promptings of instincts, needs, emotions, memories, and habits? I do not want to raise the question of the supposed nature of these inner entities. A certain kinship between such an explanatory system and primitive animism can scarcely be missed.
>
> The study of behavior remains securely in the company of the natural sciences so long as we take as our subject matter the observable activity of the organism, as it moves about, stands still, seizes objects, pushes and pulls. makes sounds, gestures, and so on. . . . Watching a person behave in this way is like watching any physical or biological system. We also remain within the framework of the natural sciences in explaining these observations in terms of external forces and events which act upon the organism. (p. 81)

According to the behaviorists, most notably its founder John Watson and its prime subsequent explicator, Skinner, although nonbehaviorist models of psychology differ among themselves, they are all mentalistic and essentially extranatural. To them, to become a true science, psychology would have to follow the example of the physical sciences, that is, it must become materialistic, mechanistic, and, above all, objective. To infiltrate unobservable mental processes would lead to a return to ancient mystical and magical thinking; therefore, any notions of the mind should be unequivocally discarded. Stating their views with vehemence, they tarred with the same brush all nonbehavioral approaches, whether structural or functional in orientation, as were the earlier competitors of a behavioral point of view. In their opinion, mental processes, be they of consciousness or of souls, were all unfit for science. As Heidbreder described Watson's views of his former functionalist allies at the University of Chicago (1933):

> In the eyes of behaviorism, functionalism is a timid, half-hearted, half-way measure, confusing and ineffectual. It made terms with an enemy that should have been slain. For behaviorism is opposed to all psychology that deals with consciousness. It sees the whole concept of consciousness as useless and vicious, as nothing but the survival of medieval superstition about the soul, and as utterly unworthy of scientific consideration. Its proposal is as simple as it is severe. Psychology must break with the past, discard the concept of consciousness altogether, begin at the beginning, and construct a new science. (p. 234)

The Psychoscience Story: I

Academic psychology in general is distinguished by its commitment to the methods of science. As usually conceived, this entails accepting three guiding principles: the use of objective and technically precise instruments, the application of rigorously controlled procedures in research design and analysis, and the search for basic laws that underlie both simple and complex functions. In contrast to those whose concern lies in the intricacies and difficulties of real life, academicians postpone what they know to be momentary and dubious solutions to pressing problems in order to discover the universally valid and durable principles of human behavior.

The use of objective and technically precise instruments can be seen readily in the laboratory methods preferred by psychoscientists. The perceptionist's use of the tachistoscope, the learning researcher's use of the Skinner box, and the psychophysiologist's use of the electroencephalogram all reflect the technical orientation of science.

As a method of achieving objectivity, psychoscientists anchor or operationally define their terms at the level of tangible observables, thereby avoiding ambiguous concepts. To further assure that hypotheses are clear and susceptible to empirical test, they design their experiments to eliminate or control extraneous influences that might confuse proper interpretation of results. To obtain quantitative or functional relationships among these concepts, they compare different magnitudes among variables and statistically analyze their significance. The rigor and precision demanded in methodology is paralleled by equivalent convictions at the theoretical level. Scientists accept hypotheses based on their empirical predictive accuracy, not because of their facile explanatory powers. Accurate findings must be generalizable and durable, as the laws of science, of which psychology is a part, are universal. Because scientific laws are universal, it follows that those governing simple behavior will be operative also in more complex behavior. As such, the most rapid and efficient strategy for investigating complex phenomena will be achieved by focusing research on the simpler and less intricate forms. Using this rationale, academicians engage in a systematic study of less complicated functions such as perception and learning, rather than personality as a whole. And, for convenience, they study them at the simpler animal level. These methodological and theoretical principles have been breached as often as not. Nevertheless, they have been and remain the major motivating guidelines underlying the development of the psychoscientific approach discussed in this chapter and in Chapter 10.

In its strictest form, the psychoscientific approach requires precisely anchoring all concepts and propositions to measurable properties in the empirical world. That psychological concepts are, in fact, not always formulated as operational concepts is a concession to the limits of practicality. Nevertheless, empirically unanchored speculation is anathema to psychoscientists; speculative concepts, which abound in psychoanalytic and phenomenologically oriented theories, rarely are found in psychoscientific theories. John Watson (1913), in his usual savvy and calculating manner, detailed this position clearly:

> Psychology as the behaviorist views it is a purely objective experimental branch of natural science. Its theoretical goal is the prediction and control of behavior. Introspection forms no essential part of its methods, nor is the scientific value of its data dependent upon the readiness with which they lend themselves to interpretation in terms of consciousness. The behaviorist, in his efforts to get a unitary scheme of animal response, recognizes no dividing line between man and brute. The behavior of man, with all its refinement and complexity, forms only a part of the behaviorist's total scheme of investigation. (p. 158)

Behaviorists and cognivists of a psychoscience orientation were concerned minimally with *when* and *what* is learned. The specific events that may be associated with the development of pathological behavior interested them little; what they had to say on this score frequently was a rewording of the speculations of psychoanalytic theorists. Their distinction lay in proposing a limited number of rigorously derived principles that could account for a wide variety of learned pathological behaviors and beliefs. Academics were wary of the excessive number of empirically unanchored concepts included in other approaches and proposed that all actions and thoughts—normal or pathological—could be reduced to a few objective principles and concepts. Their focus was on the *process* of learning in pathology, rather than on the *content* of what was learned; it added a precision and clarity to the study of psychological events that had been sorely lacking.

Behaviorism as a school of academic thought took hold rapidly in the United States and by the mid-1920s came to dominate American psychology, especially in its academic quarters. Its approach to the subject was appealing for it avoided, even if it did not eliminate, all those difficult, philosophical questions that had been a subject of inquiry for over 2,000 years—those invisible processes that go on *in* the mind. For behaviorists, the mind was viewed as a "black box" that contained irrelevant processes that can only lead to confused speculation, which should not be part of a science.

The cultural environment of the Americas was receptive to this new pragmatic and down-to-earth philosophy. By every gauge, it was practical, dealing with what can be seen and observed in concrete and tangible form. It enabled a troubled and worrisome society facing an economic depression and World War II to comprehend and deal with their world. Moreover, rampant anti-intellectualism existed in the American heartland, along with an aversion to the cosmopolitan and liberated thoughts of foreign nations, an acceptance of crude and simplistic solutions for approaching unknowable and frightening events. It was a time when people desired simplicity and common sense to rule. Matters were so severe in academic circles that anyone who would dare write about topics such as the mind and the unconscious were viewed with great suspicion, as fuzzy-minded radicals inclined to mystical thought. The harsh schism that separated American psychology between experimental behaviorists, on the one hand, and all others, most notably those oriented to clinical subjects, characterized the atmosphere of most American psychology departments. Human functioning and clinical matters were cast aside in favor of simple experimental work with animals, such as pigeons and rats, uncomplicated creatures that were easy to handle and simple to manipulate. These creatures also lacked a mind composed of complex thought. Behaviorism took firm hold in American universities, especially in the American heartland.

Unfolding of Key Ideas

Ivan Pavlov and Edward Lee Thorndike discovered the principles of classical conditioning and trial-and-error reward learning in the early years of this century, but researchers only slowly recognized the value of these principles as tools for understanding and modifying mental illness. Not until the early 1920s did research attempt to demonstrate conditioning procedures in the acquisition of pathological behaviors. Soon thereafter, behavior principles were applied to treatment.

Knight Dunlap (1932) proposed a habit extinction procedure termed "negative practice," a precursor of modern counterconditioning treatment techniques. Although anticipated to some degree by William James's chapter on habits in his 1890 textbook *Principles of Psychology*, Dunlap was in many ways the first systematic theorist using behavioral and learning principles (Dunlap, 1932). Even John Watson in his autobiography acknowledges that Dunlap was the person who convinced him that behavior should comprise the basic data for psychology.

The few concepts employed in these theories to account for the diverse behaviors involved in mental illness and psychotherapy was an achievement of considerable merit and made them especially attractive to psychologists tired of the obscure and complex explanatory concepts of the psychoanalytic schools. Of even greater importance was the hope that new insights regarding the development and modification of behavioral pathology could also be provided.

Focusing on Learning

Czarist Russia provided much of the early inspiration to the behaviorist movement with contributions by physiologists who were intrigued with the neurology and stimulus-response patterns of lab animals. Although, for the most part, these physiologists were not inclined to apply their findings to human behavior, it was perhaps inevitable that psychologists would generalize these data to a wide range of human behaviors and even higher mental processes. Early experiments by German and American psychologists on memory and formulations of fundamental laws of learning complemented this animal research to help lay a foundation of basic science on which later behaviorists could draw.

Ivan Mikhailovich Sechenov (1829–1905) was born in Tyoply Stan, now Sechenovo, Russia, to a retired army officer father and a peasant woman, whom the father arranged to be educated before he would marry her. At the age of 14, Ivan was sent to the Military Engineering School where he took his first science course. After a conflict erupted between him and the school's principal, he left to join the army in 1847. A similar problem with authority surfaced there as well, and Sechenov's military career was over within 18 months. The following year, using money from a small inheritance, he attended medical school at the University of Moscow. Postdoctoral training afforded him opportunities to work in the physiological laboratories of such German luminaries as *Johannes Müller, Hermann von Helmholtz*, and *Emil Dubois-Reymond*, as well as exposed him to the ideas of *Charles Darwin* and *Herbert Spencer*. He undertook further postdoctoral study with *Claude Bernard* in France. Several other career moves revolved around conflicts he had with senior faculty. These included his resignation from the Medico-Surgical Academy when they refused to hire *Ilya Mechnikov* (who later became a Nobel

Laureate) because he was Jewish and, later, his resignation from the University of St. Petersburg over academic politics.

Despite this seemingly tumultuous beginning, Sechenov had a brilliant career as a physiologist, and his experiments were extremely influential in psychology. In keeping with his German postdoctoral training, Sechenov believed that the only acceptable methodological procedure for studying psychology was through physiology, ". . . only physiology holds the key to the scientific analysis of psychical phenomena" (1935, pp. 350–351). He defined psychology as the science of the reflexes of the brain, which account for the diversity and breadth of all human behavior and mental life. In fact, he believed that all behavior, no matter how complex, no matter if it were voluntary or involuntary, was reflexive and could be explained by a sensory nerve, a central connection, and a motor nerve. No less an environmentalist than behaviorists were to be, he asserted that "the real cause of every human activity lies outside man" (p. 334).

Although most of Sechenov's work did not reach American shores for many decades, he was still a major precursor of behaviorism: It was his contention that all psychic activity must be judged on the basis of its expression "in external signs." Owing to his overseas studies, government authorities in Russia banned his views on the need to establish the physiological basis of psychological processes. Consistent with his German mentors, he asserted that cerebral events were ultimately reducible to the observable movements of the muscles, a perspective in keeping with Watson's behaviorism a half century later in the United States.

Ivan Petrovitch Pavlov's (1849–1936) most famous discoveries resulted from an unanticipated observation made during studies of digestive reflexes. In 1902, while measuring saliva secreted by dogs in response to food, he noticed that dogs salivated either at the sight of the food dish or on hearing the footsteps of the attendant who brought it in. Pavlov realized that the stimulus of the dish or the footsteps had become, through experience, a substitute or signal for the stimulus of food. He soon concluded that this signaling or learning process must play a central part in the adaptive capacity of animals. Because of his physiological orientation, however, he conceived these observations as processes of the brain. Initially, he referred to them as "psychic secretions." When he presented his findings in 1903 before the fourteenth International Congress of Medicine in Madrid, he coined the term *conditioned reflex* (cr) for the learned response and labeled the learned signal as a *conditioned stimulus* (cs). As his work progressed, Pavlov noted that conditioned reflexes persisted over long periods of disuse. Nevertheless, they could be inhibited briefly by various distractions and completely extinguished by repeated failure to follow the signal or conditioned stimulus with the usual reinforcement.

Despite Pavlov's lifelong predilection for conceptualizing these conditioning processes as physiological activities of the "higher nervous system," his work proved, to his occasional embarrassment and dismay, to be a major contribution to academic psychology. His early experiments served to replace the focus on subjective introspection traditional among psychologists at the turn of the century. In his substitution of measurable and objective reactions to stimuli, he laid the groundwork, not only for the next half century of Russian research, but for American behaviorism and modern learning theory as well.

Pavlov was the first of 11 children born in a small farming village in Ryazan, Russia, to a father who was the village priest and a mother who was the daughter of a priest. Poorly paid as priests were, the entire Pavlov family—except Ivan—had to cultivate the fields like all the peasants in the village. At the age of 10, Ivan sustained a serious head injury and suffered many subsequent years of poor health. Pavlov's father was an avid reader, and his godfather, an abbot in a nearby monastery, took charge of young Pavlov and encouraged him not only to read, but to think about his reading. Instead of allowing the eager young Pavlov to immediately discuss his readings, the abbot asked him to write down his thoughts and observations so that they could systematically examine and debate them together. Perhaps this is where Pavlov developed his passion for intellectual argumentation and his zeal for systematic observation that served him well in his later career.

New educational reforms in Russia under Czar Alexander II ensured that Pavlov, a financially poor but intellectually gifted student, could receive a formal education. After completing ecclesiastical primary and secondary school, he entered the University of St. Petersburg in 1870, focusing on the natural sciences. He was an excellent student and was scheduled to become an assistant to the professor Ilya Cyon, a physiologist well known in Russia for his vigorous beliefs in physiological mechanism and precise execution of experiments, when the university suddenly dismissed Cyon for his political activities. Pavlov entered medical school with the intent of becoming a research physiologist, not a practicing physician. Although he became a brilliant technical surgeon, he greatly disliked the sight of blood and performed his surgeries with such precision as to avoid any unnecessary trauma or disruption to the tissue.

Pavlov ran his laboratory like a well-oiled machine and demanded complete obedience, precision, and punctuality from his lab workers. Although often seeming gruff and tyrannical, Pavlov also inspired great loyalty and admiration from his workers as they recognized he held himself to the same high standards. He inculcated fledgling employees in his lab with a superb training program. A new worker would begin work by replicating an old experiment, providing the employee with intimate knowledge of the previous operations of the lab, as well as providing a check on the reliability of the original finding. If the results were similar, the apprentice could move onto something new. If the results were disparate, a third party would conduct the experiment anew to settle the issue. This system allowed each operative to know all the activities of other coworkers in the lab and be able to replace them if necessary.

Pavlov's most important contributions came from the results of his research. In addition to his studies with dogs and salivatory processes, he made many other discoveries that are relevant to the history of mental illness. For example, Pavlov came to realize that words could replace physical stimuli as signals for conditioned learning. He divided human thought into two signal-systems, stating (1928):

> Sensations, perceptions and direct impressions of the surrounding world are primary signals of reality. Words are secondary signals. They represent themselves as abstractions of reality and permit generalizations. The human brain is composed of the animal brain, the first signaling system, and the purely human part related to speech, the second signaling system. (p. 101)

Pavlov noted that under emotional distress behavior shifts from the symbols of the second signal-system to the bodily expression of the first signal-system. Not only did he recognize this regression as a part of pathology, but he also used the concept of the second signal to illustrate how verbal therapy can influence the underlying first signal system it represents. Thus, words could alter defective or malfunctioning brain processes in the neurotic individual via persuasion and suggestion.

Pavlov posited two fundamental processes in nervous system functioning: *inhibition* and *excitation,* each of which undergirded basic temperamental dispositions. Using dogs to illustrate his thesis, he recorded certain breeds as "excitable." Thus, various terrier breeds were notably alert, short-tempered, and nervous. By contrast, collies were likely "inhibited" types, as seen in their hesitant and timid disposition. Animals with a balanced excitation-inhibition temperament, such as golden retrievers and Labrador retrievers, would be friendly and sociable.

Ivan Petrovitch Pavlov

Pavlov's studies of experimentally produced neuroses in animals, another important contribution to psychological thought, was prompted directly by his acquaintance with Freud's writings. In this work, agitation and anger are created in previously cooperative animals by presenting them with conflicting or intense stimuli. These studies generated a marked enthusiasm among a small group of American psychiatrists desirous of finding a more rigorous foundation for psychodynamic theory. The investigations of *W. Horsley Gantt, Howard Liddell,* and *Jules Masserman* in the 1930s and 1940s were derived largely from an attempt to bridge the ideas of Pavlov and Freud.

Born to a merchant in 1850 in Barmen, Germany, **Hermann Ebbinghaus (1850–1909)** was educated in the local Gymnasium before he left for university studies in Bonn at the age of 17. The Franco-Prussian War interrupted his studies, and he served in the German army from 1870 to 1871. Ebbinghaus studied history and philology before switching to philosophy and receiving his doctorate in 1873 at the University of Bonn with a dissertation entitled "On Hartmann's Philosophy of the Unconscious." He spent several years in England and France supporting himself as a tutor and continued to take seminars and classes. While in Paris, Ebbinghaus was perusing a used-book stall when he came across a copy of Fechner's *Elemente der Psychophysik* (see Chapter 10) and quickly became convinced that psychology could become a natural science with objective psychophysical procedures just as Fechner had created psychophysics.

Ebbinghaus averred that psychology should be separated from its philosophical connections and should align itself with the natural sciences. No less important to him was his desire to orient psychology beyond its focus on simple sensation and physiology by turning its attention to "higher mental processes." Intrigued by learning through association, as well as problems of memory and forgetting, Ebbinghaus began to conduct well-controlled experimental studies of memory. He had a great love of poetry and was particularly intrigued by why and how people forgot poetry that they had once known by rote. Studying the process of memorizing poetry, or of any meaningful material, presented the complicating issue that varying degrees of strength exist in association between many of these words before even beginning the task of learning.

Hermann Ebbinghaus

With this "forgetting" research, Ebbinghaus found a rather steep curve of forgetting that occurred in the first day of learning and then a much slower decay over a period of days and weeks. His studies suggested that some kind of residue of the prior learning exists for a long time even though much of this information is impossible to recall. In addition to studying forgetting, Ebbinghaus also was interested in the learning curve. Ebbinghaus found that different learning situations led to different curves. Skills that are particularly difficult to learn are mastered slowly, but then new learning is simply a matter of increasing proficiency (positive acceleration). On skills that are relatively easy to learn, mastery happens quickly but then reaches a ceiling where further improvements are impossible (negative acceleration).

Not only were Ebbinghaus's contributions important to learning theories in general, but he was able to show that controlled and objective data could be collected to explain even the complex phenomenon of human memory and learning. For the first time, experimental psychologists could legitimately and systematically study higher mental processes.

Vladimir M. Bekhterev (1857–1927), a contemporary and rival of Ivan Pavlov, was a Russian physiologist, neurologist, and psychiatrist. Born in Viatka, he received his medical degree from the Military Medical Academy of St. Petersburg in 1881. Although he was interested in studying conditioned responses, he was considerably more inclined to investigate its direct application to human behavior. Bekhterev wanted to develop a complete behavioral system based on his studies of motor-conditioned response. After studying with Charcot in Paris, and later with Wundt in Leipzig from 1885 to 1886, he became professor of psychiatry at the University of Kazan, where he established the first psychophysiological laboratory in Russia, as well as a brain institute that combined research and practice of mental diseases. He returned to the Military Medical Academy in St. Petersburg in 1893 where he organized a second laboratory and was eventually appointed director. In 1907, he published a three-volume text, *Objective Psychology,* and established a psychoneurological institute. Owing to his differences with Marxist-Leninist thought, the government assumed responsibility for the institute's funding in 1917. He published *General Principles of Human Reflexology* that year, but spent the rest of his life conducting research on the concept of escape and avoidance learning, perhaps an apt preoccupation given his recent demotion.

Bekhterev did establish an objective experimental psychology in Russia. Although he agreed with the traditional Wundtian notions of the physiological objectification of subjective experience, he rejected introspection and language as appropriate study methods. This does not imply that he was solely concerned with mere physiological processes. On the contrary, he wanted to subject all psychical processes to objective scrutiny. As noted, he called his new objective psychology *reflexology*. To him, reflexology was the study of all human behavior as a biosocial discipline in that he looked for correlations between personality and the social environment, as well as the organic and the inorganic world.

Edward Lee Thorndike

Although *Edward Lee Thorndike (1874–1949)* made important contributions in areas as diverse as educational psychology and psychometrics, his importance to learning theories is undeniable both for his methodological and theoretical contributions. The second of four children of a lawyer turned minister, Thorndike grew up in a highly disciplined if not austere household, learning from earliest childhood to be industrious and moralistic. Entering Wesleyan at the age of 17 and graduating in 1895, Thorndike studied with William James for a year at Harvard and then left to work with James McKeen Cattell at Columbia University. He had little access to the child subjects he initially planned for his dissertation work and instead conducted research on what he did have available: animals. He published his doctoral dissertation, "Animal Intelligence: An Experimental Study of the Associative Processes in Animals," in 1898. This work served as the basis for his classic 1911 monograph, *Animal Intelligence*. For this research, Thorndike placed dogs, cats, and chickens in small puzzle boxes. The animals had to figure out how to escape by pulling strings or pressing buttons; if successful, they were rewarded with food. Thorndike found that although an animal usually achieved the correct response initially through trial and error, when placed in the box again, it performed the correct maneuver more quickly. This process of making a response, then being rewarded, and consequently learning to perform the response rapidly was what came later to be known as instrumental learning. The converse of this happens when the animal is not rewarded; the behavior gradually disappears.

Early in his career, Thorndike was characterized as a contentious and combative man, a feisty young person inclined to challenge the psychological establishment. In later years, he was viewed as a gentle and retiring man, having concluded that controversy was unproductive and being disinclined to face the critical attacks that began to plague him following his creative early achievements. Central to his thinking was the value he gave to quantitative analyses, be it in animal experimentation or in measuring vocational achievement and educational intelligence, two fields of later life interest. As he noted, "Whatever exists, exists in some amount." To know anything thoroughly, for Thorndike, meant knowing its quantity as well as its quality. Much of his later professional work involved constructing procedures that would make the data he collected both objectively and quantitatively calculable.

Thorndike proposed two laws of behavior: the *law of effect* and the *law of exercise*. He stressed the signal importance of reward and punishment in learning, formulating his *law of effect* succinctly in the following statement (1905):

> Any act which in a given situation produces satisfaction becomes associated with that situation, so that when the situation recurs the act is more likely than before to recur also. Conversely, any act which in a given situation produces discomfort becomes dissociated from that situation, so that when the situation recurs the act is less likely than before to recur. (p. 243)

Later in his career, Thorndike modified this law by abandoning the punishment component, but the law has remained a basic fundamental building block of operant conditioning used by virtually all learning theorists. The *law of exercise* states:

> Any response to a situation will, all other things being equal, be more strongly connected with the situation in proportion to the number of times it has been connected with that situation and to the average vigor and duration of the connection. (1913, p. 188)

Initiating the Behavioral Revolution

The behaviorist school of thought emerged in full form in 1919 when John Watson wrote his *Psychology from the Standpoint of a Behaviorist.* He based his whole system on a few simple and pet notions derived from conditioned learning. He condemned the mentalistic conceptions of competitive schools, such as structuralism and functionalism, and in his mischievous assault on conventional psychology judged it to have given exaggerated importance to the nervous system. Not only did he perceive the operations of this "inner bodily structure" to be the product of gratuitous speculation, but he judged these organs to compose a "mystery box" into which other psychologies pushed difficult problems, thereby creating the illusion that they had been explained.

A key orientation of the behavioral approach was its focus on practical human affairs. Especially significant was the importance infancy received as the foundation of learning and acquired behaviors. Behaviorism was more than a mere school of psychology, but a crusade in which all things of life were achievable through careful experiment and subsequent manipulation. More than any of the other mental science cults that came to characterize the field, behaviorism was the most aggressively expansive and controlling, drumming up a vast and blind following with a shallow and ritualized set of doctrines.

For behaviorists, learning concepts sufficiently explained psychic pathology. This belief was based on the assumption that laws demonstrated in simple laboratory settings could be generalized to more complex behavior. Accordingly, mental illness was perceived to be only a complicated pattern of learned maladaptive responses; all patterns of response—normal or abnormal—could be derived from a few basic laws of learning.

The following excerpt illustrates the basic learning model as applied to mental illness (Eysenck, 1959):

> How, then, does modern learning theory look upon neurosis? In the first place, it would claim that neurotic symptoms are learned patterns of behavior which for some reason or other are inadaptive.
>
> The point . . . on which the theory here advocated breaks decisively with psychoanalytic thought of any description is on this. Freudian theory regards neurotic symptoms as adaptive mechanisms which are evidence of repression; they are "the visible upshot of unconscious causes." Learning theory does not postulate any such "unconscious causes," but regards neurotic symptoms as simple learned habits; there is no neurosis underlying the symptom, but merely the symptom itself. Get rid of the symptom and you have eliminated the neuroses. (p. 72)

Most behavior theorists define pathology either as socially maladaptive or socially deficient behavior. In contrast to most theorists of other schools, who associate mental illness exclusively with undesirable feelings or irrational actions, behaviorists place equal stress on *absent behaviors,* indicating that patients have failed to learn social skills and attitudes for effective functioning in their cultural group. Their position differs from that of neuroscientists, who define mental illness as physical disease or dysfunction; it differs also from psychoanalytic theorists, who believe that pathology is defined best in terms of unconscious processes; and it differs from the cognitivists, who base their definition on subjective misinterpretations and erroneous beliefs.

Although other psychologists were thinking along the same lines at the time, John Broadus Watson is generally considered the founder of behaviorism with the publication of his article *Psychology as the Behaviorist Views It* in 1913. He was a vocal force in popularizing these ideas in the United States. However, if Watson popularized behaviorism, B. F. Skinner radicalized it in the 1950s by ensconcing behaviorism even more deeply into Western culture and thought.

John Broadus Watson (1878–1958) was the youngest of four children born on a farm outside Greenville, South Carolina, to a religiously fundamentalist mother and a hard-drinking and periodically irresponsible father. His mother encouraged him from an early age to pursue a career in theology. Despite a restrictive upbringing, Watson's independent and rebellious spirit got him into frequent trouble, including two arrests for fighting and firing a gun inside the city limits, all before his sixteenth birthday. Watson entered Furman University at the age of 16 and although he was an able and talented enough student, by his own admission, he rarely put forth much effort in his studies. He planned to attend Princeton Theological Seminary on completion of his last term, until his rebellious antics changed the course of his life. One of Watson's favorite professors threatened to fail any student who turned in their final paper with the pages backward. Watson

John Broadus Watson

couldn't resist such a dare and was forced to spend an extra year at Furman. This extra year was not wasted, however, as he used this time to earn his master's degree. In addition, his mother died during this year, eliminating the outside forces pushing him toward a profession in the ministry and his interests drifted instead toward philosophy and psychology.

Watson attended the University of Chicago where he idolized the functionalist *James Rowland Angell* (see Chapter 13), but found a more comfortable niche in a biological approach to psychology. Growing up in the country gave him a distinct advantage in handling the lab animals. Watson became the youngest student to earn a PhD at the University of Chicago, completing his work in only three years. This breakneck pace, combined with his outside jobs, led to an almost inevitable breakdown in which he suffered from persistent insomnia and severe anxiety attacks.

He recovered quickly after a long overdue vacation and had the luxury of choosing from among several job offers in both psychology and neurology. He decided to stay at the University of Chicago as an assistant in experimental psychology. He quickly was promoted to assistant professor, but at the age of 30 was lured away by an associate professorship and much larger salary at Johns Hopkins University. Within two years, he was promoted to chairman of the department and editor of the *Psychological Review* when the old chair (James Mark Baldwin) was forced to resign over a scandal. Tired of answering questions about the relevance of his research to "real" psychology or the study of human consciousness, in 1913—in his characteristically rebellious way—Watson published an article entitled "Psychology as the Behaviorist Views It" in the *Psychological Review*. This inflammatory article demanded that psychology abandon introspection as a method of investigation, the approach that reflected the functionalist views of his Chicago mentors, and instead, should embrace the objective and empirical focus on overt behavior. In essence, he asserted that psychology should become the science of behavior, instead of the science of conscious experience. By behavior, Watson did not mean strictly simple acts, but complex tasks that were relevant to daily living and had practical applications, as he had been taught by the functionalists at Chicago.

The next year, Watson published *Behavior: An Introduction to Comparative Psychology*, which expounded greatly on his new ideas for the field of psychology. He was elected president of the American Psychological Association in 1915. In his acceptance speech, Watson reported how he had became acquainted with the conditioned reflex studies of Pavlov and his Russian contemporary V. M. Bekhterev, and saw how this method could circumvent introspective reports and give him the overt and objective data he sought. From that point onward, and with each succeeding publication, Watson made the conditioned reflex a central concept in behaviorism. He rejected Pavlov's physiological orientation, however. He had no interest in the inner structure or processes of the organism, stating that concepts defined at the level of behavior sufficiently accounted for all learning processes. Watson argued further that learning alone accounts for behavior and personality; this contention gave psychologists a new sense of importance and independence, but it separated psychology further than before from the mainstream of biological thought. His insistence on the absolute power of the environment on the person can be clearly seen in his now famous statement:

> Give me a dozen healthy infants, well-formed, and my own special world to bring them up in and I'll guarantee to take any one at random and train him to become any type of specialist I might select—doctor, lawyer, artist, merchant chief and, yes, even beggerman and thief, regardless of his talents, penchants, tendencies, abilities, vocations, and race of his ancestors. (1930, p. 104)

Watson was perhaps the first psychologist to apply learning principles to in-duce a *neurotic fear* response, as well as to provide a method for its extinction. In collaboration with his graduate student, and soon-to-be wife, *Rosalie Rayner,* Watson set out to produce a learned fear of white rats in an 11-month-old child named Albert. Prior research showed that sudden loud noises naturally elicited trembling and crying reactions in the youngster, whereas the sight of a white rat had no such effect. They arranged to place Albert and the white rat in close proximity; when Albert extended his hand to touch the furry animal, they im-mediately sounded the loud noise. After seven such pairings over two separate sessions, they recorded that the mere presence of the white rat produced a fear response in Albert. The once neutral stimulus of the rat now evoked a neurotic reaction comprising both avoidant behavior and tearfulness. In addition, Albert exhibited *stimulus generalization,* that is, his learned fear response extended to a sealskin coat, a rabbit, and a dog, objects with which he had no prior experi-ences of a frightening nature.

Subsequent to the Albert study, Watson guided the work of another research associate, *Mary Cover Jones,* who tried two ways of extinguishing a child's fear of white furry animals. The child, dubbed Little Peter, exhibited less fear when he observed other children calmly handling a white rat. By introducing several such fearless children as models for Peter to observe, Jones was the first to demonstrate empirically the contemporary behavior modification technique of *model imitation.* In another study with Peter, Jones progressively exposed the child to a formerly feared white rabbit by a series of graduated steps that brought him into closer and closer contact with the animal; in due course, Peter was able to fondle the rabbit calmly. By following a course of progressive toleration of what previously produced anxiety, Jones's technique led to the now well-established behavioral procedure termed *desensitization.*

As brilliant and meteoric as was the rise of Watson's academic career, its end was accomplished with no less aplomb and flash. In 1920, Watson di-vorced his first wife to marry his graduate student, Rosalie Rayner, a recent graduate of Vassar and daughter of a prominent Baltimore family. This scan-dal was evidently too much for Baltimore society of the 1920s and the Johns Hopkins administration forced Watson to resign his post, abruptly ending his already distinguished academic career at the age of 42. Watson moved to New York, was befriended by the sociologist W. I. Thomas, and was invited to join the J. Walter Thompson advertising agency on a trial basis. He excelled there, and within four years, he was their highest paid vice-president. He continued to lecture on behaviorist psychology and also wrote on popular psychology topics including a book with his wife that became the first com-mercially successful child-rearing guide. The method he advocated was as nightmarish as any distopian novel could dream up; strict schedules, con-trolled environments, and no signs of physical affection. He never reentered the field of academic psychology; instead he pursued a highly successful busi-ness career.

Burrhus Frederic Skinner's (1904–1990) skills as an inventor came in handy in his lab where he constructed an operant conditioning apparatus, what Clark Hull later called, the "Skinner Box." Skinner placed a hungry animal, such as a rat or later a pigeon, in the box and when it performed an arbitrary response (pressing a lever or pecking an illuminated disc) reinforced the action with a pellet of food. The term *operant conditioning* comes from the fact that the animal "operates" on its environment to get a reward. Skinner's apparatus insulated the rat from external noises, and further refinements allowed a rat to run its experiment and return to the beginning without human handling. With additional fine tuning and tinkering, Skinner chanced on a method for cumulative recording that drew a curve of the change in the rate of response of a rat pressing a lever. A roll of paper would move beneath the box at a continuous speed and a pen point would move higher by a fixed amount with each successive response so that few responses would yield a flat curve and more responses would yield a steeper slope. After completing his dissertation, "The Concept of the Reflex," in 1931, he accepted a postdoctoral position and eventually a Junior Fellowship at Harvard and continued his lever box experiments and further developed his science of operant conditioning.

Some of these later experiments yielded important discoveries dealing with the contingencies of reinforcement such as an extinction curve, which happens when a response has been regularly reinforced and then suddenly ceased (as when Skinner's pellet-dispensing mechanism accidentally broke). The rat continued to elicit the response at a very high rate in a frustrated manner, then the response slowed with a few bursts of response until an eventual flattening of the curve occurred and the rat no longer exhibited a response. The response had been extinguished.

Skinner was the eldest son of an attorney for the Erie Railroad and a socially well-to-do mother in Susquehanna, Pennsylvania. His graduating senior class had only eight members and young Fred Skinner, as he was known, stood apart from his classmates not only as an intellectually gifted student but also as a keen inventor and builder. He was constantly tinkering with mechanical devices and voraciously consumed books about inventive people. At 18, Skinner left home to attend Hamilton College in another small town: Clinton, New York.

While in college, Skinner wrote several short stories, some of which Robert Frost read and commented on. Encouraged by Frost's words of praise, and despite his parents' fears that having a writer in the family would socially ruin them, Skinner resolved to become a writer after finishing college.

Skinner quickly became disenchanted with the possibilities presented by a literary career, and after a small experiment with a bohemian lifestyle in Greenwich Village, enrolled in Harvard to study psychology in 1928. Even before this, he had been greatly impressed by Bertrand Russell, and through Russell's work, John Watson. He then looked to Pavlov for guidance in developing an experimental method. Skinner came to firmly believe that if you can control the environment, order will begin to emerge in behavior.

In 1936, Skinner moved to the University of Minnesota and by the early 1940s had begun research on the effects of different schedules of reinforcement. One Friday afternoon, Skinner realized he only had a few pellets of food for his animals and decided to ration the food by reinforcing only intermittent responses instead of every response. To his surprise, he found that this type of reinforcement spurred his subjects to respond even more frequently than if rewarded after every response. This in turn inspired a wave of new research by Skinner and his students on the effects of schedules of reinforcement. In 1945, he accepted a position as chairman of the Department of Psychology at Indiana University and in 1957, Ferster and Skinner published *Schedules of Reinforcement,* which reported on millions of responses that they had recorded. In 1951, Skinner published a paper "How to Teach Animals" describing a process he termed *shaping,* whereby he could train an animal to complete a complex task (e.g., teaching a pigeon to choose a playing card from a deck).

Burrhus Frederic Skinner

Not to be outdone by his behavioral forerunner Watson, Skinner was by nature a provocateur, an unabashedly egotistic and controversial personality. He enjoyed eliciting vehement and personal attacks by others; he met his match when he contended with Noam Chomsky (described in Chapter 10). A showman and popularizer, Skinner became an effective publicist for his cause, a TV personality who enjoyed tweaking others and confronting what he judged to be their naive superstitious beliefs. In his novel, *Walden II* (1948), he sought to demonstrate how, by controlling behavior through reinforcements, he could ultimately produce a happy society; this book became a favorite and popular novel of utopian thinking in undergraduate English literature classes, despite its somewhat coarse literary talent. In his autobiography, he presented himself as having been a troublesome and rambunctious child who invariably did what he wished, caring little about his impact on others, a behavioral characteristic he manifested throughout his life. In my many extended conversations with him, I—along with many others—encountered Skinner as not merely an iconoclast and curmudgeon, but as a person of strong narcissistic and minor sociopathic inclinations. His forte was offending others and eliciting their outrage. He led a group of equally contentious younger behaviorists for several decades, most of whom had no doubt about the absolute correctness of their views.

Not surprisingly, the practical and social implications of Skinner's work became popular in academic psychoscientific circles. Unlike many psychologists, who identified few financial opportunities in their studies, Skinner became keenly aware of the economic possibilities of his efforts and made significant attempts to commercially develop them. His ideas ranged from pigeon-guided missiles, to machines that monitored babies, to teaching machines, and to his novel *Walden II*. His novel described an imaginary community where a perfectly harmonious and blissful populace was completely controlled using the principles of operant conditioning. Not especially popular when first written, it became a counterculture best seller in the 1960s and 1970s. Of his several economically viable ideas, the baby-tending machine was probably the most successful. He constructed this device after the birth of his second daughter, Deborah; it built a measure of ease in his wife's duties and made sure that Debbie was warm, dry, and entertained. The box provided a controlled environment for the child to live in; it had filtered air that was warmed to an ideal temperature and was filled with entertaining and stimulating toys. The *air-crib* was marketed as a freedom tool to relieve parents from tedious responsibilities, freedom for children from restrictive clothing and blankets, as well as limiting exposure to free-floating viruses. Skinner had the following to say about his daughter's experience in the crib:

> Predictions and tales of dire consequences have not been supported. Deborah broke her leg in a skiing accident but presumably not because of "the box." Otherwise she has had remarkably good health. She is now in college, interested in art and music, from Bach to Beatle, and she usually beats me at chess. (1967, p. 403)

Skinner disavowed the necessity for theory, and the simplicity of his formulations reflects his conviction that all behavior—normal or pathological—can be reduced to a few objective principles and concepts, known as operant conditioning. This first pure behavior theory had an auspicious beginning in the field of behavior therapy; however, further research was necessary to appraise Skinner's simplified formulation of mental illness. Millon (1969) made an early effort to expand on Skinner's basic concepts and to demonstrate their special utility in explaining the learning of complex personality styles or coping (instrumental) strategies.

Promoting Neobehaviorism

Although Watson's insistence on objectivity and experimentation contributed greatly to the scientific maturity of psychology, his ideas only modestly influenced the study of mental illness. For the next 30 years, neobehaviorists such as Clark Leonard Hull, Edward Chase Tolman, and Edwin Ray Guthrie devised brilliant experiments and theories of learning. Each of these men took a less adamant behavioristic position than Watson or Skinner, but retained those researchers' emphasis on objectivity and experimentation. In World War II, the neobehaviorists contributed to solving problems of mental disorder in the military. A rapprochement gradually emerged between behaviorists and clinical pathologists. In the absence of any fully convincing theory for mental illness, and on the assumption that all behavior was based on universal psychological processes, concepts drawn from learning research were applied to the problems of abnormal psychology with confidence.

The collection of individuals recognized as neobehaviorists in the 1930s and 1940s were a diverse group of American psychologists who helped the science of behaviorism blossom into full maturity. They often fought bitterly among themselves and inspired loyal and devoted followers who carried on these disputes. Despite their differences, they all shared a vision for psychology that denied the importance of the conscious mind and gave exalted status to S-R (stimulus-response) bonds and a rigorous scientific method.

Born in a log cabin near Akron, New York, in 1884, **Clark Leonard Hull (1884–1952)** was a young man with a remarkable drive to achieve and a gift for mathematics and logic. His family moved to a farm in Michigan when Hull was 3 or 4 years old. For most of his early education, he attended a one-room rural school, but he eventually enrolled in the college preparatory program at Alma College. Here he was exposed to and inspired by geometric principles that allowed him to deduce new relationships from established premises. This fascination with mathematics and the deductive method stayed with him throughout his life. Financial worries and illness plagued him throughout his education. From an early age, he worked at a host of odd jobs, including clearing trees, husking corn, splitting fence rails, and plowing fields, to earn his way. He even took a year off from high school to be an apprentice mining engineer. On graduating high school, a bout of typhoid fever contracted from eating contaminated food at his graduation dinner prevented him from entering college for a year. This illness and its consequent high fevers left him with permanent neurological deficits, particularly for remembering names.

Hull pursued engineering at Alma College, but in his second year was stricken with polio, which left him with a paralyzed leg and ruined his hopes of a future in engineering. He took off several years to recover and earn money by teaching high school before completing his undergraduate studies at the University of Michigan in psychology. In 1913, Hull was admitted to the graduate program at the University of Wisconsin where he immediately became fascinated with experimental psychology. He received his PhD 5 years later and continued on as faculty at Wisconsin.

Hull's research and contributions to psychology in the ensuing years fell into three distinctive phases. The first 10 years of his career focused on aptitude testing and statistics. While reviewing literature to prepare to teach a course in psychological testing, Hull was horrified by the paucity of scientific evidence on aptitude testing, particularly attempts to validate these instruments. He became determined to compile what was then known about aptitude testing and to further the scientific body of knowledge by validating many of these measures himself. His first major text, *Aptitude Testing,* was published in 1928, and the following year he joined the faculty of Yale University.

The second phase of Hull's career, which centered on the value of hypnosis and suggestibility, particularly in medical cures, was more short-lived. This area was in as much disarray and plagued with scientific ineptitude as aptitude testing had been. Hull felt compelled to bring some rigor and order to the subject. He began conducting experiments and encouraging his students to do the same. He published 32 papers and a book entitled *Hypnosis and Suggestibility* (1933) using experimental investigation. A former subject who claimed that being hypnotized had caused her to have a mental breakdown sued Hull and the university, which prompted Yale to halt his research.

Characteristically, a multitude of other areas piqued Hull's interest, and he began drafting a behavioristic account of psychology in earnest. This phase lasted until the end of his life. Inspired by Isaac Newton's *Principia* and Bertrand Russell and Alfred North Whitehead's *Principia Mathematica,* Hull found a model to use for a psychological system. With his engineering background and his love of mechanical workings, Hull became intrigued with the idea of humans as machines. After reading Pavlov, Hull proposed that conditioned reflexes were a mechanism that allowed people to react to environmental conditions and sought to devise a theory that extended the principles of classical conditioning to all types of learning. However, after reading Thorndike, he accepted the ideas of reinforcement based on drive reduction, adopted the law of effect, and became more of a reinforcement theorist. In 1943, he published *Principles of Behavior* and began a long process of attempting to reconcile Thorndike's law of effect and Pavlov's classical conditioning. Hull spent his remaining years refining his behavioristic theory, eventually formulating 17 postulates and 17 corollaries.

Hull may have been the most influential experimental psychologist from the 1930s through the 1950s, articulating a series of theoretical ideas with a degree of rigor and analytical detail unknown to the field both before and since. Both mathematical and deductive, his theories lent themselves readily to experimental test.

Edwin Ray Guthrie's (1886–1959) major contribution to psychology was the simplicity of his learning theory in that it relied on a single factor: S-R contiguity. Contiguity, in terms of learning theory, means simply that an association between a stimulus and response will be formed when they occur together or very close together. Guthrie did not suggest that the stimulus caused the response in any way, merely that it was present when the response happens, as if it were a cue for the response to take place. Guthrie contended that he could explain seemingly complex learning phenomena, such as extinction, forgetting, and insightful behavior by the principle that a stimulus that accompanied a response will tend to be followed by the same response when that stimulus recurs.

Several matters distinguished Guthrie from the other behaviorists, aside from his emphasis on the simplicity of learning. Most notably, in contrast to

Hull, he avoided psychological terminology and formal deductive theory. In contrast to Skinner, he did not believe that reinforcement was necessary for learning, but believed rewards prevented an S-R association from becoming unlearned. To demonstrate this latter assertion, he filmed cats escaping from puzzle boxes. The cats repeated the movement that had led to their successful escape from the last box. Hence, Guthrie argued that if a stimulus elicits a response just one time, the S-R connection is established. This became known as *one-trial learning*. The recipient of numerous honors, Guthrie served as president of the American Psychological Association in 1945 and was awarded the association's Gold Medal for distinguished contributions to the science of learning.

Neal Elgar Miller (1909–2000) was largely influenced by Hull's theories and sought to apply them to behavioral phenomena, as well as to develop them further. Hull's favorite protégé of the mid-1930s, Miller advocated a strict drive-reduction model for psychology and developed an acquired drive theory that sought to explain the acquisition of fear or anxiety through conditioning as similar to drive. Together with his Yale colleague, *John Dollard* (discussed later in this chapter), Miller developed a personality model considered among the most innovative of its time. Their stimulus-response theory held to the tenets of empiricism inherent in a behaviorist framework, yet was comprehensive enough to integrate the more abstract forces of inner drives and cultural influences promoted by competing psychodynamic and social psychological schools of thought.

Miller earned his PhD from Yale University in 1935 and became a Social Science Research Council traveling fellow. This took him to Austria, where he underwent a brief training analysis at the Vienna Institute of Psychoanalysis. On returning to the United States, Miller embarked on a career at Yale that centered largely around experimental problems on diverse issues such as drive acquisition and the effects of drugs on behavior. A gifted laboratory psychologist, he joined Yale's prestigious Institute of Human Relations, a cutting-edge interdisciplinary department dedicated to bringing about working alliances between such diverse human sciences as psychiatry, sociology, psychology, and anthropology. Here Miller met John Dollard, among other young cohorts who made up this exceptional group, and the blending of viewpoints and methodologies between these partners set the foundation for Neal Miller and Dollard's distinctive contributions. Working at Yale, the two men developed and explicated a reconceptualization of psychoanalytic phenomena in terms of a learning theory framework. Their efforts culminated first in their 1941 publication, *Social Learning and Imitation*, and later in the more comprehensive and fully explicated volume, *Personality and Psychotherapy: An Analysis in Terms of Learning, Thinking, and Culture* (1950).

Miller and Dollard's joint efforts emphasized the social contexts of learning. Drawing on the seminal works of learning theorists such as Clark Hull, Edward Thorndike, and Ivan Pavlov, they summed up Freudian speculation in terms of observable learning constructs. Preferring the concept of *drive* to the Freudian construct of *libido*, their S-R theory held that this notion was the motivating force of learning theory. Next, they studied the concept of *cue*, the discriminative stimuli in the environment that served as the "signal" to draw attention to their drive. What followed naturally was the *response*, the "action" component of these instrumental learning principles. Finally, there was the "attainment," or the *reward* inherent in this learning process. According to Miller and Dollard, psychoanalytic concepts, such as the developmental stages (e.g., oral, anal, phallic, latency), could be explained and examined in terms of a "true, objective science" (e.g., by outlining critical periods in terms of instrumental actions, such as feeding, cleanliness training, early sex training, and anger-anxiety-conflicts). Though many of the constructs inherent in this theory are not novel to either psychodynamic or behaviorist schools, what sets them apart is their support for previously speculative concepts with firm experimental grounding and observable empirical data.

Some consider Dollard and Miller's work to be inappropriately classified as behavior theory. Critics point out that the two merely translated the concepts of traditional Freudian psychoanalysis into the language of Pavlov's conditioning and Hull's learning theory. They further note that a proper application of behavioristic principles should have led the two to a new conception of mental illness. This criticism seems unjust. Dollard and Miller made no pretensions about devising a new theory. Further, they were the first modern behavior theorists willing to tackle the complex problems of mental illness, and they did so in a systematic and often brilliant fashion.

Dollard and Miller proposed, as did Freud, that intense emotional conflicts are the basis of behavior pathology. By conflict, they meant the existence of two or more mutually incompatible drives; thus, conflicts could occur between innate physiological needs, such as hunger or sex, or socially acquired emotional responses, such as fear, anger, or anxiety. They categorized the components of these conflicts as "approach" or "avoidant." For example, a college student who wished to marry his girl friend (approach) but feared parental disapproval of this desire (avoidant) would experience conflict.

Disorders, according to Dollard and Miller, will not arise unless individuals repress or are otherwise unaware of their conflict; problems take on serious proportions because unconscious conflicts are not accessible to realistic thought and intelligent resolution. The consequence of this repression is far-reaching. To stop thinking about the conflict, individuals tend to inhibit thinking about other problem areas; consequently, their overall capacity to reason and plan is impaired.

Dollard and Miller viewed symptoms of disorder as efforts to deny painful conflicts. A phobia of crowded places may cover up conflicting feelings toward others; similarly, antagonisms to women may arise in moralistic men as a cloak for disturbing sexual desires. To Dollard and Miller then, mental disorders consist of unconscious conflicts that cannot be resolved because they are not available to conscious reasoning. As a result, individuals engage in shortsighted partial resolutions that may invite more serious conflicts and complications.

Miller's later research, carried out with colleagues at Rockefeller University, showed that animals, and presumably humans as well, can learn reliably to change cardiovascular and visceral responses associated instrumentally in getting rewards. The list of such bodily responses that Miller conditioned operantly included heart rate and blood pressure changes, control of blood vessel diameters, contractions of the large intestine, and urine production by the kidneys, each modification relevant to various health conditions. These studies also demonstrated that visceral actions exhibit the same laws as do other, more voluntarily learned responses, such as skill acquisition and performance retention, as well as behavioral extinction, generalization, and discrimination.

Learning through Cognitive Processes

Behaviorism sought to account for mental phenomena without actually summoning the mind. They managed to reject the influence of the mind by claiming that notions of consciousness and thoughts were myths, that consciousness actually comprised sensations of bodily movement that were orally reported. Although this behavioristic model persisted for decades, other approaches concurrently and in intervening years had the foresight to recognize the role the mind plays as a causal agent in determining learning.

An impure, though highly promising, variant of the behavioral school is known as the "social learning" approach. It was developed initially in Neal Miller and Dollard's book, *Social Learning and Imitation* (1941), and more fully formulated as a "cognitive learning" approach in the work of Julian Rotter (1954, 1966) and Albert Bandura (1968, 1977). These theorists diverged from the behavioristic philosophy to an even greater extent than did the neobehaviorists in that they applied learning principles to explain nonbehavioral data such as cognitive expectancies and self-reinforcing thoughts. Their innovative ideas can be traced to learning theorists of a distinct cognitive persuasion such as Edward Tolman.

Born in Newton, Massachusetts, **Edward Chase Tolman (1886–1959),** the son of a manufacturing company president, was expected to join the family business with his older brother. Characteristically, neither did. Instead, both brothers attended the Massachusetts Institute of Technology and forged successful careers in science. This decision likely resulted from the tolerant and progressive atmosphere fostered in the Tolman household. The family encouraged ideas such as equal rights for women and African Americans, humanitarianism, and Unitarianism, as well as more puritan values of hard work and the Quaker values of "plain living and high thinking."

After completing his undergraduate degree in electrochemistry, Tolman followed his brother's footsteps into academia, but he did not want to compete in his brother's graduate field of chemistry and physics. He had begun reading William James and enrolled in Harvard's summer session, where he took courses in philosophy and psychology. He felt that psychology suited his talents and offered a good blend of philosophy and science; thus he enrolled at Harvard as a graduate student in philosophy and psychology. After his first year, he spent the summer in Germany in preparation for his German language requirements for his PhD and a month at Giessen with Koffka, which primed Tolman to be receptive to Gestalt concepts that became more widely known after World War I. Earning his degree in 1915, he was hired at Northwestern University as an instructor. Tolman was uncomfortable teaching and often suffered bouts of self-consciousness in front of the classroom. These qualities, coupled with some of his pacifist activities that the university administration construed as war retrenchment, earned him a quick dismissal from the faculty in 1918. Securing a position at Berkeley that year, Tolman embarked on what proved to be a fruitful and happy academic career that lasted until his retirement in 1954. He experienced a sense of freedom in the open California environment, which inspired him to develop a more reflective and cognitive approach to learning that has influenced psychologists ever since.

In what he came to term his theory of *purposive behaviorism*, Tolman asserted that lower animal species, such as rats, do not behave solely in terms of the stimuli and reinforcements they experience, but also in terms of their expectations, that is, an internalized awareness or acquired knowledge of what leads to what in certain situations. Influenced by his student and later colleague, *David Krech*, Tolman employed the term *intervening variables* to represent the internalized thought processes that occur between external stimuli and overt responses. As he and others conceived it, these intervening variables are not directly observable, but are inferred processes judged on the basis of observable data. In this manner, he sought to remain faithful to the behavioral thesis of objectivity but, as became increasingly apparent, he had opened a cognitive floodgate to the mind.

Despite his ultimate introduction of the concept of cognition, Tolman continued to consider himself a behaviorist because he asserted that "the only psychological statements that can be scientifically validated are statements about the organism's behavior, about stimulus situations, or about inferred, but objectively definable, intervening variables" (Tolman, 1952, p. 331). Today, however, most would likely classify Tolman as a cognitive behaviorist.

His cognitive conceptualization of learning differed from traditional Thorndikian or Hullian models of learning in an important way. He did not conceive learning in terms of strengthening stimulus-response connections defined by physiological foundations, nor by Watson's "mere muscle-twitchisms." Instead, he posited that learning is forming "sign-gestalt expectations," "sign-significate relations," or "hypotheses." (Tolman's neologisms were legendary.) The cognitive component of this theory did not signify that Tolman embraced introspection as a method (see Chapter 10). Instead, Tolman believed that purpose and cognition could be studied as objective, observable aspects of behavior.

Tolman believed that the brain organized knowledge in meaningful ways and that knowledge, as noted, was more than a simple collection of stimulus-response pairings. He described its structure as follows:

> [The brain] is far more like a map control room than it is like an old-fashioned telephone exchange. The stimuli, which are allowed in, are not connected by just simple one-to-one switches to the outgoing responses. Rather, the incoming impulses are usually worked over and elaborated in the central control room into a tentative, cognitive like map of the environment. And it is this tentative map, indicating routes and paths and environmental relationships, which finally determines what responses, if any, the animal will finally release. (1948, p. 192)

In his theory of purposive behaviorism, Tolman meant that behavior should be conceptualized at the molar level as goal-directed or purposeful. Strict behaviorists of the time rejected the notion that any animal, humans included, could engage in such directed behavior. Instead, they argued that all behavior was deterministic, meaning that it was fully determined by past influences rather than future aims. Tolman argued that even simple behaviors, such as rats searching for food, was purposive and an abstract, long-term goal that could not be understood by simple stimulus-reward connections. Tolman was thereby fully open to notions of *motivation* and *incentives*.

Although few of his many doctoral students continued to conduct Tolmanian research or employ his concepts after they left Berkeley, many dedicated their books to him and judged him to have been much more correct than his erstwhile rivals such as Hull or Skinner. Students, colleagues, and even his professional rivals admired him enormously.

Departing from the view that people were motivated by physiologically based impulses, **Julian Rotter (1916–   )** conceptualized behaviors as motivated by expectancies, leading them to seek out positive reinforcement and stimulation while avoiding negative or unpleasant stimulation. Hence, a person's behavior cannot be understood as merely an automatic response to a set of stimuli. Instead, each person brings a unique life history of learning and expectations into the equation as well. Change a person's expectancies about an event and subsequent changes in behavior will result.

Rotter was the third son of Jewish immigrant parents in Brooklyn, New York. Like many others of his generation, Rotter was profoundly affected by the Great Depression, which not only raised his awareness of social injustice, but also his understanding of the effect of situational environments on people. By the end of high school, he had begun reading books by Freud and Adler. When he entered Brooklyn College, he attended Adler's seminars and meetings of the Society of Individual Psychology, which met in Adler's home. He completed a master's degree at the University of Iowa under Kurt Lewin (see

Chapter 12) and accepted an internship in clinical psychology (extremely rare for that time) at Worcester State Hospital in Massachusetts. In 1939, he started work on his PhD in clinical psychology at Indiana University. Completing the degree in 1941, Rotter became one of the first clinical psychologists to be trained in what became labeled in later years as the traditional model. After serving in the Army during World War II, he joined the faculty at Ohio State University where he began to conceptualize his social and cognitive learning theory, ultimately published in 1954 in *Social Learning Theory and Clinical Psychology*. In 1963, he left Ohio to become the director of clinical training at the University of Connecticut.

Although an experimentally oriented behaviorist in his early years, Rotter also was a practicing clinician, well versed in the methodology of treatment. He observed that patients' psychological outlooks were shaped largely by their key life experiences, some of which were gratifying and others painful. He concluded that these experiences were akin to what behaviorists termed positive and negative reinforcements. Moreover, he asserted that people developed strong *generalized expectancies* about which life events and behaviors would likely lead to positive or negative outcomes. Rotter then led students to conduct a series of experiments to refine a general theoretical model for how life experiences generate attitudes and expectancies that shape a person's future outlook.

Rotter proposed three concepts basic to his social and cognitively oriented model of learning: *behavior potential, expectancy, and reinforcement value.* Behavior potential (BP) referred to the thesis that behaviors that most frequently led to positive reinforcements (rewarding experiences) in the past have the greatest potential for occurring again. In any situation, individuals choose from among the many behavior options that are present, the behavior that has the highest potential for positive reinforcement. The second concept, expectancy (E), was defined as the probability held by individuals that a particular reinforcement will occur as a function of a specific behavior on their part—the likelihood, as they view it, that what they do will prove rewarding. For a particular behavior potential to remain high, individuals must continue to expect that it will lead to positive reinforcement. Reinforcement value (RV) is the desirability of an outcome of behavior. As people have their own life experiences, the reinforcement value for an outcome is different for every person. Using these three components, Rotter developed an equation to explain behavior: $BP = f(E \text{ \& } RV)$, meaning that the likelihood of eliciting a particular behavior is a function of the probability that a certain behavior will lead to a certain outcome and how desirable the person perceives that outcome to be.

Born in the small hamlet of Mundare in Alberta, Canada, **Albert Bandura (1925–   )** quickly learned how to become self-directed in seeking out educational opportunities. With only two teachers serving his entire high school, students were left largely to pursue their own studies and discover their own interests. Bandura spent the summer after high school graduation in the Yukon, filling holes to protect the Alaska Highway from sinking. While there, he mingled with some extremely interesting characters who helped him develop an appreciation for everyday and ordinary mental illness. The other workers on the highway were a colorful group, mainly "on the lam" from creditors or the government, who had a penchant for home-brewed vodka. After completing his bachelor's degree in psychology at the University of British Columbia, he pursued a master's and a doctorate at the University of Iowa, working under the experimental guidance of Kenneth Spence and the clinical direction of Isidore Farber. He then joined the faculty at Stanford University where he has remained since 1952.

Albert Bandura

Partly owing to the freedom afforded him at Stanford, and partly because of his own curiosity and diversity of interests, Bandura pursued multiple areas of research that covered a wide array of innovative psychological themes. Among them were concepts such as *vicarious conditioning* and *self-reinforcement systems*. The first pertains to the fact that people can learn their beliefs and attitudes simply by observing the experiences and feelings of others; for example, if a youngster happened to glance out the window and see a neighborhood dog chasing another child, the observing youngster might learn to fear that dog even though he had no frightening experience with it himself. The second concept refers to the fact that persons reinforce their attitudes and emotions simply by thinking about them; moreover, repetitive self-reinforcements often supplant the objective reinforcements of reality. Bandura stated this thesis as follows:

> Until recently, self-reinforcing behavior has been virtually ignored in psychological theorizing and experimentation, perhaps because of the common preoccupation with animal learning. Unlike human subjects, who continually engage in self-evaluative and self-reinforcing behavior, rats or chimpanzees are disinclined to pat themselves on the back for commendable performances, or to berate themselves for getting lost in cul-de-sacs. By contrast, people typically make self-reinforcement contingent on performing in ways they have come to value as an index of personal merit. They often set themselves relatively explicit criteria of achievement; failure to meet them is considered undeserving of reward and may elicit self-denial or even self-punishment. Conversely, individuals tend to reward themselves generously when they attain or exceed their self-imposed standards. Self-administered positive and negative stimuli may thus serve both as powerful incentives for learning and as effective reinforcers in maintaining behavior in humans. (1974, p. 859)

Contained within this line of research was the idea of promoting the effects of behavior modification therapies through imitative modeling. According to

Bandura, direct selective positive reinforcement is an exceedingly difficult and time-inefficient method for advancing the acquisition of new adaptive learnings. Effective though such operant learning procedures may be for strengthening and building responses that already exist in patients' behavioral repertoire, they demand extremely ingenious and time-consuming manipulations to generate new response patterns. Rather than struggle through this tiresome and at best unreliable procedure, the task of forming new responses can be abbreviated and accelerated by arranging real-life or therapist-modeling conditions in which the desired activity is seen or is performed. Such modeled sequences may be designed in combination with reinforcement; thus, in a typical procedure, patients obtain a reward when they imitate an act performed by a real or enacted model.

Arthur Wilbur Staats (1924–   ) attempted to integrate Gestalt cognitive principles into a social behavioristic theory, stressing learned configurations of small responses. He also developed an innovative application for learning theory when he incorporated affective, conditioned states, calling it the A-R-D theory, shorthand for attitude, reinforcement, and directive processes. Although others before Staats had shown that attitudes influenced learning and that learning was more easily achieved when it was congruent with their attitude, Staats considered cognitive attitudes as having an especially strong influence on learning, serving as a major reinforcer just as food can be. Attitudes can also have positive or negative valences. He argued that most adult behavior is incited not by basic physiological needs but by attitudes.

Staats was born in New York, the youngest of four children, into a radically thinking, atheistic but Jewish ethnic, vegetarian, and economically poor family. Although he always scored very high on standardized tests, he consistently underperformed in school and preferred to engross himself in the independent thought and reading that was typical in his family.

Staats hypothesized on a variety of topics and resurrected some older ideas of prior learning theorists. His contributions ranged from new ideas about the formation of language hierarchies to experiments on conditioning personality characteristics. Significantly, Staats introduced the concept of the self into his brand of behaviorism. He conceptualized the self as an array of responses to diverse introspective components such as body image and personal achievements. This perceived self could even become a stimulus, and reactions to the self could mediate overt behavior.

Generating Behavior Therapies

With the exception of the work of a few scattered pioneers, behavior modification therapy rose to the status of a major treatment alternative only 40 years ago; it has faltered in recent years as a consequence of the growth of cognitive therapeutic approaches, discussed in Chapter 10. Differences in theory and technique exist among adherents of the traditional behavioral approach to treatment; but they share certain important beliefs.

Behaviorists argue that therapy procedures should consist of the systematic application of experimentally derived and corroborated principles. They avoid loosely formulated techniques derived from unverifiable clinical observations, which they contend typify the methodology of other treatment approaches. Behavior therapists subscribe in common to the concepts and methods of learning research. This orientation reflects both their desire to adhere to scientific principles and their belief that mental disorders are learned behaviors that are socially maladaptive or deficient. According to this view, whatever has been learned, adaptive or maladaptive, can be unlearned by the therapeutic application of the same principles and conditions that led to its initial acquisition. To achieve the goals of treatment, therapists must first specify the maladaptive behaviors (overt symptoms) and the environmental conditions (stimuli and reinforcements) that sustain them. Afterward, therapists can arrange a program of learning procedures tailored specifically to the elimination of the maladaptive responses and to the institution of adaptive ones.

A feature that most clearly distinguishes pure behavior therapies from other approaches is their commitment to an action-suppressive process. Behaviorists consider emotional ventilation and insight, the bedrock of other schools of therapy, to be of dubious value; they not only view these two procedures as time-consuming digressions, but often consider them to be counterproductive, that is, to strengthen rather than weaken maladaptive behaviors. In their view, the task of therapy is to achieve as directly as possible changes in real-life action, not greater self-understanding or affective expression.

During the late 1950s, stimulated largely by Skinner's provocative writings, the coalescence of learning and psychotherapy took a new turn. Instead of merely restating accepted forms of treatment in the vernacular of learning concepts, as Dollard and Miller (1950) did, investigators began to use principles that were first derived in behavioral learning research to create entirely new forms of therapy.

Many academic "learning" psychologists performed clinical psychological services during World War II. On their return to academia, several sought to bridge these two fields, which provided a fresh momentum to the behavioral movement. The hope was that learning principles might furnish a firm scientific basis for the nebulous concepts of therapy and that clinical processes might provide a new source of data to enrich the narrow sphere within which learning research had long been confined. The first of these integrative efforts limited itself to translating therapeutic processes into the language of learning theory. Although these writings suggested a new way of conceptualizing and explaining traditional forms of therapy, they suggested no new techniques for executing therapy. Since its earliest conceptualization, behavior therapy has transitioned through several cycles of being intolerant and rejecting of cognitive and other psychological influences and being more accepting of them as an integral part of understanding human behavior.

After receiving his PhD from Harvard University in 1903, Knight Dunlap spent two years at Berkeley before accepting a position at Johns Hopkins

University. At Harvard, he greatly impressed Hugo Münsterberg with his knack for building laboratory equipment. While at Johns Hopkins, Dunlap published "Habits," a monograph that demonstrated the interrelationship between learning and cognition, as well as many other important critiques on instincts and consciousness. Although eventually assuming the duties of the chair of the department at Johns Hopkins after John B. Watson's forced resignation, Dunlap spent most of his career in Watson's shadow. Nevertheless, Dunlap and Watson mutually influenced each other while they worked together, and it is likely that Dunlap helped Watson abandon introspection as the method for psychological investigation and pursue practical applications of the theories he was developing.

Dunlap was critical of Watson, particularly when it came to Watson's rejection of cognitive influences on behavior. Instead, Dunlap proposed a neuropsychological model that viewed consciousness as correlated with neural circuits that had connections to the motor system. Although he agreed with the traditional behaviorist view that the content of analysis of consciousness was irrelevant, he felt that conscious experiences could be studied scientifically as a process. Considering that current psychology has moved in the direction of Dunlap's conceptualization of a cognitive behaviorism, it is curious that Watson and not Dunlap remains an esteemed and dominant figure in psychological history. Dunlap can fairly be called the "forgotten man" of psychology.

John Dollard (1900–1980) received his PhD in sociology from the University of Chicago and received further training at the Berlin Psychoanalytic Institute. He dedicated his career, spent largely at Yale University's Institute for Human Relations, toward unifying the social sciences of anthropology, sociology, and psychology.

Collaboratively with Neal Miller, he proposed as complete a theory of personality as any early learning theorist could have formulated. In essence, Dollard and Miller translated the concepts of traditional Freudian psychoanalysis into the language of Pavlovian and Hullian learning theory. They proposed, as did Freud, that intense emotional conflicts are the basis of behavior pathology. By conflict, they meant the existence of two or more mutually incompatible drives.

Based on earlier experimental research by two psychologists in the late 1930s, *Norman R. F. Maier* with dogs and *Howard S. Liddell* with sheep and pigs, **Jules Masserman (1912–1990),** a psychiatrist by training, sought to connect the findings of experimentally induced neuroses explicitly to psychoanalytic concepts. Arranging learning conditions that produced severe conflicts in cats, he recorded not only their consequent and extreme startle reactions to incidental stimuli but also their physiological disturbances, notably tachycardia, irregular breathing, and profuse perspiration. Like Maier and Liddell, Masserman then took a major step in attempting to treat his animals. For example, by increasing a cat's desire to achieve one of a pair of competing drives, he was able to overcome its state of immobility. Similarly, he introduced cat "models" that demonstrated normal behaviors and served as exemplars for disturbed animals. Most successful among his therapeutic techniques were procedures that enabled cats to achieve mastery over a feared situation, such as being able in a conflict setting to have full control over when it would receive a desired reinforcement. Ultimately, these animals showed a marked reduction of neurotic behaviors, such that they could not be distinguished from their counterparts who had not been disturbed.

Born in Waterbury, Connecticut, **Andrew Salter (1914–1970)** earned an advanced degree from New York University and was a highly influential consulting psychologist. He firmly believed in the role of conditioning and sought to build therapeutic methods on the scientific bedrock of Pavlov's conditioning research in his book, *Conditioned Reflex Therapy* (1949). Ranging across a broad variety of mental disorders, such as stuttering, shyness, anxiety, masochism, and the psychopathic personality, he grounded his well-organized techniques in what he termed therapy for personality habits.

Salter was perhaps the first behavior theorist to identify personal assertiveness as an important positive goal for his patients. Although adhering rigidly to Pavlovian conceptions of cortical excitation and inhibition, he encouraged inhibited individuals to vent their emotions to others in a spontaneous and open manner. He suggested that his patients express their feelings verbally, that is, tell people when they felt good, bad, angry, or annoyed. Furthermore, Salter recommended that they should openly disagree with others and speak out when they felt unjustly treated or overlooked.

Although Joseph Wolpe and Hans J. Eysenck developed their ideas independently of one another, they are sufficiently similar to warrant considering them in sequence. Both rejected Dollard and Miller's acceptance of the basic tenets of Freudian psychoanalytic theory. Yet, despite their claim to have formulated a new basis for explaining mental illness, their systems are strikingly similar to those of Dollard and Miller. The essential difference is that Eysenck and Wolpe presented an alternative to the Freudian hypothetical constructs of unconscious conflict and impulse. Their replacement, however, is an equally ill-defined hypothetical construct: an innate physiological disposition to anxiety.

Wolpe and Eysenck proposed that mental disorders are learned when intense anxiety becomes associated improperly with various environmental conditions. If anxiety is experienced in situations in which no objective threat exists, individuals will acquire a maladaptive fear response. So far, this formulation is not unlike what Freudian theorists proposed. The difference concerns the source of anxiety. Freudians located anxiety in unconscious conflicts, whereas Eysenck and Wolpe attributed it to an innate physiological disposition to anxiety. Eysenck stated his position as follows (1959):

> . . . different children have different types of autonomic system, and the same amount of noise produces quite unequal amounts of autonomic upheaval in

different children. Consequently, autonomic reactivity must also be considered; the more labile or reactive the child, the more likely he is to produce strongly conditioned fear reactions, anxieties and phobias . . . the person (is) almost predestined to suffer from anxieties, conditioned fears . . . and so forth. (p. 69)

By introducing the notion of an innate anxiety disposition, Eysenck and Wolpe introduced a concept into their theory that is as difficult to define behaviorally as is the concept of the unconscious. As a result, they muddied the waters of their behavioral theory as much as if they had invoked the unconscious. Innate differences in anxiety proneness may exist, but pure behaviorists would be certain to reject their inclusion in a behavior theory.

Born in Johannesburg, South Africa, **Joseph Wolpe (1915–1997),** the son of Jewish immigrants from Europe, received his medical degree from the University of the Witwatersrand. As a medical officer in the South African army during World War II, he worked with patients suffering from what was then called "war neurosis" (more recently referred to as Post-Traumatic Stress Disorder). This syndrome was most often treated with drug therapy and was largely unsuccessful in helping these anxiety-ridden patients overcome their painful memories. Wolpe began to search for new methods to treat them. After the war, he conducted research on cats to see if he could devise a way for them to unlearn the feline equivalent of neurosis. He induced this neurosis by means of electric shocks accompanied by certain sights and sounds. Wolpe found that by gradually and systematically exposing the cats to their feared stimuli while giving them their food rations, the cats would seem to unlearn the connections between the stimulus and the anxiety.

Essentially, this followed the classical conditioning paradigm originated in Pavlov's research in conceiving neurotic behaviors to be simple conditioned fear responses. Extending his findings to humans, Wolpe recognized that although situations that elicit intense and opposing responses may cause anxiety, conflict was neither necessary for such neurotic responses nor the most common reason for its development. To Wolpe, anxiety stemmed most frequently from the unfortunate conjunction of a neutral stimulus with a painful psychological or physical event. Once a concurrence of this nature occurs, the conditioned anxiety may be further conditioned to an ever-widening array of events that are either similar to or happen by mere coincidence to be present during the original situation. Anxiety reactions may spread, therefore, both to stimuli that are alike and to those that bear little resemblance to the conditions in the initial event. He noted further that the neurotic response itself is often a mere repetition of the complex of behaviors, including anxiety, that people happened to be experiencing and doing at the time of the original conditioning. Subsequently, other symptoms may become attached to the syndromal picture of anxiety by virtue of their often entirely coincidental concurrence at times of anxiety reduction.

Wolpe labeled his new therapeutic technique *systematic desensitization,* a method of presenting imagined events on an anxiety hierarchy while the patient maintains a learned relaxation response. This was an effort to counteract the discomforting and inhibitory effects of fear-producing stimuli by interposing and associating a relaxation response to these stimuli. The hope was that by repeated counterconditioning, the fear response would be replaced by its antagonist, relaxation. Not only are the discomforts of fear eliminated, but patients may now acquire adaptive responses that had previously been blocked.

Born in Berlin during World War I, much of **Hans Jurgen Eysenck's (1916–1997)** childhood was spent living with his maternal grandmother. Both of his parents were theatrical performers who spent much of their time traveling. His parents' relationship ended in divorce and his mother remarried a Jewish movie producer. When Hitler became chancellor of Germany, his mother and stepfather immigrated to France. Wanting to attend university, but not wanting to join Hitler's SS, a condition for admission, Eysenck also left for France and eventually settled in England. He was admitted to University College, London, to study physics, but soon discovered he did not have the prerequisite courses he needed. All other sciences were full; by default Eysenck was placed in psychology, a field he had never heard of before. Sir Cyril Burt (see Chapter 14), head of the psychology department, quickly caught Eysenck's interest, however, and inspired his future influential career.

Hans Jurgen Eysenck

After receiving his PhD in 1942 from University College, by delivering a dissertation on the aesthetic properties of visual figures, he secured a research position at the Mill Hill Emergency Hospital, which provided psychiatric services to the British armed forces during World War II. He published over 30 research papers on topics ranging from diagnosis to personality differences and social attitudes during his four years at Mill Hill. His success there led to an appointment at Maudsley Hospital as director of the psychology department, which gained status as a graduate department of psychology within the University of London in 1950.

Acerbic and confrontational, Eysenck's powerful commitment and tireless energies helped propel the psychology division at the Institute of Psychiatry to one of the world's top psychology departments. In his lifetime, he wrote 61 books and published more than 1,000 journal articles, reviews, and chapters, as well as making innumerable appearances on television and radio. He possessed diverse interests and talents and wrote prolifically on dozens of topics, including his important contribution to the dimensions of personality, discussed in Chapter 13.

Eysenck became a well-known public figure owing to several popular books that he wrote and his many interviews and appearances on radio and television. His forthrightness led him to become a polemical figure in England, especially in British psychological circles. Innumerable anecdotes about him, which expressed a gamut of intense and contrasting feelings, ranged from derogatory vituperation to idolatric veneration. One of his first and best-known published articles reviewed evidence on the therapeutic efficacy of psychotherapy. It initiated his controversial career, quickly arousing intense antagonism from therapists the world over. Follow-up studies on this crucial topic raised serious questions about which studies Eysenck had selected to illustrate his views and how he had interpreted the data; these researchers arrived at strikingly different conclusions than those Eysenck put forth.

Eysenck believed that learning models of neuroses must recognize the possibility that some anxieties and fears are based on a biologically anchored and innate sensitivity to certain noxious objects. He suggested the probable development of an evolutionary mechanism by which organisms became biologically prepared to react to certain stimuli with fear. For example, there was survival value in a disposition to fear darkness, poisonous snakes, certain insects, and high places. Conditioned neurotic fears that were based on these evolved survival phobias might not obey the ordinary principles of learning for their extinction. Evolutionary preparedness might also explain why certain phobias tend to be restricted to a small class of events when conditioning theory would predict that *any* stimulus should be able to be made fearsome by learned associations. To Eysenck, biological preparedness suggested that only neurologically wired-in response tendencies will display this difficult-to-extinguish form of neurotic anxiety.

Not surprisingly, Eysenck advocated a behavior therapy approach to treating symptoms rather than "talk-based" therapies that assumed unconscious processes at work in creating disorders. To Eysenck, the symptoms alone constituted the neurosis. Therefore, therapies that used principles of extinction, desensitization, reciprocal inhibition, and reinforcement to treat the symptoms, should also change the person's behaviors and attitudes. The Institute of Psychiatry treated many of its patients with behavior therapy and conducted many experiments that examined the results. Eysenck wrote extensively on these results and eventually founded the journal *Behavior Research and Therapy* and edited it for 18 years. As with other successful scientists, he was burdened with increasing administrative responsibilities, though he considered faculty and committee meetings to be a waste of everyone's time, and strenuously avoided them.

Eysenck's points broke decisively with other theoretical models. Whereas Freudian theory regarded neurotic symptoms as adaptive mechanisms that are the "visible upshot of unconscious causes," Eysenck rejected such unconscious causes, regarding neurotic symptoms as simple learned habits; to him there was no neurosis underlying the symptom, but merely the symptom itself. "Get rid of the symptom, and you have eliminated the neuroses," was Eysenck's favorite phrase.

My personal contact with Eysenck, though limited and infrequent, gave me the impression of a person of forthright directness, a nakedness of ambition, and extremist views, which seemed totally lacking in ambivalence or irony. He was literal-minded in his antipsychoanalytic thinking, insisting that no psychologist was safe from the archaic notions that characterized analytic thought, especially in the United States. He made it sound as if psychoanalysis was little different than Stalin's communism. I once suggested to him that however deficient analysis may have been, no matter how sloppy and scattershot its foundations might be, it still served as a stimulus of important therapeutic ideas and imaginative theorizing. His rebuttal achieved a refreshing, if not an amusing quality as he argued in favor of and insisted on "psychological purity," whatever that meant.

Underneath his fevered criticisms and personal style of attack was an enormous ambition, as if he wanted to conquer all of psychology, which he had already accomplished in England. Whatever his shortcomings, he was a force, as were Watson and Skinner before him, a thinker of considerable intellect and conviction seeking to create a true science for psychology. Although intellectually impressive, few who knew him were blind to the negative side of his character. Perhaps I was romanticizing a dying figure when I last met him, reading humane dimensions into his personhood, but I was impressed by his self-possession, his lack of self-pity, and his utter seriousness in making assertions that many found questionable, if not reprehensible (e.g., smoking is merely a correlate, not a cause of cancer, the disease that ultimately killed him).

Comments and Reflections

One may question the behaviorists' habit of translating complex psychological processes into tangible and observable phenomena. It is difficult when reading behavioristic analyses to wonder whether they have explained anything of substance when they say, for example, that verbal communications are merely the mechanisms and expressions of oral behavior. Is anything really added to an understanding of these translations when all one has done is simply translate them into more concrete terminology? Such translations may create the illusion of explaining things scientifically when, in fact, all that has been provided are terminological formulas for substituting observables instead of providing explanations, much less understandings. Behaviorism merely substitutes an illusion of science when it deals with complex phenomena that do not lend themselves to mechanical and tangible actions. Unless a phenomenon can be rephrased in terms of explicit physical processes, that is, explanations analyzed into particular sensory and muscular activities, behaviorists consider it to be somehow unreal. Perhaps this accounts in part for their preference to work with animals; here there is no need even to pretend to provide an explanatory schema for the complex inner psychological processes that characterize human thought. This may also account for behaviorists' lukewarm attitude toward such psychological subjects as intelligence, which cannot readily be formulated in specific physical and bodily actions. They dismiss topics such as these as vague and nebulous, unworthy of scientific inquiry. One might also question the behaviorists' rejection of the concept of consciousness; many flatly deny that conscious events even occur and regard those who wish to deal with these processes as victims of an illusion. Their dread of the supernatural has led them to take so narrow a position that they have jettisoned many major topics that are valid subjects of psychological study.

Behaviorists point to the advantages inherent in their approach. First, they argue that the principles that guide their methods are anchored to scientific laboratory data that can be tested and revised, if necessary, in an objective and systematic fashion. Moreover, the correspondence between behavior procedures and basic research will enable therapists of this persuasion to translate new laboratory data into novel treatment approaches, facilitating the development of alternative empirically grounded therapeutic techniques. Second, because behaviorists focus their efforts on clearly delimited and carefully defined symptom problems, they believe they will accumulate a body of quantitative data concerning the efficacy of their approach, with specific and identifiable syndromes. These data can then be used as baselines for comparison of alternative treatment techniques. Third, if behavioral methods can be shown to be of equal or superior efficacy to other treatment approaches, their benefits will be twofold since they achieve their results in far fewer sessions than others do. This advantage is especially significant for patients in lower socioeconomic groups who can ill afford the greater expense and time involved in more traditional therapies. Fourth, behavior therapy can be carried out by persons who are appreciably less sophisticated psychologically than those who perform other types of therapy. The need for more therapists in our society is great, and the expediency and economy of employing' hospital nurses and attendants, as well as parents, teachers, and other auxiliary persons, cannot be readily overlooked.

These theorists borrow their concepts from experimental learning research; as such, one would expect their work to be subject to little scientific faulting. The failure to live up to this expectation demonstrates the difficulty of transferring concepts from one field to another. Borrowing concepts from another field may be no more than a specious ennoblement of one's efforts, a cloak of falsely appropriated prestige that duly impresses the naive. One might ask, for example, whether the laboratory-based concepts borrowed from the prestigious field of learning research are genuinely applicable to understanding and treating mental disorders, or whether they are merely bandied about in an allegorical and superficial manner. Scientific sounding terminology may be no more than a set of flimsy analogies, offering no new explanatory powers or insights; old wine in new bottles is still old wine.

There is reason to suspect, further, that the "basic" laws of learning are not so basic after all; much dissent exists among learning theorists as to which concepts and laws are basic. Examination of the literature on learning exposes marked disagreements on even the simplest conditioning processes. Can laws of learning be applied to highly complex clinical processes when the existence of these laws in simple situations is still a matter of dispute?

Another criticism of behavior theories in mental illness is their failure to formulate concepts dealing with the development of disorders. What little they say on this matter is usually a rewording of psychoanalytic theories. Where they strike out on their own, as do the Skinnerians, they appear preoccupied with *how* behavior is learned, and not with *when* and *what* is learned. The Skinnerian focus on the process rather than the content of learning may have added an important dimension to the study of mental illness. But without referencing the kinds of experience that lead to pathological learning, behavioral theories create a sterile and artificial person, an empty creature who behaves according to vacant and abstract principles. By reducing the reality of experience to abstract stimuli and responses, mental illness becomes a barren pattern of mechanical reactions. Sentimental and unscientific as these objections may appear, they bring home the point that an explanation of real behavior requires more than a set of abstract principles. Though these principles may be basic, they remain static until the content and meaning of experience fill them out.

Nonbehavioral therapists do not accept the contentions of behaviorists. They note numerous disadvantages and objections. They raise questions about whether the sparse language of learning theories—stimuli, conditioning, response, and reinforcement—is a sufficiently sensitive conceptual instrument for dealing with the subtle and complex processes of pathological development and treatment. Although learning and environmental events may be central to understanding therapeutic interactions, forcing these processes into the meager verbal formulations of behavior theories may blunt rather than sharpen the clinician's powers of observation and analysis.

Further, most behavior modification procedures include elements that are incidental to the theoretically formulated plan of therapy. In Wolpe's desensitization method, is therapeutic gain entirely a function of counterconditioning or is it at least in part attributable to therapists' personalities and enthusiasm and their powers of suggestion? Perhaps the most vigorously argued criticism of behavior therapy contends that these procedures deal only with superficial and narrowly defined symptoms; they ignore not only the underlying causes of overt symptoms, but many important although difficult-to-define syndromes such as existential anxiety or identity crises. Because deeper and more pervasive difficulties are left untouched, behavior therapy is considered a technique of markedly limited utility. Moreover, critics argue that new symptoms, perhaps different in form and content from those removed by behavior therapy, will inevitably appear since their underlying functions have not been resolved. In short, the ostensible benefits of behavior methods are either limited, temporary, or illusory.

Nevertheless, behavior modification techniques have been subjected to more systematic research, despite their limited history, than all other psychological treatment approaches. This reflects, in part, the strong academic orientation of those who practice behavior therapy.

On the debit side of the ledger, behavioral approaches have not demonstrated efficacy with diffuse and pervasive pathological impairments such as personality patterns or maladaptive coping strategies, no less existential crises. Many of these difficult-to-pinpoint problems simply do not lend themselves to the sharply focused procedures of behavior therapy. Although advances in treatment methodology may ultimately bring these forms of disturbed functioning within the purview of behavior treatment, for the present they seem more suitably handled by other therapeutic approaches.

10

Scrutinizing Introspections and Rebuilding Cognitions

Psychoanalytic and cognitive approaches to treatment are similar in many respects. Both gather their data in naturalistic settings, deriving their concepts primarily from clinical observation and occasionally from experimental research. Both recognize that their concepts and hypotheses are crude approximations of complex processes, but they contend that less rigorous notions are appropriate in the early stages of a science; thus, methodological quantification and conceptual precision are not devalued, but *de-emphasized* because they may be premature given current knowledge. The major distinction between psychoanalytic and cognitive schools of clinical thought lies in their respective emphasis on unconscious versus conscious processes. Psychoanalytic theorists believe that the most important aspects of functioning are those factors that people cannot or will not say about themselves. In contrast, cognitivists believe that people's introspective reports, taken at their face value, are most significant.

The Psychoscience Story: II

Cognitivists stress that individuals react to the world only in terms of their phenomenological and unique perception of it (see Chapter 4). No matter how transformed or unconsciously distorted it may be, people's way of perceiving events determines their behavior. Concepts and propositions must be formulated, therefore, not in terms of objective realities or unconscious processes, but in accordance with how individuals actually perceive events. Concepts must not disassemble these subjective experiences into depersonalized or abstract categories.

The phenomenon of consciousness, another facet of the *cognitive revolution* of the past two or three decades in psychology, has been one of the most controversial topics in both psychological and philosophical literature. Numerous knotty questions have been raised about the appropriate methods for obtaining conscious data. No one doubts that awareness of external events and of self exists, but how can theorists categorize, measure, or even sense cognitive reality as experienced or as people report it? For example, clinical observers must adopt an empathic attitude, a sensing in one's self of what another may be experiencing. But this method is justly suspect, fraught with the observer's countertransference distortions and insensitivities. To obviate this difficulty, clinical cognitivists assume that individuals' verbal statements accurately reflect their phenomenal reality. Any datum that represents individuals' portrayals of their experience is grist for the cognitivist's mill.

Critics have lodged serious complaints against current cognitive and historic introspective methods. Are there not deliberate omissions and inaccuracies in verbal reports? How can a scientific theory be founded on subjective reports whose meaning varies from person to person? Do not run-of-the-mill respondents, no less patients, repress and deny the most crucial elements of their experiences? And, if significant events are distorted, hidden, or forgotten, of what value are the remaining data? How then can researchers accept introspective and cognitive reports at their face value as the data for a scientific theory?

Several have offered counterarguments in defense of cognitive methods, albeit in part to right the wrong of behaviorism and to resuscitate the sphere of consciousness. They admit to the limitations of self-reports. However, cognitivists contend that individuals' verbal reports reveal the most important influences on their behavior. Is it not simple efficiency, they argue, to ask people directly what they are experiencing or what is disturbing them? Are their reports more prone to error than an observer's speculations gathered from the odds and ends of a case history study? Are they less reliable than deductions drawn from dreams and free associations? The fact that some verbal reports, retrospective recollections, and currently stated feelings are misleading is no reason to dismiss them as useless; they summarize events in terms closest to an individual's experience of them and often embody knowledge not otherwise available.

These pro-and-con stances miss the point. Conscious reports are an important source of data, but they are only one of many sources. No argument need exist between proponents of one method or another. Each method reflects a decision as to which source of data will weigh more in either the construction of a theory or the planning of a therapy. Theories or therapies using different types of data are complementary frames of reference for investigating a science or the problems of personality and mental illness. A useful task for the future is not choosing from among alternative sources of data, but in establishing connections among them.

Most cognitivists avoid formal theorizing for fear that individuals' unique and highly personal attributes will be forced into obscure cosmic airs or molds of abstraction. Their work reflects common everyday experiences and their directly related conceptions of psychic functioning. For example, Festinger's notion of cognitive dissonance (see Chapter 12) proposed that psychic discomfort results when a person maintains two attitudes or beliefs that are inconsistent with each other. This discomfort can be therapeutically reduced by a variety of means designed to establish consonance, that is, consistency between these beliefs. However, individuals will experience intense and perhaps unresolvable discomfort when dissonance arises between cognitive beliefs that are of special importance to them. Most clinical cognitivists believe this occurs when people's personal sense of self runs counter to the judgments of significant others. Disorder of this sort stems from an estrangement from self, an incongruence between attitudes people feel or believe are true or right for themselves, but which others have told them are false or wrong. This dissonance, in turn, leads to intense anxiety, which produces serious defensive reactions that further invalidate the sense of self and alienate people from their natural feelings. At its worst, individuals may experience a state of *nothingness*, that is, a sense of inner emptiness and purposelessness, perhaps instigating parasuicidal or suicidal actions.

The cognitive approach reflects the Kantian tradition in which individuals actively impose meaning on life experiences, developing a schemata, or belief system, for organizing their physical and social world. As theorists have described it, people form significant cognitive structures that categorize and organize these schemas into more complex hierarchies. Dysfunctional feelings and behaviors reflect the operation of consistently biased schemas and result in repetitive perceptual and interpersonal errors. Notably, the cognitive approach based its ideas on the impact of attributional biases rather than on motivational or unconscious ones. Hence, therapeutic change requires the reorientation of faulty assumptions, misperceptions, and erroneous expectancies.

Unfolding of Key Ideas

Few fields have gained as much ground in the past two or three decades as the cognitive sciences. Along with the increasing significance of personality disorders and rapid growth of the neurosciences, there has been an explosion of both theoretical and empirical work centered on the role of cognitive processes in the understanding and treatment of psychopathological conditions.

The emergence of psychoscience occurred less than a century and a half ago in the study of sensory reactions to physical stimuli. A number of German experimental physicists first noted the relationship between the magnitude or frequency of an environmental stimulus, such as a sound wave, and the experience people "sensed" in reaction to it. At the same time, physiologists were uncovering the structure of the internal sense organs that accounted for these sensations. These experimentalists devised systematic procedures that enabled them to quantify sensory responses to physical stimuli. The University of Leipzig established a psychological laboratory to seek scientific evidence for the view that the mind could be measured and that psychology could move from metaphysical speculation into science. The procedure of controlled introspection went beyond the study of the simple and pure stimuli that early German psychophysicists investigated. In what was termed a "science of conscious experience," experimenters systematically recorded reactions to complex and impure stimuli, recognizing that consciousness was more than a product of simple sensations.

Introspecting and Structuring

It is often assumed that psychoscience originated with the founding of Wundt's Leipzig laboratory. Not quite. The movement toward observing psychological phenomena was under way well before being housed in formal experimental laboratories. Although the laboratory at Leipzig became the focal point of this evolving science, variations preceded it along different lines of development. Comparisons between laboratory psychology and armchair psychology did not reflect the difference between observation and no observation, or between careful observation and poor observation, but rather signified a difference between two radical and distinct ways of observing. Acute observers from earlier periods, such as Locke in England, used keen observations they already had made. What they saw occurred spontaneously, and only later did they carefully note or remember it. Earlier observers, despite best intentions, acquired limited experiences and suffered faulty memories, both of which may have influenced their selection and recording of observations and recollections.

The distinguishing mark of the psychological laboratory is that it set out, from the very first, to acquire specific observations that researchers judged relevant in achieving particular conclusions instead of simply using what had happened in the past or at the current moment. Thus, experimental psychology was a technique of *acquiring* observations that would rule out as much as possible the incidental and personal factors of life experience. Experimenters began by formulating questions with a definite intent and focus, seeking to highlight, as much as possible, the most pertinent aspects of what they sought to observe. They repeatedly made observations to increase their precision and to minimize the effect of chance events. Moreover, they systematically manipulated conditions for observation. The larger context within which these observations occurred was controlled as rigorously as possible to reduce extraneous influences. In time, they subjected their observations to quantitative and statistical analysis, scrupulously recording both negative and positive results. In this way, observations would be minimally affected by the peculiarities of the moment or by researchers' expectancies, their particular preferences or disinclinations, and their motives for undertaking the studies. Basically, the experimental method became a set of procedures that protected investigators from extraneous influences, including their own biases.

The history of experimental observation is often traced to an astronomer at the end of the eighteenth century who noted that the observations he reported differed repeatedly from those of his assistant. Other astronomers, shortly thereafter, set out to compare the results of several observers, noting that there were not only frequent but characteristic discrepancies. Essentially, typical individual differences existed among observers, an individual difference phenomenon that came to be called the *personal equation*. These variations in observations of simple physical phenomena, such as human astronomical recordings, gradually led investigators to systematically study the relationship between psychological observations and objective physical phenomena, what came to be called *psychophysics*.

Scientists discussed in this section used introspective methods to explain psychophysics, the measurable relationship between physical phenomena and the psychic experience and recording of them. It became the core tradition of German experimental psychological research. The primary objective of this line of inquiry began with an effort to define *absolute thresholds*, or what the minimum magnitude of a stimulus must be for the subject to perceive it; a second goal was to establish *differential thresholds*, or how far apart two stimuli need to be for someone to perceive them as different. More than just a system of measurement, psychophysics was also a philosophy of the functional relation between the mind and the body. Ernst Weber in his experiments established a foundation for the work of Gustav Fechner, who is considered by many to be the founder of psychophysics. Fechner's later fascination with mysticism caused him to fall out of favor with scholars, and Wilhelm Wundt was given credit for being the founder of the new science of psychology. This new science grew out of the philosophical study of phenomenology, established the methodology of introspection, and gave rise to cognitive science and cognitive therapies, much later and in current favor.

Ernst Heinrich Weber's (1795–1878) most significant contribution to psychology was being the first scientist to quantitatively measure mental or psychical processes using introspection and self-report. He was a professor of anatomy and physiology at the University of Leipzig for much of his career. Most of his work centered on the systematic study of the sensation of touch, which was published in his groundbreaking *De Subtilitate Tactus* in 1834 and *Der Tastsinn und das Gemeingefühl* ("The Sense of Touch and Common Sensibility") in 1846. These texts represented the first research monographs in experimental psychology. His extensive experimentation led to the discovery of the *just noticeable difference* (j.n.d.) or the minimum change for multiple sensations such as touch, temperature, pitch, weight, and length of lines. For many senses, it was not only that people could notice a difference between two stimuli, but that they could identify a specific ratio or proportion of change in a stimulus. For example, he found the ratio to be 1:30 for weight, but 1:160 for tones. In other words, "In comparing objects and observing the distinction between them, we perceive not the difference between objects, but the ratio of this difference to the magnitude of the objects compared" (1846, p. 117).

Gustav Theodor Fechner (1801–1887) was the son of a highly progressive pastor in the Kingdom of Saxony who, unlike others in his profession at the time preached without a wig "because Jesus did not wear a wig." Historians have recorded that the young Fechner was a rebellious child, disinclined to follow any of his family's traditions, especially those of religious preaching. Precocious in his studies, Fechner was highly inattentive to what he saw as useless and boring work. He ultimately gravitated to medical studies at Leipzig University, but showed a special interest only in physiology and mathematics. Although he passed the exams for his doctorate, he resisted completing the practical hands-on aspects of this program owing to his disinclination to see himself practicing everyday medicine and surgery. Throughout this period, Fechner aimed toward an academic rather than a medical career. He taught physics at Leipzig in his early 20s and translated several published works on that subject as well as on chemistry. Scattered and desultory by virtue of his diverse interests, he began a pharmacological journal, published a text on electromagnetism, and two volumes on chemistry. He achieved the rank of professor of physics in 1834 and became a member of Leipzig's musically oriented and intellectual social world. Owing to personal and scientific conflicts, he was undone by the internecine struggles of the university and was forced to resign his chair in physics. Following a brief visual illness of likely psychosomatic character, he turned his attentions, even more than before, toward new and interesting directions.

His major work explored the relationship between the mind and body by quantifying the relationships between physical stimuli and the mental experiences of the stimuli. He believed that lawful relationships existed between physics and psychology, and he spent much of his career exploring this relationship. This eventually led him to see the importance of obtaining quantitative physical measurements of conscious sensations, thereby launching the field of psychophysics. By 1860, he published his *Elements of Psychophysics,* where he defined psychophysics as the "functionally dependent relations of body and soul, or more generally, of the material and the mental, of the physical and psychological worlds" (1860/1966, p. 7). In the intervening years he developed his own methods of measurement and began conducting experiments on lifted-weights, as well as recording and manipulating audio and visual stimuli.

Wilhelm Maximilian Wundt's (1832–1920) career spanned over 60 years and he published over 50,000 pages of scientific writing; it was his first achievement, however, the establishment of experimental psychology is his most memorable and influential contribution. In 1879, he opened a psychological laboratory at the University of Leipzig to furnish scientific evidence for the measurement of the mind. In these experiments, he initiated the study of the complex response that came to be called *perception.*

Wundt was born in Neckarau near Mannheim, Germany, into a family resplendent with distinguished scholars on both sides, from historians to scientists, theologians, economists, and physicians. His father, however, was an ordinary Lutheran pastor. Despite what would seem to be a discouraging environment for fostering a young scholarly mind, Wilhelm was isolated for much of his early life. His only living brother was older and away at school; his only companion was a feeble-minded boy with limited speech and for whom Wilhelm was responsible. With no real opportunities to learn to play and possessing a temperament that ran toward the humorless and serious, Wilhelm grew into a shy and reserved man who disliked undertaking new experiences and meeting new people.

His maternal grandfather took an interest in Wilhelm's education and started him on a strict regimen and schedule of learning. He formed an attachment to a vicar who was his father's assistant and who shared a room with Wilhelm. The vicar took responsibility for schooling him; Wilhelm was deeply upset when the vicar moved to a neighboring town. The family was never wealthy; after his father's early death, his mother had difficulty supporting the family. Needing to earn his own living, Wilhelm studied to become a physician at the University of Heidelberg. He quickly realized that medicine was not his calling, but that academia was, and obtained his doctorate in physiology. The subject was almost irrelevant for Wundt as long as it enabled him to pursue scholarly study, a lifelong dream. Appointed von Helmholtz's assistant in 1858, Wundt left after a few uninspired years, tired of the drudgery of drilling students on laboratory fundamentals. Having lost interest in pursuing pure physiological research, he gradually developed a growing interest in positivistic philosophy.

Perhaps owing to the drudgery of his earlier work, Wundt carried into his later career a tendency to overlook matters of emphasis and clarity of thought, subordinating his efforts in favor of absolute detail. He was so keenly aware of the need to hedge speculations that many described him as a man who never said a foolish thing, nor anything brilliant either. Industrious, logical, and systematic, he was well suited by training and habit to the task of careful experimentation for which psychology, no longer the handmaiden of metaphysical speculation, was in great need.

Wundt came to realize the value of controlled introspection as a potential tool for advancing an experimental psychology. Wundt's conceptualization of the method of introspection is often misunderstood. He did not believe that immediate experience was to be trusted over mediated experience. On the contrary, he believed that unaided introspection or self-observation (*Selbstbeobachtung*) had plagued prior psychophysical studies. What was needed was a method of introspection that laboratory equipment (*innere Wahrnehmung*) assisted and made more precise. His ultimate goal with the introspective method was to make internal perceptions as precise as external perceptions. Subjects often needed to provide only a "yes" or "no" response, not a detailed description of inner events. Wundt initially restricted introspection to sensation or the raw sensory content of an event, divested of any interpretation or meaning imparted by the subject. This essentially eliminated what would be considered mentalistic introspection.

By the time Wundt arrived at Leipzig in 1875, he was already a well-published and well-regarded author of books and articles on psychology, physics,

Wilhelm Maximilian Wundt

and physiology. He initiated plans for a laboratory the following year and by 1879, when the laboratory officially opened, Wundt had already begun conducting research.

Leipzig soon became the Mecca for students who wished to study this new approach to psychology—a model of research that had broken sharply from its roots in speculative philosophy. Not an offshoot of the science of physiology, this model represented a novel and daring effort to approach mental processes by the experimental and quantitative techniques that characterized other branches of science. The psychology Wundt led at Leipzig in the 1880s and 1890s was a new approach for rigorous and imaginative young persons who believed that the mind could be both measured and manipulated experimentally. These novices considered themselves to be pioneers on the frontiers of science, throwing themselves into their tasks with zest and vigor. They became trained introspectionists as they sought to develop techniques for a minute analysis of different elements of sensation and perception. Enriching their work beyond simple physiological processes, they extended their studies into complex functions such as cognition and feelings. When they finally left Leipzig, heading to other German universities, as well as to those in the United States, most carried with them enough of the Leipzig model to establish Wundtian laboratories of their own.

Wundt was tireless in training other psychologists in his methodology and was steadfast in his critique of their observations until all traces of outside distractions or beliefs were removed. Part of the vast influence of the laboratory was that Wundt trained dozens of future experimental psychologists in Leipzig from all over the world: distant Europeans, Asians, and, in particular, numerous Americans (most of the first generation of young psychologists before 1900). All returned to their native countries to establish laboratories based on Wundt's model. Some of the more prominent Americans who studied under Wundt included James, Hall, Titchener, Cattell, and Angell. Although many psychologists received their initial training in scientific psychology from Wundt, only a few spent the rest of their careers as loyal followers. Instead, most were inspired by his ideas, using them to implement their own.

Although not the first to approach psychology from a formal cognitive perspective, **David Katz (1884–1953)** was perhaps the first proponent of *experimental phenomenology* in the twentieth century. Born in Kassel, in the Prussian province of Hessen-Nassau, David Katz was the seventh of eight children. From a young age, Katz was deeply fascinated by art museums and theater productions, an interest that persisted throughout his life and influenced his choice of phenomena to study. He received his PhD in 1906 from Göttingen, and he remained at the Göttingen laboratory for 18 years until becoming a professor in Rostock in 1919. Owing to his Jewish heritage, he was obliged to leave Nazi Germany in 1933, first heading to England, and then four years later accepting a permanent academic position in Stockholm. Despite his career's vast scope in both time and range of topics, Katz consistently pursued the cognitive approach in his studies.

Some of Katz's earliest work dealt with color constancy in children's drawings; he soon discovered glaring deficits in the literature of visual phenomena. Although Gestalt psychologists (discussed later in this chapter) made the study of visual phenomena a central concern, Katz's studies predated their work by several years. Katz's *The World of Color* (1911/1935), was highly regarded for its cognitive understanding of how color takes various forms. In it, Katz argued, among other things, for the existence of *brightness constancy*. This phenomenon can be described by noting that if a white disk is in shadow, the observer perceives that the disk is actually lighter than a photometer would read, suggesting that the observer makes allowances for the object being in shadow. This example argues strongly for a cognitive component to perception; according to Katz, perception could not be predicted from a simple sensation.

Edward Bradford Titchener (1867–1927), one of Wundt's students, remained faithful to many of Wundt's ideas on his appointment to Cornell University in 1892. He became an influential figure in American psychology for more than 20 years during which he espoused a *core-context theory* of perception. To Titchener, the core of perception comprised immediate sensations fused with residual images of past sensations. The unique context of an individual's past experiences gave meaning to this core. Combined, the core and context accounted for the meaningfulness of perception.

Edward Bradford Titchener

Titchener was born in the south of England into a poor family, but his academic giftedness earned him scholarships to Malvern College and eventually to Brasenose College at Oxford where he earned a BA in philosophy. Titchener was proud of both his family and his British citizenship. At Oxford, he studied Hume and Locke but, despite a lack of psychology coursework, found himself drawn to Wundt. He left for Germany and enrolled at Leipzig, earning his PhD in two years. Even before leaving for Germany, Titchener had translated Wundt's *Physiologische Psychologie* into English. Throughout his career, he continued to translate Wundt's works, as well as other German texts, in addition to publishing many of his own books.

Having become the director of the psychology laboratory at Cornell University in 1892, Titchener worked consciously and effectively in the Wundtian tradition. He quickly became the recognized representative of Wundt's point of view, despite an occasional deviation on one or another minor matter. Many believed that Titchener strove the most valiantly in the Americas to establish the new experimental psychology, a task he carried out with the zeal of a prophet. His role in the United States was unique and extraordinary. Although he seemed committed to remain an alien in his adopted country, he was a dominant influence that prevailed for almost two decades and was strongly opposed to the many distinctly American movements that sought to assert themselves. His former student and historian, E. G. Boring, wrote the following on his death:

> The death of no other psychologist could so alter the psychological picture in America . . . he was a cardinal point in the national systematic orientation. The clear-cut opposition between behaviorism and its allies on the one hand, and something else, on the other, remains clear only when the opposition is between behaviorism and Titchener, mental tests and Titchener, or applied psychology and Titchener. His death thus, in a sense, creates a classificatory chaos in American systematic psychology. (1929, p. 490)

Titchener was never inclined in the slightest degree to become Americanized, although he arrived in the United States when he was only 25 and remained until his death some 35 years later. His two years at Leipzig under Wundt had fully Germanized him, even though he grew up proud of his British heritage. He was so flamboyant in his Germanic style that he was often mistaken for a German. He preserved the Germanic university professorial manner with punctilious devotion to the ceremonial qualities that characterized German university culture (wearing a commencement gown to his daily classroom lectures). Moreover, not only did he find his American surroundings incompatible, but he actively withdrew from or opposed many aspects that typified American university lifestyles. He viewed the emerging field of applied psychology, including industrial consulting and the study of mental testing, to be second-rate activities that deviated from his conception of pure science. As the leader of the *structuralist* movement, he fulminated against the schools of functionalism (Chapter 13) and behaviorism (Chapter 9), which rose and prospered in his later years. Moreover, he resigned from the American Psychological Association to establish his own group, known as the *experimentalists*, the membership of which was determined solely by Titchener's invitation and its papers and discussions limited to topics that met with his approval. Distinguished in manner and style, Titchener's pride led to an eccentric narcissism, an almost humorous stereotype of the self-important professor, amusingly characterized in tales by his many adoring students.

Titchener's system was based on rigorously constructing the elements of sensation, the building blocks of experience. This method came to be known as *structuralism: what* components achieved consciousness rather than *how* or *why* it was achieved. Titchener was concerned with normal adults, as they were the only ones capable of producing reliable introspection. In his opinion, animals, young children, and pathological adults could not produce trustworthy introspective results. He was concerned, not with the individual mind, but with the generalized mind. This emphasis is clear in the following passage from *A Beginner's Psychology:*

> The world of psychology contains looks and tones and feels; it is the world of dark and light, of noise and silence, of rough and smooth, its space is sometimes large and sometimes small, as everyone knows who in adult life has gone back to his childhood's home; its time is sometimes short and sometimes long; it has no invariables. It contains all the thoughts, emotions, memories, imaginations, volitions that you naturally ascribe to mind. (1916, p. 9)

As discussed in Chapter 13 and later in this chapter, members of the American functionalist and the German Gestalt schools of psychology concurrently developed differing views of the perceiver. They regarded context as a preestablished purpose or attitude that preceded the perceptual act and actively directed the individual's attention toward selected elements of the stimulus field. In their contentions, individuals did not passively receive a stimulus and then give it meaning. Rather, perception was purposeful or meaningful immediately because of the perceiver's expectation or set. In their view, the adaptive function of past experiences shaped the perception of reality; it also established a logic and experimental basis for the observation that psychic pathology leads to clinically relevant perceptual distortions.

Observing Gestalt Perceptions

The Gestalt movement began in Germany in 1910 when a group of young psychologists became convinced that the Wundtian explanations of sensory elements and their combinations were grossly inadequate. In their view, perceived movement was not simply a composition of visual sensations, nor a mosaic of parts that were then fused or compounded; these explanations did not represent the fluidity and unity of immediate experiences in the natural world. For example, they noted that numerous objects are experienced as rectangular when only rarely were they projected on the retina as rectangular in actual form. We experience picture frames, doors, tabletops, and windows as rectangular when they are not seen as such. Further, they observed that a black object in bright sunlight is judged as black and a white object in a dark shadow as white, even when physical conditions are such that the same amount of light is reflected from both objects. A man is seen as the same height whether he is 5 or 20 yards away, though in one case the retinal image is 8 times larger than the other. The character of reality, in their judgment, is contextual, in which perceptions form an immediate gestalt, such that the experience portrays the intrinsic qualities as they are in reality. Experiences are not perceived as assemblages of elements, but as unified wholes, not scattered and piecemeal sensations, but as real objects, such as trees, buildings, or clouds. The gestalt of perception is not a composition of elements, not merely a series of parts, but a unified whole.

Max Wertheimer, Kurt Koffka, and Wolfgang Köhler formed the triumvirate of Gestalt psychology. The three worked together in 1910 in Friedrich Schumann's laboratory at the University of Frankfurt where Wertheimer, likely influenced by David Katz's earliest publications, initiated his first investigations into a psychological understanding of the perception of movement. The three young Gestaltists served as each other's subjects in these early experiments and inspired each other's work.

The behaviorists (Chapter 9) proposed that the introspective study of conscious experience be replaced by the analysis of behaviors into component conditioned and reinforced actions. By contrast, the Gestaltists were not disposed to jettison the study of conscious experience, but sought to abandon the structuralists' inclination to dismember meaningful experiences into meaningless elements. To them, a collection of elements deprived of their natural bond could not be simply plastered together by unintelligible or random association. They believed that relevant psychological data could be obtained by introspection gained from direct experience, but that their analyses must proceed from their entirety down to their parts, which remain meaningful because of their intrinsic part in the whole.

Max Wertheimer (1880–1943) was raised in Prague, the second son of a father who was a prominent educator and a mother who was an accomplished violinist; he entered the University of Prague with the goal of studying law. Drawn more to philosophy, he later attended the University of Berlin, where he first worked with Carl Stumpf and Friedrich Schumann. In 1903, he spent a year at Würzburg and wrote a dissertation under Oswald Külpe on lie detection in criminal proceedings. After many years of research during which he met and worked with younger colleagues, Kurt Koffka and Wolfgang Köhler, he was called to the chair in philosophy and psychology at the University of Frankfurt in 1929. A Jew, Wertheimer emigrated from Germany to the United States in 1933, and taught for the rest of his career at the New School of Social Research in New York, an institution whose faculty was composed largely of exiled European scholars.

In the summer of 1910, Wertheimer, traveling by train on his vacation from Austria to the German Rhine, noticed that many stationary objects such as fences and buildings appeared to be moving at the speed of the train. Certainly others had noticed this phenomenon before, but he began to question *why* they appeared to move. He got off the train at Frankfurt and bought a device to gauge variable motion known as a stroboscope. In his hotel room, he experimented by projecting successive images of a horse and child. At the correct projection rate, it appeared as though the horse was trotting and the child walking. He questioned how it was that humans perceive this movement. The next day he contacted one of his former Berlin instructors, Friedrich Schumann, who had recently been appointed to the University of Frankfurt and was an expert on space perception. Although he didn't have an answer for Wertheimer, Schumann gave him access to his lab, including a new tachistoscope he had developed to flash visual images for fractions of a second, as well as two of his young colleagues, Koffka and Köhler, to assist with his experi-

Max Wertheimer

mentation. Both Koffka and Köhler, as well as Koffka's wife, served as subjects in Wertheimer's early experiments on the now famous *phi phenomenon*. In these studies, the tachistoscope projected a vertical white line on a black background followed by a horizontal white line on the same background. When alternated at a certain speed, the line appeared to move from one position to the other. Wertheimer followed up with another experiment by flashing a light through two narrow slits in a screen in rapid succession. When the lights were flashed 50 to 60 milliseconds apart, there was apparent movement (phi phenomenon); when the interval was shorter, the lights appeared to be on continuously and when the interval was longer, they appeared to be successive events. The notion that the whole perceptual experience had unique properties not shared by the individual components became the basis of the Gestalt movement.

Wertheimer's vision was extensive, ranging from studies and papers on ethics, democracy, truth, and philosophical concerns such as the meaning of truth. Notable beyond his fertile early experiments on perception was his work on the psychology of thinking in his book, *Productive Thinking* (1945). This later work contributed to ideas related to problem-solving methods and creative thought. Many of these notions anticipated the current fascination with cognitive processes and computer modeling. Here gestaltist concerns regarding insight and thinking could be profitably introduced to further enrich contemporary research.

The three founders of the Gestalt movement could not have been more different in style and appearance. Wertheimer was of Jewish descent, raised and educated in Prague. Though bald in adulthood, he had boyish features and a large Bismarckian mustache that covered a substantial area of his face. He was an articulate, fluent, and exciting speaker, rich in ideas that pressed forward in a rapid, humorous, and cheerful stream. Despite his oral facility, he had great difficulty in transcribing his thoughts to paper, racing from one idea to another, unable to limit and focus them, almost to the point of having writer's block. He was a poetic and musically gifted man whose joviality and personal magnetism entranced others.

By contrast, Koffka was a true Berliner, half Jewish, thin, small with a somber face and expression, introverted, and insecure. Uncomfortable at the lectern, he was an uninspiring speaker, but endearing to his students owing to his honesty, clarity of ideas, and personal thoughtfulness. In contrast to Wertheimer, Koffka was highly adept at his writing desk, drafting scholarly and systematic expositions of his creative ideas.

The third member of the Gestalt triumvirate, Köhler, was born in Estonia and reared in Germany. Stereotypically German, he was formal, militaristic, and arrogant; his features were neat, though his nose was bony and sharp, his hair thick and short, neatly parted down the middle. He was an inventive and painstaking researcher, clearly the most skillful of the three. Although he was a strong administrator, firm of resolve and highly ethical, his writing surprisingly was warm, relaxed, and fluent.

As mentioned earlier, because of the vicious anti-Semitism in Nazi Germany, Wertheimer left Frankfurt for the United States where he taught for the rest of his career. Koffka achieved a professorship at the University of Giessen, but was enticed to the United States to become a professor at Smith College, where he remained for the rest of his life. Only Köhler gained a major status in Germany following his early work on the Canary Islands, becoming the head of the Psychological Institute at the University of Berlin at age 34. After trying to restrain the Nazi influence on his Institute and courageously protecting his Jewish colleagues in the process, he resigned the post in 1935, came to the United States, and spent the rest of his career at Swarthmore College in Pennsylvania.

Kurt Koffka (1886–1941) was born in Berlin and expected to follow his father into the legal profession but was drawn to philosophy at the University of Berlin. Later shifting to psychology, he studied under Stumpf, earning his doctorate in 1909. After working with Oswald Külpe at Würzburg, he joined Wertheimer and Köhler at the University of Frankfurt. A 10-year period as professor at the University of Giessen followed. Koffka immigrated to the United States in 1924, much earlier than either Wertheimer or Köhler. Perhaps he anticipated the consequences of the rise of Nazism, or perhaps a year spent in Edinburgh as a student made his English proficiency marketable in America. After several visiting professorships, he was permanently appointed to that position at Smith College in 1927.

Koffka's earliest work displayed the new Gestalt theories and defined how he conceptualized and executed his ideas. Studying the inheritance of certain mental and behavioral tendencies, gross and fine motor coordinations, and the learning of perception among children, all within a Gestalt framework, he published *Die Grundlagen der psychischen Entwicklung* in 1921 (translated as

The Growth of the Mind in 1924). In this book, Koffka reviewed all that was then known about mental development and learning from a Gestalt point of view. Central to his thesis was a masterful and scathing criticism of the behaviorist position that learning consisted of random associations bonded by rewards. To Koffka, learning was a process of organization and reorganization that precedes any token of reinforcement. He drew on Kohler's studies of problem solving by apes, as well as comparable findings of problem solving by children. He offered a neurophysiological speculation that neuronal energy fields intrinsic to brain functioning (an idea akin to Donald Hebb's cell assembly notions a decade or so later) effectively construct a "good gestalt." As Koffka envisaged it, an underlying neurophysiological basis existed for both learning and memory; they composed neural traces in the brain, that is neural "residuals" embedded by experience. Unlike simple behaviorist association, which asserted that new experiences are merely added to earlier ones, Koffka believed that new experiences reorganize earlier experiences, which then create an entirely new composite of learned experience. This view resembles that of neurosurgical theorist Kurt Goldstein concerning cerebral reorganization among the brain-injured (see Chapter 6) or Jean Piaget's developmental views on child maturation, to be discussed later in this chapter.

Wolfgang Köhler (1887–1967) was born to a well-off Prussian family in Talinn, Estonia, though his family moved back to Germany when he was six. His early education was at German gymnasiums and his collegiate studies were first at universities in Tübingen and Bonn; he completed his doctoral training under Carl Stumpf at the University of Berlin in 1909. In addition to Stumpf, Köhler's physics professor, Max Planck, greatly influenced him, and he strove to follow in his footsteps by contributing to a psychological field theory. His use of modern physical concepts lent considerable respectability and credibility to the Gestalt ideas that Köhler later proposed.

The phi phenomenon work he had done with Wertheimer and Koffka greatly inspired Köhler, and he soon began testing Gestalt principles in animals. He conducted some of his earlier work on chickens. Köhler placed kernels of corn on two different cards, one a medium shade of gray with loose kernels and the other a dark gray card with the kernels glued down. The chickens quickly began to peck at only the kernels on the medium gray card. The dark gray card was then replaced with a light gray card. Traditional S-R (stimulus-response) learning theory would predict that the chickens would continue pecking at the medium gray card, the original stimulus in the S-R task. Instead, however, the chickens switched to pecking at the light gray card, suggesting that what they learned was a relationship of pecking at the lighter of two cards rather than responding in a simple S-R bond.

Köhler soon moved on to more complex studies with anthropoid apes on Tenerife in the Canary Islands. He arrived in 1913 and expected to return home to Germany the following year, but the outbreak of World War I kept him on the Spanish island until 1920. This time was far from wasted. Köhler penned an important research report entitled *Intelligenzprüfung an Menschenaffen* in 1917, which was translated into English (1925b) as *The Mentality of Apes.*

The core concept that came out of the studies with apes was insight into problem solving. In this report, Köhler described the process of seeing the relationship between things to solve a problem. He described experiments with caged chimpanzees, in which he would suspend a banana from the ceiling just out of a chimpanzee's reach. He also placed a box in the cage with the chimpanzee. Many of the animals solved the problem by moving the box beneath the banana and climbing on the box to reach it. In similar experiments, chimpanzees figured out how to break off a branch from a shrub to rake a banana closer to them or even join two sticks together to make a longer one to reach the fruit. Köhler argued that this meant the animal had to see the relationship instead of solving the problem through random trial and error.

In 1935, the Nazis instructed Köhler to discharge all Jews on his staff at the Berlin Institute of Psychology. He wrote a scathing letter to a newspaper in Berlin and then resigned from his post, leaving Germany for the United States and Swarthmore College. The psychology department at Swarthmore became a magnet for a series of young faculty members who later achieved notable distinction in the field. Though he retired in the late 1950s, Köhler continued to be actively involved in research.

Köhler enjoyed a prosperous career in the United States, becoming the only Gestaltist to be elected president of the American Psychological Association. As a humanist and distinguished scholar, Köhler wrote passionately on his social views in *The Place of Value in a World of Facts* (1938), and presented the William James lectures at Harvard and the Gifford lectures at Edinburgh. Among his many contributions were the restoration of perceptual study and the role of cognitive processes in learning. Although he and his Gestalt colleagues flourished for only a brief time in Germany, they laid the groundwork for the cognitive revolution in psychology.

Studying Cognitive Development

From its earliest incarnations, psychology has been concerned with human development. Sigmund Freud and Jean Piaget had perhaps the greatest impact in these pursuits, but others, such as Charles Darwin and G. Stanley Hall, also offered insights into children's intellectual development.

More than two centuries ago, *Jean Jacques Rousseau* (see Chapter 4) proposed a theory of development based on the idea that children repeated stages in the history of "the race." He suggested that they should be permitted, like little savages, to mature first before learning to act in a civilized manner. With the emergence of evolutionary ideas and embryological studies, the German researcher, *Fritz Muller* in the mid-nineteenth century recorded similarities between the embryos of various species, despite their considerable differences in adult appearance. This led the German biologist, *Ernst Haeckel*, in the late nineteenth century, to propose that the uniformities in embryological development suggested a biogenic natural law of recapitulation, as stated in the phrase *ontogeny recapitulates phylogeny*, a theme picked up by G. *Stanley Hall* (see Chapter 13) in his theoretical and experimental studies of children and adolescents.

Stanley Hall actively promoted systematic research on children's educational growth at the turn of the century at Clark University. Not only an academic, Hall became the leader in forming the National Association for the Study of Childhood in 1893. Not long thereafter, *Edward Lee Thorndike* (Chapter 9) and *John Dewey* (Chapter 13) undertook leadership roles in advancing childhood studies and educational theory. Another major academic of the period was **James Mark Baldwin (1861–1934)** whose developmental theories were oriented to the exploration of cognitive maturation and anticipated many of the themes that Jean Piaget later formulated. In the early twentieth century, the efforts of *Lawrence K. Frank* (Chapter 14), the child welfare benefactor, were instrumental in helping to establish numerous research institutes for the study of children. Diverse academic programs were started at Teachers College of Columbia University, the University of Minnesota, the University of Iowa, Stanford University, Harvard, and elsewhere. Yale University programs were notably productive in relating psychoanalytic notions from an experimental developmental framework; *Robert* and *Pauline Sears* led these initially, and subsequently continued their work at the Iowa Child Welfare Research Station, and later at Harvard and Stanford. Similarly, Yale was the center of **Arnold Gesell's (1880–1961)** systematic observational research on infant maturation. Other distinguished academics sustained by the generosity of Frank's largesse in their developmental studies, from physiological to social, included *Kurt Lewin* at Iowa (Chapter 12) and *Erik Erikson* at Berkeley and Harvard (Chapter 8).

Jean Piaget's (1896–1980) cognitive terminology has remained largely intact throughout the last half century with terms like *structures, accommodations, assimilation,* and *schemata* still being widely used. Although Piaget may be the most influential thinker in this realm, his ideas might have remained largely unknown had Lawrence Kohlberg not brought Piaget's ideas to the attention of American psychologists in the mid-twentieth century. Psychologists began doing empirical research to investigate Piaget's theories, with frustratingly inconsistent results. These issues are by no means settled and are still hotly debated and researched, with cognitive development throughout the life span remaining a central area in the general field of cognitive psychology.

Piaget was born at Neuchâtel in Switzerland. His father, a scholar of medieval literature, taught him to organize and study the world in a systematic manner. His mother, as Piaget described her, was "very intelligent, energetic, and fundamentally a very kind person; her rather neurotic temperament, however makes our family life somewhat troublesome" (1952, pp. 237–238). He attributes much of his early seriousness and scholarliness to his mother's mental

Jean Piaget

illness; it was Piaget's way of imitating his father and taking refuge in an orderly world of reality and scientific study. At the age of 10, after publishing an article on an albino sparrow he had witnessed in the park, Piaget became an assistant to a specialist who studied mollusks at a natural history museum. By the age of 15, he had become enough of an expert in the field to begin publishing a series of articles on the mollusks of Switzerland and other countries. After receiving an offer to become a curator of a mollusk collection, he was compelled to reveal his age and admit that he still had two years to study for his baccalaureate degree. He later received a baccalaureate and a doctorate in the sciences with a thesis on a group of mollusks.

Although it would have been logical for Piaget to pursue the natural sciences, he chose to explore philosophy and set out to gain experience in a psychology laboratory. He eventually found his way to the Sorbonne in Paris where he was given access to Binet's laboratory (see Chapter 14) and was asked to standardize a set of cognitive tests on Parisian schoolchildren. Thus began the heart of Piaget's body of research on the cognitive development of normal children.

If any word characterized Piaget's approach to his studies, it would be *painstaking;* yet he was also playful with a twinkle in his eye. A tall and slender youth, he preferred to let his hair fall across his forehead. He hid his genial and owlish face behind large horn-rimmed glasses. His high forehead was invariably under a beret with his long hair flowing to either side, a curved pipe centered on one side or another of an ever-smiling mouth. He was most assuredly a warm and gentle figure, well-experienced and kindly in relating to children. From his youth until his 80s, Piaget spent most of his time with young children, watching them play, playing with them, telling them stories, and asking them questions.

Piaget is perhaps best known for his conceptualization of the four stages of cognitive development from infancy to adulthood: Sensorimotor, Preoperational, Concrete Operations, and Formal Operations. *The Sensorimotor Stage* (birth to 2 years) is a period of remarkably rapid growth and development in the infant's cognitive structure based primarily on direct sensory and motor activities rather than on abstract thought. During the *Preoperational Stage* (2 to 7 years), children begin to think symbolically by developing the capacity for mental imagery and language. At this stage, thinking is still egocentric, in that children are incapable of seeing another person's point of view; and although they can repeat or rerun old actions in their minds, they are not able to imagine new actions that they have not yet done or seen before. During this stage, language begins to develop although it is different from the conception of language that adults possess. In the *Concrete Operations Stage* (7 to 12 years), children consolidate and organize many of the disparate conceptualizations that they formed in prior stages. Children can begin to perform mental operations such as transforming a situation or manipulating an object, but they can only reason about concrete or real physical things. In the *Formal Operations Stage* (12 years and above), children can finally ponder problems in the abstract without needing concrete representations. This stage is the basis of adult thought, although not all adults attain this stage. Representative tasks include being able to juggle several hypotheses at once and entertain a world of possible outcomes, not simply obvious and realistic ones. By this age, children can reason about abstractions such as mathematical symbols and words, making it possible to solve operations such as algebra and logic puzzles.

According to Piaget's theory, a child's mind is not just an adult's mind in miniature. It passes through stages of first being tied to sensory and bodily stimulation and only gradually learns to play with abstract ideas and hypotheses. What is common to all stages of Piaget's theory is that knowledge is an *active* process.

Piaget's theories were not always popular and universally accepted. When Piaget first became known to American psychologists, behaviorism was still at its zenith. Remarkably, despite the philosophical climate, his early translated works were widely read and others soon began to test his hypotheses. Several sociologists and psychologists were interested in testing the hypothesis that children move from animistic thinking to logical thinking. Many of these early efforts did not support Piaget's theories, including Margaret Mead's investigations of Samoan children, as well as other investigations that studied children from non-Western cultures. Many investigators thought that his ideas were culturally bound. Two decades followed with little interest in Piaget's theories. Luckily, Piaget continued his work and continued publishing in French. It was nearly 20 years later before another of his works was translated into English, but this time, his theories were more fully developed and the zeitgeist of psychology had changed to a cognitive approach that was highly receptive to his ideas.

Lawrence Kohlberg (1927–1987) is best known for his contributions to a theory of moral development; much of his work is based on Piaget's theories. Born in Bronxville, New York, to wealthy parents, Kohlberg attended prestigious schools. Much to everyone's surprise, he joined the merchant marine after high school and following the close of World War II. His ship helped smuggle Jewish refugees into Palestine by running a British blockade. The moral dilemma between breaking the law and the desire for establishing a Jewish homeland set the path for much of Kohlberg's later psychological research. After returning to the United States, he earned his bachelor's degree and doctorate at the University of Chicago; he wrote his dissertation on moral judgment in adolescents. More than the conclusions that adolescents drew from moral dilemmas, what fascinated Kohlberg was the process they used to resolve them. This line of research led him to theorize three moral stages with six levels.

In Hunt's descriptive characterization (1993), Kohlberg would have made a good clergyman; he was warm, humorous, earnest and thoughtful, passionate, and profoundly concerned about moral questions for his entire life. An archetypal intellectual professor, his hair was invariably disheveled, his clothes baggy and rumpled, his briefcase overfull and scuffed. Kohlberg attracted numerous followers and admirers; he also had many detractors who did not see moral development as following a neat upward and sequential progression. Similarly, critics found his proposals to be heavily biased in favor of the developmental experiences of men as contrasted to women. He advocated that women were likely to approach moral issues with a direct and caring response, and a desire to strengthen personal relationships; by contrast, men were more inclined to approach these matters at a formal distance and with legalistic concepts, such as justice and equity.

According to Millon (1990), two factors beyond the intrinsic genetic trait potentials of advanced social organisms have special significance in affecting their social survival. First, other members of the species play a critical part in providing postnatal nurturing and complex role models. Second, and no less relevant, is the high level of diversity and unpredictability of the ecological habitats of humans. This requires numerous, multifaceted, and flexible response alternatives, either preprogrammed genetically or acquired subsequently through early learning. Humans exhibit unusual adaptive pliancy, acquiring a wide repertoire of cognitive styles or alternate modes of functioning for dealing both with predictable and novel environmental circumstances. The malleability of early potentials for diverse learning diminishes as maturation progresses. Consequently, adaptive styles acquired in childhood and usually suitable for comparable later environments become increasingly immutable, resisting modification and relearning. Problems arise in new ecological settings when these deeply ingrained behavior patterns persist despite their lessened appropriateness. Simply stated, what was learned and once adaptive, may no longer fit. Perhaps more important than environmental diversity, then, is the divergence between the circumstances of original learning and those of later life. This schism has become more problematic as humans have progressed from stable and traditional to fluid and inconstant modern societies.

From the viewpoint of survival logic, it is both efficient and adaptive to preprogram or train the young of a species with traits that fit the ecological habitats of their parents. This wisdom rests on the usually safe assumption that consistency, if not identicalness, will characterize the ecological conditions of both parents and their offspring. Evolution is spurred when this continuity assumption fails; that is, when formerly stable environments undergo significant change. Radical shifts of this character could result in the extinction of a species. It is more typical, however, for environments to change gradually, resulting in modest, yet inexorable redistributions of a species' gene frequencies. Genes subserving competencies that prove suited to the new conditions become proportionately more common. Ultimately, the features they engender will come to typify either a new variant of, or a successor to, the earlier species.

Analyzing Linguistics

Many theorists have proposed hypotheses about the development of language. During much of the twentieth century, a behavioristic S-R theory of language development was dominant. It speculated that children predominantly acquire language by receiving reinforcement for imitating certain sounds that they hear from their parents. In Skinner's 1957 *Verbal Behavior*, he categorized two different styles of verbal emissions. The first, called *mands*, are responses that anticipate a particular outcome, such as when children say "eat," expecting their parent to give them food. The second, called *tacts*, are verbal symbols representing an object, such as when children say "peas" when they spy a green can in the pantry. To Skinner, even the most complex linguistic expressions can be understood in terms of simple stimulus, response, and reinforcement. The theorists covered in this section did much to turn attention toward what a child says spontaneously rather than forcing a rigid S-R framework onto language development.

George Armitage Miller (1920–   ), a prankish, whimsical, mischievous, yet inventive and courageous thinker, has been called "the single most effective leader in the emergence of cognitive psychology" (Baars, 1986). He combined brilliant academic achievements with personal characteristics that made him a charming communicator in the movement. He is also largely credited for making Chomsky's work (discussed later in this chapter) accessible to psychologists and for making its implications to cognitive psychology more evident. A native of Charleston, West Virginia, Miller entered college with a negative feeling about psychology. His Christian Science upbringing disposed him to view psychology and its portrayals of the mind to be the work of the devil (a comment he recorded with tongue-in-cheek in his memoir). After obtaining a bachelor's degree in English and a master's degree in speech from the University of Alabama, Miller found himself increasingly drawn to psychology because of its relationship with speech pathology. After a brief stint as a speech instructor, Miller began graduate psychology studies at Harvard. During World War II, his skills as a speech therapist made him a valuable asset at Harvard's Psychoacoustic Laboratory where he worked on voice communication systems for the military. When he returned to his Harvard studies, the Psychology Department had split into two separate and distinct factions, Social Relations and traditional Psychology, a change that ended his plans to become a clinician and cemented his involvement in experimental psychology. His academic career began at a time when behaviorists held all the dominant positions of power, wrote all the textbooks, received all the honors, and controlled all the money in psychology departments. Despite this indoctrination, he realized from the start that psychology could be based on other models. His dissertation on the intelligibility of speech in noise, based on his work for the military, relied on mathematical Markov models. This formulation led him later to turn to information theory approaches to human communication.

Miller's move away from behaviorism was not immediate; his first—and influential—textbook, *Language and Communication* (1951), had a distinct behavioristic bias. It was not until the late 1950s that he realized that he could not continue on the path of behaviorism. After working briefly with the psycholinguist Noam Chomsky, Miller returned to Harvard reconsidering his views about psychological research. As he recorded in his memoir:

> I realized I was acutely unhappy with the narrow conception of psychology that defined the Harvard department. I had just spent a year romping wildly in the sunshine. The prospect of going back to a world bounded at one end by psychophysics and at the other by operant conditioning was simply intolerable. I decided that either Harvard would have to let me create something resembling the interactive excitement of the Stanford Center or else I was going to leave. (1989)

In 1960, he cofounded, with *Jerome Bruner,* the Center for Cognitive Studies at Harvard. They chose the term *cognitive* to differentiate them from behaviorists, rather than to exclude other factors such as emotions or volition. They intended to put the "mental" aspects back into psychology. Miller continued to do research on psycholinguistics but also delved into information theory, statistical learning theory, and the new field of computer simulation. He moved from Harvard to Rockefeller University and then to Princeton, where he has concentrated on lectures in psychology. He has abandoned his earlier work on behavioristic themes in favor of the study, not only of higher mental processes, but of ideas that promote human welfare.

Miller is one of the most congenial and good-natured psychologists of his time, with a quick wit and no evidence of acidity or malevolence. Though his early work was impressive, it was fortunate and courageous of him to have left his behavioristic orientation for a more personally gratifying and professionally significant career as a cognitivist. His experimental beliefs and talents seem to have been overpowered by more worldly abilities and considerations, a direction that his erstwhile colleague Chomsky adopted, though with appreciably less cheer and geniality.

Noam Chomsky (1928–), revered by some as one of the greatest minds of the twentieth century and reviled by others, is perhaps known as much for his political views and activism as for his brilliant and revolutionary contributions to the study of linguistics. He was born in Philadelphia; his father, a Hebrew scholar working with historical languages, introduced him to linguistics. At the University of Pennsylvania, his interest blossomed as Professor Zelig S. Harris suggested that Chomsky try to diagram a systematic structure of language. Chomsky chose Hebrew and completed his undergraduate and master's theses in 1949 and 1950. He revised these papers into a publication entitled *The Logical Structure of Linguistic Theory*, which he attempted to have published in 1966; however, numerous publishers rejected it. The manuscript circulated for several years, finally being published in 1975. By then, Chomsky had moved first to Harvard as a Junior Fellow, where he pursued interests in philosophy and logic, and then on to the Massachusetts Institute of Technology, where he became a linguistics professor.

A series of lecture notes entitled *Syntactic Structures* (1957) launched Chomsky's celebrated, if not notorious, career. The revolutionary implications of Chomsky's ideas were not immediately apparent, for it appeared only to be a scathing assault on the then leading linguist in the United States, Leonard Bloomfield of the University of Chicago. Bloomfield had articulated a comprehensive taxonomical structure for linguistics based on the explicit form of script writing and oral sounds emanating from speech. Akin to behaviorists, most notably B. F. Skinner, many judged Bloomfield's linguistics to have brought a degree of scientific rigor to what had previously been considered a soft field in humanities studies.

Noam Chomsky

According to Chomsky, however, Bloomfield and his followers had locked themselves tightly to surface expressions of language and essentially were merely describing what they recorded. Language, to Chomsky, was not a surface phenomenon at all, but an intrinsic grammatical structure inherent in human biological endowment. What was so exciting about this work was Chomsky's refutation of superficial theories of grammatical structure that were popular at the time. In their stead, he outlined a system of transformational grammar that contained the sounds and words of a sentence based on the deep structure that provided meaning for a sentence. The meaning of a sentence could then be converted by transformation rules back into its surface structure. Especially novel was Chomsky's proposal that all children are born with an innate knowledge of the principles of grammatical structure for language, hence explaining the amazing alacrity at which children can learn any language. Robert Lees reviewed Chomsky's ideas in an issue of *Language* and quickly became Chomsky's first disciple.

The editor of *Language* then asked Chomsky to write a review of Skinner's recently completed *Verbal Behavior*. Chomsky's review proved to be more influential than Skinner's book, perhaps the most devastating and influential review written in contemporary psychological science. In it, he argued that Skinner had not arrived at a valid method for objectively studying verbal behavior. Chomsky asserted that Skinner had merely covered up complex verbal processes with pseudoscientific terms. As with his attack on Bloomfield, Chomsky noted that the infinite number of ways in which language is structured and expressed could not reflect any known behavioristic training sequence: It had to be the product of an intrinsic or natural human endowment. He pointed out that children of different levels of intelligence, raised in diverse cultural environments, acquired language at the same pace, even though few if any had been reinforced in a systematic fashion. Children naturally followed an inborn and common human grammatical structure with an implicit set of rules, rather than mechanically imitating what they heard. Further, Chomsky considered it preposterous to speak of language as a process by which learning through reinforcement could have shaped the infinite variety of novel verbal behavior that young children utter and comprehend. In his view, fundamental grammatical rules must already exist within children's maturational capabilities, essentially hardwired in the nervous system. Thus, language was a basic human and universal function that did not need reinforcement with M&M pellets. His review effectively criticized all aspects of behaviorism as a method for analyzing psychological phenomena. It led others, in turn, to use his basic arguments to condemn behavioristic theory in many other spheres of psychological science and provided much-needed ammunition that led to the antibehavioral cognitive revolution.

Despite his seemingly calm professorial style, Chomsky's critics have accused him of setting himself up as a guru or cult leader, even though he has frequently and consistently alienated many of his followers. Despite surface impressions to the contrary, his writings slash and cut, apparently envenomed by an intense if not vicious and acerbic sarcasm. He habitually repeats his verbal attacks using words such as murder, massacre, and atrocity again and again, until they cumulate to a devastating pitch. Chomsky has directed his assaults not only to his scientific confreres, but to much of the world-out-there, a place he sees as illiberal, undemocratic, vile, malignant, and deeply disheartening.

Computerizing Information

With the advent of computer science, it is not surprising that psychologists turned their attentions to the new and exciting possibilities that a computer metaphor afforded. Others had long since been involved in exploring how humans solved problems and made decisions, but computers and computer models opened possibilities that had never existed for exploring new theories. Computers signified an entirely new conceptual shift from a behavioral stimulus-response human to one that had inputs and output responses. Notions about memory matured into present conceptualizations of encoding and event storage. No longer were individuals passive receivers of information in which material is organized in a linear way by associative bonds. Instead, they are active organizers of information using hierarchical schemas and sophisticated systems. Computers naturally led cognitive psychologists to explore the notion of artificial intelligence as well. Not only could knowledge of human thinking help program computers to think, but powerful computers could actually further cognitive science's understanding of how humans think. Herbert Simon and Allen Newell made significant contributions to these areas throughout their careers, but particularly during the 1950s at the Rand Corporation.

At the end of World War II, a number of different thinkers and researchers began to explore the intricacies of higher mental processes. Mathematicians and philosophical logicians began to formulate human communication via a field with the name *information theory.* Similarly, with the emergence of computers, numerous engineering scientists began to design machinery that could produce a primitive form of human thinking and problem solving. Psycholinguists and philosophers began to formulate symbolic systems to represent language acquisition. Noted as well were the emergence of cognitive psychology and the broad-ranging new field of cognitive science. Early work of mathematicians such as *John von Neumann* and *Norbert Weiner* extended the possibility of using symbols to represent complex communications and institute a new form of language with which the computer could perform operations that paralleled human reasoning.

Like many others in this chapter, **Herbert A. Simon (1916–2001),** was intrigued by what he learned from the new mathematical and computer innovators, and it led him to a career that bridged diverse fields. After graduating from the University of Chicago with a bachelor's degree in economics in 1936, he first pursued political science and public administration. He completed his PhD at the University of Chicago in 1943 and, among other ventures, began work on new applications of mathematics to economics. He then introduced what was called the "Hawkins-Simon" condition of nonnegative square matrices and eventually won a Nobel Prize in economics in 1978 for his work on decision making in organizations. While working in public administration at what is now Carnegie-Mellon University, he turned to computer science and psychology. In the early 1950s, computers were just becoming viable devices, and Simon became a pioneer in artificial intelligence as well as computational modeling of psychological processes. He believed that the goal of artificial intelligence was twofold: first, to use the power of the computer to *enhance* human thinking; and second, to use it to better understand *how* humans think. By the mid-1950s, Simon and two colleagues, including Allen Newell (see following section), discovered that they could program a computer to simulate human thinking. Their program, Logic Theorist, discerned the steps involved in proofs for a theorem. They also began programming simulations of short-term memory and eventually programmed computers to perform such complex tasks as playing chess and to simulate other human problem-solving tasks.

In what came to be called *information processing,* Simon and his colleagues began to manipulate and transform data from different sources into symbolic representations. They could then systematically manipulate and evaluate them either to solve problems or to add them to extant memory and retrieve them later as needed. The ability to program computers to fulfill these tasks resulted from careful studies of how humans actually performed them. Simon spent a large part of his career discovering how humans make decisions. This research led him to make a distinction between limited short-term memory and extensive long-term memory. Simon recognized that when making most decisions, we have to rely on our limited and narrow scope of short-term memory. He measured these limitations by the number of familiar items or "chunks" that one can hold at any one time. Information is not processed as discrete entities or in single strands, but as larger chunks of similar or equivalent data. Simon believed that as one gained more experience, smaller chunks were collected together and then experienced as single larger chunks.

Herbert Simon and **Allen Newell (1927–1992),** a brilliant graduate student of his, became fast friends and collaborators for close to 40 years, working together on innumerable projects. Although he had varied interests, the main thrust of Newell's research centered on artificial intelligence with computer simulation as the primary method for understanding how the human mind worked. Some of the worthy tangents he pursued included computer hardware architectures, the psychology of human-computer interactions, and development of computer networking for Carnegie-Mellon University, where he spent most of his career.

The rapid rise of cognitive psychology in the mid-1960s called for writing a comprehensive summary and analysis to move it further forward. **Ulric Neisser (1928–   )** undertook this task in his text, *Cognitive Psychology* (1967). Born in Germany, Neisser studied in the United States and received both his bachelor's degree and doctorate from Harvard. For the next two decades, he served on the faculties of Brandeis, University of Pennsylvania, MIT, Cornell, and Emory, which provided him with diverse experiences, sufficient to write several integrative books. One of his most innovative contributions was the constructionist thesis that earlier information-processing notions were fundamentally deficient in their formulations because they assumed that people "receiving the message" were too passive or neutral in dealing with incoming messages. To him, information processing comprised an interaction between people "searching" and the characteristics of their environmental inputs.

Neisser had strong reservations also about the implications of computer programs that dealt with artificial intelligence. In contrast with Simon, Neisser believed that computers and the human mind could not be considered fundamentally alike. He asserted that the computer was single-minded, nondistractible, and unemotional, and that its mode of information processing was far removed from real life cognitive-emotional and purposeful behavior. Though computers could process simple symbols and calculate their relationships in a manner far more rapidly than humans, they lack understanding of what they are doing, nor do they consider any of the more intuitive and unconscious elements that operate in human decision making. Further, computer processes cannot demonstrate, as yet, any creative or innovative thinking activity. Lacking human emotions, the cognitive processes of computers are dry and restricted compared with the way humans think and feel.

Reorienting Cognitions Therapeutically

Cognitively oriented therapists exhibit three factors in common that set them apart from other schools of thought. First, unlike behaviorists and in common with psychoanalytic therapists, cognitivists emphasize internal processes that mediate overt actions. They conceive psychic pathology in terms of enduring and pervasive traits that shape and give consistency to behavior. No matter how widely generalized and consistent certain behaviors may be, they are simply surface derivatives of these inner mediators. Thus, cognitivists focus their therapeutic efforts on internal dispositions of feeling and behavior, but especially thought.

Second, cognitivists differ from both behavior and psychoanalytic therapists in the events and processes that they consider central to the pathogenesis and treatment of pathology. Behaviorists emphasize the role of environmental events such as stimuli and reinforcements; psychoanalytic therapists consider unconscious forces to be crucial. Consequently, behaviorists seek to alter pathology by manipulating stimulus events and reinforcement contingencies, and psychoanalytic therapists attempt to uproot and reconstruct the elements of the unconscious. In contrast to both, cognitivists concern themselves with the data of conscious attitudes and expectations, believing that these cognitive processes are crucial to the development and perpetuation of pathology. Cognitive therapy, then, is directed to the reorientation of consciously discordant assumptions and erroneous beliefs, and not to the modification of isolated behaviors or to disgorging the past and its associated unconscious derivatives.

Third, given their emphasis on conscious beliefs and expectations, cognitive therapists tend to follow an insight-expressive treatment process, similar to that of analytic therapists, rather than an action-suppressive process. Nevertheless, the cognitive focus of therapists differs, at least in theory, from that of analytic therapists. Cognitivists attend to dissonant interpersonal assumptions and self-perceptions that can be consciously acknowledged by examining the patient's everyday relationships and activities. In contrast, analytic therapists view consciously acknowledged attitudes to be superficial verbalizations that cloak hidden beliefs and emotions; to them, therapy should bring into awareness repressed materials that resist conscious examination. Cognitivists consider psychoanalytic depth probing to be unnecessary and time consuming. They believe that a reorientation of patients' conscious assumptions and feelings, without exploring their historical origins or dissolving their unconscious roots, is sufficient to enable patients to rectify their difficulties and find a more constructive outlook on life.

Cognitive therapies seek to address how patients perceive life events, focus their attention, process information, organize their thoughts, and communicate their reactions and ideas to others. These approaches provide some of the most useful indices to clinicians about patients' distinctive way of functioning. By synthesizing these data, it may be possible to identify such general features as constricted thought, cognitive distractibility, and impoverished thinking.

Patients may be viewed as inept, irresponsible, or sick, and therefore unwilling or unable to choose the course they must take for their own well-being. Therapists not only assume authority for deciding the objectives of treatment, but also confront patients with the irrationalities of their thinking; moreover, they may employ intimidating tactics to indoctrinate patients with a universally beneficial value system.

The philosophies, goals, and therapeutic procedures that differentiate cognitive style approaches make it difficult to group these therapies as a unit. Despite these substantive differences, however, certain merits and criticisms may be assigned to all of these methods. First, cognitive therapists are usually active in the treatment process, encouraging patients to alter their self-defeating perceptions and cognitions instead of allowing them to work things out for themselves. In contrast to the more humanistic and existential therapists (see Chapter 4), they tend to prejudge patients' cognitive errors in accord with a fixed philosophy, such as rationality. Seemingly, they seek to inculcate a set of alternative beliefs. Their plan is to reorient patients' misguided attitudes, whatever these may be, toward whatever direction appears to be more constructive. Although many subscribe to principles of learning, cognitive therapists differ from behavior therapists in that treatment focuses, not on overt symptom behaviors, but on internal mediating processes (expectancies, assumptions) that create and perpetuate these behaviors.

The work of **Paul Dubois (1848–1918)** predates what we customarily consider the beginnings of cognitive therapy, but his views on the treatment of the mentally ill, particularly the less severe variants, undeniably formed the basis for later theorists. Dubois was a psychiatrist and professor of neuropathology at the University of Bern. In his major work, *The Psychic Treatment of Mental Disease* (1908), Dubois encouraged other psychiatrists to spend more time talking with their patients and less time prescribing various bromides and rest cures. He optimistically believed that his patients could recover, and his self-confidence inspired his patients to wellness. Dubois believed that the goal of treatment should be "to make the patient master of himself." He meant that patients could achieve happiness by exerting self-control. Further, Dubois theorized that the best way to achieve a high degree of self-control was by rationally appealing to reason and intellect. He accomplished this by first discussing with patients the issues and problems that they were experiencing. He helped patients recognize the false beliefs and premises that were creating their problems and the injurious habits that were propagating their difficulties. By using reason and encouragement, patients could learn to control their symptoms so that they were no longer incapacitating.

George Alexander Kelly's (1905–1967) work has been labeled everything from dialectical materialism theory to behavioral theory to Zen Buddhist theory. Even psychoanalysts have claimed him as kin. Although Kelly's personal construct theory does not fit neatly into any one box, his work has been extremely influential to other cognitive therapists and thinkers. His contributions can be thought of as a forerunner to theories of cognitive therapy, despite Kelly's assertion: "It seems perfectly clear to me that personal construct theory is not a cognitive theory" (Maher, 1969, p. 216).

Kelly was born in Perth, Kansas, and soon left with his parents in a covered wagon to claim land in Eastern Colorado. His early schooling was sporadic but he completed a BA in physics and mathematics, a bachelor's degree in education from Edinburgh University, and a PhD in psychology at Iowa. He worked for many years with a traveling clinic that provided services to rural communities in the Kansas dust bowl, eventually accepting several academic appointments, most notably at Ohio State University. His theory of personal constructs grew out of his therapeutic experiences with patients during the Great Depression and out of his frustration at the ineffectiveness of using psychoanalytic and behavioral techniques with them. Instead, he began to search for new and inventive ways of helping his patients make meaningful life changes.

His major theoretical work, the two-volume *The Psychology of Personal Constructs*, was published in 1955 and contains much of his pioneering work. To understand personal constructs, it is important to recognize that Kelly believed humans live in two basic worlds. The first world exists outside human understanding: the primary world. The second world is the way we interpret the primary world in our representations or constructs, which are translations of an unknowable world. In other words, we can only know the primary world through our own interpretations of it. We can never experience it directly. Therefore, reality is a relative rather than an absolute concept. Each person brings his or her own *constructive alternativism* or unique way of making sense of experiences, rendering all constructions merely interpretations and opinions rather than facts. Logically then, Kelly believed that scientists invented the world instead of discovering some absolute truth that is out there waiting to be uncovered by someone with the right archeological tools and approach.

Kelly's use of the term *personal construct* can be understood as the way in which a person interprets, construes, or attaches meaning to some aspect of the world. Kelly believed that ordinary people acted much like scientists in that they possess theories or personal constructs that they test and use to predict and control their world. Constructs are helpful in that they allow people to anticipate the future because events that are connected with a construct keep reoccurring. People grow as their constructs evolve and become a complex web with varying degrees of incompatibility or integration with each other. Kelly was fundamentally optimistic about humans' capacity to change their constructs. Under nonthreatening conditions that encouraged experimentation, people could validate their constructs and modify them when necessary. Although most people work toward constructs with greater and greater validity, some tenaciously hang onto constructs in the face of overwhelming evidence to the contrary, which can lead to pathology.

Although Kelly often asserted that his was not a cognitive theory, most historians have characterized his work as such. Also notable are Kelly's various views regarding the therapeutic process, as illustrated in the following quote from a paper written toward the end of his career:

> And in this theory, then, the task of the therapist is to join with his client in exploring, by the only means available to man—by behavior—the implications of the constructions he has devised for understanding reality. From this point of view therapy becomes an experimental process in which the scientists are the client and his therapist. Moreover, the answers at which they arrive during the course of formal therapy are never the final answers. (1965, p. 220)

Highly aroused emotions greatly impair cognitive functions, according to **Albert Ellis (1913–   ).** In what he speaks of as "emotional behavior," Ellis states that emotions are in control rather than cognitions, with the consequence that behaviors are frequently unrealistic and neurotic. During emotional episodes, efforts to act rationally are likely to fail. To Ellis, the time to

Albert Ellis

control emotions is when reason can have the upper hand. Ellis believes people can learn and rehearse strategies for cognitive control. Like other cognitive theorists, he maintains that people can learn effective cognitive strategies by profiting from past mistakes or by anticipating problems and preventing them. People can learn both from direct experience and vicariously, by observing how others handle difficult situations. Most important is that people can rehearse self-instructions, or what Ellis terms *self-verbalizations.*

Albert Ellis was born in Pittsburgh, Pennsylvania, and raised in New York City. A kidney disorder forced him to turn his attentions from sports to books as a youngster, and his parent's rocky relationship stimulated a lifelong interest in understanding other people. The Depression dampened his hopes of becoming a self-made millionaire, allowing him time to write novels, so he turned his attention to business, earning a degree in business administration from the City University of New York. He began writing short stories, novels, plays, and essays in his spare time but could not interest a publisher. He began to write extensively on what he called the "sex-family revolution" and soon friends were asking for advice on the topic. Discovering he had a talent and passion for counseling as well as writing, he entered Columbia's clinical psychology program in 1942. By the time he earned his doctorate in 1947, Ellis was convinced of the power and effectiveness of psychoanalysis and began a training analysis. Without a medical degree, he was hard-pressed to find an analyst willing to train him. He finally completed his training with Karen Horney's group and began to practice her semiclassical psychoanalytic approach.

Despite the difficulties of his childhood—having an irresponsible father and an indifferent mother, undergoing a series of problematic hospitalizations, and being treated as something of a sissy insofar as athletic and social activities were involved—Ellis became a committed problem solver, especially in overcoming his earlier misfortunes. He ultimately became an energetic self-made and confirmed narcissist, with considerable achievements. He is now among the most celebrated twentieth-century psychologists, working long hours, maintaining a vigorous schedule well into his upper 80s, lean and trim, inclined to a ready demonic grin, charming, quick-witted, yet invariably sarcastic.

Ellis became disenchanted with psychoanalysis, discovering that his patients progressed just as quickly when he saw them once a week as when he saw them daily. He also found that his patients made more progress when he took a more active role in the therapy such as giving direct interpretations and advice. After contemplating how he had worked through his own issues earlier in life, he recalled how reading and practicing the philosophies of Bertrand Russell and Spinoza, among others, had helped him. Exploring alternatives to his practice, Ellis concluded that his patients' troubling emotions stemmed from their persistent habit of unrealistic, illogical, inflexible, and childish thinking. The therapist's task was therefore to unmask the patient's self-defeating thoughts and to institute in their stead logical and self-helping attitudes. He adopted a vigorous confrontational style and assumed a forthright and unequivocal attack on the patient's irrational ideas, pounding away, as he put it, time and again at the patient's illogical thoughts. By 1955, he had shifted completely away from psychoanalysis and toward a tactic of challenging his patients' irrational beliefs and persuading them to adopt more rational ones in their stead.

Ellis's theories and style developed over the years, and by 1958, he published *How to Live with a Neurotic*, the first publication on what he termed *Rational Emotive Therapy* (RET; more recently renamed Rational Emotive Behavior Therapy, or REBT). Among his novel ideas was the confrontation-directive group. Here, therapists assume an authoritarian role and patients, at least implicitly, are considered to be inept, irresponsible, or sick—unable or unwilling to choose for themselves what their goals should be. Not only do therapists take an active part in deciding treatment objectives, but they employ persuasive or commanding tactics to influence patients to adopt an appropriate system of values. Ellis believes that a confrontational approach is better than one characterized by sympathy and warmth. He found that a sensitive and caring approach pleased his patients and made them feel good but inclined them to remain dependent and needy and, therefore, even less confident than before to deal with the reality of their world.

Patients, by reiterating their unrealistic and self-defeating beliefs in a self-dialogue, constantly reaffirm their irrationality and aggravate their distress. To overcome these implicit but pernicious attitudes, therapists must confront patients with them, and induce them to think about them consciously and concertedly, as well as to attack them forcefully and unequivocally until they no longer influence their behavior. By revealing and assailing these beliefs and by commanding patients to engage in activities that run counter to them, their hold on patients' lives is broken and new directions become possible.

Tracing his ideas to Adler's writings, Ellis's approach in REBT is that people are too harsh with themselves, tending to blame and judge their actions more severely than necessary. Underlying these destructive attitudes, according to Ellis, is the tendency of patients to blame themselves for their limitations and wrongdoings; to subscribe to the false and self-defeating assumption that they are "no good and therefore deserve to suffer." The principal goal of therapy is to challenge and destroy this belief, to liberate patients, to free them from such irrational notions as shame and sin and to live life to the fullest, despite social shortcomings or the disapproval of others.

Assorted colleagues of Ellis have spoken of him as a difficult person with whom to work, aggressive, flamboyantly assertive, domineering, invariably putting his intelligence in the service of a need to control and shine. Some have said they constantly argued with him, sometimes violently, but ultimately submitted to the force of his persuasiveness, compromising or shifting the terms of disagreements. Others handled the less glamorous aspects of his awesome work schedule, leaving him free to participate in more rewarding activities. At some level, they judged him to be both the most tortured and the most contented of psychotherapists. Seen by many as the prototype of a mysterious genius, he expresses his views articulately and intensely in his writings, lectures, and, indeed in much of his life. One can picture him sitting in a chair, surrounded by mesmerized neophytes, talking in an insistent and prophetic manner, conveying the feeling that the entire world has been reduced for the moment to the here and now. He has an enormous physical and intellectual charm that attracts women and disciples. An excellent critic, acute, wide-ranging, alert both to the texture and meaning of psychological phenomena, he is well aware of the personal impact of his ideas. Now in his 90s, he remains thin, wiry, as flexible as a sculptural mobile, quick and nervous in all of his movements, still charming, even when devastating and putting others down.

Ellis (1970) has outlined 12 irrational beliefs that create unrealistic standards by which patients typically live. Among the most pernicious are: (1) It is essential that a person be loved or approved by virtually everyone; (2) one must be perfectly competent, adequate, and achieving to be considered worthwhile; (3) some people are wicked or villainous and therefore should be blamed and punished; (4) unhappiness is caused by outside circumstances and a person has no control over them; (5) it is easier to avoid certain difficulties and responsibilities than to face them; (6) a person should be dependent on others and should have someone stronger on whom to rely; and (7) there is always a right or perfect solution to every problem, and it must be found or the results will be catastrophic.

Some cognitive therapists are neither directive nor nondirective in their treatment goals or style of therapeutic interaction. Rather, therapist and patient agree that the latter possesses attitudes that promote and perpetuate difficulties in life. These therapists are more active in the treatment process than those who follow the humanistic philosophy; they encourage patients to alter their self-defeating perceptions and cognitions instead of allowing them to work things out for themselves. Many do not prejudge the patient's problem in accord with a fixed philosophy such as "integrity" or "rationality"; they have no particular "axe to grind," no set of beliefs they seek to inculcate. Rather, they plan merely to reorient the patient's misguided attitudes, whatever these may be, toward whatever direction may prove constructive, given the patient's personal life circumstances.

Although subscribing to learning principles, these therapists differ from behavior therapists in that treatment is focused not on overt symptom behaviors, but on those internal mediating processes (perceptions and attitudes), that create and perpetuate these behaviors. These approaches have recently begun to gain favor among many professionals as they bridge the gap between laboratory learning principles and the primary vehicle of most therapies: verbal discussion. Several formal systems have been proposed along these lines.

Julian Rotter's cognitive learning approach, described in Chapter 9, proposes in its therapeutic model to alter the patient's expectancies (cognitive anticipations) that particular forms of behavior are followed by positive or negative reinforcements of varying strengths. Maladaptive behaviors stem from erroneous expectancies, learned largely as a consequence of faulty past reinforcements that generalize into current situations and relationships. Therapy is viewed as a specially arranged process of unlearning and relearning that is no different in its fundamental character and principles from that of other learning settings. In fact, as Rotter notes, formal therapy, despite its concentration and focus, is often a less efficient vehicle for change than repetitive everyday experiences. This is because it is limited to a few hours a week at most and takes place in a setting that is appreciably different from the one to which its effects must be generalized.

Therapeutic processes are designed to change maladjustive reinforcement-expectancies, or as Rotter has put it (1954):

> . . . lowering the expectancy that a particular behavior or behaviors will lead to gratifications or increasing the expectancy that alternate or new behaviors

would lead to greater gratification in the same situation or situations. In general learning terms we might say we have the choice of either weakening the inadequate response, strengthening the correct or adequate response, or doing both. (p. 338)

The most important therapeutic goal is strengthening the expectancy that problems can be resolved, which Rotter formulates as follows:

It is the purpose of therapy not to solve all of the patient's problems, but rather to increase the patient's ability to solve his own problems. . . . From a social learning point of view, one of the most important aspects of treatment, particularly face to face treatment, is to reinforce in the patient the expectancy that problems are solvable by looking for alternative solutions. (1954, p. 342)

Aaron Timothy Beck

Aaron Timothy Beck (1921–   ) has been a prominent and insightful contributor to cognitive therapy, especially as applied to a wide range of the Axis I clinical syndromes. More recently, he and his associates have addressed the subject of personality, articulating *cognitive schemas* that shape the experiences and behaviors of numerous personality disorders. In a manner similar to Millon (1990; see Chapters 13 and 14), Beck anchors his guiding theoretical model to evolution. He speculates on how the prototypes of personality may be derived from our phylogenetic heritage. He views what may be conceived as genetically determined strategies that have facilitated survival and reproduction through natural selection. Derivatives of these evolutionary strategies may be identified, according to Beck, in exaggerated form among the Axis I clinical syndromes, and in less dramatic expression among the personality disorders. He characterizes his theory of the origins of disorders and the appropriate treatment in the following:

This new approach—cognitive therapy—suggests that the individual's problems are derived largely from certain distortions of reality based on erroneous premises and assumptions. These incorrect conceptions originated in defective learning during the person's cognitive development. Regardless of their origin, it is relatively simple to state the formula for treatment: The therapist helps a patient to unravel his distortions in thinking and to learn alternative, more realistic ways to formulate his experiences. (1976, p. 3)

Central to Beck's approach is the concept of *schema*, that is, specific rules that govern information processing and behavior. The concept of schemata derives originally from Kant's writings. More recently, Piagetian psychologists and other cognitive network theorists have used it to represent tacit internal structures that reflect abstractions about the stimulus world and their relationships. These schemata are stored in memory as generalizations or prototypes of specific life experiences; they serve as a template that provides an orientation, focus, and meaning for all sources of incoming information. Despite their unconscious character, they direct attention to aspects of ongoing experiences important for survival and adaptation. In effect, these broad-ranging schemata orient conscious cognitive processes such as attention, encoding, retrieval, and inference. Importantly, schemata incorporate not only cognitive, but emotional and affective valences as well. No less significant, schemata relate to self and serve as a gauge for appraising and valuing aspects of it.

Schemata may be classified into categories, such as personal, familial, and cultural. They are inferred directly from behavior or from interviews and history taking. To Beck, the disentangling and clarification of these schemata lie at the heart of therapeutic work. They persist, despite their dysfunctional consequences, because they enable patients to extract short-term benefits from them, thereby diverting them from pursuing more effective, long-term solutions. Beck avers that an important treatment consideration is recognizing that cognitive restructuring will inevitably evoke problematic anxieties because patients are forced to reexamine or reframe their schemata.

Although Beck is fully acquainted with the role of both self-schemata and interpersonal-schemata, he emphasizes the former. He specifically details distorting cognitive schemata for each of the personality disorders in a manner that provides a basis for planning cognitive therapy.

Beck outlined the following origin of dysfunctional beliefs (A. T. Beck & Freeman, 1990):

> Given that the personality patterns (cognition, affect, and motivation) of people with personality disorders deviate from those of other people, the question arises: How do these patterns develop? In order to address this question—although briefly—we need to return to the nature-nurture interaction. Individuals with a particularly strong sensitivity to rejection, abandonment, or thwarting may develop intense fears and beliefs about the catastrophic meaning of such events. A patient, predisposed by nature to overreact to the more commonplace kinds of rejection in childhood, may develop a negative self-image ("I am unlovable"). This image may be reinforced if the rejection is particularly powerful, or occurs at a particularly vulnerable time, or is repeated. With repetition, the belief becomes structuralized . . .
>
> The way people process data about themselves and others is influenced by their beliefs and the other components of their cognitive organization. When there is a disorder of some type—a symptom syndrome (Axis I) or a personality disorder (Axis II)—the orderly utilization of these data becomes systematically biased in a dysfunctional way. This bias in interpretation and the consequent behavior is shaped by dysfunctional beliefs. (pp. 29–30)

Beck was born in Providence, Rhode Island. Frequently sickly, he underwent surgical procedures several times, each of which intensified his strong aversion to physical pain. The sight of blood typically made him feel queasy or actually caused him to faint. Beck has written that this fear motivated his interest in a medical career as a way of confronting and overcoming his aversion. Forcing himself to see blood and experience surgical procedures as a medical student enabled him to vanquish his terrible discomfort and dispel his fears; he later extended this procedure to other realms in which he suffered phobias. By subduing these disabling symptoms, he proved to himself that they simply were immature and unrealistic, enabling him to gradually "reason them away."

Beck had a lifelong interest in psychiatry as a career. He graduated magna cum laude from Brown University in 1942 before going on to Yale's medical school. Although his original interest was psychiatry, in medical school he became dissatisfied with its then current approaches and decided to pursue a career in neurology, which seemed to possess a higher degree of precision. During his residency in neurology at the Cushing Veterans Administration Hospital in Framingham, he completed a mandatory rotation in psychiatry, which reawakened his interest in the field and he became intrigued with its newer developments. Following medical school and several years at Valley Forge Army Hospital during the Korean War, Beck attended and graduated from the Philadelphia Psychoanalytic Institute in 1956. After spending several years conducting long-term psychotherapy, he joined the Department of Psychiatry at the University of Pennsylvania. He focused his early research efforts largely on testing psychoanalytic theories of depression, but when his studies failed to support his hypotheses, he explored a more cognitive explanation of the disorder. His inquiries found that most depressed patients had a broad negative view of themselves and the world-at-large, as well as their own future. Beck reasoned that these "negative cognitive distortions," as he put them, could be corrected by applying logic and the rules of evidence to reorient the erroneous beliefs with reality. His eventually applied these cognitive investigations to a broad range of disorders, from anxiety, to substance abuse, to personality.

With over 375 articles and 15 books to his credit, Beck's work became immensely influential. Psychiatric colleagues, however, ignored his earliest efforts; many in the medical community considered him to be a pariah in their profession. It was the psychologists rather than the psychiatrists who found his ideas congenial and consonant with their growing awareness of the then emerging cognitive revolution.

In his person, Beck is almost the opposite of his fellow distinguished cognitive therapist, Albert Ellis. He is personally reserved, writing and speaking in an easy, calm, and controlled manner, none of it exhibiting the cutting incisiveness and rhetorical flashiness of Ellis. Now in his 80s, Beck remains one of the most charming and generous therapists I have met. Handsome with his gray hair and ever-present red bow tie, he evidences sensitiveness and thoughtfulness, as well as a suggestion of quiet boldness and adventurism. He is not an ideological talker; conversations with him do not feature an exchange of ideas or theories. He prefers to talk about people and events in a personal and casual way, never nasty, malicious, or self-aggrandizing. What vanity he might possess, which may in fact be enormous, is to be found in his work and his ideas. Much subtler, suaver, and more diplomatic than Ellis, he comfortably plays the part of an elder statesman. A most agile and disciplined mind, basing his ideas on reason and logical persuasion, he is a superb teacher, stimulating students by exemplifying therapeutic interactions. Though not free of the ravages of his psychoanalytic origin, that early training appears to have enhanced his thinking rather than disfigure it. Though personal recognition has primarily come from psychologists, not psychiatrists, he has never been backbiting or critical of his medical confreres, but instead is invariably scrupulous and reflective, almost paternal.

Beck is not a self-promoter, but a thoughtful, considerate, and creative man. He fully recognizes that he owes many of his ideas, first, to his early indoctrination in psychoanalysis and, subsequently, to his reading of numerous works by psychological thinkers, such as those mentioned earlier in this chapter. Although he was unaware specifically of Ellis's ideas, their approaches to modifying distorting and illogical thinking are similar. Beck's approach and his personal style are gentler and nonconfrontational; he also has sought to provide research-based evidence and a broad theoretical schema as a foundation and context for his cognitive model. Moreover, he is open-minded and receptive to using and recommending other therapeutic techniques to bolster and extend the efficacy of his cognitive approach.

Cognitive approaches to the treatment of mental disorders have become more than merely the mainstream of "talking therapies" today. More than a third of all therapists speak of themselves as cognitive in orientation, the others employ cognitive techniques periodically. Now white-haired, lean, and bent over, Beck has become the primary leader of this approach nationally and internationally. Beck has been fortunate in the number and quality of his disciples, many of whom have made significant contributions to the cognitive model on their own. Following in the footsteps of Sigmund Freud and his daughter Anna, Beck, for the past two decades, has had the help of his daughter Judith, a psychologist, in carrying out his clinical and research work.

Comments and Reflections

Although psychoscientists have been primarily interested in general laws of behavior and thinking, several principles derived from their work have proved useful in describing and modifying mental illness. Perceptual studies have demonstrated the distorting effects of preestablished attitudes and needs. Conditioning in learning research has become a central concept for understanding how maladaptive behavior is acquired. The procedure of extinction has become a model for eliminating these maladaptive behaviors.

Several objections have been raised against psychoscientifically oriented approaches to mental pathology. For example, certain classic types of mental disorders appear in all cultures. How can one account for this uniformity without postulating some universal underlying disease? To this question, academics reply that classic textbook cases are figments of a theorist's imagination; moreover, uniformity in diagnostic classification is a psychiatric fiction because classification is highly unreliable, and most nosological systems are constantly revised and rarely hold up under research analysis. Whatever regularities are found, psychoscientists account for, by similarities in patterns of conditioning. Once individuals are identified as mentally ill, they are exposed to a uniform set of conditions that shape their behavior (e.g., restriction of privileges, threats of shock therapy, decreases in social relationships, hospital atmospheres, and so on). Regularities observed among these patients are a product, therefore, of common learning experiences, not common diseases.

The philosophies, goals, and therapeutic procedures that differentiate the several cognitive approaches described in this chapter make it difficult to group and evaluate their therapies as a unit. Despite their substantive differences, however, certain merits and criticisms may be assigned to all these methods.

The following merits are ascribed by proponents of the cognitive school. The language of cognitive discourse represents events in terms that are meaningful to patients rather than in the obscure vernacular of psychoanalytic therapies or the overly objectivized terminology of behavioral schools. Consequently, patients understand what is going on in the consulting room and can readily translate into reality what they have learned. Discussions at the cognitive level, then, facilitate both the acquisition of insight and its application to current realities.

Cognitive therapies are carried out in a face-to-face interpersonal interaction that resembles normal extratherapeutic relationships to a greater degree than those of other therapeutic schools. Consequently, what is learned in the setting of cognitive treatment should more readily generalize to the natural interpersonal settings for which they are ultimately intended.

Cognitive approaches focus on internal mediating processes that underlie behavior. Consequently, they are more efficient instruments for solving pervasive or complex difficulties than are behavior therapies, which deal primarily with isolated or well-circumscribed symptoms. Similarly, cognitive therapies can grapple with such nebulous symptom clusters as *existential dilemmas* and *identity crises* that are further obscured by the conceptual schema of psychoanalytic schools and resist formulation in the overly precise language of behavior therapies.

Among the criticisms leveled at cognitive approaches, many cognitivists (as do existentialists and humanists) formulate vague and unsystematized procedures, presenting a discursive mélange of sporadic recommendations for conducting therapy. Although these recommendations are cloaked in pretentious semantics and specious social philosophies, on careful analysis, they prove to possess no more substance than those of supportive reassurance and persuasion. Critics note that all psychotherapies employ the processes that cognitive therapists consider essential; thus, cognitivists make a virtue out of the commonplace.

Cognitive therapies fail to deal with the historical course and the unconscious roots of mental illness. According to psychoanalytic therapists, consciously acknowledged attitudes and feelings, which characterize the data of cognitive therapy, are superficial verbalizations that cloak deeper motives and emotions. As they see it, unless patients come to grips with these hidden events, true insight will constantly be subverted and therapeutic progress will be blunted or illusory.

Cognitive approaches may be especially limited in psychotic cases and those with marked anxiety; they are similarly inapplicable for patients who are unable to face or analyze their attitudes and expectancies. These procedures appear best suited for relatively stable and moderately intelligent adults whose functional capacities are sufficiently intact to enable them to engage in calm self-exploration or symbolic verbal discourse.

PART VI

SOCIOCULTURAL STORIES

CHAPTER

11

Unveiling the Social and Anthropological World

Psychological characteristics emanate from our deep immersion in time and culture, and our difficulties often derive from our inability to discern the many profound effects that influence us through societal institutions. Over a decade ago, Tom Wicker, a well-regarded *New York Times* columnist, captured this phenomenon in a graphic article (1987, p. 3):

> When a solar-powered water pump was provided for a well in India, the village headman took it over and sold the water, until stopped. The new liquid abundance attracted hordes of unwanted nomads. Village boys who had drawn water in buckets had nothing to do, and some became criminals. The gap between rich and poor widened, since the poor had no land to benefit from irrigation. Finally, village women broke the pump, so they could gather again around the well that had been the center of their social lives.

Though such a simple, straightforward intervention may be effective within the context of a small, rural community, few forms of contemporary sociocultural dynamics can so readily be mended. Educational and technological advances, as well as other cultural progressions, are largely welcomed in modern Western societies but would be too powerful to be turned aside or nullified, no less reversed, even if such actions were desirable.

The Sociocultural Story: I

The sociocultural orientation to the mind represents a striking departure from most other traditions. Instead of the individual being the prime focus, the wider social setting that impinges on people and that the people then influence takes center stage. Support for a public health approach to physical disorders has grown consistently since the mid-1800s. And, with success in overcoming diseases such as tuberculosis and yellow fever, it was merely a matter of time before a social-preventive approach began to interest professionals concerned with mental disorders. Beginning in the late nineteenth century, theoretical and practical innovations emerged to reflect this changing orientation, which led to a full manifestation of new paradigms by the mid-twentieth century. The public health model supplanted the clinical model in many mental health settings, along with a shift toward preventive programs and a renewed concern for the underprivileged. These social and community approaches did not have their origins in psychiatric and psychological thought, but reflected the demands of public spokespersons, on the one hand, and the compelling data of anthropological and sociological theorists, on the other.

It stands to reason that a sociocultural approach would emerge to answer mental health needs. Historically, cultural traditions give meaning and order to social life; define the tasks and responsibilities of existence; and guide group members with a system of shared beliefs, values, and goals. Such cultural forces provide a common framework of formative influences to set limits and establish guidelines for members of a social group. These traditions, transmitted from parents to children, provide the young with a blueprint for organizing thoughts, behaviors, and aspirations.

Thus, the institutions, traditions, and values that compose the cultural context of societal living shape the mind. Methods by which social rules and regulations are transmitted between people and from generation to generation are often highly charged and erratic, entailing persuasion, seduction, coercion, deception, and threat. Feelings of anxiety and resentment are generated as a function of environmental stress, leaving pathological residues that linger and distort future relations. Nevertheless, it is not cultural and social conditions that directly shape the mind or cause mental illness; rather, they are the context within which the more direct and immediate experiences of interpersonal and family life take place. They not only color, but may degrade personal relationships, establishing maladaptive styles of coping and pathogenic models for imitation.

This exploration of early conceptualizations of the sociocultural orientation focuses on thinkers concerned with public experiences that members of a societal group share in common. In a sense, these forces characterize "society as the patient." Lawrence K. Frank suggested the following proposal more than 60 years ago (1936):

> Instead of thinking in terms of a multiplicity of so-called social problems, each demanding special attention and a different remedy, we can view all of them as different symptoms of the same disease. That would be a real gain even if we cannot entirely agree upon the exact nature of the disease. If, for example, we could regard crime, mental disorders, family disorganization, juvenile delinquency, prostitution and sex offenses, and much that now passes as the result of pathological processes (e.g., gastric ulcer) as evidence, not of individual wickedness, incompetence, perversity or pathology, but as human reactions to cultural disintegration, a forward step would be taken. (p. 42)

Few scholars could rationally argue against the observation that the organization, consistency, and strength of a particular culture's institutions are reflected among its members in great measure through the individuals' psychic structure and interpersonal cohesion. In much the same way as the paired strands of the DNA double helix unwind and select environmental nutrients to duplicate the discarded partner, so, too, does each culture fashion its constituent members to fit an existing template. Those societies whose customs and institutions are fixed and resolute will generally display a psychic composition of structured and definitive citizenry, and those societies whose values and practices are fluid and inconsistent will likely evolve in its residents' deficits in psychic solidity and stability.

Though it would be naive to state that sociocultural factors are directly responsible for individual pathology, responsible scientists would be lax in ignoring the role of cultural dynamics in the well-being of individuals, and consequently, society. Whether one is inclined, for example, to attribute the increased incidence in youthful affective disorders to the waxing and waning of population parameters, it is both intuitively and observationally self-evident that sweeping cultural changes can affect innumerable social practices. Among those social practices most evidently affected by cultural dynamics are those of an immediate and personal nature, such as patterns of child nurturing and rearing, marital affiliation, family cohesion, leisure style, and entertainment content.

Commentators of the social scene have voiced the notion that many of the mind's pathological patterns observed today can best be ascribed to the perverse, chaotic, or frayed conditions of cultural life. They have characterized these demographic conditions in phrases such as "the age of anxiety," "growing up absurd," and "the lonely crowd." It is not within the scope of this chapter to elaborate the themes implied in these slogans; a brief description of conditions of contemporary life will suggest what these writers are saying.

Our amorphous cultural state is mirrored in the interpersonal vacillations and affective instabilities that typify the longitudinal affective distress seen in patients presenting with what is called a *borderline personality*. Central to today's culture are an increased pace of social change and the growing pervasiveness of ambiguous and discordant customs to which children are expected to subscribe. Under the cumulative impact of rapid industrialization, immigration, urbanization, mobility, technology, and mass communication, a steady erosion of traditional values and standards has ensued. Instead of a simple and coherent body of practices and beliefs, children are confronted with constantly shifting styles and increasingly questioned norms whose durability is uncertain and precarious.

Woven into the fabric of traditional and organized societies are standards designed to enculturate and indoctrinate the young, as well as a kind of insurance against cultural system defects and failures. Extended families, church leaders, schoolteachers, and neighbors frequently provide nurturance and role models to children experiencing troubled parental relationships. By such cultural assurances, many otherwise disenfranchised children find support and affection, enabling them to be receptive to their society's established body of norms and values. Youths subject to any of these diffusing and divisive forces must find one or another of these culturally sanctioned sources of surrogate modeling and sustenance to give structure and direction to their emerging capacities and impulses. Without such bolstering, maturing potentials are likely to remain inchoate or scattered. Without such role models to emulate, such youngsters are left to their own devices to master the complexities of their varied and changing worlds, to control the intense aggressive and sexual urges that well up within them, to channel their fantasies, and to pursue the goals to which they aspire. Many become victims of their own growth, unable to discipline their impulses or find acceptable means for expressing their desires. Scattered and unguided, they are unable to fashion a clear sense of personal identity, a consistent direction for feelings and attitudes, a coherent purpose to existence. They become "other-directed" persons who vacillate at every turn, are overly responsive to fleeting stimuli, and shift from one erratic course to another. Without the restitutive and remedial power of beneficent parental surrogates, they fail to establish internalized values to anchor themselves and guide their future.

The impact of much of what has been described might be substantially lessened if concurrent or subsequent personal encounters and social customs were compensatory or restitutive, that is, if they repaired the destabilizing and destructive effects of problematic experiences. Whereas the cultural institutions of most societies have retained practices that furnish reparative stabilizing and cohering experiences that remedy disturbed parent-child relationships, the converse appears to be the case in Western societies today. The changes of the past four to five decades have not only fostered psychic diffusion and splintering, but have also eliminated psychically restorative institutions and customs, thereby increasing both the incidence and exacerbation of typical forms of recent mental pathology. Without social mentors and practices to provide undergirding, focus, and correction, the diffusing or divisive consequences of unfavorable earlier experiences take firm root and unyielding form, displaying their structural weaknesses in clinical signs under the press of even modestly stressful events.

A by-product of the rapid expansion of knowledge and education is that many traditional institutions of our society—such as religion, which formerly served as a refuge to many—have lost much of their historic power as a source of nurturance and control in the contemporary world. Similarly, and in a more general way, the frequency with which families in Western society relocate has caused a wide range of psychically diffusing problems. Each move not only threatens stability, but leads people to jettison a network of partially internalized role models and community institutions furnished in church, school, and friendships. Thus, the psychic structure and cohesion that could have been solidified to give direction and meaning to what are otherwise disparate elements of existence are undone. Children who move to distant settings feel isolated and lonely, and deprived of opportunities to develop a consistent foundation of social customs and a coherent sense of self. This circumstance may undermine the faith they may have had in the merits of adhering to a stable set of values and behaviors. Beyond being merely *anomic* in Emile Durkheim's sense of lacking socially sanctioned means for achieving culturally encouraged goals, these youngsters have incorporated neither the approved customs and practices nor the institutional aspirations and values of their society. In effect, they are both behaviorally normless and existentially purposeless.

It is the thesis of the sociocultural orientation not only to view society as the patient, but to understand normality and pathology of individual community members as part of the form and function of the cultural and societal environment in which they live.

Unfolding of Key Ideas

Though the peak developments of the sociocultural perspective are associated primarily with the zeitgeist of the latter eighteenth to the first half of the twentieth centuries, elements of this trend in psychological thought may be traced to those ancient philosophers who laid the cornerstone for Western philosophy. Indeed, suggestions of sociocultural influence on psychology and psychiatry emerge throughout the history of humanity. Although much of the emphasis in ideas discussed thus far has been on the individual, social and contextual themes pervade our inquiry throughout the history of humankind.

The ancient Greek philosopher *Plato* was one of the earliest proponents of a humane mental health paradigm. He outlined many of the conflicts occurring within the individual's psyche (foreshadowing psychodynamic developments of the late nineteenth and early twentieth centuries) and also explained numerous environmental and social stressors. The *Republic* contends that mental characteristics stem in large part from children's early interactions both within the family and in their educational setting. Thus, according to Plato, societal factors could influence the developmental course of individual children in any number of ways. Perhaps even more relevant to the current sociocultural discussion, however, is the overarching theme of the *Republic*, namely, whether it is better to live justly or unjustly. Thus, a central morality undergirds Plato's argument along with the assumption that an essential, objective human Good may ultimately lead all humans to universal truth and happiness. The central goal of philosophy, according to Plato, is to find that Good.

Plato's pupil, *Aristotle*, though intrigued by his mentor's abstract, pure speculation of that somewhat intangible human Good, preferred to use rational observation and empirical means to focus on the world as it appeared to the senses. The essential difference in these two philosophies, in terms of sociological content, was in the means of observation. Plato believed wholeheartedly in what he termed the *Forms* (similarities that are universal to any class of object, e.g., a chair, by which we recognize it as such) without interference by human sensorial apparatus. Aristotle believed in an empiricism that relied *precisely* on the human senses and direct observation. Though largely a scholar of science and medicine, his perspective on social and political matters followed this empirical logic, concentrating on what is *directly observable* to the senses. Thus, whereas Plato speculated about an abstract utopian society when picturing civilization in its purest form, Aristotle reflected on what the senses found to be *real* civilization and culture in its imperfect form. He speculated only that there must be a greater purpose to the collected lives of humankind. These real, observable interactions among people were approximations leading toward eventual perfection by transcending the everyday, real, observable world. Some 15 centuries later, Thomas Aquinas (see Chapter 2), in his efforts to bring ancient philosophical perspectives into acceptance with Christian theology, revisited these themes in "A Summary of Theology," bringing to light once again the concepts of *existences* and *essences*, this time as a means of describing the differences between body and soul. Again, the underlying theme was for humankind, in a unified manner, to be able to transcend existence in its common, mundane form, in the search for the greater good.

Theorizing about Society in Europe

Though the study of societal factors in human life dates back to prehistoric times, the turn of the nineteenth century in Europe saw the earliest formalization of what we now refer to as *sociology*, a hybrid science. Leaders in this field combined abstract (e.g., philosophy, evolution) and concrete (e.g., biology, physics) disciplines to posit views of humanity beyond the scope of the individual's characterological makeup. Evolutionary principles, in large part, heavily influenced these theorists, and several of them proposed that some societies were more advanced than others, demonstrating collective qualities that put them ahead of more primitive social structures. Many of these thinkers shared a belief in a *collective mind* (variously referred to by these and later thinkers as *Weltgeist*, "*collective unconscious*," etc.). This terminology acknowledged the humanlike personality, or at least dimensions of personality, of a particular society, anticipating, in some ways, later innovations of psychological (e.g., Jung) and political/philosophical (e.g., Marx) theorists. Some of these innovators described these civilizations in terms much like modern personological formulations. Later in this era, several of these theorists wrote of a society's decompensatory factors, demonstrating how a loss of balance within a community, perhaps by virtue of a charismatic but ill-intentioned leader, could contribute significantly to a marked societal pathology, perhaps contributing to epidemics of individual mental health difficulties.

Many authorities in social psychology consider the philosophy of **Georg Wilhelm Friedrich Hegel (1770–1831)** to be the forerunner of all theorists whose concepts transcend the individual and who consider the social mind to be an entity in its own right. Hegel introduced the notion that, ideally, a World Mind (or Spirit), directs the evolutionary process of humankind and society dialectically; individuals are simply agents in this larger body. To him, personal freedom was synonymous with group submission, and the larger social group (e.g., the state, a political party, or a social class), was what needed to be fostered, nurtured, and encouraged.

Born in Stuttgart, Germany, Hegel originally planned to pursue a career in the ministry, fulfilling his father's wishes. Graduating from the Theological Seminary in 1793, Hegel suddenly changed his mind regarding this career path. Maintaining a burning interest in the works of Rousseau (see Chapter 3), Hegel turned to matters more political and philosophical, first working as a tutor and then, after receiving a substantial inheritance following his father's death, pursuing an academic career. Though his contributions to a rational philosophy are numerous, perhaps his most notable idea within social theory was that of a *Volksgeist*, or collective characteristic or mental unity of a society.

Georg Wilhelm Friedrich Hegel

Vast sectors of philosophy and psychology were attuned to Hegelian ideas and responded with either major social movements or psychological theories. Indeed, Carl Gustav Jung's constructs composing the collective unconscious were closely related to, if not directly influenced by Hegel's notion of Voltgeist. More directly, however, *Karl Marx* read and absorbed

Hegel's ideas and put these notions to work in his writings on communism. He viewed each social class as an entity with its own consciousness and spirit. Where these two men differed, however, was in the underpinnings of the dialectical process that drove this evolutionary progression: Hegel identified *reason* as the essential driving power; Marx sharply denied this, pointing instead to the *real social forces of life* as the true motivator. Whereas Hegel chose to concentrate on the philosophical and rational, looking at social motion from above, Marx pointed to oppression of the working class and the ensuing hampering of human potential, as well as other societal and economic institutions. He argued that change must be indigenous, and the meaning of social and historical developments derived directly from social facts.

Known today as the father of French Positivist thought, **Auguste Comte (1798–1857)** first coined the terms *sociology* and *altruism*, outlining these and many other social concepts in his *Course in Positive Philosophy* (1842) and *System of Positive Policy* (1854). According to Comte, benevolent, altruistic drives coexisted with individualistic, egocentric instincts, a concept that helped him compose a "science of ethics," an idea he toiled with throughout his life, finally formalizing it in 1852. As much scientist as a philosopher of subjective reason, Comte came to be best known for ordering the sciences into classifications that differentiated the concrete and the abstract disciplines, seeking to outline the progressive development and emergence of these disciplines. Of particular interest was the classification of *Psychics*: a group of abstract sciences comprised first of the biological, then the sociological, and finally, the moral/individualistic. He wrestled late in life with a "true final science," essentially a hybrid of these three psychic sciences, which he planned to label *la morale positive*, a discipline that would closely resemble what we now term *psychology*. His relatively early death two years prior to his projected publishing date for these proposals prevented them from being fully explicated; only fragments of his ideas were salvageable at the time of his death in 1857. The following quote represents his thoughts on this matter:

> Positive morality is to live for others. Personality, characterized by egoism, conflicts with sociality, or altruism, and each individual undergoes three stages of human life: (1) the personal (self-love); (2) the domestic (love of family); and (3) the social, or one that achieves the "subordination of self-love to social feeling." (1908, p. 101)

Karl Marx (1818–1883) was the eldest son of a father who practiced law in the Rhenish city of Trier and rose to be the head of the regional legal bar. His mother and father were descended from long lines of rabbis in Germany and Holland. Although the family had suffered grievous civil limitations under the French Regime, they achieved equal rights as citizens following Napoleon's early liberal proposals. Following Napoleon's defeats, however, the Rhineland was given to Prussia and Jews again were deprived of their civil rights. In 1817, Marx's father decided to convert to the liberal Lutheran Church, an act of protective expediency that regained the family a measure of security. The young Marx was exposed to the world of learning and letters via his father's guidance, although he found his father's conversion and subservience to governmental authority to be embarrassingly unacceptable.

At age 17, Marx was admitted to the faculty of law at the University at Prague, later transferring to the University of Berlin where Hegel's stature remained prominent despite his earlier death. Although Marx perceived himself as a future professor of philosophy, his close mentor at Berlin was dismissed for his antireligious and liberal views before Marx was able to complete his doctoral dissertation. Although Marx had achieved recognition in bohemian quarters, his prospects for the career he originally anticipated were poor. Moving to Paris in his mid-20s, Marx plunged into a study of reformist and socialist theories that had been inaccessible to him in Germany. Importantly, he established a lifelong friendship with Friedrich Engels, the son of a successful textile manufacturer who had become a socialist owing to his revulsion observing the conditions of life he had seen among those working in one of his father's enterprises. During this period, Marx completed his own conversion to socialism and began to write, alone and in collaboration with Engels, the early works that served to define his philosophical and political ideology. Owing to his outspoken revolutionary status, the French government offered Marx the choice of either moving to a distant province or leaving the country entirely.

In 1849, Marx emigrated from France to London, England, and never returned to Europe. Marx, for years an obscure scholar who haunted the British Museum, suddenly became an object to several of the intelligence services of Europe that combed the world for revolutionaries and subversives. Although some viewed Marx's major work, *Das Kapital* (1867), as a manifesto of the new communist movement, it failed to attract much attention at first among Continental socialists; it was almost 10 years before this work was translated into Russian, French, and Italian.

From a psychological viewpoint, Marx's central contribution was his indictment of *alienation* in the lives of modern human beings. He joined many others of that period, not only in criticizing the economic conditions of life, but in seeking a future of social integration and constructive enlightenment. In his view, humankind and society had been sundered and had to be made whole again. People needed to rationally reconstruct a future in which what had been dismembered and separated could be reunited into a harmonious whole.

Coming initially from a vastly different philosophical and sociological perspective, Darwin strongly influenced **Herbert Spencer (1820–1903)** (see Chapter 13), who proposed a laissez-faire societal policy as the key component of future evolution. Psychologically, he averred that social pain brings about death, and that humans naturally pursue pleasurable experiences, thereby anticipating the later work of Edward Lee Thorndike and his "Law of Effect" at the turn of the twentieth century (see Chapter 9).

Born in Derby, Great Britain, in 1820, Spencer was the eldest of nine children, and the only one to survive to adulthood. Nothing in his life is comparable to the rich texture of tragedy and tribulation that Karl Marx encountered. Being sickly and weak as a child, Spencer did not attend regular school until he was 13, but was educated by his father at home. He then moved to the city of Bath where an uncle, a clergyman known as a social reformer and Christian dissenter, guided his further studies. His education, however, focused heavily on science, with languages and humanities being almost totally neglected. He started as a biologist, but soon turned to engineering, working for four years during the construction of the London and Birmingham Railway. He became recognized as a philosopher when he moved beyond engineering to consider problems of psychology and sociology in his later works. Many sociological historians see Spencer as an advocate and successor to Comte's organicist/evolutionary approach, despite Spencer's many differences in opinion. Although themes of the two men were similar, their focus differed. Comte, in Spencer's view, was interested in abstract constructs regarding society, environment, and the resultant mental states, whereas Spencer pursued the study of tangible realities—what actually *was*. Comte, in other words, pursued a subjective science, whereas Spencer's position (in his opinion) was distinctly objective.

In his biological studies, Spencer asserted that the perpetual law of nature changes all forms, but invariably, from simple to complex. Ultimately, according to Spencer, initial differences in this progression would balance and even it out. The State would wither away, and what would emerge would be a rational, liberal society that would demonstrate consensus in its directions. Its objectives would effectively eliminate all forms of prejudice. In his later years, Spencer declared that the time was ripe for the expansion of individuality, and that the laissez-faire principle of individual liberty was imperative. Only in such circumstances would people be able to evolve to fit the demands of modern society; those entrenched in controlled, outdated regulatory modes would be left behind, a view radically different from that held by Marx.

An imaginative scholar with an extraordinarily fertile imagination, **Georg Simmel (1858–1918)** tried to contrast his views with those of both Kant and Spencer. He posited that society comprised a web of patterned interactions; it was the task of sociology to study the forms in which these interactions develop in diverse cultural settings and historical periods. As he put it, "Society is merely the name for a number of individuals connected by interaction." Larger social systems—the state, the clan, the city, the trade union, the family—are only formal crystallizations of these interactions, even though they may attain superordinate qualities that can confront individuals as if they were alien powers.

Born in the heart of Berlin, Simmel lived his life at the intersection of many movements, influenced by the crosscurrents of multiple intellectual, political, social, and moral activities. He was the modern urban man, the youngest of seven children of a prosperous Jewish businessman who had converted to Christianity. Although he had roots in a secure family, he always experienced the sense of being an insecure and marginal person. Tied deeply to the intellectual milieu of Berlin, the anti-Semitism that disfigured much of academic life in Germany caused him to receive rather shabby treatment from the powers of academia. Some of his difficulty may be traced, however, to the breadth of his knowledge and his refusal to be restricted by any of the existing disciplinary boundaries in the academic community. As some have commented, his originality, sparkling intellect, and ability to move with effortlessness from one topic to another unsettled the spirits and confronted the narrow-minded perspective of many of his academic colleagues.

Despite the many rebuffs that Simmel received from his academic peers, he did not see himself as an embittered outsider. He actively participated in the intellectual and cultural life of Berlin, frequenting its fashionable salons and attending the meetings of philosophers and sociologists; many in the world of arts and letters befriended him. By good fortune, he was free of financial worry, and did not suffer the indignities that beset many of the more peripheral and economically straitened members of the German professoriate. His wife was a philosopher in her own right who published on diverse topics such as religion and sexuality.

Simmel was an exciting speaker, somewhat of a showman as he addressed numerous academic and public audiences, thinking extemporaneously with a series of sparkling and dazzling ideas. His writings tackled diverse matters of culture, society, and economics. He asserted that economic exchange can be understood best as a form of social interaction in which significant meanings and their quantitative gauges are conveyed among "actors" of different levels of economic competence and success. He recognized the multifaceted qualities of individuals such that personality variations within a single individual are manifested differently depending on the location of the individual's social position in diverse functional settings, such as familial, occupational, or religious. Noting that small groups permit individuals to interact directly with one another, he recognized that once a group exceeds a modestly limited size, interactions are usually mediated through formal arrangements and social hierarchies. No large group could function, in his opinion, without differentiated status positions, the creation of offices, and the delegation of tasks and responsibilities. Large groups become, therefore, minisocieties of unequals. He spoke here of the "quantitative aspects of a group," addressing the variable qualities of dyadic and triadic social interactions, and characterizing the strategies that can be enacted effectively in these systems.

Simmel posited a gallery of social types to complement his proposals of the several forms of social groups. He described in great psychological detail such types as "the stranger," "the adventurer," "the man in the middle," "the poor," and "the renegade." These social types and their psychic elaborations may well have served as models for the social psychoanalytic theorists of the following generation (e.g., Erich Fromm and Wilhelm Reich). In each case, social types are assigned a position by virtue of their specific and bounded interactive relationships, each expected to perform its assigned role. Characterizing the *stranger*, Simmel described a person who does not belong to, or is not fully part of, a group, yet is an element of the group. By virtue of that limited place in group affairs, the person can therefore, play a role that no other member of the group can play. Not committed to the group's central purposes, the stranger can take positions that reflect a degree of objectivity. The stranger may also be called on to be a confidant to the group's members because he or she is not likely to share these confidences with others. Similarly, the stranger may serve and be a better judge than full members of the group when dealing with conflicting parties because of not being closely connected to either of the contenders. The stranger can be an ideal intermediary, as well as an objective trafficker of group members' emotions. Given Simmel's own outsider status in much of his academic activities, he may have understood the stranger's role with special expertise. In describing this and other social types he proposed, his portrayal was insightful and eloquent.

The French sociologist **Emile Durkheim (1858–1917)** was perhaps the greatest social scientist in his country's history, a scholar credited with bridging the gap between science and humanity prior to the development of modern cultural concepts. Durkheim, descended from a long lineage of rabbis, was groomed to follow his forebears and entered training at a young age in Hebrew, Old Testament, and Talmudic studies, but abandoned these pursuits and became an agnostic. He received good marks in his early schooling, but he became bored during his preparatory years for university study, and was equally disappointed in the university itself, as he graduated second from last in his class. In later years, he declared that university literary training was at fault for the backwardness of the sciences of society. Despite this belligerent attitude toward his education, Durkheim excelled as an academic and found that his later teaching duties substantially augmented his scholarly pursuits. During World War I, Durkheim worked feverishly in the social sciences. With a penchant for patriotism, he sought to understand the destructive character of national mentalities that seek to gain world domination. The war's destructive power, however, may have been too much for Durkheim; he lost many of his favorite students, as well as his only son, during the retreat from Serbia in late 1915. Though he remained patriotic, his health failed, and he passed away two years later at the age of 59.

Durkheim's primary theme throughout his career was social solidarity, the ways and means employed by a social unit to hold its members together and avoid individual alienation. Around the turn of the century, Durkheim proposed the concept of *anomie* to signify a widespread disintegration of a society's standards and norms. When a high degree of anomie occurred, the rules that previously guided social behavior would lose their power to maintain group solidarity and individual direction. Durkheim was particularly intrigued by the relationship between anomie and suicide, as recorded in the following quotes (1897/1951):

> Egoistic suicide results from man's no longer finding a basis for existence in life; altruistic suicide, because this basis for existence appears to man situated beyond life itself. The third sort of suicide . . . results from man's activity lacking regulation and his consequent sufferings. (p. 258)
>
> . . . excessive individuation leads to suicide, insufficient individuation has the same effect. When man has become detached from society, he encounters less resistance to suicide in himself, and he does so likewise when social integration is too strong. (p. 217)

On the basis of his studies, he concluded that suicide is infrequent when the standards of a society are firm and unchanging; conversely what he called *anomic suicide* rose sharply at times of active social change. Although Durkheim's specific thesis has long been challenged, it stimulated others to explore the connection between social events and mental disorders. Thus, by 1922, a major annual section of the meetings of the American Sociological Society was devoted specifically to this topic.

Max Weber (1864–1920) conceived sociology to be the science of social action, not simply a static, social/structural concept. Whereas Durkheim focused on the cohesion of social structures and Marx was preoccupied with the conflict between social classes, Weber primarily addressed the subjective meaning that humans attach to their mutual goals. More than many social thinkers of his day, Weber was beset by inner psychological torment, conflicts, and turmoil as he struggled to find a meaningful and humane direction for his thoughts. These tensions derived largely from the complicated web of his personal family relationships and his efforts to separate from the stultifying atmosphere of the German hierarchical political system of his day. Weber's parents descended from a line of Protestants who had been refugees from Catholic persecution. A precocious yet shy, sickly, and withdrawn youngster, Weber's early teachers complained about his lack of respect for their authority and his rebellious attitude toward discipline. His father, a rigid disciplinarian, ruled the household with a strong authoritarian hand; young Max fought back where he could, at school. He was an avid reader and consumer of a vast and diverse literature even before entering university studies. His mother's brother, along with his wife, soon became a second set of parents to him and later guided him. His uncle and aunt were unalloyed liberals who had refused the compromises that had directed Weber's father's career, mavericks at odds with the dominant mores of the day.

Weber was sensitive to the dysfunctions of a bureaucracy, its unwieldy structure, its inability to account for troubled responsibilities and, most problematical, its stultifying effect on the individual. He spoke of its inevitable

depersonalization of life. As he described it, the more bureaucracy deperson-
alizes itself, the more it succeeds in excluding love, hatred, and every other
purely personal feeling from the execution of official tasks. Whereas in the
past, rulers' achievements were gained by sympathy, favor, and gratitude,
modern bureaucracies required for their sustaining apparatus the emotionally
detached and rigorously focused professional expert.

In Weber's discussion of authority relationships, he distinguished three
modes of role legitimacy. The first type, the *rational-legal authority*, is anchored
in a bureaucracy's impersonal rules that have been legally enacted or contrac-
tually established. The second mode, termed *traditional authority*, is found in
simpler and earlier cultures where leadership is not codified by impersonal
rules, but inheres in persons who either inherit it or are invested with it by so-
called higher authorities. The third variant, termed *charismatic authority*, rests
on the appeal of leaders who attract allegiance owing to their virtuosity, such
as gained by their extraordinary competence or heroism.

Americanizing Sociological Thought

Carrying on the traditions of its European counterparts, the early American
school of sociological thought, which came into prominence in tandem with
the later European social thinkers at the turn of the twentieth century, shared
with its predecessors an affinity with evolutionary principles and the notion of
the importance of understanding the relationship between individuals and
their social context. The American school's perspective differed, however, in
its emphasis. Whereas the European schools concentrated largely on the character of the society-at-large, the Americans focused on individuals' functions
in the surrounding culture. In this model, the individual was the most important subject for the study of sociocultural processes. However, no individual
(or an individual's behaviors, as seen in such processes as language) could be
meaningfully understood without considering the larger framework of the society within which that person functioned.

Always a marginal man in life, **Thorstein Veblen (1857–1929),** wrote
with great sensitivity about the anatomy of competition in society, proposing
innovative theories of how social changes and growth occur. Born on a frontier farm in Wisconsin, he was the sixth of twelve children born to Norwegian
immigrants who had come to America 10 years before his birth. Despite his
Norwegian heritage, his paternal ancestry could be traced to early rabbinical
drifters from various parts of the Continent. Settling first in Wisconsin and
then Minnesota, the family encountered innumerable obstacles, similar to
those that their ancestors had experienced in Norway. A hatred of speculators
and shyster lawyers ran deep in the family tradition and found expression in
much of Veblen's later writings. Through hard work, thrift, and single-minded
devotion to the agricultural tasks they faced, the family ultimately achieved a

measure of success, given the limitations inherent in the dour and pious lifestyle of their Lutheran religion.

Taking after his father, young Veblen demonstrated a precocious intelligence, invariably maintaining an unusual degree of independence that remained fixed and clear throughout his life. Guided toward self-improvement through education, Veblen's father encouraged all his children to pursue advanced learning. Having been essentially insulated on the family farm until college, young Veblen remained an outsider, terribly awkward socially, yet a voracious and successfully independent reader of moral philosophy and political economy. His career proved desultory, first at Johns Hopkins for initial graduate training and later at Yale where he achieved a PhD. Nevertheless, after this, he wandered aimlessly for years before drifting into a minor position at Cornell, where he wrote papers on economics. He moved on to the University of Chicago where he ultimately found a congenial group of colleagues, most notably *John Dewey* in psychology and philosophy. Veblen remained unorthodox in his thinking, his teaching, and especially in his personal lifestyle. His Chicago period was noted by wide-ranging and imaginative papers, such as, *Why Is Economics Not an Evolutionary Science?* A single-minded iconoclast who enjoyed demolishing accepted ideas in economics and the social sciences, his teaching approach proved to be extremely unconventional, so much so as to discourage students, perhaps intentionally, from taking his courses. Rambling in personal style and disorganized in his teaching, his days at Chicago were numbered, and he left in 1906 for a comparable position at Stanford University. There he generated nuggets at the cutting edge of theory, employing arcane facts overlooked by others of his day.

Though not considered a thinker of the first rank, Veblen produced work that stimulated social and economic theory for many years. His best-known contribution was *The Theory of the Leisure Class* (1934), which elucidated the social-psychological roots of motivation and the consequences of competitive lifestyles. He illustrated with unmatched clarity the conspicuous consumption and display of luxurious lifestyles that signified life's past deprivations. He sought to trace how the modes of contemporary thought influenced social and occupational positions. Throughout, and beyond his personal maladaptations, he was an intensely serious moralist whose subtle scholarship was shrouded under the cover of a playful cynicism that diverted his readers while subverting their fruitless social aspirations.

Having never published a book during his lifetime, the social philosopher and pragmatist **George Herbert Mead (1863–1931)** achieved notoriety through his famous and influential course at the University of Chicago entitled "Social Psychology." His theories centered on the notion that the mind and self have no particular social emergents, and that the advent of language in vocal form was necessary for humans to ascend the evolutionary ladder. The individual self, behaviorally, then, is only understood through the context of the larger group's behavior, as all individual acts are integrated within a larger social framework.

Mead viewed individual psychology as intelligible only through social processes, which took precedence over individual experience. He described two levels of the social process of communication, the first being the "conversation of gestures," and the second, the "conversation of significant gestures," or *language*, commenting as follows (1934):

> What is the basic mechanism whereby the social process goes on? It is the mechanism of gesture, which makes possible the appropriate responses to one another's behavior of the different individual organisms involved in the social process. Within any given social act, an adjustment is effected, by means of gestures, of the actions of one organism involved to the actions of another. . . . The field of operation of gestures is the field within which the rise and development of human intelligence has taken place through the process of the symbolization of experience which gestures—especially vocal gestures—have made possible. (pp. 13–14)

Although born in Pennsylvania, **Robert Ezra Park (1864–1944)** grew up in the Midwest. The son of a prosperous businessman, he attended the University of Minnesota and later the University of Michigan, where he was exposed to the reformist ideas of a young inspiring teacher, John Dewey. Rather than turn to an academic life, he followed another mentor, a newspaperman of distinction, Franklin Ford, and concluded that a career in journalism would enable him to play a significant role in influencing the social mores of society. He committed himself to move progress steadily forward through public opinion publications that focused on the crucial social events of the day. In contrast to his academically oriented peers, he resisted indulging in what he considered to be utopian dreams and blueprints.

Park had an unusual sensitivity for a white man to the social and human problems of African Americans, called Negroes in his day. He continued to focus on racial issues throughout his career. He often worked with *Booker T. Washington*, president of Tuskegee Institute, helping him write about the miseries of the Negro poor and the suffering of Europe's underclasses.

Late in life, in 1914, Park embarked again on an academic career. He wrote extensively on the concept of *social distance*, a notion Simmel had proposed in Berlin, which struck him as crucial to understanding race relations. The distance concept referred to the degree of intimacy that prevailed between groups and measured the extent of influence that each had over the other. The greater the social distance between groups, the less they influenced each other reciprocally.

As Coser (1971) has noted, Park was perpetually curious and open to novel experiences, whether on the racial frontier or in the wilderness of cities. Deeply committed to reform and the improvement of the human condition, he came to believe that trained and disciplined observers of the passing social scene were what was most needed. As he wrote, sociologists were to be super-reporters conveying the events of society more accurately and detached than would the average journalist.

The father of what may be termed *introspectionist sociology*, **Charles Horton Cooley (1864–1929)** is perhaps best known for the concept of the "looking-glass self." In his work, *Human Nature and the Social Order* (1902/1922), Cooley formulated a social psychological theory outlining the thesis that individuals and society are really collective components and distributive aspects of the same basic phenomenon: Individuals make up a society and society is made up of individuals.

Although his first book dealt with the relationship of self to others, subsequent writings dealt with social classes and social processes. Like most other sociologists of his time, evolutionary thought heavily influenced Cooley, who derived his propositions from theories of child development and proposed an "organic theory of society," stated as follows:

> . . . it is a complex of forms or processes each of which is living and growing by interaction with others, the whole being so unified that what takes place in one part affects all the rest. It is a vast tissue of reciprocal activity. (1918, p. 10)

Another advocate of the idea of a group mind, **William McDougall (1871–1938),** an English-born psychologist who spent many of his most prolific years in the United States, was among the first to promote the term, *social psychology*, titling one of his landmark texts *An Introduction to Social Psychology* (1908). Here, McDougall attempted to formulate a *hormic* theory of psychology; that is, one where the individual, with a degree of foresight, acts purposively and with the energy necessary to achieve specific goals within a social context. McDougall refuted the most popular schools of the day—behaviorism and structuralism—and dismissed them as simplistic, reductionistic, and materialistic. Like many late-nineteenth-century social and functionalist thinkers, he preferred evolutionary and purposive explanations of human behavior

William McDougall

and believed that *instinct* was the root of behavior. The essence of mind, then, was to govern "present action by anticipation of the future in the light of past experience" (1923, p. 195).

A Lancashire-born Anglo-Scotsman, McDougall was trained in medicine before turning his attention to philosophy and anthropology. He held lectureships at both Cambridge and Oxford from 1898 and was appointed Professor of Psychology at Harvard University in 1920, moving on to Duke University from 1928 until his death in 1938. Growing up within an affluent household,

McDougall was exposed to the best of traditional education, yet was a robust and independent thinker with a strong sarcastic streak. An ardent critic of the most accepted psychological thought of the day and a proponent of a rather unpopular physiological and instinctual approach to social theory, as well as being intellectually superior to most of his peers, McDougall was both revered and disavowed throughout his career. Restless, undoctrinaire, acerbic, and confrontational, McDougall evidenced a combative intelligence rare in the so-ciological field of his day.

McDougall believed, like William James, that instinct initiates human so-cial interaction, but only for a fraction of a second. From there on, social forces and experience impinged on that instinct, modifying it into the form typically observed in its human contexts; McDougall termed this product a *sentiment*. Sentiment resulted from the effects of thought (of both self and others) on the base of instincts; it was the organized emotional structure that emerged around that instinct. He attributed the social character of instincts to the human mind's tendency to be molded by the environment; the pure human mind, devoid of its social context, was an abstract concept that did not exist. McDougall proposed a number of seminal ideas concerning personality, suggesting temperament types based on his sentiments concept (discussed in Chapter 13). Central to McDougall's psychology, however, was his concept of *sympathy*, writing: "Sympathy . . . is the cement that binds animal societies to-gether, renders the actions of all members of a group harmonious, and allows them to reap some of the prime advantages of social life" (1936, pp. 79–80).

To McDougall, sociology's task was to explore and fully elucidate the *group mind*, defined as a collective spirit identifying a particular society or nation. This collective mind comprised, but was different from, the sum total of the thought and behavior of its member individuals' minds and spirits. Devoid of social participation, conditions that humanity considers to be essential to life—tradition, continuity, customs, self-consciousness, and group spirit—are all products of the individual's mutual participation in a larger social structure.

A follower of the anthropologist Bronislaw Malinowski (discussed later in this chapter), **Talcott Parsons (1902–1979)** was notable for his functionalist approach to sociology and his emphasis on the homeostatic nature of societal functions. He was born in Colorado and educated at Amherst College, as well as internationally at the London School of Economics and the University of Heidelberg (where he received his PhD in 1927). He acquired an academic post at Harvard University in 1931, a position he maintained until his death. Par-sons, who originally studied biology, drew the analogy of a society being much like a biological organism seeking a stable state of equilibrium, with its parts understood only as elements in the context of a society's entirety. He developed this theme throughout his career, formulating it into a theory that sought to place the social sciences as part of a unified science of human action.

Parsons' views subjected him to a great deal of controversy. Not only did his postulates appear to validate inequality of individuals, but his view on locus of control, which he placed outside the individual and imparted to the structures of society, went against the grain of psychodynamic thought, then a dominant force in psychological theory. In more recent times, however, Parsonian sociology has experienced a renaissance of interest. In current debates over modernism, postmodernism, and globalization, Parsons' theories occupy a central seat in the neofunctionalist realm. What is now brought to the fore when discussing Parsonian sociology is what was an often-neglected facet of his work: his emphasis on societal values and the (at least partial) level of free choice individuals experience.

Born in Philadelphia as Meyer Schkolnick to immigrant Jewish parents, **Robert King Merton (1910–2003)** spent his childhood in the slums of South Philadelphia as an avid learner and library patron, as well as a gang member, a fact he admitted to a colleague many years later (though he commented that gangs were more ritualistic than dangerous in his era). He carried his given name for the first 14 years of his life, living in an apartment above his father's milk, butter, and egg store, until the building burned down, casting the family into complete disarray for a period. As a teenager, he performed magic tricks and adopted the stage name of Robert Merlin, but after a friend suggested that the ancient Wizard's name was hackneyed, he modified it to Merton, with the concurrence of his Americanized mother. Explaining his inclination to pursue a life of social thought, he told his colleagues at a conference that his seemingly deprived South Philadelphia slum upbringing provided him with enviable "social capital" that enabled him to develop a deep understanding of the foundations of society and the causes of *anomie*, a concept that intrigued him for many years.

A tall, pipe-smoking scholar, he displayed an extraordinary range of interests and knowledge and was alarmingly well informed about matters ranging from baseball averages to Kant's philosophy. He also had a ready inclination to converse comfortably about any topic at any length and detail. Merton's most widely known book, *Social Theory and Social Structure* (1957), went well beyond the confines of sociology and revealed the depth of his curiosity and the breadth of his prodigious research. In my periodic conversations with him, he showed a special interest in *serendipity* and pondered the workings of chance opportunities and their role in advancing all forms of scientific progress. He was especially attentive to the sociology of scientific advances, focusing our discussions on the interaction of cognitive and cultural influences in numerous and diverse disciplines. He viewed his contributions to be of "theories in the middle range," that is, distanced from grand and abstractly speculative doctrines, yet avoiding those picayunish inquiries that yielded what he judged to be trivial data. He preferred conceptual ideas that would open new lines of inquiry. His own writings, he said, were in essay form, allowing him to explore incidental and side commentary in preference to the tight and narrow focus of scientific papers. He drew on psychoanalytic concepts such as manifest and latent terms, often applying them to the sociological character of science. By latent function, he meant the unintended and often unrecognized consequences of a social idea or action. He contrasted this with manifest function concepts, by which he meant those that achieve their explicit and intended consequences. No less important to him was his concept of *self-fulfilling prophecies*, in which the believer acts in a way that helps generate the expected consequence—a consequence that would not likely have occurred without that expectancy.

An enthusiastic adherent to Durkheim's writings, Merton advanced the earlier theorist's concept of anomie at a time of great social change. Writing just after the huge turn-of-the-century influx of immigrants following World War I and the Great Depression, and prior to World War II, Merton's themes were vibrant reflections of a unique period of society. Though much of the rest of the world viewed the United States as the "land of opportunity," its instability during this period meant that opportunities were not equally available to all members. Although the goals of prosperity, success, and happiness remained universal constants, the means of achieving such goals were largely bound to highly limited opportunities, many of which required specialized training and higher education.

Robert King Merton

In expanding the concept of anomie, Merton (1938) posited, in his *strain theory*, that two sociocultural elements exist: culturally derived goals and aspirations, and socially acceptable means of achieving such goals. Successful societal function, in Merton's view, required striking a balance between these two elements, with all members of a society seeking goals by legitimate and acceptable means.

Merton proposed five adaptational modes to answer the strain caused by restricted access to socially sanctioned means and goals. The first of these, which Merton considered to be the most important, was *conformity*, the most common adaptation, in which societal members accepted and followed the goals and means prescribed by society, though they would not always attain their goals. The second, *innovation*, was an adaptive strategy whereby individuals had few legitimate means to achieve goals, so they would design their own means (whether within societal standards or not). *Ritualism*, the third strategy, involved individuals' abandoning goals in favor of their current lifestyle. *Retreatism* occurred when both goals and means were forsaken, and individuals escaped into an unproductive, often substance-ridden lifestyle. Finally, *rebellion* involved outright rejection of cultural goals and legitimate means, and replacement with the individual's own goals and means, often revolutionary in character.

In mid-century America, sociology began to achieve a status akin to psychoanalysis in its seeming ability to provide explanations for everything. Interestingly, both Merton and **David Riesman (1909–2002)**were analysands of the social analyst Erich Fromm. For a period in the 1960s, Riesman was perhaps the most publicly recognized sociologist of the time. This was unusual because he began his career as a lawyer, serving a clerkship under Supreme Court Justice Louis Brandeis, and later becoming a deputy assistant district attorney in New York and a professor of law at the University of Chicago, before moving on to the Social Relations faculty at Harvard. In two of his best-known works, *The Lonely Crowd* (1950) and *Faces in the Crowd* (1952), Riesman sought to justify bridging fields by explicating the interface between social history and personality character styles. He had an enormous influence on bright students, many of whom used their enormous talents to enter politics. His love of genuine argument was impressive and sometimes endearing, especially those disputes characterized by running duels with his young adversaries.

The three social character types that Riesman identified were termed "tradition-directed," "inner-directed," and "other-directed." Each represented a source of direction for individuals as they sought to find a place in the sun by adopting an identity to counter their alienation from society. The *tradition-directed* type rigorously followed ancient rules and customs. Tradition was considered to be a period of slow growth and change in which what had worked as a way of life in the past was assumed to work also in the present. Persons from later eras modeled their ancestors in coping with current problems. *Inner-directed* persons were self-motivated and goal-oriented individuals. They reflected a society in which change had begun to occur and in which earlier solutions to life's stressors no longer worked as well as in the past. During these periods, parents and other agents of society gave children a set of principles by which they could develop for themselves solutions to life's problems. These internalized principles, according to Riesman, enabled the individual to be effective by employing inner means of direction. Riesman described *other-directed* characters as conformists who looked constantly to others for acceptance and love. According to Riesman, the essential feature in other-directed societies is that the source of direction came from one's own contemporaries. Impersonal influences, however, need not be known directly, but internalized through the impact of an all-pervasive media in rapidly changing societies such as in mid- and late-twentieth-century America. No fixed rules exist in such societies to guide one's behavior consistently and reliably; one must constantly adjust and readjust to uncover responses that could enable adequate adaptations. There are many voices "out there," but none that one can employ with trust and assurance. This corresponds to the sense of loneliness in a crowd of many.

The themes that Riesman portrayed alerted other theorists of a more psychological orientation to characterize the so-called epidemic of what came to be called the *borderline personality* (Millon, 1987). These clinical cases lack an inner self; they reflect society's constantly changing customs of behaving and thinking. Riesman's inspiring books signified a collective social neurosis; his works gained great popularity in the 1960s and 1970s, as exhibited in subsequent titles such as *Organization Man, One-Dimensional Man, Closing of the American Mind,* and *Bobos in Paradise.*

Among the many incisive critics of American society, as well as researchers of sociology in mid-twentieth century, is **C. Wright Mills (1916–1962),** educated at the University of Minnesota and a faculty member of Columbia University for several years before his untimely death. Central to his work was a social interactionist approach based initially on the writings of Max Weber. Especially impressive were his classic and best-known books, *White Collar: The American Middle Class* (1953) and *Power Elite* (1956). Here he presented a pessimistic analysis of the station of blue- and white-collar workers, their roles, and the meaning they gave to their labors. He demonstrated effectively that blue-collar workers rarely are satisfied with their jobs, viewing their efforts as having little value other than achieving modest monetary compensation. He also saw that those in white-collar managerial positions, who control and direct groups of others, consider themselves to be servants of large and impersonal organizations. Mills recorded the vast increase in recent years of white-collar jobs and spoke of how this growth affected other sectors of society, especially by increasing the power of bureaucracies that have come to dominate industrial society. Describing the interests that guide the new "science of management," Mills asserted that this so-called science has proved to be at heart an elaborate scheme to deceive and manipulate both blue- and middle-range white-collar workers.

Mills came from a rough strain; he grew up on the streets of Chicago and seemed to enjoy a good brawl. Unlike many sociologists of his time, he fought not out of vanity or self-aggrandizement but for his opinions and principles. His natural skepticism and contentiousness made him a bad risk for political orthodoxy, and he quickly became impatient with doctrinaire and simplified political ideas. He was constantly on the alert for sham and pomposity and, in a sharp but often good-natured way, he loved to cut phonies down to size. Despite his tough stance on social matters, he was, at heart, sweet and gentle, almost without rancor or malice. Despite his obvious large gifts, he seemed to be drawn into questionable and debatable positions. Even when disagreeing with some of his more dramatic and extreme stances, one had to admire the originality of his thinking and his lack of caution in publicizing his convictions.

A gifted writer with a talent for frank and forthright expression, Mills devoted his later writings to vigorous social criticism rather than to conventional academic texts. Fellow sociologists found him to be an intriguing and charming conversationalist, but they regarded Mills as not only irrepressible, but impetuous and inclined to draw conclusions in a spur-of-the-moment manner. Despite his brilliant insights, he enjoyed the public image of being a free and unencumbered spirit, inclined to pursue unorthodox beliefs while disdaining conventional public and professional social norms.

Amitai W. Etzioni (1929–   ) is another vigorous voice in contemporary sociology. Born in Germany, Etzioni spent several decades on the faculties of Hebrew University in Israel and Columbia University in the United States, most recently voicing his numerous critical evaluations as a professor at George Washington University. Among his best-known books are *The Active Society* (1968), *A Comparative Analysis of Complex Organizations* (1961), and *Genetic Fix* (1973). An active and outspoken writer in publications beyond academia, Etzioni is among the most fertile analysts of social policy implications in the late twentieth century. He argued vigorously that an ideal society can guide social change to achieve humane social goals. His more futuristic writings present sociological analyses of issues involved in genetic counseling, recording many of the positive and negative consequences of genetic intervention.

Etzioni's more academic studies attempt to interweave the concepts of power with those of involvement to form a structural typology of bureaucratic organizations. He specifies three power types: coercive, remunerative, and normative. He then interdigitates these with three types of involvement: alienative, calculative, and moral, each signifying degrees of commitment on the part of its participants. In this cross-classification, Etzioni outlines nine types of compliance relationships, of which only three are described as congruent or advantageous in an organization. Influenced by the thinking of Robert Merton, his work has signified a steady effort to build a middle-range theory of social organizations and their psychological consequences.

Pondering Cultural Anthropology

Cultural anthropologists, around the same time as their American sociologist contemporaries, began focusing their attention on personality processes and their relation to cultural variables. Although their focus was similar to that of the sociological thinkers, their approach differed significantly. Whereas pioneers in the sociological schools just discussed held to classical evolutionary paradigms, which compared societies on the basis of advancement, most anthropologists discarded this perspective. Beginning with Franz Boas, the notion of *cultural relativism* became central to their thinking. Instead of viewing one culture as more advanced than another, according to this perspective, it would be more useful, they said, to look at how different cultures evolve *in response to the demands of their particular environment and situations.* Thus, it would be faulty to claim that Western society in the United States is more advanced than a Bushman tribe in Africa; each has advanced as was necessary. The other deviation from the sociological tradition was that anthropologists emphasized empirical investigation, largely based on direct field observations instead of on the more philosophical reflections that characterized the work of their sociologist cousins.

The German-born **Franz Boas (1858–1942)** introduced the concept of cultural relativism to the body of anthropological knowledge. The term suggested that all world populations had a complete and fully developed culture,

Franz Boas

which argued against his nineteenth-century forerunners' view of society's evolution from savagery to culture. Best known for his work with the Kwakiutl Indians of Vancouver and British Columbia, Canada, Boas, who immigrated to the United States in 1887, later assumed an instructor's position at Clark University and eventually became the first professor of anthropology at Columbia University in 1899. He taught many of the next generation of "culture-personality" anthropologists (notably Alfred Kroeber, Edward Sapir, Margaret Mead, and Ruth Benedict, to be discussed shortly). Boas's attention to scientific, empirical rigor, as well as his alternate hypotheses regarding cultural development, established him as the founder of the American school of anthropology.

Boas was born in Westphalia, Prussia, to a middle-class Jewish family who did not practice their religion but held a strong affinity for Judaic culture and identity. His parents' background and liberal orientation, combined with his mother's strong emphasis on education, set the stage for the young Boas, who quickly became sensitized to the destructive power of anti-Semitism. He began thinking in terms that led to many of his later ideas refuting popular notions of the inherent superiority of specific individuals, races, and cultures. Boas excelled in all sciences throughout his academic career, eventually earning a doctoral degree in physics from the University of Keil in 1881. He took from his early education the ideal of scientific rigor and methodology and applied it to all subsequent work. In 1883, Boas embarked on his first scientific expedition, which began his lifelong interest in anthropology and human culture. Returning from a subsequent journey to the Kwakiutl tribes of British Columbia, he stopped in New York City and decided to settle there. At this time, he turned his attention fully to the field of anthropology, taking on the academic posts mentioned previously as well as becoming curator of anthropology at the American Museum of Natural History.

Uncomfortable with the idea of applying generalizations to culture (as well as other scientific disciplines), Boas vigorously pursued the idea of cultural relativity. He was among the first to emphasize that all aspects of a given culture must be understood if the observer is to have any understanding of that particular culture. Within any given culture large enough to have notable individual differences, then, was the variability of human capacity to develop (Boas, 1929). He asserted that numerous social tendencies could be separated and studied:

Thus the solidarity of social groups and their antagonism toward the outsider; the forms and motives for coordination and subordination; imitation of, and resistance to, outside influences; competition between individuals and between groups; division of labor; amalgamation and segregation; attitudes toward the supernatural—to mention a few—may be investigated. (1938, p. 675)

Boas's view was incompatible with popular evolutionary principles that modifications happen universally; instead, it assumed that no superior states of culture existed, and that each society's particular means of adaptation are the result of its unique environment and history. Cultural relativists, then, following Boas's lead, emphasized that parsimonious natural laws could not be applied directly to cultures and their complex structures encompassing unique biology, environment, migratory habits, disease history, communicability with other cultures, and nutrition concerns. It would be much more important for anthropologists, according to the cultural relativists such as Boas, to understand the history and development within societies before attempting to generalize between societies about humankind's evolution.

Alfred Louis Kroeber (1876–1960) was Boas's first student to receive a doctoral degree under his tutelage; unlike his mentor, however, his background was in the humanities, not science. A literary person, Kroeber, having earned a master's degree in English in 1897 prior to pursuing anthropology, wrote over 500 books and articles throughout his professional career. He was among the first to promote the understanding of contemporary humanity and culture through archaeological methods, whereas until then, archaeology concerned itself almost exclusively with classifying prehistoric artifacts. To Kroeber, what was vital to the conception of a given culture was its history in the context of humanity, and the most effective tool to accomplish this goal was archaeology, though he never considered himself an archaeologist.

Alfred Louis Kroeber

Born in New Jersey and raised in New York City, Kroeber benefited from the prosperity his German-Jewish immigrant father achieved in his wholesale clock business, as well as the family's regard for quality education. He attended one of the finest preparatory schools in the city, then moved on to Columbia for his college degrees. First attracted to literature, he earned his bachelor's and master's in English, then came under the influence of Franz Boas and decided to pursue his doctorate in anthropology after being one of only three to take Boas's seminar in American Indian languages. While pursuing this last degree, he spent a brief time as the curator at the Academy of Sciences in San Francisco, then joined the faculty of the University of California, Berkeley, and regained his curator position following graduation in 1901. He eventually became the director of the Academy of Sciences Museum and held his Berkeley position, earning full professorship by 1919, until his retirement in 1946.

Also a cultural relativist, Kroeber maintained Boas's relativist contentions that all cultures are civilized and that there is no particular hierarchy of stages of civilization—all are equally civilized relative to their particular ecological and historical challenges. Kroeber extended this argument, in his study of the *superorganic*, to assert that civilization is an entity beyond and separate from the individuals who carry it. The individual does not hold an inherent historical value beyond being an illustration of greater historical concepts, and whereas individual minds do exist, they respond cumulatively only on a physiological level. What was essentially human about individuals was not passed on organically, but superorganically; that is, social life comprised learned interactions passed on by culture, not just by pure organic components. Civilization is the only ethnic/cultural existence, then, and the only historical entity that could not be transcended.

The renowned linguist and anthropologist **Edward Sapir (1884–1939)** was born in Germany and, at the age of 5, immigrated to the United States with his family, first to Richmond, Virginia, then to New York's Lower East Side. Most frequently thought of as a linguist, Sapir's interests extended well into cultural behaviorism and personality development. Brought up in an Orthodox Jewish household, Sapir let go of what he considered to be the restrictions of orthodoxy as a young man, though he held onto the worldviews of the orthodox Judaic tradition throughout his life. Sapir's schooling was difficult, as his family was very poor, but he managed to earn a Pulitzer fellowship to Columbia University. After his undergraduate studies, Franz Boas and Alfred Kroeber stirred his interests in unwritten languages and anthropology. Following the completion of his master's degree, he embarked on his first field studies of the Wishram on the lower Columbia River, before pursuing the grammar of the Takelma language of Oregon for his doctoral dissertation in 1907.

An unusually versatile academician, Sapir's interests included psychology and psychiatry, sociology, religion, ethnology, and folklore, in addition to his specialization in linguistics. He had an astounding memory and could recall huge quantities of highly detailed information whenever he sought to provide an illustration for a thought or theory he had advanced. As with many persons of extraordinary ability, he read profusely in numerous areas of literature and science. After holding a brief but productive post at the University of Pennsylvania in Philadelphia, Sapir became chief of the newly formed Division of Anthropology of the Geological Survey of Canada in Ottowa. Here his interests in cultural psychology began to grow. Despite many unique field opportunities and a string of publications expounding underlying and governing principles of sociocultural processes of Western tribal life, he found himself alone among his peers. His first wife died following a lengthy illness, and he moved on to the University of Chicago in 1925, where his interests in humankind and society further flourished. He remarried, wrote prodigiously in both linguistics and cultural psychology, and became a renowned lecturer until 1931, when he was offered the opportunity to establish the Department of Anthropology at Yale University. He also took up poetry while maintaining his studies of linguistics, contributing pieces to many noteworthy poetry magazines until his death in 1939.

A cornerstone of Sapir's work was his view that language is dynamic, changing as societies change and reflecting the experiences of a culture by its distinct modes of expression. These gradual changes were what Sapir termed the *Language Drift*. Without language, reality may fail to adjust, since the real world is based largely on the language habits of a group, a view he voiced as follows (1929):

> Human beings do not live in the objective world alone, nor alone in the world of social activity as ordinarily understood, but are very much at the mercy of the particular language which has become the medium of expression for their society. . . . The fact of the matter is that the "real world" is to a large extent unconsciously built up on the language habits of the group. . . . We see and hear and otherwise experience very largely as we do because the language habits of our community predispose certain choices of interpretation. (pp. 209–210)

Bronislaw Malinowski's (1884–1942) studies began with the individual. Born in Krakow, Poland, to a cultured Jewish family, the young Malinowski was groomed to be an intellectual from a very early age. He earned a doctorate in mathematics, philosophy, and physics in 1908 from the University of Krakow, and then became ill. During this prolonged illness, Malinowski, who had abandoned a potential career in mathematics to recuperate, read Sir James Fraser's *The Golden Bough* and became enthralled with the field of anthropology. He traveled to England to pursue graduate studies in this area at the London School of Economics, lecturing there starting in 1913 and earning a doctorate in science in 1916. His early field career centered largely around the Mailu and Trobiand Islands of New Guinea. While in New Guinea, he discredited Freud's Oedipus theory when he discovered evidence suggesting that an individual's psychology was contingent on the person's cultural context. He became a teacher of prominence, loved and revered as well as hated by many in the field. After a lectureship at the London school, he taught at the University of Melbourne, Australia, then returned to the School of Economics in London, his alma mater, and later became chair of anthropology at the University of London.

Malinowski developed and applied a new ethnographic model of observation known as *participant-observation*, where the field worker becomes an active member of the society being studied. This methodology had the advantage of giving the participant an insider view of the society, as well as the more scientific, objective perspective of the investigator. He was credited by some as the founder of the field of social anthropology known as *functionalism*, follow-ing the use of this construct in the fields of psychology and economics. This perspective asserts that there exists a well-balanced system composed of inter-locking components of society, all forming an integrated whole where modifi-cation or action within one component affects all the others. He described his approach as:

> ... the explanation of anthropological facts at all levels of development by their function, by the part which they play within the integral system of culture, by the manner in which they are related to each other within the system, and by the way in which this system is related to the physical surroundings. It aims at the understanding of culture, rather than at conjectural reconstructions of its evolution of past historical events. (1944, p. 864)

The cultural relativist **Ruth Fulton Benedict (1887–1948)** studied under both Alfred Kroeber and Franz Boas, and later mentored and then partnered with Margaret Mead. Benedict supported the view that culture, rather than instinct, molded personality. Enduring temperamental facts such as heredity, individual differences, and physiology contributed to forging personality, but Benedict believed that culture singled out traits as either advantageous or un-desirable; in effect, culture created the larger canvas onto which the individual was portrayed. Coming under fire from her colleagues at several junctures in her career, her relativist views (like those of Boas and others before) differed significantly from those subscribing to a more evolutionary persuasion. Bene-dict's controversial views regarding culture's effect on personality, however, ul-timately became well accepted as social and cultural truisms.

Born in 1887 in New York City, Benedict came from old American farming stock, dating back to the Revolutionary War. Her father, a doctor, died from an infection-based fever, and this early loss shaped Benedict's keen sensitivity to loss and death throughout her life. Leading a poor and arduous childhood, Benedict moved around the country with her mother and her younger sister, liv-ing on her mother's negligible teacher's salary. Despite the family's needy situa-tion, Ruth attended Vassar College on scholarship. She majored in English literature, but found that this subject did not imbue her life with intellectual or social meaning. She discovered anthropology and was exposed to the work of Franz Boas 10 years after graduation. Here, she found a vocation that resonated with her desire to explore different peoples, societies, and historical periods. Following her training and fieldwork (which was made difficult by a lifelong hearing impediment), she accepted a post at Columbia University. Through the 1920s, Benedict published frequently and became a highly respected scholar, but it was not until 1934 that she gained prominence with her book, *Patterns of Culture* (1934), from which the following is excerpted:

> Patterning of culture cannot be ignored as if it were an unimportant detail. The whole, as modern science is insisting in many fields, is not merely the sum of all its parts, but the result of a unique arrangement and interrelation of the

parts that has brought about a new entity. . . . Cultures, likewise, are more than the sum of their traits. We may know all about the distribution of a tribe's form of marriage, ritual dances, and puberty initiations, and yet understand nothing of the culture as a whole which has used these elements to its own purpose. (pp. 2–3)

Like her contemporaries, Benedict was interested in the dynamics of culture and personality, but extended her interests to describe the personality of entire cultures. Borrowing from Friedrich Nietzsche's study of Greek tragedy, Benedict characterized such civilizations as the Kwakiutl and the Dobu as "Dionysian," noting their propensity for excess, debauchery, consumption, and revelry. At the opposite extreme were the Zuni, an "Apollonian" society, who were moderate, civil, and peaceful by comparison. On another dimension, she characterized further societal traits with a clearly pathological dimension: The Dobu, with their preoccupation with sorcery and their suspicious nature, were "paranoid," whereas the Kwakiutls' boastfulness earned them the characterization of "megalomaniacs" (the Zuni escaped such pathological depictions). These descriptions, though frequently apt, were criticized as generalizations. Without a doubt (and especially as uncovered by future fieldworkers), peaceable factions of the Kwakiutl and Dobu also existed, as well as pathologically deviant, drunk, and violent members of the Zuni. However, Benedict contended that such portrayals were not pathological. Just as her relativist mentor Franz Boas would profess, she contended that what may be pathological to one culture was adaptive in another. Nevertheless, many regarded her depictions of whole cultures as dis-

Ruth Fulton Benedict

turbed or sick as regrettably extreme and deeply troubling. These views missed Benedict's essentially humanistic message of acceptance of differences. Besides being one of the first female anthropologists of her era whose works shaped much of cultural anthropology and humanistic psychology, Benedict championed cultural relativism and was an outspoken opponent of ethnocentrism and racism.

The psychiatrist and anthropologist **Abram Kardiner (1891–1981)** attempted to reconcile Freudian psychoanalysis with culture. He may be credited, more than any other, with detaching Freudian theory from its narrow Western perspective and its emphasis on the sex drive. Once an apprentice under Freud, Kardiner recognized the clinical usefulness of classical psychoanalysis but also its inherent culture-bound constructs and the likely influence of Freud's own childhood. In 1936, he organized a major seminar at the

New York Psychoanalytic Institute in which both psychoanalysts and anthropologists (including Ruth Benedict and Edward Sapir) came together to study the interface of different cultures with psychoanalytic theory and practice. The event, which expanded and moved to Columbia University in the following year, produced several major publications. The two most outstanding works were *The Individual and His Society* (1939), which was based on the seminar, and (with Ralph Linton) *The Psychological Frontiers of Society* (1945), which explored techniques for studying reciprocal relations between culture and personality.

Kardiner was born in New York City of immigrant Jewish parents, attended the City College of New York, where he graduated in 1912, earned a medical degree at Cornell University in 1917, and began an apprenticeship under Sigmund Freud in Europe following World War I. Returning to the United States in 1922, he joined the New York Psychoanalytic Institute's faculty, a post he held for many years. He took another position at Cornell to teach psychiatry the following year, which he held for 6 years before establishing a similar post at Columbia University. Besides his professorships, Kardiner was engaged primarily in psychoanalytic practice, and during this period his interest in the interrelationship of personality and culture developed. One of his early interests was the role of the individual on the initiation and perpetuation of cultural institutions. It was also during these early years in academia that Kardiner first explored the notions regarding traditional psychoanalysis and culture, which eventually led to the seminars aimed at overhauling the culture-bound aspects of Freudian theory. Kardiner remained with Columbia University, where he held posts in both anthropology and psychiatry until 1961; he then moved to Emory University until his retirement in 1968.

Kardiner's culture-adaptive approach emphasized how individuals responded to and related with their specific culture and environment. He derived three concrete, interrelated constructs for studying the interrelationship of culture and personality. The first, *primary institution*, referred to any convention or establishment that directly affected the daily care of infants and children. Schools, churches, day-care institutions, hospitals, and families were all examples of this concept. These institutions differed significantly from one community to another, and even more so between cultures. The second was the *secondary institution*, which referred to macrolevel cultural constructs such as religion, politics, and society-at-large; these, too, exhibited vast differences between cultures. Third, Kardiner described the *basic personality structure*, which included the adaptive tools unique to an individual, but which shared common characteristics among all members of a particular society.

The American anthropologist and linguist **Benjamin Lee Whorf (1897–1941),** a descendent of old Provincetown, New England, settlers who immigrated to the new country soon after the Pilgrims, was born in Winthrop, Massachusetts, the eldest of three brothers. His father was a commercial artist with wide interests in visual and performing arts; all three sons excelled in these endeavors. The two younger brothers both pursued the arts and became famous in their own right, whereas Benjamin, intrigued by the chemicals his father routinely used in his photography hobby, decided to pursue a degree in chemical engineering at the Massachusetts Institute of Technology. He remained in this profession throughout his life, working as a fire prevention specialist for an insurance company and producing scholarly works in science and philosophy at a rate akin to that of full-time professors. Although throughout, he remained Sapir's student and colleague, he turned down offers for professorships, maintaining that his work in the corporate world offered him a superior financial situation and more freedom to pursue the interests he preferred.

Whorf examined the core of the tribal languages of the Aztec, Mayan, and Hopi (the third under the influence of Sapir), as well as Indian folklore and ethnology. Through these studies, he established his central, simple core concept: the meaning inherent in a language is absolutely vital to the study of linguistics, and categories of meaning differ between cultures. In his view, language reflects and constrains thought; therefore, thought became unique to each culture.

Whorf's central theory was referred to as *linguistic relativism,* which marked him as a determinist. His assertion that language frames experience is well expressed in the following:

> The linguistic system (in other words, the grammar) of each language is not merely a reproducing instrument for voicing ideas but rather is itself the shaper of ideas, the program and guide for the individual's mental activity, for his analysis of impressions, for his synthesis of his mental stock in trade. (1952, p. 21)

In his short but colorful career, Whorf's writing style (probably influenced by his family's artistic flair) exhibited an exciting, novel-like character, and though he was primarily a linguist, his writings are just as valuable for their descriptive cultural portrayals. His career was shortened by an extended illness that proved fatal: Whorf died at the age of 44 years.

Another student of Franz Boas (and his assistant, Ruth Benedict), **Margaret Mead (1901–1978)** is perhaps the figure in anthropology most responsible for imbuing the field with a human face. Though a self-proclaimed expatriate of psychology as a profession, Mead, who abandoned psychology to pursue anthropology following her master's degree from Columbia in 1924, did so because, by her account, anthropology dealt with human beings more tangibly than did the experimental schools of psychology in the early twentieth century. Raised near Philadelphia in an academically oriented family, Mead began her college education in the Midwest, but soon opted for the more sophisticated environment of New York City and Barnard College, a school affiliated with Columbia University. Originally planning on a career as a poet and writer, she recognized the unlikelihood of commercial success and began to explore meaningful substitutes. Attracted at first to psychology, Mead came under the influence of Boas and Benedict while attending Columbia; they directed her to pursue anthropological studies aimed at disproving the "biological determinism" thesis. Her efforts, which involved comparing Freudian sexual developmental stages between Western and non-Western societies, culminated in a groundbreaking study of the maturation of adolescent Samoan girls, *Coming of Age in Samoa: A Psychological Study of Primitive Youth for Western Civilization* (1928). This controversial publication, which asserted that young girls experienced smoother transitions to adulthood as a function of the society's sexual permissiveness in childhood, launched her career and established Mead as an advocate for more liberal societal points of view, as well as demonstrating a living example of cultural relativism.

Margaret Mead's Samoan studies were an early attempt toward her central career goal, which was to uncover and identify cultural determinants of personality. In this study, as well as in many subsequent studies in New Guinea, Bali, and American Indian regions, she demonstrated how an ingrained culture creates personality patterns. This became especially evident when comparing two non-Westernized, nonmodernized cultures. For example, whereas the Samoans demonstrated their open, permissive, and free attitudes toward the raising of adolescents, which Mead perceived to have culminated in well-adjusted young adults who were relatively free from typical conflict, the Manus (of New Guinea) showed considerable differences. Possessed of extremely high regard for authority, these people were aggressive, driven, and oriented toward surpassing their parents' standard of living. Intense emphasis was placed on the association and passing on of characteristics and traits from fathers to sons, which established something akin to a caste system. Success was largely predicated by the father's role with male progeny, and those who did not succeed were presumed to have families who did not give them a "good start." Typical of this society, then, were potent feelings, conflict between personalities, and enduring societal friction, as indicated in the following excerpt (1930/1962):

> In Manus we find three main types of personality, the aggressive, violent, overbearing type found in older rich men and in the children whom they are fostering and who have not yet reached marriageable age, the definitely assured but less articulately aggressive type found in young men who have not yet attained economic security but who were given a good start in childhood and the immature children of these men; and the mild unaggressive meek type—the older unsuccessful men who were presumably given a bad start or who have very little natural ability, and their children. (p. 233)

Gender roles played a significant role in Mead's studies. Beginning with her Samoan studies, Mead noted considerable differences between the development of personality in adolescent girls in this so-called primitive society and that of American girls of the same age. In the Manus of New Guinea, she noted an emphasis on male success and competition that closely resembled Western mandates, yet this male dynamic lay in the *maintenance* of social castes, rather than in a true upward-mobility striving. In another New Guinea culture, the Tchambuli, the gender roles were entirely reversed, with women taking on more brisk, physically challenging roles, and men assuming household chores. In the Arapesh, yet another New Guinea society, men and women were considered equal, each actively taking care of children and maintaining an egalitarian partnership. Mead's research not only demonstrated a true psychological logic, but challenged (and perhaps dislodged) the popular Freudian biological notions regarding sex roles.

Margaret Mead

Although Franz Boas introduced the notion of cultural relativism and Ruth Benedict may have done much of the early exploration of the topic, Mead was the anthropological pioneer most responsible for translating this concept from theory into living examples. Mead also was largely responsible for bridging anthropology and sociology with psychology. Mead and her third husband, Gregory Bateson (see Chapter 12), may be regarded as crossover figures largely responsible for psychology's recognition of socioenvironmental factors, as well as the enculturated character of personality development. Collaborating with psychologists and related mental health researchers throughout her life, Mead was undoubtedly a key figure in the expansion of the sociocultural perspective. Despite recent posthumous criticism for her methodological failures to adequately account for each culture's distinctive history, Mead brought a depth of cultural awareness to many branches of psychology and psychiatry.

The Belgium-born **Claude Levi-Strauss (1908–1990)** was perhaps best known for his development of *structural anthropology*. Structure, according to Levi-Strauss, did not refer to concrete manifestations of reality, but instead, to cognitive models of perceived reality. Born into a Jewish-turned-agnostic French family in Brussels, Levi-Strauss was an avid student of geology from a very young age but turned his attention to the social sciences by adolescence, finding a keen interest in both Marxism and psychoanalysis. Though never intending to pursue the vocation, he took a degree in law from the University of Paris in 1932, only to turn to sociology and anthropology as a professor two years later. Struck early in his career by the vitality and dynamics of so-called primitive people in the interior of Brazil, he altered his notion of lesser-developed societies from that of ignorance and inertia to one much more sophisticated and adaptive. Following his fieldwork in the Bororo, Nambikwara, and the Tupi, he returned to France until the outbreak of World War II, when he migrated first to Martinique, followed by Puerto Rico, and finally New York, where colleagues had arranged for his employment at the New School for Social Research. Following the war, he returned to France, where he published his landmark book on kinship, *The Elementary Structures* (1949/1969), joined the faculty of the University of Paris, and was appointed to the position of secretary general of the International Council of Social Sciences, which he held until 1960.

Levi-Strauss's work may be broadly classified as possessing three elements: (1) social anthropology (inclusive of his "alliance theory"); (2) cognition and mental processes; and (3) mythology and its structural aspects. The first area is diverse, and his alliance theory is perhaps the best-known aspect. Levi-Strauss proposed that marriage, rather than ancestral descent, is the most important factor in creating social solidarity and, ultimately, survival of a society. According to Levi-Strauss, processes of exchange between families ensure a cooperative flow between members of society. In his second facet, cognitions, Levi-Strauss asserted that human mental processes are the same between cultures, yet manifestations may be extremely different. Third, Levi-Strauss's work in mythology suggested structured regularities of human thought, which, when evolved into sustained structures, would also be comparable across cultures.

A notable impact in the United States was the work of **Erving Goffman (1922–1982),** whose contributions on the sociology of interaction provided a powerful voice in the 1960s for the lay and anthropological world in a series of books, notably *Encounters* (1961b), *Asylums* (1961a), *Behavior in Public Places* (1976), and *Interaction Ritual* (1967). Born in Canada, the son of modestly educated Jewish immigrants, he began his studies at the University of Toronto, then moved to graduate work at the University of Chicago where he completed his doctorate in 1953. Along with other critics of mental institutions in the mid-twentieth century, such as *Thomas Szasz*, the analyst, *Thomas Scheff*, the sociologist, and *Ronald Laing*, the English psychiatrist, Goffman wrote bitterly and incisively about the horrors of asylums, especially his judgment that these institutions subjected inmates to degradations and abasements that led them to withdraw from all social and psychological supports that had once sustained them in life. As he portrayed these institutions, he noted that they not only restricted their patient's lives, but infantilized and desecrated them, so that patients, like prison inmates, felt that institution time was time wasted and taken from their lives, and that the duration of their stay was an exile from living.

Relying less on formal scientific methods than on his keen observation of contemporary life, Goffman wrote on subjects ranging from the way people behave in public to the horrors and anguish of institutionalization, as well as to the many absurd if not comedic aspects of conventional social life. Speaking of "gender advertisements," he noted that women are consistently subordinated to men in films and television dramas, that they are treated as children; saved from serious talk; allowed to look, dress, and behave immaturely; and encouraged to posture themselves in absurd and clowning ways. As an ethnographer, Goffman addressed routine social interactions such as gossip and gestures in which people strive to enact socially designated identities, an assigned form of theatrical everyday behavior. In his *The Presentation of Self in Everyday Life* (1981) Goffman coined the term "dramaturgy" to explain how we stage-manage the images we convey of ourselves to others. Popular in intent, much of Goffman's writing cared little about its systematic relationship to abstract academic theories. His perceptive analyses of human relationships will likely endure far longer than the writings of most other social anthropologists.

Researching Epidemiology

Recent articles in major newspapers and popular national magazines have asked questions such as the following about mental health, violence, and criminality: What proportion of murders is related to drug trafficking? How often do suicide victims act out immediately after a marital split, loss of a job, or any other personal crisis? Are teenagers who randomly shoot others likely to be mentally ill or have they been prompted by the degradations of their social and community life?

No one, say public and mental health authorities, has accurate answers to these and other critical questions about the thousands of emotionally driven or violent behaviors that occur annually in the United States, even though this knowledge could assist health and judicial agencies in establishing wiser preventive policies and programs. Although it is surprising that no national data-gathering systems exist, periodic regional, academic, and civic efforts have been made in this past century.

Epidemiological research shows that the admission rate for all forms of mental illness is substantially higher in urban than in rural areas. Furthermore, the larger the city and the more centrally congested and overpopulated the region within it, the higher the incidence. Many attribute differences between urban and rural rates primarily to the more benign environment of country life and to the ability of rural dwellers to care for their mentally ill at home. Other interpretations are possible; however, they lack sufficient data regarding their validity.

The higher rates found within the central and congested tracts of a city, compared with the more peripheral regions, appear to apply only to larger urban centers. The higher rates of mental illness in central city areas likely occur because these communities usually are poverty stricken, physically decayed, and socially disorganized. Not only do these regions breed conditions conducive to pathology, but they tend to attract and serve as a haven of anonymity for the unstable and ineffectual who drift into their midst from other regions of society.

Epidemiological studies indicate also that married persons have a lower incidence of mental disorder than single people, especially single men, who in turn have lower rates than those who are divorced. These findings have been interpreted several ways; the two most common assert that marriage protects the individual from distresses associated with loneliness and disaffection, and that those inclined to mental illness either are ill-disposed or incapable of establishing a marital relationship or precipitate difficulties that lead to a breakup. Both explanations seem reasonable and, together, are likely to account for the obtained findings.

Single individuals who possess serious emotional difficulties are not likely to desire the involvements of close personal relationships. Because they are ill equipped or disinclined, single men may avoid the pursuit of a wife, or be ineffectual in their courtship attempts. Single men have a higher rate of serious emotional difficulties than single women. The lower rate for single women may occur because women in our society usually assume a passive role in courtship. In contrast to the disturbed man, who must assume initiative, the disturbed woman may be pursued and involved even though she may have initially been disinclined toward marriage.

Several factors may explain the high rate of mental illness among divorced persons. Emotionally impaired individuals are likely to provoke conflict with their mates, thereby increasing the likelihood of divorce. Once cut off from support and cast into isolation and disaffiliation, their pathological dispositions may be precipitated into a manifest disorder. In summary, then, different incidence rates associated with marital status probably reflect both initial dispositions to pathology and the effects of lost affection and affiliation.

Numerous demographic studies have sought to demonstrate relationships between socioeconomic conditions and prevalence and type of mental disorder. Despite a sprinkling of negative data, two findings appear to hold up fairly consistently. First, members of the lowest socioeconomic class are diagnosed as severely impaired more often than those of the upper classes. Second, the manifest patterns of mental illness differ among these classes.

Two well-controlled early studies, the first based in New Haven, Connecticut, the other in New York City, offer evidence that both the prevalence (overall presence) and incidence (rate of occurrence) of serious disorders is greatest among the lowest socioeconomic class, whereas the prevalence of milder (neurotic) disorders is greatest among the higher social classes; no difference appears to exist between classes in the incidence of milder disorders. These data are not merely a result of the proportion of the overall population that fall within these class categories (e.g., the lowest socioeconomic class accounts for 20% of the general population, but 40% of the psychiatric population).

Analysis of type of pathology found most frequently among the various social strata indicates that apathy and social detachment (traditionally diagnosed as schizophrenia), as well as the more aggressive and antisocial tendencies (traditionally diagnosed as sociopathic disturbances), characterize the mentally ill of the lower classes. Feelings of interpersonal anxiety, inadequacy, and guilt (traditionally diagnosed as neuroses and depressive disorders) are found most often in the middle and upper classes.

Organizing Socially Responsive Therapies

Cultural diversity and gender issues challenge psychotherapists in their work in Western societies. Increasingly, clinicians in many of the major cities in the United States encounter problems they have rarely come across in earlier training: *Pa-Feng*, a phobic fear of wind and cold that occurs in Chinese patients; *Hwa-Byung*, a suppressed anger syndrome suffered by Koreans; *Latah*, a Malaysian and Indonesian psychosis that leads to uncontrollable mimicking of other people. Psychotherapists refer to these kinds of mental disorders as *culture-bound syndromes*. They see such disorders increasingly often, as they treat rapidly growing numbers of immigrant populations, but the conditions are frequently misdiagnosed or confused with other perplexing syndromes. Although Western-trained therapists face their own culture-bound syndromes, such as borderline personalities and anorexia nervosa, only recently are they coming to learn and address patients' ethnicity and country of origin so as to understand and treat them ethically and successfully.

As in the past, the United States continues to be enriched by its growing diversity of ethnic and racial minorities. Also of significance is the enriching character of the feminist movement. And of no less relevance are issues associated with the flourishing openness of the gay-lesbian subculture.

Minority/Cultural Diversity.   An immigration transformation is rapidly occurring in American society. Close to 80% of those entering the United States and its labor force are minorities, drawn from a vast arena of other countries and cultures. Further, because the fertility rate of the dominant American culture has been declining, and the newborn population of ethnic/racial minorities continues to grow, minority groups will become the numerical majority in the United States, perhaps by mid-century. This trend calls for an important reassessment of traditional therapeutic attitudes and responsibilities. Psychotherapists are now being prepared for diverse patient populations with appreciably different cultural values and social experiences than those that have typified mental health practice in earlier years.

Several major racial/ethnic groups must be given serious consideration in mental health plans.

African Americans currently compose this country's second largest, and relatively distinct minority group, numbering over 30 million persons, or slightly more than 12% of the population. Despite significant intracultural differences among them, African Americans as a whole, owing to the superficial element of a darker skin, have been subjected to generations of social injustice, if not oppression. The effects of this historical prejudice, combined with problematic current life circumstances (lower economic and educational opportunities), dispose many to high levels of psychosocial stress.

Hispanic Americans, today the largest minority population in the United States, are an unusually diverse group, comprising numerous subcultures from

Mexico, Puerto Rico, Cuba, South and Central America, as well as others. Hispanics are also the fastest growing racial/ethnic group in the country, with approximately 35 million residing here at the turn of the twenty-first century. Marked differences in cultural values and outlooks add to the considerable heterogeneity within each Hispanic subgroup. Demographically, the Hispanic population as a whole tends to be less educated, younger, and poorer than the larger society, and more likely to live in congested inner cities. The stresses of this life setting, added to their linguistic minority status, contribute significantly to their vulnerability to psychosocial problems that call for therapeutic services.

Like Hispanics, *Asian Americans* include several major subcultures, including Japanese, Chinese, Filipino, Korean, Vietnamese, Cambodians, Malaysians, and others. This broad-based minority group comprises the third largest racial/ethnic population in the United States, now numbering over 7 million persons, and growing. Each subgroup features different levels of acculturation, ranging from third-generation professionals of high status and income, to recent immigrants struggling with language difficulties and problematic employment. As with other minority groups, a large proportion of these individuals have been subjected to societal discrimination and misunderstanding.

Native Americans include American Indians, Eskimos, and Aleuts. Representing tribes dispersed throughout the continent, Native Americans are culturally diverse, as well as heterogeneous in terms of their opportunities to assimilate within the wider society. A recent census reports that their population numbers roughly 2 million, with only about 20% living on reservations. A notably young population, Native Americans fall near to the low end of the educational, economic, and political power spectrum in the United States. Their poverty levels, unemployment, poor health care, shortened life expectancy, substance abuse, and suicide rate contribute significantly to the stresses they endure that require therapeutic assistance.

Consider the value system of the dominant "white American male culture" with those of the minority groups identified in the preceding paragraphs. The dominant white culture strongly encourages individualism. Therapists stress that a primary goal of treatment should be increased self-esteem and self-actualization as patients learn to act in an independent and autonomous fashion and to carry major responsibility for the course of their own lives. By contrast, persons from several, perhaps most, minority groups, regularly deemphasize individualism. American Indians value the collective group or tribe, rather than the separate worth of each person; what is best for the group takes precedence over what is best for the individual. Similarly, many Hispanic subcultures emphasize the role of the family, not that of the individual. Therapists need to recognize that an individualistic focus reflects the dominant white-male value system, which is not culturally universal.

The core unit in the dominant society is the nuclear family; here, parents live alone with their children, while other significant relatives (aunts, uncles, grandparents) live separately in independent family units. Many racial/ethnic subgroups, however, live in extended family systems, with diverse relatives of all ages living together or in close proximity. Family therapy in the dominant social system tends to include only members of the nuclear family; other relatives are rarely brought into treatment. As a result, the central role that grandparents play in the family may be overlooked in treating Asian American families.

As a consequence of the diversity of racial/ethnic value systems, the primary orientation of many established therapeutic schools of thought may not prove relevant or suitable. Many of the therapeutic theories in use today originated in Europe and hence reflect an English/European cultural perspective, with its implicit goals, values, and attitudes. The suitability of psychodynamic therapy with some minority groups is questionable owing to its focus on the key role of the individual. The desire to aid the person "to know oneself" and to recognize that the patient's problem inheres within, which requires working through unconscious mental distortions, contrasts sharply with minority patient values and experiences. For these patients, primary attention may best be placed on the key role of sociocultural factors, such as racism, poverty, and social marginality. Similarly, the orientation in cognitive approaches stresses thought distortions that undermine a person's effective functioning; in fact, the troublesome cognitions of a minority patient may represent the awful, but actual, realities experienced in everyday life. Similarly, humanistic modalities orient patients toward achieving psychic growth and self-esteem, but such an emphasis may cause considerable conflict or guilt for patients who come from cultural groups that are grounded in the importance of the collective, the family, or a traditional community.

Feminist Issues.   Although the United States has benefited greatly these past four decades by the emergence of the feminist movement, especially as manifested in an increase in women's rights and opportunities, this valued progress has been a mixed blessing for some. It wasn't until some years after the first women's rights convention at Seneca Falls in 1848 that an independent movement was established in the United States to set the foundation for achieving a woman's right to vote in the twentieth century. Progress has been slow, but over the past several decades women have made significant strides toward achieving equality with men. Although a full measure of parity has yet to be attained, numerous intrapersonal and interpersonal complications have arisen in the course of this progression.

For both men and women, a deep struggle exists between the wish for mastery and self-determination, on the one hand, and the wish for protection and security, on the other. The feminist movement has sought to facilitate the development of women's autonomy, self-assertion, and psychic independence. This same ideal, however, is often experienced as a threat when it opposes the female tradition of possessing protection from the uncertainties of a complex and competitive world. Success and achievement, therefore, can be sources of discomfort, if not anxiety, because they may threaten to disrupt the fulfillment of conflicting life-nurturing needs. Despite the worthy values of the feminist movement, many women have not been socialized to learn professional skills or to master competitive tasks. Behaviors that run contrary to traditional feminine roles are a special problem for women who often regard their efforts at autonomy and achievement as a sign of rebelliousness, if not deviance in contemporary society.

Therapists have observed that women, in efforts to compete with men, often anticipate troublesome social consequences for their effort. Whereas men assume that success will lead to further opportunities and cultural rewards, women are often in conflict about achievement. They may feel guilty about surpassing their mothers, fear losing a less successful male partner, and incur consequent anxieties about aloneness in a less-than-accepting world. Historically, women have shaped their identity to be pleasing to men, and to downgrade their own abilities and confidence. It has been difficult, therefore, for them to integrate a sense of work achievement as a source of self-identity; in achievement, some women may be depriving themselves of a traditional component of their self-esteem. Moreover, the questioning attitudes of a larger society that makes aspiration a dubious motive in women often complicates ambition. These attitudes can only create inner conflicts that may undermine a woman's ability to pursue clear-cut goals.

For some, the conception of self in the liberated woman appears to mirror what has historically typified men; that is, it is based on the need to separate oneself from the mother, the prime caretaker, the person of one's childhood who is tender, empathic, warm, and intimate. By jettisoning the mother's role and adopting the father's, women often develop a sense of separateness from others, a developmental trend in which they may deny their own tenderness and empathic sensitivity. No longer responsive to the needs of others, women may begin to feel alienated from themselves, isolated from that which may be more congruent with their inherent maternal orientation. Male bravado and chauvinism may be an attractive concept in the abstract, but it may prove a deep source of personal alienation among those women who take it seriously.

No therapist would wish to return to the days when women were encouraged to be quiet and sedate, to be seen and not heard, to be obedient and passive. But on the other hand, effective therapists must recognize that this cultural transition in society may create internalized conflicts for many women who will seek their guidance and support. There is little doubt that part of the conflict that women face stems from a social system sharply divided in its attitudes. In a society in which women are denied equal access to opportunities and resources, therapists must help resolve conflicts in those able women who struggle with role-breaking efforts to synthesize their deeper emotional needs with their desire for autonomy and independence.

Several contrasting orientations in feminist therapy have come to the foreground within the past two or three decades. One, termed *radical feminism*, attributes the struggle for women as deriving from the unequal distribution of power that exists within society. Radical feminist therapists believe that they should encourage women to assert themselves and gain increasing power in all of society's institutions. Its most significant form is the "empowerment model" of therapy. A second group of feminist therapies, termed *gender-role treatment*, seeks to have patients understand that men and women have been socialized differently. The focus here is not to foster sociocultural change, but to resocialize women patients. The task is to make female clients more androgynous, and thereby facilitate a broadening of their personal development and outlook. A third model, termed *women-centered therapy*, asserts that differences in the psychological makeup of women and men are fundamental and not due solely to cultural socialization. Therapists of this persuasion seek to positively interpret "genuine" female traits, rather than judge them as misguided, troublesome, or as signifying deficiencies. Hence, they honor as desirable such behaviors as cooperation, altruism, and empathy; and they facilitate their patients' increased valuation of their essential femaleness.

Gay/Lesbian Considerations. There is a growing receptiveness and open-mindedness in the United States today toward the diverse forms of gender proclivity and sexual preference. Although this trend has numerous benefits for many, problematic residuals remain for some that may call for therapeutic action.

Although gay men and lesbian women comprise 10% to 15% of the overall population in the United States, their status, until recently, has been that of "an invisible minority." Pervasive negative attitudes within society and insufficient professional training have prevented the delivery of thoughtful and sensitive therapeutic services to this group. The trend toward greater knowledge and more egalitarian attitudes has only recently led to increased knowledge and skills necessary to work effectively with these patients.

Gay people, both men and women, experience a unique position among the socially rejected groups in that they are reared largely in nongay families who fail to provide adequate models of self-respect and self-esteem and rarely show acceptance and affirmation for their progeny's socially problematic identity. Homophobia is commonplace and characterizes how most families and others react to gay people. Moreover, gay men and lesbian women often grow up learning rejecting and hostile attitudes toward same-sex intimacies, just as do nongays. This internalization of homophobia is distressing for many gays and further complicates their already troubled self-identity.

Homoerotic attachments were viewed in a highly tolerant manner in classical Greece. It was not until the sixteenth century when intense conflicts arose between Protestants and Catholics that legal action against same-sex behaviors became prominent. By the seventeenth century, same-sex relationships were viewed as a "crime against nature," and were classified with other forms of socially reprehensible behavior. The American colonies not only discouraged same-sex intimacies, but instituted legal prohibitions against such activities, often identified as a form of sodomy. Although legal punishment has abated in current times, considerable social and religious discrimination remains in many quarters today.

Promising signs have begun to emerge in the past few decades. For example, the American Psychiatric Association declassified homosexuality as a mental illness in 1973, followed in turn by a similar move on the part of the American Psychological Association in 1975. Most significantly, mental health professionals now treat the run-of-the-mill problems of gay men and lesbian women, whatever their source or character, instead of concentrating their efforts on reversing their sexual orientation. These promising changes are encouraging, but they do not necessarily reflect an increased sensitivity on the part of practitioners. Research suggests that many mental health professionals carry with them archaic heterosexist assumptions. They not only maintain traditional stereotypes about gay people, but are uninformed about gay and lesbian lifestyles and harbor distorted beliefs concerning the issues that arise in these patients' lives. Moreover, traditional homophobic assumptions invariably confound therapeutic work with complex transference and countertransference issues.

The problems gay persons present are not unexpected. Not untypical is a young person who might visit a therapist because he has been degraded or beaten by his family, thrown out of his home, and is now homeless. Isolation is the most frequent presenting problem among young gays. Youngsters report having no one to talk to and feeling alone in most social situations, especially within the family, at school, or in church or temple. Such isolation is usually associated with their fear of discovery and the constant need to hide. Even when a network of gay social companions is available, they may sense that others are interested only in exploiting them. Not to be overlooked is a sense of deep emotional isolation, the belief that one cannot trust bonding or attaching to others, owing to the assumption that the gay lifestyle tends to be transient and incidental, rather than genuine and enduring. Lacking a consistent and appropriate role model, many young gays demonstrate an appalling ignorance about what it is to be gay, frequently believing the worst stereotypes about homosexuals—and therefore about themselves.

Over a third of gay persons in therapy have suffered violence at the hands of others. A high percentage of suicide attempts exists during the teenage years as the early crisis of homosexual inclinations becomes inescapable. It is not until they move beyond the narrow confines of their early life settings—as they leave their communities, enter college, or find distant jobs—that these young people begin to make contact with a more sophisticated and gay-oriented community. Nevertheless, many remain troubled and in conflict.

Coping with stigmatization is not an easy task because the AIDS virus has been so closely and unjustly identified with homosexuality in the United States. Developing a close alliance with a single other person is perhaps a gay person's most important coping strategy. But the problems of being stigmatized, the feelings of internal dissonance, and the need to deceive and hide one's inclination remain serious parts of the everyday life of many young gays.

There is no reason to believe that gay people, as a group, are less well-adjusted than their heterosexual counterparts, but specific factors typify the problems that they experience when difficulties have arisen. Isolation, family rejection, abuse, and deep identity conflicts represent the problems for which they seek guidance. The task of therapists is not invariably complex. Many individuals simply need access to accurate information; others need opportunities for socialization with a wider network of peers than can be achieved in same-sex settings. Of course, it is difficult for gay people to actualize themselves in a social context of public rejection. Moreover, gay and lesbian individuals need support before they can fully express themselves and their individuality. Therapists must also learn to feel comfortable with their own sexuality and seek to rid themselves of homophobic feelings if they are to work openly and honestly with gay and lesbian patients. Most importantly, they must help their patients reject homophobic stereotypes and conflicts, enabling them to develop a healthier attitude toward their own genuine feelings and authentic identities.

For all the issues discussed in this section on minority, feminist, and gay/lesbian perspectives, most of the standard therapeutic approaches discussed in this book can be carefully examined to reorient underlying biases and assumptions. Thus, they may prove useful if applied with an informed sensitivity to patients' special life conditions.

Comments and Reflections

From a mundane and practical viewpoint, most mental health practitioners use their professional skills today in the larger social community rather than in inpatient settings. Their clients are no longer severely disturbed state hospital psychotics but ambulatory individuals seen in private offices or mental health community clinics. These clients are beset with economic stressors, social inadequacies, or family and marital conflicts, which are typically reported in symptoms such as anxiety, depression, or alcoholism.

The readiness to accept or dismiss sociocultural issues seems as closely related to partisan and political views as to any other factor. Interprofessional jurisdictional issues as well as intraprofessional concerns also hamper progress. Sociologists, social workers, social psychologists, and public health experts have raised serious questions about other mental health professionals' fitness for leading social mental health programs. Alarm rises when the language employed by leaders of the movement suggests treatment of a collectivity as a massive experiment in social engineering. Implications have been seen in these suggestions of everything from an Orwellian threat to an extreme rightist plot. That a sociocultural perspective has been able to develop at all, despite divergent opinions, conflicting value systems, and sinister implications is largely a result of the enormity of unmet mental health needs and the determined, though awkward, effort of a group of professions to realign their focus to meet these needs.

Correlations between sociocultural variables and mental illness do not necessarily indicate that these social variables have caused the psychological disturbance; the effect may go the other way. Thus, it is just as likely that already disturbed individuals will gravitate toward socially pathological settings, as that these settings produce disturbances in previously healthy individuals.

Further, the effects of a social condition can be evaluated only in terms relevant to the personal life of the individual; we cannot assume that usual conceptions of unfortunate events are effectively experienced as such by an individual. Divorce, for example, may be felt as a crushing personal loss to one individual, but a relief from unbearable anguish to another. In the first case, divorce may be pathogenic; in the second, it may be productive of mental health. Similarly, we normally assume that a high socioeconomic status provides a person with a sense of security and comfort; it may be productive, however, of indolence and irresponsibility, conditions conducive to occupational ineptitude or mental illness. The significance of any social variable must always be appraised in light of the individual's personal life. Judgments about social conditions will tend to be gross oversimplifications if they fail to be viewed from this context.

It is commonly believed that substantial differences in the prevalence of mental illness exist between cultures. Some assert that serious disorders arise less frequently among homogeneous and well-integrated primitive cultures than in those characterized by technological complexities, cultural heterogeneity, and intergroup conflict. Some investigators have come to a more discriminating conclusion. Although the beliefs and customs of a social group color overt symptomatology, the basic severe mental illnesses appear to be found with equal frequency throughout the world. Reported prevalence of mental disorder in many societies is spuriously low since these groups may lack facilities for identifying and caring for those who are ill. In sum, then, there is evidence that cultural factors affect the form of expression but not necessarily the frequency of mental illness.

The obstacles confronting investigators engaged in the design, the execution, or the interpretation of sociocultural studies of mental illness are formidable. Numerous questions have been raised about the methodological adequacy of earlier research and the likelihood that these studies will prove more fruitful in the future.

Because it is impossible to design an experiment in which relevant sociocultural variables can systematically be controlled or manipulated, it is impossible to establish unequivocal cause-effect relationships among these variables and mental illness. Investigators cannot arrange, no less subvert and abuse, a social group for purposes of scientific study; research in this field must, therefore, continue to be naturalistic and correlational. The problem with naturalistic studies is the difficulty of inferring causality; correlations do not provide a secure base for determining which factors were cause and which were effect. Correlations between socioeconomic class and mental illness may signify both that deteriorated social conditions produce mental disorders and that mental disorders result in deteriorated social conditions.

The perennial problem of unreliable and nonuniform diagnostic criteria plagues investigators in this research area even more than in other fields of mental illness. We know that the basis for assigning one or another diagnostic label varies tremendously from community to community and from state to state. Such unreliability is extremely serious in this field since the purpose of research is to compare prevalence rates among different sociocultural communities. If the criteria among regions vary, comparable figures cannot be achieved.

Despite these and other methodological complications, such as the high frequency of geographic and socioeconomic mobility in our society, a sufficient body of well-executed research indicates that sociocultural factors contribute to the course and shape of mental illness. Definitive conclusions indicating the specific factors that influence particular features of pathology will be achieved only with more sophisticated and ingenious research.

CHAPTER

12

Exploring and Enhancing Interpersonal Relationships

Following Sigmund Freud's seminal work, psychoanalytic theories began a shift from biological determinism toward a sociocultural orientation. Whereas Freud's classical analytic approach emphasized the libidinous instincts of the id, ego analysts such as Hartmann and Erikson focused on the instinctual reservoir of the ego's socially adaptive behaviors. The neo-analytic social theorists and the object relations approaches to therapy advanced another logical step from the individual's character to the person's pattern of interrelationships. In addition to their psychodynamic predecessors, relational approaches also moved beyond individuals' specific symptoms to behavioral patterns that focus on their interactions with others. To the socially oriented psychologist and the relational therapist, it is how we structure and change everyday relationships that matters most.

The Sociocultural Story: II

Although distinct disciplines today, sociology and psychology evolved from similar theoretical backgrounds (e.g., interest in social attitudes). Many of the authors described in Chapter 11 wrote about the individual and about society and culture. Some claimed to be ancestors of both sociology and social psychology. Others were hostile toward psychology, asserting that sociology should maintain its proprietary interests as a separate discipline, distinct from what began to emerge as social psychology, the latter being focused on individual behavior albeit in a social context. Critics felt that sociologists, by contrast, should focus on social groups; the concept of *group mind* became popular. Social psychology, though considered a distinct branch of psychological study, continues to overlap and intersect with other social sciences. Social psychology does not possess any specific or unifying theoretical point of view, as do other realms of psychology. Social psychologists have been unable to identify a common denominator or attribute that clearly distinguishes the topics of social psychology from fields that fall within the larger provinces of general psychology, sociology, and anthropology—or even economics or linguistics.

Several beliefs also distinguish social psychology theorists and relational therapists from similar, individually oriented figures of the past. First, social psychologists contend that the critical determinants of pathology do not arise from the biological properties of the instincts; to them, instincts have significance only in terms of their interpersonal consequences. They either reject or reinterpret Freudian stages of psychosexual development to reflect their interpersonal character. The early characterologists and Freudian dissidents began this journey away from pure biological determinism by replacing Freud's biologically based oral stage with a concentration on the relationship between parent and child in which the child experienced the interpersonal aspects of dependency. In a similar manner, they translated the anal stage to signify a period when the child learns interpersonal obedience or assertiveness.

Second, these theorists rejected the Freudian view that adult pathology could be understood simply as a repetition of earlier developmental difficulties. Although they recognized that early experience could possibly influence later behavior, they believed that later difficulties often were autonomous of their original source. They noted that intervening experiences modulated early experiences, that adaptive reactions often lead to new difficulties, and that these, in turn, bring forth new defenses. By adulthood, they posited, extensive and diffusive experiences would evolve that were far removed from the original childhood difficulties. Because they made no simple connection between childhood experience and adult pathology, these theorists shifted their focus to adult problems; the past was of value only to the extent that it could shed light on the present.

Third, the shift in focus to adult experience diminished the interest in the unconscious, which harbored residues of the past and increased the interest in conscious attitudes of adulthood. Theorists recognized that conscious attitudes shaped, in great measure, the individual's way of perceiving and organizing everyday life; these attitudes transformed the world of objective reality to suit established ways of thinking. This interest in consciousness is also a critical distinction between the orientations of the psychoanalytic and phenomenological approaches (see Chapter 4).

Modern *relational therapies,* as they have recently been labeled, have roots in the cultural and anthropological ideas discussed in Chapter 11 and with the social psychologists who gained prominence in the first half of the twentieth century, such as Kurt Lewin and Fritz Heider. However, the figure who laid the cornerstone for the therapeutic models derived from the social approach was the Freudian dissident Alfred Adler. As discussed in Chapter 7, Adler noted that the individual's social role was more integral to the formation of pathology than was the libidinal drive. Not only did a particular disorder, say, a phobia or hypochondriasis, excuse patients from unfavorable tasks, but their disability allowed for cloaked manipulation of others. Social interaction, then, fulfilled patients' power and superiority strivings resulting from the dependence and inferiority universally inherent in early childhood experience. According to Adler, these basic feelings of inferiority would lead either to a healthy personality striving for self-improvement and orientation toward positive social change or to a pathological personality struggling irrationally for power and triumph. These compensatory strivings, acquired by all individuals as a reaction to the restrictions imposed by their more powerful parents, led to a general pattern of behavior that Adler called the "style of life."

Modern-day relational therapies fall into several general categories. These approaches were rooted in social psychology theories that focused on the constructs of society and context, instead of ascribing all human dynamics to the individual. The field of social work originated in the same era, with the establishment of settlement houses and social change programs aimed at correcting social ills and empowering individuals to live effectively within their social communities. Similarly, *group therapy*, as its name implies, congregated patients together for treatment in groups typically ranging from 4 to 12 members, who were led by either one or two therapists. *Family therapy*, as is also self-evident, gathered the larger family unit for treatment, instead of the single patient (though one family member is often referred to as the "identified" patient). Finally, *interpersonal therapy* engaged one patient at a time in a dyadic patient-therapist medium, while focusing on the patient's relationships with others.

Few characterizations of American life are more apt than those that portray society as upwardly mobile. Stated differently, the American culture has maximized the opportunity of its members to progress, to succeed, and to achieve material rewards that were once considered the province only of the aristocracy and well-to-do. With certain notable and distressing exceptions, young people have been free to rise, by dint of their wits and their talents, above the socioeconomic status of their parents. Implicit in this well-publicized option to succeed, however, is the expectancy that everyone will pursue that opportunity and will be measured by the extent to which they succeed. Thus, society not only promotes ambition but expects each of its members to meet the challenge. Each aspiring individual, then, must make a precarious choice: Along with the promised rewards of success are the devastating consequences of failure.

Pathogenic feelings such as guilt for having let others down, self-devaluation for one's limitations and self-recrimination for failures well up within many members of society. People have been well trained to compete and to seek public achievements without examining their aims, their inevitable frustrations, and their limited rewards.

Furthermore, large segments of our society find themselves out of the mainstream of American life. Isolated by social prejudice or economic deprivation, they struggle less with the problem of achieving in a changing society than with attaining the bare necessities of survival. To them, the question is not which of the changing social values they should pursue but whether any social values are worthy of pursuit. Thus, many young African-Americans reject outright the idea of finding a niche in American society; they question whether a country that has preached equality, but has degraded their parents and deprived them of their rights and opportunities, is worth saving at all. Deteriorating and alienated communities feed on themselves; not only do they perpetuate their decay by destroying the initiative and promise of their young, but they attract the outcast and unstable individuals who drift into their midst.

Nevertheless, harsh cultural and social conditions rarely cause mental illness, but they serve as a context within which the direct and immediate experiences of interpersonal life occur. They color and degrade personal relationships and establish maladaptive and pathogenic models for imitation.

Although transformations in family patterns and relationships have evolved fairly continuously over the past century, the speed and nature of transitions since World War II have been so radical as to break the smooth line of earlier trends. Hence, many children today no longer have a clear sense of either the character or the purpose of their fathers' work activities, much less a detailed image of the concrete actions that compose that work. Beyond the little there is of the father's daily routines to model oneself after, mothers of young children have shifted their activities increasingly outside the home, seeking career fulfillment or needing dual incomes to sustain family aspirations. Not only are everyday adult activities no longer available for direct observation and modeling, but traditional gender roles, once distinct and valued, have become blurred and questionable. Today, children have little opportunity to observe and emulate actions that the larger society rewards and esteems. What real and important people do cannot be learned from parents who return from a day's work too preoccupied or exhausted to share their esoteric activities. Lost, then, are the crystallizing and focusing effects of identifiable and stable role models that give structure and direction to maturing psychic processes. This loss contributes significantly to the undifferentiated and diffuse personality organization characteristic of many young persons today.

With the growing dissolution of the traditional family structure has come a marked increase in parental separation, divorce, and remarriage. Children subject to persistent parental bickering and family restructuring not only are exposed to changing and destructive models for imitative learning but develop the internal schisms that typify Western youth at the turn of the twenty-first century. The stability of life, so necessary for the acquisition of a consistent pattern of feeling and thinking, is shattered when erratic conditions or marked controversy prevail. Children may be apprehensive that they will totally lose a parent through divorce; dissension may lead to the undermining of one parent by the other; and a nasty and cruel competition for the loyalty and affections of children may ensue. Constantly dragged into the arena of parental schisms, children not only lose a sense of security and stability, but are subjected to paradoxical behaviors and contradictory role models. Raised in such settings, children suffer the constant threat of family dissolution and often must mediate conflicts between the parents. Forced to switch sides and divide loyalties, children cannot be individuals but must internalize opposing attitudes and emotions to satisfy antagonistic parental desires and expectations. The roles children must assume to placate parents are markedly divergent: As long as the parents remain at odds, children persist with intrinsically irreconcilable behaviors, thoughts, and emotions.

For many children, divorce not only undermines the sense that one can count on things to endure, but often dislodges formerly secure and crucial internalizations within one's psychic self, upsetting the fusions and integrations that evolved among parental models and standards. Alienated from parental attachments, as well as often disillusioned and cynical, they may totally jettison these internalized structures. Moreover, the confidence that one can depend in the future on a previously internalized belief or precept may now be seriously undermined. Devoid of stabilizing internalizations, such youngsters may come to prefer the attractions of momentary and passing encounters of high salience and affective power. Unable to gauge what to expect from their environment, how can they be sure that things that are true today will be there tomorrow? Have they not experienced capriciousness when things appeared stable? Unlike children who can predict their fate—good, bad, or indifferent—such youngsters cannot fathom what the future will bring. At any moment, and for no apparent reason, they may receive the kindness and support they crave; equally possible, and for equally unfathomable reasons, they may experience hostility and rejection. Having no way to determine which action will bring security and stability, such youngsters vacillate, feeling hostility, guilt, compliance, assertion, and so on. Unable to predict whether their parents will be critical or affectionate, they must be ready for hostility when most might expect commendation, assume humiliation when most would anticipate reward. Eternally "on edge" emotions build up, raw to the touch, ready to react impulsively and unpredictably at the slightest provocation.

Other advances in contemporary society have stamped deep and distinct affectively loaded impressions as well as erratic and contradictory ones. The rapidly moving, emotionally intense, and interpersonally capricious TV role models, displayed in swiftly progressing half-hour vignettes that encompass a lifetime, add to the impact of disparate, highly charged, and largely inimical value standards and behavior models. Children incorporate not only a multiplicity of selves, but an assemblage of unintegrated and discordant roles, displayed indecisively and fitfully, especially among those youngsters bereft of secure moorings and internal gyroscopes. The striking images created by this modern-day flickering parental surrogate have replaced all other sources of cultural guidance for many. By age 18, American children will have spent more time watching TV than in going to school or relating directly to their parents.

Television may be pabulum for those with comfortably internalized models of real human relationships, but for those who live in a world of diffuse values and standards, or one that has discarded parental precepts and norms, these substitute prototypes are especially powerful, even idealized and romanticized. In TV characters and story plots, vulnerable children observe successful "life stories" that capture the attention and hold the fascination of their audiences by extolling violence, danger, agonizing dilemmas, and unpredictability— each expressed and resolved in an hour or less. These are precisely the features of social behavior and emotionality that come to characterize affective and interpersonal instabilities.

Although many people have their bearings in good order, some have submerged themselves in aimless materialism. Others remain adrift in disenchantment and meaninglessness—a state of disaffected malaise. Some have attached themselves to naive causes or cults that ostensibly provide the passion and purpose they crave to give life meaning, but even these solutions too often prove empty, if not fraudulent.

Children today are rebels without a cause. Whereas earlier generations of disaffected youth were bound together by their resentments or opposition to economic or political oppression, and motivated by discernible and worthy common causes that provided both group camaraderie and a path to action, today's middle-class youngsters have no shared causes to bring them together. Well nourished and clothed, unconstrained in an open society to follow their talents and aspirations freely, the purposelessness and emptiness they experience is essentially an internal matter, a private rather than a collective affair, with no external agents against whom they can join with others to take to the streets. These rebels without a cause, unable to forgo the material comforts of home and ineffective in externalizing their inner discontents on the larger scene, yet empty and directionless, make up a goodly share of people with mental problems. Were it not for the general political, economic, and social well-being of recent times, many would have banded together, finding some inspiration or justification to act out in concert. On the other hand, as society advances further into the troubled times of the early twenty-first century, individuals may again face a climate of economic and political change that is conducive to worthy or rebellious causes.

Unfolding of Key Ideas

The following section introduces the many thinkers and innovators of the recent past who have sensitized us to the psychic consequences and personal travails of social life. Later sections focus on the creative models of social and interpersonal therapy that have evolved to help prevent and rehabilitate these psychosocial ailments.

Flowering of Social Psychology

Social psychologists drew many of their ideas from the fertile theoretical advances of the psychodynamic and phenomenological schools, as well as from Gestalt psychology, which were at their creative height in the early twentieth century. Differing somewhat from these original sources, theorists such as Kurt Lewin, Floyd Allport, and Fritz Heider, to name a few of the more prominent, synthesized disparate views and applied these individual philosophies to the understanding of individuals in their social-contextual roles. Also differing from the anthropologists and sociologists discussed in Chapter 11, most social psychologists rejected the notion (or at least the emphasis) on a group mind construct. They opted instead to examine the role of individuals in society, and how individuals and their context and social group affect one another.

Emerging from the Gestalt psychology tradition, **Kurt Lewin (1890–1947)** was perhaps the most innovative and influential of the early social psychologists. In addition to the many creative students he mentored, Lewin is best known for *field theory*, a model that used topological concepts, a mathematical tool that portrayed events using spatial regions instead of numeric measures. He devised this structure to trace life events geographically within their socioenvironmental contexts. Branching beyond Gestalt theory, Lewin was immensely popular, owing to the importance of his work as well as his charisma and extroverted personality.

Born in Prussia (in a region now part of Poland) in 1890, Lewin grew up in a middle-class Jewish family, a birthright that, in his era of Prussian anti-Semitism, harbored many vocational limitations. Much of his later work in the United States, which focused on dismantling racial prejudice, may be attributable to this aspect of his personal background. An outgoing and energetic youth, Lewin was more socially than academically inclined until his exposure to the philosophies and sciences at the gymnasium in Berlin. Here he decided to pursue a medical degree, one of the few professional careers available to Jewish candidates. Beginning at the University of Freiburg, Lewin shifted his interest to research and academia, and pursued his doctorate at the University of Berlin. After an interruption for army duty during World War I, Lewin completed his advanced degree in 1916. During his military duty, he noted an important example of the central role of human perception; during times of peace, according to Lewin, trees, rocks, and other features of the landscape were impediments to farming, but these same objects represented invaluable assets for military defense. To Lewin, the motivational needs of the observer determined the meaning of the object.

Lewin immigrated to the United States following a brief career working at the Universities of Giessen and Berlin, and in industrial management planning, a pursuit consistent with his socialist political views. With the rise of the Nazi party, Lewin left Germany and, though an opponent of military action, participated actively in the American war effort, influencing the public to support war activities and domestic initiatives. Arriving in the United States in 1933, Lewin attained an academic post first at Cornell University, and then for several years at the University of Iowa. Following World War II, he organized what was called the Research Center for Group Dynamics, established first at the Massachusetts Institute of Technology, and later at the University of Michigan following his death in 1947.

No less important than Lewin's singular contributions was his influence on numerous seminal psychologists, first in Germany and then in the United States. His students referred to him as a charming, kind, charismatic, and exciting personality, bubbling in his enthusiastic conversations with them about their studies, generating an atmosphere that effectively caught and involved their interest. In his years as a young professor in Germany, he attracted students who became well-known future psychologists, notably Bluma Zeigarnik, Tamara Dembo, Maria Rickers-Ovsiankina, and Sibylle Escalona. During his years at the University of Iowa, his doctoral students included Ronald Lippitt, Maurice Farber, and Leon Festinger, each of whom, in turn, played a major role mentoring the doctoral studies of highly productive psychologists such as Morton Deutsch, Harold Kelley, Kurt Back, Albert Pepitone, Stanley Schachter, and myself. In turn, we mentored younger scholars such as Elliot Aronson, Robert Zajonc, Judith Rodin, Lee Ross, and Michael Antoni.

In his early Iowa years, Lewin undertook an intriguing experiment to evaluate the consequences of different styles of leadership. The study was carried out with several groups of young boys who came together regularly for after-school club meetings. Three different leadership styles were employed in a careful social interaction project. Children in groups with *autocratic* leaders tended to be submissive and docile when relating directly with the leader, behaving in a generally passive and apathetic manner. When the leader left the room, however, the boys manifested a great deal of aggressive behavior. Certain members of the group evolved as scapegoats and became repetitive objects of derision. By contrast, children with *democratic* leaders engaged in group activities in a playful and convivial atmosphere in which they manifested little aggression when the leader was not present. Those in what Lewin termed the *laissez-faire* condition behaved in a somewhat disorganized and nonconstructive manner. Members interfered with one another, imposing feelings of frustration in relating that often provoked in-group aggression. Significantly, the study demonstrated parallels with larger systems of political organization in that different styles of leadership produced divergent consequences in participant behaviors.

Because the tenor of psychology at the time was heavily animalistic and behavioral, many colleagues judged studies of Lewin's type to be fuzzy-minded and softheaded—most certainly not scientific—though they evoked the actual lives led by many during the Depression and World War II. Time has proved Lewin's great

Kurt Lewin

strength to be his ability to take the vague and nebulous social psychological ideas of the1930s and 1940s, and turn them into objective, well-controlled, and systematic experiments.

Throughout his brief 14 years in the United States, Lewin created an atmosphere for research in social psychology that became a touchstone for numerous solid and researchable studies in the field. His relationships with colleagues and students also became a model for egalitarian and good-natured socializing that had important positive implications for the future of psychology. Short of stature, heavily bespectacled, and tweedy in dress, Lewin was a classic academic figure. Despite his scholarly and invariably proper appearance, he was extremely genial and outgoing, a genius not only intellectually but in his personal, impassioned, and freewheeling style. Unusually fertile in imagination, he literally sparked with ideas, both conceptual and experimental, infusing his students with numerous rich potentials for their own creative work.

Lewin's personality theory, which was consistent with phenomenology, was an outgrowth of his concept of *life space* and the topographical model. From the perspective of the here-and-now, individuals examined their life space to plan action and internalize their "maps." From this perspective, various regions became more distinct, as particular areas came to represent the family, the community, work, sports, and so forth, and each of these regions came to form an expressed component of the entire life span and personality. Thus, people circumscribed certain behaviors to specific regions. An example might be the uncensored joke-telling behavior of a man in the locker room versus his technique of beginning a boardroom presentation with a well-placed and tasteful anecdote. In the Lewinian model of total personality, people draw a boundary around all their individual regions to represent the "me" and the "not me," as well as between the regions that compose their total personality. In Lewin's representation of a personality, the more changeable and less emotionally invested regions generally were located near the outer circumference of the personality, whereas those regions associated with stronger emotions and important constructs were closer to the center. Some aspects (e.g., "profession") could extend from the outer boundary to the center of the personality, but most could be considered either more peripheral or more central. At the nucleus of this circular representation was the Ego, a product of Freud's influence on Lewin.

Lewin's notions regarding societal group dynamics significantly affected the burgeoning field of group therapy. He introduced the notion of *feedback* as the situation where group members may evaluate the behavior and work done by others within the therapeutic setting, using themselves as a benchmark for comparison. Group discussions derived from emotional reactions, feelings toward the group or its leader, or other member disclosures became the basis for further and deeper exploration of interpersonal attitudes and behaviors. Perhaps most unique in Lewin's group notions, however, was his conception of the group as a structure similar to personality. Members fulfill certain roles in the functioning of the group, each vital to its work and survival.

Invariably, conflicts arise between the various functions (member roles) fulfilled by participants; these conflicts need to be explored and resolved to achieve balance between its functions and create maximum effectiveness in its work. In turn, the change brought about within the group as a whole would act as a force on individual members. As members fulfill their roles, stagnancy of the group could lead to individual inertia; conversely, a dynamic and healthfully functioning group encouraged personal growth. This conception of group dynamics became an important force in many variants of group therapy, including the fashionable T-Groups and Encounter Groups that were popular in the mid-twentieth century on the East and West Coasts of the United States.

Perhaps Lewin's most famous quote was, "Nothing is so practical as a good theory," and this statement is now the property of general psychology. Lewin's offspring institute, the Research Center for Group Dynamics, was a wellspring of solid theoretical guideposts that consistently served social psychology for decades, both before and after his death. It also developed practical strategies, derived from theory, to accomplish social change in diverse areas such as housing, bigotry, and discrimination. Lewin led a good life, albeit brief and weighted with more responsibilities than his energetic but persistently driven body could withstand.

Though frequently overshadowed by his younger brother Gordon (see Chapter 13) and his trait theory of personality, ***Floyd Henry Allport's (1890–1971)*** major contributions to social psychology were precursors of his brother's. The elder Allport approached social psychology from a highly individualistic orientation, concentrating heavily on behavioral and biological explanations of social phenomena. Noting that earlier elucidation of the subject relied on sociologists' applications of antiquated psychological notions, he called on the field to make greater use of the then concurrent advances in behaviorism and experimental psychology. His major publication, *Social Psychology* (1924), was a landmark volume in the systematic application of this behavioral standpoint to extant situations. Until this text appeared, sociologists rather than psychologists wrote most of the works in the discipline. In his preface, Allport stated: "There is no psychology of groups which is not essentially and entirely a psychology of individuals" (p. 4).

Allport was born in Milwaukee, Wisconsin, into a home characterized by an intellectual curiosity in science and nature, but which also maintained traditional ideological and religious beliefs, a complex of influences that carried considerable weight throughout his career. His father was an industrious physician who ran his practice from the family home; his mother was a teacher who was heavily influenced by her parents' involvement in the Free Methodist Church (Allport's maternal grandmother was one of the church's founders; his paternal grandfather was of Jewish ancestry). Allport attended Harvard University, first for his undergraduate degree, and a few years later for his doctorate. Soon after he began the doctoral program, he married, was called to duty for World War I, and returned to earn his degree under Münsterberg (see Chapter 13). Spending his academic career at the Maxwell Graduate School of Syracuse University, he taught courses in the sociopolitical arena and in the undergraduate psychology department. Though known as somewhat of a loner among his academic peers, the appointment allowed him freedom and access to both departments and their bibliographic wealth, affording Allport considerable research opportunities and resources.

Allport was an uncompromising advocate of a scientific social psychology grounded in experimental studies, many of which dealt with classic problems such as performance variations in the presence of others. Although his data could not be analyzed by high-powered statistical procedures in common use today, Allport recorded a wide variety of quantitative gauges to illustrate the impact of social interaction and its potential facilitative or deleterious effects. Although a behaviorist at heart, he came to believe that introspection had a valued place in any social psychology that dealt with human behavior. In his later years, however, he concluded that group effects could not be reducible to the elements of individual responses.

In his adolescent years, the Austrian **Fritz Heider (1896–1988)** was an aspiring painter, an interest that led to his embarking on a career in perceptual psychology. Earning his doctoral degree at Graz in 1920, Heider moved to Berlin where he became acquainted with the works of Kohler, Wertheimer, and Lewin and absorbed a great deal of these pioneering Gestaltists' approaches. This influence, combined with his background in perceptual functionalism, led Heider to develop the groundwork for attribution theory, or what he called *cognitive balance theory*. In his first major paper, he posited that stimuli from the environment must be interpreted through the individual's already-established inner process and organizational system. Immigrating to the United States unexpectedly during a consultation visit to Northampton, Massachusetts, Heider accepted a position at Smith College, a position he held from 1930 to 1947, when he moved to the University of Kansas until his retirement.

Considered the father of attribution theory, Heider's person-perception research included the examination of the relationship between attitudes and cognitive organization. He noted that human subjectivity tends to color an otherwise neutral perception of an individual or a group similarly to another associated entity that already holds an assigned subjective attitude. For example, a violent criminal's siblings would be perceived negatively by virtue of a simple association, even if they were inherently peaceable, law-abiding individuals. Conversely, professors would look more favorably on average students by virtue of their camaraderie with higher-achieving cohorts. In essence, people would develop a certain attitude or predisposition to others based on their relations, associations, or identification with the individual or group, regardless of their direct association with that person or group. Inherent in this notion was the basis of his balance theory; any number of entities (e.g., persons, inanimate objects) always held a configuration of specific relations, which took on the qualities of "like," "dislike," and "belonging."

Heider initially proposed his concept of attribution as early as 1927, when both Gestaltists and philosophical phenomenologists influenced his ideas. In line with the latter's conceptions, Heider asserted that attributions of causality are not determined by objective realities, but by what people believe to be the causes of events. Thus, personal perceptions, not external reality, gauged attributions. Heider noted that people attribute greater confidence and personal warmth to good-looking people than to homely people; likewise, research subjects who received false reports on how well they did on a task attributed success on these tasks to their own efforts and abilities. By contrast, when they received false reports of failure, they attributed their lack of success to inadequacies in the tools, distracting noises, or other external causes.

Heider extended his theories into the realm of social psychology in his major publication, *The Psychology of Interpersonal Relations* (1958). One of the major themes of the book was understanding "common-sense psychology." Heider implied that if one could encapsulate the understanding of a common human being, it would be possible to predict that person's expectations and actions with reasonable precision. Arguing that scientific psychology has much to learn from the intuition and experience-based truths of everyday people, Heider adopted a kind of *functionalist subjectivism*, preferring the analysis of parables and fictional plots to traditional laboratory experimentation as the key to understanding human experience.

Kurt Lewin's student, **Leon Festinger (1919–1990),** graduated with his PhD from the University of Iowa in the early 1940s and developed a social psychological model he termed *Cognitive Dissonance Theory.* Early in his career, Festinger served as a senior statistician for a committee selecting and training aircraft pilots and accepted academic appointments at Massachusetts Institute of Technology, Universities of Michigan and Minnesota, Stanford University, and the New School for Social Research. While retaining a focus on social behavior, Festinger's ideas also encompassed cognitive processing, social compliance, perception, paleontology, and the history of early civilizations.

Raised in Brooklyn, New York, the son of Jewish immigrants from Eastern Europe, Festinger attended the City College of New York. He wandered through a variety of majors, settling by happenstance on psychology, where he became acquainted with Lewin's work under the guidance of one of his professors. Festinger became one of Lewin's first graduate students at Iowa. His interests ranged broadly from social experimentation to studies with the behaviorist, Kenneth Spence, in which he carried out a learning study on taste preferences in rats. Other examples signifying the range and diversity of his interests include his development of the first nonparametric statistical test and a mathematical decision theory, the latter part of his dissertation.

After serving in World War II, Festinger joined Lewin at the newly established Research Center for Group Dynamics at MIT. He remained there from

1945 to 1948 and played a key role in mentoring immensely talented graduate students. They spoke of him as extraordinarily intelligent, if somewhat distractible in focus and interests. Nevertheless, they characterized him as an inspiring and exhilarating mentor. He engaged them in intense intellectual discussions, and his diverse research as well as the weekly presence of distinguished visitors provided a sense of repetitive excitement.

Like his mentor, Lewin, Festinger treated his students as equals; his egalitarian style manifested itself in many ways. He insisted that they always call him by his first name and included them in his many gatherings and parties at his home, where the convivial atmosphere included the singing of international songs and vigorous group dancing. His extraordinary ability to master new material and to raise intriguing questions that had not been previously explored elicited the interest of distinguished scholars from numerous academic, political, and cultural disciplines. As one of his former students explained, Festinger discovered things no one knew before and made connections between them that were highly original, always with an elegance that led one to see that his thinking was not only superb scientifically but beautiful aesthetically. Hunt has recorded (1993) that Festinger wore Lewin's mantle following the latter's early death, thanks largely to his superb intellect, the excitement he brought to his teaching, and his daring and imaginative research studies. Not only did he emulate Lewin's boldness, but he expressed his own similar personality in doing so. Festinger was fiercely competitive, a peppery fellow of moderate size who had the tough and brash spirit of men who grew up on the tempestuous Lower East Side of New York.

Festinger's theory of cognitive dissonance dealt with the need to reduce disharmonious structures within a person's inner worldview. In this conception, the need to reduce dissonant cognitions creates motivation, as individuals seek consistency and harmony among the diverse attitudes and opinions they maintain. Further, individuals will likely display avoidant behavior toward activities or thought patterns that may increase dissonance. Although the core of his model refers to inner psychological disequilibrium, the model may be extended to the social group by means of what Festinger termed *Social Comparison Theory*. This theory posited that while cognitive dissonance existed within the individual, tactics to reduce or eliminate such disequilibrium were found not only within the cognitive set of an individual's mind; they also were a primary catalyst for reducing tensions within social peer groups. The most effective means of reducing social dissonance was to replace imbalanced elements with those that are commonly shared (Festinger, 1957).

Festinger identified many of the dynamics within and among social groups that modulate dissonance. Disagreement over some issue among social group members would easily beget increased dissonance, but mounting evidence that favored one person over another assuaged the force of dissonance. Likewise, if many members of a social group shared a belief, considering the relevance and importance of a few dissenting voices would substantially mitigate their effect, the extent of the disagreement, and the significance of the dis-agreed-on element. Reduction by a member, then, would be alleviated by shifting one's opinion, winning others over to one's opinion, or by dissociating oneself from the group. Of primary importance, according to Festinger, was the innate group tendency toward uniformity and cohesion, a natural drive that influences groups, albeit not always successfully, toward cohesive resolution.

A psychologist of interpersonal relations, **William Carl Schutz (1925–   )**, earned his PhD at the University of California at Los Angeles, taught at several major universities, and became an associate-in-residence at the Esalen Institute, an imaginative setting for personal exploration and expression in the encounter group format. Studying group compatibility and productivity throughout his career, Schutz identified several variables derived from psychoanalysis. He examined *power orientation*, a dependence-counterdependence polarity whereby individuals subscribe to (and depend on) a class-driven hierarchy and meet their individual needs by conforming to rules, obeying the leader, or becoming the leader. Individuals may also respond to a *personal orientation*, another polarity structure based on personalness versus counterpersonalness, whereby needs are met by an individual's likability, rather than status. Finally, individuals may be characterized by *assertiveness*, whereby they emphatically state their view in a balanced but vigorous manner. Within a group, compatibility depended on reciprocal or complementary patterns of individual personality stances (e.g., a balance of assertive and personally oriented members, and not too many power-oriented individuals), higher productivity with tasks requiring less time pressure and cooperation, effectiveness in matching members with positions, and efficient use of member resources.

Related to these group dynamics, Schutz identified three basic interpersonal needs: *inclusion, control,* and *affection.* The first, inclusion, essentially referred to identity, as it related to being a unique person recognized and belonging to a larger social context in a way that elicits appropriate attention of the group. Control, the second element, involved decision-making processes of people within the group, one's personal sense of authority over others and group actions and decisions, and the need to be controlled by others. The last, affection, dealt with individuals' need for emotional feelings between themselves and significant others, in dyadic form. Affection involved various levels of a love-hate polarity, and occurred only between two people, or one person and the group at large. These three elements, according to Schutz, formed the basis for predicting and explaining all interpersonal behaviors.

Numerous social psychologists carried out the innovative work that Kurt Lewin had stimulated some decades earlier. Notable among these was *Philip Zimbardo,* who conducted a series of studies simulating prison life in which subjects played the part of guards and prisoners. Zimbardo illustrated how sadistic behavior could be generated among individuals who were not predisposed to it. *Stanley Milgram* conducted a similar project reflecting obedience to authority.

He attracted a number of volunteers into a study ostensibly to study the effects of punishment on learning. The volunteers served as teachers; they were led to believe that the shocks they administered to "hidden students" were being applied to real subjects, when, in fact, no subjects existed. According to their instructions, the volunteers were to intensify their shocks when the ostensible subject performed poorly. Over 60% of the volunteers continued to administer the increasingly severe electric shock even though the fake subject shouted and screamed in agony. Milgram's study, though illustrating the phenomenon of obedience to authority, engendered intense criticism owing to the deceptions involved and the possibility of lasting harm to the study's volunteers when confronted with the reality of having carried out extremely unethical behaviors.

The crisis generated in the Zimbardo and Milgram studies raised questions about the ethics and consequences of research in social psychology that resulted in wise decisions concerning the ethics of research studies in all medical and psychological fields. *Elliot Aronson*, another young and innovative researcher, well aware of the implications of these earlier problematic studies, concluded that social psychologists were still in a singular position to have a profound and positive impact on social lives by providing an understanding to important phenomena such as conformity, prejudice, and aggression.

Founding and Elaborating Social Work

Little progress can be expected in therapy if the patient's everyday environment provides few gratifications and is filled with tension and conflict. Like the proverbial high-priced automobile that uses up gasoline faster than it can be pumped in, an unwholesome life situation may set patients back faster than therapy can move them forward. For these reasons, it may be necessary to control or modify disruptive home or work influences, or remove patients entirely from these disorganizing effects.

Beyond relief and protection, the profession of social work has helped individuals achieve positive therapeutic ends such as releasing potentials or developing social skills. The alleviation of situational stress and the exploitation of situational opportunities for constructive change constitute social workers' historic roles.

The Victorian zeitgeist influenced pioneers in social casework, just as it had affected Freud, but they disrupted the status quo in a different way. Rather than examining individuals' particular socially instilled repressions, early schools of social work examined injustices and inequities created by society-at-large. In an altruistic spirit, theorists concentrated on two major tactics to eradicate inequalities inherent in civilization: (1) They became advocates for social justice, equalities, and opportunity for everyone regardless of race, social class, religion, and so on; and (2) they worked with affected individuals and socially troubled families (they later adopted formal family therapy strategies as well) in an effort to empower them in pursuing social goals that meshed with their innate talents. Although social work is not a new field (some precursors date back to ancient times), its modern era may be traced to the early settlement houses identified in England by Jane Addams, who then established the first community home in the United States. At the same time, many of these figures not only became involved as leaders of their local community, but helped establish governing councils and legal boards at the state and federal level as well. Effective and worthy social workers approached their task from both the individual and the societal levels.

The American social work, child welfare, and public welfare pioneer **Julia Clifford Lathrop (1858–1932)** was born in Illinois. Graduating from Vassar College in 1880, Lathrop set many precedents for public welfare, not the least of which was the establishment in 1900 of the first juvenile court in the United States. In 1912, President William Howard Taft appointed her as the first leader of what is now known as the Children's Bureau.

Not limiting her scope to impoverished children, Lathrop sought, in her initial mission statement, to create opportunity and care for all children, regardless of circumstance. The new bureau was designed to gather, organize, and analyze relevant information that, until then, had been scattered about many disparate government agencies., It sought to address such issues as degeneracy, child labor, desertion, illegitimacy, infant mortality, and orphanages.

The most politically charged, pressured, and controversial issue was child labor; Lathrop, as her first investigation, wisely sidestepped this hotbed issue and explored what percentage of U.S. infants died, and why. Despite the Industrial Revolution and the nation's rising position as the leader of the modern world, the infant mortality rate in the United States was much higher than in Europe. Lathrop's findings, assessed by studying birth records (rather than working backward from infant death, which was the standard approach), uncovered a pattern of maternal and infant care characterized by underpaid fathers, overworked and uneducated mothers, and an inordinate amount of uncontrollable life hazards. She determined that sanitization, licensing of midwives, and improved prenatal care would dramatically improve the mortality rate. Over the next six years, due in large part to the efforts of this new agency, birth registration statistics and infant mortality improved tremendously.

In 1899, following a visit to the world's first-known settlement house in London, England, **Jane Addams (1860–1935)** established Hull House on Chicago's West Side. It was America's first home of this kind, and thereby laid the foundation for a rich social work tradition. The settlement house concept provided for leaders such as Addams and Lathrop to live among the residents of the community, as the

Jane Addams

facility was situated within the neighborhood it served. Hull House was located in a crowded, immigrant-driven industrial and residential neighborhood that included Italians, Russian and Polish Jews, Irish, Germans, Greeks, and Bohemians. Beyond being a settlement home for recent immigrants and poverty-stricken people, the facility provided the larger community with such services as an employment bureau, a meeting room for other community organizations, libraries, an art gallery, kindergarten and day-care facilities for working mothers, and educational programs about art and music for neighborhood residents. This facility became the model for similar organizations throughout the country. Addams became one of the most influential women of her era through her mission to better understand the disenfranchised and improve their lives. She worked extensively to elicit social change and achieve a greater balance of opportunities across socioeconomic and cultural lines. Her stance as a pacifist during World War I briefly earned her a reputation as "the most *dangerous* woman in America" by many of the self-proclaimed superpatriots of the war period, but this labeling was short-lived.

Laura Jane Addams was born in Illinois in 1860, the eighth of nine children born to an active, community-leading family. A less than vigorous young woman who was troubled by a spinal curvature (later corrected by surgery), she graduated as valedictorian from Rockford Female Seminary in 1881 (with her degree conferred one year later when the school became accredited as Rockford College for Women). Her college education, uncommon among women of the late nineteenth century, left her unmarried and without a true feeling of purpose. Over the next several years, Addams began medical training, which she dropped because of her poor health, and traveled through Europe, where she finally found her future direction in East London's Toynbee Hall, the first known settlement house. This visit solidified a vague vision of helping less fortunate people that she had considered since childhood. She and her friend Ellen Gates Starr returned to Chicago to begin a similar project in one of the city's less privileged industrial communities, renting a mansion built originally for Charles Hull. A great success, Hull House became host to over 2,000 daily visitors at its apex, and it inspired a major movement across the country, as other social workers and volunteers modeled similar projects after the Chicago project.

A devout feminist, Addams worked against the traditional paradigm of "females are social workers; males are sociologists" that pervaded both fields. Despite being qualified by traditional criteria as a sociologist, Addams (along with others who associated with her) was ignored by the American Sociological Society. Addams reacted by sponsoring "sociologist meetings" across gender and culture boundaries at Hull House. In the following decade, due largely to her lifelong commitment to poverty issues, children, and equity across culture and gender divides, the scientific, sociological, and social work communities recognized her outstanding contributions. In 1931, just four years before her death from cancer, Addams, who by then was considered the "Mother of Social Work," was awarded the Nobel Peace Prize.

Mary Ellen Richmond (1861–1928) rose through the ranks, from clerical worker to head of Baltimore's Charitable Organization Society (COS). Despite lacking an advanced degree in her field, she was among the first to establish a consistent method for stressing the personal side of social casework. Like Lathrop and Addams, Richmond was born in Illinois. She was the only child of Henry and Lavinia Richmond to survive infancy, but was sent to her grandmother's home in Baltimore at the age of three, following her mother's untimely death. After graduating from high school, she cared for an elderly aunt and developed an interest in charity work. Richmond started as an office employee of Baltimore's COS, eventually becoming a regional executive of the COS movement.

Richmond may be best known for having followed the original theory of the COS: the practice of looking outside the *material* (e.g., impoverished) factors of people in need, and looking to the more *immaterial* factors, ranging from character faults to moral factors and personality dimensions. Beyond the traditional meaning of charity, as limited to financial easing, Richmond pursued what was called "friendly visiting," and was instrumental in its evolution into "deliberate social casework," using the methodology of both clinical psychology and socioenvironmental modification.

Refining the approaches for applied social work of her day, Richmond set about establishing consistent and effective social casework. She described the individuals being helped as *clients*, foreshadowing the use of the term by the humanistic schools of psychotherapy in later decades. Richmond set about defining *Social Diagnosis*, the title of her major book (1917). Here she described the process of information gathering as a systematic but imaginative progression that enabled the "visitor" (as social caseworkers were described in this era) to conceptualize the client's difficulties in a broad, environmental context. Incorporating not only protocol social work theory, but the recent advances of clinical psychology and psychiatry, Richmond sought to uncover and work with the dynamic balance of people in their social contexts.

As noted earlier, social work has traditionally played a central role in planning and controlling extratherapeutic elements and their social opportunities. Among social workers' traditional goals are assisting either individuals or families in removing or improving deleterious economic and interpersonal conditions. More recently, however, social casework has become psychologically oriented to facilitate individuals' abilities to cope with their personal affairs, essentially functioning as individual rather than as social therapists. *Jessie Taft* and *Faye Karpf*, who adopted psychoanalyst Otto Rank's ideas and methods in the 1930s, began this movement toward psychotherapy.

The historical sequence of social work education, and hence its orientation, changed over the twentieth century. In the 1930s, the formal social work accreditation group agreed that the profession should require 2 years of graduate studies leading to a leading to a master's degree (MSW). Although support remained for undergraduate training in the field, most limited training programs were gradually phased out. Another major curriculum change occurred at the end of the 1950s. It shifted an earlier emphasis on community organization and public welfare themes toward human behavior, sociology, and clinical psychology. Increasingly, students received training with a strong therapeutic slant akin to that of psychologists and psychiatrists because of the growing market for direct treatment services in agencies that helped children, families, delinquents, and the mentally ill. Even those trained prior to the 1950s came to regard their efforts as less organization and community oriented and more related to direct patient clinical service. This change in orientation did not come about without conflict and disagreement. So-called old-timers criticized the increasing emphasis on therapeutic casework, or what came to be designated as *clinical social work*. Particularly telling was the argument that this new emphasis, however much it appealed to the growing middle-class client, was not relevant and useful to the needs and problems of poor people or minority groups.

Nevertheless, the trend toward the clinical practice of psychotherapy became increasingly strong by the mid-1960s. Two distinct directions emerged within the social work profession. One moved toward the practice of psychotherapy. The other reflected the political enthusiasm of the 1960s that aimed at poverty and racism, an approach to community needs that was deeper than mere public assistance or mental health clinics could reach. Nevertheless, the focus on high-level treatment methods grew the social work profession. Clinical social work became the draw for young future professionals who focused on a society where affluence did not solve life's difficulties, but rather appeared to lead to a pervasive malaise about personal relationships and work, as well as disorders that reflected breakdowns in responsible behavior and authority attitudes. With added training and a growing confidence in their skills, social workers helped middle- and upper-class individuals who needed to adapt to their changing life circumstances. This new direction of the field captured the imagination of a reborn profession, giving it a level of identity greater than it had in former years when it focused on poverty and social welfare.

Instituting Group Therapies

As with individual therapy, literally hundreds of techniques exist for conducting group therapy. These techniques vary in their settings, the number of individuals involved, the frequency with which the group meets, the time period of the group's existence, and the group's treatment goals and purposes. The formal organization that encompasses some 4,000 active members today is called the *American Group Psychotherapy Association*; perhaps 10 times that number employ group methods in the United States today. Its informal origins may be traced to the early Greeks and Romans, though more formal methods are largely an American and British development of the past century or so.

In the early twentieth century, a small band of therapists employed early approximations of group procedures. *Joseph Hersey Pratt*, a Boston physician, held special classes as early as 1905 for tubercular patients, advising them not only on proper habits of physical care, but on methods to deal with the emotional complications that accompanied their illness. In 1909, *L. Cody Marsh*, a minister, delivered inspirational lectures to groups of state hospital patients; he noted that if patients participated in discussions following his talks it greatly enhanced the therapeutic benefits. Jacob L. Moreno, a Viennese psychiatrist, instituted similar group discussion therapies in the 1920s, which evolved gradually into his well-known *psychodramas*. In the 1930s, Samuel R. Slavson initiated programs of activity group therapy for children between 8 and 15 years of age. Also in the 1930s, Joshua Bierer, Louis Wender, and Paul Schilder employed Adlerian and Freudian approaches in the treatment of hospital groups.

Psychotherapy groups evolved over the next several decades. Although psychoanalysis, in general, was loath in mid-century to focus its attentions on group processes, most modern group theories have borrowed psychoanalytic concepts or have otherwise been influenced by psychoanalysis. Around 1938, Alexander Wolf started a formal psychoanalytic approach to group work, with a particular interest in carrying out individual psychotherapy in the group setting. This approach emphasized recreating the family of origin for each participant. Although group dynamics can be a distraction, according to Wolf, the *group ego* can facilitate a deeper understanding of the individual's dynamics.

Other analytic schools of thought made pioneering group efforts as well. Alfred Adler (see Chapter 7) is credited as the first European psychiatrist to employ group techniques, and his disciples brought his *Individual Psychology* to the United States. Most notable was the primary Adlerian translator, Rudolph Dreikurs, who was especially enthusiastic about group methods. Adlerians viewed humans as social creatures needing support and corrective opportunities from others, and noted that many disorders stem from undue self-absorption to the neglect of social interests. They regarded group processes as an effective therapeutic setting that facilitated insights into participants' lifestyles. J. L. Moreno, mentioned earlier, developed one of the more innovative group methods, the psychodrama, in which participants acted out or dramatized life situations and used catharsis as a therapeutic process. The *client-centered therapy* modality of Carl Rogers seemed a natural fit for group therapy applications, given its emphasis on interpersonal trust. His applications of group work extended well beyond the therapy group proper to include political summits and peace workshops. Mary and Robert Goulding, working from a transactional analysis basis (see Eric Berne, later in this chapter), demonstrated early efforts at an integration of psychodrama, Gestalt, and behavioral milieus within a group paradigm. These are but a few examples of the influence of group techniques. As these developments occurred, a rapid spurt of interest became apparent in the academic literature.

Recent decades have seen the vigorous exploration and expansion of group psychotherapy modalities as viable, pragmatic, and often preferred means of personal growth and mental health improvement. In the past several years, a growing awareness has emerged of the paucity of available mental health services to meet an increasing number of patients. At the same time, many patients found that they could neither afford individual psychotherapeutic services nor be adequately covered financially by an ever-tightening managed care environment. Furthermore, bound only by the ingenuity and creativity of the clinician, groups have taken on a wide array of forms to meet the needs of an increasingly diverse patient population. Future possibilities to meet specific needs seem infinite. The manifest need for more efficient, situation-, and problem-tailored forms of therapy led to a rapid growth of group treatment methods at the end of the twentieth century.

Beyond these simple pragmatics, group therapists have contended that the semi-realistic group setting allows patients to display their problematic interpersonal transactions in a way that is out of reach to traditional dyadic therapy. Subsequently, patients can acquire new skills and strategies in a setting not unlike their natural environment. The exchanges among group participants provide numerous opportunities to observe distortions in perception and behavior that aggravate and perpetuate interpersonal difficulties. Because mutual support characterizes the group's atmosphere and intent, members can rectify these distortions and acquire more socially adaptive alternatives in their stead. Moreover, as patients express their deeper feelings and attitudes with the knowledge that fellow group members share similar experiences, they gradually achieve better self-acceptance and a greater empathic stance toward others. They also gain freedom from self-defeating interpersonal strategies and participate more effectively in social relationships.

It may not be an exaggeration to say that there are nearly as many variants of groups as there have been practitioners of the art. Over its history, there have been directive and nondirective therapists, interpretation-oriented practitioners and those who invite the patient's formulation, those who become equals in group discussions and unburden their own feelings and attitudes, as well as others who remain aloof and detached. Some therapists have employed group methods as adjuncts to concurrent individual treatment, whereas others have dispensed entirely with individual sessions. Many have recommended that group members meet in sessions without the therapist; others have opposed such meetings. There have been "closed" and "open" groups, the former maintaining the same group members through fixed periods of treatment, the latter continuing indefinitely with new members added as old members graduate. Some groups have been formed on the basis of a common problem such as delinquency or marital difficulties; others have been planned to be as diverse as possible. The sheer heterogeneity of the group construct defies simple, straightforward classification.

Parloff (1967) outlined one of the more innovative approaches to differentiate the theories of group process. Each of the three perspectives that he outlined illustrates the unique benefits of group treatment relative to other modes of therapy. The first, termed *intrapersonalists*, asserts that the group is an effective medium for dealing with intrapsychic conflicts, transference, and resistance, as patients recognize that they are not alone in experiencing such unconscious issues. The second category, *transactionalists*, characterizes the group as a unique setting for understanding how people relate to others and for group members to vicariously learn about their social selves by participating in a minisocial setting. The third differentiation is termed *intergralists*, in which the primary emphasis is on the group as a whole. From this vantage point, all members of the group share aspects of their unconscious world together, particularly their relationship to authority figures, including impulses related to aggression and intimacy.

Rejecting classical psychoanalysis in favor of more spontaneous and cathartic therapeutic breakthroughs, **Jacob Levy Moreno (1889–1974),** a Jewish Romanian psychiatrist, developed one of the most creative models of group treatment, the *psychodrama*, a method designed to stimulate the open portrayal of unconscious attitudes and emotions through spontaneous playacting. As early as 1908, Moreno, inspired by his observation of Viennese schoolchildren at play, suggested that spontaneity and creativity were central in terms of healthy interactions with others. His model was rooted in his "Theatre of Spontaneity," which he began in Vienna in 1921. Here, nonprofessional actors improvised stories based on newspaper headlines or other current events suggested by the audience, who were invited to share aspects of their experience in observing the role play. In these short-lived, intense give-and-take interactions, Moreno observed that personal issues influenced both the choice and manner of presentation of the topic, and that both participants and observers experienced a catharsis, or a release of pent-up psychological feelings. From these early discoveries and developments, psychodrama was born.

Moreno immigrated to the United States in 1925, and set up a school for psychodrama in New York. Mainstream psychiatry did not take his ideas seriously, as classical psychoanalysis still largely dominated it, but Moreno's humor and dynamic style overcame the spurs of rejection and criticism. The influence of psychodrama became readily apparent with the humanistic and group developments of the 1960s, as Moreno's innovative techniques appeared not only in drama-oriented group therapy, but throughout many other psychotherapeutic approaches.

In Moreno's psychodrama, several patients and at least one therapist enacted an unrehearsed series of scenes in which they assumed roles simulating significant people in their real lives. Patients were encouraged to relive and express with dramatic intensity feelings and thoughts that ostensibly could not be tapped or vented through everyday conversation in problematic relationships. The intent was to aid patients in discharging repressed feelings and to test out new, more liberated reactions. Moreno (or a group leader) would assume the role of director and would solicit a problem situation from one of the group participants, who would subsequently assume the role of the protagonist. The director

Jacob Levy Moreno

would then facilitate action by suggesting means of dramatizing the situation, and the other group members would assume supporting roles (or as Moreno called them, *auxiliary egos*) in the drama. At some point, the director would call for "role reversal," a technique that was intended among other goals to aid patients in gaining insight into how others view them. Thus, two patients took the role of one another and portrayed, in caricature form, the attitudes and behaviors they believed depicted the person whose role they assumed. Another frequently used technique appeared when a group member other than the protagonist sensed that what the protagonist said was less than genuine. The group member would then go up behind the protagonist and speak on that person's behalf. The protagonist had the opportunity, then, to either repeat those words in agreement or refute them. Besides these two well-known techniques, over 200 others focused on preparing patients for future difficulties, desensitizing inner fears, and bolstering skills necessary for successful resolution. Group therapy innovators frequently encounter what they call the "Moreno Problem": When trying to develop new group techniques, they often find that Moreno had already invented what they are formulating.

Most psychodrama episodes are similar to a fictional story line; and in fact, the sessions are formally divided into three stages: the "warm-up" phase, the "action" phase, and the "sharing and discussion" phase. An expository element to the story emerges as a protagonist is identified and a context is developed. Following this, a gradual buildup of events and emotions occurs until a rapid energy rise becomes apparent, and a cathartic resolution is manufactured. Just as in fiction, catharsis is followed by a denouement; that is, a period of relaxation, debriefing, and absorption.

The primary value of Moreno's psychodrama and other role-playing groups was that it simulated, more closely than conversational expression ever could, real problem situations; it readily achieved generalization from the therapeutic situation to the extratherapeutic world. Additionally, patients could be "carried away" in their role portrayals, enabling them to bring their deepest emotions and attitudes to the surface. Consequently, unconscious forces could surge forth, coming into sharp focus and could be dealt with immediately and effectively through therapeutic coactors' on-the-spot manipulations. Psychodramatic methods, then, according to their proponents, often held more power and efficiency than the pallid insight-discussion techniques for exposing and resolving deeply repressed unconscious materials.

Though Moreno lived to see the popularization of his model, he died in 1974 before its further growth in the later 1970s. His epitaph read, "Here lies the man who brought laughter back into psychiatry."

Samuel Slavson (1890–1981), undoubtedly one of the most recognizable names in the history of the group therapies largely due to his pioneering efforts in the 1930s, was not trained either in group work or psychology; rather, he was a civil engineer. He was entirely self-trained in all facets of interpersonal relations and was deeply involved with individuals and social difficulties long before he became familiar with the works of Freud. Thus, he developed his early contribution, *activity group therapy,* which he established at the Jewish Board of Guardians in the 1930s, as well as several of his other treatment methods, prior to his familiarity with psychoanalytic principles. Nevertheless, his activity group work with moderately emotionally disturbed children in a controlled play environment evoked deep psychoanalytic themes, though he did not directly interpret them. Several decades later, Slavson underwent two personal analyses by a trainee of Freud, and it was in the context of related revelations that he came to understand the relevance of psychoanalytic principles and the deeper unconscious instincts and motivations of the human psyche. Slavson is also credited with being the catalyst for the changing view of group therapy from an adjunct technique supplemental to individual therapy, to the primary modality of an individual's treatment. As he became exposed to psychoanalytic psychology, Slavson's ideas evolved and he began melding educational goals, psychodynamics, and group processes in the spirit of experiential learning.

Slavson first developed activity group therapy as a technique for remediating social difficulties in children and adolescents, and it subsequently served as a model for group programs of occupational and social rehabilitation in hospitals and outpatient clinics. Patients joined in a club-life situation to pursue common sets of activities and interests such as games, handicrafts, travel, painting, or dancing. The method was most applicable to patients either with social deficits or with those whose behaviors had been socially provocative. The outward appearance of these groups was not unlike a normal social club; it was designed, however, to expand and strengthen each patient's repertoire of adaptive and wholesome interpersonal skills.

Slavson's activity therapy contributed a systematic rationale for resolving the multiple transferences that arise in group settings. In contrast to other treatment groups, however, activity therapy made little or no attempt to expose and discuss patients' pathological attitudes and emotions; it simply provided a social behavior-learning environment. Although feelings were freely vented within broad limits, there was no effort to develop insight into the roots or character of these feelings. Rather, adaptive learning accrued by the simple process of participating and sharing in group projects, a cohesion and binding, a growing together like a symbiotic organism. Guided subtly but firmly by an observant and sympathetic therapist, patients gradually were led, it was hoped, to acquire increased social initiative and group responsibility. By quietly and indirectly discouraging untoward behaviors and by facilitating and openly rewarding constructive alternatives, therapists molded the pattern of group interaction in directions suitable to the varied growth needs of each member.

Out of pure necessity, the psychoanalyst **Alexander Wolf (1907–1997)** began the first credited psychodynamic group work in 1938. Faced with patients who needed psychotherapeutic services, but who lacked the financial ability to pay for expensive and lengthy individual psychoanalysis, Wolf began group work to avoid turning needy patients away. As he began this endeavor and became more proficient at applying classic psychoanalytic concepts to group process, it became his primary mode of therapy. However, like those analysts who followed him, Wolf emphasized that the group modality was really individual psychoanalysis of each participant within the group, with the additional advantage of interaction, rather than a group process per se.

In much the same way as analytic therapeutic models handle dyadic interaction, analytical groups take inspiration from one or another of the many varieties of psychoanalytic theory. In common with individual analytical approaches, the focus of group analysis is to expose unconscious attitudes and strategies, discharge repressed emotions, and reconstruct childhood-rooted pathological trends. This is accomplished, as in classical techniques, through free association, dream interpretation, and analysis of the complex network of multiple transference relationships that emerge between patients. Wolf expanded on these traditional analytic methods by advancing a step-by-step technique for uprooting early memories, penetrating unconscious conflicts and defenses, and working through the intricate pattern of group transference relationships. He contended that the exposure and resolution of unconscious materials and transference phenomena occurs more rapidly and thoroughly in groups than would be possible in individual analytical treatment.

Wolf stressed the re-creation of the family of origin within groups, which allowed members to recall distant early memories and unresolved issues derived from family dynamics. Reactions to specific members and the group leader, according to Wolf, gave insight and symbolic clues as to their early relationships with family members. The primary focus of psychoanalytic group therapy was initial personality regression, with the ultimate intent of strengthening the ego, from which a robust and creative process of independence would grow.

Rudolph Dreikurs (1897–1972), a student of Alfred Adler, was largely responsible for translating and conveying Adler's Individual Psychology to the United States in the early twentieth century. One of Dreikurs' earliest efforts involved the addition of "audience members" in family counseling in 1928, a technique Adler first used some six years earlier with a different population. The rationale for this addition was to complement the core of Adlerian theory; this audience, who represented the caring nature of the community, demonstrated human beings' socially constructive nature. The very presence of the community was thought to carry therapeutic value, and Dreikurs subsequently added "observer" roles to his treatment of alcoholic patients by arranging to see them in groups. This model, consistent with the Adlerian conception of humans as social entities able to thrive only in context with others, was considered to be an ideal treatment milieu and was extended to include other focused groups as well as general mental health treatment.

What evolved from this model of "observers-therapist-patient" was a unique group process that bore the trademark dynamics of Adler's Individual Psychology. Group members reflected their experience within their family constellation, exposed their perceptions of "inner inferiority," and learned from each other how to best implement compensatory, socially constructive behavior. In addition to developing the group model of Adlerian psychotherapy, Dreikurs was the primary proponent of Individual Psychology's adoption and popularization among American clinicians. To this date, the Adler Institute in Chicago, which Dreikurs founded, continues to thrive as a center of activity for this branch of psychology.

Joshua Bierer (1901–1978), another of Adler's students, left Vienna, fleeing from the Nazi invasion in 1938, and established a facility at Runwell Hospital near London where he conceived what he termed a *villa* system. In accord with Adler's ideas, Bierer believed that efficient techniques could be employed to facilitate patients' increasing independence from their therapists by inspiring an active and "self-deciding" approach to life. In 1939, he helped patients form a social club at Runwell called the "Sunnyside House," in which patients assumed leadership roles in a therapeutic community. This therapeutic group ran autonomously: Patients elected their own officers, published a magazine, and met regularly on a three-times-weekly basis.

The Mill Hill Emergency unit associated with the Maudsley Hospital in London adopted the model Bierer had established. A young psychiatric resident, **Maxwell Jones (1901–1970),** who took on a leadership role for this innovative program, carried out the notion of a therapeutic community, as Bierer initially formulated it. Jones soon became a leading figure in England, accurately assessing the existence of an inpatient culture within mental hospitals and other inpatient settings. He encouraged the development of treatment methods that were a direct outgrowth of "multipatient community living." Whereas others created milieu programs that used hospital staff as role models for the inpatients, Jones, later at the Belmont Hospital in London, became a major founder of what he described in his book *Therapeutic Community* (1953). Characterized by the *open ward* policies that emerged in the inpatient hospitals of the mid-twentieth century, Jones's therapeutic community was a further extension of his early approach with hospitalized patients.

Jones would lecture to patients three hours a week about the structures and functions of the nervous system, and how neural functions related to their experienced difficulties. This psychoeducational activity, which took place in a large group setting, demonstrated the efficiency with which patients learned to surmount social impediments in a group setting, and set a precedent for learning through group interaction. Jones noted that these inpatients, who were referred largely because of long-term social relationship difficulties, might experience significant advantages in their treatment if they would learn social interaction within the peer group of the hospital, fully inclusive of patients and staff. Funded by various ministries in 1947, Jones opened a hundred-bed unit oriented to the problems of the "chronically unemployed neurotic," a hospital unit that came to be called the Industrial Neurosis Ward.

Interestingly, Bierer's and Jones's notion of a therapeutic community was extended to work with troubled outpatients. It was judged that nonhospitalized mentally ill also could benefit from the manner with which social rehabilitation began to characterize asylums both in the Americas and in England. Thus, in 1946, *Ewen Cameron* established a day hospital at the Allan Memorial Institute in Montreal. In 1948, Bierer did likewise in a comparable social day hospital in England. This treatment concept served important social and psychiatric functions that became well established throughout England in the 1950s. This British model served, in turn, as a signal stimulus for the emergence of community approaches to psychiatry in the United States in the 1960s.

With no lack of courage or imagination, the therapeutic community, as Jones and others conceived it, not only used the patient's social environment for treatment purposes, but the context of living within the ward became the treatment itself. Therapy in the usual sense was discarded in favor of an acculturation process into an egalitarian social structure composed of doctors, nurses, ancillary staff, and patients. Traditional social-hierarchical assumptions (e.g., doctor-nurse relative power) were forsaken, and therapy consisted primarily of incidental contacts occurring naturally among patients in the day-to-day living within the ward. The acculturation process, inherently an emotional learning exercise, was proposed to be as effective as the formal analytic models that were most popular at the time. Jones's model went a step further to include a "meta-therapy" component of conquering fresh neuroses created by the stresses of being an inpatient in a hospital setting. This composite treatment scheme essentially meant that all the time spent in the residential facility was considered treatment time, and all the patient's activities needed to be integrated into a therapeutic program. Ambitious as it appeared, this strategy became immensely popular in ensuing years, serving as the model for hospital experiments in both Great Britain and the United States in the 1960s and 1970s.

Expanding Family Therapy

Family therapy modalities developed from the belief that the patient who sought therapy was often but one member of a family functioning in less than healthy ways. Interactions between family members often formed a complex of shared relational difficulties, and the *identified patient* (the family member whom others believed to be the problematic one) seemed to be merely its most dramatic symptom. What was more, positive change in one family member through individual psychotherapy might be a near impossibility, as change in one member was likely to affect the others, and that change was likely to be characterized by a more crystallized, defensive, and immovable family system.

The primary patient's daily interactions were enmeshed in a system of interlocking attitudes and behaviors that not only intensified personal pathology, but sustained the family's pathological functioning. Each member, through reciprocal perceptual and behavioral distortions, reinforced pathogenic reactions in others, thus contributing to a vicious circle of self-perpetuating responses. It follows logically from this premise that therapy had to intervene not only with the patient, but with the total family. A systemic therapy for the entire family unit was needed.

Indeed, the family unit has long been viewed as crucial to the physical and emotional well-being of the individual, as the precursors for formal family theory date back at least as far as Freud and Adler with their emphases on early experience and role within the family constellation, respectively. From a more universal standpoint, many social science disciplines acknowledge the centrality of the family unit on the individual. This concept dates back to the very beginnings of civilization, yet psychological and educational models had not advanced to help the family as a unit until the previous century. Prior to explanations of individual distress as a possible product of insufficient nurturing, families were commonly regarded as the victims of the pathological member's neurological or moral failure. As interpersonal explanations became more prevalent and accepted, the family came to be viewed more often as the perpetrator of pathology. The social work, marriage and family life education, and marriage counseling movements, begun around 1900, formed the roots of family therapy. They emphasized the family as the unit of concern, and their preventive education models were designed to indoctrinate family members toward domestic life. These efforts paved the way for their students to begin discussing family dynamics and relationships, prompting further modifications in these models toward formal family therapy, but they were characterized initially by a rampant amateurism.

Many variants of family therapy theory and technique have been posited to achieve the goal of disentangling reciprocally reinforcing pathological family relations. Generally, family therapy models involve therapists bringing several members of the family together to explore major areas of conflict that have perpetuated their difficulties. In this process, they clarify misunderstandings, dissolve barriers to communication, and neutralize areas of prejudice, hostility, guilt, and fear. These family therapists gradually disengage destructive tendencies within the family system and enable members to experiment with healthier relational patterns. By instilling sounder attitudes and behaviors, and by supporting family members as they test out new patterns, therapists work toward resolving not only the difficulties of the primary patient, but pathological trends that have taken root in all members.

Leader of the *communications* approach to family interaction, **Gregory Bateson (1904–1980)** was significantly more interested in the science of communication and in theory building than in therapy. More an anthropologist than a clinician, and hardly limited to those two fields, he was an early pioneer in the field of cybernetics, an "antipsychiatry" figure championed by the1960s' counterculture, who also studied zoology and ethnology. As a psychologically oriented anthropologist, he was strongly opposed to scientific models which reduced everything to physical materiality, and argued extensively that the "mind-matter" split, so pervasive in empirical science, was nonsensical. His books, *Steps to an Ecology of Mind* (1973) and *Mind and Nature* (1980) are testimonials to his view that "mind" is a constituent part of what we call "material reality." Within the mental health sciences, Bateson is perhaps most recognized as the inventor of the infamous double-bind theory of schizophrenia, which states that the condition was caused by incongruous and conflicting parental injunctions that created a no-win situation for the patient.

Gregory Bateson was born in Grantchester, England, in 1904, the son of an eminent and pioneering geneticist, William Bateson. After his undergraduate education at St. Johns College–Cambridge University in natural history, he traveled extensively, returning several years later to Cambridge to pursue a master's degree in anthropology, which he completed in 1930. In the next several years, he traveled to New Guinea, published his first book, *Naven* (1936), about the Iatmul people of New Guinea, and met his future wife, Margaret Mead (see Chapter 11).

Between 1953 and 1962, Bateson led a research team in a series of behavioral science studies in California, which came to be known as the "Bateson Project," and which would lead to some of the most influential works in the field of marital and family therapy. Following a grant received from the Rockefeller Foundation, Bateson and his colleagues began studying the nature of communications, specifically among schizophrenic families. Included in this group were future contributors such as Don Jackson, John Weakland, Jay Haley, and Virginia Satir. Bateson and his colleagues stressed the importance of circular causality in communication; these ideas emanated from in-depth interviews conducted with hospitalized patients at the Palo Alto Veterans Hospital. During these interviews, the pattern known as the *double-bind* emerged. Essentially, this construct involves multiple levels of family communication, usually between parent and child (or other very important familial relationships), and always contains two conflicting injunctions, one of which is abstract, implied, threatening, or a combination of these elements. Victims of this bind are confronted with an impossible directive; they must break one of the injunctions to satisfy the other, and vice versa, and they eventually perceive the world only in terms of double-binds.

Known as the Grandfather of Family Therapy, **Nathan Ackerman (1908–1971),** one of the earliest psychoanalytically oriented family therapists, anticipated the emergence of the object relations movement in psychodynamic theory in the mid-1950s, and instituted a nameless but formal technique that became one of the more well-received approaches to family treatment. Though his descendants (e.g., Salvador Minuchin) strayed much further from object relations theory into the burgeoning domain of general systems and structural family theory, Ackerman's commitment to psychoanalytic thought and practice prevented him from developing a novel conceptual model for his family work. Instead, he forged family interventions that were deeply rooted in analytic theory.

A physician by training, Ackerman was a prolific writer with broad interests, first recognized for his groundbreaking studies of the economic hardship of coal miners' families in the Great Depression, as well as concurrent studies of the psychological elements of hypertension. These early studies remain a benchmark for measuring social context effects on internal family dynamics. Combining such social and relational constructs with psychoanalytic theory, and noting the early experiential and interpersonal aspects of psychological functioning, Ackerman's primary interest turned more exclusively toward the family unit. Early in his career as a psychoanalyst, Ackerman vigorously advocated for the treatment of the whole family by including all members within each session as either the main mode of treatment or as a complement to individual therapy.

Recognizing that infants and children internalize their early perceptions and experiences with their parents, Ackerman conceived family therapy to be a replication of early gratifying and discomforting relationships between children and their parents. To him, these internalized objects formed the basis for subsequent intimate relations, particularly those that would emerge in adolescence, adulthood, and parenthood. The "unpacking," or disentangling of these early templates served as the primary task of Ackerman's family therapy. Following the traditional analytic model, therapists following this approach assumed a neutral, blank stance so as to encourage patients to transfer their intrapsychic images, which could then be exposed and remedied within the family context.

Another direct descendent of psychoanalytic thought, **Murray Bowen (1913–1990),** presented a family systems approach some considered to be the most comprehensive theory-to-therapy approach among the family therapies. Whereas early family therapists shied away from direct theory generation, Bowen made it a priority to create thought clearly derived from psychoanalytic philosophies, different enough from the original to make it comprehensive and distinct, yet also aligned with a systems orientation. Much like the Bateson Project, Bowen's initial work centered on the study of schizophrenia within families; with the infusion of his strong psychoanalytic background, the focus became oriented around pathology from an intergenerational perspective.

Originally trained as a neurosurgeon, Bowen switched his emphasis to psychiatry and became a classical psychoanalytic adherent. As a young analyst and staff member at the Menninger Clinic in the latter 1940s, Bowen began focusing on mother/child symbiosis in schizophrenia cases, eventually developing a treatment milieu at the clinic where the mother and child would stay together in small cottages for periods of up to several months. In 1954, Bowen left Kansas and joined the National Institute of Mental Health (NIMH) in

Washington, D.C., where he carried out his most famous research, observing whole families of schizophrenic patients. Not long after, he decided to leave NIMH for an academic post in the Department of Psychiatry at Georgetown. It was during the Georgetown years that the family research project gradually evolved into the comprehensive and influential theory of family therapy known as the Bowenian school.

Bowen focused on a broader set of familial interactions than did traditional psychoanalysts; he traced the multigenerational transmission of family pathology as a continuing series of problematic relationships that persist through decades. Bowen defined many concepts and clinical approaches closely associated with his model, including the concepts of intergenerational transmission, undifferentiated "family ego mass," differentiation of self, and triangulation. Perhaps the best-known development from Bowenian theory was the genogram, the schematic tracing of multiple generations of interactive patterns in families using sets of symbols to depict family members and the characteristics of their relationships. In contrast to most of his family therapy associates at the time, but in concert with general systems theory, Bowen posited that one family member could break free of the reactive processes and entrapment structures of a system. This could then cause a chain reaction likely breaking up the problematic character of the system. Much like an ecosystem's characteristic interdependence on the survival of various species of plant and animal life, the family system characteristically sought homeostasis through interdependence of its members, even if the achieved homeostasis was maladaptive. Though Bowen's model focused more on the intergenerational aspects of the system, these mutual dependency themes set the stage for other burgeoning family therapy methodologies.

The central thesis of Bowen's approach relates to the fusion that emerges among family members and results in a lack of personal individuation from the family of origin, that is, an inability to differentiate self from others. This lack of differentiation, according to Bowen, leads the individual to cut all emotional bonds with parents, which, in turn, leads to excessive fusion in new family or marital arrangements. Using genograms to outline multigenerational relationships, Bowen's goal was to assist members to become more self-differentiated and, hence, to achieve greater personal expression. Differing from most other family therapists, Bowen preferred to work with only one family member at a time, while the others either were absent or were silently observing.

Virginia Satir (1916–1988) developed a model for family therapy based on homeostasis-seeking principles first established at the Mental Research Institute (MRI; see Bateson). Though not an original theorist, Satir was an extraordinary clinician, and her influence on skills and therapeutic relationships of family therapists is equal to the written material of the theorists mentioned in this section. Beginning her family work with the Mental Research Institute in California, her core ideas, though profoundly humanistic-experiential, were notably influenced by the Bateson Project's notions of the family as a balanced system. Her working model turned more profoundly to the humanistic school after she left MRI to work at the Esalen Institute, but elements of the Bateson model persevered throughout her career.

Satir was a woman of boundless energy and high spirits. Tall and handsome, she derived great pleasure in smart, feminine clothes. There seemed to be hardly anything she could not be enthusiastic about; she was as keen on dancing as on mountaineering, on tennis as on swimming and skating. Her formulations, many lectures, and workshops were fascinating, yet almost ready-made—she often sounded more like a family therapy salesperson than a groping and reflective theorist. Most assuredly, Satir was charming

Virginia Satir

and attractive; even if one could not agree with her ideas and proposals about family life, she deeply felt her views and articulated them with great clarity and conviction.

Satir viewed the *balanced family* construct as a structure that maintained homeostasis, but that balance came at considerable cost to the individual family members. Trapped in this ultimate goal of upholding the status quo, rather than allowing for healthful family and personal growth, family members became constrained, circumscribed, and symptom-ridden. Drawing on the human potential movement, which was immensely popular during the 1960s in California, among other U.S. locales, Satir generated many innovative in-session techniques to illustrate the impact of family members on one another. Satir utilized ropes and blindfolds to illustrate the constraints in which family members restrict and trap each other. She employed other methods of a more encounter and experiential nature, along with what she termed the *family sculpture* method. Here, family members are arranged in a physical setting, using distance and body positions to illustrate the several ways in which they habitually relate to one another.

Although Satir was not theory-oriented, her work had several premises. First, she strongly emphasized the notion of the power of self-actualization, which, in turn, derived from high positive self-esteem. Next, she emphasized the clarity and character of communication patterns among family members. Additionally, she sought to expose the rules by which family members interacted with one another. Satir's concept of a healthy family was one in which individual members had positive self-esteem, and intrafamily communications were direct, honest, and clear. By contrast, Satir believed that families-in-trouble failed to encourage positive self-worth, expressed indirect and vague communications, subscribed to absolute rather than flexible rules, and functioned as a highly defensive and negative closed emotional system.

The architect of what eventually came to be known as the *structural school* of family therapy was **Salvador Minuchin (1921–   )**, who was also perhaps the most recognizable name in the family therapy domain. Beginning in the mid-1960s, Minuchin, an analytically trained child psychiatrist who was supervised late in his training by Nathan Ackerman, developed a structural approach to family treatment based on his clinical experience with delinquent children. While conducting traditional psychodynamic therapy with these youths, Minuchin noted that their difficulties appeared to stem from the dysfunctional structure of the families in which they were raised. The model that derived from these observations soon became a general framework for family treatment. As Minuchin viewed it, the therapist's mission was to alter the formal or structural relationships that existed within the family through in-session manipulations.

Originally planning a specialization in pediatrics, Minuchin, an Argentinian native, graduated with his MD from the University of Cordoba in 1947. In 1948, Minuchin volunteered as an army physician for the war with the Arab nations over Israel's statehood, after which he came to New York City to study child psychiatry at the Jewish Board of Guardians, as well as psychoanalysis at the William Alanson White Institute. After this period, Minuchin returned to Israel to work with child Holocaust survivors as well as Jewish families emigrating from the Arab nations. His interest in treating the whole family originated during this experience. On returning to the United States, Minuchin began working with low-income, adjudicated boys in New York, an experience that yielded innovative techniques specifically geared to this population. In 1965, Minuchin moved to a similar setting at the Philadelphia Child Guidance Clinic as director of the facility, an appointment he held for 10 years and that brought his thoughts into the spotlight of the burgeoning field of family therapy. Renowned for his artful and flair-filled clinical style, Minuchin built the Philadelphia center into a leading family institute, and established the groundbreaking structural theory of families, outlined in his classic 1974 text, *Families and Family Therapy*. Along with his friend Jay Haley, who joined Minuchin and his colleagues in Philadelphia in 1967, the Philadelphia team created further innovations by training paraprofessionals from local communities in a successful effort to bring the therapist closer to each family's setting.

In concert with popular systems theories, Minuchin viewed the family as a system that had a self-regulated structure somewhat impermeable to changing conditions from both within and outside itself. However, some families took on a dysfunctional characteristic, wherein the homeostasis achieved by the family's structure—which in normal families would maintain a harmonious peace—actually perpetuated suffering in its members. In his model, therapists joined with the family (became a "human member" of the family unit), and worked as collaborators. This enabled therapists to become aware of the family's interactional patterns and challenge its members to find alternate forms of communication, innovative problem-solving strategies, and new perceptions of subjective reality. The goal was to undermine the faulty family structure and replace it with healthy transactional patterns. As the structure of the family's patterns of interactions changed, so would the family members' behavior.

Focusing on Interpersonal Therapy

The *interpersonal* school of therapy, as is evident from the founding members' influences and many of its techniques, is rooted in both psychoanalytic and social psychological traditions, though its outgrowth from these schools may be seen as a broadening of the earlier schools' perspectives. Although they address the psychodynamic functioning and relational conduct of patients, they assert that behaviors for relating and transacting communications with others are the most significant. Pioneered by the theorists Harry Stack Sullivan, Timothy Leary, and Eric Berne in the mid-twentieth century, recent decades have seen a marked increase in these therapies, led by such thinkers as Donald Kiesler and Lorna Smith Benjamin.

According to the interpersonal perspective, the key problems individuals face are the result of their pattern of interactions with significant others, and stem largely from disordered, inappropriate, or inadequate communications. The result is a failure to attend to and correct these unsuccessful and self-defeating communications. After completing a past history assessment, interpersonal therapists help patients identify the persons with whom they are currently having difficulties, what these difficulties are, and whether there are ways to resolve them or make them more satisfactory. The interpersonal approach focuses on the individual's closest relationships, notably current family interactions, the family of origin, past and present love affairs and friendships, and neighborhood and work relations.

The task of interpersonal therapy is to identify and modify patients' habitual interactive and hierarchical roles in these social systems. The counseling dyad, despite its apparent uniqueness, models other communication venues, with interpersonal therapists becoming sensitive to patients' transactional styles. The evocative manner in which patients "pull" therapists' feelings and attitudes indicates how patients relate to others. This process mirrors in many ways what psychoanalysts refer to in their concepts of transference and countertransference. The following theorists represent major thinkers of the interpersonal school of therapy, from its beginnings in neo-Freudian and behaviorist traditions, to the modern-day leaders of what has become a major philosophy of therapy in its own right.

Although much of his contribution to psychology was revealed posthumously through his students, **Harry Stack Sullivan (1892–1949)** may be the father of interpersonal therapy. Following the cultural and social advances of Adler, Horney, and Fromm, Sullivan, a former psychoanalyst himself, directed most of his attention to the communication processes of human beings, emphasizing the two-way interactions within the therapeutic relationship.

Influenced first by the American psychiatrists Adolf Meyer and William Alanson White, Sullivan later adopted many of Freud's concepts on psychoanalytic processes and early childhood development. His emphasis on the interpersonal aspects of growth and his contributions to the communication process in therapy classify him properly among neo-Freudian social theorists. Because of Sullivan's exposure to the linguist Edward Sapir and the positivist philosopher Percy Bridgman, he became especially critical of the conceptually awkward and frequently obscure formulations of psychoanalysis. As a remedy, he created his own system and terminology. With few exceptions, his terminology has failed to replace Freud's. However, his highly original studies, especially regarding early development, schizophrenia, and the process of therapy, have had a marked impact on the thinking and practice of contemporary psychodynamic psychiatry.

Sullivan's therapy sought to unravel the patient's pattern of self-protective, but ultimately self-defeating interpersonal measures. Though Sullivan sometimes sought to elicit childhood memories and dream materials, he focused primarily on present interpersonal problems. He believed that the classical passive or blank-screen attitude should be replaced by a more natural expression of the therapist's real feelings and thoughts. Beyond this, he proposed that therapists simulate certain attitudes to throw patients off guard, thereby provoking interpersonally illuminating responses. In short, Sullivan tried to participate actively in an interpersonal treatment relationship, exploiting his own reactions and feigning others, both designed to uncover the patient's distortions and unconscious styles of behavior.

Sullivan was born into an impoverished Irish/American farm family in central New York. He was the only surviving child in his family, as his numerous siblings died during infancy. His childhood, without siblings or neighboring children in his rural environment, was markedly lonely and isolated. Somehow, Sullivan's family managed to save enough money to provide for his higher education. He explored the possibility of a career as a physicist, but eventually decided on psychiatry, entering the Chicago College of Medicine and Surgery, and earning his medical degree in 1917.

After serving in the army during World War I, Sullivan became associated with William Alanson White, superintendent of St. Elizabeth's Hospital in Washington, D.C. White was a founding member of what was then called the "new psychiatry" movement, which sought to explain mental disorders in other than physical terms. Sullivan became his protégé, and in addition to joining White in questioning psychoanalysis and its biological assumptions, he developed an expertise in schizophrenia. His budding interpersonal model of therapy was an outgrowth of his new environmental approach to the treatment of male schizophrenics, which he began at Sheppard and Enoch Pratt Hospital in Towson, Maryland. Rather than a simple control-custodial approach, Sullivan actively altered the patients' environment by developing a separate male ward within the psychiatric unit, and surrounding the patients with talented aides who served as positive male role models, always emphasizing the interpersonal framework of this newly established subculture.

Like Freud and Erikson, Sullivan constructed a developmental stage model. In contrast to these other theorists, however, he based his system on interpersonal communication, reflecting his belief that humankind's most distinguishing developmental feature was not sexual or adaptive capacities, but the capacity for intricate, complex communication with others. He termed the emerging structures of personality as *dynamisms* (loosely defined as reasonably permanent and characteristic processes of living activities and interpersonal transactions). Sullivan then divided this construct into two broad categories: *zonal* (physical; e.g., eating, sleeping, sexual gratification) and *interpersonal* (interactional with self, significant others, etc.). Although human beings are born with most zonal dynamisms intact, they must develop interpersonal dynamisms through experience, which become patterned and habituated through a process Sullivan called *personification*. These dynamisms are built through awareness of experience, characterized by the following modes or stages: Early "raw" experience, nonverbal in nature, is part of the *protaxic* mode; the

Harry Stack Sullivan

parataxic mode, beginning at about 9 months, involves semiverbal exchanges and semicognizance of meaning; last, the *syntaxic* mode involves commonly shared meanings and complex modes, and emerges somewhere in the second year of life. In time, a complex pattern of self-protective attitudes and behaviors develops, which Sullivan referred to as the *self-system*. This system consists of measures that produce the rewards of security and avoid the anxieties of insecurity, a concept not dissimilar from Adler's notion of neurotic safeguards. Sullivan's conception of the personality patterns that derive from the self-system's safeguards are briefly discussed in Chapter 13.

Sullivan's concern with the interpersonal aspect of pathology also led him to recognize a pathogenic source that previous theorists had overlooked: the detrimental effects of normally well-meaning but inconsistent parents. Sullivan did not view anxiety to be a product of instinctual frustration or deprivation, but a direct result of interpersonal experiences; they stemmed, first, from relationships with an anxious and malevolent mother and, later, from social ostracism, ridicule, or punishment. To Sullivan, contradictory or confusing guides for behavior not only produced anxiety, but immobilized the child. When trapped in this double-bind exchange, the child would become unable to act in a focused, nonconflictual way to others. According to Sullivan, these inconsistent parental attitudes and behaviors not only produced their own anxiety, but precluded effective interpersonal relations and effective solutions to other sources of anxiety.

The primary instrument of Sullivan's therapy is skillful interviewing. By this, Sullivan meant subtly drawing out patients' unconscious distortions through careful listening and questioning, and then suggesting that patients may harbor unwarranted preconceptions of themselves and others. The therapist might also offer tentative speculations as to how these self and interpersonal attitudes could have caused problem relationships in the past and how they may be altered in the future. Sullivan thus considered the interpersonal interview interaction, not the passive free association technique, to be the most fruitful means of disentangling the web of unconscious distortions, as well as providing suggestions to prevent its perpetuation. The fertility of Sullivan's ideas extended to a formulation of several distinct personality syndromes.

Sullivan's approach took on a distinctly interpersonal character in his practicing years, setting a standard that would influence the relational school's overall development, yet little of his work was published during his lifetime. Sullivan died unexpectedly of a cerebral hemorrhage while in Paris, France, and his students published his thoughts on interpersonal psychiatry, employing their lecture notes and tape recordings.

In the interpersonal method known as *transactional analysis*, **Eric Lennard Berne (1910–1970),** its founder, continued the progression toward the sociocultural end of the continuum by directing attention to roles patients assume. According to Berne, patient-therapist interactions provided insight into patients' characteristic interpersonal maneuvers and mirrored the several varieties of their everyday social behaviors. These maneuvers translated into caricature forms he termed "pastimes" or "games," each of which highlighted patients' unconscious strategies to defend against childish anxieties or to secure other equally immature rewards. This analytical process is akin to that contained in the analysis of transference phenomena, although Berne dramatized these operations by tagging them with clever and humorous labels (e.g., "schlemeil," "ain't it wonderful," or "do me something").

Born Eric Lennard Bernstein in Montreal, Quebec, Canada, Eric Berne was the eldest child of a general practitioner and a professional writer, both Jewish immigrants from Eastern Europe. The young Bernstein, very fond of his physician father, accompanied him on his medical rounds as a young child. Following his father's untimely death from tuberculosis when Eric was 9 years old, he began to write, which he continued to do voraciously throughout his life. It was apparent in his witty, brilliant, but sometimes indecipherable style that the trauma of losing his father resonated for many years, as his writing seemed to be aimed at pleasing his parents. With his mother's encouragement, he decided to follow his father's lead and study medicine. He went on to earn his medical degree from McGill University in 1935, moved to the United States, and shortened his name to Eric Berne. Following his psychiatric residency at Yale University School of Medicine, he trained at the New York Psychoanalytic Institute. He was appointed to Mt. Sinai Hospital, and maintained concurrent practices in New York City and his home in Norwalk, Connecticut (where he met his first of three wives), until the demands of World War II brought him to the Army Medical Corps.

Like Horney, Berne contended that contradictory character trends (or as he described them, *ego states*) coexist within the patient. However, Horney posited that a single trend would achieve global dominance, whereas Berne proposed that ego states are fluid, with one or another coming to the fore depending on the person's social interactions. Berne identified three ego states that emerge from these transactions: archaic or infantile behaviors, known as the *Child* ego state (not necessarily reflecting the patient's chronological age); critical but nurturing qualities of the patient (generally reflecting borrowed attitudes of the patient's parent or guardian figures), termed the *Parent* ego state; and finally, the patient's mature qualities (again, not related to age), termed the *Adult* ego state. This trio of inner states bore some obvious resemblance to Freud's *Id*, *Superego*, and *Ego*, respectively, but there were notable differences. In contrast to classical psychoanalysis and in concert with the emerging interpersonal schools, these ego states emphasized the social and relational aspects of functioning. There were also concrete differences between each of the ego states and their Freudian counterparts. Berne (1961) differentiated between the construct of the *Child* ego state and the *Id*: "The Child means an organized state of mind which exists or once actually existed, while Freud describes the Id as 'a chaos, a cauldron of seething excitement . . . it has no organization and no unified will'" (p. 61).

The central goal of Berne's transactional analysis was the exposure and interpretation of these conflicting ego states' unconscious attitudes and strategies. To promote insight into patients' more immature maneuvers, transactional analysts would allow their own parent, child, and adult states to transact with patients' ego states. This procedure would strengthen patients' adult state because it taught them to withstand manipulations by others that formerly evoked their child and parent trends. Consequently, patients would gain insight into the scripts and/or foolish games they played in relationships, and would reinforce adult state skills and attitudes.

Part interpersonal pioneer and part folk legend, **Timothy Leary (1920–1996)** may be best remembered as a guru of the 1960s' counterculture, while his contributions to psychology and human communication in the 1940s and 1950s are often overlooked. During his tenure as a young professor at the University of California, Berkeley and as Director of Psychological Research at the Kaiser Permanente Foundation, he noted the relative ineffectiveness of many psychotherapies and proposed character typologies based on communication styles between people. He further advocated for a new paradigm of the patient/therapist relationship characterized by a more equal, two-way, unrestrained communication between the two people, instead of the classical "expert/dependent" model.

A legend grew up around Timothy Leary, partly because he lent himself to the myth of the imaginative and rebellious revolutionary. His creative talent was large, sprawling, and essentially unrealized; his intelligence and his enthusiasm for the novel and exploratory made him contrary and at times almost destroyed him. Leary had the kind of perverse and radical sensibility that flourished in the 1960s; he was heralded in the popular, media-oriented, and freewheeling counterculture of the times. In person, he was often warm and jovial, though he had an underlying streak of rage that sometimes burst out of his usual controls. He loved to argue on popular subjects and causes, usually railing against the conservatism of the scientific and political establishment. He was drawn to ideas that had something of the intellectually forbidden about them; his assertions were often beyond the reach of reason and evidence. During his earlier years, before he indulged his drug-related eccentricities, he demonstrated his lively and piercing intelligence in his concepts and his writings. After colleagues at Harvard rejected him in the early 1960s, however, he became a truculent and angry man, intensely envious of the greater successes of some of his appreciably lesser contemporaries.

Born in Massachusetts to an Irish Catholic household, Leary's family was somewhat schismatic. His father, who left the family when Leary was a teen, was from a rebellious, pleasure-oriented family, whereas his mother's side was traditional, radically religious, and disapproving of anything frivolous. Most likely as a function of his gravitation toward the more boisterous side of the family, Leary frequently challenged traditional academia (inclusive of his high school and college experiences) in controversial but brilliant ways. Always an "A" student but continually finding his academic career in jeopardy over rule infractions, Leary eventually earned his doctorate at the University of California–Berkeley, secured a teaching post there, and married his first wife, Marianne, with whom he had two children. Marital difficulties, drinking, and Marianne's bout with postpartum depression ended in Marianne's suicide. Leary subsequently left Berkeley and moved to Europe. While in Florence, Leary met *David McClelland*, then director of Harvard University's Center for Personality Research. As a result of Leary's explanation of his theories regarding existential transaction and its more egalitarian patient/therapist relationship, he earned an appointment to Harvard and began teaching there in the spring of 1960.

While on vacation in Mexico the following summer, Leary's academic career took a dramatic, unexpected turn. He discovered *psychedelic drugs* and became so convinced of their power to catalyze the exploration of the mind that he convinced Harvard to allow him to begin controlled experiments with hallucinogenic agents. His experiments first included Harvard graduate students, then expanded to divinity students (whose involvement was quickly terminated by religious institutions) and to prisoners (who evidenced some success at self-awareness and decreased recidivism). Although scientifically controlled, these experiments were controversial, even before the substances in question (psilocybin, LSD) were declared illegal shortly after the experiments had begun. Pressures from more conservative faculty (as well as CIA involvement) led to Leary's being relieved of his Harvard position in 1963; he continued his experiments independent of university support in a mansion near New York known as "Millbrook"; the ensuing period was known as the "Millbrook years."

From here, his involvement in psychology proper diminished. He became immersed in the counterculture movement of the 1960s; the notoriety surrounding his "Turn on, tune in, and drop out" advocacy of "responsible, mind-expanding" drug use led Richard M. Nixon to declare him "the most dangerous man in America." A conversion to Hinduism, another marriage, and several severe prison sentences for minimal drug charges (leading to his escape from prison, fleeing of the United States, and his extradition in 1972) came in the ensuing years, ending with his release in 1976. Yet another marriage followed, along with his public resurfacing in movies and on the college lecture circuit, as he began espousing the Internet as the mind-expanding drug of the new generation. Leary died of inoperable prostate cancer just before the immense popularization of the World Wide Web. Only recently, however, has contemporary psychology begun to acknowledge his innovative proposals in the late 1950s and early 1960s for a relational psychotherapy.

Leary proposed that personality comprised five interpersonal levels. He outlined these levels in *Interpersonal Diagnosis of Personality* (1957), and described different modalities of interpersonal content in human behavior. The first of these, termed "Level of Public Communication: The Interpersonal Reflex," summarized behavioral aspects of interpersonal transactions. In essence, this comprised the social impact of one human being on another. The next level, "Conscious Communication: The Interpersonal Trait," comprised phenomenological attributes of interpersonal exchange. This level dealt exclusively with individuals' self-perception and their personal perception of the environment taken from subjective accounts. Third was the "Level of Private Perception: The Interpersonal Symbol," which is the unconscious level. Here, Leary described individual's indirect inferences about their imagined or symbolic selves, and the imagined figures of others who populate their preconscious realm. Next was the "Level of the Unexpressed: Significant Omissions," which represented the biophysical plane. These were themes actively avoided at the previous three stages (in action, in consciousness, and in preconsciousness), which Leary considered to be the deepest stage of functioning. Finally, the fifth level was the "Level of Values: The Ego Ideal," consisting of consciously reported ideals. Unlike the sequential deepening of the other four levels, this final level was not considered particularly deep; it simply represented individuals' self-report of expressed principles. The variants of his personality type model are described in Chapter 13.

Leary remained a controversial figure to the end, shrouded in mystery as a result of his progression from psychological scientist to counterculture guru. Recent advances in interpersonal psychology have stirred a newfound interest in the innovative constructs of his earlier career.

Donald J. Kiesler (1933–   ) developed what has been termed *interpersonal communication theory*. It centered attention on the transactions between people throughout their life experience. He observed that people transmit "evoking messages" to others through both verbal and nonverbal channels; these messages create specific *encoder-decoder* relationships. Kiesler conceptualized the emotional and personality difficulties of individuals as stemming from problematic countercommunications they unknowingly elicit from others.

Kiesler earned his PhD in 1963 at the University of Illinois and began his career working with Carl R. Rogers (see Chapter 3) at the Psychotherapy Research Group, University of Wisconsin Psychiatric Institute. Much of his research interests in his first postdoctoral years centered on the study of client-centered therapy with schizophrenic patients. In addition, he helped develop *The Experiencing Scale* (M. H. Klein, Mathieu, Gendlin, & Kiesler, 1970), a measure of patient improvement over the course of psychotherapy. This manual became a prototype for many successive psychotherapeutic process researchers. In the early 1970s, his research interest moved in the direction of communication styles as Kiesler began studying nonverbal communication patterns in psychotherapy. Another test originally published in the late 1970s, the *Impact Message Inventory* (1987), served as the groundwork for the integration of his communication theory with his ongoing research in interpersonal personality, mental illness, and psychotherapy. Since the 1980s, Kiesler has continued to be active in applying and documenting contemporary interpersonal theory to personality and psychotherapy.

Kiesler has been a quiet and unassuming, yet creative thinker, representing a new breed of interpersonal theorists, quite distinct from forerunners such as Sullivan, Berne, and Leary—learned, well trained, and thoroughly grounded in the foundations of alternative models of therapy. His work reflects a person of extraordinary intelligence and scholarship in which personal stability, thorough knowledge, and sound judgment have been applied critically to a broad range of concerns, from narrow diagnostic systems to simplistic psychotherapeutic methods.

In his highly detailed and precise analysis of the interpersonal circle formulated in 1982, Kiesler arranged his personality taxonomy in terms of two major dimensions: affiliation (love-hate) and control (dominance-submission). His formulation contained some 350 bipolar interpersonal items, 3 to 9 of which composed some 64 separate subclasses; these subclasses were then grouped into 8 two-part octants. Kiesler offered a series of translations relating the *DSM* personality disorders to their profiles in his interpersonal circle. For example, the histrionic personality fits the frenetically-gregarious octant, the dependent personality parallels the unassured-submissive octant, and the passive-aggressive matches the antagonistic-aloof octant.

In Kiesler's interpersonal therapy, the therapist is charged with assisting patients in identifying, clarifying, and establishing alternatives to supplant their established, frequently rigid, and typically self-defeating evoking style. Central, recurrent, and thematic relationships that emerge between the patient and the therapist during their sessions maximize this process. The task is to replace a patient's constricted transactional messages with communications that are more flexible and adaptive to the changing realities of life. A major priority for the therapist is to stop responding in ways akin to the way others have responded to the patient in the past. These habitual transaction cycles that are activated by the patient's behaviors and communications characteristically intensify and aggravate the patient's problematic relationships.

Lorna Smith Benjamin (1934–   ) carried on the interpersonal tradition, yet has kept it a dynamic therapeutic discipline. As is characteristic of innovative thinkers, Benjamin (1974, 1993) recognized the interplay of cognitive, affective, and intrapsychic dimensions in the articulation of her interpersonal theory. Her model encompasses much of Leary's earlier interpersonal work and Aaron Beck's cognitive attributes, as well as substantial psychodynamic elements. With this detailed and versatile model of interpersonal interaction, Benjamin brought into clear relief one of the major strengths of the interpersonal approach: It can accommodate these many dimensions as inherent parts of psychological analysis.

Lorna Smith Benjamin

Benjamin obtained her PhD at the University of Wisconsin, where she taught for 30 years until becoming a professor at the University of Utah. Her theoretical model, termed the *Structural Analysis of Social Behavior (SASB)*, emphasized not only an operational description of major interpersonal patterns, but also their impact on one's sense of self, first described in articles published in the early 1970s, and further developed in subsequent scholarly publications. Her landmark book, *Interpersonal Diagnosis and Treatment of Personality Disorders*, first published in 1993, outlined the full exegesis of the SASB approach. The SASB system has been translated into 12 different languages and has been used, in addition to its application to personality disorders, to study the mother-infant dyad, therapeutic transactions, marital interactions, psychiatric diagnosis, depression, and the nature of hallucinations.

Colleagues and students consider Lorna Benjamin to be one of the nicest persons they could ever meet, a wonderful collaborator and teacher. She has been a dedicated scholar and clinician, forthright, loyal, utterly without guile, malice, or envy. One cannot help but be struck by her intense alertness, as though she were trying to penetrate ideas or people simply by looking through them, a characteristic that one comes to associate with the power and originality of her mind. Also impressive is her unusual combination of gentleness and force, a strange and seductive quality, a firmness of tone and a strength of conviction that is manifested in a soft and almost caressing manner. Even at her most insistent—when she rejects an idea or clearly feels impatient—her eyes seem to smile benignly. She thinks with originality and has the ability to put ideas in a fresh form, a talent that comes near the upper ranges and depths of few major figures in the psychological sciences. Somewhat old fashioned in manner, she lacks affectations of style or taste often cultivated by successful intellectuals. Owing to her early training as an experimentalist, she has an uncanny eye favoring empirical evidence and systematic methodology. It is not only in the originality of her ideas but in the texture of her thinking and in her sensitive empathy for patients' lives that one recognizes the preeminent quality of her work.

Benjamin's model of interpersonal interactions was built on three orthogonal dimensions: focus on others, focus on self, and introjective focus. Each of these dimensions was organized in a circumplical framework. This schema enabled one to test and understand, on a symptom-by-symptom basis, how personality disorders could be analyzed in terms of specific social learning experiences and the social context in which they were activated. Benjamin regarded personality to be a consequence of early interactions with parents and later social learning experiences with significant others. *Copying processes* initiated by early caregiving, which lead to problematic patterns in adult interactions are key issues here. To seek reconciliation, approval, and love of the original caregiver, young adults would unwittingly emulate that early object (identification), would act as if the caregiver were still present and dominant (recapitulation), would inflict self-treatment to mirror earlier treatment by the caregiver (introjection), or combine these approaches. Central to her thesis was that adult interpersonal patterns reflect the development of instrumental interpersonal competence, recognition of the consequences of neediness and illness, emergence of a self-concept and social identity, and realization of the interpersonal consequences of expressing affect. As Benjamin put it, "every mental illness is a gift of love."

Perhaps the most detailed model of the therapeutic relationship, Benjamin's SASB bridged both psychoanalytic and interpersonal realms of functioning. Her key medium for exploring these functions was the interview process, elaborated in her recent book, *Interpersonal Reconstructive Therapy* (2003), which Benjamin believed should contain six key features. First, a collaboration had to be established in which the therapist could affirm the patient's views and responses. The task of the interviewer was to be acutely aware of the patient's behaviors, feelings, and indirect communications throughout the interview process, identifying such communications as evinced in silences, affective expressions, resistances when revisiting difficult subjects, and so on. Second, unconscious processes needed to be tracked in a free-form flow of conversation. Thus, rather than seeking to control topical progressions, the interviewer needed to permit the patient to proceed with seemingly disorganized or random digressions, identifying fantasies, metaphors, and the like. Third, the therapist had to assume the narrative story line that unfolded made sense. The basic task was to understand the interpersonal and psychoanalytic patterns that emerged in terms of where they came from and what their purposes would be. Fourth,

Benjamin referred to the achievement of *interpersonal specificity,* by which she meant gaining an awareness of patterns of interpersonal relevance as they related to dimensions such as love-hate and enmeshment-differentiation. Fifth, the therapist needed to avoid reinforcing preexisting destructive patterns. Here, Benjamin recommended that the interviewer *not* show empathy for symptomatic behaviors, nor attend actively to the gathering of symptomatic data. Lastly, Benjamin enjoined the therapist to correct "errors" as quickly as possible. To her, errors were interventions that did not conform to the previous five interviewing recommendations. Thus, in Benjamin's model, the key task was to establish a collaboration in which empathic processes may or may not be appropriate. Next, she stressed facilitating patients' recognition of their interpersonal patterns of behavior. It was equally important to block maladaptive patterns and to address patients' underlying fears and wishes. And finally, therapists had to encourage the acquisition of interpersonal behaviors that were more adaptive and more gratifying than those previously employed.

Comments and Reflections

Why do mental disorders occur? Is it a defective neurochemical, an unresolved Oedipus complex, an inability to act in accord with one's personal values, a lack of exposure to a proper regimen of positive reinforcements? Each group of theorists presented earlier in the text provides a rationale for their pet notions. Perhaps it is none of these. Instead, can it be the social environment that proves primary? Perhaps many of the components we observe in our patients merely reflect the operation of social influences, cultural mores and styles, and simple economics. Some contend that much of what we see clinically is a product of social forces that impede or facilitate mental health. Others furnish a concrete and dramatic portrayal of the operation of these forces, tracing the complex of cultural and economic influences that shape deviance.

Despite these advantages, critics of sociocultural approaches note that deeper personal problems are often bypassed and unresolved, lost in the shuffle of the many voices that compete in the struggle to gain ascendancy within the group therapies. The fluid and rapid process of group interchange may not allow for the prolonged probing needed to expose and rework the roots of problems, especially among more hesitant or retiring patients. Other critics note that the freewheeling expression of attitudes among group members can seriously undermine the security of certain patients, many of whom may withdraw from treatment before these injuries can be repaired.

The advantages and disadvantages of individual, group, and family therapies have been debated for years. Obviously, these approaches are different and can be justified on rational grounds by their exponents. Group methods save personnel time and, if effective, can expedite the treatment of a greater number of patients than can individual methods. Decisions as to their special spheres of utility cannot truly be made as few empirical studies have been made demonstrating their comparative efficacies. Therapists make their choices on the basis of theoretical or personal preferences; on these dubious grounds, some use the same treatment approach for all patients.

Among the few outcome research studies, a few satisfy certain minimal criteria of sound research design. An early study compared two groups, one receiving individual therapy only, the other receiving both individual and group therapy. The results were not notably different. Using physician judgments as a criterion, 50% of the former group was improved compared with more than 60% of the latter. In a population of hospital patients, others studied the effectiveness of four therapeutic regimens: a nontherapy control, individual therapy, group therapy, and group living with periodic group therapy. Notable in the design was the systematic differentiation and matching of patient types, the use of a battery of several objective criterion measures, and periodic follow-up evaluations. The results were complicated; the efficacy of alternative treatment techniques varied as a function of type of disorder and length of hospitalization. Essentially, all therapeutic modalities proved superior to the control group. Differences among treatment procedures were minimal, although they appeared to favor the group-living and individual therapy approaches.

In contrast to other social theorists, however, a number of interpersonal therapists (e.g., Benjamin) seek to provide testable hypotheses, not only of the features or traits of each disorder, but of their social pathogenesis. Benjamin argues that the dynamic interplay of the dimensions of functioning she articulates will give coherence to the overall mental configuration. Moreover, she demonstrates that treatment interventions can be a logical outgrowth of her brand of interpersonal assessments, hence coordinating diagnosis and therapy, a necessary element for scientific and clinical progress. To her and others of the sociocultural school, how we change everyday relationships is what matters most in therapy.

Few studies have been undertaken to tease out the process ingredients of each form of socially oriented therapy. What little has been done provides no insight into their role as factors contributing to treatment efficacy. As is true with most types of individual therapy, few systematic and properly designed research studies have been published on socially oriented treatment approaches. Stated differently, few empirical data exist from which we can judge with confidence the efficacy or mode of action of these therapies. Although social treatment proponents can cite valid reasons for the paucity of sound research (e.g., the complexity and number of variables involved; the difficulty in matching patients), they have a responsibility to show that the value of their preferred method is more than a logical or rational article of faith.

PART VII

PERSONOLOGIC STORIES

CHAPTER

13

Enlisting Evolution to Elucidate Human Adaptations

The independent lines along which clinical psychiatric practice and academic psychological research have grown account in part for the scattered and often confused state of mental health practice and theory. Although there have been occasions when the ideas and methods of one field fertilized the other, many such instances would be difficult to find. The traditional psychiatric concern with practical problems, such as classification and differential diagnosis, have resulted in the development of useful but essentially descriptive concepts and terms that have little or no relation to basic psychological processes. Although the practical need for a psychiatric taxonomy and nomenclature cannot be denied, it does rest on a hazardous and essentially nonscientific foundation.

The Personologic Story: I

Scientific history has shown repeatedly that concepts constructed without reference to fundamental or general laws are extremely fragile and likely to become quickly outmoded. On the other hand, concepts formulated in pursuit of general laws of mental functioning often have little relevance to the practical problems practitioners face. Academic researchers derive many of their ideas from studies of normal behavior; these studies concentrate on limited psychological processes such as sensation or learning and frequently are based on animal rather than human subjects. The assumption academicians make is that a thorough knowledge of these part-functions will lead to a number of basic laws from which the complex behaviors of mental pathology can be logically derived. An attempt to bring basic concepts developed through academic research in line with psychiatric problems has recently begun (see discussion in earlier chapters).

This chapter and the next, however, deal with similar efforts in the fields of clinical psychology and personology. Their historical developments have attempted to bridge the gap between basic psychology and practical psychiatry by the use of personality concepts, that is, concepts that represent broad dispositions to mental functioning. Unusual as it may seem, the conceptualization of personality processes and structure has evolved somewhat independently of their scientific measurement and psychological treatment. As a result, these chapters trace both historical lines of development separately. They do, however, share several assumptions in common.

For example, they all accept the notion of the uniqueness of each individual. In contrast to academic psychologists, clinicians and personologists are less concerned with general patterns or what are called *nomothetic* commonalities among individuals, than in the *idiographic* pattern with which diverse traits and symptoms combine in each particular individual. Their focus is not on the separate elements of functioning, but on their interaction. Also referred to as the holistic approach, it signifies a concern with the unique integration of the total personality. A second assumption clinicians and personologists share is that a continuity exists between normal and abnormal behavior. Thus, measurement is designed to establish the relative position of an individual on universal dimensions of personality functioning. Viewed in this fashion, abnormality is considered to be an extension of the study of quantitative individual differences. Diagnosis, in turn, consists of specifying the individual's unique pattern of extreme scores on a set of relevant psychological dimensions.

It may be necessary in the complex phenomena of personality to transcend traditional conceptual boundaries of psychology, more specifically to explore hypotheses that draw their principles, if not their substance, from more and widely established adjacent sciences that encompass both biological and sociological ideas. Not only may such steps bear new conceptual fruits, but they may provide a foundation that can undergird and guide the explorations of personality. Much of personology, no less psychology as a whole, remains adrift, divorced from broader spheres of scientific knowledge, isolated from firmly grounded, if not universal principles, leading investigators and theorists to continue building the patchwork quilt of concepts and data domains that characterize the field. Preoccupied with a small part of the larger puzzle of nature, or fearing accusations of reductionism, many have failed to draw on the rich possibilities that may be found in diverse realms of scholarly pursuit. With few exceptions, cohering concepts that would connect the subject of personality to those of its sister sciences have only begun to be developed in recent decades.

The psychological sciences seem trapped in horizontal refinements. A search for integrative schemas and cohesive constructs that link its seekers closely to relevant observations and laws developed in more advanced fields is needed. The goal—albeit grandiose—is to refashion the patchwork quilt into a well-tailored and aesthetic tapestry that interweaves the diverse forms in which nature expresses itself.

To take this view is not to argue that different spheres of personological inquiry should be equated, nor is it to seek a single, overarching conceptual system encompassing biology, psychology, and sociology. Arguing in favor of establishing explicit links between biopsychosocial domains calls neither for a reductionistic philosophy, a belief in substantive identicality, nor efforts to fashion them by formal logic. Rather, researchers should aspire to their substantive concordance, empirical consistency, conceptual interfacing, convergent dialogues, and mutual enlightenment. Unification in the form of integrative consonance such as described previously, should not be an aspiration limited to the diverse subjects of physical sciences, as eminent theoretical physicists are striving to construct, but is a worthy goal within the domains of personological science, as well. Particularly relevant in this regard are efforts that seek to coordinate the often separate realms that comprise it, namely: its *theories*, the *classification system* it has formulated, the *diagnostic tools* it employs, and the *therapeutic techniques* it implements. Rather than developing independently and being left to stand as autonomous and largely unconnected functions, a truly mature clinical science, such as personology, will embody all realms in an integrative schema.

Opinions differ concerning how best to define personality, normal or otherwise. There is general agreement, however, that personality is an inferred abstraction, a concept or a construct, rather than a tangible phenomenon with material existence. Problems inevitably arise, however, when professionals reify these conceptual constructs into substantive entities. To paraphrase Kendell (1975), "familiarity leads us to forget their origins in human imagination." The disorders of personality should not be construed as palpable diseases. They are man-made constructions that have been invented to facilitate scientific understanding and professional communication. Personality may be conceived as the psychological equivalent of the human body's biological system of structures and functions. The body as a whole comprises a well-organized yet open system of relatively stable structures that interconnect functionally as they process a wide range of both internal and external events in a coherent and efficient manner. The diversity of functions the body carries out is awesome in its complexity and efficacy, as is the internal organization of structures that are impressively elaborate in their intricacy and articulation. The distinctive configuration of structures and functions that have evolved ensures that the system as a whole remains both viable and stable. This is achieved by processes that maintain internal cohesion and by actions that use, control, or adapt to external forces. A biological disorder arises when one or several of the following occurs: (1) the balance and synchrony among internal components go awry; (2) a particular structure is traumatized or deteriorates with the result that it repetitively or persistently malfunctions; or (3) foreign entities such as bacteria or viruses intrude themselves, either overwhelming or insidiously undermining the system's integrity.

The construct of personality may be conceived as a psychic system of structures and functions that parallels that of the body. It is not a potpourri of unrelated traits and miscellaneous behaviors but a tightly knit organization of stable structures (e.g., internalized memories and self-images) and coordinated functions (e.g., unconscious mechanisms and cognitive processes). Given continuity in a person's constitutional equipment and a narrow band of experiences for learning behavioral alternatives, this psychic system develops an integrated pattern of characteristics and inclinations that are deeply etched, cannot be easily eradicated, and pervades every facet of the life experience. This system is the sum and substance of what the construct of personality would mean. Mirroring the body's organization, the psychic system is a distinctive configuration of interlocking perceptions, feelings, thoughts, and behaviors that provides a template and disposition for maintaining psychic viability and stability. From this perspective, the disorders of personality would be best conceived as stemming from failures in the system's dynamic pattern of adaptive competencies.

Just as physical ill health is never a simple matter of an intrusive alien virus but reflects also deficiencies in the body's capacity to cope with particular physical environments, so, too, is psychological ill health not merely a product of psychic stress alone but represents deficiencies in the personality system's capacity to cope with particular psychosocial environments. Given the increasing awareness of the complex nature of both health and disease, modern clinical scientists recognize that most physical disorders result from a dynamic and changing interplay between individuals' capacities to cope and the environment within which they live. It is the patients' overall constitutional makeup, their vitality, stamina, and immune system that serve as a substrate that inclines them to resist or succumb to potentially troublesome environmental forces.

Mental disorders should be conceived as reflecting the same interactive pattern. Here, however, it is not the immunological defenses or enzymatic capacities, but patients' personality patterns, that is, their coping skills and adaptive flexibilities that determines whether they will master or succumb to their psychosocial environment. Viewed this way, the structure and characteristics of personality become the foundation for an individual's capacity to function in a mentally healthy or ill way.

No sharp line divides normal from pathological behavior; they are relative concepts representing arbitrary points on a continuum or gradient. Not only is personality so complex that certain areas of psychological functioning operate normally while others do not, but environmental circumstances change such that behaviors and strategies that prove adaptive at one time fail to do so at another. Moreover, features differentiating normal from abnormal functioning must be extracted from a complex of signs that not only wax and wane but often develop in an insidious and unpredictable manner.

Mental pathology results from the same forces that are involved in the development of normal functioning. Important differences in the character, timing, and intensity of these influences will lead some individuals to acquire pathological mental structures and functions, whereas others develop adaptive ones. When individuals display an ability to cope with the environment in a flexible manner, and when their typical perceptions and behaviors foster increments in personal satisfaction, then they may be said to possess a normal or healthy personality. Conversely, when average or everyday responsibilities elicit inflexible or defective responses, or when an individual's perceptions and behaviors result in increments of personal discomfort or curtail opportunities to learn and to grow, a pathological or maladaptive pattern emerges.

Unfolding of Key Ideas

As described in earlier chapters, personality was appraised in ancient times by relying on the study of astrological phenomenon: By positioning the location of stars and planets astrologers attempted to judge the characteristics of persons by recording information such as the time of their birth and the dominance of star clusters seen above the horizon. The early Greeks, who turned attention from the stars to physical characteristics such as humors and an individual's facial configurations, gradually replaced these astrological and comparable animistic superstitions, attempting thereby to decode inner features of a person in what came to be termed *physiognomy*. A more recent variant of physiognomy, phrenology, became a popular pseudoscience of reading inner characteristics by the contours of a person's skull, an approach that achieved great popularity in the nineteenth century.

Other foundations of personology exist as well, beginning with its biological grounding in Darwin's evolutionary theory and moving to its applications in modern psychological thinking, notably in the school of *functionalism* and more recently, in the emergence of trait theories and personality pathology.

Elaborating Evolutionary Theory

Formulas of a psychological nature must not only coordinate with, but be anchored firmly to, observations derived specifically from modern principles of physical and biological evolution. The ideas presented in the early sections of this chapter have been grounded in this knowledge.

Drawing on evolutionary theory to articulate personological science is conjectural, if not overly extended in its speculative reach. In essence, it seeks to explicate the structure and styles of personality with reference to deficient, imbalanced, or conflicted modes of ecologic adaptation and reproductive strategy.

Ideas relating to evolution may be traced to the ancients, formulated in primitive notions by Empedocles, but these notions are only tangentially related to contemporary thinking about the concept. Aristotle also initiated a series of speculations concerning evolutionary ideas, but failed to systematize them into an orderly and universal framework. It was not until the seventeenth century that the theologian John Ray proposed an evolutionary process designed to illustrate how God provided man with increasingly appropriate habitats for daily functioning. In the next century, Immanuel Kant, Pierre Simons de Laplace, and Dagobert Cuvier noted that astronomical and geological events demonstrated convincingly that nature was not immutable, specifically that stars emerge and then disappear and that the earth's crust displayed catastrophic changes in erosion and layering. In the mid-eighteenth century, Comte de Buffon outlined a highly speculative proposal of organic development in which species ostensibly underwent chance variations, with occasional deterioration and progress from generation to generation, a view theologians roundly condemned. Goethe in Germany and Fourier in France proposed that human destiny progressed through a sequence of increasingly improved stages. Similarly, Hegel was convinced that civilization itself formed evermore sophisticated cultural designs. Erasmus Darwin, Charles Darwin's grandfather, anticipated these ideas, by suggesting that all living things undergo progressively improving transformations in their structures and functions. He also set the groundwork for a purposive conception of natural evolution, a theme Jean-Baptiste Lamarck further elaborated shortly thereafter. In Lamarck's thesis, organisms were internally driven to adapt to changes in response to environmental circumstances. More specifically, he asserted that organisms exercised their bodily capacities so they would become more adaptive to their environment. Lamarck went astray when he assumed that offspring of the exercised organisms inherited these adaptive changes. Thomas Malthus also proposed in the late eighteenth century that transformations in human populations stemmed from the radical events of the Industrial Revolution. He suggested that different members of the human race were more or less fit to cope with the environmental demands placed upon their species. Some members of a species were more fit than others in adapting to the tasks of getting food, warding off their enemies and, hence, surviving from generation to generation. The innovative British geologist, Charles Lyell, in the early nineteenth century, demonstrated that different strata of rock formations in the earth had been built upon one another at a slow and progressive pace, and that they clearly reflected different time periods, as evidenced by the changing character of the fossils they contained.

What makes **Charles Darwin's (1809–1882)** contributions so outstanding was not that he was the first to think of evolutionary progressions, but that he recognized and possessed evidence of an enormous and well-ordered nature to explicate and articulate the processes involved.

Born in Shrewsbury, England, the fifth of six children of a wealthy, sensitive, and well-respected physician, and a mother from the well-established Wedgewood pottery family, Darwin was also the grandson of the outspoken social and religious critic, Erasmus Darwin, who died some years before Charles was born. In his mid-teens, Darwin went to Edinburgh to study medicine but found the family profession to be gruesome, if not repulsive, quitting medicine after two years, and joining a group of anti-establishment intellectuals known for their radical and atheistic views.

Charles Darwin

As well-recorded in the over 200 biographies written about his life, Darwin moved on to Christ's College in Cambridge to study for the clergy in his early 20s, but found these academic studies to be no more appealing than those he experienced in Edinburgh. Keenly interested in classifying naturalistic phenomenon, he became the naturalist on the ship *Beagle,* voyaging on a wandering course around the earth for a period of five years, during which he transcribed in vast detail his botanical and anthropological observations, and ultimately accumulated a large number of preserved plants and animal specimens. Upon his return, Darwin submitted many of his botanical and zoological notes for publication, but retained several secret notebooks regarding his insights into the transmutation of species, using *Zoonomia,* a title of one of his grandfather's books as a disguise and deceptive label, lest his own radical metaphysical theory be known to others.

For more than a 20-year period Darwin continued to postpone the publication of his theory, reorganizing his notes time and again, until 1858 when he received a manuscript from **Alfred Russel Wallace (1823–1913)** detailing Wallace's own theory "on the tendency of varieties to depart." Stunned by the similarity between Wallace's observations and his own evolutionary theory, Darwin was encouraged by colleagues to quickly refine his own notes and writings, submitting them, together with Wallace's paper, as a joint publication for presentation and review, most notably in his own seminal *Origins of Species* (1859). Criticism and public arguments followed from both scientific sources and religious dissenters.

Darwin, highly sensitive to scorn and public ridicule, drew increasingly away from public forums and potential controversy, but continued to write on his themes of evolutionary progression and natural selection, the essence of his highly innovative ideas. Many decades passed before the convincing research of *Gregor Johann Mendel* in the 1860s would support Darwin's thesis. Similarly, the 1880s research of Weismann and DeVries showed clearly that generation-to-generation changes were not a function of acquired characteristics, but reflected the shifting of elements in the germ cells, which periodically underwent sudden mutations.

In *The Expression of Emotions in Man and Animals* (1867/1896), Darwin produced his most important work of a psychological nature. He examined the facial musculature of many species, including that of *homo sapiens*, noting not only anatomical similarities but also similarities in facial expression generated under similar conditions. Darwin concluded that the underlying anatomical equipment necessary for the expression of affects were essentially the same or only modestly different among mammalian species. As he saw it, evolutionary progressions included not only the anatomy of each species but their functional physiology as well. Moreover, psychological evolution was a concomitant of both anatomical and physiological evolution. Human equipment for psychological characteristics could be traced, therefore, at least in his judgment, to the primitive dispositions found in lower species.

By the latter part of the nineteenth century, Darwin's ideas increasingly influenced psychological thought. People recognized that the functions served and the tasks accomplished as humans adjusted to their changing environment. The emergence of comparative psychology, the study of species differences, the psychological school of "functionalism," as well as the investigation of individual differences in intelligence and abilities by Darwin's cousin Francis Galton (see Chapter 14), became major directions in this new field.

A well-established empiricist of the British school, **Alexander Bain (1818–1903)** reformulated his early ideas in light of Darwin's evolutionary theories. Too poor as a child to obtain a formal education, Bain worked as a weaver from the age of eleven, taught himself mathematics and managed to achieve a night study degree at Marischal College in Aberdeen. Throughout the 1850s, Bain worked as a political journalist, while writing two well-regarded textbooks in psychology.

Drawing on Darwin's findings on the role of natural selection, Bain made much of the role of physiological correlates of psychological functions. Arguing for the notion of psychophysical parallelism, he stressed the view that all psychological processes have distinct physical parallels.

In a major essay, "On the Study of Character" (1861), Bain sought to find a physiological basis for differences in psychic temperament and disposition; in his view, these characteristics reflected differences in energy currents that flowed from the brain toward the muscles. Writing in *Senses and the Intellect* (1855):

> If we were to venture, after the manner of phrenology, to specify more precisely the locality the centers of general energy, I should say the posterior part of the crown of the head . . . must be full and ample if we would expect a conspicuous display of this feature (cautiousness, firmness, and conscientiousness) of character. (p. 195)

Remember the British utilitarian and forerunner of American functional-ism, *Herbert Spencer*, whose background was discussed in some detail in Chap-ter 11. Shortly before Darwin's *Origins of Species* was published Spencer borrowed Lamarck's and Malthus' ideas and coined the phrase "survival of the fittest." Spencer also quickly incorporated Darwin's ideas in revisions of his well-regarded two-volume *Principles of Psychology* (1870), and his three-vol-ume *Principles of Sociology*, (1876). Championing Darwin's evolutionary ideas and evidence, which abounded at the time, Spencer worked at applying the implications of scientific discovery to social thought and action.

A century after Darwin, **Edward Osborne Wilson (1929–   )** desired to compare the social life of insects and animals in the hope that it would enable him to uncover common principles among all variants of societal functioning. More specifically, he created a new field of study, labeled *sociobiology*, suggest-ing that a systematic biological basis of the social behavior of disparate organ-isms exists. As he saw it, traditional social scientists focused their attentions on only one mammalian species: humans. Wilson strove to establish a basis for understanding all forms of social life. Each species, to him, represented an evolutionary experiment from which one might uncover the biological origins of human social behavior. Biologists have learned about heredity from the study of fruit flies; similarly insect social behavior may provide principles that explain human behavior. As Wilson wrote in his second sociobiologic text, *On Human Nature* (1978):

> Sociobiology is a subject based largely on comparisons of social species. Each living form can be viewed as an evolutionary experiment, a product of millions of years of interaction between genes and environment. By examining many such experiments closely, we have begun to construct and test the first general principles of genetic social evolution. It is now within our reach to apply this broad knowledge to the study of human beings. (p. 17)

Although brilliant explorations detailing the processes by which social evo-lution unfolds have taken place since Darwin's seminal contributions (as seen, for example, in comparative psychology, ecology, ethology, and, most recently, genetic research), many judge Wilson's proposals to be the first fully innova-tive extension of Darwin's fundamental proposals. The early success of socio-biologic concepts, however, gives no assurance that extrapolations from lower species can be extended to human social behavior. Comparisons across species are hazardous speculations, despite their seeming logic. This is especially true when human capacities of abstraction are features not readily found in in-stinct-driven lower species.

Bypassing the usual complications of analogies, Millon (1990) drew a rele-vant and intriguing parallel between the phylogenic evolution of a species' ge-netic composition and the ontogenic development of an individual organism's adaptive strategies (i.e., its "personality style"). At any time, a species will possess a limited set of genes that serve as trait potentials. Over succeeding generations the frequency distribution of these genes will likely change in their relative proportions depending on how well the traits they undergird contribute to the species' "fittedness" within its varying ecological habitats. In a similar fashion, individual organisms begin life with a limited subset of their species' genes and the trait potentials they subserve. Over time, the salience of these trait potentials—not the proportion of the genes themselves—will become differentially prominent as the organism interacts with its environments. It learns from these experiences which of its traits fit best, that is, most optimally suited to its ecosystem. As noted by Millon (1990), in phylogenesis, actual gene frequencies change during the generation-to-generation adaptive process, whereas in ontogenesis it is the salience or prominence of gene-based traits that changes as adaptive learning takes place. Parallel evolutionary processes occur, one within the life of a species, the other within the life of an organism. A shaping of latent potentials into adaptive and manifest styles of perceiving, feeling, thinking, and acting is evidenced in the individual organism; these distinctive ways of adaptation, engendered by the interaction of biologic endowment and social experience, comprise the elements of what is termed personality styles. It is a formative process in a single lifetime that parallels gene redistributions among species during their evolutionary history.

Proposing Adaptive Functionalism

The intellectual rationale for what came to be called the school of functionalism was provided in Charles Darwin's central theme that living organisms must adapt to the exigencies of their environment, lest they suffer degradation and extinction. As psychologists came to use this concept, they claimed that every psychological function and activity must be appraised in terms of how they relate to and foster the survival of the individual or the species.

In American psychology, functionalism made its position clear and firm by its contrast to the structuralism Titchener (Chapter 10) promulgated. The focus of functionalism was primarily on activities, that is, mental operations rather than on the mind's contents. Psychological functions were processes to be studied in their natural settings, interpreted in terms of their utility, that is, actions on the part of living organisms as they adapt to their environments. The problem that functionalism set for itself was "What do mental processes accomplish?" This meant, in contrast to structuralism's introspective observation of the elements of consciousness, a marked departure from the then prevailing ideas that Titchener emphasized. Although only one or two systematic expositions of functional psychology was explicitly written, its alliance with basic Darwinian principles were implicit in the writings of William James, Hugo Münsterberg, John Dewey, G. Stanley Hall, and James Rowland Angell.

William James (1842–1910) both precedes and follows Titchener in American psychology. He was older than Titchener by 25 years and published his major work, *The Principles of Psychology* in 1890, two years before Titchener came to Cornell University from England. Moreover, he died in 1910 when Titchener's power favoring structuralism and the introspective method was at its height. Titchener's goal was to transform psychology into a science, whereas James sought to create a psychological science.

Although not the founder of a formal school of thought, James' writings clearly reflected the ideas of Darwin and served as a seminal source for the functional movement that grew around him. He was an independent and original thinker who wandered far and wide, often into fields not above suspicion, such as religion and psychical research. In contrast to Titchener, he believed significant psychological constructs such as consciousness to be composed not of discrete units joined incidentally together, but as a flowing current, a continuous and streaming process that was always in motion, choosing, shifting, and accentuating its focus.

Born the first of five children into a well-to-do New York family of literate and unconventional parents with a strong inclination for the unusual and deviant, James' grandfather acquired substantial wealth when building the Erie Canal. His father lost a leg as a result of an accident, surgery, and infection, became an introspective recluse, developing a passionate interest in the ideas of the Swedish mystic, Emanuel Swedenborg (see Chapter 2). His mother was a devoted but hypochondriacal woman, troubled by emotional concerns, and excessively preoccupied with the health of her husband and children, contributing no doubt to the periodically sickly life of her son William. The family had the freedom to travel, which they did often, encouraging the children to acquire a facility with languages, and endowed two sons with an awesome talent for life-long scholarship in both novels and science.

In his student days, James had opportunities to become acquainted with von Helmholtz and to visit Wundt's laboratories in Germany, as well as to observe Charcot's and Janet's clinical facilities in France. Consistent with his "liberal" upbringing, he clearly preferred the free and rich imagination of French psychological thinking in contrast to the highly formal and rigorous demand of the routine research that characterized German work. He struggled throughout adolescence in a not uncommon course for those who ultimately became psychology professionals. Initially seeking a career in art, he then turned to the study of chemistry with a young professor, Charles Eliot, later president of Harvard University. He moved on to travel with the Swiss-born Harvard naturalist, Louis Agassiz, beginning studies toward a medical career. Despite persistent ailments following a trip with Agassiz to South America where he contracted an obscure tropical disease, James completed his medical degree at the age of 27. Offered a position at Harvard in 1872, he appeared to recover from his ailments, though he never became especially robust. Known as an erudite and facile teacher, he progressed from numerous early written contributions to the new science of psychology to the more traditional concerns of metaphysical philosophy. Ill-disposed to experimental

William James

work, he nevertheless established a laboratory at Harvard, but for purposes of teaching rather than research. He accepted a contract to write a textbook on psychology for the Henry Holt Company in 1878, finally completing it in 1890. The two-volume work entitled *The Principles of Psychology* and its briefer version two years later framed the subject of the new science for several decades.

Despite his tremendous influence on the development of psychological thought in the United States, James was an individual, unconnected with any formal school of thought, and he exerted his wide influence primarily through his intelligence, charm, and warmth. As Heidbreder has recorded (1933), however engrossed he became in a movement, however enthusiastic about its importance, he remained incorrigibly himself, though keenly alive to all psychological enterprises of his day, by turns sympathetic, amused, critical, and, on occasion, accepting. He never lost himself either in his enthusiasms or in his aversions, yet, he was not in any sense aloof to the causes of his time. He remained in the thick of psychology in all of its turbulent movements during its fractious youth. Although cognizant of the new experimental psychology that was carried to the United States by disciples of Wundt from Germany, he kept a proper distance from it, assimilating certain of its philosophical assertions, dismissing others owing to its rigid dogma, and never transformed from his individualistic views.

As is well known, his brother, Henry James, became a distinguished novelist in England. Both brothers had a great flair for the English language, employing vivid portrayals and felicitous phraseology in their writings. Many an intelligent critic commented that Henry was a novelist who wrote like a psychologist and William was a psychologist who wrote like a novelist. Both James attracted a loyal public and an extensive professional and lay following. William was a complicated person, writing both insightfully and honestly about his own personal struggles, seeking to exemplify the richness and inevitable struggles of everyday life. Radiant, companionable, warm, and loving, William was also episodically troubled and ill, occasionally depressed, and even suicidal.

James' two-volume *Principles* had 28 chapters and was close to 1,400 pages long. Topics were wide-ranging and of great interest, even to today's contemporary psychologists. It included chapters on "habit," "the stream of thought," "consciousness," "emotions," and "will." Another of his books, one based on his "metaphysical lectures," *The Varieties of Religious Experience: A Study in Human Nature* (1902) stimulated great public interest. James voiced a deep curiosity about matters of abnormal behavior and the influence of the subconscious mind. His lifetime interest in the unconventional and spiritual led him to found the American Society for Psychical Research. Despite his vast writings as both a psychologist and a philosopher, James sought to establish psychology as a naturalistic and secular science, always keeping his fascination with metaphysical issues in check.

James' orientation rested on his belief that everyday experiences should be the basis of psychology, a perspective akin to the forthcoming functionalist philosophy. He made extensive use of personal case histories to illustrate individuals' feelings and hopes. His philosophy was pragmatic, with a down-to-earth, practical, and everyday focus that stressed the adaptive reality of persons' lives.

In 1892, William James wrote to **Hugo Münsterberg (1863–1916)** indicating that he would like the young German psychologist ". . . to take charge of the psychological laboratory and the higher instruction in that subject in Harvard University. . . . We need something more than a safe man, we need a man of genius" (1920). Münsterberg accepted the invitation and remained at Harvard until his death. A native of the Prussian city of Danzig, Münsterberg converted to Protestantism from Judaism in his early twenties, received his doctorate under Wundt at Leipzig University in 1885 and an MD from Heidelberg University two years later. After a brief initial period at Harvard, Münsterberg developed an exemplary program in experimental psychology based on the model he saw as a student in Wundt's Leipzig laboratory. Regarded as a vain and arrogant promoter of his own ideas, he started his own psychological journal, was elected the seventh president of the American Psychological Association, and remained an ardent German patriot throughout all his years in the United States.

Throughout his career, he exerted considerable leadership in carrying forward the functionalist's idea that process rather than structure was the essence of psychological study; the mind, to him, was a dynamic and active concept that should be studied in the context of everyday life. A prodigious, if not indefatigable contributor to the popular media of his day, he addressed issues such as the causes and treatment of mental disorders, often stressing the importance of religion and the therapist's active role. He was also concerned with preventing mental disorders, focusing his scorn on what he viewed to be the pernicious effects of destructive social and legal institutions. Especially significant to his place in the history of psychology was his book, *Psychology and Industrial Efficiency* (Münsterberg, 1913), in which he framed a science that bridged modern laboratory studies and the issues of social economics, synthesized toward the end of servicing commerce and industry. In line with the functionalists' philosophy, he sought to move psychology away from the abstract academic concerns of the structuralists toward the world of everyday life, exploring such practical problems as vocational fitness and job satisfaction.

In his autobiography, **Granville Stanley Hall (1844–1924)** described his life as a "series of fads or crazes, some strong, some weak; some lasting long and recurring over and over again at different periods of life and in different forms, and others ephemeral" (1923, p. 367). Hall's diverse efforts to explore every area of human activity illustrated the essence of functionalism. Challenging the structuralist's preoccupation with the static elements of consciousness and drawing upon James' implicit process-oriented perspective and Darwin's notions of adaptation, Hall's work ranged across every application of psychological study.

Born in his grandfather's home, he was raised and educated in a rural Massachusetts' environment. At the age of 16, he was awarded a certificate that enabled him to teach in the public schools, an occupation he pursued for two years before entering Williams College, later enrolling in New York's Union Theological Seminary. Exposed to the intellectual and cultural opportunities of New York City, his experiences led him to seek a broader education than what was available at the Seminary. In 1869, at the age of 25, he traveled to Germany, became a student at the University of Bonn, and pursued further studies in philosophy at Berlin University. Returning in 1870 to the United States, he completed his final year at Union and accepted a four-year teaching assignment at Antioch College, accumulating enough funds to enroll at Harvard University where he began his studies with William James. In 1878, he became the first student to receive a doctorate in the field of psychology/philosophy. He returned to Berlin University to study with several distinguished professors, most notably von Helmholtz and Wundt. He was invited in 1881 to lecture at Johns Hopkins University and was awarded a professorship in 1884, providing courses in the "new psychology," as well as developing the first full-fledged psychological laboratory in the United States. In 1888, he was offered the presidency of a new college, Clark University in Worcester, Massachusetts. There he struggled to build both a physical campus and an academic faculty, succeeding through numerous difficult periods over 35 years until his retirement in 1923.

Hall experienced innumerable tragedies and challenges throughout his life, struggling to resolve the tension between innovation and tradition, mirroring in his own life the very essence of evolutionary progression, the theme he so ardently embraced. He sought to synthesize the old and the new, to find ways to adjust to a dynamically changing world and to track the course of life's developmental progression. His major research and scholarly projects were centered on the psychology of childhood and adolescence. Here he saw a parallel with the history of species, leading him to state that an individual's developmental history, termed *ontogeny*, recapitulates the evolutionary history of species, termed *phylogeny*. This developmental/evolutionary model was an extension of William James' emphasis on Darwin's "origins" concept. With the center for experimental child research, Hall and Clark University contributed significantly to the view that psychology was a useful discipline that had important things to say about to the problems of everyday life.

The premier philosopher of education in the first half of the twentieth century in the United States was **John Dewey (1859–1952).** Trained initially as a psychologist, his work at the University of Chicago at the turn of the century was instrumental in shifting the focus of psychology away from its own navel to that of the world-at-large.

Born in 1859, Dewey graduated from the University of Vermont at the age of 19, entered the graduate program in philosophy at Johns Hopkins, studied with G. Stanley Hall, completed a dissertation on Immanuel Kant's contributions to psychology, and accepted a teaching assignment in philosophy and psychology at the University of Michigan in 1884. Ten years later, he moved to the University of Chicago as professor and chair of the psychology and philosophy department where he remained for another ten years before taking a post as dean of the School of Education at Columbia University in New York. During his Chicago period, his primary contributions to the functionalist perspective were most clearly stated.

Dewey asserted unequivocally that psychology must be rooted in the experiences of everyday life. He opposed all efforts to dissect events introspectively into their sensorial elements, a structuralist preoccupation that he viewed to be artificial and arbitrary. To Dewey, psychology should not be an abstract academic study but an applied and useful one, such as in schooling and education. He believed fervently that education should be constructed so that children would learn by doing and by reflecting on what he or she has done. In his view, psychological studies should not be separated from their natural settings or from their social consequences.

The academic careers and philosophical perspectives of Dewey and **James Rowland Angell (1869–1949)** had much in common. Further, both were born in Burlington, Vermont, albeit ten years apart. Angell attended the University of Michigan where he studied with Dewey in a course based on James' just published *The Principles of Psychology*. He then studied for a graduate degree at Harvard under James. Prior to completing his doctorate, he accepted a position at the University of Minnesota where he stayed a year before leaving for the University of Chicago. In Chicago, his academic career again overlapped with Dewey for a decade, each contributing significantly to a functionalist philosophy for psychology. Despite failing to formally complete his doctorate, Angell became the head of the psychology department at Chicago, and later assumed the role of dean of faculty and then acting-president of the University. Owing to his administrative talents, he was offered and accepted the presidency of Yale University in 1921, where he remained until retirement in 1937.

Despite his administrative responsibilities, Angell published a highly successful text, *Psychology: An Introductory Study of the Structure and Function of Human Consciousness* (1904/1909), as well as a seminal article titled "The Province of Functional Psychology" in 1907. This paper, an extension of his presidential address at the American Psychological Association, became the clearest statement of the functionalist point of view. Although functionalism was centered at the University of Chicago owing to the presence of Dewey and Angell, both scholars believed that the orientation of functionalism should not be conceived as a school of psychology, but rather something much broader than any one scientific discipline.

For the next decade or two, psychology was characterized by the contrasting views of Titchener's structuralism and Angell's and Dewey's functionalism. It was not until 1913 that both schools of thought were rudely awakened, perhaps shocked is the more apt term, by the emergence of John Watson's behavioristic viewpoint (see Chapter 9). Watson, a former acolyte of Angell, proposed a radical new focus for psychology, vigorously anti-structuralist, but also highly dubious of his Chicago mentor's functionalist perspective.

Advocating Temperamental Functions

Like intelligence and physique, temperament comprises the raw material from which the capacities and functions of the person may be fashioned, comprising biological dispositions that are largely assumed to be unchanged throughout life. According to Gordon Allport's definition (1937): "Temperament refers to the . . . individual's emotional nature, including his susceptibility to emotional stimulation, . . . the quality of his prevailing mood; . . . these phenomenon being regarded as dependent upon constitutional make-up, and therefore largely hereditary in origin" (p. 54).

The British philosopher-psychologist **Thomas Arnold (1742–1826)** actively promoted the ideas of William Cullen (see Chapter 5), especially in his well-respected book, *Observations on Nature, Kinds, Causes, and Prevention of Insanity,* first published in 1782 and then in a second edition in 1806. He characterized some 13 dysfunctional temperaments, several of which are descriptively similar to those found in current *DSM* categories. For example, his "scheming type" is nearly like the paranoid characterization; the "vain species" or arrogant form of insanity is similar to narcissistic personality disorder. The "pathetic" or "melancholic species" is akin to the depressive personality characterization. The "impulsive species" resembles current conceptions of the obsessive-compulsive type, and a "bashful" variant parallels avoidant personality disorder.

A late nineteenth-century French psychologist, **Theodule Armand Ribot (1839–1916)** (1890) attempted to formulate temperament functions in a manner analogous to botanical classifications. In 1875, Ribot published the first edition of *La Psychologie Anglaise Contemporaine,* introducing the British work of Darwin, Spencer, and Bain to his French contemporaries. Here he evidenced the view that the functional capacities or orientations of persons must be based on physiology in order for them to be subject to the "universal laws of nature." In his second book, *La Psychology des Sentiments* (1890), he stressed Darwin's proposals on the evolution and adaptive functions of the "affective life," focusing his attention on complex drive states such as pain and pleasure. Ribot introduced the concept of *anhedonie,* a functional insensibility to either or both pain and pleasure.

In his *Revue* journal in 1892, he also wrote of the "facultative division of character types." Here he stressed two essential ingredients of character (what we speak of today as temperament), specifying that its features are innate and composed of unity and stability. By varying the intensity level of two traits, those of sensitivity and activity, Ribot sought to construct several major functional temperament types. Among those proposed were: (1) the "humble character," noted by excess sensibility and limited energy; (2) the "contemplative character," marked by keen sensibility and passive behavior; and (3) the "emotional type," combining extreme impressionability and an active disposition. Among other major categories were the "apathetic" and the "calculative" characters.

A number of temperament typologists from other European nations followed a decade or so after Ribot. Most notable among them was the Dutch philosopher-psychologist **Geradus Heymans (1857–1930).** Appointed chairman of philosophy at the University of Groningen in 1890, Heymans initiated a series of psychological investigations to establish a strong empirical grounding for his philosophical ideas. His first major work, *Laws and Elements of Scientific Thought* (1890) adopted the inductive model John Stuart Mill set forth. In contrast to his contemporaries, Heymans employed empirical procedures that, much to his surprise, led him to anti-empiricist conclusions.

Along with his psychiatric colleague, *Eduard Wiersma,* and on the basis of a series of highly sophisticated empirical studies, Heymans identified three fundamental criteria for evaluating the functional qualities of temperament: activity level, emotionality, and susceptibility to external versus internal stimulation. These criteria anticipated similar threefold schemas (each based, however, on highly dissimilar theoretical models) developed by McDougall (1908), Meumann (1910), Freud (1915/1925b), and Millon (1969). By combining these criteria, Heymans deduced eight character types, namely: (1) the "amorphous" character, reflecting the interplay of passive, nonemotional, and external susceptibility; (2) the "apathetic" character, developing from a passive, nonemotional, and internal orientation; (3) the "nervous" character, a product of a passive, emotional, and external responsiveness; (4) the "sentimental" character, who is passive, emotional, and internally impressed; (5) the "sanguine" character, noted as active, nonemotional, and externally receptive; (6) the "phlegmatic" character, typified by active, nonemotional, and internal tendencies; (7) the "choleric" character, reflecting an active, emotional, and external susceptibility; and (8) the "impassioned" character, representing an active, emotional, and internal sensitivity. The criteria Heymans developed corresponded extremely well with clinical dimensions later theorists derived, specifically the polarities of activity-passivity, pleasure-pain emotionality, and an internal, or self, responsivity versus an external, or other, responsivity. This eight-fold model became known as *Heymans' cube,* a series of his three dimensions for which he found empirical support in hereditary surveys and 100 biographies of eminent individuals.

The distinguished German psychologist **Ernst Friedrich Wilhelm Meumann (1862–1915)** proposed a major effort to construct a functional theory of temperament in his 1910 text *Intelligenz und Wille*. This son of a Protestant minister was born in Prussia and followed his father's profession during his initial studies, but withdrew from all theological activities to become an outspoken agnostic, if not atheist. Immersed in the struggles between authoritarian German thought and the emergence of vigorous social and cultural reform movements, Meumann pursued a career in philosophy and psychology, becoming a student and then an assistant to Wilhelm Wundt in the early 1890s. It was Wundt who stated later in his career that Meumann's dissertations were the most outstanding achievements in experimental psychology of that period.

His major writings on temperament and character stressed the interplay of cognitive and motivational variables. Meumann specified eight fundamental qualities of feeling. Central among them were the polarity of pleasure versus displeasure, and the two excitative modes of expression, the active and the passive. Meumann considered a number of other features to be of lesser significance, such as the ease of excitability and the intensity of affect. By combining the pleasure-displeasure and active-passive dimensions, Meumann sought to account for the four classical humors. For example, the active mode and the pleasurable quality blended to produce the sanguine temperament, an active mode merged with displeasurable feelings to form the choleric temperament, the combination of a passive mode with a pleasurable feeling accounted for the phlegmatic temperament, and the passive and displeasure amalgam created the melancholic temperament.

William McDougall, whose life history, sociologic, and social psychological contributions were described in Chapter 11, proposed a "consolidation of sentiments," a formal schema similar to Heymans. In it, he derived eight "tempers" based on different combinations of three functional dispositions: the intensity (strength and urgency), the persistency (inward versus outward expression), and the affectivity (emotional susceptibility) of behavioral impulses. Those of high intensity were viewed as active individuals, whereas those disposed to low intensity were considered to be passive. High persistency directed the person to the external world, whereas those with low persistency were oriented toward internal matters. By affectivity, McDougall meant susceptibility to pleasure and pain such that those characterized by high affectivity were particularly susceptible to these influences, whereas those of low affectivity were not. Combining these three dispositions led McDougall to form the following eight tempers: (1) the "steadfast" temper, noted by high intensity, high persistency, and low affectivity; (2) the "fickle" temper, characterized by low intensity, high persistency, and high affectivity; (3) the "unstable" temper, defined by high intensity, low persistency, and high affectivity; (4) the "despondent" temper, distinguished by high intensity, low persistency, and low affectivity; (5) the "anxious" temper, designated by low intensity, high persistency, and high affectivity; (6) the "hopeful" temper, identified by high intensity, high persistency, and high affectivity; (7) the "placid" temper, depicted by low intensity, high persistency, and low affectivity; and (8) the "sluggish" temper, specified by low intensity, low persistency, and low affectivity.

Of interest is the similarity between McDougall's temperament typology and the Heymans's characterology, especially with regard to parallels between their basic dimensions of intensity and the polarity of activity-passivity, between persistency and the internal versus external orientation, and between affectivity and the emotions of pain and pleasure. As noted earlier, other theories formulated frameworks based on essentially the same three dimensions.

C. Robert Cloninger (1945–   ) formulated a model anchored to a neurobiologic theory of temperament dispositions. His entire career has been centered at Washington University School of Medicine and the Barnes-Jewish Hospital in St. Louis. His elegant model, which seeks to draw upon genetic and neurobiologic substrates, proposes a complex theory based on the interrelationship of several trait dispositions. Central to Cloninger's formula are a series of heritable characteristics or functional dispositions, notably: novelty seeking, harm avoidance, and reward dependence. Each of these is associated with different neurobiologic systems, respectively, dopamaninergic, serotonergic, and noradrenergic. The interaction of these heritable traits influences learning experiences, processing information, mood reactions, and general adaptation. Depending on the combinations of these three core dispositions, individuals will be inclined to develop particular patterns of behavior and personality styles.

More specifically, *novelty seeking* is hypothesized to dispose individuals toward exhilaration or excitement in response to novel stimuli, which leads to the pursuit of potential rewards as well as an active avoidance of both monotony and punishment. *Harm avoidance* reflects a disposition to respond strongly to aversive stimuli, leading individuals to inhibit behaviors to avoid punishment, novelty, and frustrations. Third, *reward dependence* is hypothesized as a tendency to respond to signals of reward (e.g., verbal signals of social approval), and to resist extinction of behaviors previously associated with rewards or relief from punishment. Extending the theme of novelty seeking, for example, individuals with this disposition, but average of the other two dimensions, would be characterized as impulsive, exploratory, excitable, quicktempered, and extravagant, likely to seek out new interests, but inclined to neglect details and to become quickly distracted or bored. Anchored fundamentally to the dopamine neuromodulator, individuals who might be low in this neurobiologic substrate (e.g., under average in novelty seeking) are likely to be characterized as slow to engage in new interests, be preoccupied with narrow details, and inclined to be reflective, rigid, stoic, slow-tempered, orderly, and persistent.

Drawing on various combinations of these three functional dispositions or temperaments, Cloninger describes a series of second-order personality trait patterns, as well as third-order clusters of personality types or disorders. For example, the histrionic personality is viewed as exhibiting high novelty seeking, low harm avoidance, and high reward dependence; these derive from second-order trait patterns of being impulsive, emotionally vulnerable, and narcissistic.

Larry Siever's (1950–) theoretical model has also attempted to link neurotransmitter properties to the various personality disorders. Educated at Stanford and Harvard, he completed his residency at McLean Hospital in Massachusetts before an appointment at New York's Mt. Sinai Hospital.

In many regards, Siever's proposals concerning the temperamental under-pinning of personality functions and disorders can be traced back through history to Hippocrates' humoral thesis. However, the specificity and clarity of Siever's reasoning shows how advanced this old temperament notion has become. Although not intended to accommodate all of the particulars and complexities of the many varieties of personality disorders in the classifica-tion system, it provides a means for integrating the clinical characteristics of several of these disorders and their possible psychobiologic and developmen-tal roots.

Siever has developed a dimensional model that has major clinical syndromes at one extreme and the milder personality disorders at the other end. He proposes four major functional dispositions: *cognitive/perceptual organization, impulsivity/aggression, affective instability,* and *anxiety/inhibition.* For example, schizophrenic disorders are viewed as disturbances of a cognitive/perceptual na-ture, exhibiting themselves in thought disorders, psychotic symptoms, and so-cial isolation; the schizotypal disorder would serve as the prototype among the personality types. Disorders of impulsivity/aggression are hypothesized as result-ing in poor impulse control, particularly as evident in aggressive actions. In the more distinct clinical syndromes, Siever suggests its presence in explosive disor-ders, pathologic gambling, or kleptomania. When this dimension is more perva-sive and chronic, as in the personality disorders, the predisposition may be present in persistent self-destructive behaviors, such as in borderline and anti-social personalities. Problems of affective instability are most clearly observed in the intensity and dysregulation of mood disorders. When this inclination is more sustained over time, it may interfere with the development of stable rela-tionships and self-image, as may be manifested in borderline or histrionic per-sonality disorders. Last, the anxiety/inhibition dimension appears to be related to the Anxiety clinical syndromes (e.g., social phobia, compulsive rituals); when present at a low threshold over extended periods of development, an avoidant, compulsive, or dependent personality disorder may result.

Characterizing Maladaptive Personality Styles

The early theorists presented in this section are primarily of European origin, as were most scientific contributors in the early decades of this century. As psychological interest and talent crossed the Atlantic, and as psychoanalysis gained its preeminent status in the 1930s, 1940s, and 1950s, acquaintance with a number of the theorists discussed here faded rapidly. The loss of their contributions is unfortunate in that many of them proposed concepts that had to be rediscovered in contemporary work. Present thinking might have progressed more rapidly had their ideas been in more common use.

In Chapter 5, *Emil Kraepelin*'s career and contributions were elaborated. Best known are his books on the major psychotic syndromes, but he also developed ideas concerning "personality pathology." They are worth re-examining as a preview to the writings of Schneider and Kretschmer, to be discussed next.

Kurt Schneider (1887–1967) proposed the best-known European classification of maladaptive personalities, first published in 1923 and revised through several editions (1950). Schneider differed from many of his contemporaries, most notably Kretschmer, in that he did not view personality characterizations of pathology to be a precursor to other mental disorders but conceived it as a separate group of entities that covaried with them. A student of Kraepelin, some have justly viewed him as inheritor of Kraepelin's descriptive psychiatry; nevertheless, Schneider was at heart a philosophical disciple of Karl Jaspers (see Chapter 4) and his phenomenological perspective. Whereas Kraepelin sought to objectify the mental disorders, Schneider's intent was to more clearly elucidate the patient's inner experiences.

In the last edition of his text on psychopathologic personalities, Schneider described the following 10 variants as often seen in psychiatric work. "Hyperthymic" personalities reflect a mix of high activity, optimism, and shallowness; they tend to be uncritical, cocksure, impulsive, and undependable. Many seem unable to concentrate, and those who achieve occasional insights fail to retain them as lasting impressions. The "depressive" personalities, have a skeptical view of life, tend to take things seriously, and display little capacity for enjoyment. They are often excessively critical and deprecatory of others; at the same time, they are full of self-reproach and exhibit hypochondriacal anxieties. Schneider grouped "Insecure" personalities into two subvarieties, the "sensitives" and the "anankasts" (compulsives). These individuals ruminate excessively over everyday experience but have little capacity for expressing or discharging the feelings these thoughts stir up. Chronically unsure of themselves, they are apt to view life as a series of unfortunate events. They tend to behave in a strict and disciplined manner, holding closely to what is judged as socially correct. "Fanatic" personalities are expansive individuals inclined to be bitter, combative, and aggressive in promoting their views; they are often querulous and litigious. Among the "attention-seeking" personalities are those with heightened emotional responses, who delight in novelty and give evidence of excess enthusiasms, vivid imaginations, and a striving to be in the limelight; showy and capricious, many are boastful, and inclined to lie and distort. "Labile" personalities do not evidence a simple chronic emotionality but are characterized by abrupt and volatile mood changes, impulsive urges, sudden dislikes, and a shiftless immaturity. The "explosive" personality is characterized by being impulsively violent, disposed to be fractious, and likely to become combative without warning and without provocation. "Affectionless" personalities lack compassion and are often considered callous and cold; they appear distant or indifferent to friends and strangers alike. Historically, these patients correspond to those identified in the literature as exhibiting "moral insanity." The so-called weak willed personalities are not only docile and unassuming but are easily subjected to seduction by others and readily exploited to no good end; they are inevitably fated to trouble and disillusionment. The last of Schneider's types, the "asthenic" personality, is subject to intense hyochondriacal scrutiny and is so preoccupied with bodily functions that external events fade into the background and appear strange or unreal.

Continuing in the tradition of positing a depressive temperament set out most clearly in Kraepelin's work at the turn of the century, Kurt Schneider extended the notion of temperament in a different direction. To Schneider, who termed these individuals *depressive psychopaths*, the essential element was a persistent sense of gloom. However, unlike Kraepelin, as well as his contemporary Kretschmer, Schneider considered the depressive personality to be an extreme variant of normal personality traits, rather than a facet or expression of major affective (manic-depressive) disorder. In line with German psychiatric tradition, however, he considered inborn constitutional dispositions to be at its core, with experiential factors playing only a modifying role.

Akin to current characterizations of the *DSM-IV-TR* avoidant personality was Schneider's depiction of what he termed:

> The insecure self-distrusting psychopaths . . . a deeply rooted, inner insecurity and the lack of any robust self-confidence. Such traits are not easy to detect. The inner tangles and panics of these uncertain, self-mistrusting personalities are sometimes tightly concealed from the world outside. . . . This type is continually ridden with bad conscience and are the first to blame themselves for anything that goes wrong . . . (they) They are people forever dissatisfied with themselves through life. (1950, p. 21)

The modern trend in constitutional or structural, as opposed to functional, models of psychopathology, essentially an extension of ideas discussed in the next chapter on physiognomic thinking, began with **Ernst Kretschmer's (1888–1964)** seminal ideas and research. In his practice as a psychiatrist, Kretschmer observed a frequent association between certain physical body types and particular forms of mental disorder. Prompted by this impression, he set out to systematically categorize individuals according to their dominant physical build and to relate these categories to the two major Kraepelinian disorders of schizophrenia and manic-depressive psychosis. As a third objective, Kretschmer sought to relate physique to normal behavior dispositions.

Kretschmer, a student of Kraepelin, followed the main line of thought that numerous psychiatric forerunners proposed to the effect that manic and depressive qualities covary: in this regard he differed from his contemporary Kurt Schneider. Selecting the term "cycloid" to reflect a pattern of combined temperaments, Kretschmer perceived the depressive component to be a mixture of inborn chemical dispositions that exhibit themselves with depression at one end and mania at the other. In his experience with patients, Kretschmer recorded that he encountered those with primary hypermanic temperaments far more often than those he termed constitutional depressives. As in his formulation of the schizoid temperament, where patients may exhibit varying proportions of what he called the asthenic and hyperaesthetic temperaments, Kretschmer noted that hypomanics were likely to possess a small depressive component, whereas those of a melancholic temper would occasionally exhibit a "vein of humor." Kretschmer called this relation between hypomanic and melancholic elements in cycloid personalities the "diathetic" or "mood proportion." He described aspects of the melancholic as follows (1925):

> Tears come easily to his eyes, he can't get over even quite little things, and he grieves longer and deeper than other people over sad situations. That is to say: in the case of such individuals, it is not that the temperament itself is sad, but only that it is more easily roused by sad conditions. And what is particularly significant is this: in difficult, responsible positions, when there is any danger, in thorny, exasperating situations, and in sudden precarious crises in business, they are not nervous, irritated, or agitated, like the average man, and particularly like a great many schizophrenes. But they are unhappy. They cannot see any distance ahead, everything stands like a mountain in front of them. (p. 130)

Ernst Kretschmer may be credited (or blamed?) for a synthesis of Gall's notion relating bodily contours and structures to personality (see Chapter 14) and to Jung's characterization of extrovert and introvert personality types (see Chapter 7). In his well-documented book, *Physique and Character*, published in 1925, Kretschmer extended an observation he made that schizophrenics possessed elongated physiques and manic-depressives rounded and soft physiques, into a theory connecting body build to normal personality. In a series of studies, he demonstrated that persons with tall and slender physiques were of a schizoid or introversive temperament, whereas those of a heavier and more rotund physique were extroversive. William Sheldon (discussed next) investigated Kretschmer's hypothesis with more refined measures. He found that Kretschmer's typology was oversimplified, and that patterns relating body build to personality could take many more than two or three forms.

Kretschmer's physical classification scheme resulted in four types: the *pyknic*, which he described as a compact individual with a large, round head, large thorax and abdomen, soft and poorly muscled limbs, and a marked tendency to obesity; the *athletic*, noted for extensive muscular development and broad skeletal endowment; the *asthenic*, viewed as a fragile individual possessing thin muscularity and a frail bone structure; and the *dysplastic*, which reflected Kretschmer's recognition that the first three types may be mixed in an awkwardly constructed physique.

Kretschmer's evidence of an association between physique and psychosis, combined with his assumption of continuity between normality and pathology, led him to speculate on the existence of a general relationship between body structure and temperament. He contended that normal asthenic individuals would be introversive, timid, and lacking in personal warmth, that is, a milder variant of the withdrawn and unresponsive schizophrenics to which they were akin. He conceived normal pyknics as gregarious, friendly, and dependent in their interpersonal relations, that is, a less extreme form of the moody and socially excitable manic-depressive. That Kretschmer considered psychotic disorders to be accentuations of essentially normal personality types was a position to which the majority of his psychiatric colleagues did not subscribe.

Kretschmer's proposal of a gradated relationship between body build and behavioral disposition was an imaginative extension of his earlier constitutional ideas. Unfortunately, he offered no systematic or quantifiable evidence in support of this assertion, nor did he offer a biogenic explanation of why one individual of a particular physique remained normal while a similarly built individual succumbed to a psychosis.

Nevertheless, Kretschmer's clinical astuteness paralleled Kraepelin's. For example, he identified two polarities of sensitivity among those he characterized as possessing the "schizoid temperament": the *anaesthetic* and the *hyperaesthetic*. Those whose constitutional dispositions cluster at the anaesthetic pole anticipated by half a century the current *DSM* schizoid. The group that Kretschmer located at the hyperaesthetic end of the continuum exhibits sensibilities foreshadowed and exemplified the *DSM* avoidant pattern. Kretschmer wrote:

> In the hyperaesthetic type, there often develops a sharp antithesis: "I" and "The external world." There is a constant excited self-analysis and comparison: "How do I impress people? Who is doing me an injury? In what respect have I to forgive myself something? How shall I get through?" This is particularly true of gifted, artistic natures. . . . They are men who have a continual psychic conflict, whose life is composed of a chain of tragedies, a single thorny path of sorrow. . . .
>
> [Here] we find the qualities of nervousness, excitability, capriciousness, anxiousness, tenderness, and, above all, sensitive susceptibility. . . . He behaves shyly, or timidly, or distrustfully, or as if he were pushed in to himself. He complains of nerve troubles. He keeps anxiously away from all coarse games and brawls. . . .
>
> They are not restful in spirit, but, under the covering of a sulky silence, there always glimmers a spark of inner tension, which has the character of a complex, and springs from the accumulation of all the little everyday unpleasantness of office and family life; which get heaped up inside, which cannot be overcome, and which cannot be spoken out. (1925, pp. 167–174)

The key phrase depicting Kretschmer's hyperaesthetic, and one equally central to an understanding of the avoidant personality is: "They seek as far as possible to avoid and deaden all stimulation from the outside" (1925, p. 161).

How sharply the hyperaesthetic differs from the anaesthetic, the temperament type anticipating the *DSM* schizoid, who Kretschmer depicted as possessing "a certain psychic insensitivity, dullness . . . lack of spontaneity [and] affective imbecility" (1925, p. 156). Kretschmer portrayed the extreme anaesthetic-schizoid personality as follows:

> We feel that we are in contact with something flavorless, boring. . . . What is there in the deep under all these masks? Perhaps there is a nothing, a dark, hollow-eyed nothing—affective anemia. Behind an ever-silent facade, which twitches uncertainly with every expiring whim—nothing but broken pieces, black rubbish heaps, yawning emotional emptiness, or the cold breath of an arctic soullessness. (p. 150)

Kretschmer's descriptive language is so colorful as to mislead readers into feeling that they are reading about a lively and exciting personality rather than one devoid of affect and interpersonally numbing.

William Sheldon (1899–1979), a recipient of PhD and MD degrees at Chicago and Columbia Universities, respectively, was the best-known American constitutional theorist. A disciple of Kretschmer, Sheldon formulated a series of detailed hypotheses during his years at Harvard (Sheldon, 1940; Sheldon & Stevens, 1942) concerning the relationship between body physique, temperament, and mental pathology. Adding a degree of experimental sophistication and measurement precision to Kretschmer's work, he identified three basic dimensions in his morphological schema: (1) *endomorphy*, noted by a predominance of body roundness and softness; (2) *mesomorphy*, characterized by muscular and connective tissue dominance; and (3) *ectomorphy*, identified by a linearity and fragility of structure.

In his corresponding and imaginative typology, Sheldon also specified three temperament clusters: viscerotonia, somatotonia, and cerebrotonia. The *viscerotonic* component, which parallels endomorphy, was characterized by gregariousness, an easy expression of feeling and emotion, a love of comfort and relaxation, an avoidance of pain, and a dependence on social approval. *Somatotonia*, the counterpart to mesomorphy, was noted by assertiveness, physical energy, low anxiety, indifference to pain, courage, social callousness, and a need for action and power when troubled. *Cerebrotonia*, corresponding to ectomorphy, indicated a tendency toward restraint, self-consciousness, introversion, social awkwardness, and a desire for solitude when troubled.

How did Sheldon relate the measures of somatotype and temperament to mental pathology? He attempted at first to correlate measures of body morphology with the traditional system of psychiatric diagnosis and found that the traditional system of diagnosis was inadequate for his purposes. In particular, he rejected the conventional notion in psychiatry of discrete diagnostic categories (e.g., patients were classified as suffering either from manic-depressive psychosis, *or* paranoid schizophrenia *or* catatonic schizophrenia). Instead, he proposed that a series of continuous or gradated dimensions should be substituted for the notion of discrete disease entities. Toward this end, he developed three primary components of mental illness that coexist, in varying proportions, in each disturbed individual; these components paralleled not only his somatotype and temperament measures but also psychotic categories found in the traditional classification system.

The nonanalytic American psychiatrist **Hervey Cleckley (1921–1984)** was a Rhodes scholar best known for his study of multiple personalities, especially his best-selling co-authored book and film, *The Three Faces of Eve* (1957). More significant was his incisive and thorough clinical characterization of the antisocial personality in his book *The Mask of Sanity*, first published in 1941. Attempting to clarify problem terminologies and seeking to counter the trend of including increasingly diverse disorders under the rubric of "psychopathy," Cleckley proposed replacing the term with the label "semantic dementia" to signify what he viewed to be the syndrome's prime feature, the tendency to say one thing and to do another. More important than his proposal of a new nomenclature, which attracted little following, was Cleckley's clear description of the psychopath's primary traits—guiltlessness, incapacity for object love, impulsivity, emotional shallowness, superficial social charm, and an inability to profit from experience. The Canadian psychologist *Robert D. Hare* further developed this characterization. Important was Cleckley's assertion that psychopathic personalities are found not only in prisons but in society's most respected roles and settings. Cleckley illustrated this thesis with several examples of "successful" businessmen, scientists, physicians, and, especially, politicians. He wrote as follows (1941):

> In these personalities . . . a very deep seated disorder often exists. The true difference between them and the psychopaths who continually go to jails or to psychiatric hospitals is that they keep up a far better and more consistent outward appearance of being normal.
>
> The chief difference . . . lies perhaps in whether the mask or facade of psychobiologic health *is* extended into superficial material success. (pp. 198–199)

Articulating Personality Traits and Factors

Advances in mathematics in the late nineteenth century led to a reawakened interest in the basic units of personality. To replace the hypothetical brain faculties Gall proposed, others made efforts to construct *factors—a* set of independent elements of personality derived statistically from commonalities in behavior and test performance. C. Spearman's success in analyzing the basic factors of intelligence stimulated the extension of this method to personality study by Cyril Burt, Lloyd Thurstone, and, more recently, in the multivariate research of J. P. Guilford (see Chapter 14) as well as Raymond Cattell (discussed on the next page and in Chapter 14).

Factor and cluster analyses are statistical methods that calculate intercorrelations among a large group of variables such as traits, behaviors, symptoms, and so on. Patterns or groupings among these correlations are referred to as first-order, or primary: the elements making up these factors or clusters are interpreted to provide them with relevant psychological meaning. Second or higher order groupings may be derived from the original components by combining them into larger units; it is usually these second-order groupings that possess the scope necessary to encompass the breadth of a concept such as personality.

As with the temperament and pathology characterologists described previously, models that employ statistical analyses seek to identify the basic dispositions or underlying factors of personality through a variety of numerical methods. Once these elements have been identified, the task facing theorists is to regroup them into higher order combinations that correspond to various overt personality styles or patterns. The sequence is first analytic and then synthetic.

Fundamental questions have arisen with regard to the specification of the basic dimensions, traits, or factors in the first place. How many are there? Are they consistent with one another? Do they conflict? Although ostensibly derived on objective numerical grounds, is there no subjectivity in how the basic elements were initially selected and subsequently recombined? This is not the place to elaborate these issues, but they raise significant questions, nevertheless. For example, impressive descriptions of personality derived by numerical approaches may provide only surface characterizations. Lacking is an understanding of how these elements relate dynamically. Moreover, there is usually no basis for tracing or understanding each disorder's developmental origins, nor their pathogenic course. Interesting though they may be, ostensively objective and quantitative gauges of trait dimensions are insufficient to achieve a complete characterization of personality pathology. Finally, it would be difficult to justify a preference among alternate statistical schemas on descriptive grounds alone; extra-statistical information is needed, not only to understand the character of these disorders, but to specify why one schema is preferable to the others.

Most theorists of a statistical bent share a common British heritage. Almost all have been trained in English universities, carrying on a mathematical tradition that Spearman and Burt (see Chapter 14) began in the early part of the century. The thinkers represented in this section are the most persuasive proponents of this factorial/quantitative approach to the study of personality.

One of the earliest and most productive of those utilizing a factorial approach in constructing personality dimensions is **Raymond Cattell (1905–1997),** whose assessment studies will be further described in Chapter 14. In manner and style, Cattell appeared to be a throwback to a nineteenth-century English man of letters rather than science. An accomplished methodologist and psychometrician, Cattell was a learned and witty man, like so many of his psychometric forerunners in England, such as Spearman and

Burt. Short and well-groomed, with a neat gray Vandyke beard in his later years, Cattell's ruddy face gave the impression of being cheerful and jolly, though his tongue and mind were sharp and cutting.

Cattell's research led him to identify 16 primary factors, or source traits, which he then arranged in sets of bipolar dimensions. They include: schizothymia (reserved, detached, aloof) versus cyclothymia (outgoing, warm, sociable); dull (low intelligence, concrete thinking) versus bright (intelligent, abstract thinking); low ego strength (easily upset, emotionally unstable) versus high ego strength (mature, calm, stable); and so on.

Cattell's described second-order factor dimensions, which subsume the more narrow-range first-order factors, as follows: creativity versus conventionality, independence versus dependence, tough versus sensitive, neurotic versus stable, leadership versus followership, high anxiety versus low anxiety, and introversion versus extroversion, Cattell gave primacy to the latter two second-order factors in constructing four personality types. The first type, "high anxiety-introversion," is noted as being tense, excitable, suspicious, insecure, jealous, unstable, silent, timid, and shy. The second type, "low anxiety-introversion," tends to be phlegmatic, unshakable, trustful, adaptable, mature, calm, self-sufficient, cold, timid, unconcerned, and resourceful. The third personality type, the "high anxiety extroversion" group, is tense, excitable, insecure, suspicious, jealous, and unstable but, at the same time, sociable, enthusiastic, talkative, practical, and dependent. The last of the types, "low anxiety extraversion," is identified as being phlegmatic, confident, unshakable, adaptable, mature, calm, warm, sociable, enthusiastic, practical, and conventional. Problems arise when efforts are made to synthesize trait dimensions into a diverse set of coherent clinical types. This problem is clearly evident in Cattell's typology as the traits that cluster factorially in his work neither consolidate into clinically relevant syndromes nor generate enough variety to comprise a comprehensive classification.

Perhaps the most sophisticated of recent investigators employing the factorial structure of personality and pathology are W. John Livesley and his associates (1986, 1987, 1989, 1992). Drawing initially on descriptive characterizations found in a wide range of personality-oriented texts and articles, Livesley generated a set of 100 separate traits for the personality disorders in DSM-III. Utilizing both self-report scales and psychiatrically rated trait/behavioral items, he sought to evaluate the degree to which each trait item was prototypical of the disorder. Decomposing the correlation matrix on the basis of a principal components analysis of the 100 self-report and clinician-rated traits, he initially found that 15 interpretable factors could reliably be identified to account for a large proportion of the data's variance. Solutions with more components yielded factors with only one, usually unreliable trait-item. Conversely, solutions with fewer factors became highly complex in that many trait-items loaded on several factors, hence reducing their independence.

The most vigorous and persuasive exponents of the dimensional approach to the study of personality and its disorders are those who follow the five-factor model (FFM), most notably *Paul Costa* and *Robert McCrae*. The five-factor model derives its data primarily from studies of folk lexicals, that is, the codification of descriptive words found in the language of laypersons. Although disagreements exist regarding the labels to be used to represent the five factors, sufficient commonality exists from one context and culture to another to view them as highly reliable. Borrowing ideas Eysenck and Carl Rogers (a most unusual pairing) initially formulated, they termed these factors: *Neuroticism*, reflecting chronic levels of emotional instability and susceptibility to psychological distress; *Extraversion*, signifying a disposition to interpersonal interactions, activity, and stimulus seeking, as well as a capacity for joy; *Openness to experience*, typically featuring an appreciation for new experiences, a willingness to entertain novel ideas, as well as curiousness and imaginativeness; *Agreeableness*, representing those who are disposed to be good natured, trusting, helpful, and altruistic; and *Conscientiousness*, signifying a high degree of organization, reliability, persistence, ambitiousness, and control.

Although serious critiques of this model exist, both in its assumptions and empirical support, it can provide an interesting schema of factorial traits that could serve to characterize the *DSM* personality disorders. For example, histrionic and schizoid disorders appear to fall on opposite extremes of the extraversion factor. Agreeableness may be found among dependents and compulsives, whereas deficits in agreeableness are likely to be found among antisocials and paranoids. Low scores on conscientiousness appear to be consistently associated with antisocial and passive-aggressive (negativistic) personality disorders. Neuroticism seems especially notable among borderline personalities.

Gordon Allport, to be discussed later in this chapter, took strong exception to factor-analytic approaches to personality. To him, factors were statistical fictions or mathematical artifacts devoid of intrinsic psychological meaning. He directed his criticism particularly to the notion that factors should be uncorrelated with each other. It seemed highly improbable to Allport that a theory based on independent factors could be consistent with the highly integrated nature of the nervous system.

As described in Chapter 12, *Timothy Leary* drew inspiration from the analytic writings of Horney, Fromm, and Sullivan. Along with associates at the Kaiser Permanente Foundation, Leary constructed an interpersonal typology based on two dimensions: dominance-submission and hate-love. Utilizing gradations and permutations, Leary separated 16 behavioral segments, which he then grouped into eight distinct interpersonal types. He identified each by two variants, a mild and an extreme form; two labels designate each of the eight types, the first to signify the mild or more adaptive variant; the second, the more extreme or pathological variant.

Also noted in Chapter 12, *Donald J. Kiesler* has centered attention on the transactions that occur between individuals and others throughout their life experiences. As he has formulated it, people transmit an "evoking message" to others through various verbal and nonverbal channels; the message is intended to create a particular encoder-decoder relationship. Kiesler conceptualizes the emotional and personality difficulties of individuals as stemming from problematic counter-communications they unknowingly elicit from others.

In his highly detailed and precise analysis of the interpersonal circle formulated in 1982, Kiesler arranges his personality taxonomy in terms of two major dimensions akin to Leary's: affiliation (love-hate) and control (dominance-submission). According to his developmental perspective, children settle on a distinctive interpersonal style, role, and self-definition early in life, which then leads them repeatedly to engage others in terms of how intimate and how controlling they wish to relate to others. These relatively constant interpersonal patterns and self-presentations are repeatedly validated in subsequent interactions by the responses they elicit from others.

The classification Kiesler formulated contains 350 bipolar interpersonal items, three to nine of which define 64 subclasses that may in turn be grouped into 16 major segments. Kiesler offers a series of translations that relate the *DSM* personality disorders to their profiles in his interpersonal circle. For example, the histrionic personality fits the frenetically gregarious octant, the dependent personality parallels the unassured-submissive octant, and the passive-aggressive matches the antagonistic-aloof octant.

Illuminating Personology

Despite these pioneering efforts at partial integration, no theorists discussed thus far start out with an integrative model as they seek to locate the place and character of personality disorders. The presentation that follows represents approaches that begin at their outset with an integrative worldview, which states that "nature is one," that all facets, both cross-sectionally and longitudinally, are unified by common principles, and comprise an interwoven network of characteristics that have been segmented for either scientific or pedagogic purposes. Thus, chemistry is not merely an emergent property of physical phenomena; biological systems are not reducible to chemical and physical but are, in effect, the same thing—facets of nature expressed in different forms and processes. These formal and traditional subjects view nature from different vantage points and analyze nature employing different methodologies.

As noted throughout this book, Hippocrates was among the first clinicians to formulate a characterization of personality. Dominance among any of his four body humors resulted in distinct personality temperaments: sanguine, or hopeful; melancholic, or sad; choleric, or irascible; and phlegmatic, or apathetic. The longevity of his ancient four-part typology stems not only from its explicit recognition of a relationship between body chemistry and personality, but its success in stimulating others, as well as in describing aspects of modern personality types as well.

Following Hippocrates, personality characterizations most often took the form of facile and brilliant word portraits drawn in literature and drama.

Beginning with the almost contemporary sketches of Theophrastus in the fourth century B.C. and many centuries later in the work of Chaucer, Ben Jonson, Jean de la Bruyere, and George Eliot, the masterful descriptions in drama and fiction, free of the constraints of philosophical discipline, made the clumsy scientific characterizations of their day seem colorless and restrained. Brilliant and insightful though they were, dramatic portrayals were caricatures, not whole personalities.

Formal attempts to classify nosological systems were often problematic; not only did theorists use diverse efforts to identify the essential quality that characterized the core of each schema, but they devised different frameworks by which diverse systems would group their categories. Unfortunately, no principle existed to unify or organize the various classifications that had been proposed throughout history. One useful distinction differentiated those that focused on normal as opposed to abnormal personalities. In accord with this distinction, the following discussion separates theorists who concerned themselves this past century with nonpathological traits and types from psychiatrically oriented theorists who attended to pathological symptoms and syndromes.

William Stern (1871–1938) achieved recognition as president of the German Psychological Society in 1934 and was in the midst of conducting its annual meeting when an appointee of Hitler arrived and ordered him to vacate the chair. He was forced to migrate soon thereafter to the United States, where William McDougall found a visiting professorship for him on the faculty of Duke University. An ally of McDougall's purposive orientation, Stern believed that life was goal-directed and, free of troublesome obstructions, would follow a creative course. In many regards, his views were akin to the Gestaltists in Germany (see Chapter 10) but, in contrast to their focus on the process of perceiving, Stern's interest centered on the perceiver him or herself. To Stern, all of a person's functional dispositions were of a piece, so to speak; however, two central elements existed: self-regarding tendencies (e.g., self preservation and reproduction), and other-regarding tendencies (e.g., those connected with sympathy for fellow beings).

Born and raised in Berlin of a modest merchant family, Stern idolized his grandfather, a distinguished historian and educator, as well as a leader in the Jewish Reform movement. He studied at the University of Berlin, turning to the philosophical discipline of psychology as a career. He obtained his PhD under Moritz Lazarus, a noted linguist, and Hermann Ebbinghaus, the distinguished experimental memory psychologist. Stern began his professional academic career at the University of Breslau where he remained for 19 years, until moving in 1916 to the University of Hamburg, where he succeeded Ernst Meumann. At the age of 38, he was invited, along with Sigmund Freud and Carl Jung, to celebrate the twentieth anniversary of the founding of Clark University in the United States at which time he received an honorary doctorate. Founding the *Journal of Applied Psychology* in 1907, he also earned a worldwide reputation through his three-volume *Person und Sache* (1907). In

William Stern

1909, he began a series of works on applied psychological issues, specifically those related to education and commerce; he also wrote several books with his wife Clara, notably *Child Language* (C. Stern & Stern, 1907). In 1912, he reviewed methodologies for assessing intelligence, introducing the concept of "intelligence quotient" for the first time. Similarly, he evaluated methods for testing imagination, suggesting the use of cloud pictures for their systematic personality appraisal.

When Stern emigrated to the United States by way of Holland, American psychologists became acquainted with his well-known work in Europe primarily through Gordon Allport, who introduced Stern's "personalistic psychology" to the country. Perhaps owing to his misfortunes in Germany, Stern often appeared guarded so that his speech and thoughts were to the point and not expansive. His genius could not be hidden, however, for he did not babble or talk unnecessarily on irrelevant topics, nor did he wander into naïve or speculative theorizing. What he had to say was meager but always on a high level. His extraordinary mind was engaged in the political turmoil and its personal implications for him that still were brewing on the continent in the latter years of his life.

Stern's most clearly stated his beliefs in *Algemeine Psychologie, auf Personalistiscer Grundlage* (General Psychology, from the Personalistic Standpoint; 1935). In this text, Stern addressed several traditional content areas in psychology; for example, he contrasted his own views concerning perception from those of the gestaltists, stating that it is not the objective stimulus situation that is paramount but rather the person who forms the gestaltin. Similarly, he shared, along with Kurt Lewin, the view that ostensibly self-contained people are in actuality fully engaged, open, and immersed in their surrounding environment, rather than being an entity unto themselves. He asserted that memory was a highly personal rather than objective and unidimensional phenomenon; further, an event of 10 years ago may be experienced subjectively, owing to its special meaning, as much closer in time than an event of one year ago. Stern defined comparable subjective meanings to topics such as cognition and emotion, each reformulated to represent Stern's "personalistic principles," which he considered to be central and supreme.

The distinguished American psychologist **Gordon Willard Allport's (1897–1967)** views centered on his unceasing efforts to represent the intrinsic complexity and uniqueness of individuals. To him, the diverse elements that comprise a person's psychological make-up exhibit an underlying congruence, as Allport put it, or basic unity of style and function. Among his central concepts were those that represented such terms as *self* and *ego*.

Although Allport was invariably friendly and gracious as a person, he had an enormous reserve. He did not take a shine to the exaggerated expressions of intimacy common to many of his colleagues. Though not disposed to talk about personal things, he was always sympathetic and concerned about matters that troubled others, but in a low-keyed and reserved manner. He was a classically handsome man, much like aristocratic portraits of an earlier century, displaying soft but defined features, modest but assured in manner, as are those who feel comfortable with themselves. A sound and

Gordon Willard Allport

perceptive professor, he showed a deep interest in ideas, soaking them up as if they were merely feelings or impressions. Nevertheless, his strongly held positions often conflicted with others in psychology-at-large, as well as in his department. He seemed weary of fashionable ways of life that pushed some of his students and colleagues to the edge of their ostensibly conventional academic existence. Recognizing the complicated and complicating foibles of life, he was disposed to accommodate his colleagues' contradictions and excesses with thoughtful modulations.

Allport's writings were distinguished by a tone of urbanity and cultural awareness that combined sound scholarship with a knowledge of controversial ideas and diverse methods. He was like a writer of an earlier period, methodical, endlessly rethinking his craft, jealous of his time and the use to which he put it. His psychological talents were classical, careful in their exposition and narrative, and assured in the laying out of details, demonstrating the impression of being constantly reconstructed. He remained throughout his career a thinker and writer of major stature.

In contrast to his more analytically oriented associates, Allport stressed the importance of conscious motives and the impact of present life conditions rather than those of the unconscious or of the past. In his concept of "functional autonomy," he provided a rationale for investigators to concern themselves with contemporary motivations rather than those of childhood. Centering his concerns on the normal as opposed to the abnormal, on the human adult rather than the child or animal, Allport opposed his colleagues' focus on the experimental, part-function sciences rather than those that pertained to the dynamic processes of the uniquely integrated person. He found the concern of American psychologists with operationism, positivism, and measurement to be distracting, if not irrelevant. In his first formal treatment of what he called *personalism*, a label borrowed from his friend and early mentor, William Stern, Gordon Allport stressed the uniqueness of the individual (1937):

> The outstanding characteristic of a man is his individuality. He is a unique creation of the forces of nature. Separated spatially from all other men, he behaves throughout his own particular span of life, in his own distinctive fashion. It is not upon the cell or upon the single organ, nor upon the group, nor upon the species that nature has centered her most lavish concern, but rather upon the integral organization of life processes into the amazingly stable and self-contained system of the individual creature. (p. 3)
>
> The chief tenet of "personalistic psychology" is that every mental function is embedded in personal life. In no concrete sense is there such a thing as intelligence, space perception, color discrimination, or choice reaction: . . . nor can motives ever be studied apart from their personal setting; they represent always the striving of a total organism. (p. 18)

Allport was in favor of the study of the individual as opposed to the study of general or universal laws. This thesis derived from earlier philosophers who contrasted the idiographic, or individualistic focus, from the nomothetic, or universal focus.

Allport grew up in a Midwestern home characterized, as he described it, "by plain Protestant piety and hard work," bypassing the fact that his paternal grandfather (Alpert) had descended a century earlier from a Dutch rabbinical family. His father had been a rough-hewn businessman raised by poverty-stricken farmers who later went on to become a physician when his children were still young. Ambitious and creative, his father was unusually successful. Following his older brother, Floyd, Gordon went to Harvard where he earned a bachelor's degree in psychology and social ethics in 1919, the same year that Floyd received his PhD. Following a brief period of teaching English and sociology in Turkey, Allport returned to pursue graduate study at Harvard. On his way back to the United States, he visited briefly with Freud in Vienna, where he was taken aback by Freud's decision to immediately interpret a dream Allport presented to him, which he said represented the young man's own problematic experience. Upon completing his PhD dissertation on a study of personality traits, a subject frowned upon by the Harvard psychology faculty, he traveled for two years to Europe where he had opportunities to study in Berlin with a number of gestaltists and, most importantly, to live for a brief time in Hamburg with William Stern and his family. Returning from Europe, he was offered a position in social ethics and philosophy at Harvard, following which he joined the Dartmouth faculty for four years. When McDougall left Harvard for Duke University in 1927, Allport returned to his alma mater and remained there for the rest of his career. That Allport was a deeply ethical and socially responsible psychologist was evident in his efforts to bring numerous German scholars to the United States following the Nazi assault against intellectuals and Jews. He exerted considerable effort to relocate European colleagues in America, finding appropriate academic settings for such distinguished scholars as Kohler, Lewin, and Stern.

Allport clearly formulated his conception of personality in his first major book, *Personality: A Psychological Interpretation* (1937). Here he wrote, "Personality is the dynamic organization within the individual of those psychophysical systems that determine his unique adjustments to his environment" (p. 48). Allport explored several principles of organization by which he could encompass the many traits comprising personality into a unique pattern. Employing a hierarchical organization, he referred to *cardinal* traits, which were so pervasive and predominant as to serve as a master sentiment, as his Harvard forerunner, McDougall, might have put it. He termed the next lower level the *central* traits, those few major characteristics that have come to best typify the person. Allport termed a third level *secondary* traits, those more-or-less subsidiary, more subtle, and less pervasive features that only close and knowledgeable acquaintances might recognize.

Whereas Allport concerned himself with broad principles and abstract conceptions regarding the structure of personality, **Henry Alexander Murray (1893–1988),** his erstwhile colleague at Harvard, addressed himself to the specific content and functions of personality, that is, the functional *needs* of which personality was composed in its varied surrounding environments or *press.* Murray spelled out the many traits and specific life conditions that addressed the particulars of personality, rather than constructing the more-or-less abstract framework that Allport conceptualized. Both were committed to studying the unique configuration of traits of individuals, to the dynamically integrating qualities that gave them the essence and vitality of their lives. Their styles were complementary: Allport was more philosophical and academic, Murray more clinical and literary.

Henry Alexander Murray

Murray's intellectual style would make one think of him as a charter member of a Northeastern literary community, perhaps because he was a diligent scholar of Herman Melville, writing often and at depth about the psychological significance of Melville's characters. Knowing both Erik Erikson and Henry Murray personally, my first impression when I met Murray was that he was a taller and slimmer variant of Erikson, the distinguished ego analyst and occasional colleague of Murray's at Harvard. It was Murray's habit to sit in the middle of a large room, holding court, as it were, commenting in a magisterial manner to everyone who came in the room. He was one of the great talkers of our time; only later in his career did his verbal gifts become evident in his writings. Some spoke of him as a verbal magician owing to his easy and fluent articulateness. He invariably dominated conversations, either by designating the subject, doing most of the talking, or setting the tone, but always in a cheerful and witty manner. His mind may be described as literary rather than analytic and systematic, perhaps best characterized as a rhetoric of free-association with startling turns and contrasts.

Murray was unusually influential with a large group of brilliant students who worked with him beginning in the early 1930s. No one can be considered to be an acolyte, however, inasmuch as he did not establish a formal or systematic school of thought. Extraordinarily wide-ranging, influenced early by Jung, but subsequently a founding member of the Freudian-oriented Boston Psychoanalytic Society, Murray was initially trained as a history major at Harvard, a medical student at Columbia's Physicians and Surgeons, a neurosurgeon, who obtained a PhD in chemistry at Cambridge, and a brief research career in developmental neurobiology at Rockefeller University, before turning to psychology following an invitation at the age of 33 to join Morton Prince (see Chapter 7) at the new Harvard Psychological Clinic in 1926.

Although none of his 40 or so Harvard doctoral students and collaborators sought to pursue the vast range of topics that Murray studied, many brilliant later associates picked up one or another facet of his work in constructing their own careers. Especially notable in this regard was *David McClelland* who carried on Henry Murray's interest in social motivation, utilizing the *Thematic Apperception Test* that Murray devised with his longtime colleague, Christiana Morgan (Morgan & Murray, 1935). Other distinguished students who joined him in writing his seminal book *Explorations in Personality* (1938) included Saul Rosenzweig, Nevitt Sanford, Donald MacKinnon, Silvan Tomkins, and Robert White. With the onset of World War II, Murray left Harvard to establish an assessment service for the Office of Strategic Services; here his group carried out the difficult task of screening candidates for complex and dangerous missions, a work summarized in a book *Assessment of Men* (1948). As noted previously, he explicated several works of Herman Melville, a rich sequence of books and papers that exhibited Murray's talent and devotion to cultural topics beyond formal academic study.

Murray coined the term *personology*, describing it as follows:

> The prevailing custom in psychology is to study one function or one aspect of an episode at a time—perception, emotion, intellection or behavior—and this is as it must be. The circumscription of attention is dictated by the need for detailed information. But the psychologist who does this should recognize the he is observing merely a part of an operating totality, and this totality, in turn, is but a small temporal segment of a personality. Psychology must construct a scheme of concepts for portraying the entire course of individual development,

and thus provide a framework into which any single episode—natural or experimental—may be fitted.

The branch of psychology which principally concerns itself with the study of human lives and the factors that influence their course, which investigates individual differences and types of personality, may be termed "personology" instead of the "psychology of personality," a clumsy and tautological expression. (1938, p. 3)

As a thoroughgoing clinician, Murray believed that a full understanding of behavior called for a complete and detailed study of each individual. Clearly influenced by his friend and colleague, Gordon Allport, Murray asserted that efforts must be made to articulate the unique or idiographic features of a research subject. As will be addressed in Chapter 14, one of Murray's most notable contributions to the assessment of personality were the instruments he helped devise, especially the *Thematic Apperception Test*, which became second only to the *Rorschach* as the most widely used projective technique.

Gardner Murphy (1895–1979) contributed another dimension to the triumvirate that brought the concepts of personality to the foreground in the mid-twentieth century. As with Allport and Murray, his mind was brilliant and erudite, capable of encompassing all facets of human endeavor, knowledgeable in grand detail of the early Greek philosophers, and thoroughly sophisticated with regard to the positivist philosophy of modern science. A more dazzling and charming threesome would be difficult to find in any review of the history of personology. Many of those whose graduate careers crossed in mid-twentieth century thought of these three giants as contemporary equivalents of Socrates, Plato, and Aristotle.

Gardner Murphy

Despite his warm and open manner, Murphy often appeared preoccupied with his own thinking and research. The students who flocked around him considered him a genius, endowed with a phenomenal memory; I recall a faculty colleague commenting that if there was any trouble with Murphy it stemmed from the fact that he could never forget anything. His talents and scope were so overwhelmingly verbal and so wrapped up in the substance of his scholarship that they often acted as a barrier to personal exchange. It was never clear, however, whether this was his own doing or whether it reflected the kind of august image students had of him. He was the nearest thing to a beautiful intellectual machine that you might ever meet, one that combined extraordinary erudition with fertile and incisive thinking. Though not tolerant of loose or irrelevant conversation,

Murphy was at heart a sweet man, invariably generous, one impervious to conflict or gossip. Most notable to his students was Murphy's "performance" when he lectured. As scores of students sat in the audience, he wandered back and forth across the rostrum like a caged tiger. The feeling we had was that of attending an intellectual séance. Even though the subject at hand was often esoteric, such as some obscure aspect of Greek philosophy, students were anaesthetized into a trance-like appreciation of his wide learning, the depth and creativity of his analyses, and his bold and far-ranging generalizations, truly virtuous and substantive performances—three times a week.

As Gardner Murphy wrote in the foreword to his magnum opus, *Personality: A Biosocial Approach to Origins and Structure* (1947), his aim was to clarify the little that was known about the subject of personality and to show its potential relationship to a vast domain of nature not yet comprehended. He explored confusions about the subject and helped focus subsequent efforts to investigate them more fully and accurately. In his view, personality psychology was an active field that spread in numerous directions, a field that resisted efforts to make it stand still as a fixed and knowable subject. If his writings were successful, he anticipated that they would serve as a companion to guide future investigators.

Raised in Ohio, Murphy earned a bachelor's degree at Yale University, began graduate studies at Harvard and, following a period of service in World War I, continued his work toward a PhD at Columbia University, where he remained for 20 years through the Depression. Despite highly productive writings throughout the late 1920s and 1930s, Murphy supplemented his income by assuming a number of fellowships and lectureships at other universities. At 45, he was offered a full professorship at the College of the City of New York (CCNY), where he became mentor for hundreds of bright undergraduates, many of whom went on to receive doctorates at other universities. He was an inspiring teacher, astoundingly broad in scope, with interests spanning early Greek history, experimental social psychology, as well as personality research and theory. As with other psychologists of a broad and open-minded perspective, such as William James, he maintained an active interest in psychical research, as well as in matters of international import. He left CCNY in 1952 to assume the directorship of research at the Menninger Foundation in Kansas where he undertook taxonomic and experimental studies of psychiatric concern. Along with his wife, Lois Barclay Murphy, Gardner continued his Menninger projects until 1972 when he "retired" to become a visiting professor at George Washington University.

In 1944, Murphy was elected president of the American Psychological Association and received the gold medal of the American Psychological Foundation in 1972. The latter citation read: "To Gardner Murphy—A peerless teacher, a felicitous writer, an eclectic psychologist, of limitless range, he seeks to bring the whole of human experience to bear in understanding behavior." In writing his biography (1990), his wife Lois noted that Gardner's historical perspective enabled him to perceive relationships not seen by those involved in usual academic and laboratory routines. She spoke of his classical education, including a mastery of ancient Greek and the history of philosophy, which, together with his deep commitment to an evolutionary view of human life, made it natural for him to see each new concept in terms of its origins and logic.

In his autobiography, Murphy noted his personal "passionate need for inclusiveness." As a student of Murphy, I have sought implicitly to emulate Murphy's imaginative range and search for inclusiveness, as well as communicate the diversity and open-mindedness to scholarship that typified Murphy's intellectual life. As others wrote to Lois Murphy as she prepared his biography (1990):

> His presentation, as always, was modest, matter-of-fact, never dogmatic, and never concealing the weakness or tentativeness of the material he was discussing. Yet his staggering grasp of the subject in its finest detail, his even-handed, scholarly judgment, and his legendary skill of exposition, together with his exquisitely precise command of the English language, gave our small group the sense of having in our camp the finest intellect among his peers. (p. 15)
>
> He spoke more clearly, more precisely, more beautifully than all but a few scholars could write. He brought every field of knowledge to bear on a chosen topic, with illustrations and quotations from the arts, philosophy, and other social sciences without pretension. Yet he seemed humble almost beyond belief. (p. 17)

Theodore Millon (1928–   ), an only child of modestly educated Jewish immigrants from Eastern Europe, elaborated the personologic themes of Allport, Murray, and Murphy, and asserted that common principles underlie and bind all scientific realms of study such as physics, biology, and personology. Moreover, these principles are anchored to the process and progression of evolution. Elements of evolutionary theory operate in all aspects of scientific endeavor, from cosmogony, at one end, to human interactions, at the other. Pathological forms of human functioning are interpreted as disruptions or imbalances in those evolutionary principles that foster the functions of survival and ecologic adaptation (1990). From this viewpoint, personality maladaptations could not be fully understood by limiting attention solely to cognitive preconceptions, or unconscious repetition compulsions, or neurochemical dysfunctions. Rather, each of them represent partial expressions of evolutionary functions that have gone awry. Cognitions, unconscious structures, interpersonal styles, and neurohormonal dynamics are viewed, in this formulation, as forms of expression or as functional mechanisms that reflect fundamental evolutionary processes. Each evolutionary function is important in that it can help identify clinical domains in which pathology manifests itself, and hence becomes a useful vehicle for specifying and understanding that pathology. These manifestations and correlates are not the pathology itself, however, but expressions and mechanisms of evolutionary functions in realms cognitive, behavioral, affective, as well as biologic.

A major theme of this theory, a formulation initially termed a *biosocial-learning model* (1969) was that personality functions and their failures in mental illness developed as a result of the interplay of organismic and environmental forces; such interactions start at the time of conception and continue throughout life. Individuals with similar biological potentials emerge with different personalities and clinical syndromes depending on the experiences to which they were exposed. According to this widely shared view, a number of ways exist in which biological factors can shape, facilitate, or limit the nature of an individual's experiences and learnings. For example, individuals who possess different biological sensibilities will perceive the same objective environment differently; people register different stimuli at varying intensities in accord with their unique pattern of alertness, sensory acuity, and temperamental disposition. From this fact, significant differences in experience are shaped at the outset by individuals' biological equipment. Beyond the crucial role of these early experiences, the theory asserts that a circularity of interaction exists in which biological dispositions in young children evoke counterreactions from others that accentuate their disposition. Children play an active role, therefore, in creating their own environmental conditions which, in turn, serve as a basis for reinforcing their biological tendencies.

Using a threefold biosocial-learning framework aligned with a Skinnerian model, Millon derived "coping patterns" that foreshadowed and generated each of the "official" personality disorders in the *DSM-III*. These coping patterns represented complex forms of instrumental or functional behavior, that is, ways of achieving positive reinforcements and avoiding negative reinforcements. These strategies reflected what kinds of reinforcements individuals learned to seek or to avoid (pleasure-pain), where individuals looked to obtain them (self-others), and how they learned to behave to elicit or to escape them (active-passive). Eight basic coping or personality patterns, as well as three severe variants, emerged by combining the *nature* (positive or pleasure versus negative or pain), the *source* (self versus others), and the *instrumental behaviors* (active versus passive) engaged in to achieve various reinforcements. Describing the pathological variants of these coping behaviors in reinforcement terms merely cast them in a different conceptual language than conventionally used in past diagnostic systems.

In 1990, Millon reconceptualized the theoretical grounding of these derived personality patterns and disorders. As a result, Millon deduced that the principles and functional processes of evolution were universal phenomena, albeit expressed in nature's realms at different levels and in different manifest forms. What was gratifying in this reconceptualization was the close correspondence between the 1969 biosocial-learning theory and the key principles comprising the new 1990 evolutionary model. Additionally satisfying was that the ontogenetic theory of neuropsychological stages presented in 1969 similarly paralleled his theoretical formulations of evolutionary phylogenesis.

Wandering in his early education from economics, to sociology, to philosophy, to physics, and finally to psychology as a student of Gardner Murphy, the personologist; Kurt Goldstein, the neurologist; Ernst Kris, the psychoanalyst; and two of Kurt Lewin's early doctoral students, Maurice Farber, the social psychologist and Maria Rickers-Ovsiankina, the clinical psychologist, Millon came to believe that the widespread desire among theorists to unify science should not be limited to explicating physics; that is, it should be possible in all fields of nature that have been subdivided by habit, tradition, or pragmatics (e.g., economics, sociology, geology). He believed unification to be a worthy goal even within the newer sciences, such as personology. Efforts to coordinate the separate realms that comprise the field of the mind and, more specifically, that of mental disorders would be particularly useful. Rather than developing independently and being left to stand as autonomous and largely unconnected professional activities and goals, a truly mature mental science, one that would create a synergistic bond among its elements, would embody, five explicit elements:

1. *Universal scientific principles* that are grounded in the ubiquitous laws of nature; despite their varied forms of expression, these principles may provide an undergirding framework for guiding and constructing narrow based subject-oriented theories.
2. *Subject-oriented theories,* or explanatory and heuristic conceptual schemas of the mind and mental illness. These theories should be consistent with established knowledge in both its own and related sciences and should enable reasonably accurate propositions concerning all clinical conditions to be both deduced and understood, enabling thereby the development of a formal classification system.
3. *Classification of personality styles and pathological syndromes,* or a taxonomic nosology that has been derived logically from the theory. The taxonomy should provide a cohesive organization within which its major categories can readily be grouped and differentiated, permitting thereby the development of coordinated assessment instruments.
4. *Personality and clinical assessment instruments,* or tools that are empirically grounded and sufficiently sensitive quantitatively to enable the theory's propositions and hypotheses to be adequately investigated and evaluated. Hence, the clinical categories comprising its nosology should be able to be readily identified (diagnosed) and measured (dimensionalized), thus specifying target areas for interventions.
5. *Integrated therapeutic interventions,* or planful strategies and modalities of treatment. These interventions should accord with the theory and be oriented to modify problematic clinical characteristics, consonant with professional standards and social responsibilities.

What should be aspired to in the twenty-first century is to reintegrate a mental science that had been disconnected in the twentieth century. Just as each person is an intrinsic unity, each component of a mental science should not remain a separate element of a potpourri of unconnected parts. Bothered by ambiguity and inconsistency, Millon asserted that each element should be integrated into an overall gestalt, a coupled and synergistic unity in which the whole of the science could become more cohesive, informative and useful than its individual parts.

As Millon wrote:

> What better sphere is there within the psychological sciences to undertake such syntheses than with the subject matter of personology. Persons are the only organically integrated system in the psychological domain, evolved through the millennia and inherently created from birth as natural entities, rather than culture-bound and experience-derived gestalts. The intrinsic cohesion of persons is not merely a rhetorical construction, but an authentic substantive unity. Personologic features may often be dissonant, and may be partitioned conceptually for pragmatic or scientific purposes, but they are segments of an inseparable biopsychosocial entity, as well as a natural outgrowth of evolution's progression. (1990, p. 11)

Noted by colleagues and students as possessing a quick and broad-ranging intelligence, Millon is distinguished from many other deeply concerned professors attentive to serious social, political, and international matters by the fact that he appears, contrawise, to be invariably buoyant, if not jovial. Critics are not invariably enamored, however, finding his work to be, at times, too speculative, his writings unduly imaginative, and his creativity overly expansive.

Comments and Reflections

Despite the extensive support garnered by many early theorists favoring evolutionary themes, most schemas of psychopathology were narrow in focus, such as being limited to biological matters, or essentially cross-sectional in nature. Moreover, most have failed to come to grips with its numerous and subtle variations, especially its utility in understanding fields other than its original applications, such as in cosmogony and personology. Despite some productive lines of investigation that theorists have proposed, several problems continue to be raised concerning their applicability of its concepts and methods for understanding mental illness. Methodologically, the problem can be identified in the application of factorial techniques to the study of disorders. Kendell reported that skepticism of this tool remains high (1975):

> . . . largely because of the variety of different factor solutions that can be obtained from a single set of data and the lack of any satisfactory objective

criterion for preferring one of these to the others. The number of factors obtained and their loadings are often affected considerably by relatively small changes in the size or composition of the subject sample, or in the range of test employed. (p. 108)

Further, Blashfield (1984) noted that: ". . . deciding when to stop the process of selecting the number of factors, rotating the solutions, and interpreting the factors are all highly subjective and at the discretion of the user. Therefore, many distrust the results" (p. 108).

In addition to these methodological caveats, keep in mind a number of conceptual forewarnings regarding the structural implications of several of the approaches described in this chapter. For example, a reasonable degree of fidelity must exist between the pattern of functions and attributes of personality described and their correspondence to syndromes of mental illness. Despite the popularity of certain theories of personality, their utility for psychopathology is far from evident or universally accepted. Not only do few psychopathological entities provide evidence of a relationship to personality attributes, but many personality concepts tend to be antithetical to the predominant polythetic structure and overlapping relationships that exist among mental disorders. Neither personological nor syndromic categories consist of entirely homogeneous and discrete attributes. Rather, most clinical conditions are composed of diffuse and complex characteristics that share many attributes in common. Thus, theoretical schemas of personality may rest on characteristics or attributes that do not accord with the combinations and covariations that characterize the intrinsic structure of psychopathology. The task of combining simple personality dimensions or factors into patterns and configurations that correspond to disorders is one that may transcend the power of most theorists or investigators. This task still depends on clinical artistry or theorists' speculative powers.

In contrast to clinical signs, which usually are gauged in objective biologic measures or behavioral acts, personality *traits* characterize psychological habits and functional dispositions of broad generality and diverse expression. Personality traits often are inferred rather than observed, generalized rather than specific, and dispositional rather than consequential. Assumed to be enduring and pervasive, only certain traits display this durability and pervasiveness; that is, only some will prove resistant to the influences of changing times and circumstances. Other forms of a patient's behavior, attitude, and emotion presumably are even more transient and malleable. Further, traits that exhibit consistency and stability in one person may not be the same as those that display these features in others. Additionally, qualities most prominent or central to maintaining one person's overall psychological balance and style of functioning may differ from those of others. To illustrate, the "interpersonal conduct" trait of significance for one person may be that of being agreeable, never differing or having conflict; for another, it may be interpersonally important to maintain one's distance from people so as to avoid rejection or being humiliated; for a third individual, the influential interpersonal trait may be that of asserting one's self and dominating others.

The sources used to identify clinical traits are highly diverse, from methods designed to uncover intrapsychic processes, such as free association, dream analysis, hypnosis, and projective techniques, to phenomenological cognitive methods, such as structured interviews and self-report inventories, and to behavioral methods of direct observation and rating, some systematic, others not. It is no understatement to say that the rich vein of clinical attributes that dispositional theorists have uncovered has been a boon to clinicians, but a source of perplexity and despair to researchers. More than any other domain, dispositional data and methods produce information that is fraught with complexities and obscurities that can bewilder the most sophisticated investigator. Only part of the difficulty stems from the fact that identifying hidden traits is highly inferential. Because the dispositional structure and processes that make up psychological traits can be only partially observed and take different manifest forms in different contexts, it is difficult to identify them reliably and, hence, to assign them a standard place in one's research. Matters are made more difficult by the absence of research-based normative and prevalence data, as well as by the lack of strong validation support for their investigational tools.

14

Systematically Measuring and Integrating the Mind

In societies where the rank and file advance through hard work and merit, as opposed to inheriting positions, some system of identifying qualified and deserving candidates had to be developed. One of the earliest examples of personnel selection can be traced to the Ancient Chinese, where from 2200 B.C. until the turn of the twentieth century, a rigorous civil service exam aided in this process. This selection system evolved into a highly articulated exam that lasted 3 days and nights identifying candidates for imperial government positions by appraising not only their knowledge of history and law, but also their writing abilities, their physical abilities, and their motivation and persistence. The system eventually was employed, in a limited way, as a model for several nineteenth-century European countries to assist in choosing lower level positions in government service.

The Personologic Story: II

\ Unlike personnel selection, with its nonclinical, limited, and focused goal in the commercial and governmental world, integrative personality assessment is a comprehensive appraisal of wide-ranging purposes that gives coherence, provides a complex and interactive framework, and seeks to create an organic order among a variety of diverse psychological traits, functions, and abilities. Each person is approached as a complete mental system whose psychological attributes comprise that old chestnut: The whole is greater than the sum of its parts. The full person is appraised as an inextricably linked nexus of behaviors, cognitions, unconscious processes, and so on. Behavioral acts, self-image cognitions, defense mechanisms, indeed, each functional process and structural component, are contextualized by and interdigitated with all others to form a cohesive and organic whole. No one goal is central, nor is one trait or function segregated and made to stand on its own. Each component of the psychic configuration is recognized to have its role and significance altered by virtue of its place in the overall constellation.

In a model that parallels integrative personality assessment, integrative psychotherapy is conceived as a configuration of treatment strategies and tactics in which each intervention technique is selected not only for its efficacy in strengthening desirable personality features or in resolving notable pathological symptoms, but also for its contribution to the overall constellation of procedures of which it is but one.

Personologic integration is an important new approach in the assessment and therapy of the individual, but it is also a key component in developing a mental science. For the appraisal and treatment of a particular patient to be integrated, all of the elements of a mental science, as noted in Chapter 13, should be integrated as well (Millon, 1990).

What exactly do clinical scientists and mental health professionals mean when they say that assessment and therapy should be integrated and grounded in a coordinated theory? For example, they might say that much of what travels under the eclectic banner is merely a desire to be nice to all sides and to say that everybody is to some extent right. Eclecticism as a label has become a platitudinous buzzword, a philosophy with which open-minded people certainly would wish to ally themselves. But, an integrated mental science must signify more than that. It is not mere eclecticism. Perhaps it might be considered posteclecticism, if we may borrow a notion used to characterize modern art a century ago. Eclecticism is not a matter of choice. All mental health professionals must be eclectics, selecting the techniques that are empirically the most efficacious for the problems at hand. Moreover, therapeutic integration must transcend the coexistence of two or three potentially discordant treatment techniques. Simply piecing together the odds and ends of several methods, each possibly internally consistent but oriented to different data domains, often produces a hodgepodge that creates an illusory synthesis that cannot hold together either logically or empirically. Efforts such as these, meritorious as they may be in some regards, represent the work of peacemakers, not integrationists. Integration should be eclectic, of course, but more. *It should be a synthesized and substantive system of conceptually related and empirically coordinated parts.*

The problems that patients bring to therapists flow through a tangle of feedback loops and serially unfolding concatenations that emerge at different times in dynamic and changing configurations. As noted earlier, the significance of each component of these configurations is altered by virtue of its place in these continually evolving constellations. In parallel form, so is personologic assessment and therapy conceived as a configuration of strategies and tactics in which each instrument and technique is selected not only for its efficacy in clarifying and resolving particular pathological features, but also for its contribution to the overall constellation of procedures of which it is but one. Whether we work with partial functions that focus on behaviors, cognitions, unconscious processes, or biological defects, and the like, or whether we address contextual systems that focus on the larger environment, the family, the group, or the socioeconomic and political conditions of life, the crossover point, that is, the place that links parts to contexts, is the person. The individual is the intersecting medium that brings them together.

But the full measure of a person is more than just a crossover medium. As noted in the previous chapter, according to the personologic perspective, persons are the only organically synthesized system in the psychological domain, inherently created from birth as natural entities, rather than gestalts constructed via experience or cognitive attribution. Moreover, persons lie at the heart of the assessment and therapeutic experience; they are the substantive beings that give meaning and coherence to symptoms and traits—be they behaviors, affects, or mechanisms—as well as those beings that give life and expression to family interactions and social processes. The personologic approach contends that mental health assessors and therapists should take cognizance of the person from the start, for the parts and the contexts take on different meanings and call for different instruments and interventions in terms of the person to whom they are anchored. To focus on one social structure or one psychic form of expression without understanding its undergirding base in an integrated person is to engage in potentially misguided, if not random, clinical procedures. The history leading to the integrative model will be the focus of this chapter, beginning first with thinkers who initiated the scientific study of psychological differences among individuals.

Unfolding of Key Ideas

Not only the changing patient population of clinical practice or its recently evolved role in therapeutic theory and the *DSM* signifies the growing prominence of personologic study. In the realm of quantitative assessment and psychometrics, psychologists and psychiatrists alike have turned their skills toward the reliable identification and valid measurement of the new disorders of personality.

Efforts are now underway to bridge traditional assessment and treatment techniques with renewed personologic procedures and logic. It is a rapprochement the author strongly favors; the present chapter helps identify and foster this long overdue reconciliation of methods and perspectives. Although unconvinced (as are others) that any single domain approach (e.g., interpersonal, behavioral) is optimally fruitful, no doubt together all will engender fresh ideas and insights to guide future theoretical and empirical studies.

Taking Physiognomic Portrayals Seriously

Shakespeare, a notably perceptive observer of human character, wrote these words in *Julius Caesar*:

Let me have men about me that are fat;
Sleek-headed men and such as sleep o'nights,
Yon Cassius has a lean and hungry look;
He thinks too much; such men are dangerous. (1599, Act 1, ii, 192–195)

Observant men since times of antiquity have noted that bodily form and structure were related to particular dispositions and patterns of behavior. Hippocrates' humoral doctrine is the forerunner of these ideas. Physiognomy and phrenology may be considered the origin of more recent notions of physical characterology.

Physiognomics, the art of interpreting people's psychological characteristics from aspects of their physical characteristics, was present in ancient times, reaching its peak of study in the second century A.D. These studies assumed that inner traits of people are expressed in their outer physical features, especially the face. The great thinkers of Greece explored formal efforts to systematically interpret physiognomic characteristics, for example, in Pythagoras' sixth century B.C. writings, and later Aristotle's *Analytica Priora* (Tredennick, 1967) and *Historia Animalium*, in which he wrote (Peck, 1965): "Persons who have a large forehead are sluggish, those who have a small one are fickle; those who have a broad one are excitable, those who have a bulging one, quick tempered" (I, VIII, 891b, p. 39).

Physiognomica (Hett, 1936), also attributed to Aristotle, but more likely written by his followers, examined parallels between the physiques of men and animals, to compare different ethnic groups, and to investigate the relationship between bodily characteristics and temperamental dispositions. Among the useful signs recorded were the movements, shapes, and colors of the face; the growth of hair; the smoothness of skin; the condition of the flesh; and the general structure of the body. Sluggish movements denoted a soft disposition, quick ones a fervent temperament, a deep voice denoted courage, a high one signified cowardice. The writers were wise enough to note that it would be foolish to make a judgment on the basis of any one of these signs. Centuries later Leonardo da Vinci (1452–1519) made similar physiognomic proposals in his *Treatise on Painting*, in which he explored relationships between emotional states and overt facial expressions.

In the sixteenth century, an Italian, **Giovanni Battista Della Porta (1545–1615),** published a book entitled *De Humana Physiognomia* (1586), derived from Aristotle's writings, which included many drawings designed to show similarities between humans and animals; for example, a person who looked leonine ostensibly possessed the courage, strength, and will of a lion. This book proposed the theory that every person's head resembled a specific animal's head, thereby suggesting that the person possessed the same personal characteristics as that animal. Another work by Porta, *Natural Magik* (1558/1957), outlined similar speculations by a number of his contemporary colleagues. No less speculative was Porta's *Phytognomonica* (1588) in which he addressed matters of vegetable physiognomy, that is, the art of determining the inner nature of plants on the basis of their exterior appearance.

In his five-volume work, *Les Characteres des Passions* (1640) the eminent French physician **Marin Cureau de La Chambre (1594–1669)** wrote:

> the resemblance Man has with other Creatures . . . teacheth us that those who have any part like to those of beasts, have also their inclinations . . . that men who have anything of a feminine beauty, are naturally effeminate; and that those women who have any touch of a manly beauty, participate also of manly inclinations.

Burdened with the prejudices of his day, de La Chambre was nevertheless a highly insightful physiognomist, addressing in detail the significance to be found "in the motions of the eyes, the inflection of the voice, the color of the lips," and so on. Unfortunately, de La Chambre could not help but draw upon astrological influences, speculating on the power, especially of the moon upon the brain, "causing it to increase or decrease in volume upon whether the moon is waxing or waning" (1640).

A distinguished philosopher and jurist, **Christian Thomasius (1655–1728)** helped inaugurate the period of German enlightenment, founded the University of Halle, and asserted that philosophy should concern itself with practical matters of everyday life. A prolific author, Thomasius wrote only briefly on physiognomy, drafting an essay entitled "Recent Proposals for a New Science for Obtaining a Knowledge of Other Men's Minds" (1692). Basing his ideas on the work of de La Chambre, Thomasius recommended that observation can be most useful when obtained through personal conversation with a subject; he cautioned that observers must distinguish between genuine and affected emotions.

Another theorist of physiognomy in the late eighteenth century, **Johann Kaspar Lavater (1741–1801),** asserted unequivocally the existence of a relationship between fixed aspects of the body's surface and a person's character. In his well-received book, *Essays on Physiognomy* (1775–1778), published in four lavish volumes, Lavater claimed that physiognomy was truly a science because it offered law-like regularities and depended on empirical observation. In characterizing the trait of obstinacy, Lavater wrote:

> The higher the forehead, and the less the remainder of the countenance, the more knotty the concave forehead, the deeper sunken the eye, the less excavation there is between the forehead and the nose, the more closed the mouth, the broader the chin, the more perpendicular the long profile of the countenance—the more unyielding the obstinacy: the harsher the character. (p. 480)

Though similar in many respects to classical approaches in physiognomy, a new "scientific" model known as *phrenology* emerged in the late nineteenth century. Both approaches drew inferences about character and personality from external bodily features, physiognomy from facial structure and expression, phrenology from external formations of the skull. Their underlying assumptions, however, were quite different. Physiognomists believed that a person's inner feelings and characteristics were expressed in facial features, voice, and so on. Phrenologists made no assumptions as to the external expression of varied dispositions. Their two fundamental assumptions were unusual for its time: one, that different mental functions were located in different regions of the brain and, two, that the skull's external topography reflected the magnitude of these functions. This was the first "scientific" effort made to analyze the underlying brain structure of which character and personality might be derived.

Despite its discredited side, phrenology, as **Franz Joseph Gall (1758–1828)** proposed it, was an honest and serious attempt to construct a neurological substrate in the brain to undergird a science of character depiction. Although numerous writers such as Vesalius, Willis, and Stensen in medieval times (see Chapter 6) had speculated and explored brain structures as the center of mental functioning, Gall took this view in an original direction. Most early characterologists conceived the brain as a locale where the immaterial soul may have influenced bodily activities. Gall asserted that the brain *was* the mind, not only in an explicitly material sense, but that different regions subserved different dispositions.

Gall was a German-born physician working in Austria. The rationale that Gall presented for his procedure of measuring contour variation of the skull was not in the least illogical given the limited knowledge of anatomy in his day. Assuming a relationship between mind and brain, he proposed that brain structure and their associated functions would be reflected in outer formations of the skull. Since the brain was the most important biological organ for thought and emotion, it followed, since the brain itself could not be directly appraised, that differences in these inner dispositions would be represented best by variations in the contours of the cranium. Just as it would be logical to assume that persons with large bicep muscles are stronger than those with thin or small ones, so, too, according to Gall, would it be logical to assume that persons possessing large cranial projections would display corresponding brain dispositions to a greater extent than those who evidence smaller protuberances.

Gall identified 27 different "organs" in the brain that undergirded separate psychological tendencies. By "reading" the skull, usually by running your hands over the head, different enlarged organs could be identified. Gall went to prisons and lunatic asylums to read skulls and collect data on correlations between protubrances in certain locations and personality traits. He also began collecting the skulls of dead people as well. His obsession for skulls became widely known and many in Viennese society began to specify in their wills that Gall *not* be allowed to get possession of their skulls. Moreover, by 1802, the Catholic Church had persuaded the Austrian government to ban Gall from speaking engagements as they considered him to be heretical but, as so often happens when things become forbidden, this ban only served to fan the flames of interest in Gall's theories. Gall left for a successful European tour and eventually set up residence in France.

Gall referred to his studies of brain physiology as "organology" and "crain-oscopy," but the term *phrenology*, which his younger associate Johann Spurzheim coined, came to be its popular designation. As noted, the rationale that Gall presented for measuring contour variations of the skull was not illogical. In fact, his work signified an important advance over the naive and subjective studies of physiognomy of his time in that he sought to employ objective and quantitative methods to deduce the inner structure of the brain. He concluded, quite reasonably, that both the intensity and character of thoughts and emotions would correlate with variations in the size and shape of the brain or its encasement, the cranium. That this gross expression of personality proved invalid is not surprising when we think of the exceedingly complex structure of neuroanatomy.

Cesare Lombroso (1836–1909) became a professor at Italy's University of Turin in 1878, first in legal medicine, later in psychiatry and criminal anthropology. He was heavily influenced not only by Benedict Morel (see Chapter 5), the French positivists, and the German materialists, but also by the increasing respect given to Darwinian evolutionary theory. A proponent of criminal atavism, the theory that criminals are hereditarily degenerate, he believed that signs of degeneracy could be identified in abnormal shapes of the head, eyes, ears, or jaw. A prolific writer, he wrote books such as *The Delinquent Man* (1876) and *The Female Offender* (1895). Although many of his theories seem ludicrous today, he made a number of contributions to the field, including the study of personality characteristics and their relation to criminal behavior. His interest in the pathology of personality development spawned the growth of what came to be called *pathographies*. His theories also generated the first lie detector, based on his belief that fluctuations in heart rate and blood pressure while answering relevant questions indicated that a suspect might be lying.

To the notion that the morally depraved had cerebral deficits, Lombroso added several anthropological stigmata. Dismissing his rather primitive physical anthropological thinking, what is striking about Lombroso's exposition is how closely his speculations corresponded to modern *DSM* diagnostic criteria. He was explicit in proposing the idea of a "born delinquent," a notion similar to one implied in the *DSM*. According to Lombroso, constitutionally disposed criminal types display a notably large and projective lower jaw, outstretched ears, retreating forehead, left-handedness, robust physique, precocious sexual development, tactile insensibility, muscular agility, and so on. Behaviorally, he saw them as emotionally hyperactive, temperamentally irascible, impetuous in action and deficient in altruistic feelings. His list of stigmata parallel other aspects of *DSM* antisocial personality criteria. Most similar is the symptom cluster characterized by moral perversion from early life, as evidenced in headstrong, malicious, disobedient, irascible, lying, neglectful, and frequently violent and brutal behaviors; also noted was the narcissistic antisocial's delight in intrigue and mischief, as well as a tendency toward excesses in seeking excitement and passion.

Investigating Individual Differences Scientifically

Interest in evaluating differences among individuals has been evident since the ancient Chinese developed civil service exams. Plato recognized the need to test military aptitude to ensure an optimal match of people's abilities to their tasks. However, the scientific study of individual differences did not catch fire until the beginning of the nineteenth century. This fire was ignited in an unlikely place: astronomy. Friedrich Bessel, an astronomer, read the book *Zeitschrift für Astronomie*, which told the story of the firing of an assistant astronomer, D. Kinnebrook, from the Greenwich observatory in England on grounds of incompetence. Kinnebrook apparently observed the times of stellar transitions a second or so later than his superior. Bessel was intrigued with this occurrence and began collecting data on people's reaction times to stellar transits. To his surprise, he found that consistent differences in reaction times existed and proposed that each astronomer has a "personal equation" factor when recording stellar transit times. Soon, many physiologists began examining reaction times for a variety of tasks and psychologists became interested in measuring what they termed *mental chronometry*. The following sections describe those psychologists who began to explore the theme of individual differences in a systematic and comprehensive manner.

Although the first attempts to measure psychological differences can be traced to Thomas Wright in England, Jan Huarte y Navarro in Spain, and to Christian Thomasius in Germany, especially in the latter's system of "numerical degrees for the principal passions" in the seventeenth century, the true founding of differential psychology began with a more modern scientific thinker, **Francis Galton (1822–1911).** Galton followed a suggestion made by Quatelet, a Belgian statistician, to the effect that the principles of probability and mathematics could be applied successfully to the measurement of human attributes. At his anthropometric laboratory in London, established in 1882, Galton constructed tests that were simpler than the psychophysical measures then used, and, more importantly, focused attention on individual differences rather than group characteristics. His use of statistical difference units was original, and his exploration of psychological

Francis Galton

traits and temperament went beyond the narrow sensorimotor studies typical of his day.

Galton was the youngest of seven children of a prosperous Quaker family. Galton's father was a successful banker and his mother was a daughter of Erasmus Darwin, the grandfather of both Galton and Charles Darwin, the great evolutionary theorist. A precocious child, tutored to read at the age of 2½ by an older sister, Galton displayed a wide-ranging talent in numerous fields, most notably in mathematics. Inclined in his youth toward a career in medicine, Galton ended this aspiration in his mid-twenties following a series of stressful and disturbing hospital training experiences. Upon the death of his father in 1844, the youthful Galton's private income freed him to pursue the highly varied career path that he followed for the remainder of his life.

Although he never held a formal academic appointment, Galton supported numerous fellowships and scholarships at the University of London and became an exceptionally diverse British scientist, contributing to not only the psychological literature, but also to meteorology and photography, as well as exploration and geography. His family's wealth allowed him to pursue whatever caught his interest, which, with his boundless energy and enthusiasm, was a great many things. After beginning his medical studies, where he conducted experiments on his personal reactions to taking a variety of substances, Galton became interested in geographic exploration and left for Africa where he studied both the topography of the region as well as the indigenous people.

Some of Galton's psychometric experiments included measures of mental imagery and tests of association. In measuring mental imagery abilities, he would ask subjects to recall a scene from their everyday lives in as much detail as possible, such as the lighting, the colors, and the people present in the scene. Galton also used two types of measures to study the phenomenon of association. The first was to give a subject a stimulus word and then have them respond with an association. He measured the latency of each association, which he believed served as an index of their mental keenness. Interestingly, when he analyzed the origins of these associations, he discovered that 40% of them had roots in childhood experiences. This finding lent empirical support for the analytic technique of using word association to uncover deeply rooted unconscious thoughts that stem from childhood experiences, a procedure Carl Jung employed at the turn of the twentieth century. A second method Galton used was to have subjects allow their minds to roam freely for a certain period of time and then have them analyze the content of their thoughts, a procedure Sigmund Freud more fully developed in the early years of the twentieth century in his well-known method of free association.

Galton was also intrigued by genetics and the concept of inheriting mental abilities. He first published *Hereditary Genius* in 1869 and a second edition in 1878 in which he reported the results of his investigations into the nature/nurture debate, claiming that most mental abilities are inherited. Galton was highly aristocratic, a strong believer in nobility and the assumption that nobility was associated with intellectual brilliance. He objected strongly to democratic notions that differences in achievement could be a consequence of environmental stimulation and schooling. He wrote (1869/1972): "I have no patience with the hypothesis occasionally expressed . . . that babies are born pretty much alike. The experiences of the nursery, the school, the university, and of professional careers are a chain of proofs to the contrary" (p. 56).

James McKeen Cattell (1860–1944), despite the objections of his mentor, Wilhelm Wundt, embarked on a study of Galton's concepts. Upon returning to the United States from Leipzig, where he received his doctorate, Cattell continued the Galton tradition of studying individual differences. In his laboratories at the University of Pennsylvania established in 1890, he devised statistical procedures to obtain normative and comparative measures among individuals, coining the term "mental tests" to reflect the quantitative or psychometric method he used. He was instrumental in initiating studies on such varied subjects as reading skills, college aptitudes, and the mentally defective. However, the major figure of American psychology at that time, Edward Titchener (see Chapter 9), had unequivocally condemned tests as unscientific and, as a consequence, the development of test methodology lay dormant for almost two decades.

Cattell benefited from both German and British training, but remained a follower of Galton his entire life. After graduating from Lafayette College in 1880, where his father was a professor of Latin and Greek, he traveled throughout Europe with funds from his inheritance. On his travels, he heard Wilhelm Wundt lecture. Shortly after returning home, he won a fellowship to Johns Hopkins University to study with G. Stanley Hall (see Chapter 13), the first professor of psychology in the United States. He spent 1882 and 1883 helping Hall establish a psychological laboratory and began performing experiments on himself, which he termed his "psychometric investigations." These investigations included ingesting substances such as coffee, wine, marijuana, and other drugs and then recording the effects of them on his physiology and behaviors. He also collected data on his own reactions and behaviors on many other topics from heart rate changes while running, to his own learning curve in progress while playing billiards.

In 1883, he took his data and his designs for lab apparatuses to Leipzig and became Wilhelm Wundt's (see Chapter 10) first American assistant. He remained there for three years, until 1886 when he earned his doctorate. His American individualism clashed rather heatedly with Wundt's formal German character. Wundt believed in establishing general laws of psychology and did not appreciate Cattell's insistence in looking at individual reactions. Cattell focused on research problems that were of interest to him, and not to Wundt, such as using reaction times to measure psychological processes of perception, association, and choice.

On his way home from Germany, Cattell met Francis Galton in England and instantly became a lifelong admirer. Galton, who was at the height of his career, was busy investigating such diverse subjects as heredity, photography, sound, fingerprints, and psychological phenomena such as association and psychometrics. Later that autumn, Cattell returned to Cambridge, England, to study with Galton and to lecture. By this time, Cattell was convinced that individual differences could and should be measured, but these views were extremely unpopular in Cambridge and he left for a professorship in psychology at the University of Pennsylvania in 1888. He established a laboratory at the University of Pennsylvania and began administering many Galton-like measures to the psychology students, labeling them "mental tests" in a paper published in 1890. In 1891, Cattell left for Columbia University to establish a department of psychology and a laboratory, which he headed until 1917. For many years, he continued to administer his mental tests to all incoming students, and eventually it became known as the "Freshman Test." These tests included measures of reaction times, memory for letters, perception, and attention span. Most significantly, and for a half century, Cattell was the editor of *Science*, through which he was able to promote psychology's image as a major science. He also edited the *Biographical Directory of American Men of Science*, as well as found the American Association of University Professors, an organization that sought to strengthen the role of professors in university decision making.

A fiercely independent man, willing to pursue the life of the mind outside of the academy, Cattell spoke out against the administration of Nicholas Murray Butler, president of Columbia University, in 1913. Butler had drafted a publication, entitled *University Control*, asserting the hierarchical character of university administration. Along with others of an independent mind, Cattell favored a university led by a free association of intellects, an "unhierarchical, democratic, and anarchic organization." He asserted rather vehemently that the university should not be owned, as he put it, by a small self-perpetuating board of trustees who appointed a dictator to run it. True to his character, Butler sought to fire Cattell immediately, but a powerful faculty committee in support of Cattell's views restrained him. In 1921, Cattell collaborated with over 200 psychologists to establish The Psychological Corporation, a test development company still engaged in active research today.

In 1888, while teaching English and history at the Rugby Academy in Philadelphia, **Lightner Witmer (1867–1956)** became interested in one of his students who seemed of normal intelligence, but had great difficulty with verbal tasks including speaking and writing. Witmer wanted to help the young boy enter college and began giving him special verbal tutoring. The next year, while continuing to teach, he entered the graduate program at the University of Pennsylvania to pursue a doctorate degree in political science. Within a year, he switched his focus to psychology, in part because of the influence of Cattell who had just joined the faculty. Cattell chose Witmer as his assistant and had Witmer begin to conduct research on reaction times, a favorite topic among experimental psychologists at the time. In 1891, Witmer transferred to the University of Leipzig to study with Wundt. After completing his studies, he returned to the

University of Pennsylvania as Cattell's successor and had big plans to expand the department. In November of 1896, he published a paper in *Pediatrics* entitled "Practical work in psychology." The following month, at the fifth meeting of the American Psychological Association, he presented a paper that introduced the term "psychological clinic" for the first time. In it, Witmer stressed the importance of psychology's practical school and medical applications.

In 1907, Witmer decided he had developed enough clinical skills and expertise to expand his clinic and formally introduce this new clinical psychology profession. He saw it as focusing mostly on children, but occasionally it dealt with the difficulties of adults as well. Soon afterward, his program at the University of Pennsylvania became the major training ground for all clinical psychologists in the country. By the 1910s, a number of other clinics of a similar type sprung up around the country, mostly associated with academic settings.

Developing Psychometric Statistics

Galton's student, **Karl Pearson (1857–1936),** was given the task of developing a biometric methodology to verify Galton's primitive speculations about individual differences. Although Pearson's work was not oriented to the mental sciences, his student, **Charles Spearman (1863–1945),** took up that task.

The University of London psychology department established the era of statistical analysis and made it a highly fruitful development for all aspects of psychological research, especially the methodologies undergirding factor theories, still an attractive field today. The progression from Galton to Pearson to Spearman and then, in turn, to Cyril Burt, Raymond Cattell, and Hans Eysenck became a formidable tradition not only throughout England, but in the Americas as well.

Spearman's most notable contribution emerged in his theory of intelligence, a model that rested on several imaginative assumptions. First, and still widely accepted, though controversial, was his assertion that all intellectual activities were in part a function of a broad-based or general aptitude, called the g-factor, to which one or more additional specific (S) aptitudes might be added. Thus, arithmetic performance was a product of g, plus a specific numerical aptitude. Depending on the task to be completed, as in any component of an intelligence test, its achievement would be a product of the general factor, along with one of any number of secondary aptitudes, depending upon the nature of the task. Spearman believed that the g factor was essentially determined by heredity, whereas the specific S aptitudes were largely a product of environmental opportunities and education. Spearman hesitated to commit himself to a clear characterization of the nature of the g factor, at times implying that it represented a capacity for processing symbolic material, at other times, treating it as if it signified the ability to learn.

In the United States, **Louis Leon Thurstone (1887–1955)** synthesized Spearman's varied contributions on the one hand and Thorndike's (see

Chapter 10) on the other. Spearman stressed the primacy of a general factor, whereas Thorndike proposed a constellation of special abilities without a g factor. In two major books, *Vectors of the Mind* (1935) and *Multiple Factor Analysis* (1947), Thurstone demonstrated through his "centroid method" that the correlation matrix composed of several individual tests could be repeatedly reconstructed. His method could also determine which specific units of a large number of diverse tests could most efficiently represent what he came to term the *primary mental abilities*, notably reasoning, verbal comprehension, word fluency, rote memory, perceptual speed, number facility, and spatial perception.

Measuring Intelligence

General and vague theories of intelligence had long been in existence, but it wasn't until diagnosticians began trying to measure it that it became clear that the field needed a more specific and operationalized definition. The most popular theory of intelligence until the early 1900s was based on faculty psychology, or the idea that if individuals had a good memory, their memory faculties were well developed or if they possessed good judgment, their judgment faculties were well developed. While this theory had parsimony going for it, it was not particularly useful or enlightening. As noted previously, Spearman developed one of the first explanations based on empirical evidence, the concept of g, which was based on intercorrelations between many measures of intellectual functioning. *Edward Lee Thorndike* presented a competing model (recorded in Chapter 9) when he attempted to determine whether learning one skill would help one learn another skill more easily. Thorndike's research demonstrated that this occurred rarely, convincing him that intelligence did not have a common g or unitary construct. This lack of agreement about what intelligence really was did not slow the progression of psychologists who sought to measure it.

It remained for **Alfred Binet (1857–1911)** to bring testing out of the laboratory and into systematic public use. Binet was influenced by, but expanded on the simple measures Galton and Cattell used as they were unable to discriminate the more complex higher mental processes. Given the philosophic temper of French psychology and the support of the French Ministry of Public Instruction, Binet forsook the precise and simple measures Galton constructed and studied complex processes such as memory, imagery, comprehension, attention, and judgment. By 1905, Binet combined several of the instruments he had devised into the first formal scale of general intelligence. Binet was also interested in assessing the lower end of the distribution of intellectual abilities, focusing initially on variations in children's intellectual functioning. Binet was deeply dissatisfied with the methods for assessing intelligence that existed in his day and began studying his two daughters, Madeleine and Alice.

Binet himself had been a precocious youngster, raised by wealthy and educated Jewish parents, his father a physician, his mother a talented artist; he first decided on a career in law and obtained that degree at the age of 21 but found it uninspiring. Exposed to the ideas of Jean Charcot, the great French neurologist, Binet turned his interests toward medicine, more specifically various topics of a neurological and psychological character, especially investigations into hypnosis. In 1889, he helped found the first laboratory of physiological psychology at the Sorbonne in Paris. He continued his studies, obtaining a doctorate in science in 1894 and, together with his associates, founded one of the first journals of psychology *L'anné psycholoque.* It was during this period that Binet began observing his daughters' psychological development. He made particular note of their differences, for example, how they approached the simple acquisition of walking, one hesitating and looking for support, the other bold and vigorous. He was especially intrigued by how personality factors influenced the acquisition of verbal and performance skills.

Accepting an assignment from the Ministerial Commission for the Study of Retarded in 1904, Binet was charged with developing a concrete and objective way to assess mental differences that could differentiate normal from

Alfred Binet

abnormal children. In this first version of the Binet test, carried out with his associate, **Theodore Simon (1873–1961),** they borrowed heavily from Hermann Ebbinghaus, who had developed specific tasks that captured complex mental processes, as well as from puzzles and games Binet had used to test his children. They also adopted existing medical screening procedures for testing children entering institutions for the mentally retarded and a host of other educational and psychiatric methods. Binet purposely used tasks that would motivate children to want to try hard and do their best. He had a deep and abiding interest in children who did not do well in school or had left school. For this reason, he tried to develop tasks that were not dependent upon specific learning that took place in the classroom.

To evaluate their new measure, Binet and Simon used a sample of Paris school children (ages 3, 5, 7, 9, and 11) whose teachers had divided into groups of normal or average intelligence and of subnormal intelligence. They also obtained a sample of retarded patients from the hospital at Salpétrière. Each subject was tested individually on the 30 very brief tasks and scores were averaged for each task by each age group for the normal children. This provided Binet and Simon with an indication of how difficult a task was for a given age. They rated the task to reflect the youngest age group in which most children successfully completed the task. They then ranked the tasks from easiest to most difficult based on these ratings.

Revision, translation, and the eventual adoption of the Binet scale in the United States followed shortly thereafter. **Henry Goddard (1886–1957)** published a version in 1911. Unfortunately, Goddard's zealous attitude toward his measure prompted him to begin a training program for public school teachers to allow them to assess students who needed special attention. Within a few years, hundreds of "mental testers" were unleashed on American schools. Unfortunately, these testers had very little, if any, psychological or psychometric background. The results of many of the examinations made by these mental testers were worse than useless and served to anger parents, students, and school boards. Soon the American public in general was against the idea of using these tests to measure children's mental abilities.

Lewis M. Terman (1877–1956) began to sway public opinion back in favor of intelligence testing. Born on a farm in Indiana, Terman was twelfth in a family of 14 children. Although young Terman had to work on the farm after school and all summer long, he was an extremely bright student who was promoted to the third grade after only six months of schooling. When he was still a child, a traveling peddler sold his parents a book on phrenology, which sparked Terman's interest in individual differences. When he was fifteen, he left for Central Normal College to become a teacher. After graduating in 1895, he taught in several rural Indiana schools before getting his MA in 1903 from Indiana University, where he was exposed to G. Stanley Hall's writings. With Hall's support, Terman received a fellowship to Clark University where he began his graduate studies. When Terman decided to use mental tests in his research, he was forced to change advisors owing to Hall's mistrust of mental tests. He developed tuberculosis while at Clark and when he graduated in 1905, he chose a position in the warm climate of Southern California, first as the principal of a high school and later as a faculty member at the Los Angeles Normal College. In 1910, he joined the faculty of Stanford University where he stayed on for the remainder of his career.

Terman developed and released what he called the Stanford Revision and Extension of the Binet-Simon Intelligence test in 1916, later called the Stanford-Binet. It was in this test format that Terman adopted William Stern's (see Chapter 13) term *IQ* (intelligence quotient) for the first time as an official test designation. The Stanford-Binet emerged as the most popular of all of the intelligence tests of its day. In part, this stemmed from Terman's many years of carefully standardizing the test to meet professional insistence that tests be accurate and reliable.

Terman had a special interest in studying intellectually precocious children. He established and financially supported what turned out to be a long-term study of 1,500 gifted children (IQ scores over 135, with a range of 135–200), beginning in 1921 when the children were eleven. His coworkers continued the study after Terman's death, with 95% of the original sample continuing in the project. Terman was interested in what kind of adults gifted children became. He studied their interests, their health, their educational history, their personalities, and their family backgrounds. In 1925, a first summary of these children was published, portraying them as children who enjoyed a wide variety of activities, not just the stereotypical child interested only in books. He conducted a follow-up in 1927 to 1928 when most of these children were in high school. The results showed that their scores had changed very little; not only did they excel in school, but they were successful also in a variety of extracurricular activities. He conducted another follow-up in 1939 to 1940, when the subjects were almost thirty years of age. Results from this follow-up showed that whereas only 8% of the general population attended college, 87% of the men and 83% of the women in the gifted study had done so. Subsequent follow-ups showed that these individuals continued to achieve throughout their lives in a remarkably wide variety of professions. Robert Sears and Lee Cronbach examined the men in the study in 1972, some 50 years after its origin. In 1977, Pauline Sears and Ann Barbee examined the women from the original group. The results for both genders continued to be exceptionally impressive, both professionally and personally.

David Wechsler (1896–1981) received his PhD from Columbia University in 1925. A former student of Cattell, he helped his mentor launch The Psychological Corporation, a business-oriented psychological group. Wechsler had been in the army during World War I and had considerable testing experience. After leaving The Psychological Corporation to engage in a private practice of industrial consulting, he settled in as chief psychologist of the Bellevue Hospitals of New York City in 1932. Here, he faced the challenge of testing emotionally disturbed adults who disliked the child-oriented measures available in that day. To overcome their resistance, Wechsler set out to design an adult-oriented test, one composed of 11 subtests consisting of both verbal measures (e.g., vocabulary, general information, and comprehension) and performance scales (e.g., picture completion, block design, and object assembly). Although many of the tasks that composed the first form of his test did not originate with Wechsler, he was the first to organize them into a comprehensive single measure employing well-standardized scoring procedures. Unfortunately, the instrument's norms were generated in only one locale: New York City.

Published by The Psychological Corporation in 1939, this new test was entitled the Wechsler-Bellevue (W-B) Scale. Eventually, The Psychological Corporation carried out a more representative sample for standardization. In the 1960s, when assessing learning disabilities became the rage, discrepancies between the verbal and performance scores proved invaluable to the task of diagnosing these disorders.

Another important innovation was the abandonment of the concept of a "mental age" in favor of a simple point system in which a score of 100 indicated the average or mean score of the person's general age group. Whereas the Stanford-Binet scoring system compared adult performances to those of children and adolescents, the Wechsler scores compared adults to other adults of their own age. Operating on the assumption that intelligence is normally distributed, Wechsler identified 2% of the population as "defective" and assigned them a score of 65 and below. Similarly, he identified 2% of the population as "very superior" and assigned them a score of 128 and above.

David Wechsler

The Wechsler-Bellevue scale went through several revisions, including parallel forms and simpler versions for children (WPPSI, 1957; and WISC, 1949), as well as a variant based on army data gathered in World War II. In the 1950s, a revised W-B, the Wechsler Adult Intelligence Scale (WAIS; 1955) was released; it possessed the same composition of scales as the original test, but was normed on an accurate representative national sample. It included 10% nonwhite subjects; a broad range of occupations and social strata, and a special sample of people over 60 years of age. Successive versions of the test were published over the years, the first labeled the WAIS-R (1981) and currently, the WAIS-III (1997). Each new version represented improvements in psychometric properties, as well as superior or updated contents.

Despite his protestations against formulating a theoretical schema, **Joy Paul Guilford (1897–1987)** elaborated perhaps the most sophisticated theory of intelligence to date in what he termed the "structure-of-intellect" model. His approach was guided, however, by a strong empirical orientation based on factorially derived categories and their corresponding test measurements. In the latter phases of his career, Guilford published his magnum opus, *The Nature of Human Intelligence* (1967). Basing his model on information-processing assumptions, he constructed a three-dimensional matrix based on three elements: *processing, input,* and *products.* Under "processing," he included comprehension, remembering, and fluency of ideas. The "input" dimension included visual, symbolic, semantic, and behavioral elements. In the third set, the "product" dimensions, he included classes, relations, systems, transformations, and implications.

To represent the interrelationship among the three structural dimensions, Guilford generated a visual cube composed of four inputs, five components of processing, and six kinds of products. Overly complex, albeit the most sophisticated of intelligence models, others frequently criticized Guilford's work for its excessive rigidity and detail. Moreover, subsequent researchers who found frequent covariations and repeated difficulties in separating the multitude of components in the model questioned his factors' ostensive independence. Nevertheless, Guilford's effort represented the most articulate and creative of efforts to systematize both the elements and the operations involved in intellectual functioning.

Howard Gardner (1943–) has sought to synthesize two spheres of research associated with his early training: symbol-using cognitive capacities, based on developmental research with normal and gifted children, and neuropsychology, based on adults suffering various forms of brain damage. As a result of these efforts, he introduced a theory of "multiple intelligences" in his popular 1983 book, *Frames of Mind.* Using this theoretical model, Gardner turned his attention to the study of school reform in a research program called Project Zero.

Born in Pennsylvania, the son of refugees from Nazi Germany, Gardner initially pursued a serious music career, but turned in his postsecondary studies to psychology at Harvard University, where he has remained a faculty member since the 1970s. Central to Gardner's thinking is the view that intelligence should encompass a broader range of competencies than traditionally gauged on standard mental tests. In addition to the classical psychometric measures of verbal, logical-mathematical, and visual-spatial intelligence, Gardner added a number of other facets he judged to be significant elements representing everyday competencies. For example, he posits that bodily/kinesthetic, interpersonal, and intrapersonal skills represent major facets of intellectual functioning. He also proposed that a variety of talents, such as musical and, most recently, "naturalistic" capabilities be factored into the equation.

Numerous theorists and psychometricians other than Gardner have contributed concepts and instruments to broaden the concept of intelligence. Especially valuable were early contributions by **Jacob Getzels (1912–2001)** whose 1962 book, *Creativity and Intelligence,* challenged accepted notions by stressing the importance of creative abilities as factors in both school performance and ultimate success. He found that youngsters with creative capabilities showed more energy, were more goal oriented, evidenced emotional stability, and possessed a better sense of humor than children who often scored appreciably higher on standard intelligence tests.

Robert J. Sternberg (1949–) drew upon several prior theorists, including Getzel, in proposing his new model of intelligence. In his 1985 book, *Beyond IQ: A Triarchic Theory of Human Intelligence,* Sternberg expanded on Spearman's notion of a single general intellectual trait by subdividing it into a number of information-processing components, a structure somewhat akin to Guilford's model. However, Sternberg believed that the *Componential Theory,* as it was called, was insufficient and should be expanded further into what he termed his *Triarchic Theory* of intelligence.

Sternberg's work on intelligence followed an early career in experimental psychology, first as an undergraduate at Yale University and secondly as a graduate student at Stanford University. As his work progressed, Sternberg translated his observations and studies of cognition in intelligence as evidencing three major facets. The *first,* entitled *Analytic Intelligence,* reflected the standard definitions of intelligence, not unlike the first component in Gardner's model. Its measurement elements were comprised of analogies and puzzles, and sought to reflect how an individual's internal thinking processes operate especially to solve abstract and relatively academic problems. He called the second component *Creative Intelligence*, modeled in many of its aspects on Getzels' ideas. Its essential components involved insight, synthesis, imagination, and the ability to deal with relatively novel stimuli and unfamiliar situations. In Sternberg's thinking, creative intelligence relates to the experiential aspect of functioning and reflects how the individual utilizes internal processing style to deal inventively with external reality. He called the third facet *Practical Intelligence*, which involved the ability to perceive, comprehend, and solve real relatively concrete and familiar problems of everyday life. In his Sternberg Triarchic Abilities Test (STAT), he set out to measure all three facets of his model of intelligence. He considered the three facets to be different, but viewed their interrelationship to be crucial, not only to educational success but to success in everyday life as well. Most importantly, Sternberg believed that each of the three facets could be precisely measured and lent themselves to refinement and further development given proper educational training and inspiration.

Diagnosing Neuropsychological Disorders

Neuropsychological assessment draws its nourishment from numerous other spheres of scientific and scholarly interest, such as experimental neurology, clinical psychology, behavioral medicine, and, most recently, the new field of neuroscience. The primary focus of neuropsychological assessment is to appraise the functions of the higher centers of the nervous system as they are expressed in a variety of perceptual, cognitive, and behavioral tasks. These assessments address a number of clinical questions, such as: does the patient manifest dysfunctions representing impairments in one or another region of the higher nervous system; is the likely location of the dysfunction diffuse or focal; is the dysfunction of an acute origin and might it be progressive in character; how severe are the functional limitations consequent to the impairment; are they evident in perceptual processes, cognition, personality changes, and so on; what is the general prognosis of the individual's daily living capacities, and what might be planned to overcome or compensate for the impairments.

Lev Semenovich Vygotsky (1896–1934) was born in the Russian Republic of Belarus in the city of Gomel. His father was a bank manager, an intelligent man of wide interests and fluent in numerous foreign languages. He and his siblings referred to his mother, likewise well-educated and fluent in several languages, as the heart and soul of the family. Vygotsky was the second of eight children, evidently precocious as a youngster, demonstrating a serious maturity far beyond his years. Interested primarily in literature, philosophy, and art, he was encouraged, however, to pursue a medical career because medicine was a field in which bright Jewish students could find a secure position beyond the boundaries of their restricted settlements. Vygotsky found medicine to be rather limited and stultifying and switched to receive a degree in law, but ultimately turned his interests to those of literature, aesthetics, and language, and finally to developmental psychology. Younger associates quickly recognized him as an intriguing and knowledgeable lecturer and referred to him as the "little professor."

In 1924, Vygotsky presented his first professional psychological paper at the Second All-Russian Psychoneurological Congress in Leningrad. The new director of the Moscow Psychological Institute, K. N. Kornilov, recognized his brilliant performance and quickly invited Vygotsky to join him and others in helping restructure the institute. In 1925, he completed a doctoral dissertation, entitled "The Psychology of Art," but was unable to present a defense owing to one of his periodic bouts with tuberculosis. He attracted numerous younger associates to his work, notably **Alexander Romanovich Luria (1902–1977)** of whom more will be said, and **Aleksei Leont'ev (1904–1979),** later to become head of psychology at the University of Moscow. They joined him in advancing a number of his brilliant conceptions regarding the nature of neurologic functioning and the structure of consciousness. Vygotsky profoundly influenced younger students; many became his disciples at the University.

In later years, Luria, who became one of the most prominent neuropsychologists of the twentieth century, said that his life's work had been no more than the working out of the psychological theories that Vygotsky constructed some 40 years earlier. During Vygotsky's last few years of life, as he ultimately succumbed to the ravages of tuberculosis at the age of 38, he lectured and wrote at an almost frenetic pace, editing, translating, and writing numerous papers on topics such as the diagnosis of difficult children and the development of higher mental functions, as well as formulating a unique contribution to such concepts as *mediation* and the child's self-regulation of speech in the *Zone of Proximal Development.* Here he stressed the role of *sign* and *symbol* as comprising the essential elements of human thought and communication, establishing a solid foundation for the study of semiotics, as well as philology and literary analysis. The exciting social and cultural times in which he lived in Russia enriched his great familiarity with a wide range of intellectual disciplines. He sought to bring together diverse strands of intellectual inquiry, interweaving the sociocultural context within which people think and reason. Fortunately, unusually devoted and able disciples carried on his work.

The exceptional contributions of Russian psychology to the foundations of neuropsychology were not clearly known in the Western world until the English translation of Luria's *Higher Cortical Functions in Man* in 1966. Luria began his professional career at a crucial period in Russian history with the Bolshevik Revolution in full sway. Born in the provincial commercial center of Kazan to modestly educated Jewish parents, Luria accelerated through his academic training at an unusual speed and fashioned his own educational program with a mix of utopian socialistic thinking, philosophy, and psychological science. Caught up in the enthusiasm of the Russian Revolution, Luria sought a scientific basis for shaping the character of human events, including Jung's and Freud's ideas as potential frameworks for guiding human affairs. At the age of 22, Luria met the brilliant Vygotsky when the latter joined the Moscow Institute of Psychology. Luria had already evolved a rationale for synthesizing psychoanalysis and Marxism when he was drawn into Vygotsky's inventive ideas concerning human conflict and communication. A troika of Vygotsky, Luria, and Leont'ev began to carry out the reconstruction of all of psychology from first principles that might provide a foundation of thinking for the new Soviet system. Owing to Vygotsky's interest in social education, Luria turned his attention increasingly to the social context of cognitive development; his early work centered on educating culturally different children.

As with Vygotsky, Luria had been in psychological exile during much of the Stalinist period; though both had become known in the United States, they were cut-off temporarily from the native Russian scene, regarded at times almost as foreign figures. Luria was always impressively intelligent, but maintained a constant air of sadness and morbidity that seemed to reflect his personal misfortunes and his tragic sense of history. He would sit at times alone in a room and say nothing, looking as though he were holding on to his wisdom, perhaps because he was too fearful to speak his mind. Though gracious and friendly when you got to know him, he was a brooding and reserved figure, often closed off from easy exchange, full of some dark and inner turmoil that characterized so many Russian intellectuals in the Stalinist era.

Luria advocated separating complex functions into their simplest and testable behavioral components to specify which segments of a complex functional system were compromised. He did not translate these proposals, however, into standardized operational procedures, nor did he evaluate them with appropriate reliability and validity studies. More similar to the methods of neurology rather than psychology, his proposals and procedures were qualitative rather than quantitative. It was not until *Charles Golden* proposed methods in the late 1970s that a manual with detailed procedures and standardized examination techniques translated Luria's ideas into an operational instrument; it is known as the Luria-Nebraska Neuropsychological Battery (Golden, Purisch, & Hammeke, 1985). This popular instrument contained 269 items composed of 11 content scales, such as motor functions, visual functions, receptive and expressive language, and memory. Included also were special measures addressing pathognomic signs and left and right hemisphere scales. Although some have raised questions as to whether Luria's theoretical proposals could be fully operationalized by a battery of explicit tests, this instrument has provided a useful measure of neuropsychological functioning.

Accessing and Assessing the Mind

Psychologists' early emphasis on intelligence tests was largely a result of the limited instruments available to them during the first decades of this century.

These tools measured a rather limited part of the total range of human functioning. As the need arose to study other aspects of behavior, psychologists had to devise new methods. Unfortunately, when the call came for personality measures, the undeveloped state of personality theory could provide neither suitable concepts nor a suitable format. Instead, they adopted the psychometric procedures used with some success in intelligence testing.

Personality testing employing self-report techniques began during the First World War, but faced with critical research and indifferent if not hostile academic attitudes, languished during the 1920s and 1930s. Although this period allowed for reappraisal and consolidation of early progress with the "objective inventories" of the day, the use of the psychometric approach seemed restrictive and sterile to many psychologists who had an increasing acquaintance with psychoanalytic theory. This interest led clinically oriented psychiatrists and psychologists to search for methods that would portray the complexity of personality functioning, especially with the goal of disclosing unconscious motivational processes.

Designing Projective Techniques

The search for dynamic processes led to the discovery of the little known word-association technique Jung devised in 1905, and to the inkblot cards Rorschach constructed in 1921. Rorschach's test followed observations by Binet and his associates regarding the use of inkblots as a gauge of imagination and as a route for assessing intelligence and personality. As early as 1897, George Dearborn in the United States tried using inkblots to study the content of consciousness, as did Ernest Kirkpatrick employ them to assess the maturity of children. The possibilities of this unusual technique were especially intriguing to psychologists who were dismayed by the simple and straightforward self-report psychometric measures then available in the 1920s. Obscure though the new methods appeared, they promised to reveal the latent and unexpressed aspects of personality functioning. Its logic was novel also, for it assumed that people would display the inner dynamics and full complexity of their makeup when they attempted to interpret or project meaning on an ambiguous stimulus. As Lawrence Frank phrased it (1936):

> Coming directly to the topic of projective methods for personality study, we may say that the dynamic conception of personality as a processes of organizing experience and structuralizing life space in a field leads to the problem of how we can reveal the way an individual personality organizes experience, in order to disclose or least gain insight into that individual's private world of meanings, significances, patterns, and feelings. (p. 14)

As Frank noted, projective techniques enable clinicians to tap the private world of patients so as to reveal what they could not or would not be inclined to say about themselves, especially their unconscious inclinations. The stimulus comprising these methods is intentionally ambiguous, intended to serve as a trigger for eliciting the personal fantasies and unconscious dispositions of the patient.

The very open-endedness that makes projectives so clinically rich in turn creates interpretational ambiguities that are inherently problematic. Self-report instruments do not suffer this shortcoming, since one can embark only with difficulty on the creation of interpretive ideas on their scales without explicit constraints and limits. Self-reports, of course, suffer other limitations. Patients can only report what is known, or at least what is believed to be known, and self-image is distorted both by the inaccessibility of relevant information and interpretations of dubious validity. Just as phenomenology is not all of mentality, self-reports cannot be regarded as the all of personality assessment.

The Rorschach Inkblot. A Swiss psychiatrist, **Hermann Rorschach (1884–1922),** son of an art teacher, was interested in studying perception. As noted earlier, in Rorschach's day some believed the inkblot was a useful way to study visual imagination. In fact, many others had unsuccessfully tried to incorporate inkblots into tests before Rorschach, including Binet in his intelligence tests, but they had abandoned the idea because of the difficulties they encountered when trying to administer and interpret inkblots to large groups of youngsters. For the previous 100 years or so, children and adults all across Europe had played a popular game called *Blotto* that used inkblots as a stimulus for creating little poems or playing charades. Evidence suggests Rorschach was very fond of this game; he had even been given the nickname "Klex," short for Klecksographie (or Blotto), when he was in school.

Hermann Rorschach

Rorschach had remained friends with a classmate of his, Konrad Gehring, who became a teacher in a school near where Rorschach did his psychiatric residency at the Munsterlingen hospital beginning in 1909. Gehring had been using Blotto as a behavioral management technique to get his students to behave; if they worked hard for a period of time, they could play a game of Blotto. Gehring's students often came to the hospital to sing for patients and Rorschach became intrigued with the idea of comparing the Blotto responses of his patients to the responses of Gehring's students. In 1911, Gehring and Rorschach began experimenting with different inkblots. Also in that year, Eugen Bleuler, who had directed Rorschach's thesis on hallucinations, published his book on dementia praecox that introduced the alternative label, "schizophrenia." Rorschach discovered that a repetitive character to the perceptions of certain inkblots existed among those who had the diagnosis of schizophrenia. Although he published a report on this finding, no psychiatrist seemed interested and he therefore dropped the observation for several years.

In late 1917, Rorschach began again to systematically study the character of inkblot perceptions and a variety of psychiatric diagnoses. Syzmond Hens, another student of Bleuler's, who had given a series of inkblots to children, nonpatients, and psychiatric patients, sparked hypotheses about these relationships with the publication of his "Doctor's Thesis." Hens studied the differences in the "content" of their responses, a different approach from Rorschach's original idea of understanding how people "perceived" the blots. Rorschach began his new investigation with a set of 40 inkblots; he administered 15 of them more often than the rest. Just as he had found in 1911, the schizophrenic patients responded very differently from the other groups. Interestingly, Rorschach believed that responses to these blots were indicative of a Jungian idea of introversion-extraversion, but did not think that this procedure was linked to unconscious process and did not consider this to be what came to be judged a projective technique.

Due to his interest in perception, Rorschach focused primarily on the formal aspects of the patient's response, not its content. Thus, he began to record the number of responses, the time the patient took to respond to a blot, and whether color and movement were involved in the response. He also began to construct a set of codes that could be used to score inkblot responses. He designed the first set of scores to represent the area of the blot that was used for a response, such as D for a large detail area or a W for the whole blot. He developed another set of codes to represent the features of the blot that contributed to the response, such as C for color or F for form. Last, he created a set of codes to classify the content of the response, such as H for human or A for animal.

Within two years, Rorschach had tested enough patients to see that the inkblot test was useful for diagnostic purposes, not only for schizophrenia, but also for other psychiatric diagnoses. With Bleuler and his colleagues' encouragement, Rorschach attempted to publish a manuscript based on his findings, but publishers rejected it because of the prohibitive cost of printing the inkblots. One publisher agreed to publish the manuscript if he reduced the number of blots from the 15 most commonly used to only 6. Finally, Walter Morgenthaler, a friend and colleague of Rorschach, negotiated a contract with the House of Bircher who agreed to publish the book (Rorschach, 1921/1941) if he would reduce the number of inkblots to 10. In June of 1921, the manuscript was published; however, the blots were smaller, with slightly different colors and, most importantly, they were shaded in grays by virtue of different levels of ink saturation. Shading produced a very different stimulus than Rorschach's original blots, which were all solid colors. Rorschach was pleased with the printing errors; he saw its potential and was inspired to use the multishaded blots for further investigations. In April of the next year, Rorschach was admitted into the emergency room complaining of abdominal pains and died the next morning at the age of 37.

David Levy, an American psychiatrist, received a grant to study in Switzerland. During that year, he learned of Rorschach's work and brought a few copies of the inkblots back with him with the intent to study them with children, although he became distracted shortly thereafter from this purpose.

A graduate student at Columbia University, **Samuel J. Beck (1896–1980)** received a fellowship to study at the Institute where Levy worked. Beck was searching for a dissertation topic and Levy mentioned Rorschach's inkblots as a worthy idea. Beck was intrigued and spent three years collecting data on 150 children in what would be the first systematic investigation using the blots since Rorschach's death. He inspired another student, **Marguerite Hertz (1899–1992)** who also completed her dissertation on the Rorschach blots with a different sample later that year. Interestingly, neither Hertz nor Beck added new elements to Rorschach's original coding schema. Beck began publishing articles about his findings; by 1934, when he completed his dissertation, there was a growing interest in the Rorschach Inkblot Test in the United States. Both Beck and Hertz became well established as leaders in the movement to analyze personality via this new "projective test."

European psychologists who had been exposed only incidentally to the Rorschach test, notably **Bruno Klopfer (1900–1971),** *Zygmunt Piotrowski*, and *David Rapaport*, ultimately brought fresh ideas to the instrument. Klopfer emigrated to the United States in 1934 as a research associate in the department of Anthropology at Columbia University. Psychology students at the university encouraged him to teach an informal seminar on the Rorschach in his apartment two nights a week; one of the students, Piotrowski, who originally trained as an experimental psychologist in Poland, began a series of his own explorations into the technique. Klopfer intended to adhere closely to Rorschach's administration and scoring methods, but found that the incompleteness of the scoring system led to heated debates among the students that lasted late into the evenings regarding how a particular response should be scored. Other students from Columbia and then New York University asked Klopfer to add a second and third seminar to meet their interest. By 1935, Klopfer had begun to add several new codes to Rorschach's original system. In 1936, he published a newsletter called *The Rorschach Research Exchange*, later to be called the *Journal of Projective Techniques*, and today the *Journal of Personality Assessment*. He designed the newsletter to update people on the latest developments in the test, but also to stimulate debate and idea sharing about the test.

Within the next twenty-year period, five systems of scoring the Rorschach developed in the United States. However, many practitioners treated the test as a single entity, called the Rorschach. Mental health professionals in the 1940s, used the test as a projective measure but by no means were questions of its psychometric integrity forsaken. Researchers published numerous contradictory reports, ignoring the differences in these various scoring systems, leading critics of Freudian analysis to mistakenly assume that the Rorschach, which had little to do with Freudian theory, had no value.

Originally trained in Germany, receiving his doctorate of law at the age of 22 at Heidelberg University, **Ernest George Schachtel (1903–1975)** left his homeland following the rise of Nazi Germany in the late 1930s with many other Continental émigrés to join the faculty at the New School in New York, as well as the William Alanson White Institute as a training and supervising analyst. His most penetrating contribution was his text, entitled *Experiential Foundations of Rorschach's Test* (1966), in which he set forth a framework for a theoretical understanding of the nature of the test's data and the experiential dimensions of the testee's responses. Particularly illuminating in Schachtel's formulations was his distinction between "allocentric" and "autocentric" modes of perception, and how these modes influenced the testee's Rorschach responses.

A major thinker discussed in an earlier chapter on the ego analysts, David Rapaport, spent the better part of the 1940s at the Menninger Clinic where he oversaw both research and clinical psychological services, and assembled a group of brilliant young clinicians with whom he developed a two-volume series, *Diagnostic Psychological Testing* (1946). Although committed strongly to a cognitive and ego analytic perspective, Rapaport devised a highly sophisticated analysis of several psychological tests, most notably the Rorschach. His youngest colleague in this work was **Roy Schafer (1922–)**, at first an intern following his graduation from the City College of New York, then a staff psychologist at the Menninger Clinic and later at the Austen Riggs Center in Massachusetts. Schafer received advanced degrees at the University of Kansas and then at Clark University, following which he worked for several years at Yale and more recently in New York as a practicing psychoanalyst.

Schafer's contributions were extremely insightful, especially in clarifying the underlying, unconscious processes revealed in Rorschach responses. He most clearly formulated these processes in two books, *The Clinical Application of Psychological Tests* (1948) and *The Psychoanalytic Interpretation in Rorschach Testing* (1954). Particularly notable in Schafer's explications were the mechanisms of defense and the selective responsiveness to stimulation associated with these defenses, as understood by psychoanalytic thought. Schafer demonstrated that the Rorschach test response is not merely a score but a complex verbalized end-product of unconscious thought processes.

In 1969, **John Exner (1928–)** conducted a comparative analysis of five major scoring systems of the Rorschach. He concluded that apart from the original inkblot stimuli, little in common existed among the five. Exner set out to put together the best elements of all of the systems, stressing the elements that had the greatest empirical support and clinical utility. He was also careful to preserve Rorschach's original intent for a construct whenever possible. Exner's *Comprehensive System*, as it has become to be called, while complex and detailed, combined both the perceptual process as well as the content of each response. Whereas Rorschach's scoring system had only a handful of variables,

Exner's had over 100, making learning to score and interpret the Rorschach using his system complex and challenging. Despite its integration of demonstrable wisdoms of its 80-year history, little empirical evidence supports the view that Exner's synthesis is more valid than earlier and simpler scoring and interpretive systems. Its utility in the hands of talented assessors with a thorough knowledge of personality dynamics is unquestioned; in the hands of less sophisticated clinicians, however, the instrument is less valid.

The Thematic Apperception Test. Despite its unusual structure and rationale, mental health professionals quickly adopted projective techniques for personality assessment. In 1935, the armamentarium of projective methodology was further extended with the creation of the *Thematic Apperception Test* (TAT). Combined with similar projective devices, the Rorschach and TAT tests became the major tools available for personality assessment. Both remain in universal use, but have been criticized because their interpretive procedures are subjective and standards of scientific validation have not proved fully satisfactory.

As described in Chapter 13, *Henry Murray* was born in New York City to wealthy parents, attended Groton and majored in history at Harvard University. Murray received his medical degree from Columbia College of Physicians and Surgeons in 1915, then met Jung in Europe while completing a doctorate in biochemistry, and became interested in psychology. Although an independent thinker, he still followed many Freudian and Jungian ideas about personality development. Based on his psychodynamic beliefs, Murray formulated a needs-press theory, which provided a theoretical grounding to his development of the Thematic Apperception Test (TAT). In 1935, around the time when Klopfer began organizing his Rorschach seminars, Murray, along with his colleague Christiana Morgan, set out to construct the TAT. It consisted of 31 cards, with 30 depicting scenes and people and one blank card. The clinician usually chose 20 or fewer cards to present to the patient, selecting cards based on the patient's age, sex, and the clinical questions that needed to be answered. They asked patients to make up a story that described the events seen in the card, what led up to it, how the story ended, and characters' feelings and thoughts. The general theory that undergirded the test was that the ambiguous card stimuli would elicit unconscious fantasies from the patient. The 30 cards were chosen based on their ability to accurately evoke a variety of facets of a person's character.

Educated initially in Europe, **Leopold Bellak (1916–2000),** discussed briefly in Chapter 3, studied with Henry Murray for a master's degree at Harvard before completing his medical degree in New York. Bellak had lived in his early years under fascism, but acted later as though he had experienced every painful political movement of the time. He appeared erudite and cultured, slightly jaded and skeptical, exhibiting a sophisticated air of cosmopolitanism that was not anchored to his European roots. Out of strength or suspicion, he carried with him the beliefs of an all-knowing, urbane but rather isolated professional: Independent, intransigent, but invariably an outsider among both his psychology and psychiatry peers. He was a deeply sensitive, yet bluff and strong-willed man with much macho and classic charm. Tough, quick, and with an uncanny sense of people's problems, he created the most comprehensive and articulate system for interpreting the TAT technique. A major contributor to projective literature, as well as developer of the Children's Apperception Test (CAT; Bellak & Bellak, 1949), Bellak differed with Murray on how to interpret TAT responses, despite their earlier collaboration. Whereas Murray believed that some responses were not meaningful in many test protocols, Bellak argued that every response had value. If the interpreter was skilled, he believed that the entire protocol was "wheat," rather than "chaff."

Other Projectives.   As discussed in Chapter 9, *Julian Rotter* obtained his PhD in psychology from Indiana University in 1941, and spent his academic career first at Ohio State University and since the early 1960s at the University of Connecticut. Rotter's most important contribution to psychology came in the form of his social learning theory (1954), which influenced a wide range of disciples who incorporated his ideas into socially oriented cognitive conceptions of how learning takes place. Thus, he believed that people develop expectancies that specific behaviors will produce certain outcomes that may lead people to perceive expected outcomes, even if they do not occur. Rotter also used and systematized an earlier concept of sentence completion. The examiner instructed the test taker, prompted with the first few words of a sentence, to provide an ending for the sentence. These prompts could be in the first person (When I was a child . . .) or in the third person (People are . . .). Rotter presumed that the responses would provide information about the test taker's feelings and behaviors. Rotter's *Incomplete Sentence Blank* (ISB; Rotter & Willerman, 1947) contains 40 sentence stems that are suggestive, but vague and nonspecific in their possibilities. The ISB can be interpreted using the content of the response or a rationally derived scoring system that serves as an index of adjustment-maladjustment. ISB responses are usually scored on a seven-point rating scale based on a maladjustment level. Ratings based on these have a surprisingly high level of both reliability and validity. Despite the existence of Rotter's formal scoring system, many clinicians interpret the ISB primarily on content, using their own idiosyncratic methods.

The use of drawings is another projective method that gained popularity in the 1920s when *Florence Goodenough* developed a clinically standardized procedure for evaluating children's drawing of a man to determine their intelligence level. Several different techniques became widely used. Typically, the patient (adult or child) is given a pencil and a blank piece of paper and then provided with a set of directions to follow. One major technique is *Karen Machover's* Draw-a-Person (DAP) procedure (1949), in which the respondent draws a picture of a person of either sex, and then on another sheet of paper draws a person of the opposite gender. Machover's rules for interpreting these drawings are largely based on the clinician's experience aided by deductions suggested in line with psychoanalytic theory. Among the features judged important to Machover are the head shape and size, facial expression, conflict indicators such as shading or erasing, and clothing. Some clinicians have subjects draw significant people in their lives. Others have developed elaborate coding schemas for interpreting everything from excessive erasing, to placement of the figure on the page, drawing very short arms, and drawing the back of a head. Another well-known drawing technique is *John N. Buck*'s House-Tree-Person (HTP; Buck, 1948) test in which the respondent draws a picture of each of these objects on separate pages. Similarly, clinicians have developed elaborate coding schemas for trees and houses, taking into account the use of perspective, the size and placement of windows and door, the type of tree drawn, and the parts of the tree drawn. Despite its modest validity and reliability findings, projective drawing techniques have remained popular with clinicians, especially those who work with children.

Devising Self-Report Inventories

One gauge of scientific respectability is the degree of objectivity with which an instrument can be administered and interpreted. Thus, to many psychologists, the subjectively obscure procedures followed in the interpretation of projective tests seemed like scientific irreverence. A problem arose, however, given that objective self-report methods appeared limited, perhaps incapable of uncovering the complex of clinical features that projective techniques ostensibly could uncover.

Nevertheless, the self-report modality of assessment has become the most frequently employed technique for diagnosing and assessing the characteristics of personality. In general, these inventions are of several types. One variant includes instruments designed specifically to identify personality traits or disorders, that is, they focus attention on many of the traits or factors or pathologies commonly diagnosed today. Another group of instruments reflect or identify underlying theoretical principles or personality concepts that represent factors, dimensions, or polarities that a theorist considers as a substrate for deriving personality traits or disorders; they are conceptual scales based on statistical analyses or theory.

As noted in Chapter 13, people have sought to understand the characteristics of other persons since early antiquity, as well as attempt to devise ways to characterize them. Also, a number of early approaches to personality assessment exist, some of which have persisted until today, despite their questionable metaphysical assumptions (e.g., astrology). Despite their fallacious origins, these methods fascinate large segments of the populace in that they articulate a rationale for judging one's fellow citizens. Men and women have always been curious about "character," conjecturing in rather implausible ways the central features that they ascribe to their peers.

It is highly probable that the first systematic approach to assessment was based on astrological charts, especially those associated with one's birth date, that is, the individual's horoscope. More tangible were techniques based on observable features as depicted in facial characteristics and expressions, what is referred to as physiognomy (discussed earlier in this chapter), the art of assessing people on the basis of their physical features, primarily the face. In Greek times, Pythagoras and Aristotle and, ultimately, Porta and de La Chambre in the seventeenth century gave credence to early physiognomic methods.

As noted in Chapter 2, an early physician of Spanish origin, Juan Huarte, published the first formal book on assessment titled *Examen de Ingenios Para Las Ciencas* (1575/1594), which was later translated into English: *Discovering the Difference of Wits Among Men*. Basing his proposals on the ideas of his Spanish predecessor, Juan Luis Vives (discussed in Chapter 3), Huarte asserted that individuals differed greatly from one another in their talents, especially in terms of personality tendencies and intellectual abilities; this differentiation should guide individuals to pursue appropriate educational and vocational opportunities. Especially important to Huarte was the cognitive structure of the mind, which he divided into three qualities: understanding, memory, and imagination, which was displayed pictorially in what he termed a "psychogram." Importantly, he avoided astrology and divination's metaphysical assumptions, focusing instead on character features based on observation and behavior, such as whether an individual was inclined to be ambitious, punctilious, haughty, elated, and so on.

Thomas Wright's seventeenth-century book, *The Passions of the Minde in Generall* (1604/1971), was as sophisticated a framework as could have been conceived in its day. Notable were efforts to include how passions could be discovered, including what one would describe today as a person's primary emotions and motivations. Recognizing the impossibility of delving directly into a man's heart to determine his passions, Wright stated that one can understand passions by their "effects and external operations," especially by observing speech and action. He spelled out behavioral variations observed in gestures, voice qualities, even walking, noting such patterns of speaking as "taciturn," "rashness," "affectation," and "scoffing." De La Chambre in France and Christian Thomasius in Germany, discussed earlier in this chapter, adopted aspects of Wright's ideas. Similarly, the phrenologists Franz Gall and Johann Spurzheim whose ideas were also presented earlier in the chapter. George Heymans and his younger colleagues in the Netherlands systematically formulated efforts to catalogue and appraise emotional and personality characteristics in the early twentieth century.

Robert Woodworth (1869–1962) constructed the first formal personality instrument designed in a self-report fashion in the United States during the World War I. He devised the *Personal Data Sheet* as an economical replacement for standardized interviews to identify poor military prospects. It followed the format of an interview by asking respondents to answer simple questions about themselves. This format became a model for dozens of subsequently devised questionnaire inventories; however, with a few notable exceptions these self-report instruments failed to survive the scrutiny of scientific analyses or practical use.

Following Woodworth's early work, a number of psychologists in the mid-1930s assisted psychiatrists who sought to use self-report instruments both to differentiate and diagnose psychiatric patients. Most significant in this regard were the efforts of **Kathryn Humm (1898–1982)** and **Helen Wadsworth (1912–1996)** in their innovative empirical strategy for constructing their Humm-Wadsworth Temperament Scale (1935), a tool to identify and differentiate seven categories relevant to mental illness, namely: normal, hysteroid, manic, depressive, autistic, paranoid, and epileptoid. Their decision to select items on the basis of their actual or empirical ability to differentiate criterion groups of psychiatric patients from so-called normal subjects made their technique notable. This same strategy led *Starke Hathaway*, a psychologist, and *J. Charnley McKinley*, a psychiatrist, to develop the most popular current self-report inventory: the Minnesota Multiphasic Personality Inventory (MMPI; Hathaway & McKinley, 1943). The MMPI's popularity and success led other inventory developers trained in Minnesota's psychology department to construct the Minnesota Counseling Inventory, the California Psychological Inventory, and the Omnibus Personality Inventory, each of which borrowed numerous items from the original MMPI item pool.

Raymond Bernard Cattell, discussed in Chapter 13, devised methods of test construction that were innovative variations of the basic factor analytic approach. In his early work, he began with a list of traits that Gordon Allport and Henry Odbert had generated from adjectives compiled from an unabridged dictionary. Of all possible terms, they reduced the list to 4,504 "real traits." Based on semantic meanings, Cattell narrowed this list to 171 terms that he felt represented synonym groups. He then asked college students to rate people they knew on these terms. After calculating intercorrelations for the items, a cluster analysis revealed 36 surface traits. According to Cattell, surface traits are observable attributes that are evident in the ordinary language that individuals use to describe people's personalities. Cattell added a few extra traits that he thought were important and administered these peer-ratings again to college students as well as to military and clinical populations. Cattell further determined that fifteen distinct factors plus one factor for intelligence accounted for the variance in the ratings. To represent these surface traits as well as some other areas that Cattell thought might be profitable based on prior factorial studies, he constructed 1,800 items. Several factor analytic studies later Cattell determined that at least 16 source traits existed, 4 of which had not appeared on the previous peer-rating. To compose the scales of his 16 Personality Factor (16PF; Cattell, 1949; Cattell, Eber, & Tatsuoka,

1970) instrument, Cattell chose the items that had the highest correlation with the source trait that they were supposed to measure. In 1949, Cattell published the first edition of the 16PF. Unlike the MMPI, the 16PF had no item overlap, meaning an item could only be represented on one scale.

The devisors of the Minnesota Multiphasic Personality Inventory (MMPI) adopted the test construction model Humm and Wadsworth originated in their Temperament Scale, a well-grounded empirically anchored method for building an "objective test." They believed that whatever merit an assessment inventory possessed lay in its external validity or the accuracy of its predictions and correlates, rather than in its theoretic logic or statistical methodology. If this gauge was to be applied, the value of any instrument must be determined by the degree to which it predicted or correlated with *real* and meaningful behavior. Accordingly, the responses that individuals made about themselves on the Humm-Wadsworth test or the MMPI were not to be taken at their face value, but appraised by their correlation with external criteria. Thus, only those test items that showed a significant empirical relationship with clearly defined clinical syndromes were to be included in constructing the MMPI. The rationale underlying the test established high standards of objectivity, and also showed that simplicity in structure need not be inimical to clinical utility. As such, a firm scientific basis for psychodiagnostic assessment was established.

The prime developer of the MMPI, **Starke Rosencrans Hathaway (1903–1980),** grew up in Ohio shortly after the turn of the century. He obtained his early degrees in Ohio but moved to the University of Minnesota to complete his doctorate in 1930 after which he began a long and distinguished career as the head of psychology at the university's medical school. He joined J. Charnley McKinley, chair of the psychiatry department in the mid-1930s, in culling over 1,000 items from a variety of sources to develop a new test for psychiatric diagnoses. Hathaway was an American stereotype of the inarticulate genius: a nonintellectual craftsman, shrewd, uncannily observant and sharp, particularly about fellow psychologists and psychiatrists. Like many people endowed with special abilities, he could spot instantly a phony idea or person.

Reviewing earlier tests and texts of abnormal psychology, as well as folk customs, superstitions, political and religious attitudes, and family relationships, Hathaway and McKinley rewrote all selected items into a common vernacular to give them a measure of stylistic uniformity, ultimately coming up with more than 500 items. They administered this item pool to both a normal group and a series of criterion groups. The normal group was composed of visiting friends and relatives of patients at the University of Minnesota Hospital, some students who were about to enter the University of Minnesota, medical patients from the University of Minnesota Hospital, and governmental Work Projects Administration workers. This sample was representative of Minnesota's population in the 1930s in terms of age, sex, and marital status. The criterion groups were composed of psychiatric patients who had one of the following diagnoses: hypochondriasis, depression, hysteria, psychopathic deviate, paranoia, psychasthenia, schizophrenia, and hypomania. Later, a group of normal college women and a group of "homosexual invert men" were added. They developed item sets based on the differences between the responses of the normal group and the criterion groups. They retained in the final scales items that had significantly different true-false endorsement frequencies. Many scales went through several stages of refinement to reach the final one. The University of Minnesota Press published the test in 1943.

By the late 1980s, a committee formed to restandardize the instrument and modernize it. The challenge of revamping the test was limited by the desire to keep the vast repository of data and research about the original test applicable. The resulting effort led to the MMPI-2 (Butcher, Dahlstrom, Graham, Tellegen, & Kaemmer, 1989) as well as an adolescent form, the MMPI-A (Butcher et al., 1992). Remarkably, the first 370 items are virtually identical to the original form of the test, with some minor editorial changes. They used a sample more representative of the U.S. population in the 1980s to re-norm the MMPI-2.

Hathaway collaborated with his former student, **Paul Everett Meehl (1920–2003),** upon McKinley's death. A brilliant scholar of psychiatry, philosophy, and law, Meehl (a name of Hebrew origin, *me'il*, representing a mantle worn by High Priests) traced his eighteenth-century family roots to rabbinical scholars from the Baltic region. Together with Hathaway, Meehl, a

Paul Everett Meehl

man of great intellectual strength and gravity, sought to enrich and elaborate many original MMPI ideas, most especially its validity indicators. Working as a team, they developed several sensitive measures that strengthened the likelihood of valid MMPI protocols with scales for detecting and correcting for various response biases. In 1954, Meehl published a controversial review of assessment research, entitled *Clinical versus Statistical Prediction*, a book that asserted that statistical formulas, such as regression equations and cutoffs, were better predictors of diagnosis and outcomes than were a clinician's judgments. Outcome gauges ranged from success in college, to criminal recidivism, and which patients would benefit from psychotherapy. Not surprisingly, the book sparked a debate that played out in numerous journals over several years. Most empirical studies to this day yield results largely in support of Meehl's earlier findings. These arguments lent a great deal of support and credibility to empirically and actuarially based measures such as the MMPI, as well as other empirically validated tests (e.g., MCMI).

As with his mentor Hathaway, Meehl was an undergraduate and doctoral product of Minnesota's "dust-bowl" empiricism, and exhibited a deep commitment to a tough-minded scientific approach to clinical problems, a view enhanced by his strong background in the philosophy of science. From the very beginning of his graduate training Meehl exhibited unusual talents, evincing remarkable control of tone and subject; he had a sure touch and an easy grasp of complexities. At times he appeared self-protective, distant from those he did not know well, as though he were not sure of their regard for him and was set to ward off any unfavorable opinions. Except for occasional episodes of restraint and moodiness he was extremely sweet and gentle; when he felt at home with lifelong friends or with close colleagues in Minnesota, he was extraordinarily warm, charming, and generous. Even his occasional peculiarities and reservations added to the aura of his person. At no time did his seeming self-absorption take a cranky or ugly form. His many papers on philosophy and law, no less those on psychology, were marvelously intricate and sensitive to the complexities of these subjects, evidencing an intriguing combination of powerful thinking and philosophical sensitivity.

Meehl made diverse contributions to subjects other than the MMPI and actuarial validation. Although Meehl's biologically oriented social learning model is limited to schizophrenia, it is notable both for its elegance and specificity. He hypothesized that only a certain class of people, those with a particular genetic constitution, have any liability to schizophrenia. Meehl suggested that the varied emotional and perceptual-cognitive dysfunctions people with schizophrenia display are difficult to explain in terms of single region disorders. The widespread nature of these dysfunctions suggested the operation of a more diffuse integrative neural defect. Although a combination of different neurologic disturbances can account for this defect, Meehl opted for an explanation in terms of deficits in synaptic control. More specifically, he believed that the major problem in schizophrenia lay in a malfunctioning of the two-way mutual control system between perceptual-cognitive regions and the limbic motivation center. Meehl's proposal was that integrative neural defects are the only direct phenotypic consequences produced by the genetic disorders; given the label *schizotaxia*, it is all that can properly be spoken of as inherited. The imposition of certain social learning histories on schizotaxic individuals results in a personality organization that Meehl called the *schizotype*. Four core behavior traits, namely anhedonia, cognitive slippage, interpersonal aversiveness, and ambivalence, are not innate. However, Meehl postulated that schizotaxic individuals universally learned them, given any existing social learning regimen, from the best to the worst. If the social environment is favorable and the schizotaxic person has the good fortune of inheriting a low anxiety readiness, possesses physical vigor, and a general resistance to stress, that person will remain a well-compensated schizotype and may never manifest symptoms of clinical schizophrenia.

Theodore Millon's developed his personality inventories as operational measures of his biosocial and evolutionary theories, discussed in Chapter 13. In early 1971, Millon was directing a research supervision group composed of psychologists- and psychiatrists-in-training during their internship and residency periods at the Universities of Illinois and Chicago. All had read his *Modern Psychopathology* text (1969) and found the proposal of working together to develop instruments to identify and quantify the text's personality disorder constructs to be worthy and challenging. Concurrently, Millon became involved in the development of the *DSM-III*, helping to formulate the constructs and criteria that were to characterize its Axis II personality disorders. Progressing through several versions over a seven-year period, the end product of his self-report inventory's developmental period in 1977 was called the *Millon Clinical Multiaxial Inventory* (MCMI). The MCMI was an *objective psychodynamic* instrument in that it was composed and administered in a structured and standardized manner, but interpreted by examining the interaction of scale scores and by drawing upon clinically established relationships among cognitive processes, interpersonal behaviors, and psychodynamic forces. In this regard, it was akin to the MMPI in its item format and administrative procedures, but more like the Rorschach and TAT in its interpretive style and content.

The division between personality disorder and clinical syndrome of the MCMI scales was intended to make its diagnoses and interpretations congruent with the *DSM*'s multiaxial logic (Chapter 5). Extending his focus on personologic attributes, Millon and his associates also developed the *MACI*, an adolescent inventory for troubled and troubling teenagers (Millon, Millon, & Davis, 1993), the *MBMD*, an instrument to appraise psychological influences on the course of medical illnesses (Millon, Antoni, Millon, Meagher, & Grossman, 2001), and the *MIPS-Revised*, which was designed for use with nonclinical individuals (i.e., normal personalities; Millon, Weiss, & Millon, 2003).

Melding and Integrating Diverse Therapies

"Domain" or "modality oriented" approaches have dominated psychotherapy historically. That is, therapists identified themselves with a single-realm focus or a theoretical school (behavioral, psychoanalytic) and attempted to practice within whatever prescriptions for therapy it made. Rapid changes in the therapeutic milieu, stemming from economic pressures, conceptual shifts, and diagnostic innovations took place in the later decades of the twentieth century. For better or worse, these changes showed little sign of decelerating, and became a context to which therapists, far from reversing, were forced to adapt. Most notable here was the emergence of brief forms of treatment (Chapter 5), and an increasing awareness of cultural diversity (Chapter 11). Eclecticism and integrationism were also reactions to this situation.

Eclecticism had the virtue of humility, and integrationism had the virtues of persistence and optimism. Dogmatism, that is, adherence to established schools of therapy, appeared to derive from a fear of growth, in that growth implied the insufficiency or inadequacy of what currently existed. Epistemologically, dogmatism was found in its most obtuse form in debates concerning which treatment orientation (cognitive, behavioral, biologic, psychoanalytic) was closer to the truth, or which therapeutic method was the most intrinsically efficacious. What differentiated these narrow-focused orientations and treatment methods had little to do with their theoretical underpinnings or their empirical support. As commented in earlier chapters, their differences were akin to physicists, chemists, and biologists who argued over which of their fields was a more true representation of nature. Schisms such as these in therapy had been constructed less by philosophical considerations or pragmatic goals than by the accidents of history and professional rivalries.

Prior chapters have addressed the various narrow-band theoretical orientations (e.g., somatic therapy in Chapter 6, interpersonal therapy in Chapter 12, cognitive therapy in Chapter 10). To restate this view, the book sharpens these contrasting positions. In the narrow-band treatment models, the way to practice psychotherapy is to approach all patients as possessing essentially the same key elements to their disorder, and then to utilize one appropriately focused modality of therapy for their treatment. Many contemporary therapists still employ these models. Everything learned in the last two or three decades of the twentieth century told us that this single-focus approach was only minimally effective. Open-minded therapists came to recognize that patients differed substantially in the clinical syndromes and personality disorders they presented. Therefore, not all treatment modalities are equally effective for all patients, be it pharmacologic, or cognitive, or psychoanalytic, and so on.

The inclination of proponents of one or another modality of therapy to remain separate was only in part an expression of treatment rivalries. During the early phases of their development, innovators, quite appropriately, sought to establish a measure of effectiveness without having their investigations confounded by the intrusion of other modalities. No less important was that each treatment domain represented a single dimension in the complex of elements that patients brought to therapists. As clinicians moved away from a simple medical model to one that recognized the psychological complexity of patients' symptoms and causes, it appeared increasingly wise to mirror the patients' complexities by developing therapies that were comparably complex.

Thomas French presented the first formal recommendation of an integrative therapeutic model to mirror patients' complexities in 1933; he suggested that concepts of Freudian psychoanalysis and Pavlovian conditioning, though discrepant overtly, had many fundamental similarities. Adolf Meyer (see Chapter 5) had suggested even earlier that the potential for convergences were worthwhile pursuing; however, he believed that theoreticians should continue their separate lines of development and not attempt to bridge them prematurely.

Lawrence Kubie suggested another early integrative proposal in 1943. He recognized that several psychoanalytic techniques might readily be explained in terms of Pavlov's conditioned reflexology.

In 1936, **Saul Rosenzweig (1907–)** proposed that most effective therapies shared common factors; whereas French and Kubie attempted to bring together two separate theoretical orientations, Rosenzweig averred that treatment similarities had more to do with certain common elements of practice than with their theoretical systems. Rosenzweig suggested three common factors among effective psychotherapies: (1) therapists' personalities had most to do with treatment effectiveness rather than their preferred and habitual treatment modality; (2) interpretations provided patients with alternative modes of thought and action, as well as making their problems more understandable to them; and (3) different theoretical orientations focused on different domains, but all may be effective because of the synergistic effect any one area of functioning might have on the others.

Frederick Charles Thorne (1909–1994) received his doctorate in 1934 from Columbia University, followed shortly thereafter by a medical degree from Cornell Medical School. Seeking to synthesize both aspects of his formal education, he became one of the first of the integrative thinkers of psychotherapy. Although trained by many of the distinguished psychologists and psychiatrists of his day—Adolf Meyer, Alfred Adler, Carl Rogers—Thorne did not intend his ideas to be a compilation of established theories about therapy, but an original synthesis of his own. As he described it, he was "determined to make a fresh start right from the beginning, accepting nothing on authority alone, and to formulate an eclectic system integrating all pertinent scientific information available at this time and place" (Thorne & Pishkin, 1968, p. v).

Thorne's model regarded all forms of mental illness essentially as disorders of integration. The therapist's task was to strengthen and improve not only the re-integration of personality, but to foster increasing levels of self-actualization. In what he termed the *principle of unification,* Thorne encouraged the resolution of factors that disrupt the positive features of integration within each patient. This involved methods that optimized patients' control and organization of their lives, especially by managing the disordering effects of any affective-impulsive characteristics. No less important is that patients were to be led initially to experience a degree of "positive disintegration" so that they can then reorganize and re-integrate their previously poorly oriented psychic state. In many ways, Thorne's thesis regarding the role of re-integration anticipated ideas that became increasingly relevant to what was subsequently called the borderline personality.

The major contributor to an empirically based eclectic integration is **Arnold Lazarus (1932–)** in his "multimodal therapy." Initially trained as a behavioral therapist with Joseph Wolpe during his doctoral program in South Africa, Lazarus came to believe that clinicians should employ technique modalities from different therapy systems, without necessarily accepting the theoretical rationale with which they were usually associated. Arguing for the importance of a full psychological assessment as a prelude to intervention, Lazarus developed a seven-fold schema for evaluating each patient's difficulties. Terming this scheme the BASIC IB, it included behavior, affect, sensation, imagery, cognition, interpersonal relationships, and biology (originally listed as drugs). As with other eclectic thinkers of his time, Lazarus emphasized the matching of treatment techniques to the patient's problems. Most importantly, he asserted that clinicians should select treatments on the basis of empirical evidence for their effectiveness.

Outgoing, sociable, talkative, Lazarus stood apart from others in the behavioral tradition. He was articulate, almost to the point of eloquence, a cosmopolitan intellectual, well trained in philosophical issues, and interested in educating therapists throughout the world. His books and essays reflect his very special air of sophistication and virtuosity, full of improvisation, innovative ideas, and multiple perspectives.

Empirical or "technical" eclecticism, as Lazarus termed his approach, held that therapeutic procedures may be divorced from their generative theories without the need for either endorsing the theory or subjecting it to validation. Only the efficacy of specific techniques need be justified. Eclecticism struggled to move forward as a therapeutic philosophy in the face of stubborn difficulties, not the least of which were the availability of hundreds of competing approaches. However, by promising an independence of technique and theory, he bypassed the problem of coordinating theories and therapies. As Thorne suggested years earlier, Lazarus claimed that clinicians should avoid following or constructing a mélange of techniques based on subjective preferences. Knowledge, they both asserted, should be based not only on experimental evidence, but also on formal measurement procedures to appraise the success of each technique. Lazarus also believed that by employing experimentally derived concepts and data, clinical science may replace what he called "metaphysical" theories.

Although eschewing the role of theory in psychotherapy, Lazarus acknowledged in his two most central books, *Multimodal Behavior Therapy* (1976) and *The Practice of Multimodal Therapy* (1981), that most clinicians use a rough outline of theory to orient their treatment choices and decisions. Lazarus recognized that his own orientation derived from a mix of social learning theory, communications, and general systems syntheses, although an early preference for behavioral modalities and a later expansion into the cognitive therapies shaped his therapy. His focus on assessment through the BASIC IB model attempts to take the vague and diffuse problems of anxiety, family dysfunctions, vocational unhappiness, and the like and reduce them to specific and discrete problems.

As noted in Chapter 9, a major contribution to the history of theoretical synthesis took place in 1950 with the publication of John Dollard and Neal Miller's book *Personality and Psychotherapy*. Although this book only partially went beyond translating psychoanalytic concepts into behavioral language, it was a heroic effort to synthesize notions about neurosis and psychotherapy and to provide a theory unifying both subject domains. One of Dollard and Miller's doctoral students at Yale University, **Paul Wachtel (1940–   ),** carried his mentors' thinking forward in his book *Psychoanalysis and Behavior Therapy: Toward an Integration* (1977). Hardly naïve about the difficulty of building a theoretical syntheses between the concepts of psychoanalysis and learning theory, Wachtel asserted that integrationists would need to acknowledge the diversity within each approach, as well as the need to be specific about which elements can be integrated. Wachtel identified the virtues of both theoretical schools into a framework that could incorporate these elements in an internally consistent way. He wanted to draw upon the complementary strengths of both perspectives, hoping thereby to outline a new theory for understanding mental illness and a sound treatment strategy to effect their modification.

Wachtel evidenced a strong interest in broad cultural and social issues, writing with articulateness and sensitivity on numerous problems reflecting the cultural conditions of contemporary life. Wachtel looks as though he had been physically designed for this socially concerned and philosophical role. Short, thin, with a large head made all the more substantial by the paleness of his face; he also boasts an enormous, black, and downturned moustache. In passing conversations he sounds as if he was delivering a well-crafted speech, conveying a mix of a scold and an exhortation. We sense that there is a world out there beyond the immediate themes of any conversational topic that he wants his colleagues to turn attention toward, as if they all should address the larger and more significant matters of life.

Wachtel termed the central thesis underlying all aspects of pathologic processes—behavioral, psychoanalytic, family—as *cyclical psychodynamics*. Wachtel sought to expand the realm of his synthesis to include family systems theories in the mid-1980s (Wachtel & Wachtel, 1986). He has stated unequivocally that cyclical psychodynamics is the theoretical basis for his form of integrative therapy, As he wrote (P. Wachtel, 1977):

> In contrast to a technically eclectic approach, which might consist of a hodge-podge of techniques selected probabilistically because they have seemed to work with patients with similar characteristics, cyclical psychodynamics seeks to develop a coherent theoretical structure that can guide both clinical decision making and general principles. . . .
>
> Cyclical psychodynamic attempts to forge a new, more inclusive syntheses—a synthesis that can encompass the full range of observations address by its contributory sources and also provide a context for a wide a range of clinical interventions as can be coherently employed. (pp. 335–336)

Cyclical psychodynamics' was not a new concept, although the descriptive label is distinctively Wachtel's. Horney (1945) wrote of the tendency to foster vicious circles, and Millon (1969) spoke of self-perpetuation processes in the persistence and intensification of early learned behaviors, which set in motion negative feedback for self and from others. These cyclical processes, vicious circle tendencies, and self-perpetuation cognitions and behaviors play a key role in etiology and causal processes. P. Wachtel's original intent was to combine methods derived from different theoretical perspectives. His cyclical model has provided him with a genuine model of synthesis. As he wrote (1977), "In much of the work presently approached from a cyclical psychodynamic viewpoint, it is hard to say which is the psychodynamics part and which is the behavioral. The work, one might say, is becoming more seamless" (p. 347).

What makes the approach of **Marsha Linehan (1943–   )** so significant is the systematic and integrative nature of her analysis and treatment of one specific personality disorder, the so-called Borderline patient. We need not agree with all aspects of her developmental conception of the origins of the Borderline, nor with each specific of her treatment technique, to appreciate the care and thoroughness with which she examined and treated this particular personality. If each personality disorder and clinical syndrome were approached therapeutically in the manner in which Linehan approached the Borderline, treatment for all disorders and syndromes would likely be greatly improved.

Trained at Chicago's Loyola University in the late 1960s, Linehan soon joined the faculty of the University of Washington, where she has remained for most of her career as a professor and director of several major grants on the treatment of parasuicidal and Borderline patients. Linehan believes that the concept of personality requires us to assume that an individual's style of functioning (including patterns of action, cognitive processes, and physiological-emotional responses) is reasonably consistent over time and circumstance. More specifically, Linehan spoke of the crucial developmental circumstances that underlie the Borderline's disorder. She wrote (1993):

> The main tenet of the biosocial theory is that the core disorder in BPD is emotion dysregulation. . . . The theory asserts that Borderline individuals have difficulties in regulating several, if not all, emotions. This systemic dysregulation is produced by emotional vulnerability and by maladaptive or inadequate modulation strategies. (p. 2)

Linehan defined emotional vulnerability by referring to several characteristics; first, a very high sensitivity to emotional stimuli, second, a very intense response to stimulating emotions, and third, a slow return to an emotional baseline, once emotional arousal had occurred. In her theoretical schema, the primary source of emotional dysregulation is what she termed an *invalidating environment*. Such environments are especially destructive for young children who begin life with a high vulnerability to emotional stimuli. As she conceived it, the defining characteristic of these invalidating environments was the tendency to respond erratically and inappropriately to one's own personal experience (e.g., thoughts, feeling, sensations).

A tall, robust, and handsome woman, Linehan appears in motion all the time. Unusually intelligent, energetically driving, completely without malice or cunning, she has made innumerable and valuable proposals in her acquired role as a therapeutic thinker of innovative treatment. She has gained a considerable and justifiable repute in the latter phases of her career, a repute that has come to a scholar whose main internal dialogue is an outgrowth of her own extensive experience. Her craft of therapy was exceptionally well received in mental hospitals throughout the world in the 1990s. Nevertheless, she has skillfully withdrawn from many of the intense areas of intellectual competitiveness that characterize much of conventional psychology. As with other wise persons, she has shown a distaste for the malicious infighting that often typifies alternate schools of therapy today, remaining distinguished by her warmth, directness, and lack of pretension, as well as a complete mastery of her subject.

Marsha Linehan

Linehan's therapeutic methodology is imaginative and comprehensive. In terms of goals, the first task of therapy is to orient patients and gain their commitment to the treatment course, She uses several pretreatment sessions for diagnostic interviewing, formal history taking, and an analysis of targeted behaviors to serve as a focus for initial sessions. The first regular treatment stage is oriented toward having patients attain functional and stable lifestyle behaviors and capacities. Specific targets include the reduction of therapy-interfering behaviors, diminished quality-of-life-interfering behaviors, and increased behavioral skills. During the second stage, Linehan takes a here-and-now approach. Her theoretical model asserts that previous traumatic events, especially those invalidating environments that generated emotional dysregulation must be explored and resolved. The third stage targets patients' self respect; it is oriented to helping patients value, believe in, and validate themselves.

Especially important is what Linehan called the *validation strategy*. Three steps are involved in the acceptance of a person's own life beliefs: (1) Patients are helped to identify relevant response patterns; (2) the therapist expresses accurate empathy, showing a clear recognition of patients' perception of their experiences; and (3) the therapist communicates that these perceptions make perfect sense in the context of individuals' current situation and early life experiences.

The therapeutic facet of Millon's theoretical model of mental science (Chapter 13), termed *personality-guided synergistic therapy,* has been most fully developed in his 1999 text. Whether clinicians work with "part functions" that focus on behaviors, or cognitions, or unconscious processes, or biological defects, and the like, or whether they address contextual systems that focus on the larger environment, the family, or the group, or the socioeconomic and political conditions of life, the crossover point, that is the place that links parts to contexts, is the person. The individual's personality becomes the intersecting medium that brings all therapeutic techniques together.

The cohesion (or lack thereof) of intrinsically interwoven psychic structures and functions is what distinguishes most complex disorders of mental illness; likewise, the orchestration of diverse, yet synthesized modalities of intervention is what differentiates synergistic from other variants of integrative psychotherapy. These two parallel constructs, emerging from different traditions and conceived in different venues, reflect shared philosophical perspectives, one oriented toward the understanding of mental disorders, the other toward effecting its treatment.

Millon first recommended a synergistic procedure he called "potentiated pairings"; here, diverse treatment methods (e.g., cognitive, pharmacologic, analytic) were to be combined simultaneously to overcome problematic characteristics that might be refractory to each technique, if they were administered separately. These composites pull and push for change on many different fronts, so that the therapy becomes as multioperational and as tenacious as the disorder itself. A popular illustration of these treatment pairings is found in what is referred to as *cognitive-behavior therapy.*

Millon proposed the term "catalytic sequences" (1988) to represent procedures whose intent is to plan the order in which diverse, but coordinated treatments are executed. They comprised therapeutic arrangements and timing series that optimized the impact of changes that would be less effective if the sequential combination of these treatment techniques were otherwise arranged. In a catalytic sequence, for example, one might seek first to alter a patient's stuttering by direct behavior modification procedures, which, if achieved, would facilitate the use of cognitive methods in producing self-image changes in confidence that, in turn, may foster the utility of interpersonal techniques in effecting improvements in social relationships.

Millon recognized that no discrete boundaries existed between potentiating pairings and catalytic sequences, just as no line existed between their respective pathological analogues (i.e., adaptive inflexibilities and vicious circles). Nor should therapists be concerned about when to use one rather than another of these synergistic methods. Instead, they should be regarded as interdependent phenomena whose application was intended to foster increased flexibility and, hopefully, beneficent rather than vicious circles. Potentiated pairings and catalytic sequences represented a first-order of therapeutic synergism. The idea of a "potentiated sequence" or a "catalytic pairing" recognized that these synergistic composites may build on each other in proportion to what the tenacity of the patient's mental disorder required.

Comments and Reflections

Present knowledge about combinational assessments and integrative therapeutics has only begun to be developed in a fully systematic fashion. Much of what is contained in this chapter is clinically and theoretically driven rather than empirically validated. Many assessors and psychotherapists have shown resistance to the idea of utilizing assessment combinations and treatment modalities other than those they were trained to employ. Most mental health professionals worked long and hard to become experts in a particular assessment tool or treatment technique. Though committed to what they know and do best, they may limit their approach to methods consistent with their training. Unfortunately, most clinicians are expert in only a few of the diverse approaches to assessment and treatment and may not be open to exploring new interactive combinations that may be more suitable for the complex configuration of symptoms that many patients bring to treatment.

The inclination of proponents of one or another diagnostic tool or modality of therapy to keep to themselves is only in part an expression of professional school rivalries. During early test and treatment development, clinical innovators likely sought to establish the effectiveness of their methods without confounding them by the intrusion of other methods. Most diagnostic tools or treatment procedures focused on a single facet of the complex of features that patients bring to a clinician. Now that professionals have begun to move away from a simple disease model toward one that recognizes the complexity of patients' psychological characteristics, it has become professionally wise to mirror the patients' complexities by tools and techniques that are comparably complex. The single domain focus of the past need not be replaced, but should be combined together with others that simultaneously address facets of a patient's problems.

Certain combinational approaches have an additive effect; others possess a synergistic effect. The term *additive* describes a situation in which the combined benefits of two or more therapeutic methods are at least equal to the sum of their individual benefits. The term *synergistic* describes a situation in which the combined benefits of several treatment modalities exceed the sum of their individual components (i.e., their effects are potentiated). This chapter suggests that the several modalities covered in the book—pharmacotherapy, cognitive therapy, family therapy, psychoanalytic therapy—may be combined and integrated to achieve at least an additive, if not synergistic effect.

Some problems are evident as we reflect on integrative/ combinational treatment models. For example, if two different therapeutic approaches are employed, it is not possible without extensive research to know whether and which of the treatment methods is working. If improvement occurs, is the primary reason the effectiveness of treatment A, treatment B, treatment C, perhaps some combination, or was it by spontaneous remission? Part of the evaluation effort may be clarified by catalytic sequences. Here, different modalities may be sequentially ordered so that clinicians may determine what works and what does not.

"Modality-domains," some primarily from academic psychology and others from clinical practice, gave rise to totalistic and exclusionary sophisticated philosophies of human nature, as psychoanalysis had been. Behaviorism emerged and dominated for a time, only to eventually give way to cognitive psychology, which today may itself be considered a subdiscipline of cognitive science. Other perspectives oriented both to harder (e.g., the neurobiologic) and softer (e.g., interpersonal) levels of substantive thinking have also emerged and flourished. Each of these spawned its own schools of intervention and theoretically derived techniques (in the neurobiologic perspectives these techniques take the form of medications). For the most part, each also became submerged in the specificities of its own program and developed largely in isolation, transfixed by its own internal consistency and, so, was either not attentive to or dismissive of the advances of alternative perspectives in the same field.

A major problem with both eclecticism and the common factors approaches is that they are insufficiently theoretical. The fact that some psychotherapists are apparently loaded with good judgment and are so good at what they do begs the questions "How do they do it?" and "Why does it work?," questions that bring the insufficiency of eclectic and common factors approaches to the foreground. As noted earlier, no theory-neutral observations exist; in this sense, both eclecticism and common factors approaches suffer the problems of any inductive methodology. Once regularities or patterns have been observed again and again, their existence is clear, but not *why* they exist, what creates them, or how they work.

Any independence of theory and technique entails a clinical science that is specifically unintegrated. What would clinical science look like if the two were entirely disjointed, that is, if techniques were truly theory-free? Most importantly, no scientific basis would exist on which to choose a particular technique, only an empirical one. Deprived of the guidance of theory, clinical science would then be completely in bondage to methodology. Where empirical evidence did not exist to guide the therapist, there would be no more reason to decide between one technique and any other, for there would be no theory, however implicit, on which to base the decision or narrow the range of options. Those patients experiencing difficulties as yet unresearched would either be assigned to an experimental or control group or simply be dismissed from the office as possessing problems outside the scope of psychotherapy in its then current form.

Therapeutic techniques that have been derived from the propositions of a particular modality will be most efficacious for problems anchored primarily in that modality, for example, the treatment of phobias from a behavioral perspective, or the use of cognitive techniques to reframe a patient's distorted expectancies. However, the odds and ends of diverse schemas and perspectives no more form a theory than do several techniques, randomly chosen. Such a hodgepodge will lead only to illusory syntheses and interventions that cannot long hold together. As some have noted, the addition of relaxation training to psychodynamic therapy does not constitute integration unless relaxation itself has been integrated into psychodynamic theory as a construct and as an aim of therapy. Again, the problem is that different perspectives on human nature come with different sets of assumptions. By virtue of its internal consistency, each set of assumptions carves out its own universe of discourse, the terms and propositions of which are not readily translatable into those of any other. Like theoretical constructs, each technique is embedded in a particular perspective, a preformed body of conceptual relationships. To lift it out of that perspective is to dissociate it from the assumptive world from where it takes its meaning. If applied in another context, the technique must either be translated, or applied meaninglessly, without regard to the antecedent conditions that might justify its use or the consequences that might follow.

Compelling reasons abound why a synthesis of technique and theory might make a contribution to the success of therapy. Most clinicians are capable of grasping abstract principles of the various theoretical orientations. Most clinicians are also intuitively sensitive to what their patients need at the moment. However, especially where the theory is rich, clinicians may be able to integrate several alternative methods so that their interventions will be explicitly guided by and consonant with a unified theoretical model. All interpersonal interactions are highly contextualized, with communications taking place at many different levels. Psychotherapy is even more complex. Truly integrative synthesis, in which therapists have one mind on the patient's behaviors and communications, one mind on the diverse elements of theory, and one mind on how the patient is receiving their ideas, may require a thorough guide to human relations that therapists may not be able to access on their own.

Every change that transpires in one or another psychic sphere (traits, symptoms, thoughts, feelings, or behaviors) will have an effect on every other. The task is to identify how these spheres coordinate, and here an integrative theory can be of great value. A personality-oriented theory seeks to identify the spheres that are saliently problematic in a patient, and to facilitate an understanding of how each troublesome sphere interacts with the others.

To make a platitudinous announcement that the complex spheres comprising the personality of a patient should serve as the focus for integrative treatment or that it is the natural parallel for synergistic modes of therapy, is not enough. So, too, might it be merely sententious to speak of a "personality-guided therapy." In building a comprehensive science of nature and, more specifically, that aspect we call mental illness, we must seek to discover the principles conducive to constructive human change and from which a corresponding effective group of synergistic therapies can be implemented.

Epilogue

In this book, we have considered the many roots of mental science and its growth and development throughout history, all of which have led to the major approaches to the mind in contemporary study and practice today. Primitive people were preoccupied with unknown external spirits and, later, with the internal unknown spirit of the soul. In an early, prescientific age, what few studies existed relied on philosophical methods, notably those of the fifth century B.C. Greeks, who primarily speculated on simplistic notions of naturalistic phenomena. Until the fifteenth century or so, most efforts concentrated on metaphysical phenomena and their tenuous connection to the body. The beginnings of a humanistic sensibility evolved during the sixteenth century when a few pioneers dared to speak favorably and kindly about the welfare of the mentally ill. By the seventeenth century, attention shifted from matters of the soul toward the concept of mind. Numerous philosophical thinkers revived and drew upon early Greek ideas, most significantly Descartes, who equated soul with mind. During the eighteenth and early nineteenth centuries, advances in the physical sciences guided ideas concerning the nature of the mind, initiating efforts to construct a mental science that paralleled physics. The adoption of experimental methods from physiology further strengthened the scientific research into the nature of the mind. By the turn of the early twentieth century, several distinctive and powerful movements came to the foreground concurrently, notably psychoanalysis and behaviorism. The former probed the unseen psyche, looking into the unconscious to explain an individual's actions, thoughts, and feelings. The latter approach, repudiating introspection, sought to make the mind a purely observable natural science, rejecting all forms of what was termed *mentalism*. Although the origins of a sociological perspective preceded World War II, after that period a persuasive movement developed recognizing the impact of culture on the mind.

Throughout these years, the study of the mind grew at an irregular pace and in an unordered fashion. Its progression was full of plateaus and sudden spurts, which some described as a series of theses and antitheses, though never quite leading to a synthesis. Others have spoken of mental science as if it were a pendulum, swinging in one direction and then another, from one extreme to its opposite. Perhaps its progression can best be thought of as analogous to a spiral, the repeated recurrence of old issues, but at increasingly advanced levels of sophistication and complexity. Today efforts are underway to bridge the diverse traditions of mind study using systematic methods of measurement and integration, leading toward a synthesis referred to in this book as *personologic*. Older theories, many of which were once discarded, reappeared in new forms and interpretations. Ideas once repudiated were exonerated and discussed anew. The spiraling metaphor reflects much of what has happened in these cycles.

Despite this progression, the early twenty-first century brings with it much confusion regarding how to balance the many traditions of mental science. Although the twentieth century launched an in-depth understanding of the psyche with Freud's innovative revelations, recent critics have contended that his analytic ideas were not only a sterile interlude in the science's progression, but set it back many decades. They believe the neurochemical brain functions will bear the richest fruits for the science, made more practical by advances in psychopharmacology. On the other hand, clinicians recognize that merely pacifying patients with drugs can hardly be considered the pinnacle of mental science. And similarly, the deinstitutionalization of patients from crumbling asylums only illustrates the disoriented, if not pathetic state of professional efforts. Moreover, treatment of the mentally ill is not necessarily more humane than before. Consider the thousands of poor and downtrodden psychotics who were gassed indiscriminately in the 1930s and 1940s by an ostensibly highly advanced and scientific Germany.

How far have we progressed in our journey to understand and treat the mind? A clear light does not appear to be in sight at the end of the tunnel; perhaps the field will never achieve anything close to a finite knowledge of mental reality. It is also difficult to measure how far the field has progressed in its journey. As with most scientific endeavors, profound and puzzling questions continue to spark research and debate. Future discoveries should prove illuminating and useful.

Skepticism is the beginning of wisdom for any science. An imposing storehouse of facts and ideas are a start, but developing new directions for future inquiries is essential. Despite admonitions that workers settle down to the sober acquisition of facts, we must indulge those inclined to do what Heidbreder (1933) referred to as "riotous thinking." Facts, though suggestive, are not numerous enough to be conclusive. Obscurities and doubts are legion, thus mental scientists must turn toward speculation to generate ideas to rouse the curiosity to deal with a human race that keeps stumbling on its way to an unknown future.

Unfortunately, we cannot see into the future 100 years from now and determine who were the great pioneers of the century, and who will or should be forgotten. For the moment, this history remains messy. In the seven stories of the mental sciences that comprise this book, we attempted to represent as fairly as we can where we came from and where we are now, a hodgepodge of sorts, but one that portrays contemporary realities. Ours has been an unconventional survey and appraisal of the mental sciences in which we placed upfront the once famous, but often forgotten figures of the field. Some detractors of our approach may call what we have done an abdication of a historian's responsibilities. Never mind. There are compensatory rewards for recording what remains unclear and unfinished; it is still a story both broad in scope and inclusionary. Our review, whatever its substantive failings, will be successful if it speaks to our understanding of the present. Drawbacks and limitations aside, ours was an effort to bring you up to the twenty-first century. Some of you bring fresh eyes to the stories as you see traditions turned on their head, so to speak, viewed as they wended their ways slowly to reach modern day perspectives. Some may assert that I have permitted this or that heathen to take over the temple of mental science. Could there be any worse blasphemy than to confront the narrow-minded with legitimate alternatives, even to honor them with their different theologies?

We cannot help recognizing that the status of many of the theories, concepts, and clinical findings described in this book are sad commentaries on the reality of our desire to understand mental illness fully; what is here reflects our naive eagerness to follow one evanescent or insubstantial fad after another. Many of the approaches to our field of study have come and gone, justly or otherwise (as others have remained immutably entrenched despite impressive rebuttals or incompatible evidence), but there are encouraging signs that cumulative knowledge and a refining process may be under way. The apparent viability of recent ideas concerning mental illness is noteworthy when we consider the number of spirited, if misguided, efforts in the past to dismiss its scientific and humanitarian explorations. The achievement of the seven traditions comprising this book is all the more impressive when we recall the number of other subjects that have faded to a status more consonant with their simplistic character or have, under the weight of their scientific inefficacy, succumbed to scholarly disproof, boredom, or irrelevance. The seven areas discussed here have not only weathered mettlesome assaults, but appear to be undergoing a wide-ranging renaissance in both clinical and scientific circles.

Although the ostensible orderliness of each of the different traditions of mental science described here may appear consistent and focused, there is little to convince us that any of them has provided a definitive answer to the nature of the mind and its treatment. Each system of thought has evolved a set of guiding principles and then imposed a degree of coherence on the clinical or empirical facts that support its contentions, presenting them with at least a reasonable degree of plausibility. Among the problems we face today is that, for the most part, many traditions appear more or less at odds with each other. The more rigidly an approach fixes its lines of focus, the more narrowly it must select its supporting facts. Last, and rather sadly, the more coherent and articulate the system is formed the more likely it will become isolated and exclusionary. Confusion and conflict among alternatives will only increase because none finds universal consensus.

Some will contend that this lack of harmony indicates that the entire enterprise of understanding and treating the mind is one of humankind's most useless and wasteful efforts. They are convinced that attempts to construct a mental science is futile, that efforts have not only failed to date, but that they will always fail, that the task is, by its very nature, an impossible one. In essence, the mind is incapable of dealing with itself, with its own inner complexities and distorting lenses and intricacies. Others believe that the human mind is not defective, but that the subject is intrinsically so elusive and complex as to defy scientific understanding. At best, they say, the field can acquire miscellaneous and scattered pieces of evidence, a few fragments of logic and theory, but nowhere will we find and construct the coherent and desired structure of a science.

It would be no less than unwise to recognize that possibilities other than giving up also exist. As we view it, the study of the mind is best approached through its divergent traditions, each of which portrays only one facet of the whole subject. It is the multiplicity of perspectives that has been central to our task, providing us with converging lines of evidence that essentially point to the same key conclusions. Though the seemingly divergent approaches and traditions begin with different orientations and goals, they do focus on a common subject and furnish facts that converge on common themes and knowledge. As systems of thought, they serve as a basis for exploring different facets of the complex story of the mind. Despite initial differences, they are all directed toward the same purposes and a common concern: Understanding the mind. This proves true even of those movements that gained their impetus from earlier traditions against which they revolted. These protests moved from soul to mind, from introspection to behavior, each leading to a broadening of the field. Superceding traditions did not necessarily annihilate earlier achievements. The rise and fall of traditions did not result in chaos, but an overall pattern which, it is hoped, tended toward stability and harmony. As noted, each approach to the mind should not be regarded as a conclusive form of knowledge, but as a way of thinking by which such knowledge will continue to be produced. Each provides a partial scaffold within which the science of the mind is being constructed. They provide not only a guide, but the zeal for the work of building a science, the inspiration that will generate theories and facts. Although some achieve temporary glamour in stimulating research programs and contributors, this momentary allure should not be confused with accomplishment. Each tradition, no matter how mundane its appearance, remains at some level pertinent and useful to the study of the mind. Together, they provide a defined form and a direction of approach that would be vague and aimless without them. As noted, they also provide a zest for the adventure they set out to experience. For science to advance, it needs the joy and hope of achieving its goals, as much as it needs facts and hypotheses. The approaches to the mind in this book should not be regarded as right or wrong, nor complete achievements. Instead they reflect the major stories in the emergence of mental science, different ways and means of arriving at a finished goal, temporary but necessary components in the development of the enterprise, a sometimes muddled adventure attempting to work itself into a complete understanding of its subject.

The study of the mind and mental illness *must* incorporate a diversity of approaches. But this open-mindedness should not be an invitation to random speculations and ill-conceived notions; tolerance of diversity is not license for intellectual sloppiness or scientific incompetence. None of the approaches discussed in this book is yet a complete scientific system for understanding and treating the mind.

What troubles those who seek an ecumenical synthesis among rival approaches to understanding mental illness is not the observation that some biogenic and psychogenic authors believe this constitutional proclivity or that ordeal of early life is crucial to developing a particular mental disorder. Rather, it is when claimants couple empirically unproven or philosophically untenable assumptions with the assertion that they alone possess the sole means by which such origins of the disorders can be revealed. Perhaps it is too harsh to draw parallels, but presumptions such as these are not unlike biblical inerrantists who claim their construals of the Bible to be divine interpretations, or conservative legalists who assert that their unenlightened views correspond to the original intent of the Constitution's framers. So, too, do many self-righteous therapeutic exponents practice blindly what some have judged a hopelessly flawed craft, one in which its practitioners demonstrably can neither agree among themselves, nor discover either the data or methods by which a coherent synthesis may be fashioned among their myriad conjectures.

Signs of rapprochement in recent decades suggest that the lines of cleavage may not have been as sharp as the book's chapter topics make them appear. Distinctions may have been truer in the earliest periods, but not so much so by the latter part of the twentieth century. There are hopeful signs of reaching out and closer communication that point to future reconciliations, such as seen in the newer personologic approach. Owing to the relatively brief memories of contemporary adherents, many in the field today may have little awareness that predecessors were more open to multidisciplinary perspectives than appears to be the case. In their early and preparadigmatic stage, early theorists asked questions and offered answers that were by no means closed-minded; in fact, they were much less rigid and narrow in focus than their later disciples may have become. But one fundamental and persistent difference has always remained: the empiricist-rationalist dichotomy. Debates between Galenic and Cartesian rationalist exponents, on the one hand, and Hippocratic and Lockian empiricists, on the other, have led to repeated disagreements as to how mental illnesses should be approached, studied, characterized, and understood. Thus, today, we may ask whether the field shall follow the policy guiding the construction of the *DSM*, an empiricist-clinical approach, or assume an orientation more consistent with a rationalist-theoretical formulation?

Although integration is an important concept in the therapy of the individual case, it is also important when considering the role of psychotherapy in clinical science. For the treatment of a particular patient to be integrated, it would be helpful if each element of a clinical science were integrated as well.

As noted in previous chapters, integration should comprise more than the coexistence of two or three previously discordant approaches or techniques. Many investigators have begun to combine two or three treatment modalities to see if they improve on the effectiveness of a single approach. But combinations of techniques are in themselves meaningless because they may not be designed to deal with the specific dysfunctions of a specific patient. Combining cognitive and interpersonal modalities, for example, may muddy the water, owing to the variety of traits and symptoms that are within each patient's pathology. This combination can be appropriate and useful if, and only if, the patients treated in this combinational fashion possess dysfunctions or deficiencies in both the cognitive and interpersonal realms. It is not just the notion of modality combinations nor any theoretical synthesis that will work. Combinations will be effective if they are applied to the several dysfunctional domains of a *specific patient*. Thus, a combination of certain medications (e.g., as when treating AIDS) can be quite effective; however, other combinations, for example when two or three incidental drugs are taken off the bathroom shelf, can result in dangerous consequences.

In short, researchers cannot simply piece together the odds and ends of several theoretical schemas, each internally consistent and oriented to different clinical phenomena. Such a hodgepodge will lead only to illusory syntheses that cannot long hold together. Efforts such as these, meritorious as they may be in some regards, represent the work of peacemakers, not innovators and not integrationists. Integrative approaches to treatment should comprise a synthesized and substantive system that coordinates techniques that mirror the problematic configuration of traits (personality) and symptoms (clinical syndromes) of a specific patient. Primary attention should be given to the natural synthesis that exists within the patients themselves.

In a random integrative synthesis, therapists may lose the context and thematic logic that each of the standard modality approaches have built up over its history. In essence, a broad set of intrinsically coherent approaches could be assembled unwisely in a thoughtless effort to interweave their bits and pieces. An integrative model composed of distinct alternative models (behavioral, psychoanalytic) may be pedagogically pluralistic, but they could be a collection of incidental modalities with different conceptual networks and unconnected findings. Such integrative syntheses will not necessarily correspond to that which is inherent in nature, but merely impose a schema for interweaving what is, in fact, essentially disjoined and meaningless. Intrinsic unity cannot be invented but can be discovered in nature by focusing on the intrinsic unity of the person (i.e., the full scope of a patient's psychic being). Integration based on a person's natural order and unity avoids arbitrary efforts to synthesize disparate and disjunctive theoretical schemas. Integration cannot stem from an intellectual synthesis of different approaches but from recognizing the inherent integration that unfolds and is discovered in each patient's style of psychic functioning.

As noted in Chapter 14, integration is an important concept in considering not only the psychotherapy of the individual case but also the place of psychotherapy in mental science. For the treatment of a particular patient to be integrated, the elements of that science—theory, classification, assessment, and therapy—should be integrated as well. Murray (1983) has suggested that the field must develop new, higher order theories to help better understand the interconnections between cognitive, affective, self, and interpersonal psychic systems. Personologically oriented theorists contend that the naturally interlinked configuration of clinical elements of mental pathology can serve as a foundation and guide for contemporary psychotherapy.

What of alternative methods for generating diagnostic taxonomies of mental disorder? Distinguished philosophers consider mature sciences to progress from an observational base to one characterized by abstract concepts and theoretical systems. Diagnostic classification alone, in their opinion, does not make a scientific taxonomy; more specifically, similarity among clinical symptoms does not comprise a scientific category. The card catalog of a library, for example, is a well-organized classification but could hardly be viewed as a scientific system. The characteristic that distinguishes a scientific system is its success in grouping its elements according to theoretically consonant and explanatory propositions. This occurs when certain diagnostic attributes have been isolated and categorized and then shown to be logically or causally connected to other attributes or categories. The diagnostic classes comprising a scientific taxonomy are not, therefore, mere collections of overtly similar clinical attributes or categories, but a linked and unified pattern of known or presumed relationships among them.

If therapy and theory are to be part of a single integrated mental science, then diagnoses should prescribe certain forms of intervention, aided by a guiding theory. In an atheoretical empirical classification, such as the *DSM-IV-TR*, where diagnostic syndromes are inductive summaries of observations, rather than validated phenomena, the linkage between theory and therapy will probably be weak. Categories formed on the basis of overt similarities alone, that is, by inductive methods, risk classifying together individuals who look alike, but whose pathologies are actually radically different. As a consequence, research analyses that evaluate therapeutic efficacy will aggregate individuals who do not form homogeneous groups, thereby muddying-up research designs and affecting the magnitude of the resulting statistics in unpredictable ways. To date, it is impossible to know with certainty the extent to which the categories of the *DSM* classify ostensibly similar, but intrinsically different, groups of individuals together. Only future research will demonstrate how often the *DSM-IV-TR* fails to make key clinical distinctions. Categories today draw diagnostic boundaries with imprecision and lump together distinct mental processes that should be separated.

In reality, all patients, no matter which theory or procedure the therapist subscribes to, will, as a consequence of treatment, unlearn certain behavioral habits, alter aspects of their cognitive outlook and have elements of their unconscious world realigned. In other words, the patient is a unified natural entity, not a compartmentalized mechanism that can be subdivided in accord with certain theoretical practices; beneficial interventions at one entry point or level of focus of this unitary complex will feedback and have secondary salutary effects at other levels and points as well.

Consider also the synthesis of pharmacotherapy and psychotherapy. Early proponents of both approaches exhibited an intense rivalry and competition, if not hostility. Such treatment combinations no longer appear as much an issue today. The antagonistic atmosphere is now largely one of historic interest only. As Gerald Klerman (1991), an innovator in the synthesis of these two modalities noted, many clinicians believed that psychotherapy alone could provide "a true cure," whereas medication was seen as a palliative, at best, or an inhibitor of treatment motivation, at worst.

Mental illness experts, psychiatrists, and psychologists alike, now routinely employ treatments that combine pharmacology and psychotherapy, but they remain unprepared to deal with the interactions and diverse effects of both techniques, possessing no clear guideline for their successful implementation. As Beitman et al. has written (1992):

> In part, this stems from the fact that designing research to study the relevant variables and combined regimens . . . is such a daunting task. The list of factors to be taken into account is lengthy and would include diagnosis, severity, chronicity, treatment setting, goals, stage, and type of psychotherapy. Furthermore, research would need to control such issues as the different "active ingredients" for each modality, different mechanisms of delivery, time, course of response, outcome criteria, therapist attitude, and patient expectation. (p. 535)

Since the introduction of pharmacologic agents some five decades ago, their use has increased substantially; perhaps it is too frequently prescribed in this age of anxiety. Despite its unfortunate proliferation, professionals utilize medications in an increasingly sophisticated and problem-specific way. In parallel, the modalities and techniques of psychotherapy have not only broadened, but now are highly selective when applied to different syndromes and disorders. It is the additive, if not synergistic, advantages of combining these treatment modalities that will need to be developed and more finely tuned to specific diagnostic groups. Moreover, some suggest that combining these two modalities may reduce symptoms more quickly than either treatment alone. As a synthesized unit, the pharmacology/psychotherapy approach suggests that medications are especially helpful in dealing with somatic symptoms, whereas psychotherapy helps to strengthen cognitive outlook and social adjustment.

In closing this volume on the science of mind I should like to record a quote from the great mathematician and philosopher, Blaise Pascal, in which he stated:

Nothing stands still for us. . . . We find solid ground, a final steady base on which to build a tower that rises to infinity; but the whole foundation can crack beneath us and the earth may split open down to the abyss.

Science has been that tower, a beacon of hope these past centuries, especially to the disenfranchised and wounded of the world. But, to expand on Pascal's quote, science may prove to be a double-edged sword, with wonderful achievements and knowledge, on the one hand, and an abyss of unanticipated failures with serious consequences, on the other. Sadly, science has accentuated the worst in human nature as the world now faces the potentially devastating effects of both minor and major weapons of mass destruction. Many of today's world leaders of political, religious, and national movements have become self-righteous bullies, indifferent to the wishes, cares, and needs of others. Some have acted like petulant teenagers with little care or responsibility for their behavior, derogating all those who disagree with them and responding to a difference of opinion with a barroom punch, rather than with tolerance, respect, and an effort at a genuine, long-term peaceful resolution.

This book was begun just before and written soon after the horrific events of 9/11/01. Putting pen to paper concerning the history of the mind often stirred feelings of longing and sadness in me, the gnawing sense that events may lead to an end to our recent, perhaps unique period in history—the open, free, and humanistic democracy of Western civilization. Again we must brace ourselves to live life as many of our forefathers had in centuries past, to survive in the face of unrelenting hostility and degradation. Our extraordinary recent decades did not prepare us to face the reality that our assumption of an unblemished future might soon come to an end. The painful conflicts of these past years may merely have been a dry run for something far more devastating, a monstrous assault on humankind and civilized history that we have not begun to imagine.

We should be sympathetic to the economically wretched and inescapably anomic world of the likely perpetrators of a forthcoming holocaust. But, we cannot accept their malicious and cruel wishes to find scapegoats for their perennial economic resentments and confused ambitions. We see before us much that is reminiscent of those barbarities of the past that sought out and identified our ancestors as ostensibly justified objects for plunder and vilification. We know too well the history of the weak, poor, and mentally ill as readily employed emblems of cosmic evil, or as possessors of religious calumny and malevolence. Such pernicious attitudes regress to ancient times and are evident in the paranoid displacements of suicidal terrorists.

I fear that twenty-first century science and technology may annihilate our species. The imagery of extinction has already occurred in hateful form through reports of recent and not-so-recent systematic killings of groups designated as undesirable in Europe, the Middle East, and elsewhere. The threat of humankind's extinction is a modern version of ancient beliefs of the end of the world. These fantasies and images are readily at hand today for civilizations' enemies now possess the means to destroy one another. Ancient apocalyptic prophecies may become realities, a course of events that can lead to ultimate destruction, despair, and desolation.

What makes the present so different from the past is the blind obedience and renouncement of life that guides those involved in a religio-mystical and meaningless self-suicide. To reassert self in an ostensive resurrection of eternal life plunges a moral form of self-destruction into the ultimate annihilation of humankind. These seemingly rational religious beliefs evince the final irrationality of mind. Too many of the young of our time have become indifferent to others, indifferent to questions of principle, the whys and wherefores of life, reflecting not only a total insensitivity to their fellow human beings, but an indifference to themselves. Their corporeal existence no longer belongs to them, but to a ghostly and seductive netherworld, a world composed in reality of the void of utter nothingness.

Perhaps future mental scientists, those who understand the convoluted character of the mind, will probe this evil of humankind's destructiveness, not only to combat the awful apocalypse but, equally important, to seek alternatives to the violence the world faces, and to search for a path that may protect the species and move it toward more comprehensive and enlightened understandings.

About the Author

Theodore Millon, PhD, DSc, is Professor Emeritus of Psychology and Psychiatry at the University of Miami and Harvard Medical School. He is currently Dean and Scientific Director of the Institute for Advanced Studies in Personology and Psychopathology, and author of over 30 books on theory in psychopathology, diagnostic taxonomy, clinical assessment, and psychotherapy, including *Toward a New Personology*, *Disorders of Personality*, and *Personality-Guided Therapy*, each published by Wiley-Interscience. Notable also are his several widely employed psychodiagnostic instruments, including the *Millon Clinical Multiaxial Inventory* (MCMI-III), the

Theodore Millon

Millon Behavioral Medicine Diagnostic (MBMD), and the *Millon Index of Personality Styles* (MIPS-R). A well-regarded sculptor and graphic artist, the present text, *Masters of the Mind*, is his first extensive work devoted primarily to the history of the mental sciences. Among his many professional laurels, Professor Millon was the 2003 recipient of the American Psychological Association's singular Award for Distinguished Professional Contributions to Research.

References

Abraham, K. (1911). Notes on the psychoanalytic investigation and treatment of manic-depressive insanity and allied conditions. In *Selected papers of Karl Abraham*. London: Hogarth.

Abraham, K. (1927a). Contributions to the theory of the anal character. In *Selected papers on psychoanalysis*. London: Hogarth. (Original work published 1921)

Abraham, K. (1927b). The influence of oral eroticism on character formation. In *Selected papers on psychoanalysis*. London: Hogarth. (Original work published 1924)

Adams, H. B. (1964). Mental illness—or interpersonal behavior. *American Psychologist, 19*, 191–196.

Adler, A. (1929). *The science of living*. New York: Greenberg.

Alexander, F. G. (1930). *Analysis of the total personality*. New York: Nervous and Mental Diseases. (Original work published 1925)

Alexander, F. G., & French, T. (1946). *Psychoanalytic therapy: Principles and application*. Lincoln: University of Nebraska Press.

Alexander, F. G., & Selesnick, S. T. (1964). *The history of psychiatry: An evaluation of psychiatric thought and practice from prehistoric times to the present*. New York: Harper & Row.

Alexander, F. G., & Staub, H. (1957). *The criminal, the judge, and the public*. New York: Free Press. (Original work published 1929)

Allport, F. H. (1924). *Social psychology*. Boston: Houghton-Mifflin.

Allport, G. (1937). *Personality: A psychological interpretation*. New York: Holt.

American Psychiatric Association. (1980). *Diagnostic and statistical manual of mental disorders* (3rd ed.). Washington, DC: Author.

American Psychiatric Association. (1987). *Diagnostic and statistical manual of mental disorders* (3rd ed., rev.). Washington, DC: Author.

American Psychiatric Association. (1994). *Diagnostic and statistical manual of mental disorders* (4th ed.). Washington, DC: Author.

American Psychiatric Association. (2000). *Diagnostic and statistical manual of mental disorders: Text Revision (DSM IV-TR)*. Washington, DC: Author.

Angell, J. R. (1907). The province of functional psychology. *Psychological Review, 14*, 61–91.

Angell, J. R. (1909). *Psychology: An introductory study of the structure and function of human consciousness*. New York: Holt. (Original work published 1904)

Aquinas, T. (1915). *Summa theological* [The Fathers of the English Dominican Province, Trans.]. New York: Benzinger Brothers.

Arnold, T. (1806). *Observations on nature, kinds, causes, and prevention of insanity* (2nd ed.). London: R. Phillips. (Original work published 1782)

Aschaffenburg, G. (1922). Constitutional psychopathies. In *Handbook of medical practice, Vol. 4*. Leipzig, Germany: Barth.

Baars, B. J. (1986). *The cognitive revolution in psychology*. New York: Guilford Press.

Bacon, F. (1605). *Two books of Francis Bacon of the proficience and advancement of learning, divine and humane*. London: Henri Tomes.

Bacon, F. (1620). *Novum organum*. In E. A. Burtt (Ed.), *The English philosophers from Bacon to Mill*. New York: Modern Library.

Bacon, R. (1928). *The Opus majus of Roger Bacon*. London: H. Milford, Oxford University Press. (Original work published 1260)

Baillarger, J. (1853). De la melancholie avec stupeur. *Annales Medico-Psychologiquies, 5*, 251.

Bain, A. (1855). *Senses and the intellect*. London: Parker.

Bain, A. (1861). *On the study of character, including an estimate of phrenology*. London: Parker.

Bandura, A. (1968). A social learning interpretation of psychological dysfunctions. In P. London & D. Rosenhan (Eds.), *Foundations of abnormal psychology*. New York: Holt, Rinehart and Winston.

Bandura, A. (1974). Behavioral theories and models of man. *American Psychologist, 29*, 859–869.

Bandura, A. (1977). *Social learning theory*. Englewood Cliffs, NJ: Prentice-Hall.

Bateson, G. (1936). *Naven: A survey of the problems suggested by a composite picture of the culture of a New Guinea tribe drawn from three points of view*. Cambridge, England: Cambridge University Press.

Bateson, G. (1973). *Steps to an ecology of mind*. New York: Paladin Books.

Bateson, G. (1980). *Mind and nature—A necessary unity*. New York: Bantam Books.

Battie, W. (1758). *A treatise on madness*. London: J. Whiston & B. White.

Beck, A. T. (1976). *Cognitive therapy and the emotional disorders*. New York: International Universities Press.

Beck, A. T., & Freeman, A., & Associates (1990). *Cognitive therapy of personality disorders*. New York: Guilford Press.

Beers, C. W. (1908). *A mind that found itself: An autobiography*. New York, Longmans, Green.

Bellak, L., & Bellak, S. S. (1949). *Manual for the Children's Apperception Test*. New York: Grune & Stratton.

Bendikt, M. (1906). *Aus meinem leben*. Vienna: Konegen.

Benedict, R. F. (1934). *Patterns of culture*. Boston: Houghton-Mifflin.

Benjamin, L. S. (1974). Structural analysis of social behavior (SASB). *Psychological Review, 81*, 392–425.

Benjamin, L. S. (1993). *Interpersonal diagnosis and treatment of personality disorders*. New York: Guilford Press.

Benjamin, L. S. (2003). *Interpersonal reconstructive therapy: Promoting change in nonresponders*. New York: Guilford Press.

Berne, E. (1961). *Transactional analysis in psychotherapy*. New York: Grove Press.

Bernheim, H. (1900). *Suggestive therapeutics: A treatise on the nature and uses of hypnotism* (C. A. Herter, Trans.). New York: G. P. Putnam's Sons.

Bianchi, L. (1895). The functions of the frontal lobes (A. de Watteville, Trans.). *Brain, 18*, 497–530.

Binet, A., & Simon, T. (1905). *The Binet-Simon Intelligence Scale*. Paris.

Binet, A., & Simon, T. (1911). *The Binet-Simon Intelligence Scale* (3rd ed.). New York: Houghton-Mifflin.

Binswanger, L. (1956). Existential analysis and psychotherapy. In F. Fromm-Reichman & J. L. Moreno (Eds.), *Progress in psychotherapy* (Vol. 1). New York: Grune & Stratton.

Blashfield, R. K. (1984). *The classification of psychopathology*. New York: Plenum Press.

Bleuler, E. (1924). *Textbook of psychiatry* (A. A. Brill, Trans.). New York: Macmillan.

Bleuler, E. (1950). *Dementia praecox oder gruppe der schizophrenien*. Leipzig, Germany: Deuticke. (Original work published 1911)

Boas, F. (1929). *The mind of primitive man*. New York: Macmillan.

Boas, F. (1938). Methods of research. In F. Boas (Ed.), *General anthropology*. Boston: D. C. Heath.

Boring, E. G. (1929). *A history of experimental psychology*. New York: Appleton.

Boss, M. (1963). *Psychoanalysis and daseinsanalysis* (L. B. Lefebvre, Trans.). New York: Basic Books. (Original work published 1957)

Braid, J. (1843). *Neurhypnology: Or the rationale of nervous sleep, considered in relation with animal magnetism*. London: Churchill.

Breuer, J., & Freud, S. (1895). Studies on hysteria. In J. Strachey (Ed.), *The standard edition of the complete psychological works of Sigmund Freud* (Vol. 2, pp. 1–305). London: Hogarth Press.

Brill, A. A. (1912). *Psychoanalysis: Its theory and application*. Philadelphia: Saunders.

Brill, A. A. (1921). *Fundamental conceptions of psychoanalysis*. New York: Harcourt, Brace.

Brill, A. A. (Ed. & Trans.). (1938). *Basic writings of Sigmund Freud*. New York: Modern Library.

Briquet, P. (1859). *Traite clinique et therapeutique a l'hysterie*. Paris: J. B. Balliere & Fils.

Browne, W. A. F. (1837a). *Strong remedies for kindness in custodial care*. Edinburgh, Scotland: Black.

Browne, W. A. F. (1837b). *What asylums were, are, and ought to be*. Edinburgh, Scotland: Black.

Buck, J. N. (1948). The H-T-P *Journal of Clinical Psychology, 4*, 151–159.

Burton, R. (1621). *Anatomy of melancholy: What it is*. Oxford, England: John James Lichfield for Henry Short Cripps.

Butcher, J. N., Dahlstrom, W. G., Graham, J. R., Tellegen, A., & Kaemmer, B. (1989). *MMPI-2: Manual for administration and scoring*. Minneapolis: University of Minnesota Press.

Butcher, J. N., Williams, C. L., Graham, J. R., Archer, R. P., Tellegen, A., Ben-Porath, Y. S., et al. (1992). *MMPI-A (Minnesota Multiphasic Personality Inventory–Adolescent): Manual for administration, scoring, and interpretation*. Minneapolis: University of Minnesota Press.

Butler, J. S. (1887). *The curability of insanity: The individualized treatment of the insane*. New York: G. P. Putnam's Sons.

Caradec. L. (1860). *Topographie medico-hygiènique do departement du finistère*. Brest: Anner.

Cattell, R. B. (1949). *The Sixteen Personality Factor (16PF) Questionnaire*. Champaign, IL: Institute for Personality Testing.

Cattell, R. B., Eber, H. W., & Tatsuoka, M. M. (1970). *Handbook for the Sixteen Personality Factor Questionnaire (16PF)*. Champaign, IL: Institute for Personality and Ability Training.

Chaslin, P. (1912). *Elements de seminologie et de clinique mentale*. Paris: Asselin et Houzeau.

Chiarugi, V. (1987). *On insanity and its classification*. Canton, MA: Science History. (Original work published 1793)

Chomsky, N. (1957). *Syntactic structures.* The Hague, The Netherlands: Mouton.

Chomsky, N. (1975). *The logical structure of linguistic theories.* New York: Plenum Press.

Cleckley, H. M. (1941). *The mask of sanity.* St. Louis, MO: Mosby.

Comrie, J. D. (1922). *Selected works of Thomas Sydenham, M. D.* New York: William Wood Co. (As quoted in Goshen, 1967)

Comte, A. (1842). *Course in positive philosophy.* (Original work published 1830)

Comte, A. (1854). *System of positive policy.* (Original work published 1851)

Comte, A. (1908). *A general view of positivism.* London: George Routledge.

Cooley, C. H. (1918). *Social process.* New York: Scribner.

Cooley, C. H. (1922). *Human nature and the social order* (Rev. ed.). New York: Scribner. (Original work published 1902)

Coser, L. (1971). *The functions of social conflict.* New York: Macmillan.

Cullen, W. (1777). *First lines of the practice of physick for the use of students in the University of Edinburgh.* Edinburgh, Scotland: W. Creech.

Dandy, W. (1936). Operative experience in cases of pineal tumor. *Archives of Surgery, 33,* 19–46.

D'Aquin, J. (1791). *Philosophie de la folie.* Chambery, France: Gorrin.

D'Aquin, J. (1804). *Philosophie de la folie* (2nd ed.). Chambery, France: Cleaz.

Darwin, C. (1859). *Origin of species.* London: Dent.

Darwin, C. (1867/1896). *The expression of emotions in man and animals.* London: J. Murray.

de La Chambre, M. C. (1640). *Les characteres des passions* (Vol. 1). Paris: Asselin.

Descartes, R. (1637). *Discoures de la methode.* Leyde: I. Marie.

Descartes, R. (1913). *Meditations on the first philosophy* (J. Veitch, Trans.). London: William Blackwood & Sons.

Deutsch, A. (1948). *The shame of the states.* New York: Harcourt, Brace.

Deutsch, H. (1930). *Psychoanalyses of the neuroses.* Wien, Austria: Internationaler Psychoanlytischer Verlag.

Deutsch, H. (1942). Some forms of emotional disturbance and their relationship to schizophrenia. *Psychoanalytic Quarterly, 11,* 301–321.

Deutsch, H. (1944). *The psychology of women: A psychoanalytic interpretation.* New York: Grune.

Dix, D. L. (1843). *Appeal on behalf of the insane of Massachusetts.* Address to the Massachusetts Legislation.

Dollard, J., & Miller, N. E. (1950). *Personality and psychotherapy: An analysis in terms of learning, thinking, and culture.* New York: McGraw-Hill.

Dubois, P. (1908). *The psychic treatment of mental disorders.* New York: Funk & Wagnalls.

Dunlap, K. (1932). *Habits: Their making and unmaking.* New York: Liveright.

Durant, W. (1953). *The story of philosophy: The lives and opinions of the greater philosophers.* New York: Simon & Schuster.

Durkheim, E. (1951). *Suicide.* Glencoe, IL: Free Press. (Original work published 1897)

Earle, P. (1887). *The curability of insanity.* Philadelphia: Lippincott. (Original work published 1838)

Ellenberger, H. F. (1970). *The discovery of the unconscious: The history and evolution of dynamic psychiatry.* New York: Basic Books.

Elliott, T. (1904). On the action of adrenalin. *Journal of Physiology, 31,* xx–xxi.

Ellis, A. (1958). *How to live with a neurotic.* New York: Crown.

Ellis, A. (1970). *The essence of rational psychotherapy: A comprehensive approach to treatment.* New York: Institute for Rational Living.

Engel, G. (1960). A unified concept of health and disease. *Perspectives on Biology and Medicine, 3,* 459–485.

Erikson, E. (1975). *Life history and the historical moment.* New York: Norton.

Esquirol, J. (1816). Melancolie. In *Dictionnaire des sciences medicales.* Paris: Panckovke.

Esquirol, J. (1838). *Des maladies mentales* (Vols. 1–2). Paris: Bailliere.

Etzioni, A. W. (1961). *Comparative analysis of complex organizations.* New York: Free Press.

Etzioni, A. W. (1968). *The active society.* New York: Free Press.

Etzioni, A. W. (1973). *Genetic fix.* New York: Macmillan.

Exner, J. E. (1969). *The Rorschach systems.* New York: Grune & Stratton.

Eysenck, H. J. (1959). Learning theory and behavior therapy. *Journal of Mental Science, 105,* 61–75.

Fairbairn, W. R. D. (1952). Schizoid factors in the personality. In *An object-relations theory of the personality.* New York: Basic Books. (Original work published 1940)

Falret, J. P. (1854). De la folie circulaire. *Bulletin de l'Academie Medicale, 19,* 382–394.

Falret, J. P. (1862). *Traite pratique des maladies mentales.* Paris: Ballinger.

Fechner, G. T. (1966). *Elements of psychophysics* (Vol. 1, D. H. Howes & E. G. Boring, Eds. & H. E. Adler, Trans.). New York: Holt, Rinehart and Winston. (Original work published 1860)

Feigl, H. (1943). Logical empiricism. In D. Runces (Ed.), *Twentieth century philosophy.* New York: Philosophical Library.

Fenichel, O. (1934). *Outline of clinical psychoanalysis.* New York: Psychoanalytic Quarterly Press.

Fenichel, O. (1945). *The psychoanalytic theory of neurosis.* New York: Norton.

Ferenczi, S. (1908). *The analytic concepts of psychoneurosis* [Populäre Vorträge über Psychoanalyse]. New York: Brunner/Mazel. (From S. Ferenczi, 1926/1980, *Further contributions to the theory and technique of psycho-analysis*).

Ferenczi, S. (1920, September 10). *The further development of an active therapy in psychoanalysis.* Address delivered at the Sixth International Congress of Psycho-Analysis at The Hague. New York: Brunner/Mazel. (From S. Ferenczi, 1926/1980, *Further contributions to the theory and technique of psycho-analysis*).

Ferrier, D. (1876). *The functions of the brain.* London: Smith, Elder & Co.

Ferster, C., & Skinner, B. F. (1957). *Schedules of reinforcement.* New York: Appleton-Century-Crofts.

Festinger, L. (1957). *A theory of cognitive dissonance.* Evanston, IL: Row, Peterson.

Feuchtersleben, E. (1847). *The principles of medical psychology: Being the outlines of a course of lectures.* London: Sydenham Society.

Fisher, S., & Greenberg, R. P. (1977). *The scientific credibility of Freud's theoretical therapies.* New York: Basic Books.

Forel, A. (1937). *Out of my life and work.* New York: Norton.

Frank, L. (1936). *Projective methods.* Springfield, IL: Thomas.

Frankl, V. (1969). *Psychotherapy and existentialism.* New York: Clarion Books.

Frankl, V. (1992). *Man's search for meaning.* Boston: Beacon Press. (Original work published 1959)

French, T. N. (1933). Interrelations between psychoanalysis and the experimental work of Pavlov. *American Journal of Psychiatry, 89,* 1165–1203.

Freud, A. (1936/1966). *The ego and the mechanisms of defense.* New York: International Universities Press.

Freud, A. (1969). Difficulties on the path of psychoanalysis: A confrontation of past with present viewpoints. In *The writings of Anna Freud* (Vol. 7). New York: International Universities Press.

Freud, S. (1900). *The interpretation of dreams.* New York: Norton.

Freud, S. (1925). The instincts and their vicissitudes. In J. Strachey (Ed.), *The standard edition of the complete psychological works of Sigmund Freud* (Vol. 4, pp. 109–140). London: Hogarth Press. (Original work published 1915)

Freud, S. (1937). Analysis, terminable and interminable. *International Journal of Psychoanalysis, 18*, 373–412.

Fritsch, G., & Hitzig, E. (1960). Über die elektrische Erregbarkeit des Grosshirns. *Archiv für Anatomie und Physiologie*. In G. von Bonin (Ed.), *Some papers on the cerebral cortex* [On the electrical excitability of the cerebrum]. Springfield, IL: Charles C Thomas. (Original work published 1870)

Fromm, E. (1941). *Escape from freedom*. New York: Rinehart & Co.

Fromm, E. (1947). *Man for himself*. New York: Holt, Rinehart and Winston.

Fromm-Reichmann, F. (1950). *Principles of intensive psychotherapy*. Chicago: University of Chicago Press.

Fromm-Reichmann, F. (1953). *An intensive study of twelve cases of manic-depressive psychosis*. Washington, DC: Washington School of Psychiatry.

Galt, J. M. (1846). *The treatment of insanity*. New York: Harper.

Galton, F. (1972). *Hereditary genius*. Gloucester, MA: Peter Smith. (Original work published 1869)

Gardner, H. (1983). *Frames of mind: The theory of multiple intelligences*. New York: Basic Books.

Garzoni, T. (1586). *L'hospidale de pazzi incurabili*. Ferrara, Italy: Apresso Giulio Cesare Cagnacini & Fratelli.

Getzels, J. (1962). *Creativity and intelligence: Explorations with gifted students*. New York: Wiley.

Goffman, E. (1961a). *Asylums: Essays on the social situation of mental patients and other inmates*. New York: Walter de Gruyter.

Goffman, E. (1961b). *Encounters: Two studies in the sociology of interaction*. New York: Macmillan.

Goffman, E. (1963). *Behavior in public places: Notes on the social organization of gatherings*. New York: Free Press.

Goffman, E. (1967). *Interaction ritual: Essays on face-to-face behavior*. New York: Doubleday.

Goffman, E. (1981). *Presentation of self in everyday life*. Harmondsworth: Penguin.

Golden, C. J., Purisch, A. D., & Hammeke, T. A. (1985). *Luria-Nebraska Neuropsychological Battery*. Los Angeles: Western Psychological Services.

Goltz, F. (1881). Über die Verrichtungen des Grosshirns. *Archiv für die gesamte Neurologie und Psychiatreie, 26*, 1–49.

Goodenough, F. (1926). *The measurement of intelligence by drawings*. Yonkers-on-Hudson, NY: World Books.

Griesinger, W. (1845). *Mental pathology and therapeutics*. London: New Sydenham Society.

Griesinger, W. (1868). Introductory comments. *Archives for Psychiatry and Nervous Diseases, 1*, 12.

Griesinger, W. (1882). *Mental pathology and therapeutics* (2nd ed.). New York: W. Wood.

Grob, G. N. (1994). *The mad among us: A history of the care of America's mentally ill*. Cambridge, MA: Harvard University Press.

Gruenberg, E. (1969). How can the new diagnostic manual help? *International Journal of Psychiatry, 7*, 368–374.

Guilford, J. P. (1967). *The nature of human intelligence*. New York: McGraw-Hill.

Hall, G. S. (1923). *Life and confessions of a psychologist*. New York: Appleton.

Hartmann, H. (1927). *Die grundlagen der psychoanalse*. Leipzig, Germany: G. Thieme.

Hartmann, H. (1939). *Ego psychology and the problem of adaptation*. New York: International Universities Press.

Hartmann, H. (1964). *Essays on ego psychology: Selected problems in psychoanalytic theory*. New York: International Universities Press.

Hartmann, H., Kris, E., & Lowenstein, R. M. (1946). Comments on the formation of psychic structure. In H. Hartmann, E. Kris, & R. M. Lowenstein (Eds.), *Papers on psychoanalytic psychology: Psychological issues* (Monograph No. 14). New York: International Universities Press.

Haslam, J. (1809). *Observations on madness and melancholy.* London: J. Callow.

Haslam, J. (1810). *Illustrations of madness: Exhibiting a singular case of insanity.* London: G. Hayden.

Hathaway, S. R., & McKinley, J. C. (1943). *Manual for the Minnesota Multiphasic Personality Inventory.* New York: Psychological Corporation.

Head, H. (1920). *Studies in neurology.* London: Hodder and Stroughton.

Hebb, D. O. (1949). *The organization of behavior: A neuropsychological theory.* New York: Wiley.

Heidbreder, E. (1933). *Seven psychologies.* New York: Appleton.

Heidegger, M. (1962). *Being and time.* Oxford, England: Blackwell. (Original work published 1927)

Heider, F. (1958). *The psychology of interpersonal relations.* New York: Wiley.

Heinroth, J. C. (1818). *Lehrbuch der Störungen des Seelenlebens.* Leipzig, Germany: Thieme.

Hellpach, W. (1920). Amphithymia. *Zeitschrift fuer die gesamte Neurologie und Psychiatrie, 19,* 136–152.

Helmholtz, H. (1863). *On the sensations of tone as a physiological basis for the theory of music.* London: Longmans Green.

Helmholtz, H. (1925). Concerning the perceptions in general. In J. P. C. Southall (Ed.), *Treatise on physiological optics.* New York: Optical Society of America. (Original work published 1866)

Hempel, C. G. (1961). Introduction to problems of taxonomy. In J. Zubin (Ed.), *Field studies in the mental disorders.* New York: Grune & Stratton.

Hempel, C. G. (1965). *Aspects of scientific explanation, and other essays in the philosophy of science.* New York: Free Press.

Hett, W. S. (Ed. & Trans.). (1936). Physiognomics. In *Aristotle: Minor works.* Cambridge, MA: Harvard University Press.

Heymans, G. (1890). *Laws and elements of scientific thought.* Leiden, Holland: S. C. van Doesburgh.

Hippocrates. (1952). Hippocrates. In *Great books of the Western world: Vol. 10. Hippocrates, Galen.* Chicago: Benton.

Hitzig, E., & Fritsch, G. (1870). *Ueber die elektrische Erregbarkeit des Grosshirns* [Electric excitability of the cerebrum]. Leipzig, Germany: Veit.

Hobbes, T. (1651). *Leviathan, or the matter, forme, and power of a commonwealth, ecclesiasticall and civill.* London: Andrew Crooke.

Horney, K. (1937). *The neurotic personality of our time.* New York: Norton.

Horney, K. (1939). *New ways in psychoanalysis.* New York: Norton.

Horney, K. (1942). *Self-analysis.* New York: Norton.

Horney, K. (1945). *Our inner conflicts.* New York: Norton.

Horney, K. (1950). *Neurosis and human growth.* New York: Norton.

Huarte, J. (1594). *Examen de ingenios* [The examination of man's wits. In which, by discovering the varietie of natures, is shewed for what profession each one is apt and how far he shall profit therein]. London: Thomas Man. (Original work published 1575)

Huarte, J. (1967). *L'Examen des spirits pour les sciences ou sont monstrées les differences d'esprits, qui se trouvent parmy les homes & à quelle sorte de science chacun est proper en particulier* (C. E. Goshen, Trans). Lyons, France: Gabriel Blank. (Original work published 1668)

Hull, C. L. (1928). *Aptitude testing.* Yonkers-on-Hudson, NY: World Books.

Hull, C. L. (1933). *Hypnosis and suggestibility: An experimental approach.* New York: Appleton-Century.

Hull, C. L. (1943). *Principles of behavior.* New York: Appleton.

Hume, D. (1748). *Philosophical essays concerning human understanding.* London: A. Millar.

Humm, D. G., & Wadsworth, G. W. (1935). The Humm-Wadsworth Temperament Scale. *American Journal of Psychiatry, 92,* 163–200.

Hunt, M. M. (1993). *The story of psychology.* New York: Doubleday.

Husserl, E. (1931). *Ideas: A general introduction to pure phenomenology.* New York: Macmillan. (Original work published 1913)

Jacobson, E. (1964). *The self and the object world.* New York: International Universities Press.

James, W. (1890). *The principles of psychology* (Vols. 1–2). New York: Holt.

James, W. (1902). *The varieties of religious experience: A study in human nature: Being the Gifford lectures on natural religion delivered at Edinburgh in 1901–1902.* New York: Longmans, Green.

James, W. (1920). *Letters of William James* (Vols. 1–2). Boston: Atlantic Monthly Press.

Janet, P. (1901). *The mental state of hystericals* (C. R. Corson, Trans.). New York: Putnam's Sons.

Jaspers, K. (1913). *General psychopathology.* Manchester, England: Manchester University Press.

Jaspers, K. (1922). *Strindberg and van Gogh: An attempt of a pathographic analysis with reference to parallel cases of Swedenborg & Höblerlin.* Bern, Switzerland: Bircher. (Original work published 1910)

Jaspers, K. (1931). *Man in the modern age.* Berlin, Germany: W. de Gruyter.

Jaspers, K. (1932). *Philosophy.* Berlin, Germany: J. Springer.

Jaspers, K. (1935). *Reason and existence.* Groningen, The Netherlands: J. B. Wolters.

Jaspers, K. (1938). *Existenzphilosophie.* Berlin, Germany: W. de Gruyter.

Jaspers, K. (1946). *The question of German guilt.* New York: Dial Press.

Jaspers, K. (1963). *General psychopathology* (7th ed., J. Hoenig & M. W. Hamilton, Trans.). Chicago: University of Chicago Press.

Jones, E. (1961). *Life and works of Sigmund Freud* (L. Trinning & S. Marcus, Ed. & Abridge). New York: Basic Books. (Original work published 1953)

Jones, M. (1953). *The therapeutic community: A new treatment method in psychiatry.* New York: Basic Books.

Jung, C. G. (1907). *Psychology of dementia praecox* (A. A. Brill, Trans.). New York: Nervous and Mental Diseases.

Jung, C. G. (1916). *Psychology of the unconscious.* New York: Moffat, Yard.

Jung, C. G. (1920). *Collected papers on analytical psychology* (C. E. Long, Trans.). London: Bailliere, Tindall & Cox.

Jung, C. G. (1921). *Psychological types.* Zurich, Switzerland: Rasher Verlag.

Jung, C. G. (1939). *The integration of the personality* (G. M. Dell, Trans.). New York: Farrar & Rinehart.

Kahlbaum, K. L. (1874). *Die katatonie, oder das spannungsirresien.* Berlin, Germany: Kirschwald.

Kallmann, F. J. (1938). *The genetics of schizophrenia: A study of heredity and reproduction in the families of 1,087 schizophrenics.* New York: J. J. Augustin.

Kant, I. (1799). *Kantische blumenlese.* Liepzig: J. D. Schöpes.

Kant, I. (1891). *Kant's prolegomena and metaphysical foundations of natural science* (E. Ban, Trans). London: George Bell & Sons.

Kant, I. (1957). *Perpetual peace.* (Ed. L. W. Beck). New York: Liberal Arts Press.

Kant, I. (1991). *Critique of pure reason* (J. M. D. Meiklejohn, Trans. & introduced by A. D. Lindsey). London: J. M. Dent. (Original work published 1781)

Kaplan, A. (1964). *The conduct of inquiry.* San Francisco: Chander.

Kardiner, A. (1939). *The individual and his society: The psychodynamics of primitive social organization.* New York: Columbia University Press.

Kardiner, A., Linton, R., DuBois, C., & West, J. (1945). *The psychological frontiers of society.* New York: Columbia University Press.

Katz, D. (1935). *Der aufbau der farbwelt* [The world of color; R. B. MacLeod & C. W. Fox, Trans.]. London: Kegan Paul, Trench, Trubner. (Original work published 1911)

Kelly, G. A. (1955). *The psychology of personal constructs* (Vols. 1–2). New York: Norton.

Kelly, G. A. (1969). The psychotherapeutic relationship. In B. Maher (Ed.), *Clinical psychology and personality: The selected papers of George Kelly.* New York: Wiley. (Original work published 1965)

Kendell, R. E. (1975). *The role of diagnosis in psychiatry.* Oxford: Blackwell.

Kernberg, O. F. (1967). Borderline personality organization. *Journal of the American Psychoanalytic Association, 15,* 641–685.

Kiesler, D. J. (1982). Interpersonal theory for personality and psychotherapy. In J. C. Anchin & D. J. Kiesler (Eds.), *Handbook of interpersonal psychotherapy* (pp. 274–295). Elmsford, NY: Pergamon Press.

Kiesler, D. J. (1987). *Research manual for the Impact Message Inventory.* Palo Alto, CA: Consulting Psychologists Press.

Kiesler, D. J. (1996). *Contemporary interpersonal theory and research: Personality, psychopathology, and psychotherapy.* New York: Wiley.

Kirkebride, T. (1880). *On the construction, organization, and general arrangements of hospitals for the insane* (2nd ed.). Philadelphia: Saunders.

Klein, M. (1932). *The psycho-analysis of children.* London: Hogarth Press.

Klein, M. (1926a). Mourning and its relation to manic-depressive states. In *Love, guilt, and reparation, and other works, 1921–1945.* London: Hogarth Press.

Klein, M. (1926b). The psychological principle of early analysis. In *Love, guilt, and reparation, and other works, 1921–1945.* London: Hogarth Press.

Klein, M. H., Mathieu, P. L., Gendlin, E. T., & Kiesler, D. J. (1970). *The Experiencing Scale: Research and training manual.* Madison: Wisconsin Psychiatric Institute.

Koch, J. A. (1891). *Die psychopathischen minderwertgkeiten.* Ravensburg, Germany: Maier.

Koffka, K. (1924). *Die grundlagen der psychischen entwicklung* [The growth of mind]. New York: Harcourt, Brace. (Original work published 1921)

Köhler, W. (1925). *Intelligenzprüfung an Menschenaffen* [The mentality of apes] (E. Winter, Trans). New York: Harcourt Brace. (Original work published 1917)

Köhler, W. (1938). *The place of value in a world of facts.* New York: Liveright.

Kohut, H. (1959). Introspection, empathy, and psychoanalysis. *Journal of the American Psychoanalytic Association, 7,* 459–483.

Kohut, H. (1971). *The analysis of the self.* New York: International Universities Press.

Kohut, H. (1977). *The restoration of the self.* New York: International Universities Press.

Korsakoff, S. (1887). Psychchosis polyneuritica s. Cerebropathia psychica toxaemica (M. Victor & S. Yakovlev, Trans.). *Medizinskoje Obozrenije, 31,* 13.

Kraepelin, E. (1883). *Compendium of psychiatry.* Leipzig, Germany: Abel.

Kraepelin, E. (1896). *Psychiatrie: Ein Lehrbuch* (5th ed.). Leipzig, Germany: Barth.

Kraepelin, E. (1899). *Psychiatrie: Ein Lehrbuch* (6th ed.). Leipzig, Germany: Barth.

Kraepelin, E. (1913). *Psychiatrie: Ein lehrbuch für studirende und aerzte* (8th ed.). Liepzig, Germany: Abel.

Kraepelin, E. (1915). *Psychiatrie: Ein Lehrbuch* (8th ed.). Leipzig, Germany: Barth.

Kraepelin, E. (1920). *Hundert jahre psychiatrie.* Berlin, Germany: Springer Verlag.

Kraepelin, E. (1921). *Manic-depressive insanity and paranoia.* Edinburgh, Scotland: Livingstone.

Kraepelin, E. (1962). *One hundred years of psychiatry.* (Trans. W. Baskin). New York: Philosophical Library. (Original work published 1917)

Krafft-Ebing, R. (1879). *Lehrbuch der Psychiatrie auf klinischer girundlage.* Stuttgart, Germany: Erike.

Krafft-Ebing, R. (1937). *Psychopathia sexualis.* New York: Physicians and Surgeons Books. (Original work published 1882)

Kramer, H., & Sprenger, J. (1928). *Malleus malefacarum* [The witches' hammer] (Rev. Montagne Summers, Trans.). London: Rodker. (Original work published 1487)

Kretschmer, E. (1925). *Physique und character.* Berlin, Germany: Springer Verlag.

Kubie, L. S. (1943). Manual of emergency treatment for acute war neuroses. *War Medicine, 4,* 582–598.

Kuhn, T. (1962). *The structure of scientific revolutions.* Chicago: University of Chicago Press.

Kupfer, D. J., First, M. B., & Regier, D. A. (2002). *A research agenda for DSM-V.* Washington, DC: American Psychiatric Association.

Lashley, K. S. (1963). *Brain mechanisms and intelligence.* New York: Dover. (Original work published 1929)

Lazarus, A. A. (1976). *Multimodal behavior therapy.* New York: Springer.

Lazarus, A. A. (1981). *The practice of multimodal therapy: Systematic, comprehensive, and effective psychotherapy.* New York: McGraw-Hill.

Lazursky, A. (1908). *Outline of a science of characters.* St. Petersburg, FL: Lossky.

Leary, T. (1957). *Interpersonal diagnosis of personality.* New York: Ronald Press.

Levi-Strauss, C. (1969). *The elementary structures of kinship* (J. H. Bell, J. R. von Sturmer, & R. Needham, Eds. & Trans.). Boston: Beacon Press. (Original work published 1949)

Levy, D. M. (1941). Maternal overprotection. *Psychiatry, 4,* 393–438.

Liebault, A. A. (1866). *Du sommeil et des etates analogues consideres surtout au point du une de l'action du moral sur le physique* [Sleep and analogous states]. Paris: Masson.

Linehan, M. M. (1993). *Cognitive-behavioral therapy of borderline personality disorder.* New York: Guilford Press.

Livesley, W. J., & Jackson, D. N. (1986). The internal consistency and factorial structure of behaviours judged to be associated with *DSM-III* categories of personality disorders. *American Journal of Psychiatry, 143,* 1473–1474.

Livesley, W. J., Jackson, D. N., & Schroeder, M. L. (1989). A study of the factorial structure of personality pathology. *Journal of Personality Disorders, 3,* 292–306.

Livesley, W. J., Jackson, D. N., & Schroeder, M. L. (1992). Factorial structure of traits delineating personality disorders in clinical and general population samples. *Journal of Abnormal Psychology, 101,* 432–440.

Livesley, W. J., Reiffer, L. I., Sheldon, A. E. R., & West, M. (1987). Prototypicality of the *DSM-III* personality criteria. *Journal of Nervous and Mental Disease, 175,* 395–401.

Locke, J. (1956). *An essay concerning human understanding.* Chicago: Henry Regnery. (Original work published 1696)

Lombroso, C. (1876). *The delinquent man*. Milano, Italy: Hoepli.

Lombroso, C. (1895). *The female offender*. London: Unwin Hyman.

Lucas, K. (1917). *The conduction of the nervous impulse* (E. D. Adrian, Ed.). London: Longmans, Green.

Luria, A. R. (1966). *Higher cortical functions in man* (Trans.). New York: Basic Books.

Machover, K. (1949). *Personality projection in the drawing of the human figure*. Springfield, IL: Charles C Thomas.

Maher, B. (1969). *Clinical psychology and personality: The selected papers of George Kelly*. New York: Wiley.

Mahler, M. S. (1967). On human symbiosis and the vicissitudes of individuation. In *The selected papers of Margaret S. Mahler* (Vol. 1, pp. 77–98). New York: International Universities Press.

Mahler, M. S., Pine, F., & Bergman, A. (1975). *The psychological birth of the human infant*. New York: Basic Books.

Malinowski, B. (1944). Social anthropology. *Encyclopedia Britannica, 20*, 862–870.

Maslow, A. (1957). A philosophy for psychology. In J. Fairchild (Ed.), *Personal problems and psychological frontiers*. New York: Sheridan House.

Maslow, A. H. (1968). *Toward a psychology of being* (2nd ed.). New York: D. Van Nostrand.

Maudsley, H. (1860). *Annual board report at Cheadle Royal Hospital*. Unpublished report.

Maudsley, H. (1876). *Physiology and pathology of mind*. New York: Appleton.

May, R. R. (1969a). *Existential psychology* (2nd ed.). New York: Random House.

May, R. R. (1969b). *Love and will*. New York: Norton.

May, R. R. (1975). *The courage to create*. New York: Norton.

McDougall, W. (1908). *An introduction to social psychology*. London: Methuen.

McDougall, W. (1923). *Outline of psychology*. New York: Scribner.

McDougall, W. (1936). *Psycho-analysis and social psychology*. London: Methuen.

Mead, G. H. (1934). *Mind, self, and society*. Chicago: University of Chicago Press.

Mead, M. (1928). *Coming of age in Samoa: A psychological study of primitive youth for western civilization*. New York: Morrow.

Mead, M. (1962). *Growing up in New Guinea*. New York: Morrow. (Original work published 1930)

Meehl, P. E. (1954). *Clinical versus statistical prediction: A theoretical analysis and a review of the evidence*. Minneapolis: University of Minnesota Press.

Meehl, P. E. (1959). Some ruminations on the validation of clinical procedures. *Canadian Journal of Psychology, 13*, 102–128.

Menninger, K. (1945). *The human mind*. New York: Knopf. (Original work published 1930)

Menninger, K. (1963). *The vital balance: The life process in mental health and illness*. New York: Viking Press.

Merton, R. K. (1938). Social structure and anomie. *American Sociological Review, 3*, 672–682.

Merton, R. K. (1957). *Social theory and social structure*. Glencoe, IL: Free Press.

Mesmer, A. (1948). *Dissertation on the discovery of animal magnetism* (G. Frankau, Trans.). London: MacDonald. (Original work published 1779)

Meumann, E. (1910). *Intelligenz und wille*. Leipzig, Germany: Barth.

Meyer, A. (1906). Fundamental conceptions of dementia praecox. *British Medical Journal, 2*, 757–760.

Meyer, A. (1912). Remarks on habit disorganizations in the essential deteriorations. *Nervous and Mental Diseases Monographs, 9*, 95–109.

Meynert, T. (1884). *Textbook of psychiatry* (B. Sachs, Trans.). New York: Putnam.

Meynert, T. (1885). *Psychiatry: A clinical treatise on diseases of the fore-brain* (B. Sachs, Trans.). New York: Putnam.

Micale, M. S., & Porter, R. (1994). *Discovering the history of psychiatry*. New York: Oxford University Press.

Miller, G. A. (1951). *Language and communication*. New York: McGraw-Hill.

Miller, G. A. (1989). George A. Miller. In G. Lindzey (Ed.), *A history of psychology in autobiography* (Vol. 8). Stanford, CA: Stanford University Press.

Miller, N. E., & Dollard, J. (1941). *Social learning and imitation*. New Haven, CT: Yale University Press.

Millon, T. (1969). *Modern psychopathology: A biosocial approach to maladaptive learning and functioning*. Philadelphia: Saunders.

Millon, T. (1977). *Millon Clinical Multiaxial Inventory (MCMI)*. Minneapolis, MN: National Computer Systems.

Millon, T. (1981). *Disorders of personality: DSM-III, axis II*. New York: Wiley.

Millon, T. (1987). On the genesis and prevalence of the borderline personality disorder: A social learning thesis. *Journal of Personality Disorders, 1*, 354–372.

Millon, T. (1988). Personologic psychotherapy: Ten commandments for a posteclectic approach to integrative treatment. *Psychotherapy, 25*, 209–219.

Millon, T. (1990). *Toward a new personology: An evolutionary model*. New York: Wiley.

Millon, T. (1991). Classification in psychopathology: Rationale, alternatives, and standards. *Journal of Abnormal Psychology, 100*, 245–261.

Millon, T. (with Grossman, S., Meagher, S., Millon, C., & Everly, G.). (1999). *Personality-guided therapy*. New York: Wiley.

Millon, T., Antoni, M., Millon, C., Meagher, S., & Grossman, S. (2001). *Millon behavioral medicine diagnostic (MBMD) manual*. Minneapolis, MN: National Computer System Pearson Assessments.

Millon, T., & Davis, R. D. (1996). *Disorders of personality: DSM-IV and beyond*. New York: Wiley.

Millon, T., Davis, R. D., & Millon, C. (1997). *Millon Clinical Multiaxial Inventory (MCMI-III) manual* (2nd ed.). Minneapolis, MN: National Computer System.

Millon, T., Millon, C., & Davis, R. (1993). *Millon adolescent clinical inventory (MACI) manual*. Minneapolis, MN: National Computer System Assessments.

Millon, T., Weiss, L., & Millon, C. (2003). *Millon index of personality styles-revised (MIPS-R) manual*. Minneapolis, MN: Pearson Assessments.

Mills, C. W. (1953). *White collar: The American middle classes*. New York: Oxford University Press.

Mills, C. W. (1956). *The power elite*. New York: Oxford University Press.

Minkowski, E. (1968). *Traite d'psychopathologie*. Paris: PUF. (Original work published 1927)

Minuchin, S. (1974). *Families and family therapy*. Cambridge, MA: Harvard University Press.

Mitchell, S. W. (1894). Address to the American Medico-Psychological Association. *Journal of Nervous and Mental Diseases, 21*, 413–438.

Morel, B. A. (1857). *Traite de desgenerescences physiques intellectuelles et morales de l'espece humaine*. Paris: Bailliere.

Morgan, C. D., & Murray, H. A. (1935). A method for investigating fantasies: The thematic apperception test. *Archives of Neurology and Psychiatry, 34*, 389–406.

Münsterberg, H. (1913). *Psychology and industrial efficiency*. Boston: Houghton-Mifflin.

Murphy, G. (1930). *An historical introduction to modern psychology*. New York: Harcourt Brace.

Murphy, G. (1947). *Personality: A biosocial approach to origins and structures.* New York: Harper.

Murphy, L. B. (1990). *Gardner Murphy: Integrating, expanding and humanizing psychology.* Jefferson, NC: McFarland.

Murray, E. J. (1988). Personality disorders: A cognitive view. *Journal of Personality Disorders, 2,* 37–43.

Murray, H. A. (1938). *Explorations in personality.* New York: Oxford University Press.

Murray, H. A. (1948). *Assessment of men.* New York: Holt, Rinehart and Winston.

Nagel, E. (1965). Psychology and the philosophy of science. In B. Wolman (Ed.), *Scientific psychology* (pp. 24–43). New York: Basic Books.

Neisser, U. (1967). *Cognitive psychology.* New York: Appleton-Century-Crofts.

Noyes, A. P. (1953). *Modern clinical psychiatry* (4th ed.). Philadelphia: Saunders.

Papez, J. (1937). A proposed mechanism of emotion. *Archives of Neurology and Psychiatry, 38,* 725–743.

Paracelsus. (1941). *Von den Krankheiten, so die Vernufft berauben* (Henry Sigerist, Ed. & Gregory Zilboorg, Trans.). Baltimore: Johns Hopkins University Press. (Original work published 1567)

Parloff, M. B. (1967). Advances in analytic group therapy. In J. Marmor (Ed.), *Frontiers of psychoanalysis.* New York: Basic Books.

Pavlov, I. P. (1927). *Conditioned reflexes: An investigation of the physiological activity of the cerebral cortex.* London: Oxford University Press.

Pavlov, I. P. (1928). *Lectures on conditioned reflexes* (Vol. 1). New York: International Universities Press.

Peck, A. L. (Ed. & Trans.). (1965). *Aristotle: Historia animalium.* Cambridge, MA: Harvard University Press.

Piaget, J. (1950). *Introduction à l'épistémologie génétique.* Paris: Presses universitaires de France.

Piaget, J. (1952). *The origins of intelligence in children.* New York: International Universities Press.

Pinel, P. (1798). *Nosographie philosophique.* Paris: Richard, Caille, & Ravier.

Pinel, P. (1801). *Traite medico-philosophique de l'alienation mentale* (D. D. Davis, Trans.). London.

Popper, K. (1959). *Logic of scientific discovery.* London: Hutchinson. (Original work published 1934)

Porta, G. (1586). *De Humana physiognomia.* Apud, J. Cacchium: Vici aequensis.

Porta, G. (1588). *Phytognomonica.* Neapoli, Italy: H. Saluianum.

Porta, G. (1957). *Natural magik* (D. J. Price, Ed.). New York: Basic Books. (Original work published 1558)

Porter, R. (2002). *Madness.* New York: Oxford University Press.

Rado, S. (1956). Schizotypal organization: Preliminary report on a clinical study of schizophrenia. In S. Rado & G. E. Daniels (Eds.), *Changing concepts of psychoanalytic medicine* (pp. 225–236). New York: Grune & Stratton.

Rado, S. (1959). Obsessive behavior. In S. Arieti (Ed.), *American handbook of psychiatry* (Vol. 1). New York: Basic Books.

Rand, B. (1912). On J. Müller. In *Classical psychologists.* New York: Appleton.

Rank, O. (1924). *The trauma of birth* (Trans.). New York: Harcourt Brace.

Rank, O., & Ferenczi, S. (1923). *The development of psychoanalysis* (C. Newton, Trans.). New York: Nervous and Mental Diseases.

Rapaport, D., Gill, M., & Schafer, R. (1946). *Diagnostic psychological testing.* New York: Josiah Macy Jr. Foundation.

Ray, I. (1850). Proposal for laws covering all legal relations of the insane, civil and criminal. *American Journal of Insanity, 7,* 217.

Ray, I. (1863). *Mental hygiene.* Boston: Ticknor & Fields.

Ray, I. (1962). *Medical jurisprudence of insanity* (W. Overholser, Ed.). Cambridge, MA: Harvard University Press. (Original work published 1837)

Reich, W. (1949). *Character analysis* (3rd ed.). New York: Farrar, Straus and Giroux. (Original work published 1933)

Reik, T. (1940). *From 30 years with Freud* (R. Winston, Trans.). New York: Farrar & Rinehart.

Reik, T. (1948). *Listening with the third ear.* New York: Farrar, Straus and Giroux.

Reik, T. (1949). *Masochism in modern man* (M. H. Beigel & G. M. Kurth, Trans.). New York: Farrar, Straus and Giroux.

Reik, T. (1959). *Masochism in modern man* (2nd ed.). New York: Grove Press.

Reil, J. C. (1803). *Rhapsodieen über die Auwendung der psychischen.* Halle, Germany: Curtsche.

Ribot, T. (1890). *Psychologie des sentiments.* Paris: Delahaye and Lecrosnier.

Richmond, M. E. (1917). *Social diagnosis.* New York: Russell Sage Foundation.

Riesman, D. (1950). *The lonely crowd: A study of the changing American character.* New Haven, CT: Yale University Press.

Riesman, D. (1952). *Faces in the crowd: Individual studies in character and politics.* New Haven, CT: Yale University Press.

Roazen, P. (1976). *Freud and his followers.* London: Allen Lane.

Robinson, D. R. (1976). *An intellectual history of psychology.* New York: Macmillan.

Roccatagliata, G. (1973). *Storia de la psichiatria antica.* Milano, Italy: Hoepli.

Rogers, C. R. (1939). *The clinical treatment of the problem child.* Boston: Houghton.

Rogers, C. R. (1942). *Counseling and psychotherapy: New concepts in practice.* Boston: Houghton Mifflin.

Rogers, C. R. (1951). *Client-centered therapy: Its current practice, implications, and theory.* Boston: Houghton Mifflin.

Rogers, C. R. (1961). *On becoming a person.* Boston: Houghton Mifflin.

Rorschach, H. (1941). *Psychodiagnostics* (H. H. Verlag, Trans.). Bern, Switzerland: Bircher. (Original work published 1921)

Rosenthal, D., & Kety, S. S. (Eds.). (1968). *Transmission of schizophrenia.* Oxford, England: Pergamon Press.

Rosenzweig, S. (1936). Some implicit common factors in diverse methods of psychotherapy. *American Journal of Orthopsychiatry, 6,* 412–415.

Rotter, J. B. (1954). *Social learning and clinical psychology.* Englewood Cliffs, NJ: Prentice-Hall.

Rotter, J. B. (1966). Generalized expectancies for internal versus external control of reinforcements. *Psychological Monographs, 80,* 1–28.

Rotter, J. B., & Willerman, B. (1947). The incomplete sentences test as a method of studying personality. *Journal of Consulting Psychology, 11,* 43–48.

Rousseau, J. J. (1967). *The social contract* (L. G. Crocken, Ed.). New York: Washington Square Press. (Original work published 1762)

Rudin, E. (1934). *Dementia praecox* (3rd ed.). Berlin: Springer.

Rush, B. (1810). *Letters of Benjamin Rush.* Philadelphia: Kimber and Richardson.

Rush, B. (1812). *Medical inquiries and observations upon the diseases of the mind.* Philadelphia: Kimber and Richardson.

Russell, B. (1945). *A history of western philosophy.* New York: Simon & Schuster.

Russell, B. (1959). *Wisdom of the west.* New York: Crescent Books.

Sacher-Masoch, L. (1870). *Venus in furs.* Dresden, Germany: Dohrn.

Sachs, H. (1942). *The creative unconscious: Studies in the psychoanalysis of art.* Cambridge, MA: Science-Art.

Sachs, H. (1944). *Freud, master and friend.* Boston: Harvard University Press.

Salter, A. (1949). *Conditioned reflex therapy: The direct approach to the reconstruction of personality.* New York: Capricorn.

Sapir, E. (1929). The status of linguistics as a science. *Language, 5,* 207–214.

Sartorius. (1990). *Sources and traditions of classification in psychiatry.* Berne, Swizerland: Hogrefe & Huber.

Sartre, J. P. (1957). *Being and nothingness: An essay on phenomenological ontology* (H. Barnes, Trans.). London: Methuen. (Original work published 1943)

Sartre, J. P. (1966). *Existentialism is a humanism* (P. Mairet, Trans.). London: Methuen. (Original work published 1946)

Sauvages, F. B. (1731). *Nouvelles classes de maladies.* Paris: Avignon.

Sauvages, F. B. (1771). *Nosologie methodique dans la quelle les maladies sont rangees par classes.* Paris: Herrisant.

Schachtel, E. G. (1966). *Experiential foundations of Rorschach's test.* New York: Basic Books.

Schafer, R. (1948). *The clinical application of psychological tests.* New York: International Universities Press.

Schafer, R. (1954). *Psychoanalytic interpretation in Rorschach testing.* New York: Grune & Stratton.

Schneider, K. (1950). *Psychopathic personalities* (9th ed.). London: Cassell. (Original work published 1923)

Sechenov, I. M. (1935). *Collected works.* Moscow, USSR: State Publishing House.

Shakespeare, W. (1599). *Julius Caesar.* Stratford-Upon-Avon, England.

Shand, A. F. (1895). *The foundations of character: Being a study of the tendencies of the emotions and sentiments.* London: Macmillan.

Sheldon, W. H. (1940). *The varieties of human physique: An introduction to constitutional psychology.* New York: Harper.

Sheldon, W. H., & Stevens, S. S. (1942). *The varieties of temperament: A psychology of constitutional differences.* New York: Harper.

Sherrington, C. S. (1952). *The integrative action of the nervous system.* New Haven, CT: Yale University Press. (Original work published 1906)

Shorter, E. (1997). *A history of psychiatry: From the era of the asylum to the age of Prozac.* New York: Wiley.

Siever, L. J., & Davis, K. L. (1991). A psychobiological perspective on the personality disorders. *American Journal of Psychiatry, 148,* 1647–1658.

Skinner, B. F. (1948). *Walden two.* New York: Macmillan.

Skinner, B. F. (1951). How to teach animals. *Scientific American, 185,* 26–29.

Skinner, B. F. (1956). What is psychotic behavior. In *Theory and treatment of the psychoses.* St. Louis, MO: Washington University Press.

Skinner, B. F. (1957). *Verbal behavior.* New York: Appleton-Century-Crofts.

Skinner, B. F. (1967). Autobiography. In E. G. Boring & G. Lindzey (Eds.), *A history of psychology in autobiography* (Vol. 5). New York: Appleton-Century-Crofts.

Solomon, H. C. (1958). The American Psychiatric Association in relation to American psychiatry. *American Journal of Psychiatry, 115,* 1–9.

Spencer, H. (1870). *Principles of psychology.* London.

Spencer, H. (1876). *Principles of sociology.* London.

Spencer, H. (1899). *Principles of psychology* (Vols. 1–2). New York: Appleton.

Sperry, R. (1961). Cerebral organization and behavior. *Science, 133*, 1749–1757.

Spinoza, B. (1663). *Principles of the philosophy of Rene Descartes*. Amsterdam: Johannem Riewerts.

Spitz, R. (1951). The psychogenic diseases of infancy: An attempt at their etiologic classification. *Psychoanalytic Study of the Child, 6*, 255–278.

Spranger, E. (1925). *Lebensformen*. Halle, Germany: M. Niemeyer.

Stern, C., & Stern, W. (1907). *Child language*. Leipzig, Germany: Barth.

Stern, J. A., & MacDonald, D. G. (1965). Physiological correlates of mental disease. *Annual Review of Psychology, 16*, 225–264.

Stern, W. (1907). *Person und Sache*. Leipzig, Germany: Barth.

Stern, W. (1935). *Allgemeine psychologie auf personalistischer grundlage*. Den Haag, The Netherlands: Martinus Nijhoff.

Sternberg, R. J. (1985). *Beyond IQ: A triarchic theory of human intelligence*. New York: Cambridge University Press.

Stocking, G. W. (1965). On the limits of "presentism" and "historicism" in the historiography of the behavioral sciences. *Journal of the History of the Behavioral Sciences, 1*, 211–217.

Strachey, L. (1931). *Portraits in miniature*. London: Hogarth Press.

Szasz, T. S. (1957). A contribution to the psychology of schizophrenia. *Archives of Neurology and Psychiatry, 77*, 420–436.

Szasz, T. S. (1961). *The myth of mental illness; foundations of a theory of personal conduct*. New York: Hoeber-Harper.

Terman, L. (1916). *The Stanford revision and extension of the Binet-Simon Intelligence Test*.

Thigpen, C. H., & Cleckley, H. M. (1957). *The three faces of Eve*. New York: McGraw-Hill.

Thomasius, C. (1692). *Recent proposals for a new science for obtaining a knowledge of other men's minds*. Halle, Germany: Christopher Salfeld.

Thorndike, E. L. (1905). *The elements of psychology*. New York: A. G. Seiler.

Thorndike, E. L. (1911). *Animal intelligence*. New York: Macmillan.

Thorndike, E. L. (1913). *Educational psychology: The psychology of learning* (Vol. 2). New York: Macmillan.

Thorne, F. C. (1950). *Principles of personality counseling: An eclectic viewpoint*. Brandon, VT: Clinical Psychology.

Thorne, F. C., & Pishkin, V. (1968). The ideological survey. *Journal of Clinical Psychology, 24*, 263–268.

Thurstone, L. L. (1935). *The vectors of mind*. Chicago: University of Chicago Press.

Thurstone, L. L. (1947). *Multiple factor analysis: A development and expansion of "the vectors of the mind."* Chicago: University of Chicago Press.

Titchener, E. B. (1910). *A textbook of psychology*. New York: Macmillan.

Titchener, E. B. (1916). *A beginner's psychology*. New York: Macmillan.

Tolman, E. C. (1948). Cognitive maps in rats and men. *Psychological Review, 55*, 189–208.

Tolman, E. C. (1952). *History of psychology in autobiography* (Vol. 4, pp. 323–339). Worcester, MA: Clark University Press.

Tredennick, H. (Ed. & Trans.). (1967). *Aristotle's prior analytics*. Cambridge, MA: Harvard University Press.

Veblen, T. (1934). *The theory of the leisure class*. New York: Ronald.

Vesalius, A. (1952). *On the human brain* (C. Singer, Trans.). London: Oxford University Press. (Original work published 1543)

Vives, J. L. (1945). De subvention pauperum [The support of paupers]. *Encyclopaedia Britannica, 13*(23), 227. (Original work published 1526)

Voisin, F. (1851). *The analysis of human understanding*.

Voltaire. (1759). *Candide; or, All for the best*. London: J. Nourse.

Voltaire. (1775). *The philosophical dictionary*.

Wachtel, E. F. (1992). An integrative approach to working with troubled children and their families. *Journal of Psychotherapy Integration, 2*, 207–224.

Wachtel, P. L. (1977). *Psychoanalysis and behavior therapy: Toward an integration*. New York: Basic Books.

Wachtel, P. L., & Wachtel, E. F. (1986). *Family dynamics in individual psychotherapy: A guide to clinical strategies*. New York: Guilford Press.

Watson, J. B. (1913). Psychology as the behaviorist views it. *Psychological Review, 20*, 158–177.

Watson, J. B. (1930). *Behaviorism* (Rev. ed.). New York: Norton. (Original work published 1925)

Weber, E. H. (1978a). *De Subtilitate tactus* (The sense of touch; H. E. Ross, Trans.). New York: Academic Press. (Original work published 1834)

Weber, E. H. (1978b). *Der tastsinn und das gemeingefühl* (The sense of touch and common sensibility; D. J. Murray, Trans.). New York: Academic Press. (Original work published 1846)

Wechsler, D. (1939). *Wechsler-Bellevue Scale*. New York: Psychological Corporation.

Wechsler, D. (1949). *Wechsler Intelligence Scale for Children (WISC)*. New York: Psychological Corporation.

Wechsler, D. (1955). *Wechsler Adult Intelligence Scale (WAIS)*. New York: Psychological Corporation.

Wechsler, D. (1957). *Wechsler Preschool and Primary Scale of Intelligence (WPPSI)*. New York: Psychological Corporation.

Wechsler, D. (1981). *Wechsler Adult Intelligence Scale–Revised (WAIS-R)*. New York: Psychological Corporation.

Wechsler, D. (1997). *Wechsler Adult Intelligence Scale–Third Edition (WAIS-III)*. San Antonio, TX: Psychological Corporation.

Wertheimer, M. (1945). *Productive thinking*. New York: Harper & Row.

Weyer, J. (1991). *De praestigiis daemonum* [Witches, devils, and doctors in the Renaissance]. Binghampton, NY: Medieval & Renaissance Texts & Studies. (Original work published 1563)

Whorf, B. L. (1952). *Collected papers on metalinguistics*. Washington, DC: Government Printing Office.

Wicker, T. (1987, September 24). The pump on the well. *New York Times*, p. 23.

Williams, R. J. (1960). *The biological approach to the study of personality*. Berkeley Conference on Personality Development, Berkeley, CA.

Willis, T. (1971). *De anima brutorum* [Two discourses concerning the soul of brutes]. Gainesville, FL: Scholar's Facsimiles and Reprints. (Original work published 1672)

Willis, T. (1978). *Cerebri anatome* [The anatomy of the brain and nerves]. Birmingham, AL: Classics of Medicine Library. (Original work published 1664)

Wilson, E. O. (1975). *Sociobiology: The new synthesis*. Cambridge, MA: Belknap Press.

Wilson, E. O. (1978). *On human nature*. Cambridge, MA: Harvard University Press.

Winnicott, D. W. (1956). On transference. *International Journal of Psychoanalysis, 37*, 382–395.

Wolberg, L. R. (1967). *The technique of psychotherapy* (2nd ed.). New York: Grune & Stratton.

Woodward, S. B. (1850). The medical treatment of insanity. *American Journal of Insanity, 5*.

World Health Organization. (1990). *Manual of the international statistical classification of diseases, injuries, and causes of death* (10th ed.). Geneva, Switzerland: Author.

Wright, T. (1971). *The passions of the mind in general*. Urbana: University of Illinois Press. (Original work published 1604)

Wundt, W. M. (1896). *Lectures on human and animal psychology*. New York: Macmillan.

Wundt, W. M. (1904). *Principles of physiological psychology* (5th ed., E. Titchener, Ed.). New York: Macmillan. (Original work published 1874)

Wundt, W. M. (1907). *Outlines of psychology* (C. H. Judd, Trans.). Leipzig, Germany: Wilhelm Engelmann.

Yalom, I. D. (1975). *The theory and practice of group psychotherapy*. New York: Basic Books.

Yalom, I. D. (1980). *Existential psychotherapy*. New York: Basic Books.

Zigler, E., & Phillips, L. (1961). Psychiatric diagnosis and symptomatology. *Journal of Abnormal Social Psychology, 63*, 69–75.

Zilboorg, G., & Henry, G. W. (1941). *A history of medical psychology*. New York: Norton.

Index

Note: Bold numbers indicate major discussion of the individual.